Prentice Hall

ENCYCLOPEDIC
DICTIONARY
of
ENGLISH
USAGE

SECOND EDITION

Prentice Hall

ENCYCLOPEDIC DICTIONARY *of* ENGLISH USAGE

SECOND EDITION

N.H. MAGER • S.K. MAGER
Revised by John Domini

PRENTICE HALL
Englewood Cliffs, New Jersey 07632

Prentice-Hall International (UK) Limited, *London*
Prentice-Hall of Australia Pty. Limited, *Sydney*
Prentice-Hall Canada Inc., *Toronto*
Prentice-Hall Hispanoamericana, S.A., *Mexico*
Prentice-Hall of India Private Limited, *New Delhi*
Prentice-Hall of Japan, Inc., *Tokyo*
Simon & Schuster Asia Pte. Ltd., *Singapore*
Editora Prentice-Hall do Brasil, Ltda., *Rio de Janeiro*

10 9 8 7 6 5 4 3 2 1

Library of Congress Cataloging-in-Publication Data

Mager, N. H. (Nathan H.), 1913–
   Prentice Hall encyclopedic dictionary of English usage / N.H.
Mager and S.K. Mager. - - 2nd ed. / revised by John Domini.
      p.   cm.
   Rev. ed. of: Encyclopedic dictionary of English usage.
   ISBN 0-13-276858-5 : $27.95
   1. English language - - Usage.   2. English language - - Dictionaries.
I. Mager, Sylvia K., 1916–   . II. Domini, John, 1951–
III. Mager, N. H. (Nathan H.), 1913–   Encyclopedic dictionary of
English usage.   IV. Title.
PE1628.M23   1992
428'.003--dc20   92-22944
                                                             CIP

0-13-276858-5

PRENTICE HALL
Business Information & Publishing Division
Englewood Cliffs, NJ 07632

Simon & Schuster, A Paramount Communications Company

Printed in the United States of America

ABOUT THE AUTHORS

Nathan H. Mager was publisher of *The New York Column* newspaper, and manager of the *Civil Service Leader*, a New York State newspaper for public employees. An author, editor, and publisher for more than 40 years, Mr. Mager wrote numerous articles, and authored over 20 books (some with his wife) including THE OFFICE ENCYCLOPEDIA; THE COMPLETE LETTER WRITER; LEGAL, POLITICAL AND BUSINESS GUIDE; and HOT TO PASS COLLEGE ENTRANCE TESTS.

Sylvia K. Mager is a writer, editor, researcher, and newspaper and magazine columnist. A graduate of Hunter College, she is the author of COMPLETE GUIDE TO HOME SEWING and TODAY'S WOMAN BOOK FOR BRIDES.

John Domini has taught writing at Harvard, Lewis & Clark, and a number of other institutions. Currently, he's a member of the English Department at Linfield College in Oregon. He is the author of *Bedlam*, a book of short stories, and has published fiction and non-fiction in a wide variety of publications, among them the *New York Times* and *Sports Illustrated*.

HOW TO USE THIS BOOK

This guide is intended as a single-volume ready reference for the educated professional who needs to write. It combines elements of a dictionary, a style manual, and a grammar guide—the most in-demand elements of each. This combination makes it unlike any other reference work, and more immediately useful.

In 1974 Prentice Hall published the original edition, by Nathan and Sylvia Mager. The book proved a perennial bestseller, and an essential resource book for a wide range of working people. The present, updated edition builds on the strengths of the first.

- Like the original, this edition is *comprehensive*. It distills the essence from a wide variety of texts. Our more important sources include the style manual for the Government Printing Office, the style manuals for *The New York Times* and the University of Chicago Press, *Webster's New Collegiate Dictionary*, the *Encyclopedia Brittanica*, the *World Book Almanac*, and *Warriner's Complete English Grammar*. Of course a number of other compendiums and resources proved valuable as well. The editors express the sincerest appreciation to the innumerable compilers before them.

- Also like the original, this edition is in strict *alphabetical order*. Solutions can be found simply by looking under the name of the problem: either a specific word (for instance **adverse** or **averse**), or a subject heading (like *POSSESSIVES* or *SEXIST LANGUAGE*).

Besides following the overall system of the first edition, this update also has all the same features—outstanding for their usefulness and flexibility.

- The new guide has dozens of *subject headings*. These are listings in italicized capitals, and apply to an entire subject area. The general headings cover a wide range of issues, from technical topics such as bibliography and capitalization to more complex problems of usage, convention, and changes in language—see, for instance, the listing under *RACIST LANGUAGE*. Each listing under these headings is a miniature essay, with examples covering all the exceptions and special cases each issue raises.

- The book also lists *thousands of shorter entries*. These define and demonstrate usages for everything from irregular English verbs like **catch** and **wake** to new high-technology words like **fax** and **MTV**. The shorter entries also include troublesome expressions like **either . . . or, neither . . . nor**. Then there are capitalization rules for organizations, for instance a **court (of law)** or a **foundation**, rules of address for people like **naval officers** or an **instructor in a college or university**, and even the conventions for things like **brackets, dates** and **horse races**.

- The book once again offers hundreds of *place names*. Every nation listed in the current *World Almanac* appears here, from **Afghanistan** to **Zimbabwe**, including nations whose status remains uncertain as of 1992, such as **Armenia, Croatia,** and **Lithuania**. Also listed are the 50 American states, with their abbreviations and capitals, and all the Canadian provinces.

- In addition there is an extensive compendium of *names and references from history and literature*. These include historical figures like **Kemal Atatürk** or shapers of culture like **Euclid, Friedrich Nietzsche** and **Bob Dylan**. You will also find thumbnail definitions of cultural movements, like **Modernism**, and listing for significant artifacts of the human imagination, like **Aphrodite** and **Scaramouch**.

- Especially helpful with some of the name listings, the book offers a quick *pronunciation guide*. Pronunciation was in fact one of the principal criteria for these listings. Every word in this book poses some kind of problem—it is something a person of average (or better than average) education might need to look up or double-check. For many of the entries, the problem is simply how to say the word aloud. Indeed, in some cases, the problem is how to say the same word for different uses—like **affect** as a noun or verb. The code for this book's pronunciation guide is simple, and provided on page x.

- At the same time, there are *listings of measurements*. From **millimeter** to **mile**, from **avoirdupois** to **troy weight**, any sort of measurement that seems useful for an educated reader is here. In every case, the book provides a number of different equivalences, in a number of different numerical systems. It also provides all the appropriate abbreviations.

- Finally, the guide is carefully and thoroughly *cross-referenced*. Entries recur in different places, often more than once. Anyone wondering whether to use **Indian** or **Native American** can look in a number of places: under either of those terms, under **American** or **-American**, or under the subject heading *RACIST LANGUAGE*. The same applies to abbreviations, which in most cases are listed along with the word they represent (for example, there is an entry both for **kilowatt** and for **kw**); to perennial problems like **affect** and **effect**; and to names of places currently undergoing transition, like **Croatia, Serbia, Slovenia,** and **Yugoslavia.**

As that last point makes clear, the world has seen many changes since 1974, and this new edition has been revised and updated with an eye toward keeping it useful well into the next century. Changes are intended to emphasize flexibility and practicality.

- Words derived from **computers** and other contemporary technology are listed, along with their uses.

- New rules for words like **hopefully**, new conventions for possessives, and new suffixes like **-identify** have been added. All usage changes are listed and explained.

- New nations are listed, along with their pertinent details. This includes all the members of the old Soviet Union—the **Federated Commonwealth of Independent States.**

- Historical entries have been updated. Among the additions are women like **Frida Kahlo** and events like the **My Lai** massacre.

- New acronyms and abbreviations are listed. Also, a consistent system of punctuation has been instituted with abbreviations; see below.

- All cross-references are now indicated by the simple English word *see*, rather than the more academic *Cf.* Likewise, *for example* has replaced *e.g.*

The changes number in the thousands—clarifying, updating, and in general making the book more handy. Yet the goal remains the same as the Magers had in mind in 1974: "to create a tool with maximum usefulness." Executives and students, businesspeople and letter-writers, professors and political workers and even crossword-puzzle enthusiasts should all find something in this book to make their task easier. Anyone wondering about a word should find the answer here.

ABBREVIATIONS: A Note and a List

Abbreviations in this book take points (periods) except in special cases. The American Medical Association, for instance, is here abbreviated A.M.A., not AMA. This system of course cannot possibly apply for every organization, but for the purposes of the book it was important to be consistent.

The special cases are those abbreviations that are properly considered *acronyms*—that is, abbreviations in which points would interfere with the meaning. Examples include MTV, PG (the movie rating), and the U.S. state abbreviations: MA, for instance, stands for Massachusetts, while M.A. stands for Master of Arts.

Other than that, there are a number of standard abbreviations used throughout the text:

abbreviation	*meaning*
abbr.	abbreviation
adj.	adjective
adv.	adverb
angl.	anglicized
a/k/a	also known as
approx.	approximately
Br.	British
cap.	capitalize, for a word
	capital, for a nation
colloq.	colloquial (slang)
conj.	conjunction
esp.	especially
f.	female
fem.	feminine
fig.	figurative
Fr.	French
Ger.	German
It.	Italian
lit.	literal
m.	male
masc.	masculine
n.	noun
obs.	obsolete
org.	organization
orig.	originally
p.	past
pl.	plural
p.p.	past participle
pref.	preferred
pres. part.	present participle
pron.	pronunciation
Rus.	Russian
sing.	singular
sq.	square
usu.	usually
v.	verb

PRONUNCIATION: A Guide

This edition uses the same pronunciation guide as found in the first edition. As before, "some subtleties have been eliminated." The purpose is to provide a system that can be quickly understood by anyone who knows basic English phonetics.

How to Use This Book

Vowels
Sound
Expressed   *Webster*
By   *Phonetic*

a

ae	=	ā		as in may, day delay
a	=	a		as in map, bad, pass
ai	=	ai		as in hair
ah	=	á		as in bother, father
aw	=	ó		as in saw, all, prawn

e

ee	=	e, é	as in meat, bleed, tree
eh	=	e, eú	as in bed, elk, operate
eu	=	ëu	as in few

i

ie	=	ī	as in why, side, buy
ih	=	i, í, ú	as in tip, wish, iln

o

oh	=	ō	as in woe, snow, toad
oi	=	oi	as in coin, employ, coy
oo	=	ū	as in rule, spittoon, truth
ou	=	oú	as in now, plow, denounce

u

u	=	u̇	as in stood, soot, could
uh	=	ų	as in duchess, hurry

Consonants

wh	as in what, when, whale
sh	as in shock, shun, dish
th	as in either, then, dipthong
zh	as in division, azure

TYPICAL PROBLEMS
THIS BOOK CAN SOLVE

How to pronounce

acumen	Dachau
avoirdupois	hegira
Beowulf	subpoena
bona fide	Szechwan
Cairo, IL	viva voce

When to capitalize

a.d.	Ho Chi Minh
b.c.	professor
a.m.	soviet
the bible	state
heads of departments	union

How to abbreviate

avoirdupois	free alongside
California	House concurrent resolution
(and all American states)	kilograms
Doctor of Philosophy	monsieur
Food and Drug Administration	Spanish

Differentiate between (or among)

Abyssinia, Ethiopia, Eritrea	glasnost, perestroika
ante-, anti-	hue, brillance, color
cache, cachet, sachet	1 lb. avoirdupois and 1 lb. troy
Charlotte and Emily Bronte	sensual, sensuous
eminent, immanent	stock, common stock, preferred stock

Define, identify, or explain

antonym	footnotes
Bahai	infidel
dangling modifier	the New Deal
downsize	Postmodernism
European Community	Eisaku Sato

Indicate which to write

all right, allright, or alright	Miss, Mrs. or Ms.
caret, carat, or carrot	Native American or Indian
different from or different than	NM or N.M. (for New Mexico)
farther or further	10 or ten (SEE Numbers)
Jewish, Hebrew, Israeli	x ray, Xray, or X-ray

Provide measurements or dates for

a byte	La Boheme
a dekaliter	naught
Frankenstein	an odd-lot
one horsepower	progressive average
a knot	Eleanor, Franklin, and Theodore Roosevelt

Provide correct spelling for

accommodate	Guinea-Bissau
Albuquerque	kowtow
Charles', Charles's	Odysseus, the Odyssey, and Ulysses
cynosure, sinecure	posthaste, postdoctoral
Fyodor Dostoyevsky	snafu

. . . and answer thousands of other questions of all kinds.

Prentice Hall

ENCYCLOPEDIC DICTIONARY of ENGLISH USAGE

SECOND EDITION

A

a As an article, *a* should be used before all consonants except silent *h* : *a history, a humble proposal.* BUT *an Hispanic culture.* ALSO before a consonant sound in a vowel: *a union, a UFC station.* See also: **an.**

a. (abbr.) ampere; are (metric system); area.

A. (abbr.) altitude; atomic weight; area; absolute (temperature); angstrom.

A- bomb; A-frame. BUT: A flat; A sharp.

A.A. Alcoholics Anonymous; athletic association: *Boston A.A.*

AAA (abbr.) American Automobile Association; anti-aircraft artillery. Written without points (periods).

Aaron [AIR'n]

A.B. or **a.b.** (abbr.) able-bodied seaman.

A.B. (abbr.) Bachelor of Arts. See **B.A.** (abbr.), more common.

abacus calculating instrument. (pl.) abici or abacuses.

abattoir [ab-a-TWAR] (Fr.) slaughterhouse.

abbé [a-BAE] (Fr.) a secular ecclesiastic.

Abbot (Catholic) ADDRESS: His Excellency, The Right Reverend John Jones, Abbot of Briarcliff. SALUTATION: Your Excellency.

Abbot (Protestant) ADDRESS: The Lord Abbot of Briarcliff; The Right Reverend Abbot Brown. SALUTATION: Dear Father Abbot; My Lord Abbot.

abbreviation a shortening of a word or phrase. Abbreviated: abbr. (v.)—ated, —ating. (adj.)—able.

ABRIDGMENT shortening by selection of most important portions.

ABBREVIATIONS abbreviated: abbr. In this text, nearly all abbreviations are printed with points (periods). The only exceptions are state abbreviations (such as AL for Alabama), in which the individual letters do not each stand for a word, and acronyms like MTV. MA means Massachusetts, but M.A. means Master of Arts.

MTV and abbreviations of that kind have evolved into common *acronyms*. They are then treated as words, points omitted: *NATO, co-op, etc.*

Although styles differ, the tendency is for abbreviations to lose their points as they increase in use. Thus Government Printing Office style drops the points on almost all federal and international agencies, *The New York Times* on some, and some publishers on only a few. When an abbreviation is made up of letters from one word, it generally does not require a point, as in TV, but where two or more words are involved, *The New York Times* usually uses abbreviation points: *R.F.D.*

In most writings, abbreviations are to be avoided, but more extensive use is made of them in tabular material, headlines, indexes, and addresses. The chief factor in deciding when to use an abbreviation is reading facility—the readiness with which the reader can determine the meaning and the technical space limitations.

A number of words, particularly new ones, are so distracting to the eye or so difficult to pronounce that abbreviation is necessary. Such abbreviations are proper both in writing and in speech: *AIDS, D.D.T., R.S.V.P., V.I.P., KLM* for the Dutch airline (whose full name is Koninkli jke Luchtuaart Maatschaapi jvoor Nederland en Kolonien).

The **abbreviation point** is a period, and is used with many abbreviations. When the point occurs at the end of a sentence, it is combined with a period into one dot. Before any other punctuation mark, the point remains. Customary usage eliminates the point for abbreviations of governmental organizations.

DO NOT use the abbreviation point after: (1) chemical symbols *(H₂O)*; (2) formal signs of books *(8vo)*; (3) initial used as titles of technical publications or organizations in technical matter *(PAIS for Public Affairs Information Service)*; (4) linguistic epochs *(IE for Indo-European)*; (5) the word *per cent*; (6) contractions *(can't)*; (7) shortened forms of names *(Sam)*; (8) Roman numerals *(XIX)*; (9) letters

not used as abbreviations *(A and B met and discussed the matter.)* BUT: If *A* and *B* are abbreviations for actual names, the abbreviation point is used.

ABC's the alphabet.

abettor This spelling is pref. to *abetter*, especially in law.

abjure forswear; renounce on oath; disavow.

ADJURE charge or command; entreat or appeal to.

—able When adding this suffix to a transitive verb, drop any final silent *e* or *ate* of polysyllabic words; *abominable, rebatable, accumulable. —ible* is an alternative established by custom for some forms.

The general rule: (1) When there is a corresponding noun that ends in —*tion* preceded by *a*, the adjective ending is —*able: quotation, quotable; presentation, presentable.* (2) When there is a corresponding noun ending in —*tion* or —*sion* not preceded by *a*, the adjective ending is —*ible: expansion, expansible, extension, extensible; admission, admissible.* Words formed from them by adding the prefixes *in-, un-, non-*, also have the —*ible* ending.

able-bodied (adj.) This word also appears without hyphen: *ablebodied.*

abolition abolishing or abolishment.

aborigine [AB-oh-RIHJ-ih-nee] (pl.) —*ines.* (adj.) —*inal.*

about This word is informal for *approximately*. In use, avoid implied redundancy. NOT: *about forty to fifty.* NOT: *He estimated about 15,000 were present.* See also: **above; below; on; over; under**

about-face

above In use, avoid old-fashioned style: above listed, above-mentioned. *The example above* is pref. to *the above example,* as is *the example given above.*

abridgment pref. to *abridgement.* Abridged from, abridgement of. (adj.) —eable. SEE ALSO **abbreviation.**

abrogate [AB-roh-gaet] to annul; abolish; repeal (adj.) —gable.

abs. (abbr.) absolute; abstract.

abscess [AB-sess] infection, esp. in gums.

absence Absentee: —teeism.

absent-minded

ABSOLUTE CONSTRUCTION (nominative absolute) A literary construction in which the participial phrase is not connected with the main clause. *The facts proven incontrovertibale, he won his point.* See *DANGLING MODIFIER*

absolve [ab-SAHLV] free from an obligation, or from condemnation for sin. *He was absolved from sin after confessing.*

absorb [ab-SAWRB] to take into.

ADSORB [ad-SAWRB] to condense and hold by absorption, the

adhesion of a thin layer of molecules to the surface of a solid body.

abstemious [ab-STEE-mee-uhs] displaying habitual moderation in food and liquor.

ABSTINENT displaying forbearance from indulgence, (as in certain foods). *Total restraint, especially from intoxicating beverages, is* total abstinence.

ABSTRACT NOUN a noun that names a quality, state, or idea: *peace, freedom, whiteness.* It is also used to mean the general class *(fruit)* as opposed to the particular *(apple).* Lower-case except when a proper name is involved. In use, avoid over-reliance on abstract nouns. Concrete nouns have greater impact: *snake* rather than *reptile.*

abutting touching, sometimes with a protruding portion.

abysmal [a-BIHZ-m-l] deep; bottomless; hence, wretched.

ABBYSSAL: unfathomable (tech., water depth of 300 fathoms).

abyss bottomless or unmeasurable pit or space.

CHASM a deep, long, and narrow opening.

Abyssinia [ab-uh-SIHN-ih-uh] See **Ethiopia.**

A.C. (abbr.) athletic club.

a.c. (abbr.) alternating current.

A.C.L.U. (abbr.) American Civil Liberties Union.

academic degrees and titles John J. Poole, Doctor of Philosophy; John J. Poole, Ph.D. Professor Poole; Prof. John J. Poole, Ph.D. Degrees and titles are listed separately in this sequence; theological degrees, degrees earned in course, and honorary degrees in order of bestowal. *Reverend John J. Poole, Ph.D., LL.D.* Also correct without abbreviation point: *PhD*

academic departments Use lowercase: *department of philosophy; French department.*

academy Andover Academy or Merchant Marine Academy are each referred to as *the academy* (lowercase) on second use. Most styles capitalize a second reference to National Academy of Science, the Academy of Sciences, the French Academy, and the United States Military, Naval, and Air Force Academies, BUT NOT the service academies.

Acadia [uh-KAE-dih-uh] original name of Nova Scotia.

a cappella [ah-cah-PELL-ah] (It.) without instrumental accompaniment. Choral music is sometimes described this way.

Acapulco [ah-kah-POOL-ko] full name of Acapulco de Juárez [dae HWAH-raes]. S Mexican resort on Pacific.

accede [ak-SEED] to assume an office; assent to.

EXCEED to surpass.

ACCENT When the same multisyllabic word is both noun and adjective, the noun is usually accented on the first syllable, the adjective on the last syllable: (n.) *a legal AB-stract;* (adj.) *ab-STRACT idea.*

When the word is both a noun and a verb, the noun is usually accented on the first syllable, the verb on last syllable: *progress* (n.) [PRAHG-rehs], (v.) [proh-GREHS]. Sometimes the consonantal sound at the end is hard in the noun, soft in the verb: *use* (n.) [yoos], (v.) [yooz]; *excuse* (n.) [ex-KYOOS], (v.) [ex-ICYOOZ].

There are no firm general rules regarding accent in American English, but new words tend to follow the accent patterns of similar older words. The tendency is toward recessive accents, and toward accenting the first syllable.

accept to receive willingly. *I accept your gift.*

EXCEPT leave out, exclude, *He gave a gift to everyone except me.*

acceptance approval. In general; an act of accepting.

ACCEPTATION the meaning of a word as it is generally understood.

accepter In law, *acceptor.*

access opportunity of admission.

EXCESS too much.

accession [ak-SESH-uhn] approach; adherence; something added; reaching an office or condition.

accessory [ak-SES-oh-ree] (adj.) aiding or assisting. (n.) that which (or one who) assists or contributes. Pref. to *accessary.*

accidentally NOT *accidently.*

acclimate [AK-luh-maet pref.; also uh-KLIE-miht] Also *acclimatize* [uh-KLIE-muh-tiez].

accolade [ak-oh-LAED] a ritual embrace; award.

accompanied by, with *By* is used to indicate an additional person. *With* is used to indicate supplementary activity. *He arrived, accompanied by his valet. She introduced her fiancé and accompanied her remarks with an affectionate hug.* (adj.) —nying (n.) —iment.

accommodate —ted, —ting.

accordion NOT *accordian.*

accouchement [uh-KOOSH-mahn or mehnt] delivery in childbirth; confinement period of pregnancy.

account of . . . Using *describe* with this phrase is redundant. NOT: *An account of his adventures is described in* . . . . See also **cause.**

accouter [uh-KOOT-er]. to furnish with equipment or dress. Pref. to *accoutre.* (n.) accoutrement.

acct. (abbr.) account. Also a/c

accumulate [a-KYOO-myuh-laet] —ting.

accurate [AK-yoo-riht] —racy.

ACCUSATIVE CASE See *OBJECTIVE CASE.*

accuse of to charge with. *I accuse him of theft.*

acetate [AH-seh-taet] manmade fiber used in synthetics.

acetic [a-SEE-tihk] pertaining to or like vinegar.

    ASCETIC [a-SEHT-ihk] given to self-denial; austere.

achieve This word implies effort. AVOID: *achieving old age.*

Achilles [ah-KIHL-ees] a Homeric hero.

    ACHILLES' HEEL. Fatal flaw.

acknowledgment Pref. to *acknowledgement.* BUT: acknowledgeable.

acoustics [uh-KOOS-tihks] the science of sound; qualities that determine the clarity of sound in a room.

acquaintanceship

acquiesce [ak-wee-EHS] to accept or comply passively.

acre unit of area measure = 40469 hectare = 4,046.8726 sq. meters = 10 sq. surveyor's ch. = 160 sq. rods = 4840 sq. yds. = 43560 sq.ft = approx. 2/3 city sq. block.

acreage

acre-foot measure of water = 1 foot covering 1 acre = 325,900 gals. Also = *acre-inch.*

acrid [AK-rid] irritating; corrosive.

acrostic verse in which initial letters

of words or lines form a word or words.

acrylic [ah-CRIH-lihk] synthetic plastics, resins, oils.

act For federal, state, or foreign acts, capitalize short or popular title: *Classification Act, Economy Act, Lend-Lease Act.* BUT: *the act.*

act of God (legal term) unpreventable accident.

acting Capitalize word if part of complete capitalized title: *Acting Secretary of State.* BUT: *the acting secretary.*

activate Compare to make active, esp. through chemical treatment.

 ACTUATE [AK-tyoo-aet] to put into action; incite to activity; arouse. Implies communication of power.

acumen [a-KYOO-m'n] keenness of mind.

A.D. (abbr.) anno Domini (Lat.) "of the year of our Lord" The specific year should follow. NOT: *1964 A.D.* NOT: *the tenth century A.D.* See also: **B.C.**

ad (abbr.) advertisement. Use no point (or period).

 ADD to increase; to join to.

A.D.A. (abbr.) Americans for Democratic Action (a liberal political organization).

adagio [uh-DAHjoh] (It.) In music this word means slow, graceful. (pl.) —gios.

adapt to make suitable; to fit or suit. *He adapts himself well to new situations.* —ed, —ing. (n.) —ter, —ability, —ation. (adj.) —able, —ive. Compare to

 ADOPT to take as one's own. *They adopted a new policy.*

addendum addition; supplement. (pl.) —da.

addict [(v.) a-DIHKT or (n.) AD-ihkt] (v.) to give oneself over to; (n.) one addicted to a habit, especially to taking drugs. (adj.) —ed, —ing; —ed. (n.) —edness, —tion.

addicted to. Expression must be followed by a noun.

Addis Ababa [AHD-ihs AH-buh-buh] capital of Ethiopia.

addle confuse; muddle.

addle —brain, —head, —pate.

address [uh-DREHS] Address, lecture, and speech are in descending order of formality.

ADDRESS In general, the address should stand out clearly from the body of a letter, usually at the head. On an envelope it should be specific, complete, and have an even left margin. Principal words and abbreviations are capitalized.

 Before the name appears: *Mr., Ms., Miss, Mrs., Dr., Rev., or Hon.* After the name: *Esq., Jr., Sr., 2d,* and academic degrees. BUT: When a degree or *Esq.* follows a name, there should be no preceding title, except for some academics: *Prof. John Poole, Ph.D.*

Write out *North, South, West* and *East.* In an address, *NW., SW., NE., SE.,* indicates divisions of a city. Do not abbreviate *street* or *building* when used as part of a name: *Court Street Building;* BUT *street, avenue, place, road, square, boulevard, building, terrace,* or *court* may be abbreviated when part of an address.

Write out names of U.S. states, territories or possessions when standing alone, but abbreviate after the name of a city. Every U.S. state and territory has its official two-letter post-office abbreviation—AL, ID, CZ, PR—printed without points. The zip code should appear following the names of city and state: *New York, NY 10011.*

adduce to offer as an argument; cite (adj.) —*ced,* —*cing;* —*cible* (pref. to —*eable*).

Adenaur, Konrad [ah-dehn-OU'R] (1876-1967) West German statesman after World War II. Chancellor 1949-1963.

adept [uh-DEHPT] skilled. *She is adept with a needle. Adept in* pref. to *adept at.*

adequate sufficient.

adhere to stick; cling. (n. and adj.) —ing, —ent; (n.) —ence.

ADHERENCE mental or moral attachment.

ad hoc [ad hahk] (Lat.) for this; applied to a special purpose: *ad hoc committee.*

ad hominem (Lat.) against the man; an argument that attacks personal qualities rather than ideas.

adieu [uh-DYEU] (Fr.) farewell. (pl.) —s pref. to —x.

adj. (abbr.) adjective.

adjacent Use *... to.* NOT *... of.*

ADJECTIVE a word used to qualify a noun. Generally adjectives have no special forms to denote singular, plural, or gender, but most have comparative and superlative forms. See also: *COMPARISON.*

Nouns, pronouns, the participial forms of verbs, and some adverbs may be used as adjectives: *sink washers, frightening crowds, frightened crowds, daily duties.*

Adjectives are classified as *adherent* when they are placed before a noun; *apposite* when they are placed after a noun; *predicate* when they follow a linking verb; *objective complement* when they follow the object of a verb.

In a series of adjectives the usual order is: (1) definitive adjectives *(a, the, this);* (2) ordinal numbers *(second, third,* BUT NOT *first, last,* and *others)* (3) cardinal numbers *(seven, two);* (4) fractions *(one-half):* (5) units *(tenths, dozens);* (6) adjective of degrees *(more, least);* (7) judgment words *(true, happy, ugly);* (8) descriptive adjectives *(bright);* (9) adjectives of size *(tall, slight);* (10) adjectives of color *(blue, green).* Phrases and clauses follow the noun.

Exceptions have been established by popular usage in some forms and in cases where *of* is needed: *half of the men, half the men.*

Compound adjective forms are hyphenated for clarity when they precede the noun. *The first-class passengers.* BUT: *The scholastic standing of the school is first class.*

Adjectives (and adverbs) occur in three forms: positive, comparative (with —*er* added, or prefixed by *more*) and superlative (with —*est* added, or prefixed by *most).*

adjoining having a common boundary, contiguous.

ADJACENT near, next to, but not necessarily connected. *A road may run between adjacent farms.*

ATTACHED fastened to, connected.

Adj. Gen. adjutant, general. (pl.) adjutants general.

adjoin [a-JOIN] —ed, (adj.) —ing. Compare to

ADJOURN [a-JEHRN, NOT ad—] —ed, (adj.) —ing; (n.) —ment. See also **prologue.**

adjudge [a-JUHJ] to decide; determine; order or decree. —ed, —ging.

adjudicate [a-JOO-dih-kaet] to decide judicially. (adj.) —ting, —cable.

adjure [ajoor] to command solemnly; entreat. See **abjure.**

ad-lib (theatrical slang) to speak lines not in the script. (n.) ad lib, (pl.) ad libs; (adj.), ad-lib, —bbed, —bbing.

Adm. (abbr.) admiral. Used with a name.

administer to manage directly. (adj.) —ing, —trable, —trant. (v.) —trate, —ed. (n.) —tration.

administrate (v.) —ed, —ting. (adj.) —tive.; (n.) —tion, —tor, —torship.

Administration. Cap. when referring to specific federal agency appointed by the President: *Farmers Home Administration, Food and Drug Administration, Veterans Administration.* ALSO: the Administration. BUT: the Roosevelt administration; administration bill, policy, etc.

administrative assistant Also upper case. Current use pref. to *secretary.*

administrator In law, with lowercase *A,* a person who administers an estate. With uppercase *A,* a title, such as *Administrator of Veterans Affairs.*

admirable [AD-muh-ra-uh-b'l] See **strong opinion words.**

admiral Charles F. Hughes, rear admiral, United States Navy; the rear admiral; Admiral Hughes.

Admiralty Executive British naval authority Lord of the Executive British naval authority.

admire —red, —ring. (adj.)—ring. (n.) —rer.

admission Implies gaining rights, obligations, etc.; *admission to a fraternity.* Generally pref. to *admittance.*

admit —tted, —tting; (n.) —ttance.

admit of (archaic) *He will admit of no other solution.*

ad nauseam [ad-NAW-shee-am or -NAW-seeam] (Lat.) to the point of disgust.

adobe [uh-DOH-bee] sun-dried brick; a building made of such materials.

adopted (adj.) Refers to the child.

ADOPTIVE (adj.) Refers to the parent.

adore —red, —ring; (n.) —ration,—rer.

adulate [AD-yoo-laet] to praise or flatter obsequiously. —d, —ting. (adj.) —tory [AD-yoo-luh-tawr-ee]. (n.) —tor.

adulterate to corrupt by adding a baser substance. (adj.) —*rable.*

adv. (abbr.) adverb.

ad val. (abbr.) *ad valorem.*

ad valorem (Lat.) according to value. A tax on a percentage of the value of the taxed goods is an *ad valorem duty.*

advance (n.) progress, improvement, payment beforehand. (v. and adj.) —ced, —cing. *Advance planning is redundant.*

advancement (n.) progression; often refers to promotion. Distinguish from progress. *The student received an advancement in rating for the progress he had made in his studies.*

advantageous profitable; favorable.

ADVENTITIOUS Accidental; fortuitous.

ADVERB (adv.) a word, phrase, or clause that modifies a verb, adjective, or other adverb. It answers such questions as where, how, how much, when: *speedily, directly, only, very.*

An adjective or a noun may be used as an adverb: *a light blue dress; he was there Tuesday.*

Adverbs are classified as adverbs of time: *now, soon;* place: *here, everywhere;* manner: *softly, hurriedly:* and degree: *mostly, scarcely.* They are also classified as interrogative: *when, how (She didn't know when he came);* relative (used to introduce a sentence); negative: *not, never, hardly;* directional: *back, up, down;* and descriptive: *slowly, beautifully, brightly.* Only descriptive adverbs occur in three comparative forms. See *COMPARISON.*

With a compound verb, place an adverb between the auxiliary and the verb: *He has always slept well.* With a copulative verb, place the adverb between the subject and the complement: *He is always ready to go.* With a transitive verb, the adverb does not intervene between verb and complement: *He selected the material wisely.* NOT: *He selected wisely the material.*

Split an infinitive with an adverb only when necessary for greater clarity: *He hopes to at least see the prisoner.* See also *ADJECTIVE.*

adverbial accusative a noun not in

the genitive used as adv. in preposi-tional phrase: *The miles we walked over road and field.*

ADVERBIAL GENITIVE a noun used as an adverb, formed from the archaic genitive case, usually marked by its —s ending. *I work days.* Common adverbial genitives include words like *since, needs, and sometimes.*

ADVERBIAL CLAUSE a group of words functioning as an adverb. These may be placed (1) at the begin-ning of the sentence, either to em-phasize the main clause or to avoid piling up adverbial clauses after the main clause; or (2) after the main clause, in its natural position. *If he loves me, he will come. He will come if he loves me.*

Long or complex modifiers placed at the end of a sentence are anticli-matic and weaken the sentence.

adversary [AD-vuhr-sehr-ee] antag-onist, enemy.

adverse [(ad-VURS or AD-vurs] op-posing. *There were many adverse condi-tions to be met.*

AVERSE [a-VURS] unwilling, re-luctant. *I am averse to seeing movies about serial killers.*

advert [ad-VURT] to allude. (v.) —ed, —ing. (adj.) —ent. (n.) —ence.

advertisement [ad-WHR-tis-ment or AD-vihr-TIEZ-ment] (n.) —tiser. (v.) —tise,—tised, —sing, also —ize.

advice [ad-VIES] (n.) a recom-mended opinion. [ad-VIEZ] (v.) to

counsel, warn. See also **Inform**.

advise (v.) In use, AVOID *advise* for inform. NOT: *He advised me that it was raining.* (v.) —vising, —vised. (adj.) —visable, —vised, —visory. (n.) —vi-ser, —visability, —visedness, —vise-ment.

advisedly deliberately; after consid-eration.

INTENTIONALLY by plan.

adviser Pref. to *advisor.* BUT: *advi-sory.*

advocate to support or plead for. *He advocated free speech.* NOT: *He advo-cated that liquor be served.* (adj); —at-ing, —d; —atory; (n.) —ator, —tion.

adze [adz] an ax with cutting edge perpendicular to handle.

ae The *e* alone is used for most liga-tures in English: *aesthetic* or *esthetic; aesophagus* or *esophagus.*

A.E.C. (abbr.) Atomic Energy Com-mission.

Aegean Sea [A-JEE-'n] Sea between Greece and Turkey.

aegis [EE-jihs] shield of Zeus; com-monly, a protection.

Aeneid [ee-NEE-id] epic by Virgil.

Aeolian [ee-OH-lih-an] Greek tribe.

aeolian produced by wind. Refers to music, rock sculpture, etc.

aeolian harp stringed instrument on which the wind produces tones.

aeon [EE-ahn] extremely long period of time. *Eon* is pref.

aerate [AE-ehr-aet] Pref. to *aerify*]

aerial [ae-EER-ee-uhl, AIR-ee'l] pertaining to the air. With radio and TV, *antenna* is pref.

aerie [AE-ehr-rih] a nest. Pre. to *aery, eyry, eyrle.*

aerobics [ae-ROH-bihks] cardiovascular exercise.

aerospace the total expanse beyond the earth's surface.

Aeschylus [EHS-kih-luhs] (525-456 B.C.) Greek playwright (*Prometheus Bound*).

Aesop [EE-sahp] (c. 620-560 B.C.) Greek fabulist.

aesthete [EHS-theet] one who emphasizes appreciation of beauty. Sometimes derogatory. Pref. to *esthete.*

aesthetic [ehs-THEHT-ik] pertaining to the beautiful. More common than *esthetic.*

Afars and Issas [AHF-ahrz, ee-SAHZ], Former Fr. territory in Somalia (SEE).

A.F.B. (abbr.) Air Force Base (with name).

a few a good few, a very few. NOT: *an extremely few.*

affect (v.) to influence, change, produce an effect upon. *The fire affected all the houses.* (adj.) *affectible.*

EFFECT to bring about, fulfill. *He has effected many improvements in management.* (n.) a result, consequence. *The effect of the fire was bankruptcy to the business.*

affidavit [af-ih-DAE-viht] statement written under oath.

affiliate to correct; to associate. (adj.) —liable.

affix [Af-fihks] (n.) something added; for example, a seal. [ah-FIHKS] (v.) to join to or add. See also **prefix**.

afflict Use with *with. He is afflicted with arthritis.*

INFLICT to cause to suffer; impose. *He inflicts his presence on them.*

affluence abundance; connotes plenty.

OPULENCE riches; connotes luxury.

Afghanistan [af-GAN-ihs-stahn] a country in central Asia. Proclaimed republic 1973. Cap.: Kabul [kah-BOOL]. Native: Afghan. Currency: Afghani.

A.F.L. (abbr.) American Federation of Labor: Pref. to *A.F. of L.* Used with -*CIO*, Congress of Industrial Relations. *ALF-CIO.*

afore— combining form meaning "before": *aforecited, aforesaid.* In most cases, AVOID as pedantic.

a fortiori [ae fawr-shih-OH-ree] (Lat.) on yet firmer grounds. In logic, used to introduce a fact previously mentioned, from which it follows. *He was a millionaire; a fortiori, the expense of the trip was not a factor.*

afoul in collision. From *run foul of (U.S.).*

afraid Never use directly before a noun. NOT: *An afraid child.*

afranchise to free from bondage or obligation.

ENFRANCHISE to set free; endow with citizenship or its privileges, esp. the right of suffrage.

Africa East, East Coast, North, South-West. West Coast.

African Refers generally to the Negro race. Current usage for American Negro includes *African American, Afro-American,* and *Black. See* **American.**

Afrikaner See **Union of South Africa.**

after- combining form meaning subsequent in time or place. For example, *afterbirth, afterthought, aftereffect.*

afterward subsequently. Pref. to *afterwards* in U.S.

again [uh-GEHN, or Brit., uh-GAEN]

against [uh-GEHNST or Brit., uh-GAENST]

agate line [AG-iht or AG-at] unit used in computing newspaper advertising rates = 5 1/2 points = approx. 1/14 inch. Also: agate type.

AGE Formal use requires figures for the age of persons and animals. *Paul Jones, 37 years old; a 9-year old girl; open to 3-year olds; 22 years of age; aged 22 years, aged 42 years 10 months 3 days.* Informal use allows spelling out: *a nine-year-old.* Avoid redundancy. NOT: *aged 22 years old.*

In a text, write out numbers greater than nine; *twenty-two years old.* Ages of inanimate objects are spelled out from one to nine, but use figures for numbers greater than nine. *A six-year voyage; the record was 16 years old.*

System also applies to figures besides age: *nine inches tall, 4,012 feet deep, eight miles high, 32 feet per second.* See: **animals.**

age aged [aejd], aging (v. or adj.). Also adj. combinations: ageless, agelong, age-old, age-stricken, age-weary.

agency legal relationship between a principal who authorizes and an agent who acts for him. Cap. if part of name; cap. standing alone only if referring to a federal unit: *Chippewa Agency;* the Agency. Omit periods and spacing in abbreviations of agencies of government, unions, associations, and committees.

agency shop place of employment where employees need not join a union but pay fees equivalent to union dues.

agencywide

agenda [uh-JEHN-duh] things to be done, or a list of such things. Sing. *agendum*, but pl. form used. *The agenda was amended.*

agent provocateur subversive agent who stimulates riot or revolt in order to expose opposition.

Ages Historic: capitalize historic and geological eras that are generally recognized. *Age of Discovery, Dark Ages, Elizabethan Age, Christian Era, Renaissance, the Bronze Age.* Use *Golden Age* referring to Pericles only.
 BUT: use lowercase *age* or *era when doing so would not be confusing to the reader. Cambrian age, Colonial days, Victorian period.* DO NOT capitalize eras not yet generally recognized as such: *missile age, space age, the age of MTV.* See also *NUMBERS.*

aggravate to worsen. NOT to annoy or irritate.

agreeable to NOT *with.*

aggregate [AG-ruh-gaet] (v.) to bring parts together into a whole. (n.) the total; also a mix of rocks for cement.

aghast [uh-GAST]

agile [AJ-ihl or AJ-iel]

ago Avoid redundancy. NOT: *It is scarcely a year ago since he died.* USE: *. . . that he died.* OR: *He died a year ago.*

AGREEMENT Nearly all verbs agree with their subject in number and person, but change form only in present tense.

Exceptions to the first rule include *may, can, might,* and a few others: *he may; she may; they may; George might; a few brave women might; you might.* The one exception to the second rule is *to be: I was; you were.*
 A pronoun agrees with its antecedent in person, number and gender. See also *NUMBER, PRONOUNS.*

agriculturist Pref. to *argiculturalist.*

AGRONOMIST specialist in soils and fields.

ague [AE-gyoo] a shaking chill.

Ahkmatova, Anna [ahk-mah-TOE-vah] (1889-1966) Russian poet.

"Aida" [ah-EE-da] an opera by Verdi.

aid [aed] (n., v.) help. *Aide [aed]* often used for *assistant,* both civilian and military. *Nurse's aide.*

aide-de-camp [AED-dee-kamp] officer who is a general's personal assistant. (pl.) aides-de-camp.

aide-memoire [AEED-MAE-mwahr] notes to refresh memory.

AIDS [AEDS] Acquired Immune Deficiency Syndrome.

aigrette [AE-gret] spray of feathers.

EGRET [EE-greht] heron.

aim at *Aim for* is colloquial; *aim to be* is correct.

ain't Accepted by some authorities in the sense of "am I not" *(ain't I),* but still considered ungrammatical by most authorities. NOT accepted for *is not, are not, have not, had not.*

airbase *-blast, -blown, -borne, -bound, -brake, -brush, -burst, -cargo, -coach, -craft, -crew, -crewman, -drome, -drop, -field, -flow, -foil, - frame, -freight, -gap, -glow, -hammer, -head, -hole, -hose, -lane, - lift, -line* (aviation), *-liner, -link, -load, -mail, -man, -mark,* (n.) *-marker, -mass, -park, -path, -photo, -plane, -port* (all meanings), *-power, -scoop, -ship, -show, -sick, -sickness, -sleeve, -space, -speed, -stream, -strike, -strip, -tight, -ward, -wave, -way, -wise, -worthy* (all one word).

(adj.) air-blasted. (v.) air-condition. (n. or adj.) air-conditioning. (v.) air-cool, air-dry (use hyphens).

air bends, air duct, air embolism, air raid, air sac, air time (radio and TV), air well (all two words).

Airedale terrier [AER-dael]

Air Force Air Explorers; Air France; Air National Guard; Civil Air Patrol, Civil Patrol, the patrol; Command; Reserve; Reserve Officers' Training Corps; WAF, Women in the Air Force; Air Force Academy, the Academy.

AK (abbr.) Alaska.

a/k/a (abbr.) also known as. *Robert Zimmerman, a/k/a Bob Dylan.* Also correct without slash: aka. See **alias.**

AL (abbr.) Alabama.

Alabama [A-la-BAM-ah] U.S. state. abbr: AL. Cap.: Montgomery.

a la king in a seasoned cream sauce.

a la Marengo [ah-la mah-REHNG-goh] with mushrooms or truffles.

Alamo [AL-uh-moh] Texas fortress and battle site during War of Independence, 1836.

à la carte (Fr.) On the side.

a la mode or **a la mode** in a special fashion; with ice cream.

Alaska [uh-LAS-kuh] U.S. State. abbr.: AK. Cap. Juneau [JOO-noh].

Albania [al-BAE-nih-uh] In SW Balkans. Cap. Tirana Native: Albanian. Currency: lek, quidar.

albeit [awl-BEE-iht] even though.

Alberta province in Canada. Cap.: Edmonton.

albino [al-BIE-noh] person or animal lacking skin and hair pigment. (pl.) —s.

albumen [al-BYOO-mihn] egg white.

ALBUMIN (chem) protein found in blood; also in eggs, milk, meat.

Albuquerque [AL-buh-KUHR-kee] city in New Mexico.

Aleutian Islands [al-OO-sh'n] chain of islands extending west from Alaska.

al fresco [al FREHS-koh] (Ital.) in the open air. See **fresco.**

algebra [AL-jeh-bruh] branch of mathematics dealing with the relations and properties of numbers.

algae [AL-jee] low form of plant life. Pl. of alga [AL-juh].

Algeria [al-JEER-ih-uh] Formerly French North Africa. Proclaimed republic, 1961. Cap. Algiers [al-JEERS] Native: Algerians. Currency: dinar.

alias [AE-lih-uhs] See a/k/a; **nom de plume**.

alibi [AL-ih-bie] plea of having been elsewhere. Colloq., any excuse. *What's your alibi for last night?*

alien [AEL-yehn] strange; different; belonging to another country. (v.) —ate; (adj.) —able.

alien to Preferred to *alien from*.

alight step down; dismount; descend. (v.) —ighted.

align to line up. (n.) —ment

aliquot part [AL-uh-kwaht] a part of a number that divides the whole with no remainder.

alkali [AL-kuh-lie] acrid, soluble salts with ability to neutralize acids. (pl.) —is or —ies. Mined from *alkaline earth*.

all With singular noun, the whole; with plural noun, the total or everyone. NEVER: *all's*.

Allah [AHL-lah] Moslem God. See Islam.

all-American ALSO: all-clear, all-out, all-round (adj.); all fours, all hail, all in, (n. and adj.) all star.

allege [uh-LEHJ] to state without positive proof. As a disclaimer of responsibility for a statement, for example in libel actions., the action has no legal value.

Alleghany [AL-ee-gae-nee] the name of counties in New York, Maryland, and Virginia. In Pennsylvania, the name of mountains, a river, a city, and a county.

allegory illustrative story in which characters and events represent particular things and ideas; a sustained metaphor. See: **parable.**

allegretto [al-eh-GREHT-oh] (Ital.) not quite as quick as allegro.

allegro [al-LAE-groh] (Ital.) brisk, lively.

Allende Gassens, Salvador [ah-YEHN-dae] (1908-1973 President of Chile, 1970-1973. Died during coup.

alliances (World Wars) Allied Powers, the powers; BUT: European powers. *N.Y. Times* lowercases references to post-W.W. II alliances and allies: NATO allies, CENTO allies, Western allies. BUT cap. W.W. I and W.W. II alliances: Axis, Allied. Also any alliances where name includes Allies or Allied.

alliteration in rhetoric, repetition of the same sounds in sequence of words. *"The sad sea-sounding wastes of Lyonesse."*

all of Eliminate *of* unless followed by a pronoun: *all of us; all the books.* NOT: *all of the books.*

allot —tting; (n.) allottee.

allow of to permit.

ALLOW FOR to leave a margin.

alloy [AL-oi] combination of two or more metals.

all ready prepared. *These campers are all ready to leave.*

ALREADY previously. *But those other campers have already gone.*

all right Formal English still requires two words, no hyphen. General use allows *alright*.

all-round General use allows *all around*.

allspice [AWL-spiess] berry and aromatic leaf from allspice tree; pimento. NOT: *allspices*.

all together the group in unison.

ALTOGETHER entirely.

allude to make an indirect reference. (n.) allusion. NOT: *He alluded to Mr. Olson by name.*
Distinguish from

REFER to mention directly. *Although his statement alluded to a previous marriage, he never referred to a former wife.*

ELUDE to avoid or evade. (n.) elusion. *The criminal eluded the police for months.*

ILLUSION a fanciful but not harmful impression. *His stage sets were so clever, they created the illusion of living in Wonderland.*

DELUSION a false belief. *He is under the delusion that someone is persecuting him.*

ally [(v.) a-LIE or (n.) AL-lie] (n.) an associate. (pl.) allies.

ALLEY a narrow passageway. *There is an alley between the two buildings.* (pl.) alleys.

alma mater [al-muh MAE-ter; AHL-muh MAH-tehr]. (Lat.) foster mother; one's school.

almanac —ack is archaic.

almighty

almost closer than *nearly*. *Almost no, scarcely any, hardly any, practically no.* NOT: *almost quite.*

alone See: *PLACEMENT OF WORDS.*

along with one, in company. *He took a book along.* Meaning "approximately" is colloquial, and even in speech requires *about*. *We got home along about dinner time.*

aloof [uh-LOOF] removed; reserved.

A.L.R. (abbr.) American Law Reports.

already (adv.) *Already existing* is redundant. See **all ready.**

Alsatian [al-SAE-shun] Breed of dog.

also (adv.) Can be used in combination: *which, also, and also.* See and.

also-ran (n. and adj.) (pl.) also-rans.

altar a table for worship. *The minister stood at the altar.*

ALTER to change; modify. *She gained so much weight that her clothes had to be altered.*

alternate [AWL-tuhr-NAET] (v.) to occur in turns. (adj.) arranged by turns. *The young women sat in alternate rows.* (adv.) alternately. ALSO: (n.) a choice, a substitute. *He's my alternate for this committee.* See **alternative.**

alternative (n.) a choice between two things or among several; a substitute. (adv.) alternatively.
*They had no alternative. The alternatives are liberty and (*NOT or*) death. The only alternative is war or (*NOT and*) surrender. The (*NOT other*) alternative is to surrender. The only alternatives is to surrender are arming and (*NOT or*) fightings.*
Webster's lists *alternate* and *alternative* as synonyms.

although More formal and emphatic than *though.* Only *though* may be used as an adverb and the idiom *as though.*

altogether entirely. *This is altogether too weak to hold us.*

ALL TOGETHER all in one place. *We are all together now.*

aluminum [a-LOO-mih-nuhm]

alumnus [a-LUHM-nuhs] (pl.) alumni (masc. or both masc. and fem.); When sing. fem., alumna [-nah]. (pl. fem.) alumnae.

always (adv.) all the time.

ALL WAYS in all possible manners.

A.M. (abbr.) amplitude modulation.

a.m. (abbr.) ante meridiem, NOT meridian. When printed generally AM small caps and no points. Avoid redundancy. NOT: *9 AM in the morning* or *9 o'clock AM.*

A.M.A. (abbr.) American Medical Association; American Marketing Association; American Management Association.

amanuensis [a-man-yoo'-EHN-sihs] a secretary. (pl.) —enses.

amateur [AM-uh-chehr or AM-uh-tuhr] (n. and adj.) non-professional. See Also **Connoisseur, dilettante, novice.**

Ambassador, ambassadorial Ambassador John J. Smith; John J. Smith, Ambassador to India; the Ambassador. BUT: *a meeting for ambassadors; an ambassador of goodwill.*

ambassador (American) ADDRESS: His Excellency the American Ambassador to France; The Honorable Benjamin Franklin, American Ambassador to France. SALUTATION: Sir; Your Excellency; My dear Mr. Ambassador.

ambassador (Foreign) the Ambassador; the Senior Ambassador, His Excellency Extraordinary and Plenipotentiary; Ambassador at Large. ADDRESS: His Excellency the Ambassador of Great Britain, or His Excellency, the Rt. Hon. Sir Graham

Greer Pitt, Ambassador of Great Britain. SALUTATION: Sir; Excellency; Your Excellency; Dear Mr. Ambassador.

ambassador at large Capitalize when referring to a specific person holding official title. (pl.) ambassadors —.

ambergris [AM-behr-gree] whale product used in perfume.

ambidextrous able to use both hands with equal facility; ambidexterity. (adv. —ly. (n.) —ness.

ameliorate [uh-MEEL-yuh-raet] to make better. (adj.) —rable.

amen [AE-MEN For singing: AH-MEN].

amendment Social Security Amendments of 1954, 1954 amendments, the social security amendments, the amendments; Tobey amendment to the Constitution (U.S.). *N.Y. Times* prefers capitals when referring to a specific U.S. constitutional amendment: *First Amendment*. Spell out first to ninth, use figures for 10th and higher.

amenity [uh-MEHN-ih-tee, uh-MEE-nih-tee] civility; social nicety. (pl.) —ties.

America, Americas In use, *America* generally refers to the U.S.

Technically the term includes all of North and South America.

Similarly, *Americans* generally refers to citizens of the U.S., and *American* to things of the U.S. *American lit-*

erature means U.S. writers, like Emily Dickinson; Gabriel Garcia Marquez, from Colombia, is considered part of *Latin American literature.*

If the context makes the meaning clear, *American* may be used to refer to things of the two continents together. But for *Canadian bacon, Mexican hats,* and the like, the country of origin helps to clarify and is preferred.

-American For racial designations within the U.S., current use prefers country or continent of origin plus this suffix.

African-American refers to those of Negro race. *Afro-American* and *black* are still acceptable.

Arab-American refers to those from the Middle East and, generally, the Indian subcontinent.

Asian-American refers to those of Oriental race. *Chinese American, Japanese American,* etc. can be used when appropriate, and usually appear without hyphens.

Hispanic American, refers to those of Central or South American stock, and generally appears without hyphens.

Native Americans, without the hyphen, refers to North America's aboriginal inhabitants.

In these cases and others, designation by country or tribe of origin can be useful: *Jamaican, Pakistani, Philippine, Navajo.*

BUT such designations are also limiting, and can even be taken as derogatory, since they ignore the person's present status as a citizen of the U.S. See also ***RACIST LANGUAGE;***

SEXIST LANGUAGE, **PERSON;**
COLOR, PERSON OF.

AMERICAN American Friends Service Committee (AFSC); the committee; American Gold Star Mothers,
Inc., Gold Star Mothers, a Mother;
the American Legion; American Veterans of World War II (AMVETS); etc.

Americana [uh-mehr-ih-KAE-nuh,
uh-mehr-ihKAH-nuh] collection of
documents, facts, etc., pertaining to
U.S.

American plan in hotels, a plan in
which room and board are included
in the charges. See: **European plan.**

American Stock Exchange On Wall
Street, New York City.

America's Cup yachting race and
trophy. Without hyphen, golf match
and trophy.

amiable [AE-mih-ab'l] good na-
tured; describes person.

> AMICABLE   [AM-ih-kuh-b'l]
> friendly; describes relationship or
> event.

amicus curiae [AM-ih-kuhs KYOO-
ree-ie] (Lat.) friend of the court.
Hence, a brief entered by one not a
party to a lawsuit who may have an
interest in the result.

amid Pref. to *amidst.*

amidship the middle of a ship.

Amin, Idi [EE-dee AH-meen] (1925-
1979) Ugandan prime minister, 1971.

President for life, 1976. Executed
1979.

Amish [AHM-ish] (adj.) of an orthodox sect of the Mennonites, from Ja-
cob Amen. Also (n.) the sect.

Amnesty International Worldwide
human-rights organization. Abbr:
A.I.

amoeba [a-MEE-ba] single-cell animal (pl.) —s or —bae [—bee].

among Used with groups of three or
more. For two, use *between. He divided
the silver among his four henchmen, but
he divided the gold between his wife and
himself.* Avoid *amongst* (archaic).

amoral [ae-MAW-ral] not involving
moral principles. *"The survival of the
fit" is amoral—a law of nature.*

> IMMORAL contrary to moral prin-
> ciple. *Child abuse is immoral.*

amortization process of extinguish-
ing the value of an asset or liability as
carried in the books of a company.

amount Use for bulk, mass.

> NUMBER Use for individuals,
> units.

amour [uh-MOOR] love affair.

ampere abbr.: a

ampersand (&) Use only in names
and titles to follow form: *Baltimore &
Ohio Railroad.* B. & O.

amplitude modulation (See A.M.)
Radio reception process. See Also:
frequency modulation, FM.

19

ampoule, [am-POOL] **ampule** or **ampul** [AM-pyool] hermetically sealed vessel containing material for injection. *Ampule* most common.

amuck or **amok** [uh-MUHK] in a frenzied manner.

amyl nitrate [AM-'l NIE-traet] heart-attack relief.

an As an article, use before vowel sounds: *an AEC report, an FCC rule, an 11 year-old, an VIII class, an herbseller, an NSC request, an RFC investigation.* See also **a.**

anachronistic [uh-nak-ron-nihs-tihk] out of its proper historical time; for example, a doubloon in Las Vegas. NOT: *anachronic.*

anacoluthon [an-uh-koh-LYOO-thahn] in grammar, the abrupt shift from one uncompleted construction to another: *There's no reason to—all right, go ahead.*

Also, construction that does not follow logically from another. *If he is bright and there are books for everyone why is he not well read?* See **non sequitur.**

analogous [an-AL-oh-guhs] (adj.) similar in some attributes. (n.) **analogy** a metaphor; likeness between attributes of two things. *The kingdom of heaven is like a mustard seed.* (v.), —gize. (n.) —gist.

analyst one who analyzes: *an investment analyst.* Also abbr. form for psychoanalyst.

ANNALIST a chronicler. *A sum-mary of the year was prepared by the annalist.*

analyze to break into fundamental elements; study in detail. Pref. to Brit. *analyse.* (adj.) analytic, analytical, (adv.) —cally.

anathema [uh-NATH-uh-muh] a curse; cursed object.

ancestress USE: *ancestor.*

anchovy [an-CHOH-vee, AN-choh-vee]

Ancient Free and Accepted Mason a Mason, a Freemason.

and May be used to begin a sentence.

Joining parts of a subject signals a plural verb. *The pros and cons have been discussed.*

BUT when the parts form a unit, use the singular verb. *Dollars and cents is the chief issue. Tomorrow and tomorrow and tomorrow creeps in this petty pace.*

In a series, must connect something common to all NOT: *He often writes to his mother, talks to his wife and business associate.* It would be correct to say: *talks to his wife and telephones his business associate.*

AVOID use of *and* as a substitute for *to.* NOT: *He'll try and do it.* See **also, which.**

The use of the comma before *and* in a series—*His mother, wife, and child*—is still a matter of disagreement. The movement is away from the comma before *and.*

and/or Avoid when possible. Expression is usually best limited to business and law.

The number of the following verb is determined by the singular or plural concept. *Any check and/or cash paid* considered as one unit) *is entered in the book. Any money and/or jewelry found* (considered as various items) *are his.*

and which, and who Use only after *which* and *who: Women who work, and who also keep house, suffer enormous stress.* Verb which follows must agree in number, tense, and person with main verb in antecedent's clause; See **parallelism, parallel structure**. NOT: *Stout people of middle age and who don't work should watch their diets.*

Andean [an-DEE-'n, AN-dee'h] pertaining to the Andes [AN-dees] South American mountain system.

Andorra [an-DAWR-uh] Principality in Pyrenees mountains between France and Spain. Established 1278. Native: Andorran. Currency: Fr. franc, Span. peseta.

android [AN-droid] in science fiction, a machine-made human; a robot capable of speech and thought.

Andromeda [an-DRAHM-e-duh] Princess in Greek mythology. In astronomy, a constellation and galaxy.

anemia [a-NEE-mee-ya] condition in which red blood corpuscles are low in hemoglobin or reduced in number. (adj.) —ic.

anemone [uh-NEHM-oh-nee] white, star-shaped flowers.

Also:

SEA ANEMONE invertebrate marine animal resembling the flower.

anaesthetic [an-ehs-THET-ihk] (n.) an agent that causes loss of feeling or sensation.

aneurism [AN-yoo-rihs'm] in medicine, a permanent, blood-filled sac in an artery.

angel [AENj'l] supernatural messenger.

ANGLE [ANG-g'l] corner.

angina pectoris [an-JIE-nuh PEHK-toe-rihs] disease characterized by chest pain and feeling of suffocation.

angle hook anglemeter, anglesight, anglewing, anglewise, angleworm; angle iron.

anglicized changed to conform with English style.

Angola [an-GOH-luh] republic in SW Africa, on Atlantic. Former Portugese colony. Est. 1975. Cap.: Luanda. Native: Angolan. Currency: Kwanza.

angstrom abbr: A. Unit of length, named after Swedish physicist. 0.000 000 1 mm. =0.0001 micron =0.1 millimicron=0.000 000 004 in.

Anheuser Busch [AHN-hie-zuhr]

ANIMALS Terms used for male, female, young, and group of well-known species are listed in the table below.

Animal	Male	Female	Young
antelope	buck, bull	doe, cow	calf
bear	he-bear	she-bear	whelp
beaver	—	—	kit
bison	bull	cow	calf
bovine	bull (steer castrated)	cow	calf
cat	tom	tabby	kitten
chicken	rooster, cock (capon castrated)	hen	chick
deer	hart, stag buck, ram	doe	fawn
dog	dog	bitch	puppy
duck	drake	duck	duckling
elephant	bull	cow	calf
fox	dog	vixen, bitch	whelp, cub
goose	gander	goose	gosling
giraffe	bull	cow	calf
goat	buck, ram, billy	nannygoat	kid
horse	stallion (gelding, castrated)	mare	colt, filly (f.)
hippopotamus	bull	cow	calf
kangaroo	buck	doe	joey
lion	lion	lioness	cub
moose	bull	cow	calf
pig	hog	sow	farrow, piglet
rabbit	buck	doe	bunny
rat	buck	doe	—
reindeer	buck	cow	calf
rhinoceros	bull	cow	calf
seal	bull	cow	baby
shark	bull	cow	—
sheep	ram	ewe	lamb
swan	cob	pen	cygnet
tiger	tiger	tigress	whelp, cub
turkey	tom	hen	—
walrus	bull	cow	calf
weasel	boar	weasel	—
wolf	dog	bitch	whelp, cub

ANIMAL COLLECTIVES

ants	colony	moles	labor
apes	shrewdness	monkeys	troop
asses	pace	mules	barren
badgers	cete	nightingales	watch
bass	shoal	owls	parliament
bears	sloth	peacocks	covey
bees	swarm or colony	ponies	string
		pups	litter
birds	flock	quail	covey, bevy
bison	troop or herd	rabbits	nest
bovine	herd	ravens	unkindness
caterpillars	army	reindeer	herd
cats	clowder	rhinoceroses	crash
cattle	drove	seals	pod, trip, herd, school
chickens	peep		
colts	rag	sheep	flock, drove
crows	murder	sparrows	host
dogs	pack	squirrels	dray
doves	dule	storks	mustering
ducks	school, paddling	swine	sounder
		toads	knot
eggs	clutch	trout	hover
elephants	herd	turkeys	rafter
elk	gang	turtles	bale, bevy
finches	charm	whales	gam, herd, pod, shoal
fish	school		
foxes	skulk	wolves	pack
geese	flock, gaggle or plum, in flight, skein		
goats	trip		
hares	down or husk		
hawks	cast		
hens	brood		
hogs	drift		
horses	herd		
jellyfish	smack		
kangaroos	troop		
kittens	kindle		
larks	exaltation		
leopards	leap		
lions	pride		
locusts	host or plague		

animals' ages Usu. in figures. *I sold my 2-year-olds.*

anisette [a-nih-SEHT] (Fr., Sp., *anis*) a sweet liqueur.

anklebone (adj.) ankle-deep.

Annapolis [uh-NAP-uh-lihs] site of U.S. Naval Academy, MD.

annex (v.)[uh-NEHKS] (n.) [AN-ehks] (n.) Cap. if part of building's name; the annex.

annihilate [uh-NIE-ih-laet; -hih-laet] —lable.

anniversaries biennial (2nd); triennial (3rd); quadrennial (4th); quintennial (5th); sexennial (6th); septennial (7th); octennial (8th); novennial (9th); decennial (10th); undecennial (11th); duodecennial (12th); quindecennial (15th); jubilee (25th, and also 50th); centennial (100th); sesquicentennial (150th); bicentennial (200th); trentenary (300th); quadricentennial (400th); sexcentenary (600th); millennial (1000th).

For 100-year periods, an alternative to the —ary ending is —centenary: bicentenary, tercentenary, quadricentenary, quincentenary, sexcentenary, septingentenary, etc.

DESIGNATIONS 1st, paper, clocks; 2nd, cotton, china; 3rd, leather, crystal, glass; 4th, fruit, flowers, silk, electrical appliances; 5th, wood, silverware; 6th, sugar and candy, iron, wood; 7th, wool, copper, desk sets; 8th, bronze, pottery, linen, laces; 9th, willow, pottery, leather; 10th, tin, aluminum, diamond jewelry; 11th, steel accessories; 12th, silk, linen, pearls, gems; 13th, lace, textiles, furs; 14th, ivory, gold jewelry; 15th, crystal, watches; 16th, silver holloware; 17th, furniture; 18th, porcelain; 19th, bronze; 20th, china, platinum; 25th, silver; 30th, pearl, diamond; 35th, coral, jade; 40th, ruby; 45th, sapphire; 50th, golden; 55th, emerald; 60th and 75th, diamond.

annuity [ah-NYOO-ih-tee] sums paid annually.

annul [uh-NUHL] to cancel; make void (v. and adj.) —lling, —lled.

anomalous [a-NAHM-a-luhs] abnormal; irregular. (n.) anomaly, —lism. (adj. —listic.

anomie [an-oh-MEE] (From Fr. social science) disorientation and lack of spirit, both in a person and in society. (adj.) anomic.

anonymous [a-NAHN-ih-muhs] Abbr: anon.

anorexia [an-oh-REHK-see-ah] eating disorder involving extreme lack of appetite. Usually a psychological condition, *anorexia nervosa* [nur-VOH-sah].

another *Another person is coming.* NOT: *Another person is coming, too.* And: *She prefers some kind or other.* NOT: *She prefers some kind or another.*

answer (n. or v.)

Antarctic [ant-AHRK-tihk] The continent is Antarctica. Antarctic Circle, Antarctic Ocean, Antarctic Treaty. BUT: antarctic regions, antarctic ice.

ante- [AN-tee] prefix meaning "before." Omit the hyphen except before proper nouns and words beginning with *e*: *antebellum, antemeridian, anteroom.* See antedate.

ANTI-[AN-tih] prefix meaning against or opposite. G.P.O. hyphenates before vowels and words of more recent usage: *anti-intellectual, anti-rock'n'roll.* N.Y. *Times* prefers *antiaircraft, antisocial, antitrust.* Hyphenate before a proper noun: *anti-Freud, anti-British.* BUT: *Antichrist.*

ANTECEDENT in grammar, the word or words that are represented by a pronoun. The pronoun must agree with the noun in person, number, and gender.

The antecendent must be identified (not merely implied) whenever practical. NOT: *Notwithstanding the stenographer's fatigue, it was typed perfectly.*

See *GENERAL REFERENCE, PRONOUN*

antedate [an-tee-DAET] (v.) to fix a date earlier than the actual one. (n.) the date so used. Also (v.) to anticipate; precede.

antediluvian [-dih-LOO-vee-an] before the Deluge. (By extension) very old; antiquated.

antenna [an-TEHN-uh] (pl.) —s. In zoology, (pl.) —ae, —ee.

anthracite [AN-thrah-siet] hard coal.

anthrax [AN-thraks] an animal disease.

anti- See **ante.**

antibiotic (n. and adj.) (pl.) —s.

anticipate to do beforehand; expect. NOT *believe.*

Antietam [an-TEE-tam] Maryland site of 1862 Civil War battle.

Antigua and Barbuda [ann-TEE-gua or -ah; barr-BU-dah] island

country in Caribbean. Former Br. colony; independent 1981. Cap: St. John. Native: Antiguan, Barbudan. Currency: East Caribbean dollar.

Antilles [an-TIH-lees] group of islands in Caribbean.

antiphrasis [an-TIHF-rah-sihs] the use of a word in a sense opposite to the usual meaning, as in irony. *Putting out the garbage is a herculean task.* (pl.) —es. (adj.) —stic.

antipode [AN-tih-pohd; an-TIHP-oh-dee] two points on the earth's surface directly opposite each other. Hence, opposite; contrary. (pl.) —s. (adj.) —dal.

antithesis [an-TIHTH-uh-sihs] in rhetoric, placing contrasting phrases in sequence or parallel. *They promised food and provided famine.* Hence, any contrast. (pl.) —ses.

antonym [AN-tuh-nihm] Word with opposite meaning from another. *Bad is the antonym of good.* SEE **synonym, heteronym.**

anxious full of anxiety. NOT eager.

any, anyone, anybody, anything all take singular verbs.

anyhow, anywhere (NOT anywheres) are adverbs and single words. BUT: *any more; anybody else.*

anyone any person. BUT: *Any one of these three will do.*

anyway (adv.) in any case. *Anyway, I will try.*
    Compare to

ANY WAY *Any one way. Any way he chooses is all right.*

Anzio [AHN-tsyoh; AN-zih-oh] seacoast town south of Rome. Scene of 1944 landings and battle.

Anzus (abbr.) Australia, New Zealand, U.S. alliance.

Apache [uh-PATCH-ee] Native American tribe in SW (pl.) —s. [-eez]. In French, lowercase [uh-PASH] Paris underworld person.

apart from aside from.

apartheid [ah-PAHRT-hiet] in South Africa, separation of races by law.

apartment (Brit.) a single room.

aperitif [uh-par-uh-TEEF] an alcoholic drink served before dinner.

aphelion [uh-FEE-lih-uhn; uh-FEEL-yuhn] point on an elliptical orbit around the sun that is farthest from the sun. (For the earth, about 94,500,000 miles.)

aphid [AE-fihd] plant louse. (pl.) —s.

Aphrodite [Ah-froh-DIE-tee] Greek goddess of love and beauty.

A.P.I. (abbr.) American Petroleum Institute.

apiary [AE-pee-ehr-ee] place where bees are kept. (pl.) —ies.

apiece to each. *At the movies we got a candy bar apiece.*
Compare to

A PIECE a fragment.

apish [AEP-ish] like an ape, silly or affected.

A.P.A. (abbr.) American Psychological Association.

A.P.O. (abbr.) Army post office.

Aprocrypha [ah-PAH-krih-fah] holy writings excluded from official Bible. Hence **apocryphal** (adj.) untrue, invalidated.

apogee [AH-poh-jee] point in the orbit of an Earth satellite at which satellite is closest to the Earth. See **perigee.**

apologia [ap-oh-LOH-jih-uh] a formal apology, especially in defense of an idea. (pl.) apologias.

a posteriori [ae-pahs-TEE-rih-OH-ri] (Lat.) reasoning by generalizing principles from observed facts. See **a priori.**

apostle one who hears and teaches principles. The Twelve Apostles; the Apostle John.

APOSTATE one who has abandoned principles.

Apostles' Creed Christian statement of faith from 2nd C.

APOSTROPHE (') (1) Used to indicate the omission of letters or numbers in a contraction: *haven't; I've. '76.* BUT NOT in abbreviations: *Sgt., phone, Frisco.* (2) Used in the possessive forms of nouns: *John's, boys'. America's.* BUT NOT personal pronouns: *hers, its, theirs.* (3) Used in the plural of figures and letters: *P's and Q's, the 60's . . .* BUT: Some style books allow omission of apostrophe in such cases: *Please review the 1040s. Remember those fabulous 50s?* Conventions will differ. See also: **do's and dont's.**

The apostrophe should not be used after names of countries and other organized bodies ending in *s,* or after words more descriptive than possessive (not indicating personal possession), except when plural does not end in *s: United States control Southern States industries; Bureau of Ships report.* BUT: *Children's Hospital.* EXCEPTION: Veterans' Administration (so specified in the law).

Many common expressions technically require an apostrophe, but may appear without one, given their wide usage: *for goodness' sake, a day's pay, the sun's rays, at death's door, the earth's orbit, ten dollars' worth, stone's throw.*

See also *PRONOUNS, POSSESSIVES.*

apostrophe [uh-PAHS-troh-fee] in rhetoric, a digression or aside addressed to an absent person, a thing, or an idea. *''O judgment, thou art fled to brutish beasts.''*

apothegm [ah-PAH-theh-g'm] maxim.

apotheosis [uh-pahth-ee-OH-sihs] Literally, a rising to stature of a god; a glorification. (pl.) —oses [-seez].

appall —ed, —ing.

Appalachia [a-pah-LAE-chyah]

mountain area from Pennsylvania to Alabama, known for extreme poverty.

apparatus [ap-uh-RAE-tuhs, ap-pa-RAHT-uhs] (pl) —tuses or —tus.

apparel (n.) clothes. (v.) to dress. —ed.

apparent [uh-PAR-ehnt] —ly.

appendix Usu. lower case: appendix i, A, II, etc.; the appendix. BUT cap. when part of title: *Appendix II: Education Directory.* (pl.) —dices, —dixes; esp. med. —dices. abbr.: app., apps.

applicable [AP-lih-kuh-b'l] suitable; pertinent.

appliqué [AP-lih-KAE] ornamentation laid on in relief.

Appomattox [ap-oh-MAT-aks] river and town in Virginia. Scene of surrender ending Civil War, 1865.

apposite [AP-oh-zeht] appropriate, relevant.

appositive a word or group of words used as a noun and placed after another noun, denoting the same person or thing. Words in apposition are usu. not essential to the sentence's meaning, and are set off by commas or dashes. *Johnny, that little genius, is already reading classics like* The Scarlet Letter.

appreciate [uh-PREE-shee-AET] to recognize the worthiness of. NOT a substitute for understand, as in *I appreciate your point.* In business, increase in value. (adj.) —ciable, (n.) —ciation.

apprehend (v.) to perceive; anticipate fearfully. **apprehensible** capable of being understood.

  COMPREHEND to include; understand.

apprise [ah-PRIEZ] to inform. *Apprise me of our situation.*

  APPRIZE *(same pronunc.)* to appraise for value.

approx (abbr.) approximately.

apricot [AE-pri-kaht, AP-ri-kaht]

April April-fool (v. and adj.); BUT (n.) April fool.

a priori [AH-prih-OH-rie; AE-prie-OH-rie; AH-prie-OH-rie; AH-prih-OH-ree] (Lat.) reasoning from principles considered self-evident; denotes that which may be known through reason alone, without experiences. See **a posteriori.**

apropos [ap-roh-POH] suitably; with respect to.

aqua [AK-kwa] combining prefix meaning water: aquamarine, —meter; —plane, —tint, —tone; aqua fortis, aqua green.

aquarium (pl.) —iums pref. to —ia.

Aquarius [ah-KWAER-ee-uhs] born Jan. 21-Feb. 18. See **Zodiac.**

aquavit NOT akavit. Caraway-flavored liqueur.

aquiline [AK-kwi-lien or -lihn] curving, hooked.

Aquinas, St. Thomas [uh-KWIE-nas] (1275-1335) Italian theologian.

AR Arkansas.

Arab (adj.) of the Arabs; specif. *Arab horse.* For Arab names, See *NAMES.* See also American.

  ARABIAN of Arabia or Arabs: *Arabian desert.*

  ARABIC [AR-uh-bihk] (n.) the Arab language. (adj.) pertaining to Arabic or Arabians.

Arab League loose confederation including Egypt, Iraq, Jordan, Saudi Arabia, Syria, Lebanon, Yemen, Tunisia, Morocco, Sudan, Algeria, Kuwait, Libya, others. Founded 1975.

Arabic numerals 1,2,3, etc. See *NUMBERS, ROMAN NUMBERS.*

Arapaho [uh-RAP-uh-hoh] Native American tribe.

arbiter [AHR-bih-tehr] one empowered to settle a dispute. Arbitrator [-TRAE-t'r], according to *Webster's,* is a synonym.

arbitrage [AHR-bih-trazh] the dealing of same securities in separate markets in order to profit from price differences.

arbor garden, orchards; shaded retreat. Arborway.

arboretum [ahr-boh-REE-tuhm] park with trees and shrubs grown

for scientific or educational purposes. (pl.) —tums.

A.R.C. (abbr.) American Red Cross.

arc arced, arcing.

arcana [ahr-KAE-nah] secrets. Pl. of
arcanum (rare).

arch- [ahrch- except in *archangel*,
AHRK] combining form meaning
chief: *archbishop, archduke.*

archaic [ahr-KAE-ihk] applied to
words, indicates an early usage not
often applied in modern context.
Abbr: arch.

Archbishop (Anglican) ADDRESS:
His Grace the Lord Archbishop of
London. SALUTATION: My Lord
Archbishop; Your Grace.

Archbishop (Catholic) ADDRESS:
The Most Reverend Francis P.
Keogh, Archbishop of Baltimore,
Baltimore, Md.
   SALUTATION: Your Excellency.
Brit.: The Most Reverend Arch-
bishop Keogh (followed by postal
address). SALUTATION: Your
Grace; My Lord; My Lord Arch-
bishop.

Archdeacon ADDRESS: The Vener-
able Sidney Smith, Archdeacon of
San Francisco. SALUTATION: Ven-
erable Sir; Dear Archdeacon Smith.

arche—, archi— [AHR-kih] prefix
meaning chief (*architect*) or original,
primitive *archeology).*

archetype [AHR-kee-tiep] original;
the root form.

PROTOTYPE [PROH-toh-tiep]
Earliest manmade version.

Archimedes [ahr-kih-MEE-deeze]
(c.237-212 B.C.). Greek mathematician, inventor. *Archimedes screw* (no
apostrophe).

Archipelago [ahrk-ih-PEHL-uh-
goh] Capitalize in singular when
following a name. Philippine Archipelago; the archipelago. See **Gulag.**

architect [AHR-kih-tehtk] building
designer.

archives [AHR-kievs] can be proper
name: the Archives.

Archivist of the United States
[AHR-kih-vihst, or -kie-] the Archivist.

-archy suffix meaning form of government: *oligarchy, anarchy.*

arctic [AHRK-tihk] pertaining to
North Pole region. Arctic Circle,
Current, Ocean; arctic clothing, conditions, fox, grass, night, seas, BUT:
subarctic, the arctics, arctics (overshoes).

area Cap. if part of name: Cape
Hatteras Recreational Area; the area.
BUT: free-trade area; Metropolitan
Washington area.

arena (pl.) arenas.

Arendt, Hannah [AH-rehnt] (1906-
1975) German-American writer, philosopher. Coined phrase "banality of
evil."

Argentina [ahrjehn-TEEN-uh] republic in SE South America. Independent 1816. Cap. Buenos Aires. Native: Argentine [AHR-jehn-teen—TIEN]. Currency: peso, centavo.

Argonne [ahr-GAHN] wooded plateau along French-Belgian border. Scene of W.W.I. and W.W. II battles.

argot [AHR-goh] street slang; criminal slang. See **Language.**

aria [AH-ree-ah] sweet melody, usu. in opera.

Aries [AER-eez] Born March 20-April 19. See Zodiac.

arise (p.) arose. (p.p.) arisen. See **arouse.**

aristocrat [uh-RIHS-toh-krat, AR-ihs-tohkrat] (n. or adj.) one of a privileged or ruling class; pertaining to such a class. (adj. aristocratic [uh-riss-toh-KRAT-ihk].

Aristophanes [AR-ihs-TAH-fan-eez] (c. 450-388 B.C.) Greek comic playwright (*The Birds, The Frogs).*

Aristotle [AR-ihs-taht'l] (384-322 B.C.) Greek philosopher (*Poetics).*

Arizona [ah-rih-ZOH-nah] U.S. state. abbr: AZ. Native: Arizonian or Arizonan. Cap.: Phoenix.

Arkansas [AHR-kan-saw] U.S. state. abbr: AR. Native: Arkansan. Cap: Little Rock.

Arlington National Cemetery

arm (pl.) arms. In sing., use *weapon.*

armada [ahr-MAH-duh] fleet of military ships or airplanes.

armadillo [ahr-mah-DIHL-oh] armored mammal. (pl.) —s.

Armed Forces synonym for entire military establishment. Armed Forces Day.

Armenia [ar-MEE-nee-ah] republic in former U.S.S. R., now in Commonwealth, at E tip of Black Sea. Cap: Erevan, Yerevan [yehr-uh-VAHN]. Native: Armenian(s).

armful (pl.) —fuls.

armistice [AHRM-ihs-tihs] temporary suspension of hostilities.

Armistice Day former name of Veterans Day.

armorplate (n.) armor-clad (adj.).

Armory Springfield Armory, etc,; the armory.

arm's length an emotional distance; refers to keeping personal feelings separate. *I try to keep any dealings with my ex-wife at arm's length.* As an adj., hyphenated: *an arm's-length transaction.*

army (Lowercase) Lee's army, Red army; army mobile, mule, of occupation; occupation army.

Army American or foreign, capitalize if part of name: Clark's Fifth Army. Capitalize standing alone only referring to U.S. Army. Capitalize with *Active, Adjutant General, the Band.*

Capitalize specific groups: Gordon Highlanders, Royal Guards, etc.; Brigade, 1st, etc.; the brigade; Robinson's brigade, Command, Command and General Staff College, Company A; A Company, BUT: the company.

Confederate (referring to U.S. Civil War); the Confederates. Continental (U.S. War of Independence), Continentals Corps. Engineers (the Corps of Engineers); the Engineers, BUT: Army engineer; Field Establishment; Field Forces; Finance Department; the Department.

General of the Army, BUT the general; General Staff, the Staff; Headquarters of the, the headquarters; Hospital Corps, Medical Museum; Organized Reserves; the Reserves.

Designate a U.S. Army corps by Roman numerals: *XI Corps.*

ARMY ORGANIZATION In U.S., pentagonal organization provides an army with two or more corps, each of two or more divisions, each made up of five battle groups (larger than triangular battalions, but smaller than the regiment), each with five rifle companies plus one headquarters company plus combat support. Armored battalions are organized separately for combat support. Company formations remain as under the triangular system.

Triangular organization used prior to 1956: each corps had three divisions, with three battalions each, with three regiments each, etc. Each rifle company had three rifle squads and one weapons squad.

Squad consisted of twelve persons till 1948, nine persons afterwards.

Army, Air Force, and Naval Officers ADDRESS letters to officers in accordance with their exact ranks. However, the salutation should ignore the "lieutenant" in *lieutenant colonel*, or "lieutenant commander" and the prefixed titles to *general*, *admiral*, etc.

A retired army officer is addressed by title, followed by name and "U.S.A. Ret." A member of the armed forces who is also a doctor, a dentist, or a clergyman may be addressed either by professional rank or army rank in a personal letter, but military rank should be used in official correspondence.

Army rank is also used for administrative officials.

In writing to military or naval personnel, the serial number and tactical unit or ship should always be part of the address, followed by the post and state or an A.P.O. number, c/o Postmaster of N.Y., or San Francisco, etc. *Brigadier General James Johnson, U.S.A., Commanding Officer, 3rd Corps Area (followed by postal address); Major General Robert Ryan, U.S.A., Commanding Officer, 2nd Tank Corps.*

SALUTATION: Sir (formal), Dear Sir, Dear General, Dear Colonel, Dear Sergeant, Dear Corporal. In all written correspondence rank and rating precede the name and are written out. Again, avoid prefix title. *Dear General*, NOT *Dear Lieutenant General.*

For officers below the rank of captain in the army or air force or below lieutenant commander in the navy, use: *Dear Mr.—*. For official correspondence omit ceremonial salutations and closings.

   See also *OFFICERS.*

around Brit. use *round.*

arouse to stimulate. Usually with abstract words: *fear, suspicion, desire.*

   ROUSE Implies physical action. —from sleep.

arrant particularly guilty.

arsenal Rock Island Arsenal, etc.; the arsenal.

article in English grammar: *a, an,* and *the.*

article 15 Cap. only if title: Article 15. See *CAPITALIZATION.*

Articles of Confederation compact under which the American colonies were united, 1781-89.

artillery The weapon takes a singular verb; the military unit takes a plural verb.

artisan [AHR-tih-zan] one skilled in a craft or trade.

artist [AHR-tihst] practitioner in fine arts, masc. or fem.

   ARTISTE [ahr-TEEST] public performer, masc. or fem.

artistically [ahr-TIHS-tihk-uh-lee]

Aryan [AE-ree'n; AH-ree'n] originally, Caucasians from Middle Asia, also known as *Indo-European.* In later

racist writings, esp. Nazi propaganda, came to mean Nordic, Germanic, Gentile.

as Use only when referring to *so, the same,* or *such. The hat she wears is the same as her mother's. Welcome to my home, such as it is.* NOT: *Let those as love pigs keep them.*

as When used to mean "in the capacity of," avoid dangling modifier. NOT: *The gift was presented as president of the society.* CORRECT: *As president . . . , he presented the gift.*

as When pronoun follows, case of pronoun will affect the meaning of the sentence. *He loves her as much as I* (love her.) He loves her as much as (he loves) *me.*

   AS ARE, AS DID Avoid: *The student—as did his fellows—made a practice of breaking curfew.* Use *like all students.*

   AS FOLLOWS Not *as follow.* AS for pref. to *as to. As for me, I like spicy foods.*

   AS IF Follow with a conditional form of verb. *She acted as if he were not there.*

   AS IS Applied to merchandise sold "in present condition, subject to any present faults."

   AS OF *Effective as of this date.*

   AS PER a commercial shortening of *in accordance with;* avoid in other correspondence. *The product was made as per your specifications.*

   AS REGARDS Not a substitute for *concerning* or *regarding.* See **regard.**

AS TO Use only to emphasize a subject. *As to France, her attitude is predictable.* NOT: *As to whether France will vote for the measure, no one can say.*

as, since, because. These have one meaning in common and all may be used to introduce clauses of reason.

To avoid confusion use *since* only for its distinctive meaning: for the introduction of clauses of time, duration. *Since the rule was passed there have been no more omissions.*

As may follow *express, regard, account, consider it.* BUT NOT a substitute for *that* or *whether* after *say, believe, know, think.* NOT: *I don't know as I believe you.*

AS is usually used in a positive statement. *As long as she is here, let her stay. He is as good as the next.* NOT: *He's equally as good as...*

AVOID construction where *as as* occurs. NOT: *It is not so much as a Frenchman that he loves France, as as a gourmet.*

SO...AS Usually in negative statement. *The technique is not so difficult as it appears.* See **because.**

A.S.C.A.P. American Society of Composers, Authors and Publishers.

ascendancy domination, supremacy. NOT rising trend. *Everyone now recognized the ascendancy of the party. The party is in the ascendant.* Pref. to ascendency.

ascent (n.) rise, ascending, ascension.

ASSENT (n.) consent. Also compare: *ACCENT.*

ascertain [as-er-TAEN] to make certain. Implies investigation or experiment beyond the superficial.

ascetic See **acetic.**

A.S.E.A.N. Assoc. of Southeast Asian Nations.

Asgard [AS-gahrd] Norse home of the gods.

Ash Wednesday the first Wednesday of Lent.

Asian, Asian-American See **American.**

askance [uh-SKANSS] obliquely. Hence, with mistrust.

aspect in grammar, a function of the verb that indicates action or state. The *aspect* concerns whether the action conveyed by a verb is near its beginning or near completion, whether it's of long duration or in repetition. In English, aspect is NOT simply a matter of tense.

In English, aspect is indicated in part by the verb meaning. *Find* is momentary, while *seek* is continuing. It is also indicated by the progressive form (*I am speaking*), and by modifiers (*sit, sit down, while I was sitting*).

asphalt [ASS-fawlt, AS-falt]

asphyxiate [ass-FIHK-see-aet] die for lack of oxygen.

aspirant [as-PIE-rant or ASS-pih-rant] one who aspires.

ASPIRATE the breathed sound of *h* as in *home.* The *h* in *hour,* on the other hand, is inaspirate.

assay to test, analyze, weigh, or evaluate.

> ESSAY (v.) to try. (n.) non-fiction writing, brief and usu. interpretive.

assemblage [ah-SEHM-blihj] of people, a formal assembly; of things, a collection. IN art, work made of assembled pieces.

assembly of New York, the assembly, an assembly, a state assembly, assemblies. Capitalize specific references. Second Assembly District, 23rd Assembly District.

Assembly (United Nations) Capitalize General Assembly, the Assembly.

assemblyperson assembly line; assembly room.

assess to fix value, usually for tax purposes.

asset any item of value owned; for example property, accounts receivable, copyright. (pl.) assets.

> INTANGIBLE ASSET item of value with no physical being: goodwill, patents.

> LIQUID ASSET property owned that is readily convertible into cash: notes and accounts receivable.

> NET ASSETS value of assets less liabilities.

> WATERED ASSET property or

rights carried on the books at overstated values.

assiduity [ass-sih-DYOO-ih-tee] diligence. (adv.) assiduously [uh-SIHJ-yoo-uhs-lee].

assign to appoint, designate; apportion. In law, transfer to another; (adj.) —nable. (n.) —nation, —nor. BUT —ner is acceptable in nonlegal sense; (v.) —ned, —ning.

assignee [AS-ih-NEE]

assignation [ASS-ihg-nae-shuhn] assignment; also, appointment for a love tryst.

assimilate [uh-SIM'l-aet] to incorporate; absorb. (adj.) —lable.

assistant Capitalize if part of title, and before names. Lowercase usually for subordinate positions, and where there is more than one person with the title: *the assistant; Presidential assistant; Assistant Secretary. The assistant district attorney spoke.*

assistant attorney (pl.)—attorneys, —commissioners, —corporation counsels, —directors, —general counsels. Also —attorneys, — general, —chiefs of staff, —comptrollers general.

associate (v.) [as-SOH-shih-aet] (n. and adj.) [as-SOH-shi-hyht] association. [-sih-AE-shuhn].

associate Justice Cap. for Supreme Court.

association Capitalize if part of name; capitalize standing alone if referring to federal unit: *American Association for the Advancement of Science, the association; Federal National Mortgage Association; the Association.*

assonance [AS-oh-nans] non-rhyming resemblance of vowel sounds: *safe* and *take.*

> CONSONANCE non-rhyming resemblance of consonant sounds: *move* and *moose.*

assume [uh-SOOM] in the sense of "suppose," follow by that. *He assumes that you like him.*

> PRESUME to have a stronger belief. *I presume you are cousins.*

assure, assurance In sense of "insure," use limited to insurance business. In the sense of "provide certainty," *assure* requires the indirect object. *James assured them that credit would be available.* Can substitute *gave assurance.*

> ENSURE. to make certain.

> INSURE. to make secure or protected.

A.s.t. Atlantic standard time.

ASTERISK Used to indicate a footnote. A second footnote may be indicated by two asterisks, a third by three. etc. See *FOOTNOTES.*

> Three asterisks are used to indicate an omission of paragraphs in a quotation, or to denote passage of time. See *ELLIPSIS.*

asthma [AZ-muh] disease affecting breathing.

astigmatism [a-stihg-mah-tihz'm] Near sightedness.

Aswan Dam [ahs-WAHN] Located in Egypt.

A.T. & T. (abbr.) American Telephone & Telegraph Company

at *Where are you staying?* NOT: *Where are you staying at?*

at, in. May often be used interchangeably, in phrases giving the place of an action. BUT note:

(1) *In* refers to the interior, when the site itself is stressed.

(2) *In* usually appears before countries and sections: *in Italy.*

(3) *At* is used before business firms, office buildings: *at the First National Bank.*

(4) *In* is used before a city to leave an impression of permanence; *at* is used to suggest a temporary stay.

(5) In addresses, *in* is used before the name of city; *at,* before the street number of the residence or office.

at about Redundant. USE *at one o'clock* or *about one o'clock.*

atheism [AE-thee-ihz'm] belief that no God exists. See also **deism, gnosticism, Pantheism, Polytheism, Theism.**

> AGNOSTICISM [ag-NAH-stih-sihs'm] belief that neither existence nor nature of God can be known.

Athena [ah-THEE-nah] Greek goddess of wisdom.

athenaeum, atheneum [ath-ee-

NEE-uhm] (Lat.) library for law, poetry, and oratory; scientific or literary association.

athlete [ATH-leet]

Atlantic Cap. with Charter; Coast States; Destroyer Flotilla; Fleet; Pact; seaboard; slope; standard time; North Atlantic, South Atlantic, mid-Atlantic,. BUT: cisatlantic; transatlantic; the destroyer; the flotilla.

Atlantic shoreline the Atlantic coast; the Atlantic Seaboard; the coast.

at large DO NOT hyphenate ambassador at large, representative at large. Cap. referring to a specific person: *John J. Smith, Councilman at Large.*

atlas (pl.) atlases.

at least See *PLACEMENT OF WORDS.*

A.T.M. automated teller machine.

atm., atmosphere air surrounding earth or any planet.

TROPOSPHERE ground level to 10 miles up.

STRATOSPHERE orig. ground to 10 miles up; now 10 to 16 miles (*Websters;* 7 miles) from ground.

MESOPHERE 16 to 300 miles from ground.

EXOSPHERE 300 to 1000 miles from ground.

IONOSHERE region of several layers of electrically charged air

beginning 25 miles from ground, varying by season and time of day.

atoll [AT-awl] coral island; a reef enclosing a lagoon.

atom one of minute particles of which matter is composed.

ELECTRON particle with elementary charge of negative electricity, found within the atom, hence *subatomic.*

NEUTRON [NOO-trahn] uncharged sub-atomic particle.

PROTON [PROH-tahn] subatomic article with elementary positive charge of electricity.

MOLECULE [MAHL-ee-kyool] NOT sub-atomic. Smallest portion of a chemical substance that retains identity.

QUARK [kwark] still-hypothetical sub-atomic particle; may carry fractional electrical charge.

atomic bomb, atom bomb, A-bomb. See **hydrogen bomb, neutron bomb.**

atomic weight (at wgt.) measure of relative weight of an atom of an element, based on oxygen = 16.

atrocious [a-TROE-shuhs] brutally savage. Colloq., of poor quality or in bad taste.

attaché [at-ash-AE] diplomatic staff member. *Timothy Smith, naval attaché.*

attacked occasional euphemism for *raped.*

at the present time *Now* is pref.

attorney at law attorney at law's fee. attorney, United States. (pl.) attorneys at law.

attorney general Cap. federal title: Attorney General (U.S.). BUT attorney general of Maine, etc. SEE: Cabinet member. (pl.) attorneys general; attorneys general's cases. But Webster's also accepts *attorney generals*.

> ADDRESS: *The Honorable Louis J. Lefkowitz, Attorney General of New York.* SALUTATION: *Sir; Dear Mr. Attorney General, Dear Mr. Lefkowitz.*

attribute (v.) [uh-TRIHB-yoot] (n.) [AT-trih-byoot]

audacious [aw-DAE-shuhs].

audible [AW-dih-b-l] capable of being heard.

audience Implies listening, not merely witnessing. Thus NOT of an accident, arrest, crime, or fire.

audiofrequency , audiogram, audiometer, audiovisual.

auf Wiedersehen [ouf VEE-der-zae-'n] (Ger.) see you again.

auger [AW-ger] hole-boring tool; auger box, auger drill.

augur [AW-ger] (v.) to foretell.

aught [AWT] in mathematics, a cipher or zero. *Six times aught is aught.* BUT naught is pref.

OUGHT Should. *You ought to be in pictures.*

au gratin [oh gra-TANN, also oh GRAH-t'n] with browned covering of bread crumbs, butter, and cheese.

auk [awk] northern sea bird.

auld lang syne [ald-lang-ZIEN] (Scot.) literally, old long since. Long-ago times. Name of song sung on New Year's Eve.

au revoir [OH rih-VWAHR] (Fr.) Until we meet again.

Aurora Borcalis [aw-RAW-rah BAW-ree-AII-lihs] colored lights in night sky, near Arctic Circle. In Southern Hemisphere, **Aurora Australis.**

Auschwitz [OU-schvihtz] Nazi concentration camp in Poland. Germanization of Polish name, Oswiecim.

Austerlitz [AW-stuhr-lihts] Austrian site of Napoleonic victory, 1805.

Australia abbr.: Aus. island continent and nation, SW Pacific. Formerly British; independence, 1901. Cap.: Canberra. Native: Australian. Currency: dollar.

Austria abbr.: Aust. mid-European country, established by 1300. Cap.: Vienna [VEE-ehn-ah] (Wien). Native: Austrian. Currency: schilling.

autarky [OH-tahr-kee] economic self-sufficiency. NOT: autarchy, an autocratic rule. See **-archy.**

autism [AW-tihs'm] mental disease

marked by extreme withdrawal from reality. (adj.) autistic [aw-TIHS-tihk].

author masc. or fem. Avoid use as a verb.

authoritative [aw-THAH-rih-tae-tihv]

authority Capitalize standing alone if referring to government unit: National Shipping Authority; the Authority; Port of New York Authority, the port authority, the authority; St. Lawrence Seaway Authority of Canada, the authority; Tennessee Valley Authority, the Authority.

autobahn [AW-toh-bahn] German highway. (pl.) —s.

auto-da-fé [AW-toh-da-fae]. ceremony accompanying judgment of a heretic during the Inquisition; hence, execution, especially burning. (pl.) autos-da-fé.

automaton [aw-TOM-ih-tahn] self-moving machine. See **android, robot.** (pl.) —s or —ta.

AUTOMATION [aw-toh-MAE-shuhn] automatic operation, especially of machinery for manufacturing.

autopsy [AW-tahp-see] Post-mortem examination to determine cause of death.

auxiliary [awg-ZIHL-yair-ee] helping, supporting.
AUXILIARY VERB verb that helps or supplements another verb. *Be, have, can, may shall, will* combine

with main verbs to form verbal phrases.

avail (v.) to be of use; *availed oneself of:* made use of.

avant-garde [ah-VAHN GARD] (Fr.) (adj. or n.) experimental, innovative; or work done in such a manner; or the person who does such work. See **cutting edge.**

avenge (v.) to exact satisfaction for a wrong. By implication, a just action.

REVENGE (v.) to punish or give pain because of wrong done. By implication, an unjust overreaction.

avenue Cap. with name: Constitution Avenue, Fifth Avenue, Avenue of the Americas; the avenue.

average [AV-uhr-ihj or AV-rihj] Arithmetic mean; the sum of quantities divided by the number of quantities. $1 + 2 + 3 + 5 + 9$ divided by 5 equals the average of 4.
Compare to

MEAN the figure midway between two extremes. In the series 1, 2, 3, 5, 9, the mean is 5 $(1+9 \div 2)$.

MEDIAN point in a series where half are on each side. In the series 1, 2, 3, 5, 9 the median is 3.

GEOMETRIC MEAN the root of the product of a number of quantities where the root is the number of quantities. $2 \times 4 \times 6 \times 8 =$ the geometric mean of 2, 4, 6, and 8. The figure (4.75) is generally less than the arithmetic mean. See **harmonic mean,** mode.

MOVING AVERAGE a graph showing simple averages over a period of time; for example, Dow Jones average of stock prices.

Avignon [ah-vee-NYAWN] city in S France. 14th-C. seat of rival popes.

avocado [av-oh-KAH-doh] alligator pear. (pl.) —s.

avoirdupois [av-uhr-du-POIZ] abbr.: avdp. System of weights in English speaking countries. Based on a pound of 7000 grains or 16 ounces.

avow to acknowledge openly. *He avowed his willingness to kill.*

awake (v.)(p.) awoke.; (pres. p.) awaking; awaked, awaken, (p.p.) —ed. *Awaked* for past and *awoke* for p.p. are rare. Word suggests coming to full consciousness.

WAKE (v.) (p.) woke; (pres. p.) waking; waked, waken (p.p.) —ed. *Waked* for past and *woke* for p.p. are rarely used. Word suggests process of reaching consciousness.

award Distinguished Service Award, National Book Award, Mother of the Year Award, the award.

aweigh clear of the ground: *anchors aweigh.* BUT: *The ship is under way.*

awhile (adv.) for a short time. *We'll stay for a while* pref. to *We'll stay awhile.*

a.w.o.l. (abbr.) absent without official leave.

awry [uh-RIE] Askew; amiss.

axis (pl.) axes.

Axis, the W.W. II alliance between Germany, Italy, and Japan.

AZ Arizona.

azalea [uh ZAEL-yuhl] spring flower.

Azerbaijan [AH-zuhr-bie-ZHAHN] republic in former U.S.S.R., now in Commonwealth. N. of Iran, W of Caspian Sea. Cap. Baku [ba-KOO]. Native: Azari(s) Azerbaijani(s).

Azores [a-ZAWRZ or AE-zawrz] islands in North Atlantic.

azure [AZH-ehr] blue.

B

b Usually silent before *t: subtle, debt;* and after *m: bomb, crumb, dumb.* BUT the addition of a suffix will often cause the silent letter to be sounded: *bombed.*

B. (abbr.) Baume. Hydrometer scale.

b. (abbr.) breadth or width. Also: boils at.

B.A. (abbr.) Bachelor of Arts. See A.B.

Baader-Meinhof gang [BAE-der MIEN-hoff] German left-wing terrorists of 1970's. A/k/a Red Army Faction.

Babel [BAE-b'l; BAH-b'l] (from Bible story) chaos, confusion. Rarely lowercase.

babble [BAH-b'l] meaningless noise. Always lowercase.

baccalaureate [bak-uh-LAW-ree-eht] degree of bachelor; commencement ceremony.

bacchanal [BAK-uh-nal] (n., both masc. and fem.) (From Bacchus, Greek god of wine) an orgy or revel; also participant in party.

Bach, Johann Sebastian [bahk, YOH-hahn seh-BAHS-tee-ahn] (1685-1750) German composer

backgammon [BAK-gam'n] a board game.

back of, in back of (colloq., U.S.) Use *behind.*

back-order (n. and v.) portion of an order that cannot be filled immediately, held for future delivery.

backward(s) (adv.) Both forms are acceptable; euphony determines choice. The *s* form is preferred for manner. Only backward may be used as an adjective to modify a noun immediately following.

bade [bad] p. of bid.

badinage [bad-ih-NAHZH; BAD-ih-nahzh] banter.

badland(s) In SD and NE, cap. title of national park or area.

badly AVOID sense of "ill." *He feels badly* means his sense of touch is faulty.

Baedeker [BAE-dih-kihr] (after German writer) guidebook.

baggage baggage area, car, master, rack.

Baghdad [BAG-dad] cap. of Iraq, holy to Muslims.

baguette [bag-GEHT] (Fr.) a long narrow loaf of bread.

Bahai [bah-HAH-ee] religious system, founded 1863, emphasizing spiritual unity of humankind. (n.) Bahaism. (adj.) Bahai.

Bahamas [bah-HAH-mahs; also -HAE-] island country in SW Atlantic. Former Br. colony; independent, 1973. Cap.: Nassau [NA-saw]. Native: Bahamian. Currency: dollar.

Bahrain [buh-REIN] island country in Persian Gulf. Former Br. protectorate; independence, 1971. Cap.: Manama [mah-NA-mah] native: Bahraini. Currency: dinar.

bail (v.) to draw water. (v. or n.) legal security for appearance in court.

BALE (n.) commercial bundle (cotton, paper, hay).

baker's dozen Also called long dozen, a quantity of 13.

Baku [bah-KOO] city on Caspian Sea, cap. of Armenia.

balance Should be used only in reference to money or in bookkeeping; otherwise, use *remainder.*

balance of payments difference in a statement of national trade, investment, tourist transactions, etc. showing the amount which must be settled in gold. A favorable balance of payment indicates that the nation is to receive gold.

balance of trade difference between a nation's exports and imports. A favorable balance means exports exceed imports.

Balanchine, George [BAL-an-cheen] (1904-1983) Russian-American classical choreographer.

balding going bald is preferred.

Balearic Islands [bal-ih-AR-ihk] islands off Spain.

baleful ominous, harmful. *A baleful stare.*

Balkan States, the Balkans, [BAWL-kanz] countries on the Balkan Peninsula: Yugoslavia, Romania, Bulgaria, Greece, Albania, and part of Turkey.

balony, or baloney an expression referring to false statement. *If he says he kissed her, that's baloney.* The meat is **bologna.**

Baltic States countries on E coast of Baltic Sea; Latvia, Lithuania, Estonia (absorbed by U.S.S.R., 1940; partial independence, 1989); sometimes Finland, Poland.

balustrade [bal-uhs-TRAED, BAL-uhs-traed] banister.

banal [BAE-nal, bah-NAHL] trite; flat.

band Cap. if part of name: Marine Band, Navy Band, Sousa's Eastern Band; the band; band of Cherokees; the band.

Bangladesh [BANG-lah-dehsh] nation in SE Asia. Formerly E. Pakistan; independent, 1971. Cap.: Dhaka [DAH-kuh]. Native: Bengali. Currency: taka.

banjo (pl.) —jos or —joes.

bank Cap. if part of name and when standing alone if referring to international bank: Export-Import Bank of Washington (Eximbank), Export-Import Bank, the Bank; Farm Loan Bank of Dallas, Dallas Farm-Loan Bank; First National Bank; International World Bank, the Bank. BUT: blood bank, central reserve bank, soil bank.

bank, riverbank The left or right bank is determined as one looks downstream.

bankruptcy

bantamweight boxing weight class: under 118 pounds.

barkeeper —fight, —fly, —maid, —room, —tender (all one word); bar bit, bar business.

Baraka, Amiri [ah-MEER-ee bah-RAH-kah]. (b. 1934) African American poet and playwright, formerly LeRoi Jones.

Barbados [bahr-BAE-dohs] island country in SW Atlantic. Former Br. colony; independence 1966. Cap.: Bridgetown. Native: Barbadian. Currency: dollar.

barbarian (adj.) Used in the sense of being or belonging to a barbarian: *barbarian tribes, huts, lust.*

> BARBARIC Implies no condemnation: *barbaric simplicity, splendor, ceremonies.*

> BARBAROUS Implies condemnation: *barbarous torture, practices.*

barbed wire

barbiturate [bahr-BIHT-tyoo-raet] a drug used as sedative, hypnotic, etc. NOT barbituate.

barely by a narrow margin. *We barely arrived in time.*

> HARDLY Implies physical strain. *We hardly had the strength to get up.*

bargainer In law, bargainor.

bark See **boat.**

barley field barleycorn; barley water.

bar mitzvah [bar-MIHTS-vah] or bar mitztwa, mizvah, mitzvot. A Jewish boy who has reached his 13th birthday; also, the accompanying ceremony. (pl.) —s.

bat mitzvah or bas mitzvah. A Jewish girl who has reached 13, or the accompanying ceremony.

barnstormer —yard; barn dance.

baron [BAR-uhn] peer of the realm. Orig. position a direct gift of the king. In Britain the lowest grade of peerage. ADDRESS: The Right Honourable Lord Milford; or the Lord Milford. SALUTATION: My Lord. (adj) baronial; (n.) barony.

baron (colloq.) a powerful industrialist, financier, etc.

baroness ADDRESS: The Right Honourable the Baroness Milford; or The Lady Milford. SALUTATION: Sir.

baronet rank next below a baron but above a knight. ADDRESS: Sir Sidney Milford, Bt. (or Bart.) SALUTATION: Madam.

barracks Cap. if part of name: Carlisle Disciplinary Barracks (Leavenworth); the barracks. BUT: A barracks, barracks A, etc.

barratry illegal or grossly negligent

action of master or crew of a ship which results in loss to the owner; also the practice of stirring up lawsuits to annoy a competitor.

barre [bar] fixed handrail for ballet practice.

barrel (1) in U.S., 31-1/2 gallons or 105 dry quarts. (2) Unit of petroleum capacity = 42 U.S. gal. = 34.97 imperial gal. = 158.9 liters. (3) Unit of dry measure = 7056 cu. in. = 105 dry qt. = 3.281 bu. = 115.62 liters. (4) Unit of cranberry measure = 5826 cu. in. = 86-45/46 dry qt. = 2.709 bu. = 95.471. (5) Unit of liquid measure = 31.5 gal. = 119.2371. (6) Measure of beef, pork, fish (U.S.) = 200 lbs. = 90.72 killograms. (7) Measure of flour = 196 lbs. = 88.9 kilograms. (8) Measure of cement = 396 lbs. = 170.55 kilograms. (9) Measure of lime (U.S.) small = 180 lbs. = 81.65 kilograms; large = 280 lbs. = 127.01 kilograms.

barrel —ed, —ing.

barrio [BAH-ree-oh] (Sp.) urban neighborhood. In U.S., Hispanic section of city.

barrister See **lawyer.**

B.A.R.T. Bay Area Rapid Transit, in San Francisco.

basal forming the base.

BASIC of the essence; fundamental.

base Andrews Air Force Base; Air Force base; the base.

Basel [BAH-zehl or BAS'l] city and canton in Switzerland.

Compare to

BASIL [same pronunciations] herbal spice.

B.A.S.I.C. Beginner's All-purpose Symbolic Instruction Code; computer programming language.

basis (pl.) bases.

bas-relief [BAH-] low relief, figures slightly raised from a bass-[baes].

bass [bas] (n.) fish. [baes] (adj.) deep-toned; bass drum, bass horn, bass viol; bass bar.

basinet basket used as a cradle. NOT *bassinette.*

Bastille [bah-STEEL] Paris fortress and prison stormed at start of French Revolution. Bastille Day, July 14.

Bastogne [bahs-TOHN-y] town and W.W.II battle site in Belgium.

batblind bat-man, bat-wing; bat-eyed (adj.).

bath [bath] (n.); bathe [baethe] (v.).

bathhouse, —mat, —robe, —room, —tub; (all one word) bath towel.

bathysphere diving bell for studying deep-sea life.

baton [bah-TAHN]

battalion See *ARMY ORGANIZATION.*

battery [BAT-uhr-ee] the Battery, in New York City.

battle Cap. if part of name: the Battle of Gettysburg, of the Bulge. BUT: the battle of the sexes.

Baudelaire, Charles [BOH-dih-laer] (1821-1867) French poet (*Flowers of Evil*).

Bauhaus [BOU-hous] architectural style, begun in 1920's in Germany.

bayou [BIE-oo] a creek.

bay window a window that projects from a room in any form.
Compare to
BOW WINDOW a window that projects from a room in curved form.

Bayeux tapestry [BA-yoo] 11th-century Fr. fabricwork; depicts Battle of Hastings.

bazaar a place where goods are sold. *The church held a bazaar to raise money.*

BIZARRE strange. *Many bizarre animals roam the veldt.*

B.B.C. (abbr.) British Broadcasting Corporation.

bbl. (abbr.) barrel.

B.C. (abbr.) before Christ. In use, follows number: *610 B.C. The seventh century B.C. See* **A.D.**

bd.-ft (abbr.) board-foot. Lumber equal to 144 cu.in.

be (p.) was; (p.p.) been.

beakhead (n.); beak-shaped (adj.).

bear (v.) to carry, used formally; (p.) bore [BOHR]; bearing, borne. BUT for birth, (p.) bore, (p.p.) borne, (p.p. passive) born. *I was not born yesterday.*

beat (v.) (p.) beat, (p.p.) beaten. (n.) beater.

Beatles English rock'n'roll group, 1960s. NOT *Beetles*. With article, use as plural noun: *The Beatles' first single. The Beatles were a great influence.*
Without article, use as adjective: *She likes paisley clothes and Beatles music. Let's hear some Beatles-style harmonies.* See **Musical groups.** Names.

beau [boh] suitor; admirer. (pl.) beaux, beaus [bohz].

beauty [BYOO-tee] beautyproof; beauty-blind (adj.), beauty-clad (adj.); beauty shop.

beaver board beaverpelt.

bebop [BEE-bahp] (n. or adj.) jazz movement of 1940s and '50s. Sometimes Bop.

because literally, caused by. Assigns a reason explicitly. In use, avoid implied redundancy. *The reason was that . . .* , NOT *the reason was because. . . .*

SINCE Assigns a reason more incidentally than *because*.

AS Even more casual than *since*.

INASMUCH AS Implies a concession or qualification.

FOR Introduces a reason, evidence, or justification for what has preceded it.

become (p.) became, becoming, (p.p.) become.

bedlam [BEHD-l'm] from Bethlehem Royal Hospital, 13th-C. insane asylum near London. insanity, chaos.

Bedouin [BEHD-oo-ihn] Arab nomad; sing., pl., and adj.

beechnut —wood.

beef (colloq.) a complaint. (pl.) beefs.

beefeater —steak, —y; beef-faced (adj.); beef extract.

beermaker beer cellar, beer yeast.

Beethoven, Ludwig van [BAE-tohv'n, LOOT-vik fahn; (angl.) LUHD-wig] (1770-1827) German composer.

before [bee-fawr] before-cited, before-mentioned (adj.); beforenamed, beforehand.

beget (arch.) (p.) begot; (p.p.) begotten, begot.

begin, began, beginning Rarely used in passive voice: *The project was begun.*

behalf side; interest; defense: *On behalf of. On his behalf.*

behoove [be-HOOV] to be necessary for. *If you want to see this girl again, it behooves you to treat her nicely.*

behold (p. and p.p.) beheld.

Beirut [bae-ROOT] Cap. of Lebanon.

Belgium [BEHL-juhm] NW European country, since 1830. Cap.: Brussels, also sp. Bruxelles. Native, Belgian. Currency, franc.

Belgrade [BEL-graed or -GRAHD] capital city of Yugoslovia, (see).

believable worthy of belief and confidence.

> CREDIBLE Stresses intellectual assent. *A story is believable; his report is credible. A credible witness.*

belittle to depreciate; minimize. —ler, —ling.

Belize [beh-LEEZ] Central American country. Former Br. Honduras; independent, 1981. Cap.: Belmopan [BEHL-moh-pan] Native: Belizian. Currency: Belize dollar.

belles-lettres [behl-LEHT'R] literature for art's sake, rather than for information: poetry, fiction, drama, and esp. essays.

below anywhere on a lower plane; opposite of above.
   Compare to

> UNDER lower than, usually in terms of vertical position; also subject to: *under the umbrella; under a superior officer.* Opposite of over.

> BENEATH below or under, often suggests lower in special station (and place) or prestige. *He is beneath contempt.*

UNDERNEATH underlying, hidden.

belowstairs

belt Cap. if part of name: Corn Belt, Cotton Belt, Dairy Belt, Ice Belt, Wheat Belt. BUT: garter belt.

bench Cap. only when referring to Supreme Court.

bend (p. and pp.) bent.

bends an air-pressure disease; usu. in deep-sea divers.

beneath See **below.**

beneficent [beh-NIH-fih-sehnt]

beneficial trust See **trust.**

benefit —fited, —fiting.

Benelux countries Belgium, the Netherlands, and Luxembourg.

Bengal [behn-GAWL] area in NE Indian subcontinent. *Bengali* preferred to *Bengalese.* See **Bangladesh.**

Ben Gurion, David [GOO-ree-uhn] (1886-1973) Israeli statesman; first prime minister (1949-53, 1955-63).

benighted overtaken by darkness, esp. moral or social.

benign [bee-NIEN] gentle; having no harmful effects.

BENIGNANT [bee-NIHG-nant] More formal. *Webster's* lists as synonym.

Benin [buh-NIHN] W African country. Formerly Fr. W. Africa; achieved independence as Dahomey, 1960; became Benin, 1975. Cap.: Porto-Novo. Native: Dahomian. Currency: CFA franc.

benthoscope deep-sea observation sphere.

bentwood (n. & adj.)

benzo- combining form meaning *benzoine.* benzoate, —ic.

Beowulf [BAE-oh-woolf] (c. A.D. 700) title and hero of Anglo-Saxon epic.

Berchtesgaden [behrt-tehs-GAH-dehn] town in Bavaria, site of Hitler's mountain retreat.

bereave (p. and p.p.) bereaved. *Bereaved* implies more emotion than *bereft: The bereaved wife. She was bereft of her senses.*

Bergman, Ingmar [IHNG-mahr BUHRG-mehn] (b. 1918) Swedish film maker (*Wild Strawberries, Persona*).

beriberi [BEH-ree BEH-ree] a nutritional disorder associated with tropics.

Bering Sea [BEHR-ihng or BAIR-] N Pacific strait between Siberia and Alaska.

Berkeley city in CA.

Bermuda, Bermudas Br. island colony, SW Atlantic. A famous resort. Cap.: Hamilton. Native: Bermudian. *Bermuda shorts.*

Bernhardt, Sarah [BEHRN-hahrt] (1844-1923) Fr. actress.

berth a bunk or resting place. *She selected a lower berth on the train.*

BIRTH coming into life.

Bertillon System [behr-tee-YAHN; BURH-tihlahn] method of criminal identification based on body measurements.

beryl [BEH-rihl] silicate of gemstone.

beseech to beg; entreat. (p. and p.p.) besought, beseeched.

beside (prep.) at the side of, next to.

besides (adv.) in addition to.

besiege [bee-SEEJ] to lay siege to. Hence, pester.

bestir Always used reflexively. *He must bestir himself.* NOT: *The problem bestirred the legislature to pass a law.*

bestseller bestselling, bestdressed; bestknown (adj. best man (n.) (*Webster's*: best-seller).

bête noire [baet-NWAHR] (from Fr.) object of dread.

Betelgeuse [BEE-t'l-jooz] bright star in constellation Orion.

better (n.) person making bet; pref. to *bettor.*

betterment improvement, particularly of property. Use carefully of people. *He is on a self-betterment campaign.* NOT: *He is working for the betterment of the underprivileged.*

better than Avoid use for "more than." NOT: *There went better than a million warriors.*

between refers to two alternatives. *Differences between you and me* NOT: *between you and I. Between two players.* BUT NOT: *between each of the players* or *every player.* The usual form when two terms are specified is *between . . . and.*

Avoid repeating *between,* even in long sentences.

betweendecks betweentimes.

Bev. (abbr.) billion electron volts. Measure for atom-smashing.

bevy collective still sometimes used for young women: bevy of beauties, of ladies. Often considered sexist. See *SEXIST LANGUAGE.*

bevel —eled, —ling.

beware There is no other tense.

bf. (abbr.) boldface. Heavy, dark type.

B-flat

Bhagavadgita [BAHG-vahd-GEE-tah] (c. 400) Hindu scripture. See **Mahabharata.**

Bhopal [boh-PAHL] N Indian city, site of disastrous toxic-gas leak in 1984.

Bhutan [buh-TAHN or boo-TAN] Himalayan country. Former Br. colony; independent, 1949. Cap.: Thimphu [THIHM-boo] Native: Bhutanese. Currency: Ngultrum and Indian rupee.

bi- Prefix meaning *two* or *twice*. *Biweekly* can mean either twice a week or every other week. To avoid confusion, use *semiweekly, every other week,* etc. Also bifocal, biennium, bisexual.

bias —ed, —ing. (pl.) biases.

Bible Holy Scriptures, Scripture; Koran; Talmud; also Biblical, Koranic, Talmudic. BUT: some authorities lowercase biblical, scriptual, etc.

Bible Abbreviations for books:

OLD TESTAMENT: Gen., Exod., Liv., Num., Deut. Josh., Judg. Ruth, I and II Sam., I and II Kings., I and II Chron., Ezra, Neh., Esther, Job, Ps. or Pss., Prov., Eccles., Song of Sol. or Cant., Isa., Jer., Lam., Ezek., Dan., Hos., Joel., Amos., Obad., Jonah, Mic., Nah., Hab., Zeph., Hag., Zech., Mal.

NEW TESTAMENT: Matt., Mark, Luke, John, Acts., Rom., I and II Cor., Gal., Eph., Phil., Col., I and II Thes. I and II Tim., Titus, Philemon, Heb., Jas., I and II Pet., I, II and III John, Jude, Rev.

APOCRYPHA (Apoc.): I and II Esd., Tob. Jth., Rest of Esther, Wisd. of Sol., Eccles., Bar., Sus., Song of Three Children, Bel and Dragon. Pr. of Man., I and II Macc.

APOCALYPTIC En, Sib. Or., Assmp. M., Apoc. Bar., Ps. Sol., XII P., Bk Jub., Asc.

BIBLIOGRAPHY A list of books on a particular topic or by a particular author. In a book, place bibliography as part of reference matter following the appendix and the glossary, but preceding the index. Notation should include maximum information concisely.

PUBLISHED WORK Shirer, William L. *The Rise and Fall of the Third Reich*, New York; Simon and Schuster, 1960.

EDITED WORK. Mager, N.H. and S.K. (ed.) *Index to English*. Englewood Cliffs, N.J.: Prentice Hall, 1964.

UNPUBLISHED WORK. Weiss, Raymond. *Accuracy of Reporting in New York Metropolitan Newspapers,* unpublished study. Education Library, New York University, 1957. pp. 427-432.

ANONYMOUS WORK. *Crimes of the Soviet Union*. Author anon. New York: Freedom House, 1959.

BOOK IN A SERIES. *Statistical Abstract of the United States*, 1960. Superintendent of Documents. Washington: U.S. Government Printing Office.

WORK IN PERIODICALS. Domini, John. "Highway Trade." Southwest Review. (Southern Methodist U., Dallas TX) Vol. 73, No. 2 (Spring, 1988) pp. 180-207.

PRIVATELY PRINTED WORK. Peters, Alison. *Political Almanac*. New York: Privately printed. 1938.

For second references to articles by the same author in the same publications, use *ibid.*

When more than one work of an author appears on the list, use: Mager, N.J. *Office Encyclopedia,* New York: Pocket Books, Inc. 1955.

Complete Writer: Pocket Books, Inc. 1955.

See *FOOTNOTES.*

bicentennial Pref. to bicentenary in U.S.

biceps (pl.) same; also triceps.

bid bid, bidding. *Last year, he bid $350 just to get that piece.* (p.p.) bidden. AVOID *bade,* (arch.) (p.) AVOID sense of "attempt." NOT: *He bids to become the richest man in New Jersey.*

bid and asked price bid price is the price at which someone is willing to buy; asked price, to sell.

bide to wait. bided, biding. *I bided my time.*

bid in repossession by original owner at an auction by topping the last bid.

biennium a period of two years. (pl.) —s or biennia.

BIENNIAL every two years.

BIANNUAL ambiguous. USE *semiannual* for *twice a year.*

big Most widely used for size, amount, quantity. Emphasizes bulk, weight, or volume: *big house, nose, animal.*

GREAT Signifies importance, a high degree of distinction: *great man, great idea.* Imparts extra

meaning to quantity. *In a storage room at Auschwitz they discovered a great heap of children's shoes.*

LARGE Used for size, amount; indicates extension beyond the average: *large area, large collection.*

big board N.Y. Stock Exchange.

Big Inch, Little Inch Oil and gas pipelines.

bildungsroman [BIHL-duhngs-roh-man] (Ger.) a novel of a young person's education; hence, any coming-of-age story.

bill No caps with legislative action. The Kennedy bill. Senate bill 217, House bill 31.

billet-doux [bih-lae-DOO] (Fr.) love letter. (pl.) billets-doux.

billet — head, billetman.

billiards Takes a singular verb.

billion in U.S., 1000 millions; in Brit. a million millions. Milliard refers to 1000 million in Brit.

TRILLION In U.S., 1000 billions; in Brit., a million billions. See *NUMBERS, zillion.*

bill of fare menu. (pl.) bills of fare.

bill of lading a list of items in a shipment. abbr: B/L.

bill of rights Cap. U.S. document. BUT: GI bill of rights.

Biloxi [bih-LOHK-see] city in MS.

bimetallism use of two metals as a currency base at the same time, such as gold and silver.

binary number system system with 2 as radix (decimal system uses 10 as radix); used for computers. Thus binary 13 = 1101.

bind (p. and p.p.) bound.

binoculars [BIE- pref. to BUH] field glasses; opera glasses.

biodegradable [BIE-oh-dee-GRAE-] capable of decomposing by natural biological processes.

biomass, biome [BIE-oh-mas, -ohm] large geographic community of related plants and animals.

bionics [bie-ON-ihks] artificial systems resembling living systems. See **android, robot.**

birds'-eye, bird's nest (fig.) (n., adj., v.); bird's nest (lit.) (n.).

Bishop (Catholic) ADDRESS: The Most Reverend Joseph A. Burke, Bishop of Buffalo; or, The Right Reverend Bishop. SALUTATION: Your Excellency; Dear Bishop Burke.

Bishop (Episcopal) ADDRESS: The Right Reverend Timothy Brown, Bishop of St. Louis. SALUTATION: Right Reverend and dear Sir; My dear Bishop Brown; My dear Bishop. Right Reverent Sir.

Bishop (Methodist) ADDRESS: The Reverend Bishop Frederick Jones. SALUTATION: Dear Sir; Dear Bishop Jones.

bishorpric bishop's rank, see, diocese, or office. *Diocese* is preferred for the province of a bishop.
     Compare to

SEE seal of bishop's authority.

DIOCESE district (and population) under a bishop.

Bismarck, Otto von (1815-1898) German general and statesman; first Chancellor of unified Germany (1871-1880).

bite (p.), bit; (p.p.) bitten.

bivalve animal with two-valved shell; for example, oyster, clam.

bivouac [(v.) BIHV-wak, (n.) BIHV-ou-ak] (v.) to encamp. -uacked, -uacking. (n.) temporary encampment.

bizarre See **bazaar.**

black (n. and adj.) American of African descent; usage allows, though **African-American** is currently pref. See **Negro, -American,** *RACIST LANGUAGE.* (v.) to color black.

BLACKEN unintentional coloring or figurative use: *Blacken his reputation; city blackened by soot.*

blame —mable, —med, —ming.

blameworthy

blanc mange [blahnk-MAHNZH] molded dessert with milk.

blasé [blah-ZAE] satiated and bored.

blaspheme [BLAS-feem] to speak irreverently; revile. (n.) blasphemy [BLAS-feh-mee] (pl.) —mies. (adv.) —mous, (adj.) —mously; blasphemer [blas-FEEM-ehr].

blatant [BLAE-tant] noisy; obtrusive; bellowing.

bldg. (abbr.) building.

bleed (p. and p.p.) bled.

bleeding in textiles, loss of color in wet cloth because of improper dying or the use of poor dyes. Wet, bleeding fabrics will stain white or pale fabrics in contact with them.
    In printing, extending type or illustration beyond the edge of the type page, often leaving no margin.

blessed [BLEHS-sehd] (adj.) holy. *Blest* is poetical adj. (v.) bless, blessed, blessing.

blithe [blieth] happy, carefree. Pref. to *blithesome*. Also blithe hearted; blithe-looking (adj.).

blitzkrieg [BLIHTZ-kreeg]

blizzard See winds.

bloc group, especially of legislators: *the farm bloc*. In Europe, political factions or units combined for a purpose; also racial units: *the Central European bloc*.

blond Pref. to *blonde*, except when referring to a woman. *Ted's dog is blond. Lisa is a blonde.* Note album title: *Blonde on Blonde*.

bloom Refers to flowering; the height of a period.
    BLOSSOM Implies promise of fruit, the rising of a period. *Flowers bloom while the fruit trees blossom.*

blouse [blouz or blous]

blow (p.) blew; (p.p.) blown.

blowup enlargement, esp. of art work. (v.) to blow up.

B.L.S. (abbr.) Bureau of Labor Statistics.

blue blued, bluing.

blue-chip security of a well-established company.

blue-collar worker factory, trade, and technical workers. Contrast to white-collar worker, an office worker.

Bluegrass Region Bluegrass State (Kentucky).

blue-sky law state law designed to regulate sales of securities.

b.m. (abbr.) board measure.

B.M.E.W.S. (abbr.) Ballistic Missile Early Warning System.

B.M.T. (abbr.) Brooklyn Manhattan Transit, N.Y.C. subway.

B'Nai B'rith Jewish fraternal organization.

b.o. (abbr.) best offer; also, buyer's option.

board Capitalize if part of name;

capitalize standing alone only if referring to federal, interdepartmental, District of Columbia, or international board: Civil Aeronautics Board, the Board; Board of Education, the Board. Do not abbreviate.

boardwalk, board foot, board measure.

boarding house, boarding school.

boat generally, a *boat* is any vessel that travels on water. A *ship* is larger and capable of sea travel. In most cases, *boat* refers to a small open vessel moved by oars.

BARK three-masted vessel; square fore and aft rigging.

BRIG two-masted vessel with square sails.

CARAVEL light 15th-C. ship, Spanish or Portugese; type used by Columbus.

CATBOAT sailboat with one forward mast.

CUTTER one-master, fore- and aft-rigged.

FRIGATE 18th-C. square-rigged warship.

GALLEON 15th-16th C. three- or four-decker, usu. Sp.

GIG narrow, light racing boat.

KETCH two-masted boat with small mast (mizzen) aft.

SCHOONER two, three, or more masts; fore- and aft-rigged.

SLOOP one-master with jib stay and bow sprit.

PINNACE [PIN-nihs] small vessel with two schooner-rigged masts, plus oars.

TRIREME galley with three rows of oars.

YACHT pleasure vessel with a deck.

YAWL two-master with mizzen-mast far aft.

Cutter, Gig, Pinnace, and *Yawl* are used for smaller craft attached to seagoing vessels.

boatswain [BOH-s'n] warrant officer.

bobcat, bobsled, bobtail, bobwhite.

bobby pin, bobby-soxer.

Boccaccio, Giovanni [boh-CAH-chee-oh] (1313-1375). Italian writer (*Decameron*).

Boeing [BOH-ihng]

Boer [BOOR] South African of Dutch or Huguenot descent.

bogland —man (n.), —trot (v.); bog-eyed (adj); bog iron.

Bogota [buh-GOHT-ah] borough in New Jersey; [BOH-goh-TAH] cap. city in Colombia.

bogy [BOH-gih]. bogyman [BOO-gee-] (pl.) bogies; bogymen.

BOGEY [BOH-gih] golf score one stroke above par.

bohemian unconventional person, usu. artistic. Also cap.

Bohr, Niels [bohr, neels] (1885-1962) Danish physicist.

boilerplate news material and art work provided on stereotyped plates or mats; hence, stereotyped material.

boiler room, boiling point.

Bois de Boulogne [BWAH deh boo-LOHN(y)] a park in Paris.

boldface type Heavy, dark, type-face. (abbr.: b.f.)

Bolivar, Simon [bohl-LEE-vahr see -MOHN] (1783-1830) liberator of South American nations.

Bolivia [bohl-LIHV-ih-ah] country in central South America. Independent, 1825. Cap.: Sucre [SOO-crae], seat of govt.: La Paz [lah pahs]; Native: Bolivian. Currency: peso.

Bologna [buh-LOH-nya] city in N Italy (adj.) bolognese.

BOLOGNA [buh-LOH-nee] sandwich meat; sausage. See **balony.**

Bolshevik [BAWL-shih-vihk; Bol-] (sometimes l.c.) Bolsheviki (collective plural), bolshevism. In Russian, "the majority of the party," hence, U.S.S.R. Communist Party.

Bolshoi Theatre [bohl-SHOI] Moscow theater. Also Bolshoi Ballet.

bolt (n.) unit of (1) cloth length = 40yd.; (2) wallpaper length = 16yd., (v.) break away from; gulp.

bolt cutter, —head, —work (all one word); bolt-shaped (adj.).

bombazine [bahm-bah-ZEEN; BAHM-] twilled dress fabric of silk or cotton warp and worsted filling. Pref. to —*sine.*

bombers Better-known U.S. models include; B-17G, Flying Fortress, 1937; B-24, Liberator, 1940; B-25J, Mitchell, 1941; B-26, Marauders, 1942; B-29, Superfortress, 1943; B-52, Stratofortress, 1957; B-70 Valkryrie, 1974; F-111, fighter-bomber, 1966; B-2 Stealth bomber, 1989.

Soviet: IL-2 Stormovik; T-91, Boot, Tarzan; T-95, Bear.

British & other: (Br.) Lancaster and Vickers Valiant; (Ger.) Junkers Ju 87 and Stuka; (Jap.) Zero. See **fighter planes.**

bona fide [BOH-nuh FIED] (Lat.) (adj.) in good faith. *A bona fide original.* **Bona fides.** (n.) evidence of good faith. *He produced his bona fides.*

Bonaparte, Napolcon [BOH-nuh-pahrt] (1769-1821) French general and emperor. Brothers: Joseph, Lucien, Louis (father of Napoleon III); Jerome. Wife: Josephine.

bond a written agreement, under seal, to pay a certain sum at a certain time, usually at least one year later. Brit. debenture.

bondholder, bondman or bondsman; bond paper.

bonding process of pressing fibers into sheets or webs that adhere and hold. Also, self-binding. Hence, any process of people growing close: *male bonding, child bonding.*

bonhomie [bawn-oh-MEE] cheerful disposition.

bon mot [bawn moh] (Fr.) Witty remark. (pl.) bon mots.

bon voyage [bahn-vwa-AZH] (Fr.) a good journey.

bonsai plant [BOHN-sae] tiny Jap. tree, bush. Bonsai garden.

booby trap, booby hatch.

boogie-woogie (n. or adj.) rhythmic way of playing blues, usu. on piano. See rock and roll.

book Books of the Bible, First Book of Samuel, etc.: Good Book (synonym for Bible); book I, II, etc. BUT Book 1, when part of title: *Book 1: The Golden Legend*; book II. See **Bible.**

bookbinder, bookstore.

bookmaker professional bet-taker. Not generally used for makers of printed books.

book titles Place in quotation marks (acc. to GPO, *N.Y. Times*), or italicize (UCMS). Cap. first letters of important words, except in extensive bibliographies, tables, books of the Bible, and ancient mass.

book value (1) net assets of a company; (2) proportionate allocation of the net value of a business as shown on the company's books, applicable to each share of stock.

boondoggle —ling.

Bordeaux [bohr-DOH] Fr. city; center of wine industry.

border See **boundary.**

born, borne See **bear.**

borderland, borderline.

bore hole

Borges, Jorge Luis [BOHR-hehz, HOHR-hae] (1899-1986) Argentine writer, ("The Aleph," "The Circular Ruins").

borough [BUHR-oh] Cap. if part of name: Borough of the Bronx; the borough. *Boro* is acceptable abbr.

borscht beet or cabbage soup, Russian style.

Bosch, Hieronymous [BAHSH, hihr-AHN-ih-muhs] (c. 1450-c. 1516) Dutch painter (*Garden of Earthly Delights*).

bo's'n [BOHT-suhn] boatswain. Also bosun, bos'n.

Bosporus [BAHS-pawr-uhs] the Bosporus, also Bosphorus. Straits in Turkey at mouth of Black Sea.

Botanical Garden (National) the garden. *Botanical* pref. to *Botanic*.

both (adj.) *both men.* (pronoun) *both have happy homes.* (conj.) *Both you and I will go.*
   Both (adj.) follows a single pronoun (*They both went* BUT precedes a single noun (*Both men went*) FOLLOWS a double noun (*Tom and Jerry*

both went). NOT: *The men both went to town.*

However, after a linking verb, *both* follows a single noun. *The men were both happy.*

Both also involves two elements connected by *and: They are both strong and rich.* AVOID confusion caused by combining three elements. NOT: *They are both strong, rich, and intelligent.*

AVOID placement before a preposition. Use: *Oatmeal is pleasing in both flavor and consistency,* or *both in flavor and in consistency.* NOT: both in flavor and consistency.

In the possessive: *both's homes.*

Both takes a plural verb. *Both Tom and Jerry are here.* AVOID redundancy. Do not use with *equal, alike, agree, together.* NOT: *both are equal; both agree.*

both of Must be followed by a pronoun: *both of them.* BUT: *both girls.* NOT: *both of the girls.*

Botswana [BAHT-swa-nah] inland nation in SW Africa. Former Br. Bechuanaland; independent, 1966. Cap.: Gaberones [gah-beh-ROH-nehs] Native: Botswana. Currency: pula.

Botticelli, Sandro [boht-tee-CHEHL-lee, SAHN-droh] (1444-1510) Italian painter *(Venus Rising from Waves).*

bottom land, bottom plate.

bottom of the page Pref. to *foot of the page.*

bouillon [bool-YAHN; buhl-yuhn; buhl-yahn]. Soup.

BULLION [BUHL-yuhn] metal.

boulder large, rounded rock.

boulevard [BOOL-eh-vahrd; BUHL]. Abbr: blvd.

bound obliged; or determined. *He is bound to succeed.*

boundary a definite geographical limit. *The boundary between France and Germany.*
Compare to

> BORDER line or area extending along a boundary: *the Franco-German border.*

> EDGE a terminal line between any two areas: *the edge of a precipice.*

> FRONTIER region approaching a foreign or different area: *France's German frontier; the New Frontier.*

bouquet [boo-KAE, bohkae] bunch of flowers; aroma.

bourbon (Cap.) Fr. royal family [boor-BUHN]; (lowercase) whiskey [BUR-BUHN].

bourgeois [boor-ZHWAH-ZHWAHZ] (Fr.) (n.) one of the middle class; —oise, a woman of the middle class. (adj.) middleclass. *bourgeoisie* [boor-zhwah-SEE] (n. only) the middle class.

boutonniere [boo-tuh-NYAIR] flower worn in a buttonhole.

Boutros Ghali, Boutros [BOO-trohs GA-lee] (b. 1922) Egyptian politician, statesman; Secretary-General of U.N. starting 1992.

bovine [BOH-vien -vihn] pertaining to the ox or the cow.

bowdlerize [BOUD-lehr-ieze] (v.) to edit prudishly.

bowie knife [BOH-ih, boo-ih] large hunting knife, named after frontiersman James Bowie.

bowl, Dust Bowl, Ice Bowl, Rose Bowl; the bowl.

bow window See **bay window**.

Boxing Day Br. holiday, first weekday after Christmas.

boycott (v.) to withhold business or social intercourse as punitive measure.

Boy Scouts (org.) a Boy Scout, a Scout, the Scouts.

brace two, used in referring to game, dogs, pistols. In ref. to people, usu. contemptuous. BUT *two braces* means a pair of suspenders.

BRACE { } Used to show relationship of an inclusive element to a group of subordinate elements. Used instead of an outline or a table. Point of brace faces more inclusive term.

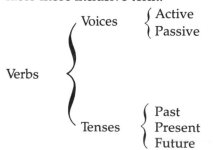

brackets [ ] Used to indicate (1) a correction; (2) a supplied omission; (3) an interpolation; (4) a comment; or (5) a warning that an error is reproduced literally.

(1) *The general [Eisenhower] ordered the invasion.* (2) *"The playing fields of Eton [an English public school] are credited with preparing many fine officers."* (3 & 4) *The meeting will be a short one [laughter], and I propose to keep it orderly [appluase].* (5) *The statue [sic] was the law of the land.* (6) In bills, contracts and other documents, used to indicate material to be omitted. (7) in mathematics, used to denote that enclosed matter is to be treated as a unit.

brag Avoid as a noun. NOT: *His brag that the team would win . . .* BUT *His brag and bluster* (one characteristic) is correct.

braggadocio [brag-uh-DOH-shee-oh] empty boasting.

Brahmin in India, highest Hindu caste. In U.S. (usu. pejorative), old, socially exclusive New England families.

Braille [brael] printing for the blind.

brake (v.) retard or stop. (n.) an overgrown area: for example, *a cane-brake.*

branch Cap. if part of name; cap. standing alone only referring to a federal or District of Columbia unit. Accounts Branch. BUT: executive, judicial, or legislative branch.

brandnew (adj.) (GPO). Spelled *brand-new* in *Webster's*.

brandyman, branywine; brandy-burnt (adj.).

brass alloy of copper and zinc.

brasier, brazier [BRAE-zhehr] a brass worker, also a pan for holding coals or one for exposing food to fire.

BRASSIER [BRASS-ee-ehr] with more brass; bolder.

BRASSIERE [bruh-ZEER] woman's undergarment.

Braun, Werner von (brawn, VUR-nuhr) (1912-1977) German-American rocket scientist.

bravado [bra-VAH-doh] swagger, simulated bravery.

brazen from bronze, but usu. used figurative: *brazen nakedness*.

Brazil largest South American country. Former Portugese colony; independent, 1822. Cap.: Brasilia. Native: Brazilian. Currency: cruzeiro [croo-ZAE-roo] Brazil nut.

breach (n.) gap. (v.) to make an opening in.

break (p.) broke. (p.p.) broken.

breathtaking

Brecht, Bertolt [brehkt, BEHR-tohlt] (1898-1956) German poet and playwright (*Mother Courage*).

breech part of a gun behind the bore; the buttocks.

breeches [BRIHCH-ehz; -ihz] (colloq.) trousers.

breed (p. and p.p.) bred; breeding.

breezeway, breeze-borne, —lifted, —swept (adj.).

Breton native of Brittany.

breviary [BREE-vih-ary; BREHV-ih-ary] book of daily prayers.

brew house, brewery, brewmaster.

Brezhnev, Leonid Ilyich [BRAEJ-nehf, LEE-uh-nihd] (1906-1982) leader (First Secretary) of Soviet Communist Party, 1964-1982; hence, head of U.S.S.R. Succeeded **Nikita Khrushchev.**

bric-a-brac [BRIHK-uh-brak] knick-nacks.

bridesmaid, bridesman.

bridge Cap. if part of name: The bridge, Arlington Memorial Bridge, Memorial Bridge. BUT: a Pennsylvania Railroad bridge.

brief short in duration. May refer to time or distance; sometimes implies incompleteness or curtailment.

In law, statement of a client's case, or of the points of a legal argument.

brig See **boat.**

brigand [BRIHG-uhnd] bandit.

Brig. Gen. (abbr.) brigadier general, brigadier generals.

brilliance brightness. *Brilliancy*

notes degrees of brightness.

brilliant cut (n.) a type of diamond. (adj.) brilliant-cut.

brimstone sulphur.

bring (p. and p.p.) brought. (pres. part.) bringing; (n.) —er. to cause to come toward or with. NOT: *bring to the enemy.* Opposite of *take.*

briquette, briquet [brih-KEHT] (n.) block of pressed coal.

British of Great Britain or the British Empire. Abbr.: Brit., Br. (n.). Britisher. More precise and forceful than **English**.

Briton native of England in Roman times. Compare to **Breton**.

British Columbia NW Canadian province. Cap., Victoria. abbr.: B.C.

British Commonwealth association of Great Britain's former colonies; established 1931.

British Honduras See **Belize**.

British Guiana See **Guyana**.

Brittany [BRIHT-n-ih] Fr: Bretagne [brehTAHN-y] region in NW France. Native: Breton.

broad wide; extended from side to side. Applies particularly to surfaces or areas: broad backs, bosom, fields, forehead, hands, mind, plains; also broad daylight, humor, outline.
    Compare to

WIDE extensive; over a great dis-

tance; to the greatest extent. Often suggests an opening. Wide distribution, mouths, range, influence, world; eyes wide open.
    Broad and *wide* are often used interchangeably, but there are different shades of meaning. *The wide plains were difficult to cross.* BUT: *Broad plains brought bountiful harvests.* ALSO: *A wide generalization covers a large area.* BUT: *A broad one neglects possible exceptions.*

broadcloth cotton material in shirts or dresses. Br., poplin.

Brobdingnag [BRAHB-dihng-nag] (from Jonathan Swift's *Gulliver's Travels*) imaginary country of giants. (adj.) Brobdingnagian. SEE **Lilliput**.

brochure [broh-SHOOR] pamphlet.

brogan [BROH-gan] a heavy, coarse shoe.

bronchial [BRAHNK-ee-uhl] (adj.) from bronchi [BRAAHNK-kie], subdivisions of the windpipe. (pl.) the bronchial tubes.

broncobuster, broncbuster one who breaks (tames) broncos.

Brontë, Charlotte [BRAHN-tee] (1816-1855) English novelist; author of *Jane Eyre*, etc. Sister of Emily Brontë.

    BRONTË, EMILY (1818-1848) author of *Wuthering Heights*. Sister of Charlotte Brontë.

Bronze Age period following Stone Age.

brooch [brohch, brooch] ornamental clip or pin.

broomstick (n.) broomtail (adj.); broom handle (n.).

Brother(s) (adherent of religious order) ADDRESS: Brother Timothy Stone, F.S.C., Superior, 121 Peach Street, etc. SALUTATION: Dear Brother; My dear Brother John.

brotherhood, brother-German; brother-in-law, (pl.) brothers-in-law.

brown study (n.) serious absorption.

Bruegel, Pieter [BROI-g'l] (c. 1525-1569) Flemish painter. Known as Pieter Bruegel The Elder.

bruit [broot] (v.) (usu. passive) to pass on rumor or bad news.
　　Compare to
　　BRUT [bruht] not sweet. Drier than extra sec.

brunet, brunette [broo-NEHT] The —ette ending is more common, and in *Webster's* it applies to both masc. and fem.

Brunei [BROO-nie] country on island of Borneo, SW Pacific. Former Br. protectorate; independent, 1984. Cap.: Bandar Seri Begawan. Native: Brunei. Currency: Brunei dollar.

brusque [bruhsk] rough, abrupt.

brussels carpet lace, sprouts. *Webster's* spelling: *Brussels carpet.*

brutal savage, cruel. Implies moral condemnation. *Only a barbarian would subject us to such brutal treatment.*

B.S. (abbr.) Bachelor of Science. B.Sc. is rare.

B.T.u. or **B.T.U.** (abbr.) British thermal unit.

bu. (abbr.) bushel.

bubble gum

buccaneer [buhk-uh-NEER] pirate.

buck male deer. Also male antelope, rabbit, rat, goat or (colloq.) sheep. Male moose and elk are bulls. See *ANIMALS.*

bucket shop unlicensed dealer or broker, esp. in securities. Orders are placed on the basis of current prices, but there is no actual selling or buying.

Buddha See **Gautama Buddha.**

Buddhism [BUHD-ihsm] religion of Gautama Buddha. Began in India c. 500 B.C.; widespread in Far East.
　　Nirvana (escape from suffering and mortality) is the Buddhist goal, attainable by "Eightfold Path:" right belief, right resolve, right word, right act, right life, right effort, right thinking, and right meditation.

budget department, estimate, message; federal budget, performance-type, President's, etc. Cap. if part of title: Budget of the United States (a publication); the Budget Bureau.

buffalo (pl.) —oes.

buffet [buh-FAE] (n.) meal in which diners serve themselves. cupboard.

BUFFET [BUHF-eht, -iht] (v.) to hit or slap. (n.) A slap.

build (p. and pp.) built; building.

building Cap. if part of name: Capitol Building, Colorado Building, House (or Senate) Office Building.

brute having animal powers and appetites. Usu. implies no condemnation: *brute force.*

brutish irrational; stupid, Implies condemnation. *The life of man is solitary, nasty, brutish, and short.*

build-up (n.). buildup (adj.).

built-in (adj.). built-up (adj.).

Bulgaria [buhl-GAR-ih-a; BUL-] republic in E Europe; independent, 1908. Cap.: Sofia. Native: Bulgarian. Currency: lev.

bullion See **bouillon.**

bull's eye

bunch AVOID use for "a lot," esp. of people.

bunkum [BUHNK-uhm] something said for show; nonsense.

bunkhouse -load.

Bunsen burner gas burner producing hot flame.

buntline rope attached to the foot of a sail.

Bunuel, Luis [boo-NWEHLL] (1900-1983) Spanish film maker (*Discreet Charm of the Bourgeoisie*).

buoy [BOO-ih; boi] (n.) moored float marking a channel, rock, or other danger. (v.) to make buoyant.

buoyant [BOI-uhnt] tending to float; hence, lightness of spirit.

burden [BUHR-d'n] a load; encumbrance.

bureau, Bureau [BYOO-roh] chest of drawers; business office; government department, or one of its subdivisions. Cap. if part of name; cap. standing alone if referring to Federal, D.C., or international unit: Bureau of Customs; Federal Bureau of Investigation; the Bureau.

bureaucracy [byoo-RAHK-ruh-sih] administration conducted by means of bureaus, hence, characterized by elaborate formal routines, red tape, etc.

bureaucrat [BYOO-ruh-krat]

burg slang for town, usu. pejorative.

burgher [buhr-guhr] freeman of late-medieval burgh; hence, any respected citizen, usu. pejorative.

burglary breaking and entering. Robbery involves taking by force.

HOLDUP robbery with a weapon.

THEFT any taking of another's property.

BURGLARIZE law-enforcement term adopted by news media.

Burkina Faso [buhr-KEE-nah-FAH-soh] W African country. Former Fr. colony; independent as **Upper Volta,** 1960; became Burkina Faso, 1984. Cap.: Oúagdougou [WAHG-uh-DOO-goo]. Native: Voltaic. Currency: CFA franc.

Burma [BUHR-muh] SE Asian country; independent, 1948. Cap.: Rangoon. Native: Burman. Currency: kyat.

burn —ed, —ing. (participial adj.) burnt, as in *burnt-out.*

burr NOT *bur.*

burst Pref. to *bust* except colloq.: *I'm busted,* meaning out of cash, or *You're busted,* meaning under arrest.

Burundi [buh-ROON-dee] Central African country. Formerly Ger. and Bel.; independent, 1962. Cap.: Bujumbura [BOO-jahm-BOO-rah] Native: Burundian. Currency: franc.

bus (pl.) buses, pres. to *busses.* busboy, busdriver, busline.

bushel abbr.: bu. Unit of dry measure (1) U.S.; 4 pecks = 32 dry qts. = 8 dry gal. = 2150.42 cu. in. (2) Brit.: 1.032 U.S. bu.=33.026 U.S. dry qt. (3) heaped (U.S.)=1.278 U.S. bu. struck measure = approx. 1 bu. struck measure = 2.747.715 cu. in.

businessman small businessman. *Business woman* is still appropriate.

bust See **burst.**

busybody

but Used (1) for *except;* (2) for *only: He had but one life to give.* (3) for *that* in *not ...but* construction: *There was not a page but had an error on it.* (4) to introduce a parallel clause: *He studied hard but he looked it.* (5) to introduce a negative clause: *He studied hard but he did not learn.*

But is considered a preposition when followed by a noun or pronoun. *Everyone was there but him.*

However, *but* is technically a conjunction, and can function that way before a noun. *Everyone was here but he (was not).*

butt unit of capacity measure equals 2 hogsheads equals 126 long gallons.

buy (n.) (colloq.) smart purchase; bargain: *a good buy.*

buyer's market: market in which supply exceeds demand.

buzz bomb, buzz saw, buzz cut.

by (adv.) *He is standing by.* (prep.) *He passed by the house.*

bygone, bylaw, byplay, bystander, byway, byword (all words n.).

by-your-leave (n., adj.), by-line, by-election, by-product; by and by, by the by, by the way.

bye bypass. *In the first round of the playoffs, the Celtics earned a bye.* Otherwords, now obs.

Byelorussia [Bie-loh-RUHSH-uh] formerly part of U.S.S.R., now in Commonwealth. A/k/a White Russia, near Poland. Cap: Minsk, also temporary cap. of Commonwealth. Native: Byelorussian(s).

by the hundred, by the dozen, by the score. BUT: by hundreds, dozens, scores.

byte [biet] (n. only) basic unit of computer memory.

Byzantine [BIH-zan-teen or BIE] from Byzantium (later Constantinople, now Istanbul) cap. of Eastern Roman Empire, later Byzantine Empire (474-1453). Also lowercase: full of intrigue and murky deals.

C

c, ck A word ending in *c* adds *k* before an Anglo-Saxon suffix: -ed, -er, -ing, or -y. *Panicky, picnicking.* This does not apply with classical suffixes: -ian, -ism, -ist, -ity, -ize. *Criticism.*

C. (abbr.) Catholic; Celsius. Centigrade may be lowercase.

C sharp C-star; C-tube.

c. (abbr.) circa (also ca.); centi. = one-hundreth (0.01); cycle (Kc. only); curie; cent, cents (also ct.).

CA California

C.A.B. (abbr.) Civil Aeronautics Board.

cabal [kuh-BAL] a secret association of a few persons.

cabala [KAB-uh-luh] esoteric doctrine or science.

cabana [kuh-BAN-uh] bathhouse.

cabdriver

Cabinet, American or foreign Cap. if part of name or standing alone: *British Cabinet: the Cabinet; the President's Cabinet: the Cabinet; Cabinet officer, member.* See **the Ministry, foreign cabinets, secretary.**

cabinetmaker, —making, —work, —worker.

cableholder —man; cable-laid (adj.); cable car, cable ship.

cacao [kuh-KAE-oh; kuh-KAH-oh] (pl.) —s. See **cocoa.**

cache [kash] hiding-place.

cachet [ka-SHAE] seal.

SACHET [sa-SHAE] pouch containing perfumed herbs.

cacodemon [kak-oh-DEE-muhn] evil spirit.

cacophony [ka-KAHF-oh-nih] discord

cactus (pl.) —ti or —uses.

cadaver [kuh-DAV-uhr or kuh-DAE-vuhr] a dead body.

caddy assistant and porter at golf game; also a tea box.

caduceus [kuh-DYOO-see-uhs] staff with separate twining snake about. Symbol of physicians and medical corps. (pl.) —cei.

Caedmon [KAD-muhn] (c. 670) Anglo-Saxon poet.

Caesar [SEE-zuhr] generic term for ruler, emperor; root of both Ger. *Kaiser* and Russ. *Czar*; after **Julius Caesar** (100-44 B.C.), Roman general and statesman, and **Augustus Caesar** (Gaius Julius Caesar Octavianus) (63 B.C.-14 A.D.).First Roman emperor (27 B.C.-14 A.D.).

caesura [seh-SUR-ah] emphatic pause.

C.A.F. (abbr.) cost and freight.

café [ka-FAE] coffee house.

café au lait [oh-LAE] (Fr.) coffee with hot milk.

    CAFE LATTE [lah-tae] coffee with steamed milk.

caffeine [kah-FEEN] stimulant alkaloid in coffee, tea, etc.

cakebaker —box, —maker.

Cairo [in Egypt, KAE-roh; in Illinois, KA-roh]

Cajun [KAE-j'n] (n. or adj.) native to Louisiana bayous.

Calais [Kah-LAE] French seaport on the English Channel.

caldron [KAWL-dr'n] large kettle. Pref. to *cauldron* in U.S.

caleche or **calash** [kuh-LESH] buggy with folding top.

Caledonian native to ancient Scotland.

calendar Cap. if part of name; House Calendar, Calendar No. 99, Calendar of Bills and Resolutions; the calendar.

calendar list of dates. Also, a smooth paper finish.

    COLANDER strainer. *Drain pasta in a colander.*

caliber Pref. to *calibre* in U.S.

California U.S. State. Abbr: CA. Cap.: Sacramento.

caliper or **calliper** [KAL-ih-pehr] measuring instrument. Usually used in plural. (pl.) —s.

calif or **caliph** [KAE-lihf, KAH-lihf] muslim ruler.

calisthenics [KAH-lih-STHEHN-ihks] exercises.

calligraphy [ka-LIHG-ra-fee] elegant penmanship.

Calliope [kuh-LIE-oh-pee] Greek muse of poetry and eloquence. Also, steam whistle musical instrument.

callus [KAL-uhs]. (n.) hardened skin. (pl.) —uses. **callous** (adj.) Feeling no emotion. **Calloused** is the adj. for skin: *calloused hands.*

calorie Usu. expresses energy value and fattening potential of food. Technically, unit of heat required to raise temperature of 1 liter of water 1 degree centigrade. (adj.) caloric.

calumny [KAL-uhm-nee] slander.

Calvary the place where Christ was crucified.

    CAVALRY soldiers on horseback.

calyx [KAE-lihks; kal-ihks] leafy part of flower. (pl.) —es or calyces [KAL-ih-seez; CAE-lih-seez].

cambist [KAM-bihst] dealer in foreign notes or money.

Cambodia SE Asian country; independent, 1953. Cap.: Phnom Penh

[P'NAHM pehn] Native: Cambodian. Currency: riel.

camel The *dromedary* (Arabian camel) has one hump; the Bactrian camel has two.

camel's-hair (adj.). camel's hair (n.).

camellia [kuh-MEHL-ih-uh, or —MEEL-yuh]

cameo [KAM-ee-oh] relief-carved stone gem. (pl.) —os.

cameraman, camera obscura. See **cinematographer.**

Cameroon [kam-ehr-OONZ] NW African country. Former Br., Fr., U.N. territory. Independence, 1960; present boundaries, 1961. Cap.: Yaounde [YUH-oon-DAE]. Currency: CFA franc.

Camp Gary, Camp David, etc.; the camp.

Camus, Albert [kah-MUE, al-BEHR] (1913-1960) Fr. writer, social reformer.

can (p.) could: *She could talk before she was a year old.* The subjunctive *could* does not require an *if* before it. *Could he have passed the test, he would have won.*

can and **may** *Can* expresses mental or physical ability; *may* expresses permission. *What is possible can be done. You may have an apple.*

Canaan [KAEN-nan]. early Biblical name for Israel. Canaanite [—iet].

Canada North American country.

Self-rule, 1837; legal independence, 1926. Cap.: Ottawa. Native: Canadian(s). Currency: dollar.

canal Cap. with name: Panama, the canal; Canal Zone; the zone.

canalboat, —man, —side.

Canal Zone U.S. leasehold in Panama, 10 mi. wide, U.S. withdrawal to be completed 1999. Abbr.: CZ.

canapé [kan-uh-PAE] an appetizer.

CANOPY [KAN-oh-pih] an overhanging covering.

Canaveral, Cape [can-AV-ehr-al] U.S. rocket-launching site in Florida. Renamed Kennedy, 1963; reverted to Canaveral, 1973.

candelabrum [can-deh-LAH-bruhm] branched candlestick. (pl.) —*bra* is pref. to —*brums*; NOT —bras.

cancel cancellation; canceler. —led, —ing.

Cancer born June 21-July 22. See **Zodiac.**

candidate [KAN-dih-daet], candidacy.

candor [KAN-der] (Br.: candour) frankness.

candy Plural forms: (same type) pieces of candy; (various types) candies.

canebrake, cane sugar.

canister

Cannes [kann] Fr. town on the Riviera; site of film festival.

cannon (sing. and collective). (pl.) —s. cannonball, —proof.

cannot One word except for emphasis.

cannot help, cannot but, cannot help but, pref. in that order.

canon [KAN-uhn] (n.) The canon of saints are those officially recognized by the Catholic Church. Hence, any ruling order approved by authority.

cantabile [kahn-TAH-bee-lae] (It.) singable.

cantaloupe [CAN-tuh-lohp]

cantata [kan-TAH-tah] dramatic choral composition.

canto [KAN-toh] division of a long poem. (pl.) —os.

canvas (n.) hemp and flax material, a common surface for artwork. Hence, any arena where art is made. *The dance floor is his canvas.*

CANVASS (v.) to solicit. (n.) solicitation; or a detailed exam.

canyon [KAN-yuhn] deep, steep-walled valley.

capable of able to.

Cape of Good Hope the cape. S tip of Africa.

Cape Kennedy See **Cape Canaveral.**

Cape Verde [kaep VUHRD] island country in SW Atlantic. Former Port. colony; independent, 1975. Cap.: Praia [PRAE-yah]. Native: Cape Verdean. Currency: escudo.

capital (n.) refers to letters, the tops of columns, and to cities: *Boston is the capital.* Abbr.: cap. Also (adj.) excellent, exemplary.

CAPITOL refers to a building.

Capital Capital City, National Capital (Washington, D.C.). BUT: the capital (state).

capital gain (or loss) profit (or loss) from sale or exchange of capital asset (asset owned in order to produce income).

CAPITALIZATION Capitalize (cap.) (1) the first word of a sentence, of an independent clause or phrase, of a direct quotation, of a line of poetry, of a formally introduced series of items. *The question is, will they work? He asked, ''Where are you going?''*
> *Whenas in silks my Julia goes,*
> *Then, then, methinks, how sweetly flows*
> *That liquefaction of her clothes.*

(2) BUT NOT the first word of a fragmentary quotation. *He objected to ''the phraseology'' not to the ideas.*
(3) Cap. the first word following a colon, an exclamation point or a question mark unless the matter following is merely supplementary. *The vote was as follows: In the affirmative, 16; in the negative, 11; not voting, 2. BUT: Revolutions are not made: they come.*
(4) Cap. proper names—*John Brown, New York, the Jones family*—

and derivatives in English. BUT there are proper nouns which have acquired common meaning: *roman type, plaster of paris, pasteurize.* These take lowercase.

(5) Cap. adjectives or common nouns which are an essential part of a proper noun: *Statue of Liberty, Amsterdam Avenue, Union Station.* BUT NOT the common noun standing alone: *the statue, the avenue, the station;* AND NOT when a common noun intervenes: *Union passenger station.*

(6) Cap. the plural forms of proper nouns; *First and P Streets.*

(7) Cap. when the common noun is used as a short form of a well-known name previously mentioned: *the Capitol, the Court* (for the Supreme Court).

(8) Cap. a title preceding a name: *Professor Jones.*

(9) Cap. eminent distinctions, titles of heads of state or of members of the diplomatic corps following a name: *Mario Cuomo, Governor of the State of New York.*

BUT NOT military titles: *Charles F. Hughes, admiral;* or scholastic titles: *Cloyd H. Marvin, president of George Washington University.*

(10) Cap. the titles of acts, articles, books, captions, chapters, editorials, essays, historical events, laws, lectures, parts of a book, poems, reports, short titles of acts, songs, television and radio programs, treaties, wars, and usually any noun followed by a numeral when used as a title.

BUT titles in a foreign language conform to the rules of that language: *Cien anos de soledad.* ALSO titles of a bill not yet enacted into law are lower case: *minimum wage bill.*

(11) When an article is part of a name or title, it is cap:

The New York Times. BUT NOT when the article is used adjectively: *the Hague Court, the Herald Tribune.* In general, lowercase the articles in reference to newspapers, periodicals, vessels, airships, trains, and firm names: *the Netherlands, the News, the Queen Mary, the U-2.*

In foreign names, articles *d', da, della, du, van,* and *von* are cap. when not preceded by a forename or title: *De Gaulle* BUT *Charles de Gaulle.* (UCMS capitalizes *Van* and *Von* in all cases.) BUT in anglicized versions, the articles in names are capitalized unless personal usage is otherwise: *Thomas De Quincey* (his usage).

(12) Cap. the full name of organized bodies and shortened names, but substitutes are regarded as common nouns and are lowercased except to indicate preeminence or distinction. *U.S. Congress, 82d Congress; U.S. Navy, the Navy, naval shipyard, naval station; Republican party.*

(13) Cap. the names of administrative, judiciary, or legislative bodies of government: *Office of Civilian Defense, Budget Bureau.* BUT NOT: general designations: *the national parliament, United States government bodies, federal court.*

(14) Cap. names of adherents of organized bodies: *a Republican, and Elk, a Communist.* BUT lowercase those with a common belief designated as a group: *liberals, democrats, conservatives, hippies.*

(15) Cap. official designations of countries, administrative divisions, regions and geographic features as nouns or adjectives, including an

area direction if part of the name: *British Commonwealth, the Commonwealth, the East, the Eastern States.* BUT: *eastern section, east* (as a direction), *the valley of the Missouri River, the river Elbe, the Indian peninsula, western Europe.*

(16) Cap. epithets and fanciful appelations: *the Bad Boys of Motown;* and vivid personifications: *When Nature wields her scepter mercilessly.*

(17) Cap. religious terms denoting the deity or a sacred book: *Heavenly Father, the Scriptures, Talmud, Exodus,, Gospel of Mark.* BUT NOT derived adjectives: *scriptural, talmudic.*

(18) Cap. calendar divisions and holidays: *Sunday, January, Thanksgiving Day.* BUT NOT the seasons: *fall, winter.*

(19) Cap. historic events and periods: *the Renaissance, the Iron Age, the Bronze Age.* See *AGES.*

(20) Cap. trade names: *Macintosh SE, Kodak.*

(21) Cap. scientific name of a phylum: *Arthopoda:* class: *Crustacea;* order: *Hypoparia;* family: *Agnostidae;* or genus: *Agnostics.* BUT NOT species. See *CLASSIFICATION OF ANIMALS AND PLANTS.* For coined terms derived from proper names, use lowercase: *menodontine.*

(22) Cap. soil names: *Bog.* and planets: *Venus.* BUT NOT *sun, moon,* and *earth* unless used with other planets.

(23) Cap. *Volume, Chapter, Book,* etc. when followed by a number that is part of a title, legend, or citation: *Book 1: The Golden Legend; Chapter 11 of the Penal Code,* BUT NOT a common noun merely because it is used with a date, number, or letter, for the purpose of reference or record: *article 1.* Lowercase *freshman, sophomore, junior,* and *senior.* (UCMS capitalizes these.)

(24) Cap. the first word following an enacting or resolving clause (usually *That*): *Resolved, That . . . and be it further. . . Provided, That . . .* But not the first word following *Whereas* in resolutions, contracts, etc.: *Whereas the law provides, etc.* (BUT U.C.M.S. always capitalizes the first word following *Whereas.*)

(25) Cap. the exclamatory *Oh!* or *O.* See **capital, capitol,** *TITLES, NAMES, SPELLING.*

Capote, Truman [kah-POH-tee]. (1924-1984). American writer (*Breakfast at Tiffany's*).

Capri [KA-prih] Island in Bay of Naples, Italy.

Capricorn [ka-prih-KAWRN] born Dec. 22-Jan. 20. See **Zodiac.**

capsule [KAP-sool, or -suhl].

caption. Title or explanation of an illustration.

captious unreasonable or unnecessary. (n.) **captiousness** peevishness.

CAVILING petty criticism.

CARPING ill-tempered criticism.

capuchin [KAP-yoo-chihn; kap-yoo-CHEEN] a hooded cloak; also a South American monkey. (cap.) an order of monks.

captivate

Caracas [kah-RAH-kahs] capital city of Venezuela.

carat measure of weight of precious stones. 3.0865 grains = 200 mgr.

KARAT measure of gold purity in 24ths; 14 karat is 10 parts alloy. Also *carat*.

CARET a mark (^) used to indicate an insertion.

CARROT the vegetable.

Caravaggio, Michelangelo [kah-rah-VAH-joh] (1573-1610) Italian painter.

caravansary [kar-ah-VAN-suh-rih] inn for caravan travelers. Hence, any gathering that seems haphazard or sprawling.

carbine [KAHR-bien] short-barreled rifle.

carburetor [KAHR-byoo-reht-er] device in which air or gas is charged with carbon compounds to create combustion.

carcass [KAHR-kuhs] dead body.

carcinogen [kar-sin-noh-jehn] Cancer-causing substance.

cardinal Cap. for title: Terrence Cardinal Cooke, Cardinal Cooke, the Cardinal. ADDRESS: His Eminence The Most Reverend Terrence Cardinal Cooke, Archbishop of New York. SALUTATION: Your Eminence; Most Reverend Sir; Dear Cardinal Cooke.

CARE (abbr.) Cooperative for American Relief Everywhere. *CARE package* (colloq.) is package from home.

Caribbean Sea [kar-eh-BEE-an; kuh-RIHB- bee-an]

caroled —ing.

carping See **captious**.

carrierborne

carryall (m. & adj.).

carte blanche [kahrt BLAHNSH] (Fr.) blank page with signature. Hence, unlimited funding or authority.

cartilage [KAHR-tih-lihj] elastic tissue composing parts of the skeleton, as in the nose.

Caruso, Enrico [kah-ROO-zoh] (1873-1921) Italian tenor.

case a particular instance, especially legal or medical: *in case of accident*; a situation involving a problem: *a case of bad blood*; an argument: *a law case*.

CASE In grammar, case means the relation of the noun or pronoun to other parts of the sentence. That is, nouns and pronouns may be subjects (nominative); objects (objective or accusative); or modifiers (possessive or genitive). Nouns or pronouns indicate their case by a change of form, inflection, or position. *He* is nominative, *him* objective, *his* genitive.

All nouns and some pronouns retain the same form in the nominative and objective cases. In these instances, the case or function is indicated by their position in the sentence. Some pronouns change form (or inflection) in all three cases: *he, him, his.*

The subject noun is always nominative case. So are nouns following a form of the verb *to be;* these are called the predicate nominative. Also in the nominative case are (1) a noun in a phrase that consists of a noun or pronoun and a participle *(the man running the show);* and (2) a noun in direct address *(Listen, you!).*

The most common examples of the objective case are the direct object (also known as the accusative case) and the indirect object (at one time called the dative case). Any noun or pronoun that functions as either must take the objective form: *I hit him; I gave the ball to her.*

Also in the objective are the subject of an infinitive, the subject of a participle, and the word before *to be: We believed him to be honest.*

Pronouns change form to show case: (1) nominative: *I, we, she, who, they;* (2) objective: *her, him, them, whom;* (3) possessive: *your, our, his, their.*

In a compound, both members must be in the same case. *She and Vera drive me crazy.* Also words or groups of words standing in opposition remains in the same case as the antecedent. *I'll take him on—him and his army.*

Expressions like *I believe* and *he thinks* between the subject and the verb do not change the case. *He is the man who I believe took the jewels.*

A relative pronoun—*who, whoever, which, whichever*—used as the subject of a clause is in the nominative case. *Return the money to whoever loaned it to her.* In a subordinate clause, the case

of the relative pronoun depends upon its use within the clause. See **aspect**.

casebook —bound, —load, —maker, -worm (all one word); case binding, case work, case worker.

casket a box. *A corpse lies in a coffin.*

cassette plastic container for recording tape.

Cassiopeia [kas-see-oh-PEE-uh] in Gr. mythology, a queen; in astronomy, a northern constellation.

cast [kast] (v.) to throw; mold; select actors in a play. (n.) the thing thrown or molded; the actors. (p. and pp.) cast; casting.

caste [kast] (n.) In Hindu religion pre-destined social standing. *lower-caste tastes.*

caster a wheel or set of wheels on furniture.

Compare to

CASTOR a type of beaver, bean, medicine. **Castor oil.**

Castro, Ruz, Fidel [KAHS-troh, Rooz, feeDEHL] (b. 1927). Prime Minister of Cuba since 1959.

casual offhand, unforeseen.

CAUSAL implying cause.

catalyst substance which affects chemical reactions. Hence, any person, event, or issue that causes change. *Her best friend's death was the catalyst for their divorce.*

catalog This spelling more common than —logue. —ed, —ing, —er.

catarrh [kuh-TAHR] inflammation of mucous membrane.

catch (p. and p.p.) caught.

catchall (n. & adj.)

CATCHUP (colloq.) (adj.) *We'll have to play catchup ball.*

categorical [kat-ih-GAWR-ih-kul] absolute, unqualified.

category [KAT-ee-goh-rih] division formed for discussion or classification. See **class.**

cater-corner Also spelled without hyphen.

caterwauling. screaming, howling.

catholic (lowercase) universal; general.

CATHOLIC (cap.) (adj.) pertaining to Roman Catholic church. (n.) Catholicism [ka-THAHL-ihsihsm].

cat's-eye (nonliteral), cat's-paw (nonliteral).

catsup Usu. spelled *ketchup.*

Caucasian (n. or adj.) the white race. A misnomer; ancient peoples of the Caucasus were not typically white. See **Aryan.**

causa mortis (Lat.) in contemplation of death: *a gift causa mortis.*

cause (n.) something that produces an effect.

REASON (n.) explanation of the cause.

cause (v.) May be followed by an infinitive: *You caused him to fail:* a noun: *You caused his failure;* or a gerund: *You caused his failing.*

cause Avoid redundancy. Use *is due to* or *The cause is.* NOT: *The cause is due to.*

cause celebre [kohz sae-LEHBR] widely publicized case.

caused by NOT caused from.

cause of . . . is that *The cause of the delay is that he was late.* NOT: *. . . is on account of his being late.* AND NOT: *. . . is due to his being late.* CORRECT: *We were delayed on account of his lateness. We were delayed due to his lateness.*

cavalcade procession. Literally, parade on horseback.

calvalryman

caveat [KAE-vee-at] beware; a warning. *Caveat emptor:* "let the buyer beware."

cavedweller, —man.

caviar

cavil —led, —ling or —lling, —ler. See **captious.**

cayenne [kie-EHN; kae-EHN] hot red pepper.

Cayuse [kie-YOOS] (Cap.) Oregonian Native Americans. (lowercase) small hardy horse.

C.B.D., c.b.d. (abbr.) cash before delivery.

C.B.S. (abbr.) Columbia Broadcasting System.

c.c. (abbr.) cubic centimeter. Also cm.

C.C.A. (abbr.) Circuit Court of Appeals.

C.D. (abbr.) compact disc.

cd.-ft (abbr.) cord-foot.

C.C.C. (abbr.) Civilian Conservation Corps; Work outfit during U.S. Great Depression, 1930s.

cease *Stop* is pref. BUT: *cease-fire* (n. and adj.).

Ceausescu Nicolae [koh-SEHS-cyoo] (1918-1989) Romanian dictator (1974-1989); executed after revolution.

cedarware, cedar-colored (adj.); cedar leaf.

cedilla. [see-DIHL-uh] mark placed under *c* to indicate soft pronunciation. Common in Fr. and Sp. See *DIACRITICAL MARKS*.

Celebes [SEHL-ee-beez or seh-LEE-beez] Indonesion island.

celebrant one who conducts a religious ceremony.

CELEBRATOR one who celebrates.

CELEBRITY well-known person.

celerity [see-LEHR-ih-tih] speed,, applied to living things.

VELOCITY speed, applied to objects.

celi- combining form meaning unmarried: *celibacy, celibate.*

cellmate, —block; cell wall.

cello [CHEH-loh] Shortened from violoncello. (pl.) —os.

Celt [SEHLT] ancient native of British Isles. Celtic.

cement [see-MEHNT] See **concrete.**

cement maker, cement-covered (adj.), cementhead (n.).

cemetery Cap. if part of name: *Arlington National Cemetery; the cemetery.*

censer [SEHN-suhr] vessel for burning incense; the person using it.

CENSOR [SEHN-suhr] one who decides on acceptability of material for publication.

CENSURE [SEHN-shoor] to condemn; criticize adversely.

census Seventeenth Decennial Census (title), Seventeenth Census (title), the census; 1950 Census of Agriculture, the census of agriculture, the census.

centare [SEHN-taer] Also centiare. Unit of area = 1.196 sq. yd. = 10.764 sq. ft. = 1 m.2 = 0.01 are. abbr.: ca.

centennial [sehn-TEN-ee-al] 100th anniversary.

CENTENARY [SEHN-tee-nehr-ih, sehn-TEHN-ehr-ih] pertaining to 100 years.

center The central point. Half is on each side, in time, space, or material. *The middle surrounds the center.* Pref. to *centre.*

centerboard, —head (printing), —line, —most, —piece; center bit, center point.

centi combining form meaning hundred or hundredth part: *centipede, centigrade.* See hecto.

centigrade [SEHNT-ih-grade] Temperature scale from 0° (freezing) to 100° (boiling). Compares with Fahrenheit for 32° (freezing) to 212° (boiling).

centigram unit of weight = 0.15432 grains = 0.01 gram. abbr.: cg.

centiliter unit of capacity = 0.3381 fluid oz. = 0.011 liter = 0.6102 cu. in. abbr. cl.

centimeter [SEHN-tih-mee-tahr] unit of length = 0.3937 in. = 0.01 m. = 10 mm. abbr.: cm.

centistere [SEHN-tih-steer] unit of volume = 0.353 cu. ft. =0.01 m.

centner 110.23 lbs. avdp.

Central African Republic country north of Congo. Formerly Fr., named Ubangi-Shari [oo-BANG-ee SHA-REE]; independent, 1960. Cap.: Bangui [BAHN-gee]. Currency: CFA franc. Native: Centrafrican.

central Asia central Europe; central states; central time, central standard time.

century The first century includes years 1 to 100. The 20th, years 1901 through 2000. Year 1900 is in the 19th century. Lowercase and spell out first through ninth centuries. Hyphenate the adjective form: *20th-century artist.*

C.E.O. in business, Chief Executive Officer.

C.F.O. Chief Financial (sometimes Finance) Officer.

C.O.O. Chief Operations (sometimes Operating) Officer.

cerebral [seh-REE-bruhl] (adj.) pertaining to the brain, physically or intellectually: *cerebral music.*

cerebrum [seh-REE-bruhm] the brain, figuratively and anatomically. Specifically, the forebrain; the seat of voluntary and conscious mental processes. (pl.) —s, —bra.

Cervantes Saavedra, Miguel de [dae ser-VAHN-taes saah-ah-VAE-thrah, mee-GAHL] (1547-1616) Spanish novelist. See Don Quixote.

Cesarean [see-ZAIR-ee-an] (var. of caesarean) birth by surgery on the uterus. Also, pertaining to Caesar.

cesium [see-zih-uhm] soft, silver metallic element.

cesspit, —pool.

Ceylon [SAE-lahn] island off SE India. See Sri Lanka.

Cezanne, Paul [sae-ZAHN] (1839-1906) Fr. Impressionist painter.

Cf. (abbr.) confer, compare.

C.F.A. (abbr.) Colonies Francaises d'Afrique.

c.f.m. (abbr.) cubic feet per minute.

C.F.S. cubic feet per second.

C.F.O. See **C.E.O.**

c.g. (abbr.) centigram.

c.-h (abbr.) candle-hour.

Chad central African nation. Formerly Fr.; independent, 1960. Cap.: Fort Lamy, a/k/a N'Djamena [n'JAH-mee-nah]. Native: Chadian or Tchadien(ne). Currency: CFA franc.

Chagall, Marc [shah-GAHL] (1887-1985) Rus. painter.

chagrin [shuh-GRIHN] mortification; shame. —ined.

chair, the Capitalize if personified.

chairman, chairperson Used for m., *chair* can be used for m. or f. Cap. if federal title: Chairman of the Federal Trade Commission, the Chairman. BUT: chairman of the board of directors, the chairperson.

chaise lounge [shaez] chair with elongated seat; divan.

chalet [sha-LAE] Swiss herdsman's mountain cottage. Hence, any house in that style.

chamber of commerce Boston

Chamber of Commerce, the chamber. BUT cap. if federal: the Chamber of Commerce of the United States, the Chamber.

chameleon [kuh-MEE-lee-uhn] lizard that can change color. Hence, a fickle person.

chamois [SHAM-mih] soft leather; or the antelope [SHAM-mih or sham-WAH]. (sing. and pl.).

chamomile [KA-moh-mie'l] herb used in tea, medicine.

Champs-Élysées [shah'n-zae-lee-ZAE] a boulevard in Paris.

chance —cy, —d, —cing.

chancellery [CHAN-seh-lehr-ih] position, court, or department of a chancellor.

chancery [CHAN-suhr-ih] in U.S., a court of equity; a court of record or office of public records.

changeable (adj). changeover (n. and adj.).

changeling in folklore, fairy child left in place of human. Hence, anyone who changes radically or abruptly.

the Channel In caps. refers to English Channel. BUT: channel 3 (TV), the channel. channeled, —ing.

chantey, chanty [SHAN-tih] (from Fr. *chantez*) a sailors' song.

chaos [KAE-ahss] complete disorder.

chapbook (n.) a little book; *chap-fallen* (adj.) downhearted.

chaparral [shahp-uh-RAL] thicket of thorny shrubs.

chaperon(e) [SHAP-uhr-ohn] person who accompanies youngsters of either sex; orig., only for unmarried women.

characters in books, plays, etc. Cap. names.. Do not place in quotation marks. *She played the role of Cleopatra.*

chapter Cap. title: *Chapter 5: Research and Development.* BUT: chapter III, the 14th chapter.

charade [shuh-RAED] guessing game in which words are acted out. Hence, any false show. *This trial is a charade.*

charge *The store is in his charge* implies responsibility. *He is in charge of the stores* implies authority.

charge d'affaires [SHAHR-ZHAY-duh-FAER] Substitute for an ambassador. (pl.) charges d'affaires.

charlatan [SHAHR-luh-tan] quack; pretentious imposter.

Charlemagne [SHAR-leh-maen] (742-814). a/k/a Charles I, Charles the Great. King of the Franks, Emperor of Europe.

charley horse

chart chart 2, A, II BUT: Chart 2, when part of legend: *Chart 2, Army strength.*

charter Cap. with name: Atlantic Charter, United Nations Charter; the charters.

chassis [SHASS-ee] body or framework of a vehicle (or machinery). (pl.) chassis [SHASS-ihs].

chasten [CHAES'n] to discipline; purify.

chastise [SHAS-tiez] to punish; suggests physical abuse.

chateau [sha-TOH] large country house. (pl.) —teaux or —s.

chauffeur [shoh-FEUR]

Chautauqua [shuh-TAW-kwah] summer educational center in N.Y. Hence (often l.c.), an educational assembly combining lectures, entertainment, and outdoor activities.

chauvinism [SHOH-vihn-ihzm] excessive patriotism. Male chauvinist. —ist, —istic, —istically. See **jingoism.**

check (n.) bank draft. (v.) to hold back. *She checked his advances.*

checkerboard, checker (at a store).

cheddar [CHEHD-ehr] a smooth cheese.

cheekbone —piece, —strap.

cheerful Applies principally to feelings. *He remained cheerful in spite of his hard luck.*

CHEERY More superficial. *Ellen sounded cheery, but she was seething.*

Chekhov, Anton [CHEH-kuhv]

(1860-1904) Rus. writer ("Lady with a Lapdog," *Uncle Vanya*).

Chelsea [CHEHL-see] a town in MA; section of N.Y.C.; borough of London.

CHEMICAL FORMULAS Use full size figures before the symbols or group of symbols to which they relate and inferior figures after the symbols. *6 Ph 5. (Ag. Cu)₂ S. AS₂ S₂.* Lower-case the names of elements and formulas: *strontium 90, oxygen.*

DO NOT use a hyphen, even in a unit modifier: *uranium 235; freon 12.* BUT U_{235}; Sr^{90};$_{92}U^{234}$.

chemotherapy [KEE-moh-THEH-rah-pee] cancer treatment.

Cheops (Gr.) or **Khufu** (Egypt) [KEE-ahps, KOO-foo] (c. 2900 B.C.) King of Egypt, pyramid builder.

Chernobyl [chehr-NOH-b'l] Refers to disaster in Russian nuclear-power facility, 1986.

cherry-colored (adj.); cherry pie, cherry pit, cherry stone.

Cherokee [chehr-oh-KEE or CHEHR-] Iroquoian Native American tribe, now in Oklahoma.

cherubic [chehr-OOB-ihk]

chesterfield the overcoat.

chestnut-colored (adj.) chestnut-red (adj.).

Chevalier, Maurice [chuh-val-YAE moh-REES] (1888-1972) Fr. actor, singer.

Cheyenne [shie-EHN, or ANN] Native American tribe. Also city in WY; river in SD.

Chiang Kai-shek [SHAHNG kie-SHEK] (1886-1975) Chinese statesman, general; president at time of Communist revolution, 1949. See **Mao Tse-Tung.**

chianti [kih-YAN-tee] Italian dry red wine.

chiaroscuro [kih-ah-roh-SKYOO-roh] drawing, painting, or film that exaggerates or emphasizes light and shade.

chic [SHEEK] stylish.

Chicano See **-American.**

chicanery [shih-KAEN-uhr-ee] trickery.

chickenpox A plural form which takes a singular verb.

chide (P.) chided or chid; —iding.

chief Cap. if referring to head of a federal agency: the Chief Intelligence office, Chief of Staff, Chief Justice. BUT: chief justice (of a state).

chiffon [SHIHF-ahn; shih-FAHN] a sheer fabric.

chiffonier [shihf-oh-NEiER] high chest of drawers.

chihuahua [chee-WAH-wah] a little dog. Also, a Mex. province.

childish Derogatory adj.; suggests immaturity.

CHILDLIKE Approving; adj. suggests sweetness.

Chile nation on W coast of South America. Independent 1818. Cap.: Santiago. Native: Chilean. Currency: peso.

chili [CHIH-lee] originally, a pepper. (pl.) -ies. Also a spicy U.S. food; derives from Sp. *chile con carne*, peppers with meat.

chimera [kih-MEE-ruh or kie-] in Gr. myth, a monster lion-goat. Hence, a foolish fancy. (adj.) chimerical [kie-MEHR-ih-kal].

China Asian country. Native: Chinese. May be used for sing. or pl., m., or f., from the mainland or Taiwan. NOT: Chinaman.

MAINLAND CHINA Peoples' Republic of China. Occupies nearly all the original Asian territory; founded by Communist revolution, 1949. Cap.: Beijing [BAE-zhihng], also Peking [PEE-kihng, PAE-] Currency: Yuan.

REPUBLIC OF CHINA on island of Taiwan (Formosa). Founded 1949. Cap: Taipei [tae-pai, -pee]. Currency: New Taiwan Yuan.

chinaware (n.), china-blue (adj.); china shop.

Chinese names See *NAMES*.

Chippewa [CHIHP-eh-wuh] Native American tribe. See **Ojibwa**. Also river in WI, falls.

chiropodist [kie-RAHP-oh-dihst] foot doctor.

chiropractor [KIE-roh-PRAC-tor] specialist in spinal manipulation and massage.

chisel in slang, (v.) to cheat in a small way. —led, —ing. (n.) the tool.

chitchat small talk. Also chitter-chatter.

chivalry [SHIHV-al-ree] dignity, spirit of knighthood.

CHIVALRIC [-rihk] Refers medieval knighthood. An emotionally neutral adj.

CHIVALROUS [- ruhs] Implies gallant, generous, etc.

chloride [KLOH-ried]

chlorine [KLOH-reen]

chlorophyll

chockablock, chock-full (adj.)

choirboy, choir master, choir meeting.

chol-, chole-, cholo- combining forms meaning bile; *cholecystectomy, choledology.*

cholera [KAHL-eh-ruh] a disease.

CHOLERIC [CAHL-ehr-ihk] quick tempered; enraged.

choose (p.) chose. (p.p.) chosen; choosing.

chophouse,   —stick, chop-chop; chop suey.

Chopin, Frederic [shoh-PAN] (1810-1849) Polish composer.

chord string of a musical instrument; also the harmonic sound produced. Hence, an emotion. *Her story strikes a chord in me.* Also, straight line intersecting a curve: *chord of an arc.*

> CORD rope, string, ribbed cloth; measure of wood (128 cu. ft.); vocal cords, spinal cord.

Chou En-lai [JOH-ehn-lie] (1898-1976) Chinese statesman.

chorus [CAWR-uhs]

Christian Christian name, etc.; Christendom, Christianity; Christianize. BUT: (v.) to christen.

Christian name first name, name "given" in baptism.

Christian Science Church of Christ Scientist; the Mother Church is in Boston. Clergy are practitioners, lecturers, or readers; never *reverend.* Cap. titles before a name: *Reader Sam Jones,* BUT *Sam Jones, reader.*

Christian Scientist Christian Science Reading Room.

Christmas *Xmas* is from *X* (Chi), the Gr. initial for Christ.

Christo [KRIHS-toh] (b. 1935) environmental artist, born in Bulgaria.

chronic of long standing; NOT necessarily bad or intense, (adv.) —ically.

chrysalis (pl.) —ises.

church Cap. if part of name of organization or building: *the Catholic Church; Westminster Church, the church.*

church calendar Cap. the words *Christmas, Easter, Lent, Whitsuntide (Pentecost).*

C.I.A. (abbr.) Central Intelligence Agency.

ciao [chow] (It.) colloq. for hello, so long.

cicatrix [SIK-uh-trihks] scar. (pl.) —trices.

El Cid [sihd] (1040-1099) Rodrigo Diaz de Bivar, Spanish hero.

c.i.f. (abbr.) cost, insurance, and freight. When added to a bill or estimate, indicates that these items are included in price.
> Compare to
>
> C.I.F.C. cost, insurance, freight, and charges or commission.
>
> C.I.F.E. . . . and exchange.
>
> C.I.F.I. . . . .and interest.

cigarette [sihg-uh-REHT, SIHG-uh-reht] This spelling pref. to *cigaret.* cigarette case, holder, maker, paper.

cigars corona; cheroot; cigarillo; Havana; panatela; stogie.

Cincinnati [sihn-sih-NAT-ee; or ih]

cinema [SIH-neh-mah] motion pictures. Cinematography refers specifically to the camera work. Cinematographer.

Cingalese See **Sri Lanka.**

cinquecento [chihnk-wee-CHEHN-to] (It.) the 1500s. In art history, Italian work of the 16th C. See **trecento.**

cinquefoil [SIHNCK-voil] five-leaved rose plant, or similar design. Pref. to *cingfoil.*

cipher [SIE-fehr] a code, or writings in code. Also a number, a symbol for naught.

circa about (when used with dates). abbr: ca., c., circ. *c. 1900; circ. 1625.*

circadian rhythm [suhr-KAE-dee-an] biological rhythms based on day's darkness and light.

Circe [SUHR-sih] in *the Odyssey,* island sorceress who turned men into beasts.

circle Cap.: Arctic Circle, Logan Circle; the circle.

circuitman, circuit breaker, circuit rider.

circuitous [suhr-KYOO-ih-tuhs] roundabout.

circumcise —cision.

circumference of a circle = π^2.

circumlocutional going in circles; going nowhere.

circumstance [SEHR-kuhm-stanss] an accompanying condition or event. (pl.) circumstances. *Under the circumstances.*

cirrhosis [suhr-ROH-sihs] liver disease.

cirrus Clouds. For pl. *cirri* is rare. (adj.) cirrous.

cite (v.) to quote. (n.) citation.

   SIGHT (n.) vision

   SITE (n.) location.

cities, sections of Cap. official or popular names: East Side, Latin Quarter, the Loop, North End, Northwest Washington, TriBeCa.

city Cap. if part of corporate or popular name: Kansas City, the two Kansas Cities, Mexico City, Twin Cities, Washington City, Windy City. BUT: city of Washington, the city government, city editor.

   Cap. when used with an official title: the City Court, City Controller Abraham Beame.

civil service Cap. only when word *Commission* follows or is implied: *the Civil Service has ruled.* BUT: *civil service employee, examination, etc.*

C.J. (abbr.) corpus juris, body of law; Chief Justice.

cl. (abbr.) centiliter.

clamor Pref. to *clamour* in U.S. (adj.) —ous.

clampdown (n. and adj.) See **crackdown.**

Clan Cap. if part of tribal name. The clan; clansman.

clandestine [klan-DEHS-tihn]

clangor (Br.) clangour. Both, clang-orous.

claque [klak] plaid applauders.

clarify to clear up; NOT to answer, unless the question is obscure. NOT: *He addressed the group to clarify questions raised.*

class a group with common characteristics. See **category**.

class1, class 2, A, II. But Class 2 when part of title: *Class 2: Leather Products.*

class book, classmate, —room; class-conscious (adj.); class consciousness, class day.

classic first-rank art or literature. With cap., means methods or style of Greeks and Romans.

CLASSICAL Generally used in contrast to *romantic*, in reference to literature, music, visual arts. Also, in methods or style of Greeks and Romans.

CLASSIFICATION OF ANIMALS AND PLANTS Kingdom, animal; phylum, (pl.) phyla, *chordata;* sub-phylum, *vertebrata;* class, *mammalia;* sub-class, *theri;* infra-class, *eutheria;* order, *Primates;* sub-order, Simiae or *Anthopoidea;* infra-order, *Hominoidea;* family, *Hominidae* (adj. *hominid);* genus, (pl.) genera, *Homo;* species, (pl.) species, *sapiens*

Capitalize the Latin scientific names of orders, families, and genera BUT NOT English derivatives and NOT names of species. In printed matter, italicize the names of genus

and species used either separately or together: *Homo sapiens.*

CLASSIFICATION OF GEOLOGI-CAL AND PALEONTOLOGICAL GROUPS Capitalize Latin scientific names and divisions.

The geological time scale is based on sedimentary strata, and divided into *eras, periods,* and *epochs.* In paleontogy, fossils are classified according to the geological scale, plus by distinguishing body types, such as *a brachiopod of the Silurian period, Paleozoic era* (430-395 million years ago). There are 4 geologic eras, from earliest to most recent the *Precambrian, Paleozoic, Mesozoic,* and *Cenozoic.* The *Paleozoic* has the most periods, from the *Cambrian* to the *Permian.* Epochs are identified only in the *Cenozoic* era, and range from the *Paleocene,* beginning 65 million years ago, to the *Holocene,* the present epoch.

classified information in U.S. government, information with a restricted circulation. Hence, any secret.

CLAUSE a group of related words containing subject and predicate.

An independent or main clause can stand alone as a complete sentence; a dependent clause cannot. A dependent or subordinate clause depends upon a word or words in the independent clause to complete its meaning.

Clauses can function as adjectives and adverbs.

Clausewitz, Karl von [KLOU-zehvihts] (1780-1831) Prussian military scientist and general.

claustrophobia [klaws-trohFOH-bih-uh] See —**phobia.**

cleanly, clearly NOT synonyms. *Cleanly* means in a clean manner. *He gutted the fish as cleanly as possible.*

Clearly means without impediment, or explicitly: *When she began to cry, I saw our dilemma clearly.*

cleave Split or split apart. (p.) clove, cleft or cleaved. (pp.) cloven, cleft, or cleaved. *Cleft palate, cloven hoof, a cleft stick.*

> CLEAVE to adhere (p. and p.p.) cleaved. *Oh dearest, cleave to me.* NOTE: same spelling, opposite meanings.

clef [klehf] in musical notation, symbol determining key.

clematis [KLEHM-at-ihs] vine.

clench Applies to parts of body, for example, jaws, nails, etc.

> CLINCH Applies to a sale, an argument. Close or finish.

Cleopatra [klee-oh-PAT-ruh] (69-30 B.C.) Egyptian queen famous for beauty and power.

clergy Titles of clergy members vary among the faiths. Accepted forms are: Anglican, priest; Bahai, chairman of the assembly; Baptist, pastor and minister; Christian Science, reader; Congregationalist, minister; Eastern Orthodox, rector; Episcopalian, rector, if of the chief church of the parish (if not chief official, vicar

[VIH-kuhr]; but all other clergymen are priests after serving six months as a deacon); Evangelical, pastor; Greek Orthodox, pastor; Jehovah's Witnesses, minister; Jewish, rabbi; Lutheran, pastor (applied to all clergy); Methodist, minister; Muslim, mulla or mullah; Presbyterian, pastor (others are minister); Reformed, pastor; Roman Catholic, pastor, priest; Seventh Day Adventist, pastor; Unitarian, minister.

Women in the clergy take the same titles, except where gender-specific. Nuns and Catholic officials are *sister.*

The title *Father* is used by Roman Catholics and most Episcopalians in addressing their clergymen.

Roman Catholics ADDRESS: The Reverend Joseph B. Hunter; Dear Father Hunter, or Dear Father; refer to Father Hunter.

Episcopalians ADDRESS: The Reverend Father Johnson, O.H.C. (without a Christian name), and refer to Father Johnson.

Some orders use the title *Father* and address Father John, The Reverend Father John, C.S.F. Lay brothers may be addressed Brother Thomas, O.H.C.

ADDRESS: The Reverend Samuel Brown or The Reverend and Mrs. Samuel Brown or (if a doctor of divinity) The Reverend Dr. Samuel Brown; The Reverend Dr. Brown.

SALUTATION: Dear Sir; Reverend Sir; Dear Mr. Brown; Dear Dr. Brown. Never "Reverend" or address as "Reverend Brown". In conversation, address as mister or doctor. This applies with all denominations.

For forms of address of other

clergy members, SEE: minister and each of the titles. Also see **Minister (Protestant), Rabbi.**

cliché [klee-shae]

clientele [klee-ahn-TEHL; klie-en-TEHL] customers or clients.

climacteric [klie-MAK-tehr-ihk or -TEHR-] a critical period of change, especially menopause.

> CLIMACTIC refers to a climax.

> CLIMATIC refers to climate.

> CLIMACTIC ORDER arrangement by rising importance. *She distributed pennies, nickels, and dimes.*

cling (p. and p.p.) clung; clinging.

clique [kleek] derogatory for a small, exclusive group. (adj.) —quy or —quey.

cloak-and-dagger (n. and adj.).

clockwise, counter-clockwise.

close-connected (adj.), close-out (adj.).

closed-circuit (adj.), closed shop.

closure [KLOH-zhuhr] In Br. Parliament, provision for limiting debate. In U.S. Senate, **cloture.** *N.Y. Times* follows Br. style.

clothe [klothe] (p. and p.p.) clothed, also clad; clothing.

> CLOTHES [klohz] May be sing. or pl. in meaning, but takes a plural verb.

clue (n.) hint, suggestion, piece of evidence. (v.) to make or provide these. *Clew* is arch., except (n.) a ball of thread or cord; or, (nautical) lower corner of a sail.

cm. (abbr.) centimeter.

c.m. (abbr.) circular mil (wire measure).

CO Colorado.

C.O. commanding officer.

Co. company. *Dombey & Co.* (pl.) Cos.

co- combining form meaning with; *coadventure, cohabit.* Use hyphenated form (1) to distinguish from other words; *co-respondent, correspondent;* (2) to safeguard against mispronunciation; *co-worker;* (3) in made words; *co-partnership;* (4) *Webster's* hyphenates *co-o* words.

coagulate [coh-AG-yoo-laet] to clot, congeal, solidify.

coalesce to grow together. —escing.

coarse not fine.

> COURSE direction of movement; path.

coast Atlantic coast; East, Gulf, West, etc.

Coastal Plain (Atlantic and Gulf).

Coast Guard, U.S. the Coast Guard; Coastguardsman Smith. BUT: a coastguardsman; a guardsman.

coat of arms (pl.) coats—.

coauthor, codefendant, coed, coeducational, cooperate, coordinate, coowner, co-partner, copilot, co-star.

cobalt bomb atomic bomb containing cobalt; produces large contaminated radioactive area.

cobblestone

COBOL Common Business Oriented Language, for computers.

coccus [KAHK-uhs] spherical bacterium. (pl.) cocci [KAHK-sie].

COCCYX end of the vertebral column.

cockscomb originally comb of a rooster.

COCKSCOMB, COXCOMB colorful plant of amaranth family.

COXCOMB red cloth strips worn by a jester; hence, a fop.

cocoa [KOH-KOH] drink, bean, or powder. BUT: coconut.

c.o.d. (abbr.) cash on delivery.

code Cap. in shortened title of a publication: District Code, Federal Criminal Code, Internal Revenue Code, Penal Code, Pennsylvania State Code, Uniform Code of Military Justice. BUT: civil code; flag code; Morse code.

code, codebook. See **cipher.**

codex manuscript book. (pl.) codices.

codicil [KAHD-ih-sihl] an addition to a will.

coerce (v.), coercible (adj.).

coffer box for storage of valuables.

COFFIN (NOT casket) the box containing the corpse.

coffin-maker, coffin-headed (adj.); coffin bone.

cogitate to think. (adj.) cogitable.

cognac [KOHN-yak] Fr. brandy.

cognate having common blood. In grammar, having the same origin. *Spanish and French are cognate languages.*

cognizance [kahg-nih-sans] apprehension; heed; notice. (adj.) —zant, —zable, [kah-niez-abl; or KAHG-nihz-abl].

cognomen [kahg-NOH-m'n] family name (originally, a third name). Sometimes a nickname, a first name.

coif [kwahf] (v.) to cut and style hair. (n.) (colloq.) a hairdo.

COIFFEUR [KWAH-feur] hairdresser.

COIFFURE [KWAH-fyoor] hairdo.

C.O.I.N. (abbr.) Air Force counter-insurgency force. See Seal.

coin-box —holder (n.); coin-operated (adj.).

coincide [koh-ihn-SIED] to occupy the same place or time; agree exactly.

co-insurance clause provision in an insurance policy limiting liability of the insurer to "no greater proportion of any loss than the amount insured bears to the percentage specified of the actual cash value of the property described at the time when such loss shall happen."

Col. (abbr.) colonel, used with name.

col. (abbr.) column.

colander [KAHL-ehn-dahr] bowl-shaped sieve. Not **calendar**.

Colette [koh-LEHT] (1873-1954) Fr. writer (*Chéri*). Real name, Sidonie Gabrielle Claudine.

coliseum [kahl-ih-SEE-uhm] any large structure for entertainments or sporting events. BUT cap. the Colosseum in Rome.

collaborate together is redundant.

collage [kahl-lazh] miscellaneous materials assembled into an artistic composition. See **assemblage.**

collate [KOH-laet] to put printed sheets in order; to gather.

   COLLATION [kahl-LAE-shuhn, koh-] formal term for light refreshments. Also, a gathering together.

collected together is redundant.

collectible Pref. to —*able* in U.S.

collection the Brady collection, etc.; the collection.

collective bargaining tactics

COLLECTIVE NOUNS Some collective nouns may be treated as either singular or plural according to the

sense intended. *The Committee approves the bill.* BUT: *The membership are active in many sports. My family are sick.* Such nouns are called mass nouns, and usually are expressed in the singular.

Some collectives are always treated as singular: apparatus, news, summons, whereabouts. *The summons is on my desk.*

Some are always treated as plural: assets, earnings, means (income), adds, promises, proceeds, quarters, savings, wages, winnings. *The day's proceeds were satisfactory.*

Some are treated as either singular or plural, according to the meaning: ethics, goods, gross, headquarters, mechanics, politics, series, species, statistics, tactics. *Ethics is taught in high school. His ethics are above reproach. Misfortunes follow them in their travels.*

Types of words treated as collectives include: (1) Certain pronouns: all, any, many, more, most, none, some, who which: *All the books are here. All the glue is here.*

(2) Units of measure: *Six months have passed. Six months is a long time to wait.*

(3) Group nouns: committee, people.

(4) Company names. The sound may determine whether a singular or plural verb is to be used: a name ending in *company* or *corporation* usually takes a singular verb.

(5) Abstract collectives. Use singular form for reference to qualities, emotions, feelings, or actions of a group: *Love is here to stay.* Use plural form when there is no generalization. *His loves are legion.*

(6) Nouns that have the same form in singular and plural: deer, sheep.

(7) Nouns which use singular forms to denote the plural: fish, duck, cannon.

(8) Abstract singulars used for concrete plurals: nobility.

(9) Nouns which derive from the material content: straw, fur, linen, silver, glass, china.

(10) Nouns which may mean all or one of a thing: *timber, cheese.*

(11) Nouns of indefinite quantity: butter, wine;

(12) Nouns which have a plural but are used in the singular as collectives: shot.

(13) Nouns of quantity: pair, fathom.

(14) Nouns of multitude: cattle, shot.

(15) Animal collectives: *flock of sheep, pride of lions,* etc. See: *ANIMALS.*

college Cap. if part of name: Linfield College, Detroit College of Business: But: the college, electoral college.

College Degrees See **B.A., M.A., Ph.D.**

collegian [KAHL-LEE-jih-an] college student.

collision meeting of two moving bodies.

colloquial applied to words used in informal writings or speech, but not suitable for formal expression. abbr.: colloq.

colloquy [KAHL-oh-kwih] mutual discourse.

Colombia nation in northern South America. Independent, 1819. Cap.: **Bogota.** Native: Columbian. Currency: peso.

COLON Used: (1) after a formal introduction;

(2) before a quotation or example;

(3) after the salutation of a business letter: *Dear Personnel Director;* (4) to separate two main clauses not joined by a conjunction, between which there is some essential logical relationship, especially when they are in antithesis. *I sow: he reaps; I'm the singer: he's a comedian;* (5) before a final summary in a sentence. *Flying is not dangerous: it is merely untried.*

(6) to introduce material that follows, in effect often replacing *as follows, that is,* or *for example. He mentioned the following passages: Section 317, p. 17; Section 819, p.141; and Section 320, p. 6;* (7) in indicating time, between the hour and the minute: *2:30 P.M.;* (8) in citations of volume and page numbers, or chapter and verse numbers: *Exodus 6: 9.*

DO NOT use a colon between a verb or preposition and its objects. NOT: *He gave books to: Tom, Dick and Harry;* or *His friends are: Mary, Jane, Alison, and Sally.*

Usually capitalize the letter following a colon but not an explanatory element following. *He has three attractive qualities: physique, intelligence, and money.*

colonial American Colonial Army, the Colonials. In real estate: *a beautiful Colonial home.* BUT: colonial times.

Colonies, the the Thirteen Colonies,

American Colonies, Original Colonies. BUT: 13 separate colonies.

colonnade

colony Crown Colony of Hong Kong; the colony.

color —rable, —rist. (Br.) *colour*. Color is composed of three elements:

HUE quality which distinguishes one color from another: red, yellow, green.

BRILLIANCE measure of light or dark in a color, on a scale which 0 is black. In red, brilliance runs from maroon to pale pink.

SATURATION measure of vividness of a color. Less vivid red would be watery, more vivid carmine.

Degrees of *coloration* are expressed as compounds, taking hyphens in adj. form: Bluish green, bluish-green feathers; iron gray, iron-gray hair; etc.

color-bearer, colorblind (*N.Y. Times*, color-blind), —fast (adj.); —man, —type (printing) (n.); color-free, color-washed (adj.); color blindness, color guard, color line (n.).

color, person of Current usage allows this as a general term. Refers to any non-white: Native American, Asian-American, etc. (pl.) persons of color.

Colored is considered pejorative, and no longer acceptable. See **-American,** *RACIST LANGUAGE.*

Colorado U.S. state. Abbr.: CO

Cap.: Denver. Native: Coloradan.

colossal [koh-lahs-'l]

COLOSSUS (pl.) —ssuses or —ssi.

column [KAHL-hum], columnist [KAHL-umnihst]. *She's hiding behind the third column. See column 2.*

column inch unit of advertising and newspaper space, 1 column wide, 1 in. deep.

Comanche [kah-MAN-chee] Great Plains Native Americans.

comatose [KAHM-uh-tohs; KOHM—] (adj.) as in a coma.

combholder, -maker, comb case; comb-toothed (adj.).

combat —ed, —bating; combatant [KAHM-ba-tihnt].

combine [(v.) kahm-BIEN, (n.) KAHM-bien] *Combined together* is redundant.

combustible

Comdr. (abbr.) commander.

come (p.) came. (p.p), come. coming.

comedy Applies to all art, not just drama. When referring to actual experience, usu. applies to particulars, rather than whole. *The wedding was a comedy of errors.* NOT: *Our national history is a comedy.* See **tragedy.**

comedian [kom-EE-diehn] —ienne (fem.).

comely [KUHM-lih] of pleasing appearance.

come-on (pl.) come-ons.

comestible food. (pl.) —s.

comforter a quilted bedcover.

comic book, comic opera

comity [KAHM-i-tih] courtesy. *Comity of nations.* Respect for one another's laws and institutions among civilized states.

COMMA. Used: (1) To indicate that a word or phrase has been omitted: *To err is human, to forgive, divine.*

(2) When two or more qualifying words modify the same word without a conjunction between them: *her small, red hat.* BUT when the first adjective modifies the combination of second adjective plus noun, no comma is used: *a large Amish barn.* The rule-of-thumb test is: Could you comfortably put *and* between the adjectives? If you could, a comma belongs.

(3) After a subordinate clause at the beginning of a sentence, especially between introductory modifying phrase and subject modified. *The sun shone all day, drying all the puddles.*

(4) Before the conjunction in a compound sentence if the second clause is complete with subject and predicate.

(5) To separate an introductory phrase from a question. The test is: Will the sentence retain its sense if the introductory phrase is omitted?

(6) To set off incidental or parenthetic words, phrases, or clauses. *Mr.*

Kennedy, the Senator from Massachusetts, repudiated the statement. BUT a phrase or clause that restricts or limits the meaning of a word is not set off by commas. *The man standing beside her is her husband.*

(7) To set off words in apposition or explanation when they are not restrictive. *Sam, the butler, opened the door.* BUT when the word in apposition restricts or limits the subject, do not use commas. *The renowned scientist Einstein developed the formula e = mc².* (There are other scientists.) BUT: *My wife, Sylvia, is here.* (I have only one wife.)

(8) Following an introductory phrase before a direct quotation: *He said, ''Now is the time.''* BUT when the quotation is the subject or object of the sentence, so that the part of the sentence that is not quoted serves as more than a mere introduction, a comma is not used: *Don't say ''Yes.''*

(9) To separate two words or figures that might otherwise be misunderstood: *September 17, 1945.*

(10) Before Jr., Sr., Esq. Ph.D., M.D., etc.: *Tom Brown, Jr.* BUT: *John Smith II* (or *2nd*).

(11) After each member of a series of three or more words, phrases, letters, or figures when *and, or,* or *nor* precedes only the last. *The flag is red, white, and blue.* BUT (usually): *She was four years one month and three days old.* (The last comma before the conjunction is called a "serial comma," and many authorities now omit it.)

(12) After a noun or noun phrase in direct address. *Gentlemen, please be seated.*

(13) Between the name and number of an organization.

(14) Inside closing quotation marks when there is no stronger punctuation and the sentence continues. *She answered "No," and perhaps meant no.* BUT: *Will you?" he demanded.*

(15) In numbers of four or more digits: *7,267.* BUT SEE exceptions under (19).

(16) In addresses, between the city and the state: *Teaneck, NJ 07666.*

(17) After the year in complete dates within a sentence: *The Declaration of Independence, first read July 2, 1776, was applauded.*

The comma is NOT used: (18) Between months and year in dates: *December 1960; 5th of May 1916. June and December 1910.*

(19) In built-up fractions, decimals, and serial numbers: *3.4196, Beekman 3-6018, 1630 Fifth Avenue, Motor No. 1013, 2800 meters.* No commas unless more than four figures.

(20) Between superior figures or letters in footnote references. *Numerous instances may be cited.[112]*

(21)Before ampersand (&): *John, Jeffreys & Jones.*

(22) To set off an adverb. NOT: *Suddenly, the monster appeared.*

(23) Before and after Jr., Sr., Esq., Ph.D., etc., within a sentence except where possession is indicated. *John Smith, Jr., Chairman; Motorola, Inc., factory.*

command capitalize with name: GHQ Far East Command, Joint Far Eastern Command, Zone of Interior Command; the command.

commandant [KAHM-uhn-DANT]

commander-in-chief (pl.) commanders-in-chief.

commence formal for *begin.* Commencement: Graduation ceremony. *The 1963 Yale commencement.*

commingle [KUH-mihng-gl] to mingle.

commiserate [KAH-mihs-uhr-aet] (v.) to show compassion.

commission Cap. if part of name; capitalize standing alone if a federal or international commission: Alaska Road Commission, Atomic Energy Commission, United Nations Human Rights Commission; the Commission.

committee. Cap. if part of a name or if an international or federal committee: the Committee of One Hundred, the Committee; the committee on Finance, the committee; Committee Print No. 32; the committee print.

commodity

common law body of law developed by custom and precedent.

Common market After 1992, European Community.

COMMON NOUNS OR ADJECTIVES In grammar, those nouns which apply to one of a class or group: *boy, sample, door.* See **PROPER NOUN.**

A common noun is used with a date, number, or letter merely to denote time or sequence, for reference or for convenience; does not form a proper name and is not cap. *This is our workroom #6.*

Commonwealth of Australia, of Massachusetts, etc.; British Commonwealth; the commonwealth.

Commonwealth of Independent States vast cooperative Eurasian organization, comprising at most 12 republics, all former states within the **U.S.S.R.** Est. 1992, under directorship of **Boris Yeltsin.** Temporary cap.: Minsk. Currency: ruble.

See member states: **Armenia, Azerbaijan, Byelorussia, Georgia, Kazakhstan, Kirghizia, Moldavia, Russia, Tadzhikistan, Turkmenistan, Ukraine, Uzbekistan.**

See also **Estonia, Latvia, Lithuania**; not in Commonwealth but formerly part of U.S.S.R.

See also **Gorbachev, Lenin, Leningrad, Stalin.**

communal [KAHM-yoo-nal, kuh-MYOO-nal]

Commune (of Paris).

communicate [kuhm-yoo-uik-KAET] (v.) a communique [kuh-myoo-nih-KAE] (n.).

Communist Party Cap. when referring to the political party, otherwise, lowercase.

communist Cap. for member of party. Communism; communist philosophy. (Pref. to *communistic*).

Comoros [KAH-muh-ROHS] island nation off SE Africa. Formerly French; independent 1975. Cap.:

Moroni [MUH-roh-nee]. Native: Comorran. Currency: CFA franc.

compact U.S. marine fisheries compact, etc.; the compact.

company Cap. if part of name; lowercase standing alone. abbr.: co. *Procter & Gamble Co.; the company.* If a government agency, *Panama Railroad Company, the Company.*

company union union sponsored by the employer.

companywide

comparable [KAHM-puhr-uh-b'l]

comparatively few NOT a comparatively few.

compare with When the objects are side by side to show their relative value. When one is said to be like the other, use *compare to. She compared John with Bill. She compared John to a horse and Bill to a mule. He compared himself with Shakespeare. He compared himself to Shakespeare.* The last sentence implies near-equality; the previous one does not imply equality.

comparison: other, else. In a comparison, two elements must appear, and the time compared must be separated from the group. NOT *He is better than any man.* BUT: *He is better than anyone else (or any other man).*

COMPARISON (adj. and adv.) An adjective or adverb changes its form to express greater or lesser degrees. The forms are positive: *big;* comparative: *bigger;* and superlative: *biggest.*

Most adjectives of three or more syllables and most adverbs use *more* and *most* or *less* and *least* to denote the comparative and superlative forms. Adding *er* or *est* to a word emphasizes the quality: using *more* or *most* emphasizes the comparison.

A few modifiers have irregular comparisons, notably: *good, well, bad, badly, far, late, little, many, much.*

More and *most* are the required forms for adverbs ending in *ly*, for words which can be used predicatively, for unusual or foreign words, and for *eager. More* and *most* forms are pref. for long modifiers, for words of more than one stressed syllable, and for words ending in *-s, -ish, -est, -ive, -or, -ile, -ed,* or *-in.*

Absolute words *(perfect, unique, extreme, complete, equal, square, chaste, pregnant)* should not be compared. For comparisons of these qualities, use *more, nearly perfect,* etc.

comparison shopper retail store employee who checks merchandise and prices at competing stores.

compass directions N, NE, E, SW, S, NNW, W, ESE, IO°N 25°W, NW by N; north, northerly, northern, northward, northeast, north, northeast, east Pennsylvania, eastern region, southern France.

BUT: West Germany, the East (region), West Coast.

In description of a tract of land, omit periods: lot *4, NE sec.2 T 6N, R 1 W.* See **points of the compass, latitude** and **longitude.**

compatible capable of living together in harmony.

compendious (adj.) Abridged. (n.) —dium, (pl.) —diums or —dia. Compendium is a brief compilation, not an exhaustive one.

compensate [KAHM-pehn-saet] (v.) compensatory [kahm-PEHN-suh-toh-ree] (adj.).

competence Pref. to —cy.

complacent [kahm-PLAE-zant] (adj.) self-satisfied. (n.) —cency.

COMPLAISANT willing to please.

complement (v.) to complete. In grammar, a word or words which follow the verb and complete the meaning of the sentence. A complement may be a direct object, an indirect object, a predicate adjective, or a predicate nominative.

COMPLIMENT (n. or v.) to praise.

SUPPLEMENT (n. or v.) something additional.

complete having attained its limit. NEVER: *more complete, most complete.* BUT: *most nearly complete.*

ENTIRE undivided; unbroken.

WHOLE is synonymous.

COMPLEX SENTENCE a sentence composed of one independent clause and one or more dependent clauses.

COMPLIMENTARY CLOSE For business letters a number of closings are appropriate: *Yours truly, Sincerely yours, Sincerely, Cordially yours, Cordially.*

For social letters, closings can reflect the writer's mood and relationship with the reader. A common, emotionally neutral close is *All the best*. Other possibilities: *As ever, Your friend, Devotedly,* and the ever-popular *Love.*

complexioned Use in combination: *dark-complexioned.*

comply with NOT comply to.

composition In printing, the setting of type; or, in law, agreement between debtor and group of creditors for partial payments in settlement.

compost [KAHM-pohst] the refuse itself, not the pile in which it biodegrades. NOT a garbage dump.

compound [KAHM-pound] (n.); [kahmPOUND] (v.).

COMPOUND SENTENCE a sentence containing two or more independent clauses.

COMPOUND-COMPLEX SENTENCE a sentence composed of two or more independent clauses and one or more dependent clauses.

comprehend to understand. —ed, —nding, —ensible.

comprehensive covering the entire field: *a comprehensive view of the subject.*

compressible

comprise consist of, contain, NOT compose. *New York City comprises five boroughs.* Pref. to —ize.

COMPOSE to create by putting together. *Cement is composed of lime, clay, and water.*

compromise

comptroller [kuhn-TROHL-uhr] controller of the funds. Cap. with government agencies: Comptroller of the Currency, the Comptroller; Comptroller of the Post Office Department, the Comptroller; Comptroller General (U.S.).

comraderie [KAHM-rad-uh-ree] (Fr.) spirit of good will.

COMPUTERS A number of neologisms having to do with computer technology have come into the language. These words tend to spring up haphazardly, and can drop out of use the same way.
  Some are acronyms, some compounds of acronyms and older words, some entirely new contructions. Some function as both nouns and verbs, some as adjectives, too. This book lists the neologisms that seem reasonably likely to last.
  See **A.T.M., BASIC, COBOL, E-mail, fax, floppy, high-tech, IBM, modem, moog synthesizer, mouse, neutron bomb, software, voicemail, word processing.**

concave [kahn-KAEV] hollow.

convex rounded; protuberant.

concept Current usage pref. to *conception.*

concerto [kahn-CHAIR-toh] (pl.) —os; in Ital. —i.

concessionaire [kahn-sehsh-uhn-AER]

conch [kahngk] shell. (pl.) —s.

concision, conciseness Both acceptable.

Concorde [kahn-COURD] Fr. passenger jet, fastest available.

concrete cement (burned clay and limestone) plus sand, mixed with gravel and/or crushed rock and set with water.

concupiscent [kahn-KYOO-pih-sehnt] (adj.) lustful. (n.) —ence.

condescend [kahn-dee-SEHND] to forego privileges or dignity of a superior position; usually implies a patronizing manner.

condolence [kahn-DOH-lehns] expression of sympathy.

conductible

conduit [KON-doo-iht]

confectionery candies.

Confederacy (of the South). Confederate States of America; Confederate Army, government, soldier.

conference Cap. if referring to governmental (U.S.) or international conference: Bretton Woods Conference, the Conference. Non-governmental: Sixth Annual Conference of Southern Methodist Churches, the conference; conference of Governors; conference of mayors; Governors' conference.

conference room

conferrable [kahn-FUHR-ra-bl] capable of being given.

Confession, Augsberg. Lutheran confession of faith, from 1530.

confidant(e) [kahn-fih-DANT] (m. and f.) a close friend.

    CONFIDENT [KAN-fih-dehnt] fully assured.

confines [KAHN-fiens] (n.) boundaries.

conflux (n.) confluence.. (adj.) —luxible.

confrere [KAHN-fraer] colleague.

Congo Central African nation, formerly Fr.; independent, 1960. Formerly Belgian Congo, now **Zaire**. Cap.: Brazzaville. Native: Congolese. Currency: CFA franc.

congratulate; —ations.

congress (convention). Cap. if part of name; cap. standing alone if international congress: International Good Roads Congress, the Congress; the National Congress of Parents and Teachers, the congress.

Congress (legislature). Cap. if referring to national congress: Congress of Bolivia, the Congress; U.S. Congress; First, Second, 11th, 82d, Congress; the Congress.

Congressional Directory the directory; First Congressional District, 11th Congressional District, etc.; the

First 11th District; the congressional district; the district; Congressional Library, the Library; Congressional Medal of Honor (See **decorations**).

BUT congressional action, Congressional committee, etc.

Congressman, —woman (U.S.) Congressman at Large; Congresswoman from Colorado; Member of Congress; Member; membership.

conjecture [cuhn-JEHK-chyoor]

CONJUGATION in grammar, the different forms of a verb, according to number, person, tense, mood, or aspect.

CONJUNCTION a word used to join words, phrases, or clauses: *and, but, nor.* See *CONNECTIVES.*

conjure [kahn-JOOR] (v.) beseech; entreat. [KUHN-jehr] to do magic. In either meaning, a *conjurer.*

Connecticut [kahn-NEHT-ih-kuht] U.S. state. Abbr.: CT. Cap: Hartford. Native: Connecticuter.

CONNECTIVES The most important connectives are conjunctions and prepositions.

Coordinate conjunctions connect elements of equal grammatical importance: *and, but, or not, for, yet.* Correlative conjunctions work in pairs to connect elements of equal rank: *either, or; neither, nor; not only, but also; both and.* Each member of this group must be followed by the same part of speech.

Conjunctive adverbs connect independent clauses and show a relation between them: *therefore, however, consequently, accordingly, furthermore, moreover, nevertheless.*

Other connectives may be used to join elements of unequal rank. These include subordinate conjunctions: *before, since, after, as, because, if, unless, until, although;* relative pronouns: *who, whom, that, which, whatever, whichever, whoever;* and relative adverbs: *how, when, where, while.* Subordinate conjunctions introduce dependent adverb clauses and join them to independent clauses. Relative pronouns introduce noun and adjective clauses and also act as pronouns within the clauses. Relative adverbs introduce subordinate clauses.

The other connective, the preposition, is used to connect its object with the word in the main clause which is modified, showing the relationship between the word and the object of the preposition: *to, of, between, in, over, under, from, for.*

connoisseur [kah-uh-SEUR] an expert in a certain field. See also: **amateur, dilettante.**

connote to suggest, imply. (n.) connotation.

DENOTE to indicate, signify explicitly. *The dollar denotes 100 cents but connotes power and materialism.*

conscious [KAHN-shush] (adj.); consciousness (n.).

consensus agreement of opinion. *Of opinion* is implied without being stated. NOT: *consensus of opinion.*

consequential following as a result; also, self-important. NOT meaning of consequence or having great consequences.

conservative cautious. In politics, tending to preserve existing conditions. See **liberal, progressive.**

REACTIONARY favoring return to old system or ideas.

conservatory school for music; open, airy room in which music may be played. (pl.) —ries.

consider *I consider her intelligent.* NOT: *to be intelligent* or *as intelligent.*

consist of applies to parts which make up the whole. *The omelet consists of vegetables and eggs.*

CONSIST IN applies to inherent qualities; introduces a definition. *Truthfulness consists in not lying.*

consolatory [kuhn-SAHL-uh-tohrih] comforting.

consommé [kayn-soh-MAE] clear soup.

consonant [KAHN-soh-nant] consistent; having agreement.

consonance See **assonance.**

CONSONANT ENDINGS When adding a suffix which begins with a vowel to either a one-syllable word ending in a single consonant or a multi-syllable word which is accented on the last syllable, double the final consonant: *sit, sitting.* BUT NOT when the final consonant is *c, h,j,q,w,x,* or *z.* EXCEPTIONS: *defer-*

ence, refer-ence, infer-ence, prefer-ence prefer-able, transfer-able, chagrin-ed, gas-eous.

Do not double the final consonant in words of more than one syllable where the accent is on any but the last syllable. BUT: *cancellation, questionnaire, crystallize.*

NOTE: Do not double the consonant if (1) the word ends in more than one consonant: *resist, resistance;* (2) the word ends in a single consonant preceded by more than one vowel; *detain, detainable;* (3) the suffix begins with a consonant: *loyal, loyalty.* A word ending in a double consonant usually retains the double consonant; *skill, skillful.*

consort [KAHN-sawt] (n.) partner; companion (v.) [kuhn-SAWRT] to associate.

conspicuous —ness.

constitution Cap. with name of country; cap. standing alone when a specific national constitution: the Constitution of the United States, the Constitution. BUT: New York constitution; the constitution, constitutional.

constitutional amendments Cap. when referred to by name or number: *First Amendment.*

constructive trust See **trust.**

construe [kuhn-STROO] See **translate.**

consul commercial representative of a foreign state, Consular. British consul; consul general, British consul general; British consulate, etc.

ADDRESS: John J. Smith, American Consul, London, England. SALUTATION: Sir; My dear Mr. Smith; Dear Mr. Smith.

consultant

consummate [kahn-SUHM-iht] (adj.) perfect. [KAHN-suh-maet] (v.) to complete. Applied to marriage or love affair, implies sexual intercourse.

cont. (abbr.) continued.

contact (v.) to get in touch with. (n.) acquaintance.

contagious communicable by contact or by contact with breath, clothing, etc. (colloq.) catching.

INFECTIOUS A synonym, though stronger.

contemplate [KAHN-tehm-plaet] (v.) to think; meditate; intend. [kahn-TEHM-pluh-tihv] (adj.) contemplative.

CONTEMPTUOUS [kahn-TEMPT-tyoo-uhs] full of contempt.

contemptible [kahn-TEHMPT-ih-bl] worthy of contempt.

content [KAHN-tehnt.] (n.) substance; material: *Table of contents.* [kahn-TEHNT] (adj.) happy. (n.) contentment.

content oneself with NOT *by.*

contest [KAHN-tehst] (n.); [kahn-TEHST] (v.).

continent Cap. only if following name: American Continent, the continent. BUT: the Continent, meaning continental Europe.

Continental Army the Army (also Continentals); Continental Congress, the Congress; Continental Divide (See **Divide**); Outer Continental Shelf, the shelf.

continual going on or recurring at short intervals: *a continual flow of trade.*

CONTINUOUS uninterrupted: *a continuous pavement.*

continuance (n.) a continuing in a state or direction. In law, adjournment to a specified time.

CONTINUATION (n.) extension; resumption.

CONTINUITY quality of being continuous.

contour [KAHN-toor] (n.) outline.

contra- prefix meaning *against: contraband, contraceptive.* Cap. for Nicaraguan guerilla opposed to Sandinista rule, 1979-89.

contract [KAHN-trakt] (n.) document [—TRAKT] (v.) to agree to; undertake. (adj.) contractible.

contraction See *ABBREVIATION.*

contractual NOT contractural.

contralto (pl.) —os.

contrary [KAHN-trehr-ee] opposed; opposite.

CONVERSE Implies expression of opposites. *It's not that she loves him, but the converse: he loves her.*

contrast [KAHN-trast] (n.) [—TRAST] (v.)

contravene [KAHN-truh-veen] to oppose; act contrary to.

control —lled, —lling, —llable.

controvertible in law, open to dispute.

contumely [KAHN-tyoo-mee-lih] (n.) insult.

convention Cap. for U.S., international, or national political: the Constitutional Convention (United States, 1787), the Convention; Democratic National Convention; 19th Annual Convention of the American Legion; Universal Postal Union Convention; International Postal Convention; Warsaw Convention. BUT: convention of 1907 (not formal name).

conversant [KAHN-vuhr-sant] acquainted; familiar.

conveyor

cool, coolly, coolheaded.

cooped up v. combination; the adj. has a hyphen.

cooperate, cooperative.

coordinate (n. or v.)

copperhead —plate, —proof, —smith, —ware, —works; copperbot-

tomed (adj.); copper-colored, copper-headed, copper-plated (adj.); copper mine, copper miner.

copyright

coquette [koh-KEHT] (n. and v.). —quetry [KOH-keht-rih].

coral [KAWR-uhl] marine skeletons forming underwater deposits.

CORRAL [kuh-RAL] enclosure for animals.

CHORAL [KOH—ruhl] Sung by a chorus or choir.

coral beaded, coral red (adj.); coral reel (n.).

Corbusier, Le [leh kohr-BWAH-see-eh] (1887-1965) Fr. architect and city planner. Real name: Edouard Jeanneret.

cord unit of volume is 127 cu. ft. or 3.625 m.3; usually 8ft. long x 4ft. x 4 ft. abbr.:cd. See chord.

cord foot unit of volume is 16 cu. ft. abbr.: cd. ft.

cordon [KAWR-d'n] line or circle of people: *a police cordon.*

C.O.R.E. (abbr.) Congress of Racial Equality.

coriolis effect (sometimes cap.) tendency of a projectile to be deflected right in the northern hemisphere, left in the southern hemisphere, by earth's rotation.

CORRELATIVE CONJUNCTION conjunctions used in pairs to connect sentence elements of equal value: *either, or; neither, nor; not only, but also; both, and.*

co-respondent [KOH-rehs-PAHN-dehnt] the third party in a divorce suit. The spelling *correspondent* is acceptable, but confusing.

CORRESPONDENT [kahr-eh-SPAHN-dehnt.]

Corneille, Pierre [kawr-NEH-y or -NAE] (1606-1684) French playwright, (*Horace*).

cornucopia (pl.) —as.

corollary [KOHR-uh-la-ree] something logically follows.

corona [kah-ROH-nuh] crownlike structure or radiation. (pl.) —nas.

coroner public official who conducts medical investigation on a dead body.

Corot, Jean Baptist Camille [koh-ROH-, zahn bah-TEEST kah-MEEY] (1796-1875) French impressionist painter.

corporal of the physical human body, as in *corporal punishment.* See **officers.**

CORPOREAL having a physical nature; tangible. *Goblins are fears given corporeal form.*

corporation (abbr., corp.) Cap. if part of name; the Corporation, if referring to unit of Federal government: Commodity Credit Corporation; Federal Deposit Insurance Corporation. BUT: Rand Corp., the

corporation; St. Lawrence Seaway Development Corporation, the corporation.

corps [cohr] Cap. if part of name; the corps (see also Reserve); Adjutant General's Corps, Army Hospital Corps, Enlisted Reserve Corps, Corps of Engineers, Army Engineers. BUT: Army engineer, diplomatic corps, hospital corpsman.

corps sing. [kohr]; pl. [KAWRZ]. See *ARMY ORGANIZATION.*

CORPSE [kawrps] dead body. (pl.) —ses.

corpulence fatness.

corpus body. Thus, corpus of knowledge, of writings. The pl. —pora, is rare.

corpuscle [KAWR-puhs'l] free floating blood or lymph cell.

corral (n. or v.) —lled, —lling. See **coral.**

correctitude propriety.

correlative [koh-REHL-uh-tihv] (n. and adj.) mutually related. In grammar, ordinarily used together: for example, *either. . . or.*

corrigible capable of being corrected.

corroborate (v.) to confirm. (adj.) —rable.

corrosible capable of being corroded. Pref. to *corrodible.*

corrosion [kuh-ROH-zhun] eating

away by chemical action. Corrosion of copper, corrosible.

> EROSION wearing away by action of water or wind.

corruptible

corsage [kawr-SAHJ]

cortege [KAWR-tehzh or -taezh] a group of followers.

Cortes [KAWR-tehz] legislatures of Portugal and Spain.

Cortes, Hernan [KAWR-tehz] (1485-1547). Sp. explorer.

cos. (abbr.) cosine.

Cosa Nostra (It.) "Our Thing." Organization of U.S. crime syndicate, alleged name of Mafia.

cosmopolitan [kahz-mah-PAH-lih-tan] (adj.) urbane; sophisticated. (n.) such a person.

cosmos the universe.

cost (p. and p.p.) cost; costing.

cost and freight term of sale including these items. abbr.: c.a.f. See **c.i.f.**

Costa Rica Central American nation; independent, 1821. Cap.: San Jose. Native: Costa Rican. Currency: colon.

—cote [kaht] suffix meaning shed or coop: *sheepcote, dovecote.*

Cote d'Or [koht-dawr] area in E. France.

coterie [KOH-tuh-ree] congenial group.

coulee [KOO-lih] solidified lava stream. In U.S., a steep-walled valley.

coulomb [koo-LAHM] unit of measure of quantity of electricity which flows in a specified period of time: 1 ampere in 1 second.

council Cap. if part of name, standing alone if federal or international unit: Boston City Council, the council; Choctaw Council, etc., the council; Federal Personnel Council, the Council; His Majesty's Privy Council, the Privy Council, the Council; Philadelphia Common Council, the council.

council a governing body, or a meeting of one: councilor, a member of a council.

> COUNSEL (n.) —or,—lor. Advice, or the one who gives advice. *They hired counsel to defend them.* (v.) counsel, —seled or —selled; —seling or —selling.

countdown (n. and adj.); count down (v.).

countenance face; implies expression.

> PHYSIOGNOMY Implies character, as revealed in features.

counter- combining prefix meaning opposite, retaliatory, or complementary. Counterclaim, counterculture.

counterpart a similar or complementary thing. NOT opposite. See **contrary.**

countess In Britain, the wife of or female equivalent of an earl. In other countries, the wife of or female equivalent of a count. The title is often territorial: *The Countess of Derby, Lady Derby; Countess Attlee, Lady Attlee.*

ADDRESS: The Right Honourable the Countess of Haddington, the Countess Haddington. SALUTATION: Madam, Dear Lady Derby.

county Cap. when part of a name: Queens County, the county; County Frederick, county of Frederick; the county sheriff.

countrywide

coup [koo, kooz] a successful blow. (pl.) coups.

COUP D'ETAT [KOO deh-tat] a sudden overthrow or subversion of government or state policy.

COUP DE GRACE [deh-GRAS] putting one out of his misery.

coupe [koo-PAE; KOOP] nearly always refers to automobile.

court (of law) Cap. if part of name of a local, state, national, or international court, U.S. court, district court, or State court; lowercase if part of the name of city or county court; cap. standing alone if referring to the Supreme Court of the U.S., to Court of Impeachment (U.S. Senate), or to an international court; Circuit Court of the United States for the Second Circuit, the circuit court, the court;

Court of Appeals of the State of Wisconsin, etc., the court of appeals, the court; Court of Claims, the court; Court of Customs and Patent Appeals,, the court; Court of Impeachment, the Senate, the Court, District Court of the United States for the Eastern District of Missouri, the district court, the court; Emergency Court of Appeals, United States, the court; International Court of Justice, the Court; Permanent Court of Arbitration, the Court; Supreme Court of Virginia, etc., the supreme court, the court; Tax Court, the court; U.S. Court of Appeals for the District of Columbia, the court. Appellate Division, Court of Appeals, Court of Claims, Court of Criminal Jurisdiction.

courtesan [KAWR-teh-zan] prostitute.

court-martial (pl.) courts-martial. Pref. to *court-martials.*

courthouse BUT: United States Court House.

courtier [KAWR-tih-ehr; KAWRT-yehr] a minor attendant at a royal court. Hence, any hanger-on or flatterer.

couturier [koo-too-RYAE] designer of high fashion, man or woman. A male dressmaker, —iere, f.

coveralls

covert [KOH-vuhrt] concealed.

covetous [KUHV-eh-tuhs] desirous of what belongs to others.

cowardice [KOU-uhr-dihs]

coxswain [KAHK-s'n]

coyote [KIE-oht; kie-OH-tee]

cozen [KUEH-zihn] cheat, defraud.

cp. (abbr.) candlepower; chemically pure.

C.P.A. (abbr.) certified public accountant.

C.P.I. (abbr.) Consumer Price Index.

Cpl. (abbr.) corporal.

c.p.m. (abbr.) cycles per minute.

C.P.R. (abbr.) Cardio-Pulmonary Resuscitation.

cr. (abbr.) credit; creditor.

Crab Nebula In astronomy, the best-known nebula, derived from a supernova noted by Chinese in 1054.

crack (slang) cocaine in rock form; ingested as smoke.

crackdown (n.); crack down (v.)

craft or horizontal union union including workers with the same skills. See **union, unionman.**

craft Meaning boat, (pl.) craft. BUT other meanings, (pl.) crafts.

craftsman, craft-work, craft union.

cranium The skull. (pl.) —niums, —nia.

crape or **crepe** the fabric. Crepe-hanger.

C ration emergency military packet of 3500 calories including meat, biscuits, coffee, and candy.

crawfish

creche [kraesh, krehsh] Christmas scene.

credence [KREE-dehns] belief.

credible worthy of belief.

CREDITABLE worthy of praise.

credit man, credit union.

credulity [kruh-DYOO-luh-tih]

Creed, Apostles' the Creed.

creek [kreek; NOT krihk]

creep (p. and p.p.) crept.

Creole white or mixed-race descendant of French or Spanish settlers of the U.S. Gulf States; also the native French language, food, cattle, cooking style.
In Latin America, native of European ancestry, usually Spanish.

crepe [kraep] crepe de chine, crepe paper. See **crape.**

crepe suzette (pl.) crepes suzette.

crepuscule [KREE-puhs'l; kree-puhs-kyool] twilight.

crescendo [kreh-sh-EHN-doh]

crestfallen —line.

Crete [kreet] Island off Greece, site of ancient civilization.

cretin [KREE-tihn] Born with congenital thyroid insufficiency, resulting in deformity and retardation. Hence, an idiot.

crime buster —busting; crime wave.

crinoline [KRIHN-oh-lihn] stiff cloth; lady's skirt.

crisis [KRIE-sihs] (pl.) —ses [seez].

crisscross —crossed.

criterion [krie-TEER-ih-uhn] standard of judgment. (pl.) criteria.

criticism judgment of a work, especially unfavorable.

   CRITIQUE [krih-TEEK] an estimate or discussion of a work, not necessarily unfavorable.

Croatia See **Yugoslavia.**

Croesus [KREE-suhs] (died c. 546 B.C.) King of Lydia renowned for his wealth.

Croix de Guerre Fr. medal.

crooked dishonest; illegal. (The word is not colloquial.)

croupier [KROO-pih-air; Fr. —pyae] person running a game of roulette.

crown Cap. if referring to ruler. BUT: crown colony, lands, etc. *The Crown* for king or queen as constitutional monarch.

crow's foot (nonliteral), crow's-nest

(nautical). BUT literally: crow's nest. *There's a crow's nest on the maple tree.* Crowfoot, crowfeet.

crucible [KROO-sih-b'l] pot for melting ores. Hence, any private trial from which a person emerges changed.

cruxifixion Cap. if referring to a specific work of art.

cruel —ler, —lest.

crux [kruhks] crucial point.

crybaby

cryogenics [CRIE-oh-JEHN-ihks] science of dealing with substances at very low temperatures. Loosely, procedure of placing the terminally ill in deep-freeze, in hopes of resuscitating later, when cures are available.

cryptic [krip-tihk] secret, hidden.

   CRYPTOGRAM

crystal —lize, —line [KRIHST-uh-lihn].

C.S.T. (abbr.) central standard time, Also, c.t.

Ct. (abbr.) Court.

CT Connecticut.

Cuba island nation in Caribbean. Former Sp. colony; independent, 1902. Cap.: Havana (La Habana). Native: Cuban(s). Currency: peso.

cubbyhole

cubic Three-dimensional; of third power; cubic content.

cubic centimeter (abbr., cc., cm³) unit of volume is 0.061 cu. in.

cubic foot (abbr.: cu. ft.) unit of volume = 1728 cu. in. = 0.037 cu. yd. = 0.028 m³.

cubic inch (abbr.: cu. in.) unit of volume is 0.000579 cu. ft. = 16.3872 cm.³.

cubic kilometer (abbr.: km³.) unit of volume = 1 billion cm³.

cubic meter (abbr.: m³.) unit (1) of volume is 1.3079428 cu. yd. = 35.31445 cu. ft. = 61,023.38 cu. in. = 1000 cu. decimeters; (2) of capacity is 264.1776 gal. = 10001.

cubic millimeter (abbr.: mm³) unit of volume = .00006 cu. in. = .001 cm³.

cubic yard (abbr.: cu. yd.) unit of volume = 27 cu. ft. = 46,656 cu. in. = 764559 m³.

Cubism [KYOO-bih-s'm] artistic movement of early 20th C.

cuckold [KUHK-uhld] (n.) man with an unfaithful wife.

crudgel —led, —ling.

cue [kyoo] a signal; also, the stick in billiards.

QUEUE [kyoo] waiting line.

Cuernavaca [kwehr-nah-VAH-kaha] resort city in Mexico.

cui bono (Lat.) *Who benefits from it?* NOT: *What is its use?*

cu. (abbr.) cubic.

cuisine [kwee-ZEEN] style of food preparation; the kitchen.

cul-de-sac blind alley.

culinary [KYOO-lih-nehr-ih] pertaining to cooking.

culminate (v.) to reach the highest point. (n.) —nation.

culottes woman's sport skirt divided into two legs.

cumulo [kyoo-myool-oh] combining form meaning to heap: *cumulative, cumulate, cumulo-nimbus clouds.*

cuneiform [kyoo-NEE-ih-fawrm] wedge-shaped characters of ancient writing. Babylonian, Asyrian, etc.

cupful (pl.) cupfuls. Pref. to *cupsful.*

cupola [KYOO-poh-lah] small structure over roof; a rounded ceiling.

Curacao [KYOO-rah-soh] island in Antilles; also, the liqueur.

curator [kyoo-RAE-tuhr] keeper, custodian.

curé [kuh-RAE] (Fr.) parish priest.

cure-all (n. and adj.).

Curie, Marie (1867-1934) and **Pierre** (1859-1906) [keu-REE] Fr. chemists.

curiosity

current (adj.) up to the minute: *the current fancy.*

CURRANT small seedless raisin of Middle East.

current (n.) Cap. if part of name: Arctic Current, Humboldt Current, Japan Current, North Equatorial Current, the current.

curriculum (pl.) —la. Pref. to —ums.

custom work, custom-tailored.

Customhouse (a specific one). BUT a custom house; customs official, customs duty.

cut (p. and p.p.) cut; *cutoff* can be n. or adj. Cut off, cut away, etc. are v. combinations.

cutting edge the most advanced development; the latest.

Cuyahoga Falls [kah-HOHG-a; HOHG-ah; kah-HAW-gah] Town in Ohio.

C.W.O. (abbr.) chief warrant officer.

cwt. (abbr.) hundredweight.

cyanide [SIE-ah-nied] strong poison.

cybernetics [sie-ber-NEHT-ihks] study of electronic devices as brains. See **android, cyborg robot.**

cyborg [SIE-bohrg] Technically, a person kept alive by mechanical devices. Informally, esp. in science fiction, an advanced form of robot.

cyclone Typhoon is a sea-based cyclone.

HURRICANE Violent tropical cyclonic system.

Cyclops mythological one-eyed giants. (pl.) —opes or —opses.

Cymric, Kymric [SIHM-rihk or KIHM-rihk] pertaining to the Celts in Wales.

cynical (adj.) faultfinding; distrustful. (n.) cynic.

SARDONIC bitter, sneering, derisive.

cynosure [SIE-noh-shoor; Br. SIHN-] a center of attraction.

SINECURE [SIHN-ih-kyoor] secure and valuable position with little responsibility.

Cyprus island nation in Mediterranean. Independent, 1960; partitioned into Greek and Turkish states, 1964. Cap.: Nicosia [nih-koh-SEE-ah]. Native: Cypriot. [-uht]. Currency: pound.

C.Z. (abbr.) Canal Zone (Panama).

czar [zahr] Pref. form: tzar (closer to the Russian). Cap. when referring to a specific monarch. —ist. Also, colloquial: one in complete charge: *baseball czar.*

Czechoslovakia [CHEHK-es-sloh-VAH-kee-ah] Central European nation. Independent, 1918. Cap.: Prague [prahg]. Native: Czech [chehk]. Currency: koruna. In 1992, Czechoslovakia voted to separate into two independent nations, Slovakia in the east (cap. Bratislava) and Czechoslovakia (cap. Prague) in the west.

D

d, dd Most one-syllable words ending in *d*, preceded by a single vowel, double the d before suffixes beginning with a vowel.

The same applies to most polysyllabic words ending in *d* with the accent on the last syllable: *reddish, bidden, baddish, bedridden*.

BUT NOT to words ending in a diphthong, a double vowel, or a vowel and *r*: *deaden, goodish, periodical, nomadic*.

d. (abbr.) died; pence; deci.

Dachau [DAHK-hou] Nazi concentration camp, W Germany.

dachshund [DAHKS-hoont] breed of dog.

dactyl in poetry, metrical foot consisting of one stressed and two unstressed syllables. (adj.) dactylic.

Dadaism, Dada [dah-dah] Early 20th-C. movement in painting and literature characterized by shock effects, esp. the renunciation of tradition and logic. (adj.) Dadaist.

Daedalus [DEH-dah-luhs] in Gr. mythology, architect and inventor. Father of Icarus.

daemon [DEE-mahn] Older variant of demon. (pl.)—s. (adj.)—ic.

daguerreotype [tuh-GAIR-oh-typ] early photograph on glass.

dahlia [DAHL-ya]

Dahomey [dug-HOH-mih] See **Benin**.

dais [DAE-ihs] speaker's platform. (pl.) daises.

Dakar [dah-KHAR] African seaport in Senegal.

Dalai Lama [DAH-lee LAH-mah] Tibetan spiritual ruler

Dali, Salvador [DAH-lee] (1904-1989) Spanish surrealist painter.

dalmation [dal-MAE-shun] breed of dog.

dam Lowercase with number or in conjunction with lock; cap. with name: Boulder Dam, Boulder Dam site.

damage (n.), -geable. (adj.).

Damascus, Syria Native: Damascene.

dame a woman of station; wife or daughter of a lord; a lady. When used as a title: *Dame Margot Fonteyn, Dame Margot*. A dame who marries below her rank retains her title: *Dr. Robert Arias and Dame Margot Fonteyn de Arisa*. See **Lady**.

damn [DAM] (v.) to condemn; bring damnation; curse. (adj.) —ably.

danger exposure to injury or evil.

RISK Implies voluntary exposure to danger.

DANGLING MODIFIER In grammar, a modifier (usually an infinitive, participial, or prepositional-gerund phrase) which does not logically relate to the sentence element it modifies.

NOT: *By submitting my application now, the Personnel Department has time to check references.* CORRECT: . . . *I am allowing the Personnel Department time to check references.*

Dante, Alighieri [DAHN-teh, ah-lih-GYEH-ree] (1265-1321) It. poet, author of *Divine Comedy.*

D.A.R. (abbr.) Daughters of the American Revolution.

Dardanelles, the Dardanelles [dahr-duhNEHLS] narrow strait between Europe and Turkey. NOT: Dardenelles Strait.

darkly (fig.) dimily; gloomily; threateningly.

DASH Printed in two widths, the "em dash" and the "en dash." The em dash, a long dash (--), is used:

(1) To mark a sudden break or dramatic change in thought or in construction. *If he leaves—the villian—she will come immediately.*

(2) Instead of commas or parentheses, if the meaning is clarified. *She had bad things to remember—death and sickness—but she did not falter.*

(3) To give emphasis to an element added to a sentence. *He spoke once—but it was enough.*

(4) Before a final clause that itemizes a series of ideas. *Wealth, good health, a happy home—what more can a man desire?*

(5) After an introductory phrase introducing a series set in separate lines (a colon is also correct here). *This is the proposal—that no further travel be permitted.*

(6) To indicate a faltering in speech or an interruption. *I—I don't know. Will you—"* he had begun when the alarm sounded.

(7) To precede the name of an author or a signautre. *"Give me liberty or give me death."—Patrick Henry.*

(8) To separate questions and answers in testimony.

(9) After a sidehead of printing. BUT NOT at the beginning of a line (except 7) or after a comma, colon, or semi-colon.

(10) To indicate a root omitted: *dash, —ed, —ing, —board.*

Use an en (short) dash (very similar to a hyphen), in combinations of figures and/or letters; *Sec. 7–A;* or to denote a period of time: *1958–60.* BUT NOT when preceded by *from* or *between.* See *HYPHENS.*

dastardly cowardly, untrustworthy. Now arch., usu. ironic.

data [DAE-ta, DAH-ta] information. Pl., but used with a sing. verb. The sing. is *datum. Data is available.*

data processing handling masses of information, nearly always by computer. See *COMPUTERS,* **word processing**.

date International Date Line—table.

dates July 1966, May 7, 1966 (BUT NOT: May, 1966; comma error); May, June, and July 1979; May and June 1956; May-September 1985; May 1,

1942-January 4, 1946; 4th of July (or Fourth); the 1st; the end of April (not a specific day). In December, 1917; Christmas 1917. See **time, weeks, months, years, decades, century, Ages**.

daub [dawb] Smear with plaster, mud, paint

daughter-in-law. Pl. daughters-in-law.

davenport. U.S., a sofa. Brit., a writing table.

da Vinci, Leonardo. See Vinci

dawnlight. dawn-gray (adj.).

Dayan, Moshe [DIE-an, MOI-shuh] (1915-1981) Israeli general, politician.

daylight-saving time. System of time adjustment designed to provide longer summer days. Set the clock ahead one hour in the spring (usually last Sunday in April), back one hour in the fall (usually in Oct.). 7 P.M. *eastern daylight time (e.d.t.)*

days

db. (abbr.) decibel.

d.c. (abbr.) direct current.

D.C. (abbr.) District of Columbia.

D.D. (abbr.) Doctor of Divinity.

D-Day World War II Allies land in Normandy: June 6, 1944.

D major D-plus-4.

D.D.S. (abbr.) Doctor of Dental Surgery.

DDT (abbr.) dichlorodiphenyltrichloroethane, an insecticide.

De-, de- Fr. preposition preceding a name. See **Le, le**.

de- combining form meaning away from: *decentralize;* down: *depose;* intensificiation: *denude;* reversal: *denationalization*.

DE Delaware.

deacon cleric or lay servant of the church who may preach and give communion; deaconate. ADDRESS: The Reverend Deacon Smith. SALUTATION: Reverend Sir.

dead letter unclaimed mail; unenforced laws.

deaf [dehf] deaf-dumb, deaf-dumbness.

deal (v.) (p. and p.p.) dealt. (n.) amount: *a great deal;* transaction: *a business deal*.

dean ADDRESS: The Very Reverend the Dean Smith; Dean Smith. SALUTATION: Very Reverend Sir; Sir.

dean of a college or university ADDRESS: Dean Norman B. Gould, School of Fine Arts, Columbia College; or Norman B. Gould, Ph.D., Dean of the School of Fine Arts, Columbia College; or Dr. Norman B. Gould, Dean of the School of Fine Arts, Columbia College. SALUTATION: Dear Sir; Dear Dean Gould; Dear Dr. Gould; Dear Mr. Gould (if he does not hold a doctor's degree).

dear (adj. and adv.); dearly (adv. only).

dear in a salutation, no affection is indicated by the term *dear*. *My dear* usu. occurs only in extremely formal salutations.

debacle [dee-BAH-kl, —bak'l] a sudden breaking up; hence, disruption, terrible defeat.

debar to exclude, prevent

DISBAR in law, to expel from the bar.

debonair [dehb-oh-nair] gay and graceful.

debris [deh-BREE; dae-BREE] rubbish; ruins.

debt [deht] —or.

Debussy, Claude Achille [deh-beu-SIH, klohd] (1862-1918) Fr. composer.

debut [DAE-byoo] orginially, a well-born young woman's first social affair; hence, any initial public appearance.

debutant [DEH-byoo-tahnt]. fem, —ante.

Dec. (abbr.) December.

deca- metric system prefix. Meaning multiplied by 10. See **deci-**.

decades Spell out or write in figures: *the nineteen-twenties; the 1950s.* When the century is omitted: *the twenties, the 20s.* Cap. special eras: *the High*

Sixties. See **years, century**.

decadence [DEHK-uh-dent] deterioration; decline. (adj.) decandent.

decagram (abbr.: dkg.) unit of weight is 0.35274 ou. avdp. = 0.32151 ou. = 10 grams.

decalog the Ten Commandments. *Webster's* spelling: *Decalogue.*

decameter (abbr: dkm.) unit of length is 10.9361 yd. = 32.8083 ft. = 393.7 in. = 10m.

decare (no abbr.) (Sing. and pl.) unit of area. 0.2471 acres = 10 ares.

decathlon [dih-KATH-lahn]

deceased [deh-SEESD] (n.) the dead.

DISEASE [dih-SEEZ] illness. Diseased: the sick.

descent proper, suitable: *decently dressed.* (n.) decency.

DESCENT Downward movement: *a descent to the ground.*

DISSENT (v.) to disagree. (n.) disagreement. *Justice Marshall, dissenting from the majority, wrote a long statement explaining that dissent.*

deci- prefix meaning "divided by ten;" one tenth. See **deca-**.

decibel (abbr. db.) unit of sound measure. Threshold of hearing is 0 decibels; a whisper is 10-20; an automobile 40-50; conversation 60; a riveter 90-100; threshold of pain 120.

decided clear-cut.

> DECISIVE that which decides an issue. *Wellington's decided superiority made possible a decisive victory.*

decigram (abbr: dg.) unit of weight. 1.5432 grains = 0.1 gram.

deciliter (abbr: dl.) unit of capacity = 0.1816 dry pt. = 0.211 liq. pt. = 0.8454 gill = 3.38147 fl. ou. = 0.1 liter; (2) unit of volume = 6.1025 cu. in.

DECIMAL SYSTEM numerical system based on radex of ten. 1 is unit; .1 is one-tenth; .01 is one-hundredth; .001 is one-thousandth. .017 is seventeen-thousandths; .117 is one hundred seventeen-thousandths; .0001 is one ten-thousandths; etc.

Use figures for numbers which contain decimals: *2.5.* Decimals without units should be preceded by 0: *0.72.* See *FRACTIONS,* **Metric system.**

decimate (v.) to kill one in ten, hence, to kill a large number. But NOT: *decimated the population by 50 percent.*

decimeter (abbr: dm.) unit of length is approx. 0.328 ft. = 3.93 in. = 0.1 m. = 10 cm.

declaration Cap. with name: Declaration of Independence, the Declaration; Declaration of Panama.

declare to make a formal, explicit statement.

declassé [dae-klass-AE] socially fallen.

declension Inflection of n. and pron., including forms for gender, number, and case.

decolleté [dae-kohl-TAE] (adj.) low-necked, of a gown. (n.) decolletage.

> DISHABILLE undressed; loosely or carelessly dressed.

> DISHEVELLED [dih-SHEH-vehld] mussed.

Decoration Day Old name for *Memorial Day.*

decorative [DEHK-oh-rae-tihv; ruh-tihv] ornamental.

decorous [DEHK-oh-ruhs] restrained; seemly.

decree See **Executive**.

decry to belittle. *To decry talent is to stifle ambition.*

> DESCRY to discover by looking. *The astronaut descried the shape of continents below.*

de Cuellar, Javier Perez See **Perez de Cuellar, Javier**.

deduce [dih-DOOS] (v.); deducible (adj.).

deductible clause in an insurance policy, provision that the first specified part of loss (for example, $500) is to be absorbed by the insured.

deduction in logic, drawing a specific conclusion from a general principle.

INDUCTION drawing a general conclusion from observation of various similar specifics.

de-emphasis (n.); —se (v.).

deer Both singular and plural. See *animals*.

defendant In legal writings, name usu. italicized: *Roe v. Wade*.

defense defense bond, defensible. Br. spelling: —ce.

Defense Establishment

deferrable

deficit [DEH-fih-siht] shortage in amount.

definite precise, exact: *a definite meaning*.

DEFINITIVE [deh-FIHN-ih-tihv] defining precisely; not alterable; final. *He wrote a definitive study*.

Degas, Hilaire (German Edgar) [deh-GAH, ehd-GAHR] (1834-1917) Fr. impressionist painter.

de Gaulle, Charles (André Joseph Marie) [dug-GOHL, sharl] (1890-1970) Fr. general, statesman, president (1958-69). De Gaulle Free French: But de Gaullist.

dehydrate (v.) to extract moisture in order to preserve. (n.) —tion

deign [daen] to allow grudgingly; condescend.

deism [DAE-ihs'm] belief in a God unknowable within the range of human experience. See **atheism**.

deity Cap. nouns denoting deity and all but relative pronouns: *the word of the Lord; His word: God, who is good*.

dejeuner [deh-zhuh-NAE] (Fr.) breakfast.

Delacroix, Eugene [Deh-lah-KWAH] (1798-1863) Fr. Romantic painter.

dekaliter (abbr: dkl.) (1) unit of capacity = 2.6418 gal. = 10.5671 liq. qts. = 10.1. (2) Unit of volume = 0.284 bu. = 1.1351 pks. = 9.081 dry qts. = 610.25 cu in.

de Kooning, Willem [dih Koo-nihng] (b. 1904) Dutch-American Abstract Expressionist painter.

Delaware U.S. state. Abbr: DE. Cap.: Dover. Native: Delawarean.

delectus personae [duh-LEHC-tuhs puhr-SOH-nae] (Lat.) choice of persons, as the right of a partner to reject other new partners. See **dramatis personae**.

delegate (n.) (to a conference) the delegate, the delegation, delegate at large. Cap. if attached to U.S. Congress.

Delhi [DEH-lee] Indian province. New Dehli is the city.

delineate (v.). —neable (adj.).

delinquent [deh-LIHN-kw'nt] (adj.) failing in duty; offending by neglect or violation. (n.) one who thus fails or offends.

delirium psychosis. (pl.) —s or deliria.

Delphi [dehl-fie] in ancient Greece, place of prophecy.

delta Mississippi River Delta, the delta.

delusion misconception; fantasy. See **allude**.

deluxe [deh-LOOKS; dee-LUHKS] (from Fr.) fine quality.

demagogue [dehm-uh-gahg] rabble rouser; implies disapproval. Rarely spelled *demagog*; demagoguery [dehm-uh GAHG-uhr-ih].

demarche [dae-MAHRSH] a diplomatic maneuver.

demimonde [DEH-mee-mohnd] (Fr.) literally "half-world." Life at fringes of society; orginally, the life of prostitutes. —aine, woman of doubtful reputation.

de minimus (Lat.) of the least; a minor error.

demise [dehm-iez] death. NOT —ize.

Democrat Member of Democratic party. Democratic National Convention. Democratic returns.

DEMONSTRATIVE ADJECTIVES adjectives that tell which or what is meant. Definite: *the, this, that, other.* Indefinite: *a, any, another, certain.*

demote (v.) to lower in rank.

demur [dee-MUHR] (v.) to object; decline. —rred, —rring, demurs.

DEMURE [dee-MYOOR] (adj.) serious, modest; prim.

demurrage a charge made for storage on merchandise not unleaded or picked up at the specified time.

demurrer in law, a plea admitting facts but denying that they create a legal cause of action.

dengué fever [DEHN-gae] painful but seldom fatal tropical viral disease carried by mosquito. Also, breakbone fever.

denier unit of yarn fineness based on weight in grams of 10,000 m. (until recently 9,000 m.). The lower the denier the finer the yarn.

denigrate [DEHN-ih-graet] to defame, blacken. See **deprecate**.

denim n. or adj.

Denmark nation on Baltic coast; since 12th C. Cap.: Copenhagen. [koh-pehn-HAE-gehn] Native: Dane. Currency: kroner.

denouement [deh-noo-MUHN] (Fr.) "unknotting." Final resolutions of a drama, following the climax.

dentifrice toothpaste. NOT *dentrifice*.

department Cap. if part of name; cap. standing alone if referring to federal or international unit: Highway Department (District of Columbia), the Department; Post Office Department, the Department.

Yale University Department of Economics, the department of economics, the department.

Lowercase before clerical, legislative, executive judicial, other departments.

departmentwide

dependent

dependent clause in grammar, a clause used as an adjective, adverb, or noun that cannot stand alone: *Because I love you . . . Although she is blind. . .*

depositary Person or institution named to hold something of value. BUT: *A diary is a depositary of secrets.*

DEPOSITORY. A place where things may be left, usu. for safekeeping.

depot [DEH-poh]. A reception, storage or classification center. BUT a railroad station is DEE-poh. Cap. if part of a name.

deprecate [DEH-preh-kaet] to belittle.

depression Cap. when referring to the 1930's: *the Great Depression, the Depression.*

deprivation [DEH-prih-VAE-shuhn]

deputy Cap. if part of capitalized title: BUT: the deputy.

deputy chief of staff (pl.) —chiefs—

de rigeur [deh-ree-GOOR] (Fr.) with strict etiquette.

derisive [deh-RIE-sihv] (adj.) mocking; scornful. (n.) derision.

DERISORY [deh-RIES-uh-ree] derisive, or inspiring derision: *a derisory recommendation.*

derivative

derring-do (n.) bravery. Arch., thus often ironic.

Descartes, Rene [dae-KAHRT] (1596-1650) Fr. mathematician and philosopher.

desalting Pref. to *desalinization,* which in turn is preferred to *desalinification.*

descend to go down. See **decent**.

descendant (n. and adj.) offspring.

DESCENDENT (adj.) going down: *in the descendent.*

descendible in law, that which can descend to an heir. —able.

description

descry to discover by looking. See **decry**.

desecrate (v.); —crable (adj.); —crater (n.).

desert [DEHZ-zuhrt] (n.) arid area.

DESERT [dih-ZUHRT] (v.) to abandon. (n.) reward or punishment, usu. pl.: *The villians got their just deserts.*

DESSERT [deh-ZUHRT] (n.) sweet course at end of a meal.

deshabille [dehz-uh-BEEL] loosely dressed. *Dishabille is pref. See* **decolleté.**

designate Chairman-designate, etc.

desist [dee-ZIHST] (v.); —ance (n.).

Des Moines [deh-MOIN] city in Iowa.

desperado [dehs-per-AE-doh; des-per-AH-doh] criminal.

desperate without hope; reckless.

DISPARATE different; distinct.

despicable [Dehs-PIH-kuh-b'l] Contemptible.

destructible

desuetude [DEHS-wee-tood] not being used. *The regulation is nullified by desuetude.*

determinedly with determination.

DETERMINATELY in a fixed way, precisely.

detour (n.) [DEE-toor]; (v.) [de-TOOR].

detractor

de trop [dee-troh] (Fr.) out of place, too much.

deus ex machina [DAE-oos ehks MAH-kee-nah] (Lat.) "god from the machine." In Roman drama, plot resolutions provided by a god-character suspended on a crane over the stage. Hence, any implausible, forced solution.

deutsche mark [DOI-cheh MAHRK] Ger. monetary unit.

Deutschland uber alles [doitsh-lahnt EE-bair AHL-less] "Germany above everything." Ger. national anthem.

device (n.) contrivance.

DEVISE (v.). to contrive; invent; or, in law, to distribute, as in a will. —sor. —see.

devil Cap. when meaning *Satan.* BUT: *That dog's a devil.*

deviltry mischief (generally benign).

devise See **device.**

DIVISOR in math, number which divides the dividend.

devotee [dehv-oh-TEE]

D.E.W. (abbr.) Distant Early Warning. DEW line.

Dewey Decimal Classification System of arranging books by subject based on numbers for each subject, 000 is general works; 100 is philosophy; 200 is religion; 300 is social science; 330 is economics; 340 is law; 370 is education; 400 is language; 500 is pure science; 600 is technology; 610 is medicine; 620 is engineering; 630 is agriculture; 650 is business; 700 is the arts; 780 is music; 790 is sports; 800 is literature; 900 is history; 910 is travel; 920 is biography.

dexter right; in heraldry, right of shield or shield bearer.

SINISTER left; in heraldry, left of the shield or bearer.

Dhahran [dah-RAHN] oil town in E Saudi Arabia.

dharma [DAHR-mah] in Hinduism, moral law governing conduct. In Buddhism, universal truth proclaimed by the Buddha.

di- prefix meaning two or double: *diacid, dichromic.*

dia-, di- prefix meaning through or between, apart, across: *diaglyph, diagonal.*

DIACRITICAL MARKS appear on some letters in foreign words to indicate a deviation from normal pronunciation.

In most daily communications in English, diacritical marks are left out. Word processing programs require special commands for placing such marks. Most typewriters do not have the necessary keys.

FRENCH uses acute é [ae], *financé*; circumflex â [ah] ê î ô û, *pâte*; (there is then no dot over the i; grave, à, è, ù, *première*; and diaceresis on ä ë ï ü, *näivete* [*nie-EEV-tae*]. The two dots of the diaeresis take the place of the customary one on the *i*, and indicate that the vowel is to be pronounced separately. The cedilla under *c, reçu, façade* [RAE-soo, fuh-SAHD] is used before *a, o,* and *u* to indicate an *s* sound. Ordinarily the French *a* is pronounced *ah*; *i* is pronounced *ee*, *j* is pronounced *y*, and *u* is pronounced as

the German *u* in *Walkure*.

GERMAN language may use an umlaut on ä, ö, ü [ue].

SPANISH. The acute á, é, í, ó, ú is used to indicate stress or to distinguish two words alike in spelling but different in meaning. A tilde makes the ñ soft; thus, cañon is pronounced *canyon*. The ñ is a separate letter in the Spanish alphabet between *n* and *o*. The diaeresis is used in combination with *u* on *güe* and *güi*, when the *u* is to be pronounced.

Common foreign words which take diacritical marks: à l'américaine, attaché, blessé, calèche, cañon, chargé, crédit mobilier, curé, doña, exposé, mañana, maté, mère, outré, passé, pâte, père, piñata, précis, raisonné, resumé, touché.

ENGLISH words may carry the diaeresis to indicate the separate sound of two adjacent vowels. *Näive, coöperate.*

diagnosis (pl.) —oses. pron. —sees.

DIAGONAL LINE as in *either/or*. See ***SLASH, VIRGULE.***

diagram —ed, —ing. (adj.) diagrammatic.

dialect a local language. (adj.) dialectal. See **language**.

dialectic or **dialectics** (n. and adj.) in logic, using opposing viewpoints to discriminate between truth and error. (pl.) —s. (adj.) —tical.

dialog Also spelled *dialogue*.

dialysis Separation. (pl.) —ses.

diameter [die-AM-uh-tuhr] Of a circle, diameter = circumference x .3182 = 2 x radius

diapason [die-uh-PAE-zn] (from music) the entire scope.

diaphragm [die-uh-fram]

diaeresis [die-er (or EER) -ruh-sihs] Pref. to *dieresis*. Pl. —ses [—seez] The mark (¨) over a letter indicating that two vowels should be pronounced separately. *aëration, coöperative*. Also, separation of one syllable into two. See *DIACRITICAL MARKS*.

diarrhea

diary [DIE-uh-rih] a daily record book.

DAIRY [DAE-ree] milk establishment.

Diaspora [die-AS-puh-ruh] dispersion of Jews after the destruction of Jerusalem, 70 B.C.

diastole [die-AST-tohl-ee] rhythmic beat of the heart; correlative to systole. (adj.) diastolic [die-as-TAHL-ihk].

dichotomy [die-KAHT-oh-mih] division into two parts. (pl. —ies.)

dictionary a publication concerned with words.

LEXICON More specialized, shorter than dictionary.

ENCYCLOPEDIA Concerned with things.

dictaphone a dictation machine. Trademark name.

dictum formal statement; a judge's opinion. (pl.) —ta.

didactic [die-DAK-tihk] (adj.) in the manner of a teacher or moralizer. (n.) —ticism.

die gambling cubes. (pl.) dice.

Dien Bien Phu [dee-EHN bee-ehn FOO] city in Vietnam, site of final French defeat, 1954.

dietary [DIE-uh-tehr-ee] *Dietitian* pref. to —*ician*.

Dietrich, Marlene [DEE-trihk, mahr-LAEN] (1904-1992) German actress and singer.

different [DIHF-ehr-ehnt] Always followed by *from*. NOT: *different than*. (adv.) differently.

differentiation [dihf-ehr-ehn-shee-AE-shuhn]

diffuse (v.); diffusible (adj.); diffuser (n.).

dig (p. and p.p.), dug; digging.

digestible

digit a number from 0 to 9; or a unit of length, 0.75 in.

dike or **dyke** lowercase: dike no. 1.

dilemma difficulty in choosing between poor solutions. NOT difficulty in finding any solution: *two horns of a dilemma*.

dilettante [dihl-un-TANT] person with superficial interests only. (pl.) —s. (n.) —*tism*. See also: **amateur, connoisseur**.

dillydally (v.) —dallied, —ies, —allying. (n.) —ier.

dimlit (adj.)

dimensions Write in figures. *1 by 2; 6 feet 2 inches by 2 feet 4 inches; 6 feet 3 inches tall; 14 years 2 months 7 days; 3 parts gin 1 part vermouth; 7 to 5; 10-to-1 shot, 2 x 8; 20-foot boat.*

dimensions of water Weight of water is important because it is the basis for many calculations involving capacity and pressures. 1 cu. in. is 0.03617 lbs.; 1 cu. ft. is 62.5 lbs.; 1 cu. ft. is 7.48052 gals.; 1.8 cu. ft. is 112.5 lbs.; 35.84 cu. ft. is 2240.01 lbs. See *NUMBERS, MEASUREMENTS*.

diminuendo of sounds, diminishing in volume. (pl.) —os.

diminishment or **diminution** [dihm-in-NYOO-shuhn]

Dinesen, Isak [DEE-neh-sehn, EE-sohk] (1885-1962) Danish writer (*Out of Africa*) Real name Karen Christence Dinesen.

dinghy [DIHNG-gee] small rowboat.

diocese [die-oh-sees or sihs] (n.); diocesan [die-AHS-eh-s'n] (adj.).

Dionysus [die-oh-NIE-suhs] Greek god of wine and ecstasy; Bacchus. NOT: *Dionysius*.

Dior, Christian [dee-OHR, Krehst-YAHN[(1905-1957) Fr. fashion designer.

diptheria [dihf-THEER-ih-uh]

diphthong [DIF-thawng] sound changing continuously from one vowel to another: *out; yoo* in *beauty*. Loosely in the ligature: *ae.* Consonantal diphthongs: $t + sh = ch; d + sh = j$.

diplomatic corps See **corps; service**.

diptych [diph-tihk] series of pictures painted on two hinged tables. From hinged writing tablet. See **tryptich**.

direct address A noun or pronoun used in direct address is in the nominative case and set off by commas. *I tell you, father, I will not be stopped.*

direct object in grammar, the person or thing directly affected by the action of the verb. *I took the book.* See *CASE*.

director Cap. if head of federal or international unit, the Director; District Director of Internal Revenue, the Director; Director of Fish and Wildlife Service, the Director; BUT director, board of directors (non-governmental).

dirigible [DIHR-ih-jih-b'l] blimp.

disadvantageous [dihs-ad-van-TAE-juhs].

disbar See **debar**.

disc, disk Use either spelling. See **CD, floppy**.

discern [dih-ZERN] (v.) to see. (adj.) discernible [dih-ZERN-ih-b'l].

discharge [(v.) dihs-CHAHRJ, (n.) [DIHS-charj]

discomfit (v.) to frustrate, over-whelm. (n.) —ure.

DISCOMFORT (v.) to make un-easy. (n.) uneasiness.

discordant [dihs-KAWRD-'nt].

discotheque [DIHS-koh-tehk] From Fr. dance club depending on re-corded music, usu. with a disc jockey. (pl.) —s.

discourse [dihs-KAWRS; DIHS-kawrs].

discreet [dihs-CREET] prudent, ju-dicious.

DISCRETE separate, discon-nected, distinct. *Light is not a con-tinuous flow, but is made up of dis-crete particles.*

discriminate (v.). —nable (adj.).

disenfranchise [dihs-ehn-FRAN-chiez] to deprive of the rights of a citi-zen.

disgraceful See **strong opinion words**.

disguise

dishabille [dihs-ah-beel] Also spelled *deshabille*. See **decolleté**.

disheveled [deh-SHEH-vihld]. See **decolleté**.

disinterested [dihs-IHN-tehr-ehs-tehd] unbiased.

UNINTERESTED not taking any interest.

INDIFFERENT lacking in feeling.

disk See **disc**.

dismissible

disparage [dihs-PAR-ihj].

dispatch NOT: *despatch*.

dispel Must be followed by an object which can be dispersed in different directions, such as suspicion, cloud, darkness. NOT: *He dispelled the report.*

dispense with to do without. Also has special legal and ecclesiastical meanings.

disperse (v.); —ible (adj.).

displacement ton See **ton**.

disposition *Disposition of funds*, pos-sessions, etc., implies distribution or utilization.

DISPOSAL *Disposal of funds*, pos-sessions, etc., implies getting rid of.

disputable [DIHS-pyoo-tuh-bl; dihs-PYOO-].

disputant [DIES-pyoo-tant].

disseminate [dih-SEH-mih-naet] to spread wide.

dissent to disagree. See **decent**.

disassociate [dihs-ah-SOH-shee-aet] (v.) to disunite; separate from. Pref. to *dissociate*. (n.) —tion.

dissoluble or **dissoluable**

dissonance [DIHS-oh-nans] discord.

distaff (arch.) woman's domain; female part of group.

distension stretching.

distill —ed, —ing, —ment.

distinct marked out.

distingué [dihs-tang-GAE] elegant in appearance.

distraught [dihs-TRAWT] confused mentally. *After the death of her child, she was distraught.*

distributable (adj.); distributor (n.).

district Cap. if part of name: District of Columbia, the District; Alexandria School District No. 4, the school district; Chicago Sanitary District, the sanitary district; 1st Naval District, naval district. BUT customs district No. 2; first assembly district; school district No. 4.

district attorney (pl.) —attorneys. ADDRESS: The Honorable Frank S. Hogan, District Attorney, New York County, Criminal Courts Building, New York, N.Y. 10013. SALUTATION: Dear Sir; Dear Mr. Hogan.

districtwide

diurnal [DIE-uhr-n'l] taking place during the day. Opposite nocturnal. See **annual**.

DAILY occurring every day.

diva [DEE-vuh] opera star; prima donna.

divers [DIE-vuhrs] (arch.) various, several.

DIVERSE [dih-VURHS; DIE-vuhrs] several, different, unlike. *They learned the same facts but reached diverse conclusions.*

divestible

divide Continental Rocky Mountain Divide, the divide.

Divine Father BUT: divine guidance, divine providence.

divisible

division Cap. if referring to federal unit: Electro-Motive Division, the division; division of General Motors.

division, Army Cap. if part of name: 21st Division (BUT spell out numbers from first to ninth), the division. See *ARMY ORGANIZATION*.

divorced from NOT *by*. Strictly, the party sued is divorced.

divorcee [dih-vawhr-SEE] a divorced person (m. or f.). ADDRESS: Divorced women choose the name they prefer to go by. Current usage prefers title *Ms.*

Djakarta See **Jakarta**.

Djibouti [ji-BOOT-tih] nation on E African coast. Former French Somaliland; independent 1977. Cap.: Djibouti. Native: Somali. Currency: franc.

D. Lit (abbr.) doctor of literature.

Dnieper [NEE-puhr (Russ.) Dneper, d'NYEH-pr]. Rus. river flowing into Black Sea.

do (p.) did. (p.p.) done.

do-all, do-gooder, do-nothing (n. and adj.)

Doberman pinscher Breed of dog.

docile [DAH-sihl] tractable.

dock no. 1 lowercase.

docket no. 66 lowercase.

doctoral

doctrinal [DAHK-trih-nal] pertaining to ruling theories.

> DOCTRINAIRE [dahk-trih-NAIR] going by the book; heedless of practical or emotional considerations.

Doctrine, Monroe the doctrine; BUT Truman doctrine.

Document Cap. if part of name: *Document No. 2.*

doe female of antelope, deer, rabbit, etc. See **buck,** *ANIMALS.*

dog days from the dog stars Sirius and Procyon, visible between July and September. Late summer; implies weariness, danger.

doggerel

dogma [DAWG-mah] ruling theory. (pl.) —mas.

dollars and cents Write in figures: *2 cents, 10 cents $4.00, $6.35, $1,000,000.* Round numbers and approximations may be spelled out: *a dollar, about a million, million-dollar robbery, forty billion.* Spell out cents when less than $1.00 except in tables: *7 cents, 98 cents, one red cent.* In tables: *7¢, 98¢.*

dolorous [DAHL-uhr-uhs; DOHL-] sorrowful.

Domesday Book [DOOMZ-dae, DOHMZ-] record of land survey by William the Conqueror, 1085-1086.

domicile [DAHM-ih-sihl], —ed [DAHM-ihsihld] Also spelled —cil.

Dominica [doh-MIH-nih-kah] island country in E Caribbean. Former Br. colony; independent, 1978. Cap.: Roseau. Native: Dominican. Currency: East Caribbean dollar.

Dominican [duh-MIHN-ihk'n]

Dominican Republic Shares Caribbean island of Hispanola with Haiti. Former Sp., Fr., Haitian; independent, 1924. Cap.: Santo Domingo. Native: Dominican(s). Currency: peso.

Dominion of Canada, of New Zealand, etc., the Dominion; BUT British dominions, a dominion, dominion status.

domino the game, although in the pl. takes a sing. verb. *Dominoes re-*

quires both skill and intelligence. (pl.) — oes.

Dona [DOH-nyah] (Sp.) Lady (lowercase) a lady.

Don Juan [dahn-JOO-an; (Sp.). dawn-WAHN] in Spanish tradition, a nobleman and lover.

Don Quixote [dawn-kee-HOH-tee] title character of 16th-century novel by **Miguel de Cervantes**.

doomsday the day of judgment.

doppelganger [DAH-puhl-GAN-gehr] (Ger.) a human double. Traditionally, seeing a doppelganger is a premonition of death.

Doppler effect apparent change in wave length of light, sound, etc. caused by change in relative position; for example, change in pitch of train sound as it moves away.

do's and don'ts sometimes *dos and donts.*

do-see-do [doh-see-DOH] a square dancing term.

dossier [DAHS-ee-ae] a record concerning person or subject.

Dostoevski or Dostoyevsky, Fedor Mikailovich [DAHS-tuh-YEHV-skih, FYAW-dehr] (1821-1881) Rus. writer (*Crime and Punishment*).

dotage [DOHT-ihj] excessive fondness; also senility.

double-crostic Word-definition

puzzle in which letters properly entered form a sentence.

double-entendre [DOOB'L ahn-TAHN-dre] expression with two meanings, of which the less obvious is indicated.

DOUBLE NEGATIVE Two negatives in a sentence may add emphasis. *No, I'll never do it!* BUT in many instances, the construction is incorrect. *No one said nothing.*

Difficulties arise particularly with the use of negative pronouns *no, none, nothing*; negative adverbs *hardly, scarcely*; negative conjunctions *but, neither, nor*; and negative verbs *doubt, deny, refrain.*

Although it is generally assumed that two negatives make a positive, the reader is often left to puzzle out the meaning. *I could hardly approve. It is scarcely possible that no one will either deny or confirm the possibility of the cabinet's fall.*

doubt Always followed by *whether* in the affirmative and by *that* in the negative and interrogative. *I doubt whether she knows. I do not doubt that he knows.*

doubtless without doubt. The word *undoubtedly* is stronger.

doughty [DOW-tee] brave.

Douglas fir tree

dour [doo'r; dow'r] sour, sullen.

dowager [DOU-wah-jihr] a widow who has inherited from her husband; an elderly lady.

dower [DOU-'r] widow's share of property.

dowry property or gift brought by a bride.

Down East (colloq.) coast of NE U.S. and SE Canada.

downsize in business, to reduce activities and/or staff for economic reasons. Colloq., but common. —zing.

downward Pref. to *downwards*. See **backward**.

dozen (abbr.: doz.) group of 12. (pl.) —s. *Dozens of cousins, two dozen eggs.* See **baker's dozen**.

D.P. (abbr.) displaced person.

dr. (abbr.) debit; debtor; dram. Doctor is cap.: Dr.

draft [draft] Pref. to *draught* except for drinking, fishing, and air currents. Br. distinguish draftsman (one who draws banking drafts) and draughtsman. U.S., draftsman.

drachma [drak-muh] Greek coin. —6 obols. (pl.) —s or —mae.

dram [dram] a small quantity.

DRAM apothecaries (dram. advp.) unit of weight is 2.1943 dr. avdp. = 0.125 ap. cz. = 2.5 dwt. = 3 scruples = 3.888 grams = 60 grains.

dram, avoirdupois (dram avdp.) unit of weight is 0.4558 dr. ap. is 0.0625 av. oz = 1.1393 divt. = 1.3672 scruples = 1.7713 grams = 27.344 grains.

dram, liquid (1) U.S. = 0.125 U.S. fl. oz. = 60 U.S. minims = 0.2256 cu. in. = 0.03125 gill = 3.6966 milliliters, (2) Brit. unit of capacity = 0.125 fl. oz. Brit. or 0.9607 U.S. liquid drams = 60 Brit. minims = 0.2167 cu. in. = 3.5514 milliliters.

drama [DRAH-muh]

dramatis personae [DRAM-uh-tihs puh-SOH-nee] (Lat.) the cast of a theatrical production.

drapery (pl.) —ies.

draw (p.) —drew. (p.p.) drawn.

drawing II, A, 3, etc. BUT Drawing 2 when part of the title: *Drawing 2—Hydroelectric Power Development*.

dream (p. and p.p.) dreamed or dreamt.

dressing room

Dreyfus, Alfred [DRAE-fuhs, DRIE-fuhs; Fr. drae-FUES] (1859-1935) French army officer, victim of anti-semitism.

drink (p.) drank. (p.p.) drunk, drunken.

drive (p.) drove. (p.p.) driven.

dropout (n.)

drought [drout] lack of rain.

drowned *He drowned.* NOT: *He was drowned.*

dry drier, driest, dryly, dryness, dryer (the machine).

drydock no. 1 Lowercase.

dry measure system for measuring volume of dry commodities based on pint of 33.60 cu. in., one bushel is 4 pecks is 32 quarts is 64 pints.

dual. double: *a dual solution, offering both money and time.*

DUEL a challenge fight between two persons.

Dubcek, Alexander [DOOB-chehk] (b. 1921) Prime Minister of Czechoslovakia during "Prague Spring," 1968, brief period of democratic socialism crushed by U.S.S.R.

ducat [DUHK-uht] coin first used c. 1150, worth approx. $2.25.

Duchamp, Marcel [DOO-shahm, mar-SEHL] (1887-1968) Fr. avant-garde painter, sculptor.

duchess female soveriegn of a duchy, or the wife or widow of a duke: the Duchess of Argyle, the Duchess.
ADDRESS: Her Grace, the Duchess of Atholl; Her Grace, the Most Noble Duchess of Atholl. SALUTATION: Your Grace; Madam.
ADDRESS: Her Royal Highness, the Duchess of Kent. SALUTATION: Madam.

duel (v.) dueled, dueling. (n.) duelist. See **dual**.

due to Avoid use of *due to* as a prepo-

sition. Use *since* or *because* where appropriate.

dufflebag

Dufy, Raoul Ernest Joseph [deu-FEE, rahOOL] (1877-1953) Fr. progressive, painter.

dugout (n. or adj.).

duke ADDRESS: His Grace, the Duke of Windsor. SALUTATION: My Lord Duke; Sir; Your Grace (for servants or retainers).

du Maurier, Daphne [deu-MAW-ryae] (b. 1907) Eng. novelist (*Rebecca*).

Dumas, Alexandre [doo-MAH]. Dumas, *père* (1802-1870), French novelist, author of *The Count of Monte Cristo*. **Dumas,** *fils* (1824-1895), French realistic playwright (*La Dame Aux Camélias*).

dumbfound to amaze. (adj.) dumbfounded.

dumdum a soft-nosed bullet which expands on impact.

dunderhead —headed.

duodenum [dyoo-oh-DEE-nuhm; dyoo-AHD-n-uhm].

Dürer, Albrecht [DYUHR-ahr, AHL-brehkt] (1471-1528) German painter and engraver.

duress [dyuhr-REHS] being under constraint.

during the time that *While* is better.

Düsseldorf [DEUSS-ehl-dawrf] city on Rhine River, Germany.

dutiful [DOO-tih-fuhl].

Duvalier, Dr. François (1907-1970) President of Haiti, 1957-1970. Son, Jean-Claude, fled revolution, 1986.

Dvorak, Anton [DVAWR-zhahk, AN-tawn] (1841-1904) Czech composer.

dwell (p.) dwelt or dwelled; (p.p.) dwelt.

d.w.t. (abbr.) deadweight tons.

dwt. (abbr.) pennyweight.

dye, dyed, dyeing.

    DIE died, dying.

Dylan, Bob [DIH-l'n] (b. 1941) Am. singer, songwriter. Real name: Robert Zimmerman.

dynamo (pl.) —os.

dynasty [DIE-nast-ee].

E

e. (abbr.) erg. Unit of energy = 1 dyne acting through distance of 1 cm.

E. (abbr.) east.

each As subject, always followed by singular verb: *Each has her own hat. Each of the men has two hats.* NOT: *Each has their own hat.* BUT in apposition, with a plural noun, *each* takes a plural verb. *The men have two hats each.*

When *each* is emphasized, it precedes the verb or part of the verbal phrase or its complement, and takes a plural pronoun. *We each have our own hats.*

When the verb is emphasized, *each* follows, and a singular pronoun is used. *Masqueraders are judged, each on his own costume.* See **between each.**

Each or *every*, when used to modify a compound subject (joined by *and*), is treated as a singular subject. *Each governor and every senator has approved the measure.*

When *each* is inserted parenthetically or in explanation between a plural or compound subject and its plural verb, the plural verb is not affected. *A, B, and C each are entitled to rebates. The Governors each want the plans enlarged.*

Each other is the pref. form for two agents, *one another* the pref. form for more than two. *The two spoke to each other. Three of us spoke to one another.* Possessive: each other's; one another's.

earl ADDRESS: The Right Honorable Earl of Athlone; or the Earl of Athlone. SALUTATION: My Lord; Sir. See **nobility.**

earl's wife See **countess, nobility, lady.**

earnest (adj.) serious. *He made an earnest effort.* (n.) guarantee of serious intention. *He provided $3000 as earnest money.*

earth Lowercase unless used with names of other planets.

EARTHEN made of earth.

EARTHLY belonging to this planet.

EARTHY containing soil; materialistic; lusty.

Earth First! radical environmental group. Always appears with exclamation point: *the Earth First! demonstrators.*

easement right for the use of land owned by another.

east, eastern. Cap. Eastern Europe (political entity), Eastern Orthodox Church (religious denomination), etc.

Cap. East Germany (political entity), Middle East, Near East, the East (section of United States), East End (London), etc.

Also the East or the Far East, (Communist, Oriental), East Orange (city name), the East Side (section of a city).

east east coast (U.S.); *N.Y. Times*

uses: East Coast (U.S.); east Pennsylvania.

eastbound, east-central, east-northwest, east-sider.

Easter first Sunday following the Paschal full moon on or after March 21; therefore, always before April 25. If Paschal full moon falls on Sunday, Easter is next Sunday. Easter-tide.

easterly, westerly, and so on. Using *-ly* in connection with direction implies either present motion or position attained because of prior motion: *a westerly course; the most northerly outpost of our expansion.*

easy May be used as adv.: *take it easy.* BUT *easily* is pref.

eat (p.) ate. (p.p.) eaten.

EDIBLE can be eaten; indicates question of healthfulness. *Are those mushrooms edible?* Opposite is *inedible.*

eavesdrop —dropper, —dropping. NOT the eaves of a house.

ebony [EH-buh-nee] (n. or adj.).

ebullience [eh-BUHL-y'ns] high spirits. Pref. to —cy.

E.C. (abbr.). European Community.

ecce homo [EHK-ae HOH-moh] (Lat.) "behold the man." BUT *Ecce Homo* when referring to Christ.

Ecclesiastes [eh-KLEE-zee-ASS-tees] See **Bible.**

echo (pl.) echoes.

éclair [AE-klair] cream-filled pastry.

éclat [AE-KLAH] notoriety; acclaim.

eclectic [ehk-LEHK-tihk] selected from many sources.

ecology the interrelationship of organisms and environment. NOT environment itself.

Ecotopia [EHK-oh-TOH-pee-ah] fictional community in harmony with nature. See **Utopia.**

ectomorph [EHK-toh-mawrf] person with body type tending to thinness. Ectomorphy, the body type itself. (adj.) —phic.

ENDOMORPH [EHN-doh-] person with body tending to fat.

MESOMORPH [MEHZ-oh-] person with body of medium build.

ecru [ehk-roo; AE-kroo] beige color.

Ecuador [EHK-wah-dawr] country in NE South America. Independent, 1830. Cap.: Quito. Native: Ecuadoran(s). Currency: sucre.

eczema [EHK-seh-muh] (pl.) —mas or —mata.

ed., eds. (abbr.) edition, editions.

edema [uh-DEE-muh] body swelling, usually due to excess fluid. Pref. to oedema. (pl.) —mas, edemata.

edge, edgeways, edgewise. See **boundary.**

edible. See **ert.**

Edinburgh [EHD'n-BUHR-oh; —buhr'h] cap. city of Scotland.

e.d.t. (abbr.) eastern daylight time.

educate (v.); —cable, —cative (adj.).

educe (v.) to bring out something latent. (adj.) —cible.

eerie Pref. to *eery*.

E.E.C. (abbr.) European Economic Community, or Common Market. See **European Community.**

effect [eh-FEHKT] (v.) to cause, bring about. *Ms. Schroeder has effected many improvements since she became president.*

> AFFECT (v.) to influence. *Her voice affected me deeply.*
>
> EFFECT (n.) result, consequence. *The effect of the change in price was a run on the stores.*
>
> AFFECT [AF-fehkt] (n.) emotional impact. *A great poem produces a powerful affect in the reader.*

effective producing a result: *an effective speaker.*

> EFFECT OF . . . IS PRODUCTIVE Redundant. NOT: *The effect of the new tax is to produce a new middle class.* (Delete *to produce.*)
>
> EFFECTUAL Applies to means and actions and implies the achievement of the desired effect: *effectual action.*
>
> EFFICACIOUS Applies to medicines, etc.; implies it can be effective: *an efficacious drug.*

EFFICIENT Applies to persons, machines, organizations; implies energy and competence.

effectuate to put into effect.

effervesce, effervescent.

effluvium [eh-FLOO-vee-uhm] something that flows out. (pl.) effluvia or —ums.

e.g. (abbr.) *exempli gratia.* (Lat.) "for instance." Always precede with comma or semi-colon.

egoism excessive love of self; egocentricity, egotism. Opposite of *altruism.*

egregious [ee-GREE-juhs, —jih-uhs] outstanding, usually for bad qualities, as term of contempt: *An egregious liar . . .*

egret [EE-greht] the bird. See **aigrette.**

Egypt African nation on Mediterranean coast. Ancient empire; independent of British, 1922. Cap.: **Cairo** [KIE-roh]. Native: Egyptian(s). Currency: pound. See United Arab Republic.

E.H.F. (abbr.) extremely high frequency.

Eiffel Tower [ei-fehl].

Eire [AE-reh] (Gaelic) Ireland. Formerly Irish Free State.

Eisenhower, Dwight David [IES-ehn-our] (1890–1969) U.S. general and President (1953-1961).

Eisenstadt, Sergey [IES-ehn-staht, sehr-GAE] (1898–1948) Russ. film maker (*Potemkin*).

either, or [EE-thuhr; EI-thuhr] Use to distinguish two choices, NOT more than two. NOT: *either of the NATO nations.* In U.S., *either* can mean *both: Curtains at either end of the room.*

either . . . or, neither . . . nor A complete alternative should follow each of the words, and the alternatives should be in structural balance. *The men wanted either more days off or higher wages.* NOT: *The men wanted either to have more days off or higher wages.*

Usually takes a singular verb, but where a subject contains a plural, a plural verb is acceptable, especially where pl. applies to both. *Neither of the men are coming. Are either coming?*

eke out to stretch out the usefulness of something by adding to it. *He was able to eke out a living by taking part-time work.* NOT: *He was able to eke out a living from his menial job.*

élan [ae-LAHNN] enthusiasm.

Elbe [EAL-buh] river in middle Europe, flows to North Sea.

elder, eldest *Webster's* lists as synonym for *older, oldest.*

-elect elected, but not yet installed in office: *president-elect.* Cap. titles preceding names, and when standing alone in references to government office: *Senator-elect John J. Smith; the Sentator-elect.* See **suffix**.

elective in academics, an optional course. Opposite of *required*.

electoral college the electors.

electric, electrical *Webster's* lists as synonyms.

    ELECTRO- combining form meaning electric: *electro-optics, electro-osmosis, electrocution.*

electrolyte chemical substance that conducts electricity; negative ions move toward an anode while positive ions move toward a cathode. Electrolysis.

electromagnetic radiation

electromotive force (abbr.: e.m.f.) pressure under which electricity flows, measured in volts.

electron negatively charged physical particle ($-1/1840$ of mass of hydrogen atom) which orbits around nucleus of atom. See **atom**.

electronics (n.) branch of physics which deals with electrons, especially with their action in gases and vacuum tubes. Field covers radio, TV, computers, flow of electrons, etc. (adj.) electronic.

elegy [ehl-eh-JEE] (n.) poem of mourning. (adj.) elegiac [-JIE-ak or JEE-ak].

    EULOGY commentary on or praise of the deceased.

elemental of the elements; primal: *elemental spirit; drive.*

    ELEMENTARY pertaining to basic

components, great principles, or a single element: *elementary school.*

elf (pl.) elves. (adj.) elfin.

elicit to draw out. *They tried to elicit more information.*

ILLICIT unlawful or prohibited: *an illicit love affair.*

Elizabeth II (b. 1926) Queen of England since 1950. The Queen, the Crown, Her Most Gracious Majesty, Her Majesty.

ell Br. unit of cloth length = 45 in. = 1/32 bolt.

ellipse [eh-LIHPS] a plane curve, roughly egg-shaped.

ELLIPSIS omission of word or words, in quotation, indicated by three dots in the middle of a sentence or four dots at the end of a sentence. When a complete paragraph or more is omitted, three asterisks (***) may be inserted as a separate line, or a complete line of dots may be made.
''When in the course of human events it becomes necessary . . . to assume, among the powers . . .''
***
'' . . . therefore, the Representatives of the United States of America, . . . do . . . solemnly publish and declare, That these United colonies are, and of Right ought to be Free . . .''
(pl.) —ses.

elliptic usually refers to ellipse.

ELLIPTICAL usually refers to ellipsis.

ELLIPTICAL CLAUSES When parts of a dependent clause are omitted, the reader is presumed to understand the missing elements. However, the writer should be certain that the modifiers in the incomplete clauses identify, both logically and grammatically, the subject of the main clause. *She is rich and I* [am] *poor, so why tax me?*

In **parallel construction**, corresponding portions of expressions may be omitted, esp. (1) parts of the verb *be: He is there and I here;* (2) compound verbs: *She cannot love him or leave him;* (3) subject after *than: No greater love is possible than* [the love] *she gives.* But NOT if tense, voice, or number changes.

El Niño current [NEEN-nyoh] major S Pacific current, affects U.S. weather pattern.

El Salvador [ehl sal-vah-DOHR] Central American republic; independent, 1821. Cap.: San [sahn] Salvador. Native: Salvadoran(s). Currency: colon.

else other; additional to. Possessive: everyone else's.

elude to escape capture. See **allude.**

em measure of type = width equal to the height of the line. An em of 12 pt. type = 12 points = 1/6 in.

E-mail electronic mail; correspondence via computer.

Emancipation Proclamation

embargo prohibition of commerce or freight. (pl.) —oes.

embarrass, embarrassment.

embassy British Embassy, etc., the Embassy; BUT embassy when standing alone, consulate.

embed Pref. to *imbed*. (p.) —dded.

emblematic Pref. to —*cal*.

embolism [EHM-boh-lih′m] obstruction in artery.

embrasure [ehm-BRAE-zhyehr] recess for a door or window.

embryo [EHM-bree-oh] (pl.) —os.

emend (v.) to correct, especially in a literary work. (n.) —ation.

emerge [ee-MERJ] to rise out of. *The submarine emerged from the water. . . . emerge from poverty.*

   IMMERSE to disappear, to plunge into. *He immersed himself in work.*

emergence coming into notice.

   EMERGENCY situation requiring immediate help.

emeritus [ee-MEHR-iht-uhs] retired, with title: Dr. John Smith, professor emeritus (or emeritus professor) of literature. NOT professor of literature emeritus.

e.m.f. (abbr.) electromotive force.

emigrant (n.) person who leaves a country. (v.) emigrate.

   IMMIGRANT (n.) person who comes into a country. (v.) immigrate.

EMIGRÉ [ae-mee-GRAE] political emigrant.

REFUGEE political emigrant who has suffered great hardships or losses.

eminent Prominent. See **immanent**.

eminent domain power of a state, subject to payment, to acquire private property for public use.

emir, emeer [eh-MEER] (Arab.) military commander. (Turk.) title of dignity.

emollient [ee-MAHL-ih-ehnt, -yehnt] a soothing medication: *emollient for a burn.*

   EMOLUMENT [ee-MAHL-yoo-mehnt] remuneration. *She received a salary and other emoluments, including room and board.*

emotive expressing emotions.

emotional arousing emotions; prone to emotion.

emperor Cap. when part of a title or referring to a specific person: Emperor Haile Selassie; the Emperor.

emphysema [ehm-fih-SEE-mah] breathing disorder; bronchitis.

empire Ethiopian, etc., the Empire; BUT *an empire.*

empirical [ehm-PIHR-ih-kal] (adj.) depending on experience or observation. Pref. to empiric. (n.) empiricism.

employ Stresses the use of a person's services.

HIRE Stresses the act of engaging a persons's services.

emptor (Lat.) buyer. *Caveat emptor:* Buyer beware.

empyrean [ehm-pih-REE-an] (n.) highest heaven.

en measure of type. Half an **em**.

en- prefix meaning *in.*

encephal- prefix meaning of the brain. *Encephalitis.*

enclasp

enclave [AHN-claev] smaller territory enclosed within a larger, somehow foreign one.

enclose (n.) enclosure. AVOID *enclosed herewith.* (*Herewith* is superfluous.) AVOID *enclosed please find.* (Trite, archaic commercialese.)

encumber [ehn-CUHM-bur] (v.); encumbrance (n.).

encyclopedia See **dictionary.**

endeavor Br. spelling: —our.

ended For references to the past. *The period ended* [last] *Dec. 31.*

ENDING For references to the future: *Period ending* [next] *Dec. 31.*

endemic habitually prevalent; native.

EPIDEMIC temporarily widespread.

PANDEMIC affecting all people.

—e endings in adj. Drop the final *e* when adding *y: wave, wavy.* EXCEPT: to avoid confusion with another word: *hole, holey; for nouns ending in -ue: glue, gluey.* Nouns ending in *y* take *ey: clay, clayey.*

endive [EHN-dieve, AHN-deev] variety of lettuce.

endocrine [EHN-doh-krien; -krihn, -kreen] (adj.) secreting internally: *endocrine glands; system.*

endomorph person tending to fat. See **ectomorph.**

endorphin [ehn-DOHR-fin] chemical produced in body by strenuous exercise.

endorse (v.) to transfer title by signing on the back of a negotiable instrument, esp. a check.

Also, to express approval. *They endorsed the product.* (n.) endorsement. In insurance, addition to a policy.

endurable [ehn-DYOOR-uh-b'l]

endways Pref. to —*wise.*

enforce (v.) to give force to; execute. *Enforce the law.* Do not confuse with *force.* (adj.) enforceable. (n.) —ment.

enfranchise to set free; admit to citizenship. NOT —ize.

engine Used for steam-driven (except turbines), rocket-driven, some gasoline-driven and electrical devices.

MOTOR used for gas-driven or electrical devices.

engine company Bethesda Engine Company; engine company No. 6; No. 6 engine company; the company.

Engineer officer of Engineer Corps; Chief of Engineers.

engineer's chain. (abbr.: ch.) unit in length = 100 ft. = 30.48 m.

engineer's link (abbr. li.) unit of length 1/100 chain = 12 in. = 0.3048 m.

England [IHNG-l'nd] originally, the SE section of the larger of the two principal British Isles. Usu. refers to whole of **Great Britain**.

For most situations, *British* may be substituted. BUT: *English language, history, fair play, gentleman; the word of an Englishman.*

Also see **British, Scotland, United Kingdom, Wales.**

engross [ehn-GROHS] to absorb; occupy fully. (adj.) engrossed.

enhance to intensify; advance; make greater.

enjoin to command, forbid. Usu. *enjoined from.*

en masse [ehn mass] all together.

enmesh

ennui [ahn-WEE] (Fr.) boredom.

enough Pref. as noun and as adjective of amount only, regardless of kind or quality. *I've had enough.*

SUFFICIENT Pref. as an adjective. As an adverb, rare and more formal.

enroll —ed, —ing, —ment.

Ens. (abbr.) ensign [EHN-sihn]. See *OFFICERS.*

ensure (v.) to make sure. Spelling pref. for most uses.

INSURE (v.) to assure against loss by a contingent event, as in life insurance.

ASSURE (v.) to convince, make confident.

entente [ahn-TAHNT] friendly agreement; also those who join in an entente.

enterprise (pl.) —s; —sing.

enthrall —lled, —lling.

entire, —ty [ehn-TIE'r; -tee] *Entirely complete* is redundant.

entity an existing thing.

NONENTITY a thing or person of no consequence. In philosophy, a thing that does not exist.

entomology [ehn-toh-MAHL-ohjih] study of insects.

ETYMOLOGY [eht-ih-MAHL-ohjih] study of the history of words; the derivation of a word.

ETIOLOGY [ee-tee-AHL-ohjih] science of causes, especially of diseases.

entr'acte [ahn-TRAKT] in theater, a short performance between acts; hence, any brief diversion.

entrechat [AHN-trih-SHAH] (Fr.) a ballet leap.

entree, entrée [AHN-trae] main course of a meal; (Fr.) an entrance. *His recommendation was my entrée into the exciting world of publishing.*

entrepot [AHN-treh-poh] warehouse.

entrepreneur [AHN-tur-preh-NUR] person who assumes ownership, management, and risk of a business.

entropy [EHN-troh-pee] theory from thermodynamics. Energy always increases beyond its capacity to be made useful; hence, everything eventually turns to waste.

entrust to give into the charge of, or place in charge of something. NOT merely trust, or place trust in.

entry, entrant Either may be used for a person who enters a contest.

entwine

ENUMERATION Place numbers in an enumeration in parenthesis. *He wanted (1) cash payment, (2) a large house, and (3) a guaranteed income.*

When the enumeration is formally introduced, cap. the first word in each section of some length. *He listed their assets: (1) Cash in the bank; (2) A large house on Duane Street; and (3) A guaranteed income of $40,000 a year.* BUT do not cap. brief items. Cap. the first word in each element of an enumeration if it is presented in a sentence style, but do not cap. brief items.

Enumerations within a sentence take normal punctuation, using commas between simple elements and semicolons between long elements. If enumerated items are not complete sentences, omit the closing periods. Avoid ending a line with a division mark.

Use a **dash** to set off added defining or enumerating elements: *these Indians—Apache, Shawnee, and Mohawk—had depended on treaties signed before 1900.* Use a dash to set off a phrase on a separate line. *I say—(1) That they are poor workers. (2) That they should be retired.*

Complicated enumerations should be replaced by two or more sentences.

enunciate [ee-NUHN-see-aet; -sih-aet] (v.); —ciation (n.).

envelop [ehn-VEHL-uhp] (v.) to surround. *Fog enveloped me.*

ENVELOPE [EHN-veh-lohp; AHN-veh-lohp] (n.) a wrapper. *Place the letter in a No. 10 envelope.*

environs [ehn-VIE-ruhnz] (n.) suburbs; surroundings. (There is no singular.) (v.) to environ: to surround.

envoy [EHN-voi] a messenger; diplomat ranking between ambassador and minister: Envoy Extraordinary and Minister Plenipotentiary.

Also, postscript to a poem, essay, or book.

Eolian See **aeolian.**

e.o.m. (abbr.) end of month. A term of payment.

eon division of geological time. Variant of *aeon.*

-eous, -ious If preceded by *c,* sound *c* as *sh: precious.*

épée [ae-PAE] pointed sword with no cutting edges.

epicurean [ehp-ihkyoor-EE-uhn]

epidemic See **endemic.**

epigram (n.) pithy, memorable statement. (adj.) —mmatic.

ANAGRAM scrambled spelling to create new words.

epilogue Pref. to —log.

Epiphany [eh-PIHF-uh-nih] Christian holy day celebrating the coming of the Magi, Jan. 6.

episcopal, Episcopal (adj.) Lowercase pertains to bishops; cap. to Episcopal Church. (n.) Episcopalian.

epistemology [eh-PIH-steh-MAH-loh-jee] study of nature and validity of human knowledge.

epitome [eh-PIHT-ohmee] a part that typefies the whole. NOT: the high point.

epoch [EHP-ahk] period marking a distinct development.

Epstein-Barr virus lymph cancer.

equal *Equally as* is redundant. Use: *He is as good as you. He is equally good.* —ed, equaling.

equilibrium (pl.) —iums, equilibria (scientific).

Equitorial Guinea coastal island country off W Africa. Former Sp. colony; independent, 1968. Cap.: Malabo [mah-la-BOH] Native: Guinean(s). Currency: Bipkwele.

equivalence Pref. to —cy.

equivocal [ee-KWIHV-oh-kuhl] questionable, ambiguous.

eradicate (v.); —cable (adj.).

erasable [ee-RAES-uh-bl] able to be erased.

IRASCIBLE [ih-RAS-ih-b'l] quick-tempered.

ere long, ere now

Erewhon [EH-reh-wahn] imaginary utopia (*nowhere* spelled backward). 1872 Samuel Butler novel.

ergo [uhr-goh] (Lat.) therefore; (arch.) often facetious.

Eriksson, Leif [EHR-ihk-s'n, Laef] Also Ericson. (c. 1000) Norwegian discoverer of Vinland, North America, somewhere between Labrador and New Jersey.

Erin Go Bragh [brah] (battle cry, Gaelic) Ireland forever.

Eritrea [ehr-ree-TRAE-uh] in NE

Africa, on Red Sea. Province of **Ethiopia** since 1950; at war to achieve independence since 1961. Cap.: Asmara.

erosion

errant wandering. *The batter went down before an errant pitch.* Also, *erring.*

ARRANT (arch.) confirmed: *an arrant fool.*

errata [air-AH-tuh]. Sing. erratum. The plural refers to a list of errors and may take a singular verb.

errorproof

erstwhile (arch.) formerly.

erudite [AIR-oo-diet; AIR-yoo-diet] learned.

eruption a bursting out of something confined: *a volcanic eruption, a skin eruption.*

IRRUPTION a bursting in or invasion. *An irruption of children into the study made work impossible.*

eschew [ehs-CHOO] to shun.

escrow [ehs-KROH, EHS-kroh] an agreement to place property in the hands of a third party until certain acts are performed. *Hold the money in escrow.*

escudo. (abbr.: Esc.) monetary unit of Portugal and former colonies. (pl.) —os.

Eskimo (pl.) —s.

esoteric private; understood only by the initiated.

EXOTIC of foreign origin.

esophagus [ee-SAH-fuh-guhs] (pl.) —i [jie].

especially Separates the preeminent. See **special.**

espionage [EHS-pih-oh-nahzh] spying.

esplanade [ehs-pluh-NAED, NAHD] walkway.

espresso (It.) strong, steam-brewed coffee.

Esquire [ehs-KWIER; EHS-kwier]. (abbr.: Esq.) Used after surname where there is no title (Sir, Dr., Prof., etc.), to denote a gentleman: John Jones, Esq. NOT Mr. John Jones, Esq. Nearly always ironic or an affectation.

essay (v.) to attempt.

ASSAY to test.

essence spirit; intrinsic quality.

SUBSTANCE materials; tangible quantities.

essential absolutely necessary. *Light is essential for plant growth.*

INDISPENSABLE cannot be spared. *No man is indispensable to a well-run organization.*

NECESSARY required; compulsory. *At least $5000 in capital is necessary.*

REQUISITE Required. *He lacked the requisite energy.*

These four words can be used interchangeably.

E.S.T. (abbr.) Eastern Standard Time.

esthete [EHS-theet] Also spelled *aesthete.*

estimate an approximation of value or cost.

estivate spend the summer. Opposite of *hibernate:* spend the winter.

Estonia [eh-STOH-nee-ah] Baltic country. Russian territory till 1920, then independent till 1940, when it again became part of U.S.S.R. Newly independent, 1991. Cap.: Tallinn [TAL-lihn]. Native: Estonian. Currency: ruble.

estuary [EHS-tyoo-ehr-ih] where the tide meets a river.

e.s.u. (abbr.) electrostatic unit.

e.t. (abbr.) eastern time.

et al. (*et alia,* Latin) And others.

etc., et cetera, and so forth Generally informal. Always preceded by comma or semicolon.

ethics Applies usually to public behavior.

MORALS Applies usually to private acts.

Ethiopia [EE-thih-OH-pih-ah] African nation on the Red Sea. Formerly Abyssinia. Native: Ethiopian. Cap.,

Addis Ababa. Currency: Birr. See **Eritrea.**

etiology See **entomology.**

Etna, Aetna [EHT-nah] volcano in NE Sicily.

étude [AE-tyood] musical practice piece.

etymology See **entomology.**

Euclid [YOO-klihd] (c. 300 B.C.) Greek mathematician. Hence, geometry; euclidean.

eugenics [yoo-JEHN-ihk] science of human improvement by genetic means.

eulogy. See **elegy.**

euphemism a mild or acceptable term substituted for a disagreeable one: *underprivileged* for *poor; passing away* for *dying.* (adj.) —mistic. (v.) —mize.

EUPHUISM affectation in literary style, characteristic of Elizabethan Age.

euphony [YOO-fah-nee] harmony of sound.

Euphrates [yoo-FRAE-teez] river flowing from E Turkey to Persian Gulf; site of ancient Babylonia, Assyria, etc.

Eurasian of mixed European and Asiatic descent.

Euratom European Atomic Energy Community.

European Community (abbr.: E.C.). Western European free trade zone, with standardized currency. Twelve original members, 1992: Belgium, Denmark, France, Germany, Greece, Ireland, Italy, Luxembourg, Netherlands, Portugal, Spain, United Kingdom. 60 affiliate nations.

European Economic Community (E.E.C.), or Common Market, and European Free Trade Association (E.F.T.A.) were earlier, less comprehensive organizations.

European plan hotel charges covering rooms only.

AMERICAN PLAN charges including meals.

CONTINENTAL PLAN charges including continental breakfast of roll, coffee, sometimes juice.

eustachian tube [yoo-STAE-kih-an] tube connecting the middle ear and nasal cavities. NOT spelled *eustacian*.

euthanasia [YOO-than-AE-sha] mercy killing.

evacuate (v.); —cuable (adj.).

evaluate (v.); —uable (adj.).

evanescent [ehv-uh-NEHS-ehnt] fleeting.

evasion an illegitimate avoidance; evasiveness.

AVOIDANCE keeping clear of.

evenness

ever always; at any time; in any case.

everybody, everyone take singular verb and pronoun.

evidently [EHV-ih-dehnt-lee] obviously; as is clear from the evidence. NOT *seemingly.*

APPARENTLY clear, manifest, visible.

evince [ee-VIHNS] to display; exhibit; give evidence of.

evolution [ehv-uh-LOO-shuhn].

-ex, -ix. Plural form in Latin is —*ices,* in English, —*exes:* index, indexes, indices. Scientific and technical words tend toward Latin; popular words toward English.

exacerbate [ehg-ZASS-ehr-baet] to irritate.

exactly precisely, accurately.

JUST almost; nearly. Also, precisely: *just right.*

exaggerate

ex cathedra [ehks-kuh-THEE-druh] (Lat.) from the seat of authority.

exceed (v.) to go beyond. (adj., adv.) —ing, —ingly: more than the average; extraordinary.

EXCESSIVE more than enough. (adv.) —ly.

In spite of his excessive spending, he was not exceeding his ability to pay.

excellent AVOID use with more or most. See **strong opinion words.**

except Stronger than *but*

excepting Use only with *not. Everyone makes mistakes, not excepting the people who write guidebooks.*

excerpt [EHK-suhrpt] (n.) extract.

EXCLAMATION POINT Designates surprise, intense emotion: *No! Please! God!* Should be used sparingly. Excessive use is equivalent to overexcited speech, and can undermine intended impact.

Place inside parentheses and quotation marks where sentence ends within same.

excommunicate (v.); —**cable** (adj.).

execrate [EHKS-ih-kraet] (v.) to curse.

EXECRABLE [-kruh-b'l] detestable.

Executive (President of the United States) Executive Order No. 100, Executive Decree 100, BUT Executive decree, order; Document No. 91; Executive Mansion, the mansion; the White House; Executive Office, the Office. BUT Executive power.

executive agreement, branch, communication, department, document, paper.

executor [ehk-SEHK-yoo-tawr] in law, the agent of an estate. (pl.) —s.

exegesis [ehk-see-JEE-sihs] detailed explanation, especially of Scriptures. (pl.) exegeses.

exemplary [ekg-ZEHM-pla-ree] serving as an example.

exhale [ehks-HAEL] (v.). exhalation [-ha-LAE-shuhn] (n.).

exhaustible

exhibit 2, A, III etc. Cap. when part of title. *Exhibit 2: Capital Expenditures 1990–94.*

exhilarate [ehgs-ZIHL-ur-raet] to gladden.

exigency [EHK-sihjehn-sih] urgent requirement.

exiguous [ihg-ZIHG-yoo-uhs] scanty, diminutive.

existentialism philosophy that existence is a state of mind, and therefore must be asserted by exercise of free will. Absolute value systems do not exist. See **Sartre.**

ex officio [ehks-uh-FISH-ih-oh] (n.). ex-officio (adj.). by virtue of an office.

exorbitant

exotic foreign. See **esoteric.**

exoskeleton [EHK-soh-] hard shell on insects, etc.

expansible or **expandable**

ex parte [ehks PAHRT-ee] (n. and adj.) (Lat.) in the interest of one side only: *an ex parte legal action.*

expatriate NOT *expatriot.*

expect May be used idiomatically for *expect to find that. I expect he will make the grade.*

expediency Pref. to —ce.

expedite (v.) to speed up. (adj.) expeditious.

expert [(n.) EHKS-puhrt; (v.) ehks-PUHRT].

expiate [EHK-spih-aet] to atone for. (adj.) —iable, (n.) —iation.

expletive [EHKS-plih-tihv] Usu. an obscene exclamation. In grammar, filler word used to introduce an intransitive verb. *There* are two people. *It* is time to go.

explicit detailed; plain; unmistakeable: *explicit instructions.*

EXPRESS firm and put into words: *our express intention.* Also, expressed.

All imply definite, specific terms put into words.

exponent [ehks-POH-nehnt] one who interprets or represents.

exposé [ehks-poh-ZAE] (n.) exposure of something discreditable.

EXPOSE [ehks-POHZ] (v.) to lay open.

ex post facto [ehks-pohst-FAK-toh] after the fact; retroactive: *an ex post facto law is not enforcible.*

expressible

expressway, express train.

exquisite [EHKS-kwih-siht]

extend to increase; reach out. Sometimes, to give: *extend an invitation.*

(adj.) extendible, extensible.

extent [ehk-STEHNT] range: *the full extent of the law.*

EXTANT [EHKS-tant] in existence.

external outside and apart. Opposite of *internal.*

eterminate (v.); —nable (adj.).

extol, extoll [ehks-TOHL] (v.) to praise. —ed, —ing.

extract [(n.) EHKS-trakt; (v.) ehks-TRAKT].

extraneous [ehks-TRAE-nee-uhs] coming from the outside; not pertinent.

extrasensory perception (abbr.: ESP) unexplainable perception beyond the five senses, such as telepathy.

extravaganza [ehk-strav-uh-GAN-zah] spectacular dramatic or musical composition.

extricate [EHKS-trih-kaet] (v.) to free from difficulties. (adj.) —cable.

extrinsic (adj.) inessential. Opposite of *intrinsic.* See **extraneous.**

Exxon Valdez disaster Alaskan oil spill, 1989. Also *Valdez spill.*

eye (v.) eyed; eyeing. Eyeglasses.

EYRIE, AERIE a nest.

Ezekiel [ee-ZEEK-yehl] (600–549 B.C.) Biblical prophet.

F

f. (abbr.) feminiine.

F. (abbr.) Fahrenheit [FAR-uhn-hiet, FEHR-]. Scale of heat measurement named for G.D. Fahrenheit.

To convert centigrade to Fahrenheit, multiply centigrade degrees by 9, divide by 5, add 32. To convert Fahrenheit to centigrade, subtract 32 and multiply by 5/9.

$32°F = 0°C$ (freezing); $70°F = 21.1°C$ (room temperature); $110°F = 43.3°C$ (bath); $212°F = 100°C$ (boiling).

See **Réaumur, temperature.**

F flat, F sharp; F-horn.

F. number, in photography, the focal number. Means focal length of lens divided by effective diameter. The brighter the light, the higher F. number required.

fabricate to construct or put together. Stresses skill.

MANUFACTURE Stresses labor.

fabulous [FAB-yuh-luhs] excellent; very good. Also, like a fable; hence, incredible.

facade [fa-SAHD] The cedilla is used in the best form: *façade.*

facetious [fuh-SEE-shuhs] humorous.

factbook (n.); —finding (adj.) (GPO spells as one word).

factituous [fak-TIHSH-uhs] sham; artificial.

factious [FAK-shuhsh] Seditious, quarrelsome.

faculty In U.S., the teaching staff, in Brit., one of the university departments: *Faculty of Law.* (pl.) faculties (more than one school). Unless sing. is indicated *(the faculty),* sing. or pl. verb may be used.

fait accompli. [feht uh-KAHN-plee] (Fr.) a deed presumably irrevocable; accomplished.

faker [FAEK-ehr] swindler; fraud.

FAKIR (fuh-KEER; FAEK-ehr] in Hindu religion, a beggar and wonder-worker

falderal See **folderol.**

fall (p.) fell; (p.p.) fallen; falling.

fallible [FAH-ih-b'l] subject to error.

fallout

fallopian tubes [fah-LOH-pee-an].

falsetto [fawl-SEHT-oh] artifical high voice. (pl.) —os.

fancies Both sing. and pl. form.

Faneuil Hall [FAN'l, FAN-y'l] historic Boston building. From Peter Faneuil (1700-1743), American merchant.

-fangle used usu. with *new: some new-fangled technique.*

Fannie Mae Federal National Mortgage Association, which buys mortgages from banks at a small discount. Fanny Maes are the bonds. *N.Y. Times: Fanny May.*

fantasia [fan-TAH-zih-uh; fan-TAE-zih-uh] composition unrestricted by a set form.

 FANTASY fanciful invention; vision.

F.A.O. (abbr.) Food and Agriculture Organization (United Nations).

faraway —fetched, —flung, —seeing, —off, —reaching (adj.) (all one word); far cry.

far from the madding crowd (NOT maddening)

farsightedness vision disorder. See *nearsightedness; shortsightedness.*

farther Use for physical distance. *They moved farther into the jungle.*

 FURTHER Use for time, quantity, or degree, and as a verb. *Let's carry the discussion one stage further. A fair deal will further both our ends.*

f.a.s. (abbr.) free alongside. Includes all risks and costs to delivery alongside ship. See *c.i.f.*

fasces [FASS-eez] bundle of sticks, symbol of authority for Roman magistrates; the symbol of **Fascism.**

Fascism [FA-shihsm] originally, Italian totalitarian movement, 1919-1945,

under **Benito Mussolini.** Hence, any repressive rule.

 May be lowercase: Fascist, fascist.

fastidious Over-careful; too clean.

fathom (abbr.: fath.) unit of depth 6 ft. or 8 spans, 1.829 m. Orig. an arm's length: *a seven-fathom line.*

fatherland, father-in-law, father-confessor.

Father (clerical title) Use in direct address and in a second written reference to a Roman Catholic priest, or to a Protestant Episcopal clergyman: The Rev. John J. Smith, Father Smith.

Father's Day third Sunday in June.

faultfinder, —finding; —line.

fauna [FAW-nuh] the realm of animals. May take sing. or pl. verb. (pl.) —s or —ae. See **flora.**

Faust, Dr. Johann [FOUST, YOH-Hahn] (died c. 1540) Ger. astrologer-magician. Gave name to famous story of a man who sells his soul to Satan (a play by Christopher Marlowe, 1604; a novel by Thomas Mann, 1947).

 Faustian bargain, etc.

faux pas [foh-pah] sing. and pl. (Fr.) "false step;" an offense against good taste or propriety.

fax [faks] (n. or v.) transmission of exact facsimiles, via combination of copying and communications technology. Current usage colloq. *I got* *your fax. He faxed me the figures this morning.*

faze (v.) to disconcert.

PHASE (n.) transitory state.

F.B.I. (abbr.) Federal Bureau of Investigation.

F.C.A. (abbr.) Farm Credit Administration.

F.C.C. (abbr.) Federal Communications Commission.

F.D.A. (abbr.) Food and Drug Administration.

F.D.I.C. (abbr.) Federal Deposit Insurance Corporation.

feasible capable of being accomplished.

Feast of the Passover, the Passover Pesach. Eight-day Jewish festival of deliverance from Egyptian bondage, occurring in March or April.

febrile [FEE-brihl; FEB-rihl] feverish.

February [FEB-roo-ahr-ih]

feces [FEE-sees] excrement. fecal.

fecund [FEE-kuhnd] fruitful in offspring.

FERTILE capable of reproducing.

federal Cap. when used in titles as synonym for United States or other sovereign power: Federal District (Mexico); Federal government (of any national government); Federal grand jury, the grand jury; Federal land bank (See **bank**); Federal Personnel Council (See **council**); Federal Register (publication), the Register; Federal Reserve Bank (See Bank); Federal Reserve Board, the Board, Federal Reserve; Federal System, the System; Federal Reserve Board Regulation W, BUT regulation W.

federal court See **court**.

Federated Commonwealth of Independent States Former U.S.S.R. Proper name: **Commonwealth of Independent States**.

fedora [feh-DOH-ruh] wide-brimmed felt hat.

fed-up (adj.) Also, fed up.

feed (p. and p.p.) fed; feeding.

feel Meaning "I am ill," *I feel bad* (NOT *badly*) is correct. (*I feel badly* means *My sense of touch is impaired.*) (p. and p.p.) felt.

felicitate [feh-LIH-sih-taet] to make matters easier; express a wish for happiness. See **congratulate**.

Fellini, Federico [FEH-lee-nee, feh-deh-REE-koh] (b. 1920) It. film maker (*La Strada, 8 1/2*).

fellow, fellowship (academic) lowercase with name: *a teaching fellow at Johns Hopkins* BUT: *N.Y. TIMES, a Nieman Fellow, Nieman Fellowship in Journalism.*

—fellow, bedfellow, schoolfellow, playfellow.

felony [FEH-luh-nee] serious crime punishable by imprisonment. See **misdemeanor.**

female, male (n. or adj.) Neutral terms; scientific.

WOMAN, MAN (n.) Less formal, still neutral.

AVOID certain older words for *woman* that now have unflattering connotations: *lady, gentlewoman.* See **SEXIST LANGUAGE.**

ferret. (v.) to search out. —eted, —eting.

fervid intense, implying feverish or vehement.

FERVENT Intense, implying spiritual, warm.

festal pertaining to a festival: *festal day.*

FESTIVE Like a festival: *festive mood, meal.*

fete [faet] (Fr.) a celebration, festival.

fetid [FEHT-ihd] stinking.

fetish [FEHT-ihsh] irrational obsession.

feudal [FYOO-d'l].

few Takes a plural verb. *A few, comparatively few.* NOT *a comparatively few, very few, a very few.*

FEWER Refers to numbers. *He has fewer cases now.*

LESS Refers to quantity or degree. *He earns less on his new job.*

SMALLER Refers to size.

SOME When followed by a number, means "approximately:" *some 20 or so.*

Feynman, Richard P. (b. 1918) American scientist and writer. Winner of Nobel Prize for Physics, 1965.

F.H.A. (abbr.) Federal Housing Administration; Farmers Home Administration.

F.H.L.B.B. (abbr.) Federal Home Loan Bank Board.

fiancé, fiancée [fee-ahn-SAE] In French, the single *e* is masculine, the double *e* feminine. English usage allows double *e* for both.

fiasco [fee-ASS-koh] dramatic and ridiculous failure. (pl.) —oes or —os.

fiber glass But *Fiberglass* is a trademark.

F.I.C.A. (abbr.) Federal Insurance Contributions Act.

fictitious [fihk-TIH-shuhs] imaginary.

FICTIONAL imaginary; also, pertaining to fiction.

FACTIONAL pertaining to factions or cliques. See **factious.**

fidget —eted, —eting.

fiducial [fih-DYOO-shal] founded on trust, esp. religious.

FIDUCIARY (-shih-ehr-ih] of the nature of a trust; pertains esp. to financial matters.

—fied Nouns ending in *y* change *y*

to *i* or add *i* in forming an adjective, except when noun provides a convenient connecting syllable: *countrified, bountiful.*

fiery [FIER-ih]

F.I.F.O. inventory system in which merchandise first in is counted first out. Assumes all stock is recent, and thus valued at current market prices. See L.I.F.O. (last in, first out).

fifty-fifty

fig. (abbr.) figure; also, figuratively.

fight (p. and p.p.) fought; fighting. Use fight *against*, or *on the side of.*

fighter planes Better-known U.S. models include: P-38; P-51 Mustang (W.W. II); F-86 Sabre (Korean War); F-III (Vietnam).
    British: Sopwith Camel (W.W.I); Spitfire, Hurricane (W.W. II).
    French: Spad (W.W. I); Mirage (Middle East conflicts, 1970's).
    Japanese: Zero (W.W. II).
    Soviet: MiG-15 (Korea); MiG-23.

figurehead , figure-eight (adj.); figure eight (n.).

figure 2, A No cap. for illustration; BUT Figure 2, when part of a legend: *Figure 2, —Market scenes.*

Fiji [FEE-jee] island nation in SW Pacific. Former Br. colony; independent, 1970. Cap.: Suva. Native: Fiji or Fijian. Currency: dollar.

filet mignon [fee-LEH meen-YAWN]

(Fr.) steak from the ends of the fillet of beef.

    CHATEAUBRIAND (shaht-OH-bree-AHN] steak from center of the fillet; often served with butter and lemon.

filibuster (n. and v.) delaying speech in a parliamentary body.

filigree [FIHL-ih-gree] wire ornamental work.

FILING Two systems of alphabetical order are recognized: dictionary order and directory order. Dictionary order recognizes all existing letters, ignoring spaces or word divisions; directory order considers each word as a unit listing identical words in order of the second word. Thus dictionary would list: *American, Americanization, American states.* Directory system would alphabetize: *American, American states, Americanization.*

    In both cases, punctuation is disregarded. Numbers and abbreviations are alphabetized as if they were spelled out. But some directories place all initials at the beginning of each letter: *aaa, AZC Co., Abraham & Co.*

    In similar spellings, the shorter word precedes the longer: *John, Johns, Johnson.* Company names, corporations, and organizations are listed by the first word (initials are placed at the end): *James Worth, Inc.* under *J. Worth, J. J. Co.* But individuals are listed by their last or family names. *Brown, James; Brown, T. M. Co.; Brown Water Works.* Identical names are listed in alphabetical order of state, city, name streets, numbered streets.

In directories, government departments are listed under the government having jurisdiction: *New York State, Department of Conservation.* Geographical-alphabetical listings (used for mailing lists) file alphabetically by state, then city, then postal zone where appropriate, then name.

Zip code order lists are filed under state then numerically by zip number.

Compound names and names with a prefix present special problems. *Webster's* ignores prefixes in alphabetizing, as does this text.

But the American Library Association follows a set style: (1) The prefix is considered part of the name in *A, Ap, Fitz, M', Mac, Mc, O', Saint, San.*

(2) BUT names beginning with a prepostion, or article or a contraction or both vary with the country where the person is a resident. In general, follow the name style indicated by the person: *De La Rue, De Morgan, Du Maurier, Le Gallienne, Van Buren.*

(3) Alphabetize with the prefix all names beginning with *Le, De, De La, Du,* and *Van* all French names where the prefix consists of an article or a contraction of an article and a preposition: *Des Esse, Du Souleur, Le Sage.*

(4) Also all Italian names where the prefix consists of an article: *La Farra, Il Gotti.*

(5) Also Scandinavian names of romance language origin when the prefix consists of an article (but cross-reference).

(6) In cases not specified, enter under the name following the prefix and refer from the name beginning with a prefix. Thus: French names which begin with a prefix that consists of a preposition, *de;* German names, Scandinavian names when the prefix consists of a prepostition, *av or af* (the equivalent of the German *von):* Hallstrom, *Cunman Johannes af; Linne, Carl von.* Also Spanish and Portuguese names, with rare exceptions: *Rio, Antonio del; Ripo, Domingo le.*

A married woman's name may still be filed under her husband's name, but it is currently more common for her to retain her maiden name. That name may be cross-refernced with her husband's: *Shriver, Maria (Schwarzeneggar).* Compound names made up of surnames of husband and wife are treated as two words and filed under the first word.

Spanish women customarily add to their own surnames the name of their husbands, connecting the two by the preposition *de,* but dropping the part which refers to the mother's surname. File these as compound words: *Molina y Vedia de Bastianini, Delfina,* (Her father's name was Octavia T. Molina, her mother's name was Manuella Vedia de Molina, her own maiden name was Defina Molina y Vedia, and her husband's name was Rene Bastianini.) Cross-refer to *Bastianini* and *Vedia.* In Portugal and Brazil, the style is similar to the Spanish but less consistent. File under the last (husband's) surname rather than the compound. In Dutch, the wife's name is a hyphenated compound of husband's name followed by wife's maiden name; *Ammers-Kullen, Jo van.* Cross refer to *Kullen.* In Italian, the wife's name is a compound of husband's and wife's maiden name, either one of which may precede. File as used and cross-refer.

Arabic, Persian, and Turkish names prior to 1900 are a compound of given name, the word *ibn* (son) or *aku* (brother), and patronymic name: *Abu al Ala Mohammad-ibnZakarya*. Hebrew names prior to 1800 are compounds of given name, *ben* (son) and patronymic name: *Itzhak-ben-Zvi*. File under *Ben-Zvi*. Hebrew articles *ha* and *he* are never capitalized: *Judah ha-Levi*.

Japanese names are filed under the family name followed by the given name: *Noguchi, Hideyo*; except in cases of well-known pseudonymns: *Jippensh Ikku*. Chinese names are listed under the family name (given first) separated from the given name by a comma: *Sun, Yat-sen*; but are usually written without the comma: *Sun Yat-sen*. In modern works, names may follow Western style.

Saints are generally alphabetized under their forename in the long Latin form: *Benedictus, Saint*; except Biblical saints, who are alphabetized by their forenames in English: *James, Saint, Apostle*. Modern saints are filed by vernacular name: *Luigi Conzaga, Saint* with cross reference from *Ignatius Loyola, Saint* and *Ignacio de Loyola, Saint*. Popes and kings who have achieved sainthood are filed according to the rules for popes and kings. Popes are filed under Latin pontifical name followed by title: *Pius XI, Pope*, with cross reference from *Pio* and *Ratti, Achille*. A patriarch is listed under the name under which he was known in his own country: *Cyrillus,*

Saint, Patriarch of Alexandria. A cardinal is listed according to the custom at the time and place of elevation: *Richelieu Armand Jean du Plessis, duc de, Cardinal*. An ecclesiastical prince is listed under his forename in the vernacular: *Neithard Prince-Bishop of Bamberg*. A bishop or an archbishop is listed under his surname: *Waitz, Siegmund, Prince-Archbishop of Sakburg*. Where there are several bishops etc. of the same name in one see, include a number.

File names of sovereigns and rulers under their forenames: *James I Napoleon III, Harun al-Rashid*. Consorts follow the same style: *Albert, consort of Victoria; Marie Antoinette* (under M). Except Ming and Ching dynasties, Chinese emperors are filed under the name of the dynasty followed by the temple name given posthumously: *T'ang Hsuan-tsung, Emperor of China*. Ming and Ch'ing emperors who are known by reign titles are so filed: *Hangwu, Emperor of China*; with cross references from personal name, name of dynasty, and temple names. Edicts, proclamations, and laws issued under a ruler's name are filed under the name of the country. Princes and members of a royal family are filed under their forename (but Russian families include family names). Nobles are listed under their latest title unless they are better known under a family name or an earlier title: *Wellington, Arthur Wellesly, 1st duke of; Scott, Sir Walter, bart.; Landseer, Sir Edwin Henry; Campbell Dame Jane Mary; Cordon, Lord George; Russell, Hon. Harriet*.

fillet [FIH-leht, fih-LAE] strip of lean

meat. BUT: *filet mignon, filet de sole.*

filly See **foal.**

finagle [fih-NAE-gl] (v.) (from card-playing) to cheat, use devious methods, shirk work. (n.) finagler.

finale [feh-NAH-lae] the concluding piece.

finalize *Finish* or *complete* are pref.

finance [fih-NANS; fie-NANS; FIE-nans].

financier [fihn-un-SEER; fie-nan-SEER; fih-NAN-sih-ehr].

find (p. and p.p.) found.

fin de siècle [FAN duh see-EHK'l] (Fr.) (adj.) end of the century. Characteristic of Paris at the end of the 19th century; hence, decadent.

finesse [fih-NESS] delicate skill. Also, a play in bridge.

finger unit of length = 0.125 yd. = 4.5 ins. sometimes 3/4 inch to 1 inch.

Finland Scandinavian country. Formerly Russian; independent, 1917. Cap: Helsinki. Native: Finn. Currency: markkaa.

fiord, fjord [fyawrd] canyon-like Scandinavian ocean inlets.

firearms

first (adv., adj., or n.) first floor; First Lady.

firstly Adv. only: *firstly, secondly, finally.*

1st Lt. (abbr.) first lieutenant.

1st Sgt. (abbr.) first sergeant.

First World War (W.W.I) See **War.**

fiscal year arbitrary year for accounting purposes. For the U.S. government, July 1 to June 30. See **year.**

fission [FIHSH-uhn] nuclear reaction necessary for conversion to power.

fix Use noun form to mean *a predicament* is colloq.: *He's in some fix.* —ed, —edly, —edness.

fizz, fizzed, fizzing.

FL (abbr.) Florida.

flaccid [FLAH-sihd] flabby.

flag, U.S. Cap. Old Flag, Old Glory, Stars and Stripes, Star-Spangled Banner.

flags, foreign Cap. Hammer & Sickle (U.S.S.R.), Maple Leaf (Canada). Tricolor (French), Union Jack (British).

flair instinctive taste and aptitude: *a flair for dressing.*

FLARE incandenscent signal fired into the air.

flambeau [flam-BOH] flaming torch. (pl.) —s or —x.

flameproof, flamethrower.

flamingo species of long-legged, aquatic bird. (pl.) —os.

flammable

flatulence intestinal gas. Pref. to —cy.

Flaubert, Gustave [floh-BAIR, gues-TAV]. (1821-1880) Fr. writer (*Madame Bovary*).

flaunt to display ostentatiously. *She flaunted her wealth before the neighbors who had snubbed her when she was poor.*

FLOUT to insult, scorn, mock. *She flouted common standards of decency.*

flautist [FLAWT-ihst] flute player. Also *flutist* (FLOOT-).

flaxen (adj.) Pref. to flax.

fledge [flehj] to acquire feathers necessary for flight.

flee (p. and p.p.) fled, fleeing.

FLY, FLEW, FLOWN, FLYING.

Both verbs can mean run away from danger.

fleet Cap. if part of name: *Atlantic Fleet, Grand Fleet, High Seas Fleet, Naval Reserve Fleet, 6th Fleet; the fleet.*

fleshly worldly, unspiritual; bodily; sensual.

FLESHY containing flesh; plump.

fleur-de-lis [fleur-duh-LEE] stylized lily, symbol of French monarchy. *N.Y. Times,* uses no hyphens. (pl.) *fleur-de-lis.*

flimflam, illegal subterfuge, con-game. flimflammer.

fling (p. and p.p.) flung; flinging.

flock birds, sheep, Christian congregation. (pl.) —s.

flophouse

floppy (n.) floppy disk. A computer disk kept separate from main unit and inserted for use; holds limited data.

HARD DISK computer storage built into main unit; can contain far more data than floppy.

flora plant life. (pl.) —s or —ae. See **fauna**.

Florence [FLAHR-ehns]; (It.) Firenze (fee-REHN-tsae] It. city on Arno River; noted for Renaissance art.

Florida, U.S. State. (abbr.: FL). Cap.: Tallahassee. Native: Floridian.

flotation [floh-TAE-shuhn] process of floating.

flotsam [FLAHT-suhm] objects found afloat; wreckage.

JETSAM [JEHT-suhm] objects thrown off a ship and later washed ashore.

flow chart diagram of production-plant sequence, showing transformation of materials to finished product. Hence, outline of any transformational process.

flux (n.) fluid discharge; copious flow. (adj.) fluxible.

fly (p.) flew; (p.p.) flown; flying. (n.) flyer. See **flee.**

fly-leaf blank page at beginning or end of book.

F.M. (abbr.) frequency modulation.

F.M.B. (abbr.) Federal Maritime Board.

F.N.M.A. (abbr.) Federal National Mortgage Association. See **Fannie Mae.**

foal (m. and f.); colt (m.); filly (f.). All young horses.

f.o.b. (abbr.) free on board. Term of sale including all costs and risks to point mentioned.

focus (pl.) focuses or —ci; focused; —cusing.

foist (v.) to pass off something spurious as worthy; insert surreptitiously.

—fold combining form meaning "times as many": *tenfold.*

foderol [FAWL-deh-RAWL] old song refrain; a bit of nonsense. Also *falderal* (FAL-deh-RAL] .

folk (sing. and pl.) *Folks* is colloquial.

follow-up, followup.

font [fahnt] in printing, type size and style.

Fontainebleau [FAHN-tn-bloh]

community near Paris, residence of former French kings.

foolscap (arch.) sheets of paper.

foot (abbr.: ft.) (pl.) feet. Unit of length. 12 in. = 1/3 yd. 1.515 links = 0.3048006 m. *A 17-foot boat; a 6-footer; about 7 feet; 12 footpounds; a ten-foot wall.*

FOOTNOTES Footnotes rarely appear outside of longer academic papers (a senior thesis or a doctoral dissertation), and authorative texts on history, biography, or social issues. Business books will carry them occasionally, but business reports almost never.

Such notes are indicated by superior figures or symbols in the text, placed after the punctuation mark. Numbers are used consecutively and written as superior figures. Symbols may be used instead, such as * (asterisk), or † (dagger). Footnotes may be placed at the bottom of the page or at the end of the work; if they appear at the end, footnotes are segregated by chapters, newly numbered from one at the beginning of each chapter. All footnotes take a paragraph indentation.

The first mention of a work is given with full detail except where the author or title is mentioned immediately before the footnote in the text. In the second mention of the same work, eliminate the author's initials.

U.C.M.S. is most widely accepted in listing references. In a footnote or bibliography, the form is highly standardized.

For books:

(1) AUTHOR, FIRST NAME OR INITIALS FIRST, FOLLOWED BY A COMMA. Omit listing degrees unless relevant to the work. A pseudonym is followed by a true name in brackets; if the pseudonym is acknowledged, this is noted by *(pseudonym)* following the name. If there are three authors, all are cited, if more than three, the first is cited followed by *et al*. Editors of compilations are treated as authors.

(2) TITLE, UNDERLINED AND FOLLOWED BY A COMMA. If part of a whole published work, the facts of publication are included, with the numbers of volumes noted, followed by a semicolon. The title should follow exactly the style of the book title page except that punctuation must be added to clarify the elements shown on different lines and in different type sizes. The titles of holy books are neither underlined nor quoted. Capitalize the first and last words of titles, and all verbs, nouns, adjectives, and adverbs; or capitalize only the first word and all proper nouns and adjectives. Titles in French, Italian, and Spanish require capitalization for the first word and for all proper nouns. Titles in German require capitalization for all nouns and words used as nouns and adjectives derived from personal names. A part of a work followed by a number should be abbreviated. Capitalize *Bk., Fig., MS, Vol.*

(3) FACTS OF PUBLICATION. All in parenthesis. Include edition, if more than one, followed by semicolon; place of publication, followed by semicolon; publisher, followed by comma; date of publication, followed by comma; volume number in cap. Roman numerals, followed by comma; page number, followed by period. When a serial publication has no volume number, give the year number, but place this outside the parenthesis. If some element differs from the rest of the items, place the reference to this edition after the volume number, not after the title. The words and abbreviations *infra, supra, passim, et al and ca.* should be underlined to indicate that they would be printed in italics.

For Periodical References:

1. author (first name or initials first) followed by comma;

2. title of article in quotation marks;

3. name of periodical underlined followed by comma;

4. date of the periodical followed by comma;

5. volume number of the periodical in capitals. Roman numerals followed by comma;

6. month and year of publication followed by comma;

7. page numbers. Where only both volume and page numbers are given, they need not be identified, but if one is given or other designations are made, all must be identified. Legal publications use a special style: volume, journal, page, and date in parenthesis: 6. *Yale Law Rev. 1321 (1927).*

When references to the same work follow consecutively, use *ibid.* (the same) for as much of the reference as can be carried forward. When the reference is to material cited previously, but not immediately prior, use *loc. cit.*

(in the place or passage cited) or *op. cit.* (in the work cited).

For volume, book, part, or division of a modern work, use capital Roman numerals. For introductory material, page numbers, use lowercase Roman numerals. For periodical numbers and page numbers, use Arabic numerals.

EXAMPLES:

1. W.L. Shirer, *The Rise and Fall of the Third Reich* (New York; Simon & Schuster, 1960), p. 37.

2. Shirer, op. cit. p. 47.

3. A Manual of Style, 11th ed. (Chicago; University of Chicago Press, 1940), p. 140.

4. J.F. Wharton, "The Plight of the Promising Play," *Saturday Review*, XLIV, No. 17 (1961), 9.

5. *The New York Times*, CXXI, June 28, 1973. p. 8, col. 2.

6. Wharton, loc. cit., *supra* note 4.

Abbreviate a designation followed by a number: *Vol. 111, sec. 2;* except parts of a play; *Act 1, scene 2, line 7.*

for See **because.**

for- prefix meaning out, away, refusal: *forbear.*

FORE— prefix meaning before: *fore-ordainn.*

forbear to refrain, avoid. *Forbear from asking further.*

FOREBEAR ancestor. *One of his forebears fought in the Revolution.*

forbid (p.) forbade or forbad; (p.p.) forbidden; forbidding.

force(s) Cap. if part of name: the force(s); Active Forces, Air Force (See **Air Force**); Armed Forces (synonym for overall Military Establishment); Army Field Forces; the Field Forces; Navy Battle Force (See **Navy**); 7th Task Force; the task force, task force report; United Nations Emergency Force, the Emergency Force. BUT United Nations police force.

force majeure (Fr.) an irresistible force. In law, the act of a greater power which excuses fulfilling a contract.

forceful Use is abstract: *forceful personality, forceful argument.*

FORCIBLE Use is concrete: *forcible invasion.*

forceps Pl. usually the same, or —ses.

fore and aft lengthwise on a vessel; contrasted with *athwart. Fore* is toward the bow or forward end, *aft* toward the stern or rear.

fore-, See **for-.**

forearm, forehead, forenoon, foresee, forestall (—STAWL).

forecast Pref. to —ed. for p. and p.p.

forecastle [FOHK-s'l] on board ship, crews' quarters.

foregone what has gone before: *foregone conclusion;* or renounced: *His rights forgone, the Duke fled to America.*

foreign cabinets Foreign Office, the

Office; Minister of Foreign Affairs, the Minister; Ministry of Foreign Affairs, the Ministry; Premier; Prime Minister.

foreign service Cap. the Service and preceding officer; Officer Corps, BUT the corps; Reserve officer, Reserve Officer Corps, and the Reserve Corps; BUT the corps; Staff officer, the Staff officer, Staff Officer Corps, the Staff Corps, BUT the corps.

forensic of the law: *forensic medicine.*

forest Cap. if part of name: the national forest, the forest; Angeles National Forest. Black Forest, Coconino and Prescott National Forests. BUT state and national forests.

foreword material at the front of a book. Also, preface.

forfeit [FAWR-fiht] .

forget (p.) forgot; (p.p.) forgotten; forgettable.

forget-me-not (pl.) —nots.

forgo, forego forego *Webster's* lists both to mean "refrain from."

form 2, A, II But Form 2, when part of title: *Form 1040: Individual Income Tax Return.* BUT *withholding tax form.*

former Refers to the first of two. Not used when three or more are involved. See *latter.* Pref. to *ex-* in most cases.

formerly in time past. *He was formerly an artist.*

FORMALLY in accordance with form. *She was formally introduced to her lover's wife.*

formidable [FAWR-mih-duh-b'l; -MIHD-].

Formosa [fawr-MOH-suh] island in SE China Sea. See **Taiwan.**

formula [FAWR-myuh-luh] (pl.) —s, or —lae.

forsake (p.) forsook; (p.p.) forsaken; forsaking.

forswear to renounce under oath; or to swear falsely.

forsythia [fawr-SIHTH-ee-uh] yellow spring flowers.

fort Cap. and spell out when part of a name: Fort McHenry, etc.; the fort. BUT abbr. (Ft.) in lists, tables, etc.

forté [fawrt] a strong point; (FOHR-tae] musical term.

fortissimo [fohr-TEESS-ee-moh] (It.) in music, very loud.

fortitude strength in adversity.

fortnight [FAWRT-niet] two weeks.

fortuitous undesigned, accidental. Not always fortunate.

forum a public meeting for open discussion.

DISCUSSION talk for purposes of finding solution.

SYMPOSIUM presentation of various viewpoints on a single subject.

DEBATE formal public argument between opposing points of view.

forward near the front, advanced in position; (of a person) overready; of the future; or the direction, towards.

FORWARDS Contrast to *backwards, sideways.*

fossil [FAH-sihl] preserved remains, impressions, footprints of an animal or plant of past ages, found in the earth.

Foucault pendulum [foo-CAW(l)] device for demonstrating Earth's rotation, from Fr. scientist Jean-Bernard Foucault (1819-1868).

foul, foully.

foundation Cap. if part of name; cap. standing alone if referring to federal unit: Chemical Foundation, the foundation; Infantile Paralysis Foundation, the foundation; National Science Foundation; Russell Sage Foundation, the foundation.

Founding Fathers (colonial).

fountainhead the source of anything.

four 4, Roman IV; fourth 4th; **fourteen,** Roman XIL or XIIII, fourteenth; **forty,** 40, XL or XXXX, fortieth, 40th; forty-one, XLI; forty-first; four hundred.

Fourth Estate the Press. The other three: Lords Spiritual, Lords Temporal, and the Commons.

Fourth of July Also called "the Fourth."

fourscore eighty.

foyer [FOI-yehr] lobby.

fox Fem.: *vixen* or *she-fox*. See *ANIMALS.* The v. is usu. *outfox.*

F.P.C. (abbr.) Federal Power Commission.

f.p.m. (abbr.) feet per minute.

F.P.O. (abbr.) fleet post office.

f.p.s. (abbr.) feet per second. In filmmaking, frames per second.

Fr. (abbr.) France, French.

fracas [FRAE-kuhs; FRAK-ahz] brawl. (pl.) —ases.

FRACTIONS In general, follow the style of numerals, spelling out one to nine. (Some styles include ten.) Spell out a fraction when it appears by itself in a text: *one-half gallon, ten-hundredths* (NOT ten one-hundredths). BUT use numbers when fractions apply with a full number and in ages, dimensions, measures, sizes, etc.: *3 1/2 x 6 inches, 6 1/2-pound bird, 1/4, 2/3, 7/8.* Do not use comma in fractions of four or more digits: *3/1787.* Use only one hyphen in spelling out: *one-seventh; one thirty-seventh.* Fractions which modify a noun of distance drop the final *s: three-tenth feet.*

fragile [FRA-jihl] easily broken. Meaning can be physical or psychological.

France (abbr.: Fr.) largest nation in Western Europe; established by 8th C. Cap.: Paris. Native: French. Currency: franc. French-minded; French Army.

Frances (f.) —cis (m.).

Francesca, Piero della [dee-lah frahn-CHEHS-kah, PYEH-roh] (1420-1492) It. painter.

franchise tax tax on the right to conduct business, esp. corporate franchise tax.

Franco, Francisco [FRAHN-koh] (1892-1975) Spanish general, dictator. Caudillo (leader): 1939-1973.

François [fran-SWAH].

francs and centimes Spell out when written with figures. *8 francs; 1,000,000 francs, 25 centimes.*

frangible [FRAN-jih-b'l] breakable.

Frankenstein [FRANK-'n-stein] 1818 novel by Mary Wollstonecroft Shelley. The name was that of the scientist who builds the monster, not the monster itself.

Frankfurt [FRANK-fehrt] district and city in Germany.

frappé [frap-PAE] iced and whipped; a milk shake.

fraternal organizations Cap. names: *Odd Fellow;* cap. titles of officers: *Sachem, Grand Regent.*

Frau [frou] (Ger.) Mrs.

FRAULEIN (FROI-lien] (Ger.) Miss; young lady.

freedman one freed from slavery.

FREEMAN not a slave, in a state which permits slavery.

Freemason member, Ancient and Fraternal Order of Masons.

free trade area

freeboard, freestyle; free-form; free will.

free association (n.) psychiatric procedure. (v. and adj.) free-associating.

free verse verse without meter or rhyme. See **verse.**

freeze (p.) froze; (p.p.) frozen; freezing.

freight [fraet.], freight house, freight room.

French cuff, French door, French-fried potatoes.

frenetic [freh-NEH-tihk] frenzied; frantic.

frequency modulation (FM) radio reception process; involves varying frequency wave. See **amplitude modulation.**

frère

fresco [FREH-skoh] painting on fresh plaster. (pl.) —oes. See **al fresco.**

freshman name of college class, or member. Rarely cap.

Freud, Sigmund [froid, SIG-muhnd] (1856-1939) Austrian neurologist, founder of psychoanalysis.

F.R.G. (abbr.) Federal Republic of Germany. See **West Germany**.

friable [FRIE-uh-b'l] capable of being crumbled. See **fryable**.

friar mendicant monk who lives outside a monastery.

> MONK male member of a religious order, usually segregated in a monastery.

fricassee [frihk-uh-SEE]

frieze [freez] in architecture, esp. classical, a decorative outside panel. NOT spelled *freeze*.

frogman skindiver, esp. for military operations.

frontier frontiersman. See **boundary**.

frontispiece [FRUHN-tihs-pees] illustration facing the first or title page of a book.

fructose [FROOK-tohs] simple fruit or honey sugar. See **sucrose**.

fruition [froo-IHSH-uhn] attainment of thing desired; coming to fruit.

F.R.S. (abbr.) Federal Reserve System.

fryable [FRIE-uh-b'l] able to be fried. See **friable**.

fryer used for a chicken, instead of frier.

ft. (abbr.) foot.

ft. b.m. (abbr.) feet board measure.

ft.-c. (abbr.) foot-candle.

F.T.C. (abbr.) Federal Trade Commission.

Ft.-l (abbr.) foot-lambert.

ft.-lb. (abbr.) foot-pound.

fuchsia [FYOO-shuh] a decorative shrub. Also, the pink color of its flowers.

fuel fuel injection, line, oil. (v.) —led, —ling.

fugue [fyoog] highly systematic musical composition.

Fuhrer [fe-rehr] (Ger.) leader. Title for Adolf Hitler.

—ful (pl.) spoonfuls, mouthfuls. NOT spoonsful.

fulcrum [FUHL-kr'm] support upon which a lever turns. (pl.) —s or —cra.

fulfill —ed, —ing, —ment.

full-fashioned shaped on a flat knitting frame; applies to hose, sweaters, and underwear shaped to form-fit.

fullness

fulsome offensive; foul; insincere. NOT full.

fund Cap. if part of name; cap.

standing alone if referring to international or United Nations fund: Common Market Fund, the Fund; International Monetary Fund, the Fund; Rockefeller Endowment Fund, the fund: BUT: civil service retirement fund, mutual security fund, insurance fund.

funeral (n.) observance for the dead. (adj.) funereal, funerary.

fungus (pl.) fungi (FUHN-gee, -jee) (adj.) fungous.

funnel funneled, —ling. Br. ll.

funny humorous; also, strange. *She gave me a funny look.*

furbelow [FUHR-bee-loh] ruffle; frill.

furlong (abbr.: fur.) unit of length = 0.125 statute mi. = 10 chains = 40 rods = 220 yd. = 201.168 m.

furor [FYOO-rohr] in a person, rage, fit; in a crowd, excitement, commotion.

further See **farther**.

fuse use this spelling for all meanings.

fuselage [fyoo-zehl-LAHZH; FYOO-z'lihj].

fusillade [FYOOS-zih-LAED] a rapidly repeated or simultaneous discharge, usually of firearms.

fustian [FUHS-chuhn] corduroy, velveteen; also, verbal bombast.

futures in commodity trading, contract for delivery of specified commodities at specified future dates.

G

g Usually silent before *m* or n: *gnat, phlegm, sign.* BUT the addition of a suffix will often cause the letter to be sounded: *phlegmatic.*

g (abbr.) gram, gravity. 3 g = three times the force of gravity.

—g Words ending in single vowel and *g* double the *g* before a suffix beginning with a vowel: *bigger, begging, zig-zagging.*

G-1 Personnel; G-2, Intelligence; G-3, Operations and Training; G-4, Supply and Evacuation. (Sections of U.S. Armed Forces.)

G major, G-force, G-man, G minor, G sharp.

GA Georgia (U.S. state)

gabfest

Gabon [gah-BAWN] Central African nation on Atlantic Coast. Formerly Fr.; independent, 1960. Cap.: Libreville [lih-bruh-VEEL]. Native: Gabonese. Currency: CFA franc.

Gaea [JEE-uh] Greek Earth-Mother goddess. Also *Gaia.*

Gael (n.) one of Celtic inhabitants of Ireland, Scotland, and Isle of Man; native language: Gaelic [GAEL-ihk]. (adj.)

gala [GAE-luh; GAH-luh] festival; celebration.

Galapagos [guh-LAE-pah-gus; -LAP-ah-] Sometimes Colon Arrchipelago. Pacific island group known for primitive animals.

galaxy [GAL-ak-see] galactic.

Galilee [gal-ih-LEE] region in Israel where Jesus lived. *Galilean.*

Galileo [gah-lih-LAE-oh] common reference for Galileo Galilei [gah-lih-LAE], It. scientist (1564-1642).

gallant [GAL-lahnt] stately; noble. [gal-LAHNT] courtesously attentive to women.

galley (pl.) —eys.

Gallic [GAH-lihk] characteristically French; from *Gallia* (Gaul), Latin name for France. Rarely *Gaulish.*

Gallipoli [gah-LIHP-oh-lee] Turkish seaport, site of 1915 W.W. I battle.

gallon (abbr.: gal.) unit of capacity. (1) U.S. = 0.82368 Brit. gal. = 4 U.S. qts. = 8 U.S. pt. = 32 U.S. gills = 128 fl. oz. = 231 cu. in. = 3.78531. (2) Brit. or Imperial = 1.20094 U.S. gal. = 4 qt. Brit. = 8 pt. Brit. = 160 fl. oz. = 277.42 cu. in. 4.5460.

gallop running gait of a horse. —oped, —oping.

gallows (pl.) —ses.

galoshes [guh-LAH-shihs] overshoes.

GALLUSES [GAL-luh-sihs] (arch.) suspenders.

galvanize to plate with zinc.

Gambia, The [GAM-bih-uh] nation on NW African coast. Formerly Br.; independent, 1960. Cap.: Banjul [BAHN-jool]. Native: Gambian. Currency: Dalasi.

gambit chess term meaning an opening sacrifice. Hence, any clever ploy.

gambol [GAM-buhl] (v.) to frolic, play. —ed, —ing.

    GAMBLE [GAM-b'l] to wager.

game As an adj., it can mean "plucky" or "willing." For animals, any animal hunted.

gamma ray penetrating electromagnetic radiation.

gamut [GAM-uht] the entire range of notes, prices, or choices.

gamy [GAEM-ih]

Gandhi, Mohandas Karamachand [GAHN-dee, MOH-huhn-dahs, KUHR-uhm-chuhns] (1869-1948) Mahatma [muh-HAHT-muh; (angl.) -HAT-] Hindu nationalist, ascetic and non-violent. Assassinated.

G.A.O. (abbr.) General Accounting Office.

gaol jail. Spelling is obsolete in U.S.

garble to scramble or mutilate facts or language.

garçon [gahr-SAWNN] (Fr.) boy, waiter. (pl.) —s.

García Marquez, Gabriel [gahr-SEE-ah, MAHR-kehz, GAH-bree-EHL] (b. 1925) Colombian writer; *(100 Years of Solitude)*; Nobel prize, 1982.

gargoyle [GAR-goi'l] the sculpture; hence, anything ugly or monstrous.

Garibaldi, Giuseppe [GAR-ih-BAL-dih, joo-SEHP-pae] (1807-1882) It. revolutionary patriot.

garnishment warning or legal proceeding attaching money or goods against payment to a debtor.

garret [GAH-reht] an attic; suggests poverty.

garrote [guh-ROHT] (n. or v.) strangulation; or, to strangle.

garrulity [guh-ROOL-uh-tee], garrulousness [GAR-uhl-luhs-nehs] talkativeness.

gaseous [GAS-ee-uhs]

G.A.T.T. (abbr.) General Agreement on Tariffs and Trade.

Gatun [gah-TOON] dam, town, lake on Panama Canal.

gauche [gohsh] awkward, especially in social intercourse.

gaucho [GOU-choh] (Span.) Cowboy. (pl.) —os.

gauge [gaej] measure. BUT *gage is perf.* for a few technical uses.

Gauguin, Eugène Henri Paul [goh-

GAN] (1848-1903) Fr. painter.

Gaul See **Gallic**.

Gautama Buddha [GAH-uh-tah-mah, BUHD-dah] (c. 563-483 B.C.) Indian philosopher, founder of Buddhism.

Gautier, Theophile [GOH-tyae, TAE-aw-feel] (1811-1872) Fr. writer. (*Mademoiselle de Maupin*).

G.A.W. (abbr.) guaranteed annual wage.

gay Use for *homosexual* is colloq. —er, —est; gaily, gaiety.

Gaza [GAH-zuh] Arab, Ghazze. Palestinian Arab refugee area, including a seaport, in Israel on the Mediterranean.

gazetteer a geographical dictionary.

G.c.t. (abbr.) Greenwich civil time.

Gdansk [gih-DANSK] Baltic seaport now in Poland. Former German Danzig [DAN-zihg]; a cultural and political center.

Geiger counter

geisha [GAE-shuh] Japanese girl trained to entertain men. *Geisha girl* is redundant. (pl.) geisha or —s.

gelatin

Gemini [JEH-mih-nie] born May 21 - June 20. See **Zodiac**.

gendarme [ZHAN-dahrm] French police.

gender In English grammer, the property of nouns and pronouns relating to the sex of the object named, masculine, feminine, or neuter.

For problems of gender in language, See **Sexist Language**.

genealogy [jeen-ee-AH-loh-gee] ancestry of a family or person; also, the study of family pedigrees.

General Assembly (United Nations), the Assembly.

General Order No. 14, General Orders, No. 14; a general order.

generalissimo (obs.) commander of combined forces. (pl.) —os.

GENERAL REFERENCE Use of *this, it, which,* or other indefinite pronoun as reference to implied or previously established subject. *Night after night I stand crying outside her window. This can't go on.*

The pronoun must have a specific referent and a specific function. NOT: *Henry James claimed he suffered a sexual dysfunction which helped him write. This is often the case.*

Genghis Khan, Jenghiz Khahn [JEHNG-gihs, KAHN] (1162-1227) Mongol conqueror.

genie [JEEN-ee] also *djinn. supernatural spirit. (pl.) genies or ginii [JEE-neeie].*

genitive case Possessive case: *Tom's book; a dog's life.*

genius great inborn mental or creative power. (pl.) geniuses.

TALENT a natural capacity.

genre [ZHAHN-'r] (n. or adj.) in the arts, a definable type. *She writes in the science fiction genre. At first the painting looks like a genre piece, the children before the fireplace.*

BUT major movements such as *Romanticism* or *Dadaism* (See both) are more than genres.

genteel polite; well bred. (adv.) —lly.

gentile [JEHN-tile] an outsider. Used by Jews to distinguish a non-Jew, by Muslims, a non-Moslem.

genuine [JEH-yoo-ihn] not spurious; of verifiable origin: *genuine diamond, genuine Stradivarius.* Also sincere; true.

AUTHENTIC authoritative; trustworthy: *authentic document, relic.*

genus [JEE-nuhs] (pl.) genera [JEH-neh-rah] scientific division of living things into families, themselves divided into species. Names are written in italics with the first letter capitalized, except medical terms.

In a list, or in second reference to species of the same genus, abbreviate the genus: *Lepomis gibosus, L. megolatis.* See **Classification of Animals and Plants**.

geodesic dome [jee-oh-DEE-sihk] from *geode*, semi-spherical structure invented by R. Buckminster Fuller (1895-1983).

geographical terms Cap. if part of name; lowercase in general sense: *rivers of Virginia and Maryland, Erie Ba-*

sin. See specific place names: **street**, etc.

geometric mean See **average**.

Georgia U.S. state, abbr.: GA. Cap.: Atlanta. Native: Georgian.

Georgia republic in former U.S.S.R., part of Commonwealth of Independent States, 1992. E of Black Sea, N of Turkey. Cap.: Tbilisi [TIH-fluhs, tuh-FLEES]. Native: Georgian(s).

geriatrics [jeh-ree-AH-trihk] study of old age. Use as synonym for *the elderly* is colloq. and derogatory. (adj.) —tric.

German measles rubella.

germane [jur-MAEN] appropriate or relevant.

Germany nation in N Central Europe. Established by 9th C., unified 1867, split into East and West Germany 1945. (East, the *German Democratic Republic*; West, the *Federated Republic of Germany*). West Germany was in **NATO**. Cap.: Bonn. East Germany was in **Warsaw Pact**. Cap.: East Berlin. Two countries reunified 1990. (pl.) Germanys. Native: German(s). Cap.: Berlin. Currency: Deutsch Mark.

gerund in grammar, a verbal noun in the form of the present participle, thus ending in *-ing*. (adj.) gerundive.

There are two tense forms. Present: *Hating him gave her courage.* Perfect: *She can't help John's having cared for her.* Can function as adjective: *a living memorial.*

Gestalt [geh-STAHLT] (n. or adj.) Can be lowercase. In psychology, personality as a pattern of interactive parts. Hence, any distinct pattern or context.

Gestapo [geh-STAH-poh] Nazi police force.

get (p.) got; p.p. gotten.

Gethsemane [gehth-SEHM-uh-nee] scene of Jesus' arrest.

geyser [GIE-sehr] erupting hot spring.

Ghali, Boutros See **Boutros Ghali.**

Ghana [GAH-nah] republic in W Africa. Formerly Br.; independent 1957. Cap.: Accra. Native: Ghanaian(s). Currency: Cedi.

gherkin [GUHR-kihn] small cucumber used for pickling.

ghetto orginally a Jewish quarter, decreed by law. (pl.) —os.

ghoul [gool] evil being that feeds on the dead; grave robber.

G.I. (abbr.) general issue; Government issue. Hence, U.S. soldier. G.I. bill of rights. (pl.) G.I.'s.

gibberish [JIHB-ehr-ihsh] foolish chatter.

gibbet [JiH-beht] gallows where executed hung in chains.

gibe [JIEB] (n. or v.) taunt.

JIBE (v.) to agree. In sailing, to change direction abruptly.

Gide, André [zheed] (1869-1951) Fr. novelist. (*The Counterfeiters*).

gigolo [JIHG-uh-loh] paid male escort.

gild to paint in gold.

GUILD an association with similar interests, especially trade or vocation.

gill [jihl] unit of capacity. (1) U.S. = 1/8 qt. = 1/4 pt. = 4 fl. oz. = 7.2188 cu. in. = 0.1183 l. (2) Br. gill = 1.20094 U.S. = 1/8 qt. Br. = 1/4 pt. Br. = 8.6694 cu. in. = 0.1421. (pl.) —s.

Giotto [JAWT-toh] Giotto di Bondone [dee bohn-DOH-nae] (c. 1276-1337) Florentine painter, architect.

gird (p.) —ed, or girt; —ing.

Girl Scouts (organization) a Girl Scout; a Scout.

gist [jihst] main point.

Gitmo See **Guantanamo Bay.**

give (p.) gave; (p.p.) given; giving.

giveaway (n. and adj.) Sometimes give-away; give-and-take.

glacé [glas-SAY] (Fr.) candied; iced. Also, a glistening lustrous effect in finished fabics. —eed, —eing.

glacier [GLAE-shehr] (n.), glacial [GLAE-shal] (adj.).

gladiolus [glad-ee-OH-luhs] (sing. and pl.), or (pl.) —luses. Also, *gladiola.*

glamour [GLAM-ehr] Also, *glamor.* (v.) glamorize.

glasnost [GLAHS-nohst] (n.) Also cap. Russian for "openness." General term for liberal reforms in U.S.S.R. after 1985. See **Mikhail Gorbachev, perestroika.**

glassful (pl.) glassfuls.

glaucoma [glaw-KOH-muh] condition of the eye causing impairment of vision or blindness.

glazework, glaze wheel.

glazier [GLAE-shehr] glass worker.

glissade [glih-SAHD] in ballet, a glide; also in skiing.

glossary appendix defining unfamiliar words.

VOCABULARY stock of words available for use.

Gloucester [GLAW-stehr] town in Massachusetts.

glucose [GLOO-kohs] Also, dextrose. Sugars in honey, fruit, and animal blood, more complex than **fructose.**

gluey

G.m.t. (abbr.) Greenwich mean time. Also, G.m.a.t., Greenwich mean astronomical time.

gneiss [nies] rock similar to granite. —ic, —oid.

gnomic [NOH-mihk, NOHM-ihk] containing maxims.

gnosticism [NAHS-tih-sih-s'm] belief that knowledge brings emancipation from matter. (adj.) gnostic. See **atheism, deism.**

G.N.P. (abbr.) Gross National Product.

gnu [noo, or nyoo] African antelope.

go (p.) went; (p.p.) gone; going.

gobbledygook unnecessary long words and circumlocution. Usually refers to language of law or bureaucracy.

go-between (pl.) go-betweens.

God Capitalize. Most authorities cap. personal pronouns: *He, Him, His;* BUT lowercase relative pronouns: *who, whom, whose.*

Godard, Jean-Luc [goh-DAHR] (b. 1930) Fr. film maker. (*Weekend*).

Goebbels, Joseph Paul [GEH-bels] (1897-1945) Nazi propagandist.

—goer concertgoer, playgoer, theatregoer, etc.

Goering, Hermann Wilhelm [GEHR-ihng] Sometimes *Goring.* (1893-1946) Nazi general and politician.

Goethe, von, Johann Wolfgang [fawn GEU-teh, YOU-hahn VAWLFgahng] (1749-1832) German writer (*The Sorrows of Young Werther*) and philosopher.

go-getter go ahead.

Gogh, Vincent van [vahn KAWK; (angl.) vahn GOH] (1853-1890) Dutch Impressionist painter.

Gogol, Nikolai Vasilievich [GAW-guhl] (1809-1852) Rus. writer (*The Overcoat*).

goings-on (pl.)

Golden Age, Golden Rule.

Golgotha [GAWL-guh-thuh] Calvary, where Christ was crucified. Also, a burial place.

Goliath [guh-LIE-uhth]

—gon combining form meaning closed geometric plane figure: polygon (many sides and angles); trigon, triangle (3 sides and angles); tetragon, quadrangle, quadrilateral (4); pentagon (5); hexagon (6); heptagon (7); octagon or octangle (8); nonagon (9); decagon (10); undecagon (11); dodecagon (12). (adj.) —gonal.

gonad [GAHN-ad] sexual gland, male or female.

gondola [GAHN-duh-luh]

gondolier [gahn-duh-LEER]

good-by, goodby, good-bye, good-bye.

Good Friday Christian holy day commemorating the Crucifixion.

good will (n. or adj.) of a transaction or a person, often spelled *goodwill* or *good-will. A good-will gesture.*

googol Figure 1 followed by 100 zeros = 10^{100}.

Gorbachev, Mikhail Sergeyevich [GOHR-bah-chehv or -CHAHV, mee-KAEL] (b. 1931) General Secretary of U.S.S.R. Communist Party, thus leader of country, 1985.

Initiated liberal reforms known as **glasnost** and **perestroika**.

Resigned, 1991, and helped dismantle U.S.S.R., establish **Commonwealth of Independent States** in its place.

Gorgonzola [gawr-gahn-ZOH-luh] It. cheese.

gorilla [goh-RIHL-luh]

Goring, Herman Wilhelm See **Goering**.

gospel Cap if referring to the first four books of the New Testament; BUT *gospel truth.*

gossamer [GAHSS-uh-mehr].

gossip (v.) —ed, —ing. (adj.) —y. (n.) gossip, gossips.

Gotham New York City. Can refer to any large city.

Gothic orginally, 12th C. through 15th; Gothic novel, 18th-19th C.; Gothic revival (architecture), 19th C.

Gotterdammerung [GOHT-tur-DAH-mur-ruhng] (Ger.) "Twilight of the gods;" the end of the world in

Norse myth. Hence, any apocalyptic event. Also, opera by **Richard Wagner**.

gouache [goo-AHSH] watercolor painting technique.

Gouda [GOU-dah] hard eyeless cheese from S Netherlands. Also l.c.

gourd [gohrd or goord] vine-growing plants: melon, squash, pumpkin, etc. Also, the hollowed, dried rind of plants.

gourmand [GOOR-mand] a lover of eating; a greedy eater.

> GOURMET [GOOR-mae] a connoisseur of food and drink.

Government, government (abbr.: govt.) Cap. British Government, Soviet Government, the Government; Canal Zone Government, the government; Government (U.S.) department, officials, publications, (U.S. Government); National and State Governments; Government Printing Office. (See **office**.)
> Lower case: Churchill government, Communist government, European governments, Federal government, State government, municipal government; island, military government; seat of government; Territorial government.

Governor of a State the Governor; Governor of the Federal Reserve Board, the Governor; Governor of the Panama Canal, the Governor; Governor of Wisconsin, the Governor; State Governor(s); Governors' conference; a Governor. ADDRESS:

His Excellency Mario Cuomo, The Governor of New York, etc.; or The Honorable the Governor of New York, Albany. N.Y.
> SALUTATION: Sir; Dear Sir; Dear Governor Cuomo.

governor general Governor General of Canada, the Governor General. (pl.) governors general.

g.p.m. (abbr.) gallons per minute. g.p.s. (abbr.) per second.

G.P.U. See **M.V.D.**

gr. (abbr.) grain, gross, gram.

gr. wt. (abbr.) gross weight.

gradation [grae-DAE-shuhn]

gradc, market See **market grades**.

gradual [GRAD-joo-uhl]

graduate (n.) one who has completed a school course. As verb, active form is preferred to the passive. *She graduated from* pref. to *was graduated from.*

grain unit of weight = 1/5760 troy lb. = 1/7000 avoirdupois lb. = 0.05 scruple = 64.799 milligrams.

gram (abbr.: g.) unit of weight in the metric system = 0.03215 oz. sp. = 1/1000 kilogram = 15.432 grains = 0.03527 ou. Based on weight of 1 cc. of pure water at 4° centigrade.

gram calorie, small calorie unit of heat required to raise 1 gram of water 1 degree centigrade. See **calorie**.

GRAMMAR Grammatical problems are addressed throughout the text. This entry provides a brief and partial overview to help users find solutions to particular problems.

MAIN NOUN: case, collective nouns, general reference, nouns, number, person, plurals, pronoun; nominative absolute, predicative nominative, subject of a sentence.

OBJECT NOUN: case, collective nouns, nouns, number, person, plurals, pronoun; accusative case, objective case, predicate.

SENTENCE: complex, compound, clause, linking verb, placement of words, tense, verb; also phrase, preposition.

VERB: auxiliary verb, clause, linking verb, mood, number, participle, person, tense, verb; also aspect, be.

MODIFICATION: adjectives, adverbs, hyphens, number, participle, placement of words, possessives, prefixes and suffixes; also color, predicate complement, preposition.

Many brief entries directly address problem words: *as, each, hopefully, I, that, was,* etc.

Grand Guignol [grahn GEEN-yohl] (Fr.) violent, horrific drama.

grand mal [grahn mahl] convulsive epilespy.

Grange, the (National)

grant-in-aid a government grant. (pl.) grants-in-aid.

graph 2, A, II BUT capitalize Graph 2, when part of title: *Graph 2. —Production Levels.*

gratis [GRAE-tihs or GRAT-ihs] without recompense; free. *The service was gratis.*

gratuitous [gruh-too-ih-tuhs] freely given; also, (derogatory) uncalled for. *Gratuitous advice, coinage.*

grave (p.p.) graven.

grave, accent (`) [GRAHV] In French, an open *e*, pronounced "eh." In English (archaic, poetic), used on any vowel to indicate stress. *Time's wingèd chariot.*

gray Pref. to *grey* in U.S.

great See **big**.

Great Basin Great Beyond, Great Divide, Great White Way (See **Nicknames**); Great Lakes, the lakes; Great Plains, BUT southern Great Plains; Great War (See **War**).

Great Britain specifically, the largest of the British Isles, containing England, Scotland, and Wales. Also, the nation, officially known as the United Kingdom.

COMMONWEALTH OF BRITISH NATIONS Australia, Canada, etc. Includes nearly every former Br. colony, all now autonomous nations.

great circle in navigation, the shortest distance between two points on earth, allowing for earth's curvature.

Great Lakes Erie, Ontario, Huron, Michigan, Superior.

Greater Los Angeles, Greater New York.

Greco, El (1541-1614) Greek-Spanish painter. Actual name, Domenikos Theotokopoulos.

Greece nation in SE Europe, on Mediterranean. Ancient democracy; independent from Turkey, 1829. Cap.: Athens. Native: Greek. Currency: drachma. See **Hellenes**.

> GRECIAN Usu. refers to facial features or architecture.

> GRECO Combining form. *Greco-Roman.*

> GREEK For ordinary usage: *Greek islands, church, history.*

Greenpeace worldwide environmental organization.

Greenwich mean time [GRIHN- or GREHN-ihch] (abbr.: G.m.t.) time on the zero meridian, which runs through Greenwich, England. London time is Greenwich mean time. New York time is 5 hours earlier, Tokyo time 9 hours later.

Greenwich Village [GREHN-ich] area in lower Manhattan, New York City. Noted for artistic population and unconventionality.

Grenada [greh-NAH-dah; -NAE-] island country in Caribbean. Former Br. colony; independent, 1974. Cap.: St. George's. Native: Grenadian. Currency: East Caribbean dollar.

grey *Gray* is pref. BUT *greyhound.*

grid metal grating or plate. See **grille**.

> GRIDDLE flat pan for cooking cakes. See *grill.*

> GRIDIRON metal plate or grid used for broiling food. (colloq.) football field.

griffin, gryphon monster part lion, part eagle. Also, racehorse in its first race. See **hippogriff**.

grill (v.) to broil. (n.) broiler.

> GRILLE lattice. *An iron grille ran across the porch.*

grimace [grih-MAES] (n. and v.) —cer, —ced, —cing.

grimy [GRIE-mee]

grind (p. and p.p.) ground; grinding.

gringo among Spanish Americans, contemptuous term for a foreigner, especially English or American. (pl.) —os.

grippe, grip [GRIHP] influenza.

grisly (adj.) inspiring horror.

> GRIZZLY the bear.

Gris-Nez, Cape [GREE-nae] cape in France; point on European mainland nearest Britain.

Gromyko, Andrei [groh-MEE-koh, UHN-drya] (1909-1982) Rus. economist, diplomat.

grosbeak [GROHS-beek] species of finch.

gross 12 doz. = 144.

    GREAT GROSS 12 gross = 1728.

Gross National Product (abbr.: G.N.P.) value of all goods and services produced in a nation each year.

gross-minded, (adj.), gross weight, (n.).

group Military Advisory Group, the group; Standing Group. See *ARMY ORGANIZATION.*

group 2, II, A BUT cap. Group 2 when part of title: *Group II: List of Countries by States.*

GROUP NOUNS such as flock, family, crowd take a singular verb except where the sense is plural. *The football team were given letters.*

groups triad (3); tetrad (4); pentad (5); hexad (6); heptad (7); ogdoad (8).

grouse (n.), (sing. and pl.) bird. (v.) to complain.

grovel [GRUHV'L] —ling, —led.

grow (p.) grew; (p.p.) grown.

grown-up, grownup

growth rate for a nation, annual percentage increase in G.N.P.

gruel [GROO-uhl] (n.) a thin porridge.

    GRUELLING (adj.) punishing; trying one's endurance.

gruesome repulsive; grisly.

Gruyere [groo-YEHR] cheese made chiefly in Switzerland.

G.S.A. (abbr.) General Services Administration.

G.T.C. order Good till cancelled order, especially to a stockbroker, or for advertising.

Guadalcanal [GWAH-dal-cah-NAL] SW Pacific island, site of 1942 W.W. II battle.

Guadeloupe [gwahd-LOOP] islands in French West Indies.

    GUADELUPE North Mexico mountains and river.

Guam [GWAHM] (no abbr.) U.S. territory in central Pacific; U.S. naval base. Native: Guamanian.

guano [GWAH-noh] dung of seafowl used as fertilizer.

Guantanamo Bay [gwahn-TAH-nah-moh] site of former U.S. naval base, SE Cuba. In slang, **Gitmo.**

guarantee, guaranty *Guarantee* is more common as verb, and as noun for the security or pledge offered. *The agency guaranteed his mortgage to the bank. The bank holds a guarantee from the government agency on his mortgage.*

    Guarantor is the one who offers security.

    Guaranty is more common as noun, for the act of guaranteeing or offering security. *The certificate of guaranty is good until the mortgage is completely repaid.*

guaranteed annual wage (abbr.: G.A.W.).

guardsman See **Coast Guard; National**.

Guatemala [GWAH-teh-MAH-lah] Central American nation. Independent, 1839. Cap.: Guatamala City. Native: Guatemalan. Currency: East Caribbean dollar.

gubernatorial [goo-behr-nuh-TAWR-ee-uh] of the state governor or government.

Guernica [gehr-NEE-kah] city in NE Spain bombed during Spanish Civil War, 1937; subject of painting by **Picasso**.

guerilla, guerrilla [guhr-IHL-uh] (n. and adj.) small-scale, irregular warfare; also, combatants in such a war, often untrained. Distinguished from larger conflict between trained armies. Hence, any subversive activity, such as guerilla theater.

GORILLA an ape.

guffaw [guhf-FAW] loud burst of laughter.

Guevara, Ernesto "Che" [gwah-VAH-rah, "CHAE"] (1932-1967) Argentine-born Cuban revolutionary.

Guiana [gee-AH-nah] area along N coast of South America. Includes former Dutch, British, French colonies.

guidon [GIE-dun] small flag, military banner. See **pendant**.

Guignol See **Grand Guignol**.

guild organized trade group. See **gild**.

guillotine [GIHL-oh-teen] Fr. beheading machine.

Guinea [GIHN-ih] NW African nation on Atlantic coast. Formerly Fr.; independent since 1958. Also, region from Gambia to the Cameroons. Cap.: Conakry. Native: Guinean. Currency: Guinea franc.

Guinea-Bissau [BIH-sou] nation in NW Africa, on Atlantic coast. Formerly Portugese; independent, 1974. Cap.: Bissau. Native: Guyanese. Currency: Peso.

guinea hen, guinea pig.

Gulag [GOO-lahg] common term for Soviet concentration-camp system, established under **Josef Stalin.** *The Gulag Archipelago*, novel by **Aleksandr Solzhenitsyn**.

gulden [GOOL-dehn] Dutch and early German coin.

Gulf Coast States gulf coast; Gulf of Mexico, the gulf; Gulf States; Gulf Stream, the stream.

gullible

guns Use figures for caliber: .22 rifle; .45 caliver revolver; .410-gauge shotgun; 7.3-inch gun.

gunwale [guhn-el] Sometimes *gummel*. Part of vessel where topsides and deck meet.

guru [GOO-roo] Hindu spiritual teacher. Hence, any teacher.

Gutenberg, Johann [GOO-tehn-be-hrk, YOH-hahn] (1400-1468) Ger. inventor of printing with movable type, 1440. The town is sometimes written *Guttenberg*.

Guyana [gee-ANN-uh] country in NE South America. Formerly British Guiana; independent, 1966. Cap.: Georgetown. Native: Guyanese. Currency: Dollar.

gymnasium (pl.) —s or —ia.

gynecology [GIE-neh-KAHL-uh-jee]

gypsy

gyrate [JIE-raet] (v.)

gyroscope [JIE-roh-skohp] spinning disk which rotates on perpendicular axis, used to control torque.

H

h Silent in nihilism, philharmonic and other multisyllable words where the syllable is not accented. *H* is usually aspirate (sounded with a breath) as in *have, home, behave,* more heavily so before vowels and *w.*

h. (abbr.) hecto = 100 in the metric system.

H-bar, H-beam, H-bomb, H-hour, H-piece.

ha. (abbr.) hectare.

habeus corpus [HAE-bee-uhs KOHR-puhs] (Lat.) writ of law used, most importantly, to correct violations of personal liberty.

habitué [huh-biht-yoo-AE] frequent visitor or resident.

hacienda [hah-see-EHN-dah] (Sp.) house

had better *He had better be here. He had better have been here.* NOT: *He had better been here.*

Haggada in Judaism, Exodus story told at Passover meal.

The Hague city in the Netherlands, site of international court. Spell: *the Hague Court, the Second Hague Conference.*

Haifa [HIE-fah] Mediterranean seaport in Israel. Also, Jaffa, Joppa.

Haile Selassie [HIE-lee sih-LAH-sih]

(1892–1975) Ethiopian statesman; last Emperor.

hailstone, hailstorm; hail fellow.

hairdresser, hairline, hairsplitting; hair ribbon, hair trigger.

hairdo (pl.)—dos.

Haiti [HAET-ee] Caribbean nation, shares island of Hispaniola with Dominican Republic. Formerly independent, 1804. Cap.: Port-au-Prince. Native: Haitian. Currency: gourde.

halcyon days [HAL-see-ohn] (from ancient fable, 14 days around December 21) a period of success.

hale (adj.) healthy. *Hale and hearty.* (v., rare) synonym for *hail;* also, compel. *He hailed a cab* pref. to *He haled a cab.*

half (1) *cut in half* is pref. to more correct *cut in halves;* (2) (v.) halve; (3) *a yard and a half* is pref. to *one and a half yards,* even when written *1 1/2 yards.* The verb of a mixed number is singular: *Seven and a half tons is here;* (4) half again as much is 150 percent.

half past

halfback (football), halfbreed, half-hearted, halfpenny, half-tone (printing), half-track, halfway; half-and-half (n. and adj.), half-afraid, half-alive, half-baked, half-hourly, half-mast, half-ripe, half-strength, half-witted (adj.); half-truth (n.).

half hour, half load, half measure, half mile, half moon, half nelson, half past, half speed.

hallmark, hallway.

hallelujah [hal-luh-LOO-yuh]

Halley's Comet [HAL-lee] comet that orbits Earth every 76 years, named for English astronomer Edmond Halley (1656–1742). In this century appeared 1910, 1986.

Halloween, Hallowe'en

halyerd [HAL-yuhrd] a hoist for flags.

Hammarskjold, Dag [HAHM-ahr-shuld, dahg] (1905–1961) Swedish statesman, U.N. Secretary-General, 1953–61.

Hammurabi [hahm-uh-RAH-bee] (c. 1955–1913 B.C.). King of Babylon, famed as lawgiver.

hamstring, hamstrung.

hand unit of length = 4 in. = 10.16 centimeters.

handmade, BUT hand-tailored, hand-tooled.

handicap —pped, —pping.

handkerchief [HANG-kuh-chihf].

hand-me-down (pl.) -downs.

hanged refers only to people so killed; otherwise, *hung.*

hanger-on (colloquial) for dependent. (pl.) hangers-on.

hanker (for) have a craving (for); also, *hanker after.*

Hanukkah, Hanukka, Chanukah [HAH-nuh-kah] Heb. word for Jewish festival of lights, in December.

happen into, happen to Acceptable, though stilted. *I happened into the shop. I happen to know.*

happy-go-lucky

hara-kiri [HAR-uh KIHR-ih] Jap. ritual suicide.

harass [nearly always huh-RASS] harrassment.

harbor master —side.

hard (adj. and adv., except in sense of "scarce") *I worked very hard.* BUT: *I had hardly enough myself.*

hard-and-fast rule

hard disk computer storage built into unit. See **floppy.**

hard-pressed hard-hearted, hard-set, hard-won, (adj.); hard rubber, hard shell, hard up, hard work.

hardly Followed by *when. He had hardly been seated when the curtain rose,* NOT *. . . than the curtain rose.* AVOID double negatives. NOT: *He saved hardly nothing.*

harebrain (n.); —brained (adj.).

harem [HAE-rehm]

harken, hearken

Harlequin [HAHR-lih-kihn; -kwihn]. also lowercase

harmony in music, a group of notes forming a pleasing chord. adj., *harmonic*.

> MELODY a series of notes in expressive succession.

harnessmaker, harness-making (adj.); harness race.

hart male deer, esp. red deer. Also stag, buck. See *ANIMALS*.

> DOE female deer; female for other animals. Also, hind.

harum-scarum (adj. or adv.) reckless.

has-been (n.).

has got meaning "possesses" is redundant.

hashish Pref. to —sheesh.

hauteur [haw-tuer] haughtiness of manner.

Havel, Vaclav [HAH-v'l, VAH-clahv] (b. 1936) Czechoslovakian playwright and politician. President, 1990-92.

have-not (n. and adj.).

havoc —cked, —king.

Hawaii [hah-WIE-ee] chain of islands in central Pacific; formerly Sandwich Islands, U.S. state; abbr.: HI. Capital: Honolulu. Native: Hawaiian.

hazelnut, hazel-eyed (adj.)

H.B. (with number) (abbr.) House bill.

H. Con. Ra. (with number) (abbr.) House concurrent resolution.

H. Doc. (with number) (abbr.) House document.

Head of state department ADDRESS: The Secretary of State, Commonwealth of Pennsylvania; or The Honorable John J. Jones, Secretary of State. SALUTATION: Sir; Dear Sir; Dear Mr. Jones; Dear Mr. Secretary.

headache, headband, head-on (adj.); head tax.

headquarters (abbr.: H.Q.) Alaska Command Headquarters, the command headquarters; 4th Regiment Headquarters, regimental headquarters; 2nd Division Headquarters, division headquarters.

healthcraft, healthful. BUT: health foods, health nut.

> HEALTHY Generally refers to physical health. BUT *healthy influence* or . . . *climate* have more general meaning.

heaps Use a singular verb except when followed by *of. There is heaps more work to do. There are heaps of dishes.*

hear (p. and p.p.) heard.

hearken, harken

heartache, heartbeat, heartbreak;

halfhearted; lionhearted, soft-hearted; heart-throbbing, heart-weary (adj.).

heave (p.p.) *heaved* is pref. to *hove*; heaved to, hove to.

heaven Cap. Deity *I thank Heaven.* Lowercase place: *I'm in heaven.* The plural *heavens* is pref. for the sky.

heavenly bodies Names are not capitalized unless used in connection with the names of planets or stars that are always capitalized: *sun, earth, moon, stars, polestar, lodestar.* BUT: *studying Mercury, the Sun, Mars, the Earth.*

Nicknames in English are always capitalized: *the Milky Way, the Great Bear, the Dog Star.*

Heavenly Father the Almighty, Thee, Thou, He, Him. Current usage avoids male identification when possible. In the Protestant Doxology, the lyrics no longer read *Praise God from whom all blessings flow. / Praise Him . . . / Praise Him . . .* Instead, the song now repeats *Praise God* in each line.

heaven's sake NOT *heavens' sake.*

heavenward, heaven-sent (adj.).

Hebrew the language and, in literary or historical contexts, the people. (adj.) Hebraic. See **Jew.**

hecatomb [HEHK-uh-tahm] (from public sacrifice of 100 oxen) a great slaughter.

hectare (abbr:) unit of area = 2.471

acres = 1 hm.2 = 100 acres = 10,000 m².

hectic [HEHK-tihk] at a high pitch of excitement.

hecto-, hect- prefix meaning hundred. See **centi-.**

hectogram. (abbr: hg.) unit of weight = 100 g. = 3.5274 oz. = 0.1 kg.

hectoliter (abbr: hl.) unit of (1) capacity = 100 liters. = 2.838 bu. = 2 bu. 3.35 pk. = 26.418 gal.; (2) volume = 6102.5 cu. in. = 0.1 m.³

hectometer (abbr: hm.) unit of length = 100 m. = 109.361 yd. = 328.083 ft.

—hedron combining form meaning sides of a solid: polyhedron (many); trihedron (3); tetrahedron (4); pentahedron (5); hexahedron (6); cube (6 equal); cuboid (approx. cube); heptahedron (7); octahedron (8); decahedron (10); dodecahedron (12); icosahedron (20); tetrahexahedron (24 equal triangular); trisoctahedron (24 equal). (adj.) trihedral, etc.; prismatic.

Hegel, George Wilhelm Friedrich [HAE-gehl] (1770–1831) Ger. philosopher.

hegemony [hee-JEHM-oh-nih, HEHJ-eh-moh-nih] leadership, especially of a government or state.

hegira [hee-JIE-ruh; HEHj-ih-ruh]. Also hejira, hijrah. Mohammed's escape from persecution in Mecca,

A.D. 622, Moslem yr. 1. Hence, any journey, esp. a flight from trouble.

height [hiet] NOT *heighth*.

Heimlich maneuver [HIEM-lihk] maneuver to relieve choking.

heinous [HAE-nuhs] infamous; odious.

heir (m. & f.) one who inherits anything (characteristics, etc.).

HEIRESS (f.) Usually used in connection with wealth.

heir apparent heir regardless of any possible new developments (usually the oldest son).

heir presumptive heir subject to birth of a more legitimate heir; for example, the oldest daughter where a son might be born and would inherit.

helicopter [HEHL-ih-kahp-tihr].

helio-, heli- prefix meaning the sun: *heliocentric, heliograph*.

heliotrope [HEE-lih-oh-trohp] lavendar flower.

heliotropism movement toward sun.

APHELIOTROPISM movement away from sun.

helium [HEE-lee-uhm] (abbr: He) gaseous element first found in the sun's atmosphere.

helix [HEE-lihks] a spiral. pl. helices [HEH-].

hell BUT Cap. *Hades.*

Hellenic [hehl-EHN-ihk] (from Hellas [HEHL-as], classical name for Greece) in modern times, used for pro-Greek feeling. (adj.) Hellene, (n.) Hellenism (v.); Hellenize. See **Greece.**

hellbent, —bound, —box, (printing), —bred, —cat, —diver, —fire, —hole, —hound (all one word); hellred (adj.).

Hells Canyon NO apostrophe.

helter-skelter

hem-, hema-, hemato-, hemo- [HEEM] combining prefixes meaning blood: *hemastatic, hematoblast, hemoglobin.*

hematoma [hem-uh-TOH-muh]. Bloody tumor.

hemi-. Prefix meaning half: *hemisphere, hemiatrophy.*

hemisphere Eastern Hemisphere, Western; the hemisphere.

hemoglobin [HEE-moh-glohbihn] red blood corpuscles.

hemorrhage internal blood discharge caused by injury. —ing.

hence from this place, time, or source.

THENCE from that place, time, or source.

WHENCE from what place or source.

WHITHER to what place.

All are archaic. The preposition *from* or *to* is understood and should not be repeated. *Go hence immediately. Whence you have come concerns me not.* NOT: *Go from hence.*

henceforth, henceforward

hepatitis [HEH-peh-TIE-tihs] viral infection of the liver.

her, hers *This book of hers. Your and our and her courses. His house and hers. The law aplied to you and yours, her and hers, me and mine.* See **him.**

her, she as personification. Avoid except where traditional, or in poetic context. NOT: *The nation deserves the best we can give her.* BUT *she* and *her* may be used for a ship, the Queen, and other nouns of traditional gender.

herb [uhrb] seed plant used in medicine and cooking. (adj.) herbal.

herbacious [huhr-BAE-shuhs] of an herb or a leaf.

Herculaneum [huhr-kyoo-LAE-nee-uhm] ancient Italian city, buried along with **Pompeii** *(see)* by eruption of Mt. Vesuvius, 79 A.D.

Herculean [huh-KYOO-lih-an] pertaining to Hercules; requiring great strength; difficult.

hereabout —after, —by, —from, —in, —inabove, —inafter, —of, —on, —to, —tofore, —unto, —upon, —with (all one word). With all these constructions, a simple *here* is often better.

hernia [HIHR-nee-ah] protrusion of organ from its normal cavity. (adj.) herniated [-AE-tehd].

Herr (Ger.) Mister. pl. Herren.

herringbone

hesitation Pref. to *hesitancy* or *hesitance. Hesitancy* indicates a tendency to hesitate. *After a moment of hesitation, he drove ahead.* BUT: *There was a hesitancy in all his decisions after he learned of this disability.*

hew (p. and p.p.) hewed, sometimes hewn.

H.E.W. (abbr.) Department of Health, Education, and Welfare. Formed as cabinet-level federal agency, 1953. Education jurisdiction transferred to new *Department of Education*, 1979. Remainder of H.E.W. reformed as *Department of Health and Human Services*, 1980.

hexagon regular six-sided polygon. Area = diameter of inscribed circle × 0.860.

hexameter [hehks-AM-ee-tehr] in poetry, verse of six metrical feet.

H.F. (abbr.) high frequency.

hg. (abbr.) hectogram.

HI. Hawaii.

hiatus [hie-AE-tuhs] a gap. In grammar, slight pause between two vowels, each distinctly sounded: *egoism* (pl.)—es or hiatus. See **diaeresis.**

Hiawatha [hie-uh-WAHTH-uh].

hiccup or hiccough [HIHK-uhp] —uping, —uped.

hide (p.) hid; (p.p.) hidden.

hideaway (n. and adj.), hide-and-seek (n. & adj.).

hie (arch.) hurry, (p.) hied, hieing.

hierarchy [HIE-uhr-ahr-kee] order of importance or rule.

High Church, High Commissioner, High Court (See **Supreme Court**), High Holy Days (Jewish).

higher-up (n.) (pl.) higher-ups.

highfalutin

highlight (n. and v.).

Highness title of address to member of a royal family. *Your Highness is followed by you and your. Your Royal Highness is correct in your decision regarding your voyage.*

high school Cap. if part of name: Jefferson High School. BUT: the high school.

high tech. Both n. and adj., both with and without hyphen. *We feature a high tech (or high-tech) light show.*

highways U.S. 40, U.S. No. 40, U.S. Highway No. 40; Route 40; State Route 9; the highway. Sunset Parkway; East River Drive.

hijack —ed, —ing; —er.

hi-fi high fidelity.

hijirah See **hegira.**

hilarious [hih-LAIR-ih-uhs; HIE-].

hillbilly

him Informally, *him* may be used after *is* or *than. It's him or me, but rather me than him.* FORMALLY: *It is he or I, but rather I than he.* See **PREDICATE NOMINATIVE.**

Himalayas [hih-mah-LAE-yuh or hih-MAHL-yuhz].

hindmost NOT *hindermost.*

hindrance [HIHN-druhnss].

Hindu one of the native races of India. The language is Hindi, the religion Hinduism. Hindustan [hihn-doo-STAHN] is in N India; (adj.) Hindustani. See **India.**

hinge hinging.

Hippocratic oath [hihp-uh-KRAT-ihk] code of medical ethics. From Greek scientist and doctor Hippocrates, (c. 460–357 B.C.)

hippogriff, —gryph monster part horse, part **griffin.**

hippopotamus (pl.) —*muses* is pref. to —*mi.*

hire Applied to labor, automobiles, halls.

    RENT Applied to buildings, equipment, halls.

    CHARTER Applied to vessels, buses, planes.

hiring hall employment agency, esp. in maritime, music, and printing trade.

Hirohito [hee-roh-HEE-toh] (1901–1989) Jap. Emperor during W.W. II and after (1926–1989).

Hiroshima [hee-RAWSH-mah] city in Japan where first A-bomb was dropped, 1945.

His Excellency The Duke of Athol, etc.; His Excellency, Their Excellencies. Similarly, His Majesty, His Royal Highness.

Hispanola, —niola [hihs-pahn-YOH-lah] Caribbean island containing Dominican Republic and Haiti.

historic [hihs-TAHR-ihk] worthy of a place in history. A *historic event* is momentous, rare, memorable.

HISTORICAL part of history. A *historical event* took place in the past.

HISTORICITY historical existence.

Historic Events the Reformation; the Renaissance; the Restoration (also, the English Restoration); the Revolution (American, 1776; French, 1789; English, 1688). See *AGES*.

hit (p. and p.p.) hit; hitting; hitter.

hit-and-miss, hit-and-run, hit-or-miss (all adj.).

hitchhiker —hiking.

hither, thither here and there. Poetical use only.

hitherto until now.

H.I.V. Human Immunodeficiency Virus. Infection often a precursor to **AIDS** (see). *HIV-positive.*

H.J. Res. (with number) (abbr.) House joint resolution.

hl. (abbr.) hectoliter.

hm. (abbr.) hectometer.

hoarfrost

hobbyhorse

hobgoblin

Ho Chi Minh [hoh chee MEEN, MIHN] (1890–1970) President of North Vietnam (Communist Vietnam) 1945–1970, during the wars with France, South Vietnam and the U.S. See **Vietnam.**

HO CHI MINH CITY former Saigon (See)

hocus-pocus

hodgepodge a mixture, in a derogatory sense.

hoe hoeable, hoeing.

hogshead (abbr.: hhd.) Unit of capacity. (1) U.S. = 1/2 butt = 63 U.S. gal. = 2 liquid bbl. = 238.476 l.; (2) Brit. = 52.4 imperial gal.

hoi polloi [hoi puh-LOI] (Gr.) the many. Ordinary people; rabble.

hoist *Hoist with his own petard:* killed with his own weapon. —ed, —ing, —er. See **petard.**

Holbein, Hans [HAWL-bien]. Father (1465–1524), son (1497–1543). Ger. painters.

hold (p. and p.p.) held; holding.

hold in abeyance *Suspend action* is pref.

hold steady is idiomatically correct for *hold steadily.*

hold up (v.), holdup (n. and adj.). *A holdup man holds up the victim of a holdup.*

hole-in-one (n. and adj.)

holidays can refer to individual days; extended weekends. Also, general term for period from Thanksgiving through New Year's. *Watch what you eat during the holidays.*

> VACATION extended time away from work. In academics, summertime.

holidays and special days Admission Day, April Fools Day, Arbor Day, Armed Forces Day, Christmas Day, Christmas Eve, Columbus Day, D-Day, D-plus-4 day, Father's Day, Flag Day, Fourth of July, Halloween, Inauguration Day, Independence Day, Labor Day, Memorial Day, Mother's Day, New Year's Day, New Year's Eve, Presidents Day (combining Washington's and Lincoln's birthdays), Thanksgiving Day, Veterans Day. BUT: election day; primary day, your birthday.

Holland the Netherlands.

holy sacred.

HOLEY full of holes.

HOLLY [HAH-lee] the Christmas plant.

WHOLLY [HOH-lee] completely.

Holy Scriptures Holy Writ. See **Bible.**

home A place where a person or family lives.

> HOUSE a structure suitable for a home.

home Naval Home, Soldier's Home; the home.

homely plain, simple. Hence, ugly.

homeo- combining form meaning "like:" *homeopathy* [hoh-mee-AHP-uh-thee] (medical system which uses medicines that produce like symptoms), *homeomorphism* (like crystalline forms in unlike chemicals). See **homo-.**

homeward

homicide [HAHM-ih-sied] killing of a human being.

> MANSLAUGHTER unlawful homicide without malice.

> MURDER killing with malice and premeditation.

homo-, hom- combining form meaning "same or equal:" *homonyms, homosexual.*

homogeneity [hoh-mohjehn-EE-uh-tee] (n.) things that have the same nature. (adj.) homogeneous [HOH-moh-GEE-nee-uhs].

homogenized milk

homonyms words having the same sound but different meanings: *bark* (of a tree), *bark* (of a dog); *rite, right, wright.*

heteronyms words spelled alike but with different sound and sense; *sow* [sou] (pig); *sow* [soh] (seed).

SYNONYMS words with identical meaning (rare). Hence, words with similar meanings.

ANTONYMS words with opposite meanings.

homo sapiens [HOH-moh-SAE-pee-uhnz] (Lat., "the knowing man") the human species.

Hon. (abbr.) Honorable. Title preceding Christian name or initials of a public official, especially a judge: *the Hon. John Collins* or *the Hon. J.T. Collins.* NOT: *the Hon. Mr. Collins.*

Honduras Central American country; independent, 1821. Cap.: Tegucigalpa [teh-GOO-sih-GAL-pah]. Native: Honduran. Currency: lempira.

honeycomb

Hong Kong [HAHNG-kahng] Brit. crown colony island, plus adjacent mainland, in SE China. Reverts to Chinese control, 1997. Currency: dollar.

hoof (pl.) —s is pref. to *hooves.*

Hoover Dam also Boulder Dam, on Colorado River between Nevada and Arizona.

hopefully Until recently, this adverb could refer only to a specific action. *He spoke hopefully. She looked up hopefully.*

Now it may address more general desires. *Hopefully, I'll get that job. Hopefully, the new Soviet Commonwealth will embrace freedom of the press.* BUT more direct expressions may be stronger: *I hope I'll get that job.*

Hopi [HOH-pee] Native Americans of SW.

horror-struck, horrorstruck.

hors de combat [AWR-duh-kohm-BAH] (Fr.) out of action.

hors d'oeuvre [awr-duhv'r] (Fr.) appetizer.

horse For cavalry, plural is *horse.* (adj.) horsey, horsy.

horsepower measure of power = 33,000 ft. lbs. per sec. = 0.746 kilowats = 4241 B.t.u.

horseraces Cap. names: *Kentucky Derby.*

hose Plural for stocking, *hose*; for rubber tube, *hoses.*

hosiery [HOH-zhuhr-ee].

hospitable [HAHS-piht-ab'l].

hospital Cap. if part of name; otherwise, the hospital. BUT naval (marine or Army) hospital.

host (m. & f.); hostess (f.).

hostile [HAHS-tihl].

hotelkeeper

houri [HOOR-ih or HOUR-ih] Muslim nymph.

house houseful; (pl.) —ful-s. See **home.**

house Cap. if part of name: Johnson house (private residence); Lee House (hotel); House of Representatives; the House (U.S.); House of the Woods (palace), the house; House Office Building (See **building**); Ohio (State) House, the house. The White House. BUT both Houses, lower (or upper) House (Congress).

hover [HUHV-ehr].

however Stress is usually placed on the word that precedes *however* in the sentence. *also, But . . . however* is redundant.

Hoxho, Enver [HAHDZ-hah] (1906–1985) Albanian soldier, Communist dictator 1945–1985.

hp. (abbr.) horsepower.

hp. -hr. (abbr.) horsepower-hour.

hr. (abbr.) hour.

H. Rept. (with number) (abbr.) House report.

H. Res. (with number) (abbr.) House resolution.

hubris [HYOO-brihs] (Gr.) overweening pride.

hue See **color.**

Hue [HWAE] seaport in Vietnam, site of 1968 battle.

human pertaining to people: *the human race.* Avoid as a noun; use *human being.* —ism, —istic, —itarian, —ity, —kind, —ly.

HUMANE —having tenderness, compassion: *humane character, actions.*

humbly [HUHM-blee].

humdrum

humpty-dumpty

humus [HYOO-muhs] organic part of soil, brown or black, formed by decomposition.

HUMMUS [HUH-muhs] Arab food, ground chickpeas.

hundred = 100 = C. Several or many hundred; hundreds of books. One hundred, one hundred and one, one hundredth, one hundred and first, two hundred, two hundredth. See **million.**

hundredfold, —weight, hundred-percenter, hundred-pounder.

hundredweight (abbr.: cwt.) unit of weight = 1/20 ton; gross or long = 112 lbs. = 50.802 kgs. net or short = 100 lbs. = 45.359 kg. *20 hundredweights,* BUT *a few hundredweight.*

hung p.p. of *hang;* but persons are *hanged.*

Hungary nation in E Europe. Medieval kingdom; independent again 1867. Cap.: Budapest. Native: Hungarian. Currency: forint.

hunger-mad, hunger-worn (adj.)

hung-up (adj.); hung jury (n.).

Hurricane Carol

hurt (p. and p.p.) hurt.

hush up (v.) *Would you please just hush up?* (n., adj.), hush-up. Also, hush-hush; hush money.

hussar [huh-ZAHR] European cavalryman, 17th–19th C.

Hussein, Ibn [hoo-SAEYN] (b. 1935) King of Jordan since 1952.

hussy [HUHZ-ee] disreputable woman.

huzza [huh-ZAH] Hurrah!

hybrid cross-breed.

hydrangea [hie-DRAN-jee-uh].

hydrofoil [HIE-druh-FOI'l] underwater fin on a boat. Also, the boat.

hydrogen bomb

hydrometer instrument for measuring specific gravity.

HYGROMETER instrument for measuring moisture content.

hydropathy [hie-DRAHP-uhthee] treatment of diseases by copious use of water, internally and externally.

hyena [hie-EE-nuh].

hygiene [HIE-jeen] (n.) hygienic [hiejih-EHN-ihk] (adj.).

hymns Cap. principal words in titles and place titles in quotation marks.

hyper- combining form meaning above, over, extra: *hyper-Dorian, hyperacidity, hypermeter.*

HYPO- combining form meaning under, less than normal: *hypodermic, hypoplasia.*

hyphen The verb is *hyphenate.*

HYPHENS In general, compound two or more words to express a literal or figurative unit that would not be clearly expressed if the words were left unconnected.

Hyphenate: (1) To avoid doubling a vowel or tripling a consonant: *anti-inflation, brass-smith.* BUT do not hyphenate after a short prefix: *co-, coordinate; de-, deemphasise; pre-, pro-, re-.*

(2) When the vowel end of the prefix and the vowel beginning of the base word create a diphthong: *co-author.*

(3) When lack of a hyphen may create confusion in pronunciation or meaning: *co-op, coworker, re-formation, recover.*

(4) When the prefix is duplicated: *re-direct examination.*

(5) To join a prefix to a capitalized word: *pre-Victorian, un-American.*

(6) Where the terms are repetitive or conflicting: *walkie-talkie, pitter-patter, young-old.*

(7) To join a capital letter to a noun or participle: *u-turn, I-beam.*

(8) In chemical formulas: *Cr-Ni-Mo.*

(9) In technical compounds: *candle-hour*.

(10) In improvised compounds: *to blue-pencil*.

(11) In unit modifiers (in this text called adjectives) formed of an adjective or a noun plus a present or past participle: *a slow-rising elevator*.

(12) Unit modifiers formed of a present or past participle or a preposition not governing a following noun: *double-twisted cord, self-winding watch, lying-in hospital, hard-of-hearing class.* BUT NOT when the meaning is clear without the hyphen: *child welfare program, flood control project.*

(13) Unit modifiers made up of a verb plus a noun or pronoun: *make-believe, has-been, be-all.*

(14) Any adjective phrases made up of words not normally considered a unit which might be ambiguous: *high-school building, matter-of-fact manner, second-class citizen, Spanish-speaking, community.* BUT NOT when the phrase is made up of two words normally considered a single unit, especially those expressing chemical, geographical or political ideas: *North American customs* (U.C.M.S. hyphenates Latin-American), *New York traffic, Old English cheese, civil service jobs, family welfare studies, public school enrollment, social security payments, social service studies;* and foreign expressions: *laissez faire policies.*

(15) A compound of which the base word is derived from a transitive verb: *wage-earner, fun-loving, office-holder.* BUT expressions formed of a transitive or intransitive verb as the first word are written as two words: *frying pan.*

(16) Although G.P.O. usually makes one word of agency compounds, U.C.M.S. hyphenates such compounds ending in *collector, dealer, driver, hunter, maker, etc.: toy-maker, book-critic, gun-dealer.* BUT commonly used words in this category are always treated as one word: *bookkeeper, bookdealer, bookmaker, copyholder, dressmaker, proofreader, serviceman, shopgirl, taxpayer, washerwoman.*

(17) Usually, hyphenate compounds beginning with *mother, father, brother, sister, daughter, parent, fellow, foster: sister-city, fellow-members.* BUT compounds with a distinct unit meaning are written as one word: *fatherland, fellowship.*

(18) Hyphenate compounds beginning with *cross: cross-purpose;* with *great: great-grandfather;* with *life: life-giving,* BUT NOT: *lifeline, lifelong, lifetime,* and similar unit ideas; with *self: self-respect,* BUT NOT *selfless, selfsame,* and other unit ideas; with *half* and *quarter: half-mile, quarter-final,* BUT NOT *halfpenny, halftone, quarterback, quartermaster;* with *master: master-plumber,* BUT NOT *mastermind, masterpiece;* with *vice: vice-president,* BUT NOT *viceroy, vicerregent;* with *ultra: ultra-elegant,* BUT NOT *ultra microscopic, ultra montane, ultraviolet;* with *quasi: quasi-judicial.*

(19) Hyphenate compounds of *god: sun-god; like* (if the base word has more than one syllable): *Spanish-like.*

(20) Titles in which the last element is *elect* or *designate: governor-elect.*

(21) Spelled-out fractions: *three-fifths, five-sevenths.*

(22) Also hyphenate the following compounds: *after-years, bas-relief, blood-feud, blood-relation, courtmartial,*

loan-word, object-lesson, sea-level, sense-perception, thought-process, title-page, trade-mark, trade-union, well-being, well-nigh.

(23) A compound containing another compound is separated with an en (short) dash between the parts: *New Orleans-Nashville run.*

(24) When multiple compounds have a common unit, the common unit may be omitted: *6- and 7-year olds, third- and fourth-year students.*

The following compounds may be made single words:

(1) Two nouns making a third: *fishmonger.*

(2) A short verb and an adverb: *blowout, showdown.*

(3) A one-syllable noun prefix, especially most compounds of *book, eve, horse, house, mill, play, room, school, shop, snow, way, wood,* and *work;* BUT when the two components constitute a commonly accepted special meaning, write as two words: *tailor shop, bond house, book work, case work, field work.*

(4) Words beginning with *non,* BUT *non-civil service, non-European, non-pressed, non-tumor bearing, non sequitur.*

(5) Words ending in *store* or *fold,* if preceded by a one syllable word: *drugstore, twofold;* BUT these compounds are written as two words if preceded by words of more than one syllable: *tailor store, grocery store, twenty fold.*

(6) Compounds ending in *berry, blossom, boat, book, borne, bound, brained bush, collector, dealer, driver, fish, flower, grower, hearted, holder, house, helper, keeping, light, like, maker, man, master, mate, mill, mistress, mon-*

ger, piece, power, proof room, shop, skin (when preceded by a one-syllable word), *smith, stone, store, tail, tight, time, word, weed, wide, wise, woman, wood, work, worker, working, worm, writer, writing, yard;* BUT NOT if preceded by a long or unwieldy word and if no confusion would result from writing as two words: *encyclopedia maker.*

(7) Compounds ending with *one,* beginning with *any, every, no,* and *some,* BUT NOT when meaning a single or particular person or thing: *any one of these three.* Also, write *no one* to avoid confusion.

(8) All personal pronouns: *himself.*

(9) Compass directions of two points: *northeast;* BUT hyphenate when three points are combined: *north-northeast.*

(10) Technical terms in anthropology: *shortheaded.*

Separate words:

(1) A predicate adjective or predicate noun when the second element is a participle. *The problem was price fixing; the cost was price fixed.*

(2) Compounds in the predicate modifier where the first element is in the comparative or superlative. *The merchandise was of a better class.* BUT: *lighter-than-air craft, higher-than-market price, bestseller* (n.) are exceptions.

(3) Compounds which are combinations of an adverb and an adjective or an adverb and a participle: *a never ending flow.*

(4) Compounds where the first element is an adverb ending in —ly: *eagerly awaited arrival.*

(5) Compounds where the first two words in a three-element modifier are adverbs.

(6) Compounds where a unit modifier contains a number or a letter as a second element: *Class II railroads;*

(7) Compounds which have an element in quotation marks: *''blue sky'' laws;*

(8) Compounds where colors are separate words: *bluish green;* BUT hyphenate compound colors when used as unit modifiers: *bluish-green paper.*

(9) Independent adjective preceding a noun: *big gray houses.*

(10) Civil or military titles denoting single office: *sergeant at arms, attorney general.* BUT not if two offices are involved: *secretary-treasurer* but not *vice president.*

(11) A modifier with one element in the possessive case: *a week's pay* — except when used in a figurative sense: *cat's-paw.*

(12) Technical and chemical terms: *carbon monoxide poisoning.*

(13) Many elements usually hyphenated or written as one word, when preceded by words of two or more syllables: *grocery store, seventeen fold.*

(14) Two-word compounds containing an apostrophe: *science teacher's text.*

hypotenuse [hie-PAHT-eh-nuhs]

hypoxia insufficiency of oxygen at high altitudes.

I

-i Plurals made by -i are usually pronounced *ee*, except for Latin and Greek words with singular ending in -*us* or -*os*, which are pronounced *ei*: *bacilli*. But the plurals of some Latin words have irregular endings: *hiatus, corpus, octopus, virus, callus*. When in doubt, use the -*uses* form for plural.

I Nominative case: *I am. It is I.* BUT: *Between you and me.*

I-bar, I-beam, I-iron, I-nail.

IA Iowa.

I.A.E.A. (abbr.) International Atomic Energy Agency.

iamb [EI-am] poetic foot consisting of an unaccented and accented syllable: *upset.* (pl.) —s. See scansion.

Iberia [ie-BEER-ih-ah] European peninsula containing Spain and Portugal; also ancient region now Georgia, Commonwealth of Independent States.

ibex [IE-behks] Old World goat (pl.) ibexes or ibex.

ibidem (abbr.: ibid.) (Lat.) "in the same place." Used in citations to avoid repetition of a source. See *FOOTNOTES.*

ibis [IE-bihs] wading bird. (pl.) ibises.

IBM International Business Machine Corporation.

Ibsen, Henrik [IHB-sehn] (1828–1906) Norwegian playwright *(The Wild Duck, Hedda Gabler).*

I.C.A. (abbr.) International Cooperation Administration.

Icarus [IK-uh-ruhs] in Gr. mythology, son of Daedalus whose wax wings melted when he flew too close to sun.

I.C.B.M. (abbr.) intercontinental ballistic missile, range exceeding 5000 mi.

I.C.C. (abbr.) Interstate Commerce Commission.

iced tea [EIS TEE].

Iceland island nation in N Atlantic, since 10th C. Cap.: Reykjavik. Native: Icelander. Currency: krona. (adj.) Icelandic.

I Ching [ih jihng] ancient Chinese fortune-telling hexagrams.

iconoclast [ie-KAHN-oh-klast] idol smasher; a rebel.

—ics, —ic. Most branches of study have -*ics* endings: *classics, dynamics, physics.* But a few take -*ic*: *logic, music, rhetoric.*
  Words ending in -*ic* and those used strictly for a branch of study take the singular. *Magic* (or *mathematics* or *metaphysics*) *is an interesting subject.* But in a general sense, the plural verb is required. *Her ethics are strong but her mathematics is weak.*

ID Idaho.

I.D.A. (abbr.) International Development Association (of the World Bank).

Idaho U.S. state. Abbr.: ID. Capital: Boise. Native: Idahoan.

idée fixe [EE-dae feeks] a dominating idea.

idem (abbr.: id.) (lat.) "the same." In a citation, the same source.

identical to, identical with

-identify suffix to indicate association: *Western congresspeople are generally timber-identify.* Not common usage.

ideology [ihd-ee-AHL-uhjee, ie-dee-].

id est. (abbr.: i.e.) (Lat.) "that is." Always precede by a comma or a semicolon.

idiom in grammar, an accepted form of expression not necessarily in accord with grammatical rules or with ordinary meaning of words used. *She made friends with them.*

idiot See **mental retardation.**

idiot savant [sah-VAHNT] mentally retarded person with one outstanding developed faculty, such as math or painting. NOT a **savant.**

idiosyncracy [ih-dee-oh-SIHN-kra-see] (n.) peculiarity, individuality. —cratic (adj.).

idleheaded

idyl, idyll [IE-dihl] description of rustic life. (adj.) idyllic.

i.e. See **id est.**

—ie, —ei. Use *i* before *e* except after *c*, or when sounded like *a*, as in *neighbor* and *weigh.* BUT: *either, seize, seizure, neither, either, height, sleight, their, weird.*

I.F. (abbr.) intermediate frequency.

if Use to introduce a subjunctive clause of condition or supposition. Use *whether* where an alternative is indicated, expressed, or understood. *Tell us whether you sent the package (or not).*

If must be followed by present or past tense. *If* also may be omitted as understood. *Were I to go, he would object.* See **SUBJUNCTIVE MOOD, was, were.**

I.F.C. International Finance Corporation.

igneous [IHG-nee-uhs] a rock type, crystalline.

ignitible or **ignitable**

ignominy [IHG-no-mih-nih] (n.) disgrace. (adj.) ignominious [ihg-noh-MIHN-ih-uhs].

ignoramus [ihg-noh-RAE-muhs] (pl.) —uses.

ikon Use *icon.*

IL Illinois.

I.L.A. (abbr.) International Long-shoreman's Association.

Île-de-France or **Isle-de-France** [eel-deh-FRAHNNS] region around Paris.

I.L.G.W.U. (abbr.) International Ladies' Garment Workers Union.

Iliad [IHL-ee-ihd] Homer's epic about war against Troy (Ilium).

ill-advised, ill-born, ill-bred, ill-fated (all adj.); ill-treat (v.); ill breeding, ill fame, ill health, ill will (all n.).

Illinois [ihl-ih-NOI] U.S. state. (abr.: IL). Cap.: Springfield. Native; Illinoisan.

illusion [ih-LOO-shuhn] something unreal; figment of imagination. (adj.) illusive, illusory. See **allusion, delusion.**

illustrate [IHL-uhs-traet; ih-LUHS-traet] (v.); illustrative (adj.).

I.L.O. (abbr.) International Labor Organization.

Il Trovatore [eel troh-vuh-TOH-reh] opera by Giuseppe Verdi.

imagery [IHM-ihj-rih].

imam [ihm-MAHM] head of a Muslim community.

imbed Use *embed.*

imbibe (v.); —bable (adj.).

imbroglio [ihm-BROH-lyoh] complication; confusion; struggle.

imbue with to saturate, inspire.

> INFUSE INTO to pour into.

> INSTILL INTO to infuse gradually.

> INCULCATE WITH to impress upon by repetition.

imitate, —tator (n.); —table (adj.).

immanent [IHM-uh-nehnt] intrinsic, indwelling. *God is immanent in nature.* (n.) immanence.

> IMMINENT threatening to occur immediately. *Rain was imminent, so we sought shelter.*

> EMINENT [EH-mih-]prominent, lofty: *An eminent physician.*

immaterial not material, unimportant.

immediately Avoid using for *as soon as.* NOT: *He will call you immediately he comes in.*

immersible capable of being plunged into liquid. See **emerge.**

immigrate (v.); immigrant (n.). See **emigrate.**

imminent [IHM-mih-nehnt]. See immanent.

immobile [ihm-MOH-bihl].

immoral See **amoral.**

impact Colloq., often used as a verb with *on,* meaning "effect." *Will this impact on my career?* In formal usage, a noun only. *Will this have an impact on my career?*

impale [ihm-PAEL] Pref. to *em—*.

impanel —led, —ling.

impassable (from passable) cannot be passed. *The road was impassable.*

> IMPASSIVE without feeling or, esp., without showing emotion. *His face was impassive.*

impasse [ihm-PAS; IHM-pas] a blind alley; predicament from which escape is impossible; direction without a future.

impecunious [im-peh-KYOO-nee-uhs] without money.

impel —lled; —llable (adj.).

impenitence Pref. to —cy.

imperceptible

imperil NOT *em—*. —led, —lling.

impermeable [ihm-PUHR-mee-uh-b'l].

impermissible

impersonate (v.); —nable (adj.); —tor (n.).

impersuasible

imperturbable [im-puh-TUHRB-uh-b'l] incapable of being disturbed.

impetus (pl.) —tuses.

impinge to encroach. —ging.

impious [IHM-pih-uhs] irreverent.

implausible

implicate (v.); —cable (adj.).

imply to suggest. (adj.) implicit, opposite of *explicit*.

> INFER to conclude. *When she asked "Can you afford it?," she implied that he did not have enough money. He inferred that she was offering to pay.*

impolitic not good policy. (adv.) —icly.

import (n.) meaning, significance. (v.) to bring in.

> PURPORT (v.) to suggest, imply. (n.) intention, purpose.

important essentials is redundant.

importune [ihm-pawr-TYOON] to pester; urge. (adj.) importunate [ihm-PAWR-tchoo-niht] pressing, begging.

impotent [IHM-poh-tehnt].

impracticable not capable of being accomplished; infeasible.

> IMPRACTICAL not conforming with reality; theoretical.

impresario [ihm-prae-SAR-ih-oh] (pl.) —os.

impress [IHM-prehs] (n.) mark, stamp.

impressible

impromptu (pl.) —us.

impugn [ihm-PYOON] to criticize as false.

impuissant [ihm-PYOO-ihs-sahnt] weak; powerless.

in- prefix meaning in, into, on, within: *innate, inside;* also meaning not: *incest, intangible, inept.* Usu. with latinate words.

UN- a form of *not,* usu. with English words: *unmasked, untouched, unspeakable.*

IL- a form of *in-* meaning not: *illegitimate;* or meaning the word "in:" *illuminate.*

IM- a form of *in-* meaning not: *immaterial;* or in: *imbue.*

IR- a form of *in-* meaning not: *irresponsible.*

IN Indiana.

inacceptable *Un-* is pref.

inaccessible

inadequate not equal to the need.

inadmissable

inadvertence Pref. to —cy it.

inadvisable Pref. to *un-.*

inalienable [ihn-AEL-yehn-uh-bl, pref. to -AEL-ih-] incapable of being surrendered. In U.S. Declaration of Independence, the word is *unalienable,* an archaic form.

inamorato (m.) lover; (pl.) —tos. (f.) inamorata; (pl.) —as.

inane [ihn-AEN] empty; pointless.

inanimate

inapprehensible

inapt inappropriate; unskilled. See **inept.**

inartistic, unartistic.

inasmuch, inasmuch as, insofar; in-and-out, in-flight or inflight (adj.), in-law or inlaw (n.); in re, in situ.

inasmuch as See **because.**

inaudible

inaugurate [ihn-AW-gyoo-raet] to install; initiate.

incarnadine [ihn-KAHR-nuh-dihn] fleshcolored; by extension, blood red.

incarnation embodiment of a spirit, ideal, in human flesh. *The incarnation of murder.* NOT: *The incarnation of a murderer.*

incase Br. spelling is *en-.*

incessant

inch (abbr.: in.) unit of length = 1,000 mils. = 2.54 centimeters = 1/12 foot = 1/36 yard.

inch worm, inch-pound; inch-deep, inch-long (adj.).

inchoate [ihn-KOH-iht; -aet] (adj.) just begun; incomplete, elementary. NOT related to chaos.

in.-lb. (abbr.) inch-pound.

Inc. (abbr.) incorporated.

incident, incidental *Incident* implies a closer and more certain relationship than *incidental. Old age and its incident illnesses . . . The incidental expenses of old age.*

inclose Use *en-* except for legal purposes.

include Refers to a part of the contents.

COMPOSE, COMPRISE Refer to the whole contents.

incombustible

incommensurable having no common measure; of a ratio not expressed in whole numbers.

incommunicative refusing or not inclined to talk; reserved. Also *uncommunicative.*

incomparable [ihn-KAHM-puh-ruh-bl] peerless.

incompatible not harmonious.

incompetence In legal use, often spelled —cy.

incomplete But *uncompleted.*

incomprehensible

inconceivable

inconsolable Pref. to *un-*.

incontrollable *Un-* is pref.

incontrovertible

incorporate (v.); —rable (adj.).

incorrigible

incorruptible

incredible beyond belief. See **strong opinion words.**

INCREDULOUS skeptical. *The reporter was incredulous; he could not believe such an incredible story.*

incredulity [ihn-crehd-DYOOL-ih-tih].

incriminate [ihn-KRIHM-uh-naet].

incrust (v.); —station (n.). Br. encrust, incrustation.

incubus evil spirit which lies upon a sleeper; nightmare; a burden. (pl.) —bi or —buses. See **obsession.**

inculcate [ihn-KUHL-kaet] to teach by repetition. See **imbue.**

IMPRESS to leave an impression on the mind.

incunabula [ihn-kyoo-NAHB-yoo-luh] infancy, beginnings; also, books printed before 1500 A.D.

incur —rred, —rring.

Ind. (abbr.) Indiana, India; lowercase stands for *independent.*

IND (abbr.) Independent Subway System, N.Y.C.

indecorous [ihn-DEHK-oh-ruhs].

indefatigable [ihn-dee-FAT-ih-guh-b'l].

indefensible

INDEFINITE PRONOUNS pronouns which do not specify a person: *anyone, each, either, everyone, none, someone.*

When used to modify a noun they are indefinite adjectives. All except *neither* and *none* take a singular verb when followed by *of* plus a plural noun. *Everyone of them is guilty.* A plural verb is also acceptable, but a plural pronoun then must follow. *Each of the women were in favor, and they so voted.* See *GENERAL REFERENCE.*

indenture Deed between two or more persons in which each assumes specific obligations.

indescribable

indestructible

index (pl.) indexes. Scientific, *indices.*

India Central Asian nation, ancient empire, later under British rule. Independent, 1948. Cap.: New Delhi. Native: Indian. Currency: rupee. See **Hindu.**

India ink, india paper, india rubber.

Indian Current usage pref. Native American.

Collectives: Shawnee Tribe, the tribe; Easter (or Lower) Band of Cherokee, the band; Five Civilized Tribes, the tribes; the Six Nations (Iroquois Confederacy).

Indian summer mild weather in October or November.

Indiana U.S. state. Abbr.: IN. Cap.:

Indianapolis. Native: Indianian. Nickname: Hoosier.

indicate. When followed by an explanatory clause, use *that. He indicated that he would go.*

indict [ihn-DIET] (v.) to accuse. *After the grand jury indicted him for larceny, he engaged an attorney.* (adj.) —able. (n.) —ment.

CONVICT (v.) to find guilty of an accusation.

INDITE (v.) to compose or put into writing. *He was told to indite the resolution.*

indifferent to not interested in.

indigestible

indigo (pl.) —os. indigo-blue (adj.).

INDIRECT OBJECT noun which receives the action of a verb only indirectly, usu., but not always after a preposition. *He threw the ball to* (indirect object:) *me.*

Verbs like *give, pay, send,* and *write* take an indirect object not essential to the meaning of the verb but indicating person or thing affected. *Pay* her *the money. Read* him *the letter.* See **direct object, objective case,** *CASE.*

indirect discourse in writing, reporting what was said without direct quotation. *The senator argued against more defense spending. She began to cry and plead for him to stay.*

indiscernible [IHN-dih-ZUHR-nih-bl] imperceptible.

indiscreet lacking discretion.

indiscriminate without restraint. See **undiscriminating.**

indispensible See **essential.**

indisposed unfit.

UNDISPOSED not disposed of.

indisputable [ihn-dihs-PYOO-tuh-bl].

indissoluble not capable of being dissolved or annulled. (adv.) indissolubly. See **soluble.**

individual Use only for contrast with a group. *The sole individual opposed to the measure . . .* NOT: *Any individual* (anyone) *can win.* See **special.**

indivisable

Indochina Formerly French Indochina, is now independent Cambodia, Laos, and Vietnam. More generally, the term can include Thailand, Burma, Malaysia, etc.

Indonesia island nation in SW Pacific. Former Dutch colony, independent, 1949. Cap.: Djakarta [juh-KAHRT-uh]. Native: Indonesian. Currency: rupiah.

indubitable [ihn-DYOO-bih-tuh-b'l] (adj.) too evident to doubt. (adv.) —bly.

induction drawing a generalization from known cases.

DEDUCTION drawing a conclusion from general principles.

indurate [IHN-dyoo-rht] hardened.

industrywide

ineffaceable Pref. to **un-.**

ineffective —fectual. See **effective.**

ineligible

inept not fit; inappropriate; absurd.

INAPT unskilled; not suitable.

inequity unfairness.

INIQUITY sin.

inertia, inertial

inescapable Also spelled *un-.*

inessential Usually spelled *un-.*

inestimable NOT *un-,* except in Br. use.

inexhaustible

inexlicable [ihn-EHKS-plih-kuh-b'l].

inexpressible

infallible

infamous [IHN-fuh-muhs] Notoriously evil.

infant In general usage, under 1 year.

BABY Generally under 6.

CHILD Generally under 12; in law, legitimate offspring.

infanta [een-FAHN-tah] daughter or

daughter-in-law of king of Spain or Portugal.

infantile See **childish.**

infeasible

infer (v.) to deduce. (p.) —rred, (adj.) —erible, (n.) —erence. See **imply.**

inferno (pl.) —os.

infidel an unbeliever, especially by Muslims of Christians or Jews, and by Christians of Muslims. In modern usage, one who believes in no God. See **gentile.**

> HEATHEN especially one ignorant of Christianity. Suggests adherence to idolatry.

> PAGAN especially one who ignores Biblical ethics. Now one who is not Christian, Mohamedan, or Jew.

INFINITIVE form of a verb taking the auxiliary *to: to see, to bake, to divorce.*

Infinitives function like a noun but at the same time perform verbal functions, taking an object and verb modifiers. *My goal was to take her home. To go boldly where no one has gone before.*

Infinitives have two tense forms, present and perfect, and have no subject when standing alone as an infinitive: *To see, to have seen.*

See *SPLIT INFINITIVES.*

inflection in pronunciation, accent or stress. In grammar, changes in a word to make it conform in person, number, tense.

inflexible

inflict *He inflicted himself upon them . .*

> AFFLICT *My attempts at playing guitar afflicted them. They were afflicted with a contagious disease.*

inform (v.) to communicate. See also **advise.**

informer, informant An informer gives information against another; an informant merely provides information.

infrared wave lengths longer than visible light but shorter than radio waves.

infringe (v.) to damage, weaken, violate. Common use allows combination with *on, upon.* (adj.) —able, —ging.

> IMPINGE (v.) to strike sharply, encroach: *impinge upon, on.* (n.) impingement.

—ing Both the gerund (noun form of a verb) and the participle are usually formed by adding —*ing. Racing* (gerund) *was his hobby. The racing* (participle) *group . . .*

AVOID using a modifying pronoun unless necessary. *He was certain of being elected.* NOT: *of his being elected.*

ingenious [ihn-JEEN-yuhs] resourceful, showing ingenuity: *an ingenious invention.*

> INGENUE [ahn-zhae-NYOO] a naive girl, or the actress playing such a part. (pl.) —ues.

INGENUOUS [ihn-JEHN-yoo-uhs] artless, free from dissimulation: *an ingenuous young lady.*

ingrained

ingratiate [ihn-GRAE-shih-aet] to bring oneself into the favor of another. In the reflexive used with *with*. *I tried to ingratiate myself with my superiors.*

inherent [ihn-HEER-'nt] (adj.) firmly fixed by nature. (v.) inhere. (n.) inherence, —cy, (pl.) —cies (especially for an attribute).

inhibition [ihn-hih-BIHSH-'n].

inimitable

initiate (v.); —iator (n.).

initiative (n.) the first step, or the ability to take it. *He took the initiative in denouncing the program.*

injustice

in lieu of *In place of* or *instead of* are pref.

innocuous [ih-NAHK-yoo-uhs] (adj.) harmless. (adv.) —ly, (n.) —ness.

innuendo (pl.) —oes.

—ino combining form, from Spanish, used to form noun of adjective: *albino, bambino.*

inoculate

in order that Follow with *may* or *might, shall* or *should. In order that he*

might be able to rest comfortably . . .

input (v. or n.) *Let's input this file. I didn't have any input on that decision.* Colloq., but widely used. See **output.**

inquietude uneasiness.

inquire. (v.) Pref. to *en-.* (n.) inquiry [ihn-KWIER-ee; IHN-kwih-rih].

Inquisition, Spanish the Inquisition. Catholic tribunal est. late 15th C., noted for torture and executions, in search of Jews, witches, Muslims. Hence, any punishing and unfair questioning.

in re (Lat.) in the matter of; concerning.

in rem (Lat.) a thing. In law, an action *in rem* is against a property rather than against a person.

insanitary See **unsanitary.**

insatiable [ihn-SAE-shih-b'l] hungry or needy in the extreme; incapable of being satisfied.

insidious full of plots; intended to entrap; sly.

INVIDIOUS tending to create envy, ill will.

insensible

insignia Pl. of insigne; nearly always used.

insofar as

insoluble cannot be dissolved; or cannot be solved.

INSOLVABLE, UNSOLVABLE Pref. for "cannot be solved."

insomuch (adv.) AVOID.

insouciance [ihn-SOO-see-anss] indifference.

inspire inspire ambition in; inspire a person with ambition.

install —ed, —ing; (n.) —ment, installation.

installment plan Br. hire purchase plan.

instill *Into* should follow. *He inspires hope. He instills hope into every man.* —lled, —lling. See **imbue.**

institute Cap. if part of name; cap. standing alone if referring to government or international organization: National Cancer Institute, the Cancer Institute, the institute; National Institute of Health; the Institute of International Law, the Institute; Woman's Institute, the institute.

institution Cap. if part of name; cap. standing alone if referring to federal unit: Carnegie Institution, the institution; Smithsonian Institution, the Institution.

instructor in a college or university. ADDRESS: Gerald Fitzgerald, Ph.D., English Department, Boston University, or Dr. Gerald Fitzgerald, English Department, Boston University.

If the instructor does not hold a doctorate: Mr. Robert B. Cadugan,

Department of Physics, Rutgers University.

SALUTATION: Dear Sir, Dear Dr. Fitzgerald, Dear Professor Fitzgerald, Dear Mr. Cadugen.

insubstantial *un-* is pref.

insufficient (adj.) Should qualify a quality, quantity, or amount. *There were an insufficient number of people.* NOT: *There were insufficient people present.*

insular [IHN-suh-luhr] of or like an island; isolated.

insulin [IHN-suh-lihn].

insupportable Pref. to *un-*.

insuppressible

insure Against a loss.

ENSURE to make certain.

ASSURE to convince; give confidence to.

insusceptible NOT *un-*

integer a whole number: *3, 66, 421.*

INTEGRAL [IHN-teh-gruhl] of an integer; also, whole, complete; essential.

integrate (v.); —tion (n.).

integrity [ihn-TEHG-rih-tee] quality of being complete; soundness; honesty.

intelligent having a high mental capacity.

INTELLECTUAL [ihn-t'l-EHKchoo-uhl] relating to a high degree of knowledge and understanding.

intelligentsia [ihn-tehl-uh-JEHNT-see-uh] (It.) the intellectual class. In former U.S.S.R., —siya [ihn-tehl-ih-GEHNT-tsihuh] the professional and highly educated classes.

intelligible capable of being understood.

intense in an extreme degree: *intense sunlight.*

INTENSIVE Applies to concentrated effort for a limited objective. *Intensive farming requires large quantities of fertilizer on a small area.*

INTENSIVES adverbs and auxiliary verbs used to emphasize a verb: *do, too, very, terribly. I do know him.*

INTENSIVE PRONOUNS Himself, herself, myself, yourself, itself are used to emphasize another noun or pronoun. *I, myself, will call the teacher.* See *REFLEXIVE PRONOUNS.*

intentionally See **advisedly.**

inter alia (Lat.) "among other things." *Inter alios,* "other persons."

interceptor

intercoastal waterway See **waterway.**

interdepartmental

INTERJECTION In grammar, an ejaculatory word: *O, Oh, lo, say, ah.* Set off with commas or follow with an exclamation point.

interment burial.

INTERNMENT detention.

intermittent going on and off.

intern graduate medical student in a hospital; also, detained alien.

international banks (See **bank**); international date line, international law, international Morse code (See **code**); International Geophysical Year (See **year**).

International Court of Justice See **court.**

International Ladies' Garment Workers' Union. Abbr.: I.L.G.W.U.

internecine [ihn-tehr-NEE-sihn, -sien] mutually destructive; deadly within small group. NOT intramural, intertribal, internal.

interpolate [ihn-TUHR-pohl-aet] (v.) change a text by adding new material; insert between other things (n.) —ation.

interpretive Pref. to *interpretative.*

interruptible

interstate between states.

INTRASTATE within a state.

Interstate Commerce Commission. abbr.: I.C.C.

interstice [ihn-TUHR-stihs] space between close things; a crevice. (pl.) —ces. [stihseez].

intestate [ihn-TEHS-taet] without a will. *He died intestate.*

in the amount of *For* is pref.

in the course of Use *during* or *when.*

in the event that *If* is pref.

intimacy

intimidate (v.); —dation, —dator (n.).

in to Can indicate joining. *She came in to the club . . ., the family . . ., play. The suspect turned himself in to the police.*

INTO Indicates motion, coming from outside *She came into the room, theater, house.*

in toto entirely. NOT "on the whole." Usually in negative sense. *She rejected the plan in toto.*

Intracoastal Waterway, the waterway. See **waterway.**

intractable not easily governed.

intransigent (n. and adj.) refusing compromise. See **recalcitrant.**

INTRANSITIVE VERBS Verbs that do not take a direct object. *Go in peace. She walked for miles.* See *TRANSITIVE VERBS, VERBS.*

intrastate See **interstate.**

intrigue [ihn-TREEG] (v.) to cheat; entangle; (n.) puzzle; plot.

introduction See **preface.**

intrude to thrust in, or force in or upon.

OBTRUDE to thrust out; expel.

inure [ihn-YOOR] (v.) to accustom; accept something undesirable.

invaluable priceless; of value beyond counting. AVOID use for *valuable.*

UNVALUABLE of no value.

UNVALUED not greatly wanted; also, not yet appraised.

inveigh (against) [ihn-VAE] (v.) to dispute (with words); rail bitterly.

INVECTIVE (n.) violent denunciation.

inveigle [ihn-VEE-g'l; in-VAE-g'l] (v.) to lead astray by deceit.

invincible

invited guest Redundant except in contrast to paying guest.

invoice formal bill giving quantity, prices, shipping charges.

inward See **backward.**

ion [EI-uhn] electrically charged atom. See **electrolyte.**

Ionesco, Eugène [ie-ohn-EHS-koh, ee-] (b. 1912) French-Romanian playwright.

Ionic [ie-AHN-ihk] style of architecture, derived from classical Greek.

ion propulsion use of recoil from ejection of high-velocity charged particles as a propellant, especially in space.

IOU (abbr., usu. no periods) I owe you.

Iowa U.S. state. abbr.: IA. Cap.: Des Moines. Native: Iowan.

ipse dixit (Lat.) "so he says." An individual's unsupported testimony.

I.Q. (abbr.) intelligent quotient. A measure of aptitude (usually verbal and numerical) based on a comparison with normal mental age (= 100), but always quoted plus or minus 10. A boy of 120 months with a mental age (M.A.) of 144 months has an I.Q. of 120, plus or minus 10.

Iran [ie-RAN] Middle Eastern nation, formerly Persia. Cap.: Teheran (Tehran). Native: Iranian. Currency: rials.

Iraq [ie-RAK] Middle Eastern nation, formerly Mesopotamia and Persia. Cap.: Baghdad. Natives: Iraqui(s). Currency: dinars.

irascible [ei-RAS-ihbl; ih-] prone to anger.

Ireland island nation just W of England. Formerly Br.; independent, 1922. Cap.: Dublin. Native: Irishman, Irish. Currency: pound. See **Eire.**

iridescent having a rainbowlike play of colors.

Iron Curtain, the curtain. Eastern Europe, and former Soviet Union, 1945–1990. From speech by Winston Churchill, 1946.

Iroquois [IHR-uh-kwoi] Originally Five Nations of Indians, comprising Mohawk, Oneida, Onondaga, Cayuga, and Seneca (1772). Later expanded.

irreconcilable [ihr-EHK-ahn-SIEL-un-b'l].

irredeemable

irreducible

irrefutable [ihr-REHF-yoo-tuh-b'l; ihr-ree-FYOOT-uh-b'l] cannot be proven false.

irregardless Incorrect. Do not use. Instead use *regardless.*

IRREGULAR VERBS There are 227 irregular verbs in English, most of them noted in this text.

Regular verbs form the past tense and past participle by adding *-ed,* the present participle by adding *-ing.* See ***VERBS.***

irrelevance (n.) Pref. to —cy.

irremediable [ihr-ruh-MEED-ee-uh-b'l] incurable.

irremissible unpardonable, inescapable.

irremovable may not be removed.

irreparable [ihr-REHP-uhr-a-b'l].

irrepressible

irresistible

irrespective of without regard to.

irresponsible

irreversible

irrigation district See **district, project.**

irruption See **eruption.**

I.R.S. (abbr.) Internal Revenue Service.

I.R.T. (abbr.) Interborough Rapid Transit, N.Y.C.

is, are *Two times three is* (or *are*) *six. What is wanted are two horses. (Two horses is the subject.) One and one are two. His goods, his money, and his reputation are at stake.* See *NUMBER.*

Isaiah [ei-ZAE-ah] Old Testament book and prophet.

—ise See **—ize.**

—ism suffix meaning an act, state, process or doctrine: *Hinduism, Marxism, realism, spiritualism.*

　　—ITY suffix meaning the quality of being: *reality, spirituality.*

Ishmael [IHSH-mae-uhl] in the Old Testament, outcast son of Abraham; hence, any wanderer or social outcast. In Islam, founder of the race of Muhammed.

Islam the Moslem religion, founded by Mohammed in 7th C. Rooted in uncompromising monotheism: ("There is no god but Allah") and strict adherence to religious practices. Also, the population or geo-graphic area which embraces this belief. See **Allah, Mohammedan, Moslem.**

is of the opinion that *Believes* is pref.

isolate [EI-soh-laet].

isosceles [ie-SAHS-eh-leez] a triangle with two equal sides.

isotope form of an element distinguished by atomic weight and different radioactive transformations.

　　ISOTROPE (adj.) having the same properties in all directions.

　　ISOTYPE (n.) in statistics, graphic presentation in which a figure represents a unit quantity, other quantities being represented by additional figures or fractions of figures.

Israel [IHZ-rae-ehl; IHZ-rih-ehl]. nation on E Mediterranean coast. Native: Israeli. Ancient kingdom; under British rule 1917–48. Established as free Jewish state 1948. Cap.: Jerusalem. Currency: shekel. Native born Jewish Israeli, Sabra. See **Jew, Palestine.**

Issas See Afars and Issacs.

issued, issuing, issueless.

Istanbul [ihs-tan-BOOL] Turkish city on strait between Black Sea and the Mediterranean. Formerly Constantinople, Byzantium. See **Byzantine.**

isthmus [IHS- or IHSTH-muhs] (pl.) —uses.

it (pronoun) Used to refer to things without gender and as an indefinite pronoun.

it . . . it. Avoid use of both expletive and personal pronoun in the same sentence. NOT: *It is their idea that it should be done.*

ITALICS the form of a typeface approximating handwriting. Used in printing for differentiation of material, emphasis, foreign words, formulas, scientific names, vessels, the title of a book (if not in quotation marks), publication, or law case, and sometimes for the name of a fictitious character.
Also the words *Resolved, Resolved further, Provided, ordered*, etc., and letters used as symbols, but NOT for chemical elements.

Italy nation in S Europe. Center of Roman Empire; unified as republic, 1870. Cap.: Rome. Native: Italian. Currency: lira.

I-T-E Circuit Breaker From inverse time element.

itinerary [ei-TIHN-uhr-ehr-ee] outline of a route.

its possessive of *it.*

it's contraction for *it is.*

itself See **intensives**, *REFLEXIVE PRONOUN.*

I.T.U. (abbr.) International Telecommunications Union

Ivory Coast nation in NW Africa on Atlantic coast. Formerly Fr.; independent, 1960. Cap.: Abidjan. Natives: Ivoriens. Currency: CFA franc.

Ivy League Harvard, Princeton, Yale, Dartmouth, Columbia, Cornell, Brown, and University of Pennsylvania.

Iwo Jima [EE-woh JEE-mah] island in SW Pacific, site of 1945 W.W. II battle.

—ize American English prefers this spelling to —ise, except words ending in *—mise: chemise, surmise.*

Izvestiya [ihz-VEH-stee-yah] U.S.S.R. newspaper.

J

J-bolt

jabot [zhah-BOH] lace decoration on clothing.

jackanapes [JAK-uh-naeps] a monkey; also, a conceited, impudent person.

jack-in-the-box, jack-in-the-pulpit, jack-of-all-trades, jack-o'-lantern.

Jacobean [jak-uh-BEE-uhn] of James I of England, or his era.

Jacques [zhahk]; character in *As You Like It* [JAE-kweez].

jaguar [JAG-wahr].

jai alai [HIE (ah)-LIE] court game resembling squash, played between teams of two.

Jakarta [juh-KAHR-tah] Also Djakarta. Capital city of Indonesia on Java Island, formerly Batavia.

jalopy

jamb (n.) upright piece forming the side of a door, etc.

Jamaica island nation in West Indies. Formerly Br.; independent, 1962. Cap.: Kingston. Native: Jamaican. Currency: dollar.

James, St. James's, Court of St. James's; St. James's Palace; King James Version of the Bible.

Japan island nation in W Pacific. Es-tablished since 12th C. Cap.: Tokyo [TOHK-yoh]. Native: Japanese. Currency: yen. See **Nippon.**

jasmine [JAZ-mihn].

jato (abbr.) jet-assisted takeoff.

jaywalker

jealous of Or use . . . *about.*

Jeanne d' Arc [zhahn DAHRK] (1412–1431) Fr. saint and heroine. Joan of Arc, the Maid of Orleans.

Jehovah [jeh-HOH-vuh], Jehovah's Witnesses.

jejune [jee-JOON] meagre, uninteresting.

jellybean

jeopardy (n.); (v.) —dize.

jerry-built constructed only for temporary use.

Jesuit [JEHZ-yoo-iht].

jetsam See **flotsam.**

Jew descendant of the tribe of Judah, or one whose religion is Judaism. (adj.) Jewish. *Hebrew, Hebraic* is usually used of the ancient people and their language. See **Hebrew.**

ISRAELI citizen of Israel. Sabra, native-born Israeli; Israelite, inhabitant of ancient Israel. Semite, one of the Semitic races. See **Israel.**

jewel [JOO-ehl; JYOO-ehl] —led, —ling, —ler, —ry.

jew's harp musical instrument played with mouth.

Jg. (abbr.) junior grade.

jibe [jieb] to agree; (nautical) to shift. Pref. to *gibe*.

jihad [zhih-HAHD] Muslim holy war.

Jim Crow Pertains to discrimination against African-Americans, from stereotype of Negro in 1860 play by Thomas D. Rice. *Jim Crow law, car,* etc.

jingoism [JIHNG-goh-ihzm] bellicose, chauvinistic policy in foreign affairs. (adj.) jingoist.

jinn Pl. of *jinni,* or *djinni.* See (adj.) **genie.**

job lot mixed assortment of merchandise, usually offered at a price concession.

jiujitsu See **judo.**

Joan of Arc See **Jeanne D'Arc.**

Johannesberg [joh-HAN-nihs-buhrg] city in South Africa.

John XXII (Angelo Giuseppe Ronacalli) (1881–1963) Pope, 1958–1963; oversaw major changes in Catholic dogma.

Johns Hopkins University [jahnz HAHP-kihns] university in Baltimore. NOT *John Hopkins.*

joint account (abbr.: J/A) account in the name of more than one person, any of whom may claim benefit.

Joint Chiefs of Staff, Chiefs of Staff, the joint Chiefs.

Joint Committee on Atomic Energy See **committee.**

Joliet [JOH-lee-eht] city and state prison in Illinois.

Jordan Middle Eastern nation. Under British rule, 1920–1946. Cap.: Amman [ah-MAHN]. Native: Jordanian(s). Currency: dinar.

joule (abbr. J-.) (joul). energy unit in the MKS system = the energy needed to exert a force of 1 newton over a distance of 1 metu approx. 3/4 ft. lb. = 10^7 ergs

journalese hasty, formulaic newspaper writing.

journey prolonged travel. (pl.) —eys.

journeyman, —work.

Jr. (abbr.) junior. James Smith, Jr. is distinguished from his father James Smith, Sr. Do not use without a first name or initial. No feminine equivalent to Jr. exists.

jubilation [JOO-bih-lae-shun] rejoicing.

Judaism [JOO-dae-ihz'm] See **Jew, Hebrew.**

Judea, Judaea [joo-DEE-uh] ancient region of South Israel, at times under

Persian, Greek, and Roman rule. (adj.) Judaean.

Judge title of a member of the judiciary.

> JUSTICE used in place of *judge* for Justice of the United States (Supreme Court); in New York State, for Justice of the Supreme Court, Justice of the Appellate Division, Justice of the Peace.

Distinction is based on ancient concept of difference between courts of law and courts of equity.

judge advocate (pl.) advocates.

Judge of a Federal District Court ADDRESS: The Honorable John Clark Knox, U.S. District Judge, Southern District of New York.
SALUTATION: Sir; Dear Sir; Dear Judge Knox.

judgment Pref. to *judgement*.

judicial of a court or judge.

> JUDICIOUS exhibiting good judgment.

> JUDICIARY [joo-DIHSH-ih-ehr-ee] a body of judges.

judo [JOO-doh] a martial art. Also jiujitsu [joo-JIHT-soo].

jukebox

jumbo Pl. -os.

junior not Junior or Jr., the appelation. See **freshman.**

junk bonds in finance, any bond or instrument which offers a potential

high rate of return at high risk of short-term cash loss. Often associated with shady dealings.

junk mail unsolicited 3rd class mail, esp. addressed to *Occupant* or some other unspecified receiver.

junto [JUHN-toh] group set up for political purpose.

> JUNTA [HUHN-tah] ruling council, esp. military.

juror member of a jury.

jury-fixing (adj. or n.), jury box.

just Avoid repetition. Avoid *just exactly.* See **exactly.**

just as precisely as, in the same way as. NOT: *He was graduated just as his classmates were.*

Justice Associate of the Supreme Court. ADDRESS: The Honorable William O. Douglas, Associate Justice of the Supreme Court, Washington, D.C.; or, Mr. William O. Douglas, Associate Justice, etc.
SALUTATION: Sir; Mr. Justice; Your Honor; Dear Justice Douglas.
Chief Justice of the Supreme Court. ADDRESS: The Chief Justice, The Supreme Court, Washington, D.C.; or, The Honorable William Rehnquist, U.S. Supreme Court, etc.
SALUTATION: Sir; Mr. Chief Justice; Dear Mr. Chief Justice.

juvenile [JYOO-veh-nihl].

juxta- prefix meaning near: *juxtaposition, juxta-articular.*

K

K. (abbr.) Kelvin. Known as "absolute temperature," international standard temperature. Freezing point of water (O°C, 32°F) is 273.15 kelvin. See **temperature.**

k. (abbr.) kilo = one thousand; knot.

K-ration, K-term.

kaddish [KAH-dihsh] Jewish prayer for the dead.

Kafka, Franz [KAHF-kah, frahnz] (1883–1924) novelist and short-story writer. ("The Metamorphosis," *The Trial*) Native Czech Jew, wrote in German.

Kahlo, Frida [KAH-loh, FREE-dah] (c. 1907–1954) Mexican symbolist painter; wife of **Diego Rivera.**

kaleidoscope [kuh-LIE-duh-skohp] instrument of loose colored glass and mirrors which creates variety of patterns; hence, any changing scene.

Kalif Use *Caliph.*

Kalinin, Mikhail [kah-LEE-neen, mee-KIEy] (1875–1946) Soviet Russian statesman. City, Kalinin, in W central Common Wealth of Independent States on Volga River; formerly Tver.

kamikaze [kahm-ih-KAH-zee] Japanese suicide planes used in W.W. II.

kangaroo court an unauthorized court, usually created to circumvent normal justice.

Kansas U.S. state. Abbr.: KS. Cap.: Topeka. Native: Kansan.

Kansas City, MO (also KS) Pl. Kansas Citys.

Kant, Immanuel [kahnt, ih-MAH-noo-ihl] (1724–1804) Ger. philosopher. (adj.) Kantian, (n.) —ianism.

kapok [KAE-pahk] seed fiber of silk tree.

karat See **carat.**

Kathmandu [KAT-man-doo] Also **Katmandu.** Cap. of Nepal.

Kazakhstan [kah-ZAHK-stahn] republic in former U.S.S.R.. (SEE); part of **Commonwealth of Independent States** (SEE). In central Asia, bordering China. Cap.: Alma-Ata [AL-muh uh-TAH]. Native: Kazakh(s).

kc. (abbr.) kilocycle.

keen, keenness, keenly, keener.

keep (p. and p.p.) kept; keepsake, keepworthy.

keg, nail unit of weight = 100 lbs. = 45.359 kg.

kelpie or **kelpy** water sprite, usually in shape of horse.

kelvin. See **K.** A temperature scale.

Kemal, Atatürk, Mustafa [kee-MAHL-A-TA-tuhrk] Original name

Mustafa [moo-STAH-fah] Demal (1881-1938). Turkish soldier, statesman, founder of present Turkish republic.

kempt Rare p.p. of *kemp*, to comb. Opposite of *unkempt*.

kennel —led, —lled.

Kentucky U.S. state. Abbr.: KY. Cap.: Frankfort. Native: Kentuckian.

Kenya [KEHN-yuh; KEEN-yuh] nation in E Africa on Indian Ocean. Formerly Br.; independent, 1963. Cap.: Nairobi [nie-ROH-bee]. Native: Kenyan. Currency: shilling.

Kenyatta, Joma [JOH-moh] (c.1891–1978) African revolutionary and statesman. First president of independent Kenya, 1964–1978.

kerneled —ing.

ketch See **boats.**

ketchup See **catsup.** Both spellings are accepted.

kettledrum, —drummer, —stitch.

Kev. (abbr.) kilo-electron volts.

key —eyd, —ing.

Keystone State nickname for Pennsylvania.

kg. (abbr.) kilogram.

KGB Soviet secret police. See **MVD.**

Khaddafy, Muammar See **Quaddafi.**

khaki [KAK-ee; KAH-kee].

Khartoum [kahr-TOOM] Pref. to *Khartum.* Cap. of Sudan.

Khmer [KEH-mehr] aboriginal people of Cambodia. (pl.) Khmers.

KHMER ROUGE Marxist Cambodian regime, 1975–1979, known for mass murder. See **Pol Pot,** the **Killing Fields.**

Khrushchev, Nikita Sergeyevitch [KROOSH-chawf, nuh-KEET-uh] (1894–1971) Soviet premier, Communist leader 1954–1963.

kibbutz Israeli communal agricultural settlement.

kidnap —ped, —ping; —per (n.).

Kierkegaard, Søren [KEE-ihr-kih-gahrd, SAW-rihn] (1813–1855) Danish existentialist philosopher.

Kiev [kee-EHF] city on the Dnieper River, Ukraine.

the Killing Fields General term for Cambodian concentration camps under **Khmer Rouge.** Oscar-winning film, 1984.

kilo- [KEEL-oh] metric system prefix meaning multiplied by 1000: kilogram, -meter, -volt, -ampere, kilowatt-hour. *Kilo* colloq. shortened form of *kilogram* or *kiloliter.*

kilocycle [KIHL-oh-SIE-kl] (abbr.: kc) 1000 cycles, especially in radio.

kilogram [KIHL-oh-gram] (abbr.: kg.) (colloq.: *kilo*) unit of weight =

2.2046 avoirdupois lb. = 2.6792 apothecaries lb. = 1000 grams.

kiloliter [KIHL-oh-lee-tehr] (abbr.: kl.) (colloq.: *kilo*) unit of (1) capacity = 28.378 bu. = 264.18 gal. = 10001; (2) volume = 1.308 cu. yd. = 35.315 cu. ft.

kilometer [KIHL-oh-mee-tehr]; kih-LOHM-eh-tehr] (abbr.: km.) unit of length = 0.621370 miles = approx. 5/8 mi. = 1093.611 yds. = 3280 ft., 10 in. = 1000 m.

kilostere unit of volume = 1308 cu. yds. = 1000 m^3. = 1000 steres.

kiloton measure of explosive power = 1000 tons of TNT.

kilowatt-hour unit of measure = 1000 watts used per hour.

kimono [kuh-MOH-nuh] (pl.) —os. (adj.) —ed.

kin relatives, collectively. *Kith* is archaic.

kindheart, —hearted.

kind *Of what kind are these oranges? This kind of apple. These kinds of apples.*

kind of class or variety of. Use as *somewhat* is colloq.: *kind of sloppy; kind of a drag.*

kindergarten

kindly Avoid use for *please.* NOT: *Kindly give me some peaches.*

kindred [KIHN-drihd] relationship; relations.

King (or any member of the Royal Family) ADDRESS: To His Royal Highness George; or The King's Most Excellent Majesty; or His Most Gracious Majesty, King George. SALUTATION: Your Royal Highness, Sir.

kingly of or worthy of a king.

REGAL of the office or majesty of a king or queen: *regal bearing.*

ROYAL of the person of a king, queen, or crown.

SOVEREIGN of highest power.

kinfolk, —man, —people, —woman. Pref. to kinsfolk.

Kinshasa [kihn-SHAH-suh] formerly Leopoldville, cap. of **Zaire.**

kiosk [KEE-ahsk] outdoor newsstand.

Kirghizia [kihr-GEE-zhee-uh] republic in former **U.S.S.R.**; now part of **Commonwealth of Independent States.** In SE central Asia, bordering Pakistan and China. Cap.: Frunze [FROON-zuh]. Native: Kirghizi(s).

Kiribati [kih-rih-BAH-tee] island nation in middle Pacific. Formerly Br.; independent, 1971. Separated from neighboring **Tuvalu,** 1978. Cap.: Tarawa. Native: Kiribati. Currency: Australian dollar.

kiss-off (n. and adj.).

kitchenmaid, —man, —ware, —wife, —work.

kl. (abbr.) kiloliter.

Klansman, —woman.

Klee, Paul [klae] (1879–1940) Swiss modern painter.

km. (abbr.) kilometer. km.^{2}: square km. km.^{3}: cubic km.

knapsack, —sacked, —sacking.

knee-jerk reflex

kneel (p. and p.p.) knelt, kneeled.

knickknack

knife (pl.) knives; (v.) —fed, —fing.

knifeboard, knife edge, knife grinder.

knight-errant (pl.) knights-errant.

knit (p.p.) knit or -tted. The long form is used for individual needle works. BUT: *factory knit goods.*

knock-kneed, knockkneed (adj.).

knoll [nohl].

Knossos, Gnossus [NOH-suhs] city in ancient **Crete.**

knot (abbr.: k.) unit of speed = 1 nautical mile (6080.2 ft.) per hour. *Speed of 30 knots, NOT 30 knots per hour.*

know (p.) knew; (p.p.) known.

know-how, know-it-all, know-nothing (all n. and adj.).

knowledgeable

Kobe [KOH-beh] city in **Japan.**

kohlrabi [KOHL-rah-bee] large-stemmed cabbage.

kopek [KOH-pehk] 1/100th ruble. See **U.S.S.R.**

Koran [koh-RAHN; KAW-rahn] or **Qur'an** Islamic holy book. (adj.) Koranic, koranic.

Korea [kaw-REE-uh] two nations since 1948, on peninsula off NE China. Native: Korean. Divided roughly by 38th parallel.

> NORTH KOREA Cap.: Pyongyang [pyahng-yahng]. Currency: won.

> SOUTH KOREA Cap.: Seoul (soul). Currency: won.

Kosygin, Aleksei Nikolaevich [kuh-SIH-gin, uh-LYEHK-syae-ih] (1904–1980) Premier, U.S.S.R., 1964–1980; shared power with **Leonid Brezhnev.**

kowtow [kou-TOU] Pref. to *kowtow.*

K ration U.S. Army food ration. See **C ration.**

krona Swedish currency. (pl.) kroner.

krone Danish, Norwegian currency. (pl.) kroner.

KS Kansas.

kt. (abbr.) carat, kiloton.

Kublai Khan [koo-blie KAHN] (1216–94) Mongol conqueror, Emperor of China.

Ku Klux Klan [KOO kluhks klan], the Klan.

Kuomintang [kwoh-mihn-TAHNG] Chinese regime prior to Communist Revolution, 1949; still in power in Taiwan. NOT Kuomintang party (redundant); *tang* means party.

Kurosawa, Akira [koo-RAH-souwah, ah-KIH-rah] (b. 1910) Japanese film maker (*Ran*).

Kuwait [koo-WAET] oil-rich nation in NW corner of Persian Gulf. Formerly Br. independent, 1961. Cap.: Kuwait. Native: Kuwaiti(s). Currency: dinar.

kv. (abbr.) kilovolt.

kv.-a. (abbr.) kilovolt-ampere.

kw. (abbr.) kilowatt.

kw.-hr. (abbr.) kilowatt-hour.

KY Kentucky

L

l. (abbr.) liter, line.

L-bar, L-beam, L-block, L-square.

La, la French article preceding a name. See **Le, le.**

LA Louisiana

label —led, —ing.

La Bohème [lah boh-EHM] 1897 opera by Giacomo Puccini.

labor Br. —our. Labor Day, Brit., Labour Party.

laboratory [LAB-ruh-toh-ree] Cap. if part of name: Forest Products Laboratory, the laboratory.

laborious [luh-BAWR-ee-uhs].

labor-saving, labor union.

labyrinthine [lab-uhr-IHN-thihn] (from *labyrinth* [LAB-ih-rihnth]) maze-like.

lacerate [LASS-uhr-aet] to tear; mangle.

lachrymal, lacrimal, lacrymal of tears. (adj.) —matory, —mose.

lackadaisical

lackey (pl.) —eys.

lacquer [LAK-uhr].

lacuna [la-KYOO-nuh] in a manuscript, a gap or missing portion. (pl.) -nae [—nee].

Lady The title *Lady* is held by all peeresses under the rank of duchess, and by daughters of dukes, marquises, and earls, by the wives of knights, baronets, barons, viscounts, marquesses, knights, and lords of session.

REFER TO: (1) A peeress in her own right, or a peer's daughter: *the Countess of Cromartie, Lady Pamela Berry.* Her title does not apply to her husband. If she outranks him, refer to *the Countess of Cromartie and her husband, Col. Edward Walter Blunt Mackenzie.* (2) A widowed or divorced lady as *Nancy Viscountess Astor* or *Anne, Lady Orr Lewis.* For a second reference use *Lady Astor,* NOT *Lady Nancy Astor.* (3) A daughter of an earl, marquess, or duke is *Lady Mary Grosvenor, Lady Mary,* but NOT *Lady Grosvenor.* ADDRESS: *Lady Martha Sperling,* or *Lady Sperling,* or *The Honorable Lady Sperling.* SALUTATION: *Madam, My Lady, Your Ladyship.* See **Nobility, Lord and Lady.**

lady Connotation is sexist, and thus use should be avoided except where a matter of etiquette is involved. *Gentlemen stand behind the ladies' chairs.*

ladybug British use *ladybird.*

L.A.F.T.A. (abbr.) Latin American Free Trade Association. Members: Argentina, Bolivia, Brazil, Chile, Colombia, Ecuador, Mexico, Paraguay, Peru, Uruguay, Venezuela.

La Fontaine, Jean de [de lah fawn-

TEHN, zhahn] (1621–1695) French fable writer.

LaGuardia, Fiorello [lah-GWAHR-dih-ah, fee-aw-REHL-oh] (1882–1947) Colorful New York City mayor, 1934–1945.

laid See **lay.**

laissez faire [LEH-sae FEHR] (Fr.) "let (them) do as they please." In economics, freedom from government interference.

La Jolla [lah HOI-ah] Section of San Diego, CA.

Lake Erie, Lake of the Woods, Salt Lake; the lake.

Lakes, Great See **Great Lakes.**

lamé [lam-AE] fabric with gold or silver threads.

lame duck (n. and adj.) (nonliteral) An elected official serving an unexpired term after a successor has been chosen.

lamentable [LAM-ehn-tuh-bl] (adj.); —tably (adv.).

laminated composed of layers of material (cloth, wood).

lamppost

lamprey (pl.) —eys.

Lancelot [LAHN-seh-laht] in legend, greatest of King Arthur's knights, seducer of Queen Guinevere. Also spelled **Launcelot** [LAW-].

landing craft (abbr.: L.C.C., L.C.M., L.C.S., L.S.T., etc.) military amphibious landing vehicles, used mostly in W.W. II.

language means of communicating thought.

ARGOT [AR-goh] language of thieves and hobos, designed to hide meanings.

CANT stock phraseology of a learned group; thus, pious but thoughtless speech.

COMMERCIALESE typical advertising writing.

DIALECT local language.

GIBBERISH unintelligible language.

GOBBLEDYGOOK nonsense, circumlocution; derogatory for government or legal terminology.

IDIOM characteristic expressions of native speakers.

JARGON hybrid or technical language, difficult to understand: *computer jargon.*

JOURNALESE semi-colloquial, reportorial style.

LINGO foreign languae; word often used in a contemptuous sense.

OFFICIALESE typical government wording.

PARLANCE manner of speaking. Must be associated with a modifier: *nautical parlance.*

PATOIS [PAT-wah] dialect; often a combination of languages.

SLANG popular but unauthorized words or expressions.

VERNACULAR local or native language.

languor [LAN-gger] (n.) laziness; sleepiness. (adj.) languorous [-ruhs].

languid [LAN-gwihd]

languish [LAN-gwihsh]

lanolin [LAN-uh-lihn] wool grease used in ointments.

Laos [LAH-ohs, lous] nation in SE Asia. Formerly Fr.; independent, 1949. Cap.: Vientiane [vee-ehn-TEE-ahn]. Native: Lao, Laotian. Currency: kip.

Lao-tzu [lou tzuh] (6th C. B.C.) Chinese philosopher, founder of **Tao** religion. Also spelled *Lao-tse.*

lapis lazuli [LAP-ihs LAZ-yuh-lih; LAE-pihs—] azure blue stone of silicate and sulphur; its color.

La Rochefoucauld (Francois, Duc de) [lah RAWSH-foo-koh]. (1613–1680) Fr. writer (*Maxims*).

large Denotes extension in several directions and beyond the average. Not so emphatic as big, and more formal: *large size, large-sized, large scale, large-scale, loom large, by and large.* (adj.) —gish. (adv.) —ly.

largess, largesse [LAHR-jehs] liberal giving.

larva (pl.) —vae.

larynx (pl.) larynxes.

lascivious [luh-SIHV-ee-uhs] lewd.

laser device which amplifies light.

lasso [LASS-oh] (pl.) —os.

last Indicates that none follow; not to be confused with *latest.* NOT: *This was the last burglary in the area. The last three* pref. *the three last.* In an enumeration, *lastly.* See **late.**

last-born, last-cited (adj.).

lat. (abbr.) latitude.

late When attached to a name or title, means "dead:" *the late John Lennon, the late President.*

Comparative: *later, latter;* superlative: *latest* or *last.* The comparative form means *nearer the end,* but *latter* is also used in contrast with former. *The latter part of the 19th century. He preferred the former to the latter.*

The superlative form of *latter* is *lattermost.*

Generally, limit the use of *last* to the meaning of *final,* rather than *immediately preceding* or *latest.*

latecomer (n.) —coming (adj.); late-born (adj.)

latent [LAE-tehnt] hidden; not necessarily dormant.

latex [LAE-tehks] rubber (natural or synthetic) particles suspended in water. (pl.) latexes.

lath [lath] wood or metal strip base for plaster, tiles, etc.

lathe [laethe] machine for turning and shaping material.

Latin America comprises all of Western Hemisphere south of Texas. (adj.), Latin American. Colloq., Latino. SEE **American, L.A.F.T.A.**

latitude Figured in equal degrees of 68.703 statute miles north and south of the equator; written: *latitude 49 26'14" N.* abbr.: lat.

latter Refers to the second of two things. Opposite of: *former.* Avoid with more or less than two. See **late.**

LATER coming afterward.

Latvia nation in NE Europe, on Baltic Sea. Independent 1919–1940, then part of **U.S.S.R.** Independent again 1991. Cap.: Riga [REE-guh]. Native: Latvian. Currency: ruble.

Launcelot [LAWN-seh-laht] See **Lancelot.**

laundrymaid, laundry room.

laureate [LAWR-ee-eht] crowned with laurel, a mark of honor; hence, distinguished: *poet laureate.* (v., p.) laureled.

lavaliere [lav-uh-LEER] pendant of jewels on a chain. Also spelled *lavalier.*

Lavoisier, Antoine-Laurent [lah-VWAH-see-eh, an-TWAHN] (1743–1794) Fr. chemist and scientist.

law, Walsh-Healey law; law 176; law No. 176; copyright law; Ohm's law.

lawyer a member of the legal profession.

ATTORNEY one (usually a lawyer) empowered to do business for another. (pl.) —eys.

BARRISTER one who pleads in court.

COUNSEL a legal representative engaged especially for a particular case.

SOLICITOR in Britain, a lawyer permitted to conduct litigation but to plead only in lower courts.

lay, laid, laying a transitive verb: requires a direct object. *Lay the book on the table. I must have laid it somewhere.*

LIE, LAY, LAIN an intransitive verb: cannot take a direct object. *Lie down on the bed. I lay down on the bed. He has lain there for an hour.*

layaway plan method of selling by accepting payments in installments before delivery.

layman, layperson not a professional. Pertaining to the laity, in contrast with the clergy; hence, anyone not a doctor, lawyer, engineer, academic, or member of another specially trained class.

lb. (abbr.) pound. Use for weight only. (pl.) lbs.

lb. ap. (abbr.) pound, apothecary's.

lb. av. (abbr.) pound, avoirdupois.

l.c. (abbr.) lowercase.

Le, le Fr. article preceeding a name. Cap. preceding a name only when not preceded by a first name: *Le Fevre says . . .; Jean le Fevre.* See *FILING,* **La, la.**

lead (p. and p.p.) led.

leaderwork, leader line.

leading question in law, a question which leads a person on. NOT the most important question.

league (1) unit of length = 3 statute miles = 4.82805 km.; (2) marine league = 3 nautical mi. = 3.45 statute mi. = 5.56 km. At various times league has measured 2.4 to 4.6 miles. Square league = 4439 acres = 1796 hectares.

lean-faced, lean-looking (adj.), lean-to (n. and adj.).

leap For p. and p.p., *leaped* is pref. to *leapt.*

leapfrog

leap year a year made up of 366 days. Occurs each 4th year, excluding century years (BUT not 2000). The additional day is February 29th.

learn For p. and p.p., *learned* is pref. to *learnt.* BUT do not confuse with the adj. *learned* [LUHR-nihd].

leasehold

leave (p. and p.p.) left; leaving.

leave AVOID use when meaning "let." *Leave me alone* means "Depart and allow me to be in solitude." *Let me alone* means "Do not disturb me."

leaved Pref. to *-leafed* in *broad-leaved plant.*

leavetaking

Lebanon Middle Eastern nation on Mediterranean. Ancient kingdom, independent since 1920. Cap.: Beirut. Native: Lebanese. Currency: pound.

Lebensraum [LAE-b'nz-roum] (Ger.) living space.

leeward [LYOO-ahrd] opposite of *windward* or *weather.* The side farthest from the point from which the wind blows.

left, leftist, leftwing (adj.) In politics, means favoring social change, liberal, radical. See **Right, rightist, rightwing.**

The designations derive from the seating for the first French governments after the Revolution.

leftmost

left bank Orientation determined when facing downstream.

Left Bank the intellectual and artistic section of Paris.

left-hand *Left-hand drawer, left-handed person.*

left-handed compliment a round-about, ambiguous, clumsy, or possibly insincere compliment.

legate [LEHG-iht] a commissioned deputy; for example, an ambassador.

LEGATEE [lehg-a-TEE] one to whom a bequest is made.

legion American Legion, the Legion, a Legionnaire; French Foreign legion, the legion.

legislative assembly Cap. if part of name: Legislative Assembly of New York, the legislative assembly; the assembly of Puerto Rico, the legislative assembly, the assembly.

legislative branch clerk, session, etc.

Legislator ADDRESS: The Honorable Peter D. Smith, The State Legislature; or The Honorable Peter D. Smith, Member of Legislature, The State Capitol. SALUTATION: Sir; Dear Sir; Dear Mr. Smith.

legislature National Legislature (U.S. Congress), the Legislature; Ohio Legislature, Legislature of Ohio, the legislature.

leisure [LEE-zhoor, LEZH—].

leitmotiv or **leitmotif** [LIET-moh-teef] in music, melodic phrase associated with an idea, person, or situation. In film, a recurring image or style of shot.

Le Monde [leh MAWND] noted Fr. newspaper; translates as "The World."

lend (p. and p.p.) lent; (n.) loan. NOT *Loan me some books.*

lend-lease hyphenated in all forms.

lengthwise Pref. to —ways.

lengthy long, especially of speeches, writings, etc.

leniency Pref. to —ce. (adj.) lenient [LEEN-yehnt].

Lenin, Vladimir Ilyich [LEH-nihn] (1870–1924). Russian revolutionary and statesman. First premier of Communist **U.S.S.R.**, 1917-24. Born Ulyanov. Sometimes listed Nikolai from pen name "N. Lenin," taken from wife's name *Natalya.*

Leningrad [LEN-nihn-grahd] 1924–1991 name for city in N Russia; site of W.W. II seige. 1703–1914, **St. Petersburg,** after Czar Peter the Great; 1914–24, Petrograd. In 1991, a plebiscite restored the name *St. Petersburg.*

lens (pl.) lenses.

Lent 40-day penitence period preceding Easter.

lentissimo, lentando, lentamente, lento. Musical terms describing degrees of slowness.

Leo born July 23–Aug. 22. See **Zodiac.**

lèse-majesté [leez MAJ-ehs-tih] (Fr.) crime against sovereign power.

Lesotho [luh-SOH-toh] kingdom completely surrounded by South Africa. Formerly British Basutoland, independent, 1966. Cap.: Maseru [MAZ-eh-roo]. Native: Basatho. Currency: Maloti.

less, lesser, least; much less, much more.

-less When added to nouns, the suffix means without: *careless, headless.* When added to verbs, it means not able to or not subject to: *tireless, restless.*

let (p. and p.p.) let.

letdown (n. and adj.).

lethargy [LEHTH-ehr-gih], (adj.) lethargic [lehth-AHR-jihk].

letters illustrating shape and form: U-shape (d), A-frame, T-bone, T-rail.

letters, plural a's, b's, c's.

letup (n.) abatement.

leukemia

levee [LEHV-ee] embankment: levee no. 1.

levelheaded, level-line.

lever [LEE-vuhr; LEHV-ehr].

Levi's Can appear without the apostrophe: *Levis.*

lexicon brief dictionary, usu. for words of special use.

L.F. (abbr.) low frequency.

lf. (abbr.) in printing, *lightface.* See **bf. boldface type.** In baseball, indicates *left field.*

liable responsible, obliged; also exposed to risk. *He was liable for his partner's debts.* NOT **libel.**

APT have a tendency to.

LIKELY probable. *It is likely that he will be elected, and he is apt to vote for a liberal program. In such a case, he is liable to lose a great many followers.*

liaison [lee-ae-ZAWN, lee-AE-zn] connecting link; bond.

libel [LIE-b'l] in law, false and malicious defamation published or broadcast. NOT **liable.** See also **slander.**

liberal in politics, progressive, usu. supporting greater freedom and social equality. Opposite of **conservative.**

liberal-minded (adj.); liberal arts.

Liberia [lie-BEER-ih-uh] NW African republic, on Atlantic Ocean, independent since 1847. Cap.: Monrovia. Native: Liberian. Currency: U.S. dollar, native cent.

Liberty Bell, Liberty ship.

Liberty Island, N.Y. Formerly Bedloes Island, site of the Statue of Liberty.

libido [lih-BEE-doh] in psychology, primary creative and sexual energy; the life force. Identified by **Freud.**

Libra born Sept. 23–Oct. 22. See **Zodiac.**

Librarian of Congress, the Librarian.

library Franklin D. Roosevelt Library; the Library of Congress, the Library; Public Library, the library.

libretto [lih-BREHT-oh] (pl.) —etti, or —os [lih-BREHT-tee, —ohs].

Libya [LIHB-ih-uh] nation in N Africa, on Mediterranean. Formerly It., Br., Fr.; independent, 1952. Caps:

Tripoli and Benghazi. Native: Libyan. Currency: dinar.

license Pref. to *—ence.*

lichen [LIE-kehn, -kihn] plant of fungus and alga.

licorice [LIHK-uhr-ihsh].

Lidice [LIHD-ih-see] city in Czechoslovakia obliterated by Nazis in 1942, following assassination of party official.

lie (p.) lay; (p.p.) lain; lying. See *lay.*

LIE to tell a falsehood. (p.) lied; (p.p.) lying.

Liechtenstein [LIHK-tehn-shtien] tiny nation between Switzerland and Austria on the Rhine River. Cap.: Vaduz. Native: Lichtensteiner. Currency: Swiss franc.

lief [leef] (arch.) willingly, freely: *I would as lief; had as lief.*

lien [lee-ehn; leen] in law, a claim against property. See **lean.**

lieu [loo] stead: *in lieu of.*

lieutenant [loo-TEHN-ant; LEHT-eh-nant]; lieutenant colonel, (pl.) —colonels.

Lieutenant Governor of Idaho etc.; the Lieutenant Governor; lieutenant governorship.

Lieutenant Governor of a State ADDRESS: The Lieutenant Governor, State of New York; or The Honorable Malcolm Wilson, Lieutenant Governor of New York. SALUTA-

TION: Sir; Dear Sir; Dear Mr. Wilson.

life-belt, lifebelt, lifesaving, lifetime, life-size, life-sized (adj.); life everlasting, life mask, life net, life rate (n.).

lifestyle Current usage allows one word. As a noun: *He embodies the rock-'n'roll lifestyle.* As adj.: *These are lifestyle questions.* AVOID as clumsy substitute for *life.*

L.I.F.O. (abbr.) Last in, first out: inventory system. See F.I.F.O.

lift Br. word for elevator.

lift-off (n. and adj.).

ligature [LIHG-uh-tchehr] a binding; two or more letters printed together: *ae, fl.*

light (p. and p.p.) lighted or lit.

lightborne, —face (printing), —house, —weight (n. and adj.), —wood (all one word); light-clad, light-colored, light-footed, light-producing, light-struck (all adj.), light-year; light buoy.

lighter-than-air

light station Cap. if part of name: Watch Hill Light Station, the light station, the station.

light year unit of measure = distance light travels in 1 yr. = 6 trillion miles.

ligne unit of measure for the diameter of a watch movement = 2.2559 millimeters = approx. 1/11 inch.

likeable

likewise, like-looking (adj.), like-minded (adj.).

-like childlike, ladylike, businesslike, lifelike, tigerlike (all one word) BUT bill-like. Suffix is hyphenated when joined to most one-syllable words.

like (n.) *I never saw his like.* BUT *the likes of her* is colloquial.

like (v.) to enjoy, be attracted toward. *I like him. I like to study. I like studying. I like it that you came;* BUT NOT *I like that you came. I would like you to sing;* BUT NOT *for you to sing.*

like (adj., adv., prep.) similar: *A man like him.* DO NOT use as a mitigator: *She was pretty-like.*

like (conj.) Meaning colloq.: *The paint won't peel like the wallpaper does. Winston tastes good like a cigarette should.* Can also mean *as if* (colloq.): *He acts like he knows everything.*

likely highly probable. *It is likely that he will arrive soon.*

> LIABLE bound by law or legally answerable for an action. NOT *He is liable to arrive soon.* See **liable.**

Lilliput [LIH-lih-put] imaginary land of tiny people, from *Gulliver's Travels* by Jonathan Swift. (adj.) Lilliputian [lihl-ih-PYOO-shuhn]. See **brobdingnag.**

lilyhanded, lily-shaped, lily-white (adj.).

lima, Lima [LIE-mah] the bean, the city in Ohio. [LEE-muh] the city in Peru.

limbo (pl.) —os.

limelight —pit, —stone, —water (all one word); lime juice.

limit point which marks the end of the area specified.

> LIMITATION the end of conditions or circumstances.

limn [lihm] to draw, paint. —ed, —ing.

Limoges [lee-MOHZH] city in France; type of porcelain.

limousine [lihm-u-ZEEN].

linage, lineage [LIE-nihj] in printing, the number of lines.

> LINEAGE [LIHN-ee-ehj] descent; race; family.

line Cap. if part of name: Burlington Lines (railroad), Greyhound Line (bus); the line(s).

line, D.E.W. line; Mason-Dixon line or Mason and Dixon's line; Pinetree line; State line.

lineament [LIHN-ee-uh-ment] an outline or contour of the body or, especially, the face.

lingerie [LAN-jeh-ree; lahn-jeh-RAE].

lingo (pl.) —oes. See **language.**

link See surveyor's link, engineer's link.

LINKING VERB (copulative verb) a verb which connects a subject with a predicate by telling what the subject is. It is followed by a predicate nominative: *I am a man;* or by a predicate adjective: *She looks beautiful. He is big. The flower smells sweet.*

In addition to the verb *to be,* common linking verbs are *remain, grew, seem, keep,* and the verbs referring to the senses: *see, taste, smell, feel.*

AVOID the use of an adverb for the predicate adjective. *He feels badly* would mean his sense of touch is impaired.

Although the predicate nominative is properly in the nominative case (*It is I*) popular usage of the objective case is often permissable: *It is me;* esp. in complicated sentences.

Always use the objective case after *to be. He expected the caller to be me.* A noun or pronoun not in the genitive case after *being* is also in the objective case. *Would you like to try being me?*

links (sing. an pl.) a golf course.

Linnaeus, Linnaean (for Karl von Linne, Swedish naturalist) system of plant classification and nomenclature including genus and species.

lionheart, —hearted, —like; lion-headed, lion-maned (adj.).

lipread

lipstick

liquefy -faction.

liqueur [lih-KEUR; -KOOR] a sweet, flavored dessert brandy.

lira [LEE-rah] monetary unit of Italy. (pl.) lire.

lissome, lissom [LISS-uhm] limber; agile.

listener-in (pl) listeners-in.

litany prayer form of supplication and responses.

liter (abbr.) unit of capacity = 1.0567 liquid qt. = 0.9081 dry qt. = 61.025 cu. in. = approx. 1 dm^3.

literature [LIHT-ehr-uh-tchoor].

lithe [liethe] flexible, limber.

Lithuania [LIHTH-oo-AEN-ee-ah] nation on Baltic Sea. 16th-C. empire, later part of U.S.S.R. Independent 1920–1940, and again since 1991. Cap.: Vilnius. Native: Lithuanian. Currency: ruble.

Litt. D. or **D. Litt.** (abbr.) Doctor of Literature.

little Comparative: littler, less, lesser; superlative: littlest, least.

littleneck (n.); little-known, little-used (adj.).

littoral Pertains to a shore, especially of the sea; used in describing marine life in shallow coastal water.

livable

livelong [LIEV-lawng], —stock,

—wire (nonliteral); live load, live weight, live wire.

livelily Though rare, this is the correct adverb form before an adjective. *The dance, livelily executed . . . NOT lively.*

livid pale, bluish. Can mean flushed, red.

　　PALLID pale, wan.

living room

llama South American animal.

　　LAMA Buddhist priest.

LL.B. (abbr.) bachelor of laws.

LL.D. (abbr.) Doctor of Laws.

Llewellyn

loadstone that which attracts; magnetite. Pref. to *lodestone.*

loan (n.) Use *lend* for verb. *He would not lend me the money. He lent me the money.* BUT: *He gave me a loan.*

loath [LOHTH] (arch., adj.) reluctant. *I am loath to go.*

　　LOATHE [LOHTHE] (v.) to detest. (adj.) loathsome.

lobsterproof, lobster-tailed (adj.); lobster pot.

local Cap. for Teamsters Local Union No. 15; BUT local No. 15.

locale [loh-KALL] neighborhood.

　　LOCAL (adj.) in or from the neighborhood.

LOCUS [LOH-kuhs] place (pl.) —ci or locuses.

loch [lahk] (Scot.) lake.

loc. cit. [abbr.] loco citato (Lat.) "In the place cited."

lockerman, locker room.

locus place. (pl.) loci or locuses. See **locale.**

lodestar guiding star, especially polestar. Pref. to *loadstar.*

lodgment or **lodgement** lodging place.

Lodz [looj] city in Poland, site of controversial Jewish ghetto during Nazi occupation, 1939–45.

log. (abbr.) logarithm.

logbook, logroll.

loggerheads The expression *at loggerheads* implies a conflict, not merely a tangle. *He and I are at loggerheads over this issue.*

loggia [LOHJ-uh] open-roofed gallery. (pl.) —s.

　　LOGIA [LAH-jih-uh] Christ's words not in the Bible. Pl. of *logion,* pointed saying of a religious teacher.

logo- combining form meaning "word:" *logogram, logometric.*

Lolita [loh-LEE-tah] 1955 novel by **Vladimir Nabokov** concerning love affair between middle-aged man and 12-year-old girl. Hence, a sexually precocious young woman.

loll [lahl] droop.

long adj.: *long journey;* adv.: *we will long remember;* v.: *I long to see you.*

Longchamp [lohn-SHAHN] race track in Bois de Boulogne, near Paris.

long distance call

longitude, vertical measurement along Earth's surface; measured in degrees. 0° longitude is in Greenwich, England.

longways or **—wise,** lengthwise.

looker-on (pl.) lookers-on.

lookout (n.); look out (v.).

looseleaf, loose-limbed, loose-tongued (adj.).

lopsided, lop-eared (adj.).

loquacity [loh-KWAS-ih-tih] talkativeness.

loran (abbr.) long-range navigation.

Lord and Lady The titles *Lord* and *Lady* are applied to all members of the English peerage except dukes and duchesses. The wife of a peer takes the title corresponding to that of her husband: *duchess, marchioness, countess, viscountess, baroness.* The wife of a baronet or a knight receives the title of *Lady.* The placement of this title depends on its source.

    The daughter of a duke is *Lady Mary (Pierrepont) Wortley Montague;* the wife of a peer is *Lucie (Custin),*

Lady Duff-Gordon. The daughter of a viscount or baron married to a baronet or knight keeps her own title and keeps the title of Lady: *Hon. Anna Emily, Lady Acland.* The wife of a younger son of an earl or the son of a viscount or baron without title in her own right is *Margaret (Wilson) Montague, Hon. Mrs. Charles Montague.* A maid of honor retains her title after her marriage, unless it is merged with a higher title.

    The eldest son of a duke is called by his father's second title (*marquis* or *earl*); the younger son of a duke or a marquis is called *Lord* his first name, and his wife is *Lady* her husband's first name: *Lady George.* Daughters are *Lady Jane,* etc. Bertrand Lord Russell, *Lady Russell. Sir Tom,* NOT *Sir Brown, Lady Cynthia Brown, Dame Cynthia.* When in doubt use *Sir.*

    See **nobility** and the various titles.

Lorelei [LAWR-uh-lie] legendary German siren on the Rhine.

Loren, Sophia [law-REHN] (b. 1934) It. film actress.

Los Angeles

lose (p. and p.p.) lost; losing.

Lothario libertine; woman-chaser. (pl.) —os.

lotus (pl.) —uses.

loud May be used as adv. after *talk* and *laugh: laugh out loud.*

loudmouthed. loud-speaker (radio); loudvoiced (adj.).

Louisiana U.S. state. abbr.: LA. Cap.: Baton Rouge. Native: Louisianian.

Lourdes [lurds] Fr. town, site of miraculous visions in 1858. A famed pilgrimage center, esp. for the crippled.

louse (pl.) lice.

louver slatted panel.

Louvre [LOOV'r] art museum in Paris.

love-making, —seat (n.); —sick (adj.); love knot (n.).

low Comparative: lower; superlative: lowest, lowermost.

lowborn, low-built, low-lying, low-power, low-pressure (adj.); low frequency, low tide, low water (n.).

Low Church group in Anglican Church which holds evangelical views. Low-Churchman.

lower Cap. if part of name: Lower California (Mexico); Lower Colorado River Basin; Lower Egypt; Lower Peninsula (of Michigan); Lower House (U.S. House of Representatives). BUT: lower (or upper) House of Congress, lower Mississippi.

lower class, lowerclassman.

lowercase (abbr.: lc or l.c.) printers' term for small letters. Opposite of *upper case, capitals.* (v.) lowercase.

lox. (abbr.) liquid oxygen.

lozenge [LAHZ-ehnj]. See **shapes.**

LSD (abbr.) lysergic acid diethylamide. Hallucinogen synthesized in 1943, popularized in 1960s.

l.s.t. (abbr.) local standard time. l.t. (abbr.) local time.

L1011 large passenger jet.

Lt. (abbr.) lieutenant.

Lt. Col., Comdr., Gen., (jg) (abbr.) lieutenant colonel, commander, general, (junior grade).

Lt. Gov. (abbr.) lieutenant governor.

Ltd. (abbr.) limited. Br. for U.S. "Inc." Limited liability company, a corporation.

Luanda [loo-AHN-dah] Cap. of **Angola.**

lucent bright, clear, translucent.

lucite See **acrylic.**

Lufthansa [LOOFT-hahn-seh] German airline.

Luftwaffe [LOOFT-vah-fuh] German airforce.

lukewarm

lumberjack

lumen-hour Foot-candle hour.

Lumumba, Patrice [luh-MUHM-buh] (1925–1961) Congolese statesman, first prime minister (1960–61) of what is now **Zaire.**

lunatic loony.

lunch a casual midday meal. lunchbox, —room.

LUNCHEON a formal midday meal.

BRUNCH a late breakfast-lunch.

lunging

luster gloss, lustrous. Pref. to —tre.

lusty full of vitality. lustily.

LUSTFUL full of lust. lustfully.

Luxembourg [LUK-sehm-buhrg] small landlocked nation in NE Europe. Independent, 1866. Cap.: Luxembourg. Native: Luxembourger. Currency: franc. Pref. to *Luxemburg*.

Luxor [LUHK-sohr] town on Nile River, Egypt; ancient Thebes.

luxuriant fertile, profuse, florid.

LUXURIOUS indulging in costly dress, food, etc.

luxury [LUHK-zhyoo-ree].

lycée [lee-SAE] French secondary school.

lyceum [lie-SEE-um]. Aristotle's garden school; hence, his philosophy and followers. Also a lecture hall, literary institution, or a group which sponsors lectures. (pl.) —ms or —cea.

lying p.p. of *lie* in either sense.

lying (n. and adj.).

lymph, lymph node, lymphatic system.

lyonnaise [lie-uh-NAEZ] cooked with fried onions.

lyrics Usu. refers to words of a song. lyricist.

lyrist lyre player.

Lysenko, Trofim Denisovich [lih-SYEHN-koh troh-FEEM] (1898–1943) Russian geneticist; instituted destructive Stalinist farming and breeding practices.

M

m. (abbr.) (1) milli = one-thousandth (0.001); (2) meter; (3) merides (noon), as 12 m., BUT use 12 A.M. to avoid confusion with 12 midnight. 12 p.m. = midnight; (4) masculine.

M. (abbr.) (from the Roman numeral) thousand.

M. (abbr.) monsieur; *MM.*, messieurs.

-m, -mm- Words of one syllable ending in *m* when preceded by a single vowel (but not a diphthong or a vowel and verb) become *mm* before suffix beginning with a vowel: *hummer, drummer.* BUT: *dreamer, roomy.*

m.² (abbr.) square meter.

m.³ (abbr.) cubic meter.

ma. (abbr.) milliampere.

MA Massachusetts.

ma'am (archaic) madam contracted. See lady.

Mac or **Mc** File names *Mac* or before *M.*

macabre [muh-KAHBR] (from the dance of death) gruesome.

macaroni pasta; or (arch.) dandies. (pl.) —nis (food), —nies.

Mach number. [mahk] velocity compared to speed of sound. *Mach-2* is twice the speed of sound.

machete [mah-SHEHT-tee] heavy knife used for cutting cane or thick brush.

Machiavelli, Niccolò [mah-kyah-VEH-lee, NEE-koh-loh] (1469–1527) Florentine statesman, author of *The Prince*, classic argument for strong, pragmatic central government. (adj.) Machiavellian [mak-ee-uh-VEHL-ee-uhn], (n.) —ism.

machination [MAK-ih-naet-shun] contrivance; backstage plotting.

machine-gun, machine-finished, machine-hour, machine-made; machine shop, machine stitch, machine work.

machinist [muh-SHEEN-ihst].

machismo, macho. [mah-KEES-moh, or MAH-choh] (Sp.) exaggerated masculinity. Colloq., an adj.: *He's a macho man.*

mackeral [MAK-uhr-ehl].

mackinaw [MAK-ih-naw] (from straits between lakes Michigan and Huron) a short, heavy plaid coat.

mackintosh (from Charles Mackintosh, 1766–1843.) waterproof outer coat or cloth. Sometimes spelled macintosh.

macramé [MA-krah-mae] artwork of knotted fibers.

Madagascar island nation off E Africa. Formerly Fr.; independent,

1960. Native: Madagascan or Malagasy. Cap.: Antananarivo. Currency: franc.

madam [MAD-am] (n.) form of address to a woman. See **ma'am**. In U.S., also, the woman in charge of a brothel.

> MADAME (Mme) [MAD-am, ma-DAM] title given to a married woman in France. In English, foreign married woman. (pl.) Mesdames (Mmes) [mae-DAM].

made-over, made-up (adj.).

Madeira [muh-DEER-uh] Portuguese Atlantic Ocean Islands, famous for wines. Hence, any similar wines.

mademoiselle [mad-mwa-ZEHL, mad'm-muh-ZEHL]. (abbr.: Mlle.) (Fr.) Miss. (pl.) mesdemoiselles (abbr.: Mlles.) [maed-mwa-ZEHL].

Madras [muh-DRAS] city in S India; name of shirt or dress fabric.

maelstrom [MAEL-strahm] whirlpool.

maestro [mah-EH-stroh, MIES-troh] master in an art, especially music. (pl.) —stros.

Maeterlinck, Count Maurice [MAH-tehr-lingk, MAE-tehr-lihngk] (1862–1949) Belgian writer (*The Blue Bird*).

Mafia [MAH-fee-ah] criminal organization, originally Sicilian. Hence, lowercase, any tight-knit and dangerous group. *Chinese mafia, feminist mafia.* See **Cosa Nostra.**

magazine [MAG-a-zeen (publication) or mag-a-ZEEN (storehouse)] Italicize names of publications, but place titles of articles in quotation marks.

magdalene [MAG-duh-lehn] a reformed prostitute.

Magdalene, Mary [mag-duh-LEH-nee] in Gospels, an unmarried woman accepted into Christ's circle. Later theology argued she was a prostitute.

maggoty

the Magi [MAE-jei] (sing. and pl.) priestly caste of ancient Persia. Popularly, the three wise men of Christmas story.

Maginot Line [MAH-zhee-noh] (after French statesman, Andre Maginot) fortifications on Franco-German border believed impregnable before Nazi invasion of 1940. Hence, any dubious excess enjoying official approval.

magma mobile rock.

Magna Charta or **Carta** (M.C.) [MAG-nuh KAHR-tuh] "Great Charter" of rights between English barons and King John, 1215. Refer to *Magna Charta*, NOT *the Magna Charta.*

magna cum laude (Lat.) with high honors.

Magnani, Anna [mahn-YAH-nee] (1908–1973) Italian actress.

magnetite-spinellite [MAG-nuh-tiet SPIE-nehl-liet] black mineral.

magneto [mag-NEE-toh] magneto-electric machine.

magnolia [mag-NOH-lih-uh or -lyuh].

magnum wine bottle of two champagne quarts, usu. 52 oz.

magnum opus (Lat.) great work.

Magritte, René [mah-GREET reh-NAE] (1898–1967) French surrealist painter.

Magyar [MAG-yahr] Hungarian people and their language.

Mahabharata [mah-HAH-bah-RAH-tah] Hindu epic of dynastic struggle, from ancient oral tradition, compiled 4th C. Contains **Bhagavadgita.**

maharaja(h) [mah-HAH-RAH-juh] Indian state sovereign. His wife is a *maharani* or —*nee* [muh-hah-RAH-nee].

mahjong [mahjengg, mah-JAHNG] Chinese game.

maid of honor unmarried attendant of a bride.

MATRON OF HONOR married attendant of a bride.

Maimonides, Moses [mie-MAH-nih-dees] (1135–1204) Jewish philosopher, jurist, physician.

Maine U.S. Abbr. ME. Native, Mainer. Cap., Augusta.

maître d'hôtel [MEH-truh doh-TEHL].

maize corn; Indian corn.

MAZE labyrinth.

Majesty, Your, His, Her, Their. See **His Exellency**. Title of address for a reigning sovereign. See **Nobility.**

Maj. (abbr.) major: Maj. Gen., major general.

Majorca [muh-JAWR-kuh], Span., Mallorca [mah-YAWR-kah]. large Mediterranean Spanish island.

major-domo(s), major-leaguer, major key, major league.

major general (pl.) major generals.

majuscule [mah-JUHS-kyool] a large letter; capital. Opposite, minuscule.

make (p. and p.p.) made.

makefast —ready (printing), —shift, —up (n. and adj., all one word); makebelieve (n. and adj.).

make inquiries concerning *Ask about* is pref.

making up

mal- prefix meaning "bad:" *malediction, maladjustment.*

Malaga [MAH-lah-gah] city, province, and white wine of Spain.

Malagasy [MAL-uh-GAS-ih] See **Madagascar.**

malaise [muh-LAES] indefinite body illness or discomfort.

malapropism [MAL-uh-prop-ihz'm] (from Mrs. Malaprop in Sheridan's comedy "The Rivals.") the wrong word, used for its approximately correct sound.

Malawi [muh-LAH-wee] landlocked nation in SE Africa. Formerly Nyasaland (Br.); independent since 1964. Cap.: Lilongwe. Natives: Malawian. Currency: kwacha.

Malaya area in SE Asia, now part of Malaysia.

Malaysia Federation of SE Asian states, formerly Br., established 1963. Comprised of Malaya, Singapore, Sarawak, and Sabah (North Borneo). Singapore seceded, 1965. Cap.: Kuala Lumpur [koo-AH-lah luhm-poor]. Currency: ringgit. Natives: Malaysian, Malay.

Maldives [maul-DEEVS] island nation in Indian Ocean. Formerly Br.; independent, 1965. Cap.: Male. Natives: Maldivean. Currency: rifiyaa.

malefactor [MAL-uh-fak-tawr] evildoer.

malevolent [muh-LEHV-uh-l'nt] wishing evil.

malfeasance an improper act.

MALFEASANCE Implies performing a proper act improperly.

NONFEASANCE Implies failure to perform a necessary act.

Mali [MAH-lee] landlocked nation in NW Africa. Formerly French Senegal; independent, June 1960. Cap.: Bamako [bah-muh-KOH]. Native: Malian. Currency: CFA franc.

malinger [muh-LIHNG-ehr] to pretend illnes, usu. to escape work.

mall [mawl] originally, a shaded walk; now, a shopping area.

Mallarmé, Stéphane [mah-lahr-MAE] (1842–1898) French Symbolist poet *(The Afternoon of a Faun)*.

Malraux, André [mahl-ROH] (1901–1976) French writer *(Man's Fate)*, politician.

Malta Mediterranean island nation. Formerly Br.; independent, 1964. Cap.: Valletta. Native: Maltese. Currency: Maltese pound.

Malthus, Thomas Robert (1766–1834) English economist.

MALTHUSIAN THEORY [mal-THOO-zhan] Population expands faster than food supply, tending to keep standard of living at subsistence level.

mameluke [MAM-eh-lyook] (arch.) in Islamic countries, a slave.

mammon wealth, civil influence.

manageable

Managua [mah-NAH-gwah] capital city of **Nicaragua.**

—man Nouns or compound words ending with this form usually use —men for pl.

—mancy suffix meaning ability to foretell, divination, by specified means: aeromancy (from the air); astromancy (stars); bibliomancy (books); chiromancy, palmistry (palms); chronomancy (time); crystallomancy (crystal ball); ichthyomancy (fish); necromancy (word from the dead); oneinomancy (dreams); pyromancy (fire).

mandamus [man-DAE-muhs] in law, writ to enforce performance of a duty (pl.) —uses.

MANDATE an authoritative command, esp. to perform some act.

MANDATORY (n.) the one to whom a mandate is given.

MANDATORY (n.) mandatary. (adj.) obligatory.

mandible jaw, especially lower jaw.

Manet, Édouard [mah-NAE] (1832–1883] Fr. painter, precursor to Impressionists. NOT **Monet.**

maneuver [ma-NOO-vuhr] adroit movement or dealing.

mango (pl.) —oes.

mangy [MAEN-jee] infected with mange; shabby.

mania, —mania Alone, indicates enthusiasm, excessive but benign. *He has a mania for chocolate.*

As a combining form, indicates psychosis: dipsomania (alcoholism); kleptomania (thievery); megalomania (grandiose delusions); monomania (in one area); nymphomania (sex); pyromania (setting fires).

Schizophrenia is a more complex and general madness. See **obsession.**

maniacal [ma-NIE-uh-kal] affected with madness.

manic-depressive (n. or adj.) cyclical mental disorder.

manifest (adj.) easy to see and understand; (v.) make evident; (n.) an indication or proof; also, a passenger or cargo list for a ship or plane.

manifesto a public declaration of policy and motives: *the Communist Manifesto.* (pl.) —oes, —os.

manikin anatomical model; a little man or dwarf.

MANNEQUIN dummy or female model for costumes.

Manitoba (abbr.: Man.) province in Canada. Cap.: Winnipeg.

man of war Also spelled with hyphens. (pl.) men of war.

manly Refers to admirable qualities in a man.

MALE Refers to gender. Contrast with female.

MANNISH Refers to qualities normal in a man, esp. appearance, but applied to a woman. See **masculine.**

MASCULINE Refers to male qualities.

manpower

mansard roof [man-SARD] (from Francois Mansart, French architect) roof with double slopes, the lower much steeper.

manslaughter. Unlawful but not willful killing. See **homicide.**

mantel shelf.

MANTLE cloak.

mantelpiece

manuscript abbr.: MS. or ms.; pl., MSS. or mss.

many Takes a plural verb; *many a* takes a singular verb. *Many are chosen. Many a man prefers his own home. Many men prefer to stay.*

Maori [MAH-oh-rih; MOU-rih] Polynesian aborigines of New Zealand. (pl.) —ris.

Mao Tze-tung [MAH-oh dzuh-DOONG] (also Tse-tung, Ze-Dong) (1893–1976) Chinese Communist statesman and revolutionary. First dictator (1949–1976) of mainland People's Republic.

map 3, A, II, lowercase, BUT cap. when part of title: *Map 2: Railroads of Middle Atlantic States.*

maraschino [mahr-a-SKEE-noh] the cherry, and the liqueur distilled from it. (pl. —os).

marbleize

marchioness wife or widow of a marquis, or one of equal rank. ADDRESS: The Most Honourable, the Marchioness. SALUTATION: Madam. See **nobility, Lord and Lady.**

mare's-tail cirrus cloud with a flowing tail.

margarine [MAHR-juhr-reen] butter substitute.

marginalia [mahrjih-NAE-lih-uh] (n. pl.) marginal notes.

marijuana [mah-rih-HWAH-nah] hemp; the intoxicating properties are contained in the leaves and flowers.

Marine Corps, the corps. Cap. for the organization: *Send in the Marines;* but lowercase for individuals: *a pair of marines at the bar.* Cap. the Reserve.

Marine Officers ADDRESS: U.S.M.C. (United States Marine Corps) should follow the branch of the service in which the person addressed is engaged: *Captain Howard T. Smith, Signal Corps, U.S.M.C.* SALUTATION: See *ARMY ORGANIZATION.*

Mariner cap., NASA spacecraft designed to approach Venus.

marital pertaining to marriage.

MARTIAL pertaining to war.

markdown (n. and adj.).

Market grades and classes U.S. grade A; Western, Mixed, Malting Two-rowed (barley), Red Kidney, U.S. No. 2 Pea (beans); Prime, Choice, Good (meat); Yellow, White, Mixed, Dent (corn); Middling, Strict Good Ordinary, Strict Low Middling, Good Ordinary (cotton); Timothy Light Clover Mixed, Upland Prairie (hay); White, Red, Mixed (oats); Yellow, Black, Mixed (soybeans); Hard Red Spring, Red Durum, Durum, Hard Red Winter, White, Mixed, etc. (wheat); Grade 60s, or one-half blood (wool).

marketplace Can appear as two words.

market quotations Form: Pennsylvania Railroad, 29; gold is 107; wheat at 45; sugar, .03.

marquee tent or canopy leading to an entrance; a tent.

MARQUIS, MARQUESS [MAHR-kwihs; mahr-KEE]. nobleman ranking above earl or count and below duke.

MARQUISE [mahr-KEEZ] wife of a marquis; marchioness.

Marquez, Gabriel García. See **García Marquez, Gabriel.**

Marquis ADDRESS: The Most Honourable the Marquis of Donlan; or The Marquis of Donlan. SALUTATION: My Lord; or Sir. See **nobility, Lord and Lady.**

marriageable

Marseillaise, La [mahr-s'YAEZ] Fr. national anthem, by Claude Joseph Rouget de Lisle in Marseilles.

MARSEILLES or MARSEILLE [mahr-SAE, mahr-SAE-'y]. Fr. port on Mediterranean Sea.

MARSEILLES [mahr-SAELZ] cotton fabric similar to pique.

marshal an officer.

MARTIAL military.

martini cocktail made of gin and vermouth.

marvel —led, —ling; (adj.) —lous.

Maryland U.S. state. Abbr.: MD. Cap.: Annapolis. Native: Marylander.

masculine Use for appearance, qualities, companionship, nature, gender.

MALE (adj.) consisting of males. For choir, fertilization, sex, servant, voice. See **female, manly.**

Mason member of Ancient and Honorable Order of **Freemasons.**

Mason-Dixon line Originally surveyed 1760, to establish northern Maryland border; later marked division between free and slave states. See **line.**

masonwork

masque Spelling used for ball or entertainment. Otherwise, *mask.*

Mass Is celebrated, said, or read; High Mass is sung; the Rosary is recited.

mass measure of inertia in a body.

Massachusetts U.S. state. Abbr.: MA. Cap.: Boston. Native: Massachusettan.

massacre —cring.

masseur [muh-SEUR] male practitioner of massage. Female, masseuse [muh-SEUZ].

mass-produce (v.).

mass nouns. See *COLLECTIVE NOUNS.*

Mastroianni, Marcello [mass-troh-YAHN-ee] (b. 1924) It. film actor, producer.

master at arms (pl.) masters. Webster's spelling: *master-at-arms, masters-at-arms.*

Masters, Mates & Pilots' Association

maté [MAH-tae]. Paraguayan tea.

material [muh-TEE-ree-ehl] (n.) substance; contents.

MATERIEL [muh-tee-ree-EHL] (n.) provisions and equipment. *An army requires up-to-date materiel.*

matin morning prayers. Usu. plural, with plural verb. (pl.) matins.

matinee [mat-ih-NAE] an afternoon performance. *Matinee performance* is redundant.

matrimonial Pertains to marriage; generally.

NUPTIAL pertains to the marriage ceremony.

CONJUGAL Connotes the persons joined together for life.

CONNUBIAL Pertains to the married state.

SPOUSAL Emphasizes legal commitment, pledge at altar.

MATRONLY Emphasizes motherhood, homemaking.

MARITAL Pertaining to the married state; usu. emphasizes the husband.

matrix (pl.) matrices, matrixes.

mature [ma-TYOOR].

maturity full development; also date for payment of bill.

matutinal [muh-TYOO-tih-nal] of the morning. Opposite, nocturnal.

matza [MAHT-tzah] unleavened bread eaten by Jews during Passover. Usu., plural. (pl.) matso [-tzuh].

maudlin [MAWD-lihn] over-sentimental.

Maugham, William Somerset [MAWM] (1874–1966) English novelist (*Of Human Bondage*) and dramatist.

Maui [MAH-oo-ee, MOU-ee] Hawaiian island.

Mau Mau [mou] Anti-British guerillas in Kenya, 1950s. Hence, any subversive or terrorist outsiders.

de Maupassant, Guy [de MOH-puh-SAHNN] (1850–1893) Fr. short-story writer ("The Diamond Necklace").

Mauritania [maw-reh-TAE-nih-uh] nation in NW Africa. Formerly Fr.; independent, 1960. Cap.: Nouakchott. Native: Mauritanian. Currency: CFA franc.

Mauritius [maw-RIHSH-ih-uhs] island nation in Indian Ocean. Formerly Br.; independent, 1968. Cap.: Port Louis. Native: Mauritian. Currency: rupee.

mausoleum [maw-soh-LEE-uhm] (pl.) —s or —lea.

Mauve Decade 1891–1900.

maximum (pl.) —ms, —ma.

may *May* is the accepted form; *can* refers to ability. (p.) might. In asking permission, *may* is bolder than *might*.

     Can and *could* may also be used in asking permission, esp. where ability is not in question. *Can I have that letter?* See **can.**

Maya [MAH-yuh] Mayan Indian of Central America.

Maypole, —tide, —time; Mayday (adj.); May Day, May fly.

mayonnaise [mae-oh-NAES].

Mayor of a City. ADDRESS: The Honorable David Dinkins, Mayor of the City of New York, City Hall, New York, N.Y.; or The Mayor of the City of New York, etc.

     SALUTATION: Sir; Dear Sir; Dear Mr. Mayor; Dear Mayor Dinkins.

mayoralty [MAE-ehr-al-tih, MAIR-al-tih] office of mayor.

mb. (abbr.) millibar.

M.b.m. (abbr.) thousand (ft.) board measure.

M.B.A. (abbr.) Masters in Business Administration.

mc. (abbr.) megacycle.

M', Mc. Alphabetize as if spelled *Mac.*

M.c.t. (abbr.) thousand cubic feet.

MD Maryland.

M.D. (abbr.) doctor of medicine.

ME Maine.

me *Between you and me, . . . him and me, . . . her and me. He asked my friends and me. She gave me the book.*

mealticket, —time.

mealy-mouthed over-cautious in speaking.

mean [meen] (n.) the middle point. The Golden Mean is a hypothetical place between any two extremes. See **average.**

     MIEN [meen] (n.) demeanor, bearing. *His dejected mien suggested he had come upon misfortune.*

mean (p. and p.p.) meant; (n.) meanness.

means When referring to income, takes pl. verb: *Our means are limited.*

meantime Usually a noun: *in the meantime.* Can be adv.

     MEANWHILE Usu. adv.: *Meanwhile they left.*

measles Singular and plural forms usually take singular verb.

measuredly [MEHZH-urd-lee].

MEASUREMENT Units of measurement, time, and quantity are expressed in Arabic numbers. This especially applies in reference to age, clock time, dates, decimals, degrees of latitude and longitude, distances, market quotations, mathematical expressions, money, percentages, proportions, and sports scores.

Other than that, numbers of 10 and above are generally expressed in Arabic numerals: *3 feet by 1 foot; 4 inches by 2 feet 2 inches; about 12 yards; 1 1/4 miles; 3 ems.* BUT: *tenpenny nail, fourfold, sixfold; three-ply; six bales; two-story house; five votes; midthirties; between two and three hours;* and indefinite expressions. See *NUMBERS,* **dimensions.**

Without a number, a unit of measure is used in the possessive and takes an apostrophe. *It was a mile's hike.* But with a number, the compound form is used; *a ten-mile hike; a two-foot-deep creek,* and the singular form of the unit is used. BUT when the measure does not modify a noun, the plural form is used. *It is two feet deep. Two feet are dug.*

measurement ton. See **ton.**

meatless

medaled, medalist.

median [MEE-dee-ihn] mid-point in a series. See **average.**

meditate (v.) to use a third party to resolve disputes. —tor, —tion (n.).

medicate (v.); —cable (adj.).

medieval. [mee-dih-EE-val; mehd-ih-] pertaining to the Middle Ages. Pref. to *mediaeval.*

mediocre [mee-dih-OH-kehr] ordinary.

Mediterranean

medium (pl.) media; except when word refers to spiritualists: —ums.

meet (p. and p.p.) met.

meetinghouse

mega-, meg- prefix meaning great: *megacephalic, megalith.* Can also mean million: *megadeath,* one million deaths; *megaton,* one million tons of TNT.

megalo-, megal- combining form meaning large: *megalopolis, megalomaniac.*

mein Herr Ger. for *Sir.*

meiosis [mie-OH-sihs] (pl.) —oses. in biology, nuclear changes in cells with half the usual chromosomes present. See **mitosis.** ALSO, in rhetoric, understatement. *Some corn is grown in Iowa.* Also known as litotes.

Meir, Golda [mie-ehr] (1898–1978) Russian-American Israeli politician and statesleader. Prime Minister of Israel, 1969–1974.

melange [mae-LANZH] mixture.

melee [mae-LAE; MAE-lae] confused battle.

mellifluous [mehl-LIHF-hoo-uhs] flowing sweetly.

melodic [meh-LAHD-ik] having melody: *a melodic tune.* See **harmony.**

MELODIOUS [meh-LOH-dih-uhs] agreeable in sound: *a melodious voice.*

melody agreeable series of notes.

HARMONY pleasing combination of notes in a chord.

member Cap. if referring to Senator, Representative, Delegate, or Resident Commissioner of U.S. Congress; also Member at Large; Member of Parliament; BUT membership.

memento NOT momento. A *memento mori* is a symbol or reminder of death. (pl.) —os.

memo (usage allows this spelling) technically, abbr. for memorandum.

memorabilia (n. pl.) souvenirs.

memorandum (pl.) —dums, or —da for informal records.

menage [mae-NAZH] a household; household management.

menagerie [mehn-AZH-ehr-ee, meh-NAZH-ehr-ih] collection of wild animals. Connotes greater confusion than *zoo.*

mendacity act of a liar.

MENDICITY act of a beggar.

Mendelssohn, Felix [MEHN-dehl-suhn] (1809–1847) Ger. Romantic composer.

menial unskilled: *menial labor.* Has derogatory connotation.

menstrual [MEHN-stroo-awl] (adj.); menstruation [-AE-sh'n] (n.).

—ment (from Lat. *-mentum*) suffix meaning condition, action, state or quality, usually added to verbs to form nouns: *movement, indictment.*

mental retardation Usually defined as an IQ of 70 or less, according to standardized test.

menu [MEHN-yoo] (pl.) —s.

Mephistopheles [meh-fih-STAHF-eh-leez], also Mephisto [mee-FIHS-toh]. chief devil; makes deal with **Faust.** (adj.) Mephistophelean [meh-fihs-toh-FEE-lee-an].

meq. (abbr.) milliequivalent.

mercantile [MEHR-kihn-tihl, -tiel] pertaining to merchants and trade, or to mercantilism.

mercantile agency credit information organization.

merchandise

Merchant Marine Reserve, the Reserve. BUT: U.S. merchant marine, the merchant marine.

Mercury smallest planet; speedy Roman god. (adj.) mercurian.

meretricious like a prostitute; deceitfully ornamental.

MERITORIOUS deserving of honor.

meringue [meh-RANG] stiffened, sweetened egg white used for pie covering.

merit system employee relations program based on employment and advancement by competition, merit, or seniority.

mesa [MAE-sah] small, high plateau.

mesalliance [mae-zal-YANS, mae-ZAL-ih-ahns] marriage with a social inferior; **misalliance** pref.

mescaline [MEH-skuh-lihn] Hallucinogen derived from **peyote.**

Mesdames [mae-DAM] plural of *madame.* See **madam.**

mesdemoiselles [maed-dehm-mwah-ZEHL]. See **mademoiselle, Miss, madam.**

meso- combining form meaning intermediate, in the middle: *mesoderm, Meso-America.*

mesomorph [MEH-so-mowrf] person with body type tending to muscle mass. Condition is mesomorphy. See **ectomorph, endomorph.**

meson subatomic particle with + or — electronic charge, short life, and mass between **electron** and **proton.**

messieurs [MEHS-uhrz] (abbr.: Messrs.) Plural of *monsieur.*

mestizo person of mixed blood, usu. aboriginal and white European, esp. in Philippines and Latin America. (pl.) —s.

metal a class of substance (steel, gold, lead); *a metal bar.*

METTLE   honor;   courage; strength. *Tried his mettle.*

metaled —ing, —ize.

metamorphosis [meht-uh-MAWR-foh-sihs] change in form or substance. Cap. English title for famous 1915 story by **Franz Kafka.** (Pl.) —oses [-sees].

metaphor figure of speech that describes or illuminates by comparison. The comparison is usu. between abstract and concrete. *My hopes, those moth-eaten tatters, suddenly flapped whole and clean again.* See **simile.**

mete to apportion. meted, meting.

meteor celestial matter, heated by friction with the earth's atmosphere. meteoroid.

meteorite meteor which reaches the earth.

meteorology [MEE-tee-ohr-RAH-loh-gee] study of weather.

METROLOGY study of weights and measures.

meter. In poetry, any systematic rhythm. Divided into syllabic groups or feet. See **scansion.**

meter (abbr.: m.) unit of length = 1.093611 yd. = 3.280833 ft. = 39.37 in.

Since 1963, "a length equal to 1,656,763.83 wavelengths in a vacuum of the radiation corresponding to the transition between the level 2 P 10 and 5 D 5 of the atom krypton 86," the wave-length of an orange light.

methodical Pref. to *methodic.*

meticulous painstakingly careful of details.

metonymy [mee-TAHN-ih-mih] in rhetoric, a suggestive emblem substituted for actual term, for example, *the Crown,* instead of *the King.*

metric System Prefixes.
  milli = 1/1000 = one thousandth centi = 1/100 = one hundredth; deci = 1/10 = one tenth; deka = 10 = ten; hecto = 100 = one hundred; kilo = 1000 = one thousand

metric ton or millier. (abbr.: t.) unit of weight = 0.98421 long tons = 1.1023 short tons = 2204.622 lb. avoirdupois = 2,679.23 lb. troy = 1000 kms. See **ton.**

metric units meter (m.) for length; gram (gm.) for weight or mass; liter (l.) for capacity.

metropolis (pl.) —lises; *metropoles* is rare.

mettle courage, spirit. *Tragedy tested his mettle.* See **metal.**

Mev. (abbr.) million electron volts.

Mexico Central American nation; independent, 1821. Cap.: Mexico City (Ciudad de Mexico). Native: Mexican. (Usage may allow *Chicano;* some consider it degrading.) Currency: peso.

mezuza [meh-TZU-zah] Jewish doorway icon.

mezzo- [MEHD-zoh], Fem. mezza-

[MEHD-zah] combining form meaning middle, half, not extreme: *mezzo-soprano, mezzotint.*

MF. (abbr.) medium frequency.

mG. (abbr.) milligauss.

mg. (abbr.) milligram.

mbo. (not an abbr.) unit of conductance, reciprocal of ohm.

MI Michigan.

Michelangelo (Michelangelo Buonarroti) [mee-kehl-AHN-jehl-loh] (1475–1564) It. artist.

Michigan U.S. state. Abbr.: MI. Cap.: Lansing. Native: Michiganite. Nickname: Wolverine.

micro- combining form meaning small or millionth: *microscope, microvolt.* Oposite of *macro-, mega-.*

microbe [MIE-krohb] minute organism.

micron symbol (μ) unit of length = 0.00003937 in. = 0.03937 mil = 0.001 mm. μa., microampere; μg., microgram; μv., microvolt; μw., microwatt; etc.

mid amid.

mid- combining form meaning middle: *mid-American, mid-April, mid-ice, mid-1958, mid-Pacific, mid-Victorian.*

midcontinent region

Middle Atlantic States New York, New Jersey, Pennsylvania, Maryland, Delaware (sometimes Washington, D.C.).

Middle Ages Roughly 400–1400. "Middle" refers to period between Roman civilization and Renaissance.

Middle East Mideast, Mideastern, Middle Eastern (Asia); middle Europe; Midwest (sections of United States), Midwestern States, Midwesterner. But midwestern farmers, etc.

Midwest U.S. area between Allegheny and Rocky Mountains, north of Texas. Comprises Illinois, Indiana, Kansas, Michigan, Minnesota, Nebraska, North Dakota, Ohio, South Dakota, Wisconsin.

midnight 12 p.m.

mien See **mean.**

Mies van der Rohe, Ludwig [MEES van duhr ROH] (1886–1969) German-American modernist architect.

MiG, MIG Soviet jet fighter plane. See **fighter planes.**

mignon [mee-NYAWNN] (Fr.) delicate; graceful; petite.

migraine [MIE-graen].

mile (not abbreviated) Statute mile. Unit of length = 5280 ft. = 1760 yds. = 1.6093 km. = 0.868.

mile, nautical unit of length. (1) U.S. = 1.007 international nautical mile = 1.1515 statute mi. = 6080.20 ft. = 1.853248 km.; (2) Brit. = 6080 ft. = 1,8532 km.; (3) International Hy-drographic Bureau mile = 0.999 U.S. nautical mile = 6076.10 ft. = 1.852 km.

mileage Pref. to *milage.*

milieu [mee-LYUH] social environment.

militia Cap. if part of name; 1st Regiment Ohio Militia, Naval Militia, Militia of Ohio, Organized Militia; the militia.

militiaman

mill in U.S. currency, 0.1 cent or $0.001.

millenary pertaining to a thousand.

MILLIARY Pertaining to 1000 or to the ancient Roman mile.

MILLINERY hats.

millenium 1000 years, especially measuring Christ's reign. By extension, the end of the world. (pl.) —s or millennia.

millimeter (abbr. mm.) one thousandth meter. = 0.3937 inches.

milliard 1000 millions, in France; in U.S., usually a *billion.*

millier See **metric ton.**

milligauss (abbr. mG.).

milligram (abbr. mg.) unit of weight = 0.01543 grains = 0.001 gram.

milliliter (abbr.: ml.) unit of (1) capacity = 0.27052 fluid dram = 16.231 minims = 0.001 l.; (2) volume =

0.06102 cu. in. = approx. 1 cm³.

millimeter (abbr.: mm.) unit of length = 0.03937 in. = 0.001 meter.

millimicron (abbr.: m,u.) unit of length = 0.001 micron. = 0.000 000 03937 in.

million 1000 thousand. Two million and a half, or two and a half million. Ten million, a dozen million, a thousand million. BUT: many millions, millions of dollars. *He's worth millions.*

millionaire

milord [mih-LAWRD, mehl-AWR] (from *my lord*) an English lord or important person (used on the Continent). Also, *milady.* See **Lord and Lady.**

milquetoast [MIHLK-tohst] (n.) timid, unassertive man; from comic-strip character Caspar Milquetoast. Can also be cap.

mime [miem].

mimeograph originally a trade name (by A.B. Dick Co.) of stencil duplicating machine; now a generic term.

mimesis [mih-MEE-sihs, -MAE-] (Gr.) "imitation." A theory of art, claiming it represents or mimics experience. (adj.) mimetic.

min. (abbr.) minute.

minatory [MIHN-ah-taw-ree] menacing.

mince (v.); —ceable (adj.).

mind-blowing (adj.); —blower (n.).

minestrone [mihn-ehs-TROH-nee] It. vegetable soup.

minesweeper

miniature [MIHN-ee-uh-chuhr] (n.) a small painting; a small copy. (adj.) on a small scale.

minim A half note; anything very small.

minim (U.S. min.). unit of capacity (1) in U.S. = 1/60 fluid dram = 0.06161 ml. = 1/480 fluid oz. = 0.00376 cu. in. = 0.06161 m.; (2) Brit. = 0.96073 U.S. minim = 0.05919 ml. = approx. 1 drop.

minimize to make the least (not less) of.

minimum (pl.) —s, —ma.

minion a servant; in printing, 7-point type.

miniscule

minister See **clergy.**

minister-designate (pl.) ministers designate.

Minister (diplomatic) For foreign ministers. ADDRESS: His Excellency, the Romanian Minister, the Romanian Legation, Washington, D.C., or The Honorable George Macovescu, Minister of Romania, The Romanian Legation.

SALUTATION: Your Excellency; Sir; Dear Mr. Minister; Dear Sir.

Minister Pleninpotentiary Cap. the Minister; Minister Without Portfolio. See **foreign cabinets.**

Minister (Protestant) ADDRESS: The Reverend J.J. Jones, D.D. or Rev. J.J. Jones. SALUTATION: Reverend Sir; My dear Sir; Dear Dr. Jones; Dear Sir.

Minister (U.S.) ADDRESS: The Honorable John J. Adams, American Minister, Ottowa Can. SALUTATION: Sir; Dear Mr. Minister; Dear Sir.

the Ministry See **foreign cabinets.**

Minneapolis with St. Paul, one of "Twin Cities."

Minnesota U.S. state. Abbr.: MN. Cap.: St. Paul. Native: Minnesotan. Nickname: Gophers.

minor-leaguer, minor key, minor league.

minority less than half the group.

minority leader Cap. with name: Minority Leader Robert Dole; BUT: the minority leader (U.S. Congress).

minority of one one person.

mint Philadelphia Mint; the mint.

Minuteman Originally, a U.S. colonial militiaman, ready to fight in a minute. Now U.S. ICBM, land-based strategic missile.

minuteman, minute book, minute band, minute mark.

minutia [mih-NYOO-shih-uh] trivial, precise detail. (pl.) —iae.

mirabile dictu [mihr-RAB-ih-lee DIHK-too] (Lat.) "wonderful to relate."

miracle play dramatization of a Bible story.

Miró, Joan [mee-ROH, zhoo-AHN]. (1893–1983) Spanish artist.

mirage [mih-RAHZH].

mirthmaking

M.I.R.V. (abbr.) Multiple intercontinental reentry vehicle. A MIRV warhead.

misalliance [mihs-uh-LIE-ans] marriage to a social inferior. Pref. to **mesalliance.**

miscegenation [miss-seh-jeh-NAE-shuhn] interbreeding of races.

miscellaneous

miscellany [MIHS-sehl-ae-nee].

mischiefmaker, —making.

mischievous [MIHS-chihv-uhs].

miscreant [MIHS-kree-ehnt] rascal.

misdemeanor minor crime. See **felony.**

misled [mihs-LEHD; NOT: MIE-suhld]. p. and p.p. of *mislead.*

misogynist [mih-SAHJ-ih-nihst] woman hater; misogyny

Miss (not an abbreviation) (pl.) misses. *The Misses Brown* (formal); *The Misses Brown and Smith; Miss Brown and Miss Smith; Miss Joan and Miss Cynthia Smith.*
Do not use *Miss* as a form of address if the name is followed by an academic title. NOT: *Miss Joan Smith, Ph.D.* (British do not use *Miss* as a form of address). See **Mr., Ms.**

missilemaker, —man, —work.

mission Cap. if part of name: Gospel Mission, Mission 66, the mission. BUT diplomatic mission, Jones' mission.

Mississippi U.S. state. Abbr.: MS. Cap.: Jackson. Native: Mississippian.

missive (n.) a letter.

missile projectile.

Missouri U.S. state Abbr.: MO. Cap.: Jefferson City. Native: Missourian.

misspell

misstate

mistake (p.) mistook; (p.p.) mistaken. —nness.

Mister See **Mr.**

mistletoe [MIHS-l'toh] green semi-parasitic shrub traditional for Christmas.

mistral [MIHS-trehl; mihs-TRAHL]

cold dry wind in S France.

mistreat to abuse. In U.S., *maltreat* is malpractice.

miter (v. or n.) Pref. to —re. miter box (n.).

mitigate (v.) to moderate; meliorate. (adj.) —gable. (n.) —tor.

mitosis [mih-TOH-sihs] cell reproduction process resulting in creation of chromosomes. See **meiosis.**

mixup (n.), mix up (v.). *I'll mix up the martinis.*

mizzenmast

ml. (abbr.) milliliter.

Mlle. (abbr.) mademoiselle.

mm. (abbr.) millimeter. mm² (abbr.) square. mm³ (abbr.) cubic.

Mme. (abbr.) madame. (pl.) Mmes (abbr.) mesdames.

MN Minnesota.

mnemonic [nee-MAHN-ihk] (adj.) aiding memory.

MO Missouri

mo. (abbr.) month.

mobile [MOBH-biel] (adj.) movable. [-beel] (n.) sculpture with movable parts capable of easy movement.

mobilization [moh-bihl-ihz-AE-shuhn].

moccasin

mocha [MOH-kuh] coffee or coffee flavoring. From Red Sea port known for coffee shipments.

model —led, —ling.

Modernism movement in all arts, roughly 1890–1940. In general marked by compositional experimentation, rejection of tradition, and belief in supremacy of artistic vision. Includes **Picasso, Stravinsky**, others.

POSTMODERN Art and culture since W.W. II. Sp.: Postmodern, Post-Modern, post Modern, post-Modern.

modular [MAHD-joo-luhr].

modicum [MAHD-ih-kuhm; NOT: MOHD-] a small quantity.

IOTA Greek letter *i*; the smallest quantity.

MORSEL a bite; mouthful.

Modigliani, Amedeo [moh-deel-YAHN-ee, ahm-ae-DAE-oh] (1884–1920) It. Modernist painter noted for nudes.

modiste [moh-DEEST] (fem.) dressmaker.

modus vivendi [MOH-duhs vih-VEHN-dee] (Lat.) a way of living; an arrangement or accommodation.

Mogul [moh-GUHL, MOH-gul] of Mongolian race, esp. the conquerors of India and their descendants.

mogul a dictator or powerful person. In skiing, a bump.

Mohamma (570-632) principal prophet, founder of Islam. Adj., Mohammedan. See **Moslem**.

Mohave, Mojave [moh-HAHV-eh] desert, river, Indian tribe in SW U.S.

moiety [MOI-eh-tih] one of two equal parts; a half.

moiré [mwohr, mohr] (n.) silk material with frosted or watered appearance.

MOIRE [MAW-rae; MOH-rae] (adj.) having a watered appearance.

molasses Takes a singular verb.

mold Pref. to **mould**.

Moldavia [mohl-DAE-vee-ah] republic in former **U.S.S.R.**; part of **Commonwealth of Independent States**, 1992. In SE Europe, bordering Romania. Cap.: Kishinev [KIHSH-uh-nehf]. Native: Moldavian(s).

molecule See **atom**.

Molière [mawl-YAIR] (1622-1673) pseudonym of Jean Baptiste Poquelin, humorous French dramatist (The Miser).

mollusk

Moloch [MUH-luhk] demonic pagan deity from Old Testament.

molt Pref. to *moult*.

molten

mol. wt. (abbr.) molecular weight.

moment a short but indefinite period of time.

INSTANT a point in time. *The instant the switch was turned the bomb exploded.*

momentarily in or for a moment.

MOMENTARY lasting for a moment.

MOMENTOUS of great importance.

Mon. (abbr.) Monday.

Monaco [MAHN-ah-koh] small principality between France and Italy on the Mediterranean. Cap.: Monaco. Native: Monegasque or Monacan. Currency: franc.

monad [MOH-nad] indivisible unit, esp. in philosophy.

monarchic [muh-NAHR-kihk] of a monarchy.

Monday [MUHN-dih] (abbr. Mon.).

Mondrian, Pieter Cornelis [MAWN-dree-ahn, PEE-tuhr] (1872–1944) Du. modern painter.

Monet, Claude [maw-NEH, klohd] (1840–1926) Fr. impressionist painter. NOT **Manet.**

money $2.75; $0.27; 14 cents; $2 per 100 pounds; 2¢ to 6¢ (no spaces); £2 4s 6d; 2.5 francs; fr. 2.5; Rs. 5,278,411 (Indian rupees); 85 yen, Y190, £127; $17 million; $1.7 million or $1,700,000. BUT $750,000; $1/2 billion to $1 1/2 billion.

See individual countries for native currencies.

money rate interest rate for short-term loans.

money (n.); monied (adj.).

MONIES sums of money.

—monger [MUHNG-guhr] suffix orig. meaning salesman or trader: *fishmonger, ticketmonger.* Now suggests instigator: *scandalmonger, warmonger.* Connotes discreditable dealing.

Mongolia Central Asian nation, independent since 1921. Cap.: Ulaanbaatar [oo-LAHN bah-TAR]. Native: Mongolian. Currency: Tugrik.

mongoose (pl.) —ooses.

monitory [MAHN-ih-tawr-ee] admonishing.

monogamy [muh-NAHG-uh-mee] marriage with one person at a time. For person, monogamist. (adj.) monogamous.

monogrammed —ing.

monologue words delivered by one person on stage; a speech monopolizing a conversation. (Sp. pref. to *monolog.*) Use monologist [MAHN-ahl-oh-gihst] to refer to speaker.

SOLILOQUY speaking to oneself.

monotonous Implies sameness and boredom.

MONOTONIC in music, one tone.

monseigneur [MAWN-saen-yoor].

my lord. Fr. title for church and court dignitaries. *Monseigneur the Archbishop.* (pl.) —s.

monsieur (abbr.: M.) Fr. for Mr. or sir. pl. —s (abbr. MM. or Messrs.) [meh-SYUH, -z].

monsignor [mawn-SEEN-ayawr], (pl.) —s or —ori [mawn-see-NYOH-ree] title of honor held by Catholic prelates.

ADDRESS: The Right (or Very Reverend) Monsignor Thomas Delaney. SALUTATION: Monsignor; Right Reverend Delaney, Dear Monsignor Delaney. Italian form: Monsignore. (pl.) —ori.

montage [mahn-TAHJ] picture created by blending several other pictures or other materials.

Montana U.S. state. Abbr.: MT. Cap.: Helena. Native: Montanan.

monthlong (adj.).

MONTHS Generally abbreviated: Jan., Feb., Aug., Sept., Oct., Nov., and Dec.

Less often abbreviated: March, April, May, June or July (Mar., Apr., Je., Jy.).

monument Bunker Hill Monument, the monument; National Monument (See **National**); Washington Monument, the monument.

mood (or mode) in grammar, verb form which denotes style or manner. Imperative: *Go.* Indicative: *I am going.* Subjunctive: *If I go . . .* See *SUBJUNCTIVE MOOD.*

moog synthesizer [moog or mohg] electronic device that can reproduce, store, and distort a wide variety of sounds. (colloq.) synth, synthesizer.

moon Lowercase unless used with names of other celestial bodies.

moonlight (v.) to work at an extra job. (n.) moonlighter, moonlighting.

moose (pl.) moose.

moot (adj.) debatable, or lacking practical signifigance. A *moot court* is a mock court.

mopping-up (adj.); mopping up (v.). *This pitcher is just mopping up.*

moral (adj.) pertaining to conduct of humans as social beings. (n.) a lesson that teaches such conduct.

MORALE emotional condition.

morality play dramatized allegory, such as "Everyman."

morals See **ethics.**

morass [moh-RASS] marsh; hence, anything tangled or confusing.

moratorium period of delay. (pl.) —ia or —ums.

more and more Never follow by *than.* NOT: *The council required more and more taxes than the community would pay.* BUT . . . *required more than they could pay.*

mores [MOH-reez] (n.) social customs and manners.

more than one Though plural in

meaning, takes a singular verb. *More than one person is here.*

morgen 2.1165 acres (U.S.A.).

Mormon (from *Book of Mormon*, believed to contain divine revelations) a member of the Church of Jesus Christ of Latter-Day Saints, founded in 1830 by Joseph Smith.

Morocco NW African nation, on Mediterranean Sea. Formerly Sp. and Fr.; independent 1956. Cap.: Rabat. Native: Moroccan. Currency: dirham.

Morpheus [MAWR-fee-uhs; more properly, MAWR-fyuhs] Gr. god of dreams; hence, sleep.

morphology in grammar, study of inflectional forms, their origin, development, and functions; in biology, science of structural organic types.

morsel See **modicum**.

mortgagee the lender.

    MORTGAGER [MAWR-gihj-uhr] the person who pledges property. In law, —or.

mortgageholder, mortgage bond.

mortician [mawr-tihsh-ehn] undertaker.

    MORTUARY [MAWR-choo-air-ee] place where dead bodies are kept.

mortise [MAWR-tihs] (n.) a cavity. (v.) to cut a cavity.

Moslem or **Muslim** believer in Islam.

MUSSELMAN orthodox believer in Islam.

MUHAMMAD, MOHAMMED, MOHAMET the prophet of Islam.

mosquito (pl.) —os; pref. to —oes.

most-favored-nation (adj.).

motherhood, —land; mother-of-pearl; mother lode, mother ship.

mother-in-law (pl.) mothers-in-law.

Mother Superior ADDRESS: Reverend Mother Superior; or Reverend Mother Sophie (followed by initials designating the order); or Reverend Mother Superior Louise (without the initials designating the order); or Mother Louise, Convent of the Immaculate Conception. SALUTATION: Reverend Mother Louise; Dear Reverend Mother.

motif [moh-TEEF] theme or salient feature of a work.

motion pictures *Moving pictures* is arch.; use *movies. Cinema* or *film* usually connotes higher cultural intention.

motor. See engine.

Moulin Rouge [MOO-la'n ROO-ZH] Paris dance hall featured in paintings of **Tolouse-Lautrec,** and in 1953 film.

mountainside, —top (n.); mountain-high (adj.).

Mountain States Colorado, Wyoming, North Dakota, South Dakota; sometimes Idaho and Utah.

mountain time mountain standard time. See **time.**

mouse the computer accessory is always a noun.

mousse [mooss] a flavored frozen cream or gelatin dessert.

moustache, mustache Either spelling acceptable.

movable

movies, moviegoer, —land, —maker. See **motion pictures.**

Movie Ratings Instituted in 1968 as indication of movie content. G: for general audiences, including children. PG: children admitted, but parental guidance suggested. PG13: parents advised against allowing children under 13 to attend. R: restricted to those over 13. NC17: no one under 17 admitted.

The M rating, for Mature, is no longer used, and neither is the X rating, which indicated sexual content and full frontal nudity (it has been replaced by NC17).

The XXX rating is a marketing ploy of so-called "adult theaters," indicating explicit sexual content.

moving average See **average.**

mow (p.) mowed; (p.p.) mowed or mown; mowing.

Mozambique [moh-zam-BEEK] island nation off SE Africa. Formerly Port.; independent, 1975. Cap.: Maputo. Native: Mozambique (rare). Currency: Metical.

Mozart, Wolfgang Amadeus [MOH-tsahrt, VOLF-gahng ah-mah-DAE-uhs] (1756–1791) Austrian composer.

m.p. (abbr.) melting point.

M.P. (abbr.) military police; Member of Parliament.

m.p.h. (abbr.) miles per hour.

Mr. (abbr.) mister. Title of address for a man: *Mr. Brown, Mr. John Brown.* The pl. messrs. (abbr.), or messieurs, is archaic: *Messrs. Jones, Brown, and Smith.*

Never use *Mr.* with a title, or with honorable, reverend, or esquire, or when an academic degree follows the name: *Rev. John Law* or *John Law, D.D.; Dr. Joseph Brown* or *Joseph Brown, M.D.; The Reverend Dr. John Smith.* BUT: *John Smith, D.D.; Mr. Chairman; Mr. Secretary.*

Use Mr., Mrs., Ms., or *Miss* as appropriate, for citizens who do not have titles which replace these terms.

M.R.B.M. (abbr.) medium-range ballistic missile.

Mrs. technically, an abbr. for *mistress: Mrs. Smith, Mrs. Jones.* The pl. is also *Mrs.,* technically an abbr. for *mesdames.* BUT *Mesdames Smith and Jones* is archaic, and used only in exceptionally formal settings. Instead of *Mesdames B.O. and A.R. Jones,* use *the Mrs. Jones.*

Mrs. as a title of address takes the husband's last name: *Mrs. Jackie Kennedy* or *Mrs. Jackie Onassis; Mrs. Raisa Gorbachev.* Thus in many cases, a less objectionable title is **Ms.**

Ms. Elizabeth Taylor is a married woman keeping her maiden name; *Ms. Jackie Onassis* is a widow who happens to be identified by her former husband's name, but who has nonetheless established an adult identity of her own.

Mrs. may be used with reverend honorable, or doctor: *The Reverend Mrs. Smith.*

See: **madam, Ms.,** *SEXIST LANGUAGE.*

MS., ms. (abbr.) manuscript; MSS., mss. (abbr.) manuscripts.

M.S. (abbr.) master of science.

Ms. non-sexist form of address, replacing *Miss* or *Mrs.* Introduced in 1970 (also the name of a magazine featuring women's issues), the term is now widely accepted. It should be used in all cases when some other form of address has not been clearly indicated beforehand.

Ms. is not an abbr. for anything, and can be used either with a married name, *Ms. Jackie Onassis,* or, more commonly, a maiden name, *Ms. Jane Fonda.*

Ms. can also be used with other titles: *Reverend Ms. Nutting. See:* **Miss, Mrs.,** *SEXIST LANGUAGE.*

msec. (abbr.) millisecond, 1/1000 second.

Msgr. (abbr.) monsignor.

M. Sgt. (abbr.) master sergeant.

m.s.l. (abbr.) mean sea level.

m.s.t. (abbr.) mountain standard time.

mt. (abbr.) megaton; mountain.

MT Montana.

m.t. (abbr.) mountain time.

MTV (all caps.) Music Television, established 1980.

muchly (obs.) Use *much.*

mucilage [MYOO-sihl-ihj].

muckrake (v.); —raker (n.).

mucus (n.); mucous (adj.).

muddlehead, —headed.

mudfish, —flow; mud flat; mud hen.

mufti [MUHF-tee] *In mufti* means in civilian clothes.

muezzin [myoo-EHZ-ihn] Moslem prayer crier.

Muhammad Ali (b. 1942) American heavyweight champion, born Cassius Clay.

muleback, —man, —skinner; mule deer.

muleteer [myoo-leh-TEER] mule driver.

multiple-purpose (adj.)

multiplication Related words: double, triple, quadruple, quintuple, sextuple, septuple, octuple, nonuple, decuple.

Munchhausen, von, Baron Karl Friedrich [fawn MEUNK-hou-zehn, FREE-drhk]. (1720–1797) Ger. soldier, hunter, hero of burlesque stories by Rudolf Erich Raspe, 1785.

Muscat and Oman See **Oman.**

museum Cap. with name: Army Medical Museum, the Medical Museum, Field Museum, National Museum; National Air Museum, the Air Museum.

muses nine Greek goddesses of arts: Calliope, Clio, Erato, Euterpe, Melpomene, Plymnia, Terpsichore, Thalia, Urania.

music Cap. title of an opera: *Aida.* Cap. characters and titles of symphonies (but place nicknames in quotation marks: *"the Pastorale"),* and names of movements: *the Scherzo.*

Lowercase instrumentation added for explanation: *Sonata in F Major for piano.*

musical [MYOO-sih-kuhl] Word serves as both adj. and n.

MUSICALE [myoo-sih-KAL] (n., rare) program of music.

musical groups If the group's name is a plural, it is treated like any plural noun. *If the Ink Spots hadn't been black, they'd have become millionaires. The Platters were at their peak in "The Great Pretender."*

A singular name is treated as singular. *Aerosmith plays heavy metal. So does Van Halen. Then what is Public Enemy, a rap group, doing on the same bill?*

Either type of name, or part of a name, can be combined with a prefix to make an adjective. *I love those chiming Byrdsy guitars. They play lean and hard, Creedence-style.*

musicmaker, music room; music-mad (adj.)

Muslim See **Islam, Moslem.**

muslin a cotton cloth.

Mussolini, Benito [moos-oh-LEE-nih, bae-NEE-toh] (1883–1945) It. Fascist dictator, 1921–1945, a/k/a *Il Duce* [eel DOO-chae].

mustache, moustache

mutual [MYOO-choo-uhl] shared equally and jointly by two or more for benefit of all.

RECIPROCAL returned and given in due measure by each of two sides.

mutual defense assistance program

M.V. (abbr.) motor vessel.

MVD, KGB, NKVD various abbrs. for U.S.S.R. secret police. *KGB* is most common.

My Lai [mee lae] village in former South Vietnam, a/k/a Song My, site of civilian massacre by U.S. forces, 1968.

myopia [mie-OH-pee-uh] nearsightedness.

myriameter unit of length = 6.2137 miles = 10 km.

myrhh [muhr] fragrant, bitter plant resin of middle East; traditionally, a gift brought to infant Jesus by the Magi; signifies death.

myth story concerning supernatural beings, u‸u. designed to explain a natural phenomena. Use *mythology* for the study of such stories.

N

n Usually silent after *m* in the same syllable: *autumn, solemn.* BUT the addition of an extra syllable will often cause the silent letter to be sounded: *autumnal, solemnity.*

-n Words of one syllable ending in *n* preceded by a single vowel (but not a diphthong) double the *n* before a suffix beginning with a vowel: *running, sinning.* BUT: *darning, coining.*

Words of more than one syllable do the same if the last syllable is accented: *beginning, unplanned.* BUT: *womanish.*

n. (abbr.) noun.

N. (abbr.) normal.

N.A.A.C.P. National Association for the Advancement of Colored People.

Nabokov, Vladimir [nah-BOH-kuhv, vla-DEE-mihr] (1899–1977) Russian-American writer. See also *Lolita.*

nacre, nacré Mother of pearl and shellfish that yield it.

Nagasaki [nah-gah-SAH-kee] seaport in Japan, second target of atomic bomb, 1945.

naiad [NAE-ad, Br., NIE-] a water nymph.

nail unit of cloth length = 1/16 yd. = 2.25 in. = 1/4 span = 5.715 cm.

Nairobi [nic ROH-bee] Cap. city of Kenya.

naive [nah-EEV] (adj.) unsophisticated. (n.) naivete [nah-eev-TAE].

name namable.

Namibia SW African territory governed by South Africa. Cap.: Windhoek [vihnt-HOOK]. See **South Africa.**

name plate —sake; name-calling, namedropping (adj.).

NAMES In common usage, given names are written first, followed by a family name: *John Brown.* The first reference to a person should include the first name and any initials commonly used. BUT AVOID single initial: *J. Doe.* Additional references should be to *Mr. Doe.*

Traditionally, women in England and United States have adopted the given and family names of husband, disregarding maiden name: *Mrs. John B. Doe.* BUT nowadays it is common for women to retain their maiden name: *Ms. Mary Brown.* Women may also use the husband's name and the mother's maiden name with or without hyphenation: *Ms. Mary Doe Brown, Ms. Mary Doe-Brown.*

British Peers sign only given name with peerage designations; peeresses sign given names or initials with peerage designations. See **Lord and Lady** and **Lady.**

Bishops sign initials followed by the name of the See.

ARAB NAMES are usually made up of Arab words and follow grammatical rules. Many incorporate *the* as *al*. The article may be joined to any or both names, but *al* is usually hyphenated with the word following *al-Mutasim*. Common names are: *Abdullah (Worshipper of God), Abdel (Worshipper of the Victorious One), Haj (Pilgrim)*.

Most names have at least three or four parts: the given name, the father's and the grandfather's names, and sometimes a family name. Anglicized versions prefix *Mr.* to the last name for a second reference.

BURMESE NAMES are usually single words prefixed by a title such as U (something between *sir* and *uncle*) or Thaikin (master). In Anglicized versions the title is used in the first reference: U Thant. In second references, it is *Mr. Thant* or *Secretary General Thant*. Where more than one name is given, all references include both names: *U rin Maunp, Mr. rin Maunp*. Women's names do not change at marriage.

CHINESE NAMES. Family names appear first, but many Chinese adopt western style, at least for foreign use, putting their given names or initials first: *K.C. Wu*.

Transliteration of Chinese words is based on the Wade-Giles system, but apostrophes are omitted. *Chiang Kai-shek, General Chiang; Sun Yat-sen, Mr. Sun*.

INDONESIAN NAMES often have only one name: *Sukarno, President Sukarno*. When there is no title, the name is written *Mr. Sukarno*.

For Western contacts, a first name may be adopted, like *Achmed Sukarno*. In Bali, children are numbered.

KOREAN NAMES. Family names are usually written first. Use *Kim* in second reference to *Kim Il Sung*. Unlike Chinese, the given names are not hyphenated. Some Koreans, like *Syngman Rhee*, use western style: *Rhee* is the family name.

SPANISH NAMES are usually made up of two surnames, father's family name and the mother's family name, often joined by a *y* (and). These are sometimes hyphenated. A second reference to *José Molina Valente* is usually *Molina*, NOT *Valente*. Some individuals prefer both the mother's and father's family names for a second reference. *Gabriel García Marquez, Mr. García Marquez*.

A married woman usually adds to her own surname the name of her husband, connecting the two by the preposition *de*, but omitting the portion which refers to his mother's surname.

VIETNAMESE NAMES. Although family names appear first, use full names in second as well as in first references: *Ngo Dinh Diem* NOT *Ngo* or *Diem*.

See *FILING*, **Nobility.**

nape [NAEP], **napery** [NAE-puhr-ee].

naptha [NAF-thah; NOT: NAP-tha] volatile, often flammable liquid.

Napoleon Bonaparte, Code Napoleon; the pastry is lowercase. See **Bonaparte.**

naptime

narcissus (pl.) narcissuses or —cissi. Cap. is figure in Gr. myth.

narcissism [nahr-SIHS-ihzm] self-love. For person with this condition, use —cissist.

narcosis [nahr-KOH-sihs] (pl.) — oses [-seez].

narrative [NAR-uh-tihv], narrator [nar-RAE-tehr].

NASA [NA-suh] (abbr., no points) National Aeronautics and Space Administration.

nascent [NASS-ehnt; NAE-sehnt] coming into being.

Nasser, Col. Gamal Abdel [NAH-saer, guh-MAHL] (1918–1971) Egyptian soldier and statesman. President of United Arab Republic (Egypt), 1958–1971.

nasturtium [nuhss-TUHR-shuhm] herb with red and yellow flowers.

nation Cap. when synonym for United States; also Indian Nation, Woodstock Nation, etc. BUT: the nation, nationwide; French nation, Balkan nations.

National. Cap. in conjunction with name, like National Academy of Sciences (see **academy**), and with state institutions: National Archives; National Capital (Washington), the Capital (Washington), National Forest (see **forest**); National Gallery of Art, the National Gallery, the gallery; National Grange, the Grange; National Guard, Air National Guard, the guard, a guardsman, BUT a National Guardsman.

See also institute, legislature, monument, museum.

national. Lower-case with agency, anthem, customs, spirit, stockpile, water policy.

National Income

nationwide.

Native American Pref. to *Indian*. See **Indian, -American.**

nativity [nae-TIHV-ih-tih] birth or circumstances of birth. Cap., the birth of Christ.

NATO [NAE-toh] (abbr., no points) North Atlantic Treaty Organization.

naught, nought [nawt] a cipher, zero, nothing. *Nought* is customary in the mathematical sense, *naught* in other contexts: *Nought from six is six. He cares naught for money.* See **aught.**

Nauru [nah-OO-roo] tiny island nation in SW Pacific. Formerly U.N. Trust Territory; independent, 1974. Cap.: Yaren. Native: Nauruan. Currency: Australian dollar.

nausea [NAW-see-uh; NAW-shuh] stomach sickness, such as seasickness; by extension, extreme disgust. Use *nauseated* for a person. *He was nauseated and nauseating.*

NAUSEOUS [NAW-shuhs] disgusting.

nautical mile. One minute of longitude at the equator = 6080 feet = 1.15 miles. See **mile.**

Navaho, Navajo [NAV-uh-hoh] Native American nation now in Arizona, Utah, New Mexico. Also a mountain in Utah.

naval Cap. if part of name. Naval Academy (see **academy**); Guam Naval Base, the naval base; Naval District; Naval Home (in Philadelphia), the home; Naval Militia, the militia; Naval Reserve, the Reserve, a reservist; Naval Reserve Officer, a Reserve officer; Naval War College, the college.

Naval Shipyard, cap. if preceding or following name: Brooklyn Naval Shipyard. BUT the naval shipyard. Naval Station, cap. if preceding or following name: Key West Naval Station.

Naval Officers. See *OFFICERS*.

navel orange

navy, American or foreign. Cap. if part of name; cap. standing alone only if referring to U.S. Navy: Admiral of the Navy, the admiral; Navy Battle Force, the Battle Force, the force; Navy Hospital Corps, hospital corpsman, the corps; Navy regulation 56; Navy Scouting Force, the scouting force; Navy Seabees, a Seabee; Navy 7th Task Force (See **forces**).

Nazarene [naz-uh-REEN] Christ.

Nazi [NAHT-see; NAT-see] Abbr. for National Socialist German Workers Party (Nationalsozialistische Deutsche Arbeiterpartei), led by Adolf Hitler 1921–1945. Now, any intolerant, oppressive force or person. Nazism.

N.B. (abbr.) New Brunswick, Canada.

n.b. (abbr.) nota bene. (Lat.) Note well.

N.B.S. (abbr.) National Bureau of Standards.

NC (abbr.) North Carolina.

NC17 See **movie ratings.**

ND (abbr.) North Dakota.

NE (abbr.) northeast, Nebraska.

nearby, nearsighted, near-miss.

Near East countries bordering eastern Mediterranean Sea, a/k/a the Middle East.

nearly See **almost.**

nearsightedness vision disorder. See **shortsightedness.**

neat's-foot (adj.).

Nebraska U.S. state. (abbr.: NE) Cap.: Lincoln. Native: Nebraskan. Nickname: Cornhuskers.

Nebuchadnezzar [nehb-yuh-kuhd-NEHZ-uhr] (605–502 B.C.) King of Babylon legendary for power and opulence.

nebula [NEHB-yoo-luh] cloudlike celestial structure. (pl.) —lae. (adj.) nebular [-lehr].

NEBULOUS adj. meaning vague.

necessary [NEHS-eh-sehr-ih] (adj.);

necessarily [NEHS- or -SEHR-] (adv.). See **essential**.

necessity for NOT *necessity to.*

nectar —ed, —rine, —ous.

née (f), né (m.) [nae] Fr. for *born. Mrs. Cynthia White, née Brown.*

ne'er-do-well

Nefertiti [NEH-fuhr-TEE-tee] Queen of Egypt, 1379–1365 B.C., legendary for beauty.

NEGATIVES If put together incorrectly, negatives say the opposite of what is meant. The problem occurs most commonly in parallel clauses, where the negative may not apply to the second clause.
    Incorrect usage: *None shall come but shall see that I am right. No person may enter unless he is a member, and (each member* omitted*) must pay his dues.*
    See *DOUBLE NEGATIVE.*

neglect, negligence Both mean failure to attend to, but negligence generally connotes habitual neglect. *Neglect of duty is an offense punishable by court martial. The owner's negligence caused the building to deteriorate.*

negligée [nehg-lih-ZHAE; NEHG-].

negligible

Negro Current usage prefers **black** for American Negroes. (pl.) —oes, —s. See **African, African-American**.

    COLORED of a race other than white. Usu. pejorative, though

formal usage allows **person of color.**

Nehru, Jawaharlal [NAE-roo, juh-WAH-hahr-lahl] (1889–1964) First Prime Minister of India, 1947–1964.

neither, nor [NEE-thuhr; NIE-thur] Best used with two nouns, but may correctly refer to more. Usually takes singular verb, but when plural is indicated in one part, verb agrees with closest subject. *Neither John nor Mary knows. Neither she nor they know.*
    Neither must be followed by *nor*, except when meaning "not yet." Place *neither* before the noun modified. See **either, or.**

neo-classicism imitation of Greek and Roman style.

neologism a new expression or new meaning of an old one.

neophyte [NEE-oh-fiet] newcomer, esp. in priesthood.

Nepal [neh-PAWL] Himalaya kingdom, on NE border of India. Cap.: Kathmandu [KAHT-man-doo]. Native: Nepalese. Currency: rupee.

nepotism [NEHP-uht-ihsm] favoritism shown to relatives, especially in employment.

Neruda, Pablo [neh-ROO-dah] (1904–1973) Peruvian poet and diplomat. Nobel Prize, 1971.

nervewracking Sometimes hyphenated, or hyphenated and spelled *nerve-racking.*

nether lower, under: *nether garments.*

Netherlands coastal nation in NW Europe, since Middle Ages. Cap.: Amsterdam; seat of government, The Hague. Native: Netherlander, Dutchman, Hollander. Currency: guilder.

network a chain of radio or TV stations; hence, any group of acquaintances. In latter context, may be n. or v. *I did a lot of networking in order to get this job.*

neuralgia [nyuh-RAHL-jah] acute, paroxysmal pain.

neurosis mental disorder. (pl.) —oses [-seez].

neutron Unchanged subatomic particle.

neutron bomb still-experimental device which would destroy people and leave buildings and machinery intact.

Nevada [neh-VAD-ah, -VAH-duh] U.S. state. Abbr.: NV. Cap.: Carson City. Native: Nevadan.

nevermore, —theless; never-ending (adj.)

new Cap. if part of name: New Willard.

New Brunswick Abbr.: N.B. Province in Canada. Cap.: Fredericton.

New Caledonia [nyoo kal-eh-DOH-nyah] Fr. island near Australia. Cap.: Noumea. Currency: C.F.A. franc.

New Deal political-economic philosophy and reforms under President F.D. Roosevelt. See **N.R.A.**

New England States Maine, New Hampshire, Vermont, Rhode Island, Connecticut, Massachusetts.

newfangled

Newfoundland [noo-fuhnd-LAND] island province in Canada. Abbr.: N.F. Cap.: St. John's. Native: Newfoundlander.

    NEWFOUNDLAND [nyoo-FOUND-land] breed of dog.

New Hampshire U.S. state. Abbr.: NH. Cap.: Concord. Native: New Hampshirite.

New Jersey U.S. state Abbr.: NJ. Cap.: Trenton. Native: New Jerseyite.

newly (adv.) newlywed; BUT new-baked bread, newmown hay.

New Mexico U.S. state Abbr.: NM. Cap.: Santa Fe. Native: New Mexican.

New Orleans [noo AWR-lee-anz] city in Louisiana.

news (sing. and pl.) Takes a sing. verb.

newsboy, —caster, —letter, —making, —man, —paper, —paperboy, —paperman, —print, —reel, —room, —stand, —worthy, —writing (all one word); news editor.

newspaper titles Some include the name of the city in the title, but others do not. Follow the style set by the newspaper. *The New York Times, the Sun* (Baltimore), *The Times of London.*

New Year's Day, New Year's Eve.

New York U.S. state. Abbr.: NY. Cap.: Albany. Native: New Yorker.

New Zealand Pacific island nation near Australia. Formerly Br., independent, 1907. Cap.: Wellington. Native: New Zealander. Currency: dollar.

next of kin

nexus connection. (pl.) —es.

Ngo Dinh Diem [noh dihn dee-EHM] (1901–1963) Vietnamese politician, president at beginning of U.S. war.

NH (abbr.) New Hampshire.

niacin [NIE-a-sihn] a B-vitamin; pellagra preventative.

Niagara [nie-AG-ruh].

Nibelungenlied [NEE-buh-luhng-uhn-leed] 12th-C. German epic, used by Richard Wagner in opera. In German myth, Nibelungs are children of the mist.

Nicaragua [nihk-uh-RAH-gwuh] Central American nation. Independent, 1838; **Sandinista** revolution, 1979. Cap.: **Managua**. Native: Nicaraguan. Currency: cordoba.

Nice [NEES] resort seaport on French Riviera.

nicety [NIES-eh-tee] (n.) a special feature; a delicacy. *We could afford a va-*

cation with all the niceties.

niche [nihzh].

nickelplate (v.), nickel-plated (adj.), nickelplating (n.).

NICKNAMES Cap. when used with or for a proper name. Bay State (Massachusetts), Big Four (powers, railroads, etc.), City of Churches (Brooklyn), New Deal, Fair Deal, Keystone State (Pennsylvania), the Hub (Boston).

Niebuhr, Reinhold [NEE-boo'r, RIEN-hohlt] (1892–1971) Am. (New York City) theologian, writer.

Nietzsche, Friedrich [NEE-cheh, FREE-drihk] (1844–1900) Ger. philosopher. Nietzscheism.

Niger [NIE-juh] landlocked nation in N Africa. Formerly Fr.; independent, 1960. Cap.: Niamey [nee-AH-mae]. Native: Nigerois. Currency: CFA franc.

Nigeria [nie-JEER-ih-uh] nation on W African coast. Formerly Br.; independent, 1960. Cap.: Lagos [LAH-gohs]. Native: Nigerian. Currency: Naira.

nigh. (arch.) near.

nightingale

nihilism [NIE-uhl-ihzm] philosophy which denies any substantive ground of truth or moral principle.

Nijinsky, Waslaw [nih-ZHIHN-skee, VUHTS-lahf] (1890–1950) Rus. ballet dancer, choreographer.

nimblefooted, nimble-fingered (adj.).

nimbus halo. (pl.) —bi.

nimrod hunter.

nine, ninety, ninth, the nineties, 9, IX, nineteen, ninetieth, ninety-one.

ninepin (pl.) ninepins. The game is always plural, but takes singular verb.

Nippon old alternative name for *Japan*. (adj.) —ese.

Nisei [nee-SAE] (adj.) American-born Japanese.

nite Avoid this spelling; use *night*.

niter native soda. Pref. to Br. *nitre*.

NJ. (abbr.) New Jersey.

Nkrumah, Kwame [n'KROO-mah, KWAH-mee] (1909–1972) Ghanan writer, revolutionary, first prime minister (1957–60) and president (1960–66).

NKGB, NKVD See **KGB, MVD.**

N.L.R.B. (abbr.) National Labor Relations Board.

NM (abbr.) New Mexico.

No., Nos. (abbr.) number, numbers.

nobody —how, (adj.), —where, —wise (all one word); no-account, no-good, no-show (all n. and adj.), no-hitter (n.); no man's land.

Nobel Prize [noh-BEHL] annual awards in such fields as literature, the sciences, peacemaking. Created by Alfred Nobel, 1833–1896.

nobility. In order of rank: reigning sovereign (king and queen); member of the royal family (prince and princess); duke and duchess; marquis and marchioness; earl and countess; viscount and viscountess; baron and baroness; baronet; knight. See **Lord and Lady.**

noble NOT an adv. NOT: *You did noble.*

noblesse oblige [noh-BLEHS oh-BLEEZH] (Fr.) "nobility obliges;" rights entail responsibility.

no-fault insurance, no-fault divorce.

nohow Some grammarians accept the term, meaning *not in any way,* but Webster's calls it dialect. It is always incorrect in a double negative. *I wouldn't do it nohow.*

n.o.i.b.n. (abbr.) not otherwise indexed by name. Used in freight classification.

noisemaker

noisome poisonous; foul-smelling. NOT noisy.

nolle prosequi, nolle prosse [NAHL-ih PRAH-see-kwih] (Lat.) (n. and v.) "Unwilling to prosecute further." A criminal case abandoned by a district attorney. (v.) nol-pros. (adj.) nol-prossed, nol-prossing.

nolo contendere (Lat.) I will not

contest it. A plea in a criminal case which submits the defendant to conviction without admitting formal criminal guilt.

nomad [NOH-mad] (n.) a wanderer. (adj.) of a wandering tribe.

nom de plume [nahm-duh-PLOOM] pen name.

NOM DE GUERRE [nahm-duh-GAIR] name for a short period or single purpose.

PSEUDONYM assumed name; pen name.

ALIAS [AE-lee-uhs] assumed name, esp. for criminal purpose.

nomenclature [NOH-mehn clae-choor] system of naming.

NOMINATIVE ABSOLUTE OR ABSOLUTE a clause resembling a participial phrase which modifies a whole sentence rather than any part. It is independent and does not dangle. *All things considered* (nom. absolute), *he is a great man.*

NOMINATIVE CASE Used for subject of verbs. See *CASE.*

non- prefix meaning "not:" non-European, non-commital, non-tumor-bearing (adj.); non sequitur.

nonce the time being; a single brief occasion.

nonchalant [NAHN-shal-ahnt] (adj.) unconcerned. (n.) —ance.

non compos mentis (Lat.) not of sound mind.

none Meaning not one, takes a singular verb. *None of the candidates is qualified.*

NONE Meaning *not any,* may be treated as a plural. *None of the guests have arrived.*

nonentity [nahn-EHN-tuh-tee] person or thing of no account. Rarely spelled with hyphen, *non-entity.*

nonesuch something unique; a paragon.

nonetheless (adv.) nevertheless.

nongovernmental

nonpareil [nahn-pah-REHL] (adj.) unequalled. (n.) a printer's measure = 6 points or 1/12th inch.

noplace Do not use; incorrect.

nonplus (v.) to confuse. (adj.) —plused, —plus(s)ing.

non sequitur [nahn-SEHK-wih-tuhr] (Lat.) "does not follow." Statement that does not logically follow whatever was said previously.

noon (abbr.) 12 A.M.

noonday, —tide, —time.

no one Two words, no hyphen.

no par value stock common stock which has no face value.

nor See **or; either, or; neither, nor.**

north, northern Comparative: more northern; superlative: north-most, northernmost. See also **east-erly.**

north North Atlantic, Atlantic States, North Atlantic Treaty Organization, North Equatorial Current, North Korea, North Pole, North Star (Polaris), the North (section of United States; side in U.S. Civil War); BUT north Delaware.

North Jersey, South Jersey are exceptions to the general rule. See also **organization, treaty.**

North Carolina U.S. state. Abbr.: NC. Cap.: Raleigh. Native: North Carolinian. Nickname: *Tarheel.*

north-central region

North Dakota U.S. state. Abbr.: ND. Cap.: Bismarck. Native: North Dakotan.

northeast, northwest, northeastbound.

northerly a direction: *northerly wind, most northerly city.* BUT: *north side.* See **easterly.**

northerner BUT cap. for Union soldier in U.S. Civil War.

Northern Ireland Br. territory in NE Ireland, site of longstanding terrorism and civil unrest. Cap.: Belfast.

northward

Northwest Pacific, Northwest Territory.

Northwestern States Idaho, Montana, Oregon, Washington.

Norway Scandinavian nation, since Middle Ages. Cap.: Oslo. Native: Norwegian. Currency: krone.

no sooner Is followed by *than,* not *when. No sooner had he received a check than the creditors appeared.*

Nostradamus [nahs-trah-DAE-muhs] (1503–66) Fr. physician, astrologer; famous for predictions.

nostrum [NAHS-truhm] a quack cure.

not all, not everything Pref. to *all is not; everything is not.*

noticeable

not only . . . but, but also The first is always followed by one of the second. The sentence should be in structural balance. *She not only loved to read, but also loved to watch television.*

notorious ill-famed.

not un— May be used to express a double negative. *It is not unusual to find . . . Such things are not unheard of.*

notwithstanding

nougat [NOO-guht] candy made of nuts in sugar paste.

NOUNS (common variety) names of places, persons, things, qualities, etc.: *boy, river, keyboard, freedom.*

A proper noun is the name of a particular thing and is capitalized. Collective nouns refer to groups; concrete nouns, to specific things; abstract nouns, to general things.

Verbs must agree with the subject noun in number.

A noun preceding a gerund should be in the possessive case: *in the event of Mary's leaving . . . ; the ship's hovering nearby. . . .*

nouveau riche [noo-voh-REESH] (n. and adj.) newly rich (disparagingly). (pl.) —veaux riches.

Nova Scotia abbr.: N.S. Province of Canada (with Cape Breton Island). Cap.: Halifax.

novice a beginner. See **amateur, dilettante.**

novitiate [NOH-vihsh-ih-aet] apprentice nun; hence, novice.

now May be used as an adjective: *The now generation.*

nowhere NOT *nowheres.*

noxious [NAHK-shuhs] harmful.

NRA. National Rifle Association. In 1930s, National Recovery Administration, established as part of the **New Deal.**

N.S. (abbr.) Nova Scotia.

N.S.C. (abbr.) National Security Council.

nth [EHNTH] mathematical symbol for an unspecified number. Hence, *the nth degree,* to an extreme. Italicize *n.*

nuance [NOO-anss] subtle difference in meaning.

nucleus [NOO-klee-uhs] (pl.) —lei [-klee-ie].

nugatory [NOO-guh-toh-rih] worthless.

nuisance [NYOO-sans]

NUMBER in grammar, the distinction between singular and plural. See *VERBS.*

(1) Sing. subjects take sing. verbs; pl. subjects, pl. verbs. *I am here. They are here. I am many things. America is 50 states. The 50 sovereign states are America. Either he or she is coming. One or two are sick. She and he are coming. Everybody (no one, each) is here. All are here. The first ten of American parentage are here. Italy is one of those nations which are members; BUT Italy is the only one of those nations which is a member. The flock is nearby. What men do is their own affair. What is there for children to do? There is heaps to do.*

(2) The word *number* is itself sing. BUT: *A number of people were at the table. The number of books on the table is six.*

(3) Subjects joined by *and* take a plural verb. Subjects joined by *or* or *nor* take a singular verb.

Where a sing. and a pl. subject are joined by *or* or *nor,* the subject closest to the verb determines number. *One or two are sick.* Usage prefers a pl. subject closest to the verb.

(4) Two indefinite pronouns joined by *and* remain singular in meaning. *Anyone and everyone is here. Tomorrow and tomorrow and tomorrow creeps in its petty pace.*

(5) When a word is accepted as singular or plural in a sentence, the

same number should be retained throughout the sentence, with all verbs and pronouns agreeing. NOT: *Because Congress bases its decisions on whatever is politically expedient, they must first learn what the voters want.*

See **is, are;** *COLLECTIVE NOUNS.*

a number of Takes plural verb.

number a term used in counting; the amount of units.

NUMERAL a word or figure expressing a number.

FIGURE a symbol expressing a number. *I saw the figure 5 writ in gold.*

Numbers cardinals: one, three, twenty; ordinals: first, second, tenth; multiplicatives: single, double; arabic: 1, 7, 100; Roman: I, V, X, C, L, D.

NUMBERS The general rule is that numbers one through nine are spelled out, numbers ten or above written in figures. In business statistics or scientific work, both requiring many numbers, figures should be used in nearly every case.

Exceptions are made for percentages, decimals, dates, streets, telephone numbers, exact sums of money, numbers written with abbreviations, and pages (except preliminary pages, which are written in small Roman numerals). Other occasional exceptions are age, clock time, degrees of latitude and longitude, distance, market quotations, mathematical expressions, and proportions. See *MEASUREMENT.*

Use figures for numbers: (1) in groups of two or more numbers if any of the numbers is 10 or more: *I invited six boys and nine girls. There were 7 boys, 12 girls, and 4 parents;* (2) for isolated numbers of 10 or more; (3) with units of measurement: *7 bushels;* (4) for serial numbers: *Book 2, Exhibit 7.* Colon preceding does not affect the use.

Spell out numbers: (1) at the beginning of a sentence: *Six dollars was the price.* AVOID *$9;* (2) for serious and dignified texts: *the Thirteen Original States; the Eightieth Congress;* (3) for isolated units of time, money, or measurement under 10: *seven years;* (4) for numbers less than 100 preceding a compound modifier containing a figure: *two 1/2-inch boards* BUT *200 1-inch boards;* (5) for indefinite expressions: *the Seventies* BUT *the '70s, the 70s* are allowed; (6) for the words *million* and *billion* in large numbers, not tabulated: *$6 billion;* (7) for round numbers: *a thousand men.* (8) for fractions standing alone: *one-half.*

Occasionally, usage may allow numbers spelled out for centuries, dynasties, chapters, decades, military bodies, political divisions, or sessions of Congress.

Numbers larger than 1000, if written out, appear without extra commas or hyphens: *one thousand nine hundred and seventy.*

Cap. numbers if spelled out as part of a name: *Charles the First; Committee of One Hundred; Fourteenth Census* (See **Census**). PLURALS: *twos, threes, sevens. 2's, 3's, 7's, 42's.* AGES: *six years and three months; men between thirty and forty; a forty-one year old bridge.* See also *AGES,* **time.**

Use Arabic numbers with abbreviations, and for pages, chemical formulas, dates, decimals, degrees, dimensions, distances, fractions, market quotations, measurements, money, paces, temperature, weights, unit modifiers, time of day and years (BUT NOT in formal invitations: *On Saturday May the Twenty-sixth, at four p.m.*)

Used as modifiers, numbers are hyphenated: *a 7-hour day.*

HIGHER NUMERATION Follows two systems, one adopted by the U.S. and France, the other by Britain and Germany. In U.S., a billion is 1000 million, in Britain a million million. (Brit., 1000 million = 1 milliard). In U.S. a trillion is 1000 billion, in Britain, a million billion. Thus, where the U.S. adds three zeros, Britain adds six for each unit. The number of zeros under U.S. and British systems respectively are indicated: million 6, 6; milliard, 9, 9; billion 9, 12; trillion 12, 18.

Place a comma after each group of three numbers in a text. BUT in Spanish and German a period is used: *1.423.612.* In India, a comma appears after each two zeros.

FRACTIONS *1/1000th, one-thousandth; 2/3, two-thirds; 2/1000, two onethousandths; 23/30, twenty-three thirtieths; 21/32, twenty-one thirty-seconds; 3/4 inch, three-fourths (or three-quarters) of an inch. 0.9 ton.* POSSESSIVES: *1 month's layoff, 1 week's pay, 2 hours' work, 3 weeks' vacation.* ROMAN: See ***ROMAN NUMERALS.***

SERIAL NUMBERS *Bulletin Number 72; document 27; pages 127–129; lines 2, 3, and 4; Genesis 39:20; I-405* (the highway).

TIME In general use numerals. *3:00 p.m. or 3 a.m.;* at 2:30 *in the morning;* at 2 *o'clock; at half past three; 12 a.m.* (noon); *12 p.m.* (midnight): *o'clock* is not used with a.m. or p.m. Without a number, write a unit of time in the possessive: *a day's journey.* BUT with a unit, use the compound form: *a three-minute egg.* If the numeral is one or less than one, the possessive form may be used: *one minute's wait, a half-hour's wait.* If the numeral is more than one, the form may be *a ten-minute wait,* or *ten minutes' wait.* With an intervening adjective, the singular form of the unit is preferred: *a two-year-old horse.* BUT a plural unit, *seven days' journey, two years old,* may be used.

QUANTITY Units usually take an *of* form: *a quart of wine.* In a compound, the singular is used: *a twenty-gallon tank.* BUT in other constructions, the plural may be used: *four quarts of milk.* In weight measurements, the singular form is sometimes used, especially in Britain or Canada: *six ton of hay;* BUT the plural is preferred.

TITLES Usually cap.: *Book 5; Book Five;* BUT *abstract B pages, article 3 provisions, class II railroad, grade A milk, point 4 program, ward D beds.*

UNIT MODIFIERS: *twenty-one, twenty-first, 6-footer, 24-inch ruler, 3-week vacation, 8-hour day, 10-minute delay, 20th-century progress, 3-to-1 ratio, 5-to-4 vote, .22 caliber cartridge, 2-cent-per-pound tax, four-in-hand tie, three-and-twenty, two-sided question, multi-million-dollar fund.*

BUT *one hunded and twenty-one; 100-odd, foursome, threescore, foursquare, $20 million airfield, 2-inch* *diameter, 10-word telegram, 5-percent increase, 3-phase, 6-cycle, 115-volt; 5-gallon, 2-gallon, 1-quart cap; 2-inch, 1 1/4-inch, 1/2-inch, 1/4-inch.*

2- or 3-em quads, NOT *2 or 3 em quads; 2- to 3- and 4-ton trucks; 2- by 4-inch boards,* BUT *2 to 6 inches wide; twofold or threefold, not two- or three-fold.*

eighties, NOT *'eighties.* BUT *'20s.*

READ: *1500* as *fifteen hundred,* NOT *one thousand five hundred.*

See also **figures, foot, hundred, million, one.**

numbskull, numskull

nun See **Sister.**

nuncio [nuhn-shih-oh] permanent, official representative of the pope. (pl. —os)

nuptial [NUHP-shal]. See **matrimonial.**

Nureyev, Rudolf [nyoo-RAE-ehv] (b. 1938) Rus. ballet dancer who defected from U.S.S.R., 1961.

nutmeg the spice, the seed, the fruit.

NV Nevada.

NY New York, N.Y.C., New York City.

Nyasaland [nih-AS-uh-land] See **Malawi.**

O

—o Becomes -oes in plural: usually when word is more common in the plural: *dominoes;* or for monosyllables: *noes;* DOES NOT become -oes with rare plurals: *dos, dittos;* in words where a vowel precedes -o: *intaglios;* foreign and strange words: *albinos;* curtailed words: *photos;* multisyllable words: *archipelagos;* and proper names: *Romeos.*

oaf (pl.) —s.

Oahu Is. [oh-AH-hoo] chief island of Hawaiian group.

O.A.I.S. (abbr.) old age, invalidity, and survivors insurance (Social Security). Sometimes OASI.

oaken Use *oak.*

O.A.S. (abbr.) Organization of American States, formerly Pan American Union. Also, Organization de L'Armee Sécrète, French Secret Army Organization during war in Algeria.

oasis [oh-A-sihs] (pl.) *oases* or *oasises.*

oath (pl.) —s. [ohthz as in "clothes"].

obbligato a required musical accompaniment.

obdurate [AHB-dyoor-iht] hardened.

obeisance [oh-BAE-sehnts; —BEE-] homage, deference. Also, a bow, curtsy.

obese [oh-BEES] (adj.) fat. (n.) obesity.

obfuscate [AHB-fuhs-kaet] (v.) to make obscure.

obiter dictum [OHB-ih-tuhr DIHK-tuhm] (Lat.) incidental opinion by a judge; hence, any incidental observation. (pl.) —dicta.

object *He objects to having to go.*

OBJECTIVE CASE in grammar, the case used to denote the receiver of the action of a verb. Includes both the direct object: *I hit* the ball; and the indirect object: *I gave* him *the ball.*

Objective case also includes the object of a preposition: *I gave the ball to him;* the subject of an infinitive: *I want him to have* the ball; or the subject of a participle: *Can you imagine* him *playing the piano?* See *ACCUSATIVE CASE.*

objet d'art [ahb-JAE dahr] (pl.) objets. See **virtu.**

obligated Refers to a legal obligation.

OBLIGED Refers to a social favor. *He felt obliged to you for your courtesy and obligated for the amount of the damage.*

obligatory [ahb-LIHG-uh-toh-ree].

oblique [oh-BLEEK] (adj.) slanting, diagonal; (v.) to bend aside.

obliterate [ahb-LIHT-ehr-aet] (v.) to

destroy, erase. (adj.) —rable.

obloquy [AHB-loh-kwih] censorious speech: *described with obloquy.* Also, bad repute. (pl.) —ies.

oboe [OH-boh] (pl.) —s. oboist.

obsequious [ah-SEE-kwee-uhs] fawning.

obsequies [ahb-see-kwihz] (used only in pl.) funeral rites.

observance carrying out a custom.

OBSERVATION noticing.

observatory Cap. with name: Astrophysical Observatory; Naval Observatory, the Observatory.

obsession persistent concern, usually a delusion.

COMPLEX a system of desires and memories which exerts a strong influence on a person.

INCUBUS a nightmare.

MANIA strong misconceptions and delusions which result in insanity. See **psychopathic.**

obsolete (abbr.: obs.) no longer in use.

OBSOLESCENT becoming obsolete.

obstacle to

obstreperous [ahb-STREHP-uhr-uhs] aggressively noisy, disorderly.

obverse facing side. Opposite of *reverse.*

obviate (v.) to anticipate and dispose of or prevent.

occasion [oh-KAE-zhuhn] (n.); occasionally (adv.).

the Occident [AHK-sih-d nt] the West, esp. as opposed to the *Orient.* (adj.) occidental.

occiput [AHK-sih-puht] back of the head.

occult [ahk-KUHLT] magic, alchemy.

occur —rred, —rring, —rrence.

ocean Cap. if part of name: Antarctic Ocean, Arctic Ocean; Atlantic Ocean, North Atlantic Ocean; Pacific Ocean, Southwest Pacific Ocean. BUT: the ocean.

Oceania [oh-shee-AN-ih-ah] general term for central and southern Pacific Islands, including Melanesia, Micronesia, Polynesia, and Australia.

ocelot [ah-seh-LAHT] jungle cat.

ocher (Brit., —re.) impure yellow iron ore; its color.

octagon regular eight-sided polygon.

octave [AHK-taev, -tihv] in music, span of eight notes.

octavo [ahk-TAE-voh] (abbr.: 8vo) small-sized book, 8 pages to a printed sheet (pl.) —os.

octet. A group of eight.

octopus (pl.) octopi, octopuses.

oculist an opthalmologist.

> OCULARIST maker of artificial eyes.

> OPTHALMOLOGIST physician who treats eyes.

> OPTOMETRIST one who measures the range of vision and may prescribe eyeglasses.

> OPTICIAN one who prepares eyeglasses from a prescription.

O.D. (abbr.) officer of the day.

od. (abbr.) overdose, esp. on illegal drugs.

odalisque [oh-dah-LEESK] painting presenting sensuous woman in Middle Eastern setting; also, a harem woman.

-odd Meaning "roughly:" twenty-odd, thirty-odd, 100-odd, etc. BUT NOT ten-odd, or 100 and odd. *How many were there? Twenty-odd.* See **suffix.**

odd lot less than standard round lot. In securities, round lot is usually 100 shares of stock or 10 bonds.

oddment part of a broken set.

Odessa [oh-DEHS-ah] Black Sea port, former **U.S.S.R.** Also, a city in Texas.

Odysseus [oh-DIHS-ee-ehs] or **Ulysses.** Gr. hero of Trojan War.

> ODYSSEY [AHD-ih-see] Homer's epic; without cap., means long journey.

O.E.C.D. (abbr.) Organization for Economic Cooperation and Development.

Oedipus [EHD-ih-puhs] Gr. tragic hero who killed his father and married his mother. *Oedipus Rex* is the play.

> OEDIPUS COMPLEX Freudian psychoanalytic theory.

O.E.E.D. Organization for European Economic Development. See **European Community.**

off NOT *off of.*

-off cut-off; rip-off (colloq.) BUT *playoff* pref. to *play-off, takeoff* to *take-off,* etc.

offal [AW-fuhl] (adj.): rubbish; garbage.

Off Broadway (adj.): *an Off Broadway play.* (n.): *Off Broadway produces some excellent works.* Also: *Off-off Broadway.*

offend, offense (Br. —ce.) (v.) [aw-FEHND]; (n.) [AW-fehns].

offering in business, a product, commodity, or security offered for public sale.

office Cap. if referring to unit of government: Chicago Operations Office, the Operations Office; Executive Office, Foreign Office, General Accounting Office; New York regional office (including a branch, division, or section); the regional office; the Office of Alien Property; Office of

Chief of Naval Operations. See **foreign cabinets.**

officeholder, —seeker, —worker (all n.); office-seeking (adj.); office boy (n.).

officer Army officer, Marine officer, BUT naval and marine officers; Army, Navy, and Marine officers; Regular Army officer, Regular officer, Regular Reserve officer.

officer in charge

OFFICERS In U.S. armed forces, in order of rank, plus insignia:

ARMY. general of the armies (5 stars); general (4 stars); lieutenant general (3 stars); major general (2 stars); brigadier general (1 star); colonel (eagle); lieutenant colonel (silver leaf); major (gold leaf); captain (2 silver bars); 1st lieutenant (silver bar); 2nd lieutenant (gold bar).

Non-commissioned officers: platoon sergeant or sergeant first class (3 chevrons, 2 rockers); staff sergeant (3 chevrons, 1 rocker); sergeant (3 chevrons); corporal (2 chevrons); private 1st class (1 chevron); private; recruit.

NAVY. admiral of the fleet (5 stars); admiral (4 stars); vice-admiral (3 stars); rear admiral (2 stars); commodore (in wartime only; 1 star); captain (eagle), commander (silver leaf); lieutenant commander (gold leaf); lieutenant (2 silver bars); lieutenant (jr. grade) (silver bar); ensign (gold bar); commissioned warrant officer (silver cord device).

Non-commissioned warrant officer (gold cord device); master chief petty officer (3 chevrons, 2 rockers, 2

stars); senior chief petty officer (3 chevrons, 1 rocker, 2 stars); chief petty officer (3 chevrons, 1 rocker, 1 star); petty officer, 1st class (3 chevrons); petty officer 2nd class (2 chevrons); petty officer 3rd class (1 chevron); seaman, seaman apprentice, seaman recruit.

AIR FORCE. Commissioned officers follow style of the army.

Non-commissioned officers: warrant officer (gold stripe with blue stops); chief master sergeant (6 chevrons, 2 rockers); master sergeant (6 chevrons); technical sergeant (5 chevrons); staff sergeant (4 chevrons); airman 1st class (3 chevrons); airman 2nd class (2 chevrons); airman 3rd class (1 chevron); airman, basic.

See **Army.**

offroad, offshore, offset. BUT: off-track betting.

offspring progeny. Usu. refers to plural.

often [AW-f'n or AH-f'n].

ofttime (arch.) often.

ogre [OH-guhr] (n.) fairy-tale monster. (adj.) ogreish.

OH Ohio.

Oh! Cap. any brief expletive.

oh-oh Means "oops;" also, "uh,oh."

O. Henry Pen name of William Sydney Porter (1862–1910), American short story writer. *Oh Henry!* is the candy bar.

Ohio U.S. state. Abbr.: OH. Cap.: Columbus. Native: Ohioan. Nickname: Buckeye.

ohm (Not an abbr.) unit of electrical resistance = volts/amperes.

O.I.T. (abbr.) Office of International Trade.

Ojibwa [oh-JIHB-wah] Native American tribe, a/k/a **Chippewa.**

OK Oklahoma.

OK OK'd, OK'ing, OK's. Also O.K., okay etc.

Okeechobee Lake [oh-ka-CHOH-bee] lake in S Florida.

Okefenokee Swamp [ok-keh-fihn-NOH-kee] swamp in SE Georgia, NE Florida. Okefenokee Swamp National Wildlife Refuge.

Okinawa [oh-kih-NAH-wah] island south of Japan, site of 1945 W.W. II battle.

Oklahoma U.S. state. Abbr.: OK. Cap.: Oklahoma City. Native: Oklahoman.

old comp.: —er, —est. Among members of a family, may be elder, eldest. Hyphenate: *Vera is our eight-year-old.* See *AGE.*

Old Dominion Virginia.

Oldenburg, Claes [OHL-dihn-buhrg, klaus] (b. 1929) Swedish-American pop sculptor and artist.

old-fashioned, old-fogyish.

Old Glory the flag of the United States.

Old Guard, Members of the Old Guard, NOT: Old Guards.

oleaginous [oh-lee-AHJ-ih-nuhs] oily.

oleomargarine [oh-lee-oh-MAHR-jeh-rihn] margarine.

olfactory pertaining to sense of smell.

oligarchy [AH-lih-gahr-kee] government by a few.

olive-drab, olive-skinned (adj.); olive oil (n.).

Olympic game Olympiad. Held every four years since 1896.

Olympus —pia, —pic, —pian.

Om [OHHM] sacred syllable in Hinduism; highest mantra.

Oman sultanate on SE coast of Arabian peninsula. Formerly Muscat and Oman, independent since 18th C. Cap.: Muscat [MUH-skat]. Native: Omani. Currency: Rial Omani.

Omar Khayyam [OH-mahr kie-YAHM] (c. 1048–1122) Persian poet, astronomer, mathematician; author of the *Rubai'yat,* love poems.

omega [oh-MEH-gah] O, last letter of the Greek alphabet. *Alpha and omega* means first and last, everything.

omelet

omit -tting, omissible.

omni- combining form meaning all: *omnivorous, omniscient.*

omnibus (n.) arch. for bus; now a collection of works from a single source. (pl.) —uses. (adj.) pertaining to many things at once.

omniscient [ahm-NIHSH-'nt] all knowing.

omnivore both carnivorous and herbiverous. (pl.) —a.

on Indicates touching, contact; esp. for an upper surface: *on the bed;* or time: *on March 15.* Also continued motion: *sail on, work on.* AVOID *upon,* formal.

onto (prep.) to a position on; upon. Pref. to *on to.* See **above.**

on-and-off (n. and adj.).

on the other hand. Indicates contrast, reconciling opposites. *Just now it's rainy. On the other hand, this morning was lovely.*

ON THE CONTRARY Emphasizes difference. *The sun never came out; on the contrary, it was drizzly all day.*

once, twice, thrice.

once-over, onceover (n.).

one (pronoun) Used in two senses: (1) numerical: *One of us still cares.* (2) representing an average person: *One has to make the best of things.*

ANYONE, anyone, everyone,

someone, no one: all take singular verb.

one of Followed by a pl. noun and a pl. verb. But the antecedent of a following pronoun is the pl. noun. *One of the men who were here yesterday is sick.*

ONE OF MANY May take pl. verb, if referring to pl. persons. *One of every six doctors are specialists.*

Oneida [oh-NIE-dah] lake, city, Native Americans in NY.

onerous [AHN-er-uhs].

oneself

onetime Usually means former: *onetime governor.*

ONE-TIME Means single occasion: *a one-time opportunity.*

on hand present, available.

AT HAND, TO HAND within reach.

onionpeel, —skin (one word).

only Placement in sentence is essential to meaning. COMPARE: *Only the lady came at noon yesterday. She was the only lady who came. The lady came only at noon. The lady came at noon only yesterday.*

When meaning can be misunderstood, place *only* before the word modified.

only one Takes sing. verb. *Only one of the books was returned.*

onomatopoeia [ahn-ahm-aht-ah-PEE-ah] (n.) formation of words from sounds, or in imitation of sounds: *giggle, gobble, gabble; tintinnabulation of the bells; babble; cuckoo.* (adj.) —poetic.

Ontario (abbr.: Ont.) province of Canada. Cap.: Toronto.

on the occasion of *When* is pref.

on to *She came on to the ship.*

> ONTO *She stumbled onto a solution.* See **into, on.**

"Ontogeny recapitulates phylogeny" [ahn-TAH-juh-nee, fie-LAH-juh-nee] (from Ernst Haeckel, 19th C. Ger. zoologist) Larger changes within a species, over the course of history, mirror smaller changes within any one member of that species as it matures.

onus [OH-nuhs] resonsibility; burden; obligation.

onward Pref. to —s. See **backward(s).**

opacity, opaqueness imperviousness to light; hence (as *opacity* only), difficulty in understanding.

op. cit. (abbr.) *opere citato* (Lat.) in the work cited.

open-ended, open-end mortgage; open house, open shop.

opera bouffe [boof] (FR.) light comic opera. Also opera bouffa [boo-fuh] (It.).

> OPERA-BOUFFE (adj.) *an opera-bouffe government.*

operagoer, —going; opera house.

operas Title in quotation marks, cap. principal words.

Ophelia [oh-FEEL-yah] In Shakespeare's *Hamlet,* daughter of Polonius, in love with Hamlet, eventually driven mad and a suicide.

ophthalmologist. See **oculist.**

Oppenheimer, J. Robert [AH-pehn-HIE-mehr] (1904–1967) American scientist, leader in development of atomic bomb.

opponent [oh-POH-nehnt].

opposite from NOT *opposite than.* See **contrary.**

opposition. Cap. if referring to a specific group opposing the party in power in a foreign country: *the Opposition proposal.*

oppress —ssible, —ssor.

oppugn [oh-PYOON] (v.) to controvert.

optimism —ist, —istic.

opus [OH-puhs] work, esp. of music or literature. (pl.) opera.

or (1) *He cannot walk or ride. He can neither walk nor ride.* BUT NOT: *No one should trust them or* (use *nor*) *help them.*

(2) Where there are two negative alternatives, *or* is used to introduce the second if the negative (usually in the verb as part of the auxiliary) clearly applies to both alternatives.

Sometimes, however, the first negative does not clearly carry over to the second; either the negative does not apply to both, or the auxiliary is repeated without the negative. In these cases use *nor*. Examples:

She never played or sang again (the negative adverb *never* applies to both alternatives). *She cannot write or remember without pain* (the negative auxiliary *cannot* applies to both alternatives). *I will ask no more, nor will I go* (*no more* is the object of *say*, has no connection with the second alternative). *I will not write it myself, nor will I help him* (the auxiliary will is repeated without the negative).

(3) Avoid unnecessary repetition after *or*. COMPARE: *He came without money or tickets* (he had neither). *He came without money or without tickets* (one was missing).

(4) In a series: *I think he is either short or tall or in between. He never saw a man who was bigger or taller or fatter.*

(5) In a series of alternatives, the verb is always singular: *A, B, C, or D is coming.* See **neither, nor.**

-or See **our.**

OR Oregon.

oral [OH-rahl] spoken. See **verbal.**

AURAL [AW-ral] heard.

orangeade, —peel (n.); orange-colored, orange-red (adj.).

orangutan [oh-RANG-ih-tan] Pref. to *orang-outang.*

orate —ation, —ator, —atorical, —atory.

oratorio [awr-uh-TAWR-ee-oh] dramatic text, often from Scripture, set to music.

orchestra [AWR-kehs-truh] (n.); orchestral [awr-KEHS-tral] (adj.).

orchid [AWR-kihd].

Orderly Sgt. (abbr.) orderly sergeant.

ordinal numbers Examples: *First, fifth.*

CARDINAL NUMBERS *Examples: One, five.* See *NUMBERS.*

ordinance a local law.

ORDNANCE military equipment.

ordinarily [AWR-dih-NAR-ih-lee].

Ord. Sgt. (abbr.) ordnance sergeant.

Oregon [AWR-eh-guhn, NOT OHR-a-GAHN] U.S. state. Abbr.: OR. Cap.: Salem. Native: Oregonian. Nickname: Beaver.

organdy, organdie stiff-finished muslin.

organization Cap. if part of name; cap. standing alone if an international unit: United Nations Educational, Scientific, and Cultural Organization (UNESCO); International Labor Organization; North Atlantic Treaty Organization.

organized Cap. Marine Corps Organized Reserve, the Reserve; Organized Militia, Organized Naval Militia, the Naval Militia. BUT the militia;

Organized Reserve Corps, the reserve.

orgasm [AWR-gah-s'm] sexual climax.

the Orient [OH-ree-ehnt] Pref. to *the East* to avoid confusion with U.S. eastern states. (adj.) oriental.

orient Pref. to *orientate* in sense of adjusting, finding way.

orientation [oh-ree-ehn-TAE-shuhn] (from "facing East.") adjustment to new circumstances.

-oriented informal suffix, indicating particular audience or subject matter: *a student-oriented video, a salary-oriented discussion.*

oriole [OH-rih-ohl] bright-colored bird.

Orion [oh-RIE-uhn] Northern constellation; hunter in Gr. myth.

orison [AWR-ih-zuhn] a prayer.

ormolu gold-colored alloy of copper and zinc, used for decoration in furniture and jewelry.

oro- prefix meaning mountain; also mouth: *orogeny* (process of mountain-making); *orotund* (sound made with round mouth).

Orozco, José Clemente [oh-ROHS-koh, HOH-sae klae-MAEIN-tae] (1883–1931) Mexican painter, muralist.

Orpheus [awr-FEE-uhs] in Gr. myth,

superhuman singer and musician, husband of Eurydice.

ortho- combining form meaning straight, right: *orthography, orthogon.*

orthodontia [or-thuh-DAHN-shuh] (n.) dentistry to correct irregularities. Use —dontist when referring to such a dentist. (adj.) —dontic.

orthography [awr-THAH-greh-fih] science of writing.

orthopedic [awr-thoh-PEE-dihk] branch of medicine dealing with correction of deformities.

oscillate (v.), —llable (adj.); —tor (n.).

oscillograph [AH-sih-loh-graf] records electrical waves.

osmosis [ahs-MOH-sihs] in biology, spontaneous passage of water through a membrane. Hence, any remarkable transference.

ostensible apparent; superficial. *His ostensible frankness hid a devious scheme.*

osteopath [AHSS-tee-oh-pahth] doctor who applies theory that illness is due to mechanical defects; manipulates joints, spine, similar to **chiropractor.** Use —thy to refer to this type of medical practice.

ostracize (v.) to banish from fellowship. (adj.) —zable.

Oswiecim [awsh-VYEHN-tsehm]. See **Auschwitz.**

O.T.C. (abbr.) Organization for Trade Cooperation.

Otello Operas by Rossini (1815) and Verdi (1887).

Othello, the Moor of Venice play by Shakespeare (1604).

other, others *In this recipe basil, as in her other sauces, is essential. There were others among the children who were hungry. Not that one, but the other, is mine.*
Others as sole subject takes a plural verb. *That one horse and five others are getting away.* See **COMPARISON.**

otherwise (prep.); —worldly (adj.).

ought (n.) anything. Incorrect for *naught.*

ought (v.) *Can and ought;* NOT *ought and can.* This verb has no infinitive, no participle; it is used only as an auxiliary.

Ouija [WEE-juh] (Fr. *oui* + Ger. *ja.* trademark name for spiritualist reading board.

ounce (abbr.: oz.) (1) unit of weight. In avoirdupois system = 437.5 grains = 1/16 lb. = 28.35 grams = 0.91146 ounces troy weight.
(2)In troy and apothecaries' measure = 480 grains = 1/12 lb. = 31.10 grams = 1.097143 ounces avoirdupois.
(3) Unit of dry measure = 2.10002 cu. in. = 1/16 dry pint.
(4) In textile measurement, weight in ounces avoirdupois of 1 yard of 36 in. fabric.

(5) In leather measurement, = 1/64 in. thickness.

ounce, fluid (abbr.: fl. oz.) Unit of capacity: (1) U.S. = 1.041 Brit. fl. oz. = 1/32 liquid qt. = 1/10 liquid pt. = 1/4 gill = 8 fl. drams = 480 minims = 29.5737 cm³. = 29.5729 ml.
(2) Brit. = 0.96073 U.S. fl. oz. = 1.734 cu. in. = 28.413 cm³. = 28.4122 ml. = app. volume of 1 oz. avp. water.

-our, -or —our is Br. spelling for most U.S. —or endings: *honour, honor; colour, color.*

ours

outcast, outcropping, outdoors, outlaw (n.); out-and-out, out-of-date, out-of-state, out-of-the-way (adj.).
outdo, outrun, etc. (v.); out-Machiavelli, etc., (v.): *He's so devious he could out-Machiavelli Machiavelli.*

outermost, —wear.

out loud not to oneself. Use *aloud* for loudly, not in a whisper.

output Pref. as noun. *Our Maine plant has the best output.*

outré [OO-trae] bizare: *an outré hat.*

outside NOT *outside of.*

outstanding in finance, unpaid. *You have several bills outstanding.* Also, stock in the hands of stockholders.

outward, —bound (adj.). See **backward(s).**

ovenbaked, —ware.

over Indicates at higher level; sometimes implies motion: *carry over, move over.* See **above, below.**

overage (n.) surplus. (adj.) older.

overall (this spelling used for all meanings); overalls (garment); over-the-counter (adj.).

over- overrule, overtake, overthrow.

—over carryover, hangover, spillover, turnover.

override (v.) to trample down; also annul. *The Senate overrode the President's veto.* (n.) in business, commission paid to supervisory personnel, above that paid to the actual salesmen.

overly Use especially when speaking of virtues: *overly cautious, frank, deliberate, economical.*

overseas (adv. & adj.) *He worked overseas; an overseas job.*

Ovid [AH-vihd] (43 B.C.–A.D. 17) Roman poet.

ovum egg or egg cell. (pl.) ova.

owing to Means *as a result of.* Pref. to *due to.*

owl-eyed (adj.)

oxblood (color), oxcart, oxlike, ox team.

oxymoron [ahk-see-MAW-rahn] (from Gr. for "wise foolishness") in rhetoric, the use of two apparently contradictory terms in a single structure: *an honorable thief.*

oyez [OH-yehz; also OH-yae] Hear ye!

oyster bed, —house, —man, —shell, —woman (all one word); oyster-white (adj.); oyster catcher (bird), oyster crab (n.).

oz. (abbr.) ounce.

P

p. (abbr.) page; past tense. **pp.** (abbr.) pages.

PA Pennsylvania.

P.A. public-address system.

pace [paes] unit of length: (1) common pace = 2.5, 3, or 3.3 ft.; (2) military double time —3 ft.; (3) military quick time = 2.5 ft.

pacemaker, —making; pace-setting (adj.); pace setter.

Pacific Pacific Coast (or Slope) States; Pacific Northwest, Northwest Pacific; Pacific seaboard; Pacific slope; South Pacific; Pacific States; Pacific time, Pacific standard time (see **time**). BUT transpacific.

packhorse, packsaddle (n.); pack-laden (adj.); pack ice (n.).

packinghouse packing box.

packing list statement of contents in a package. See **manifest.**

pact Cap. with name; lower-case standing alone: Atlantic Pact, Atlantic Defense Pact, Baghdad Pact; the pact.

paddle wheel

Paderewski, Ignace [pah-de-REHF-skee een-YAHS] (1860–1941) Polish pianist, statesman.

padre [PAH-drae] (from Sp., It.) monk or priest. pl.—dres.

padrone [pad-ROH-nae] patron; master. In Italy, innkeeper; in U.S., Italian employment agent. pl. —ni [nee].

paean [PEE-an] hymn of praise or thanks.

page 2 Lowercase.

PAGINATION Books are usually compiled in the following order: (1) Title (frontispiece, if any, on back).

(2) Frontispiece, facing title page.

(3) Title page.

(4) Back of title (listing publisher, copyright information, and frequently such useful bibliographic information as list of sponsors, note of editions and printings, etc.).

(5) Dedication or letter of transmittal (on new odd page).

(6) Foreword (an introductory note written as an endorsement by a person other than the author, beginning on a new odd page).

(7) Preface, by author, on a new odd page.

(8) Contents, on a new odd page, immediately followed by list of illusrations and list of tables, as part of contents.

(9) Text, which begins with page 1.

(10) Bibliography, on a new odd page.

(11) Appendix, on a new odd page.

(12) Index, on a new odd page.

In books using a "half-title page," text begins on page 3. Page numbers belong in Arabic, except introductory material which is written in small roman numerals. See *NUMBERS, ROMAN NUMERALS.*

Pagliacci [pahl-YAT-chee] opera by Leoncavallo, 1892.

pailful (pl.) —s.

painkiller

painstaking

paintbox, —brush, —maker, —mixer, —pot (all one word); paint-stained (adj.); paint filler, paint thinner (n.).

paintings Place titles in quotation marks, and cap. principle words.

pair group of two: *one pair of socks.* Pl. *pairs* is pref. to pair: *three pairs of twins.*

PARE (v.) to cut off; trim.

PEAR (n.) the fruit.

pajamas [puh-JAH-mahs] Also *pyjamas.* Even one set takes a plural verb. *My pajamas are green.*

Pakistan [pahk-ih-STAHN; -STAN] nation on NW border of India. Formerly Br., independent, 1947. Cap.: Islamabad [ih-SLAH-mah-bahd]. Native: Pakistani. Currency: rupee.

palaver [pa-LAV-ehr; —LAHV—] in Africa, a conference.

pale palely. Also, (n.) an enclosure: *beyond the pale.*

paleface (n.); pale-blue, pale-cheeked, pale-faced (adj.).

Palestine area on E Mediterranean coast divided between Israel and Jordan. Native, *Palestinian,* refers to Arab (non-Jewish) inhabitants of Israeli territory.

PALESTINE LIBERATION ORGANIZATION. (abbr.: P.L.O.) organization dedicated to establishing Palestinian homeland.

palindrome word, phrase, etc., which is identical when read forwards or backwards: *radar, noon, Hannah;* or the first sentence ever spoken: *"Madam, I'm Adam."*

palladium (from Gr. statue of Pallas Athena) a safeguard. Also, soft metal used as gold alloy. (pl.) —ia.

pallbearer

pall-mall [pehl-mehl] a game. Cap. for London street famed for clubs. See **pell mell.**

pallid. See **livid.**

palm unit of measure: either the length of a hand (7 to 10 in.) or its width (3 to 4 in.).

palmetto variety of fan palm. (pl.) —os.

palpable [PAL-pah-b'l] easily apprehensible by the senses, particularly touch.

palsied [PAWL-zeed] paralyzed.

pan- prefix meaning every, throughout: *pan-Hellenic, pan-American, panacea.*

pan-broil

Panama [PAN-uh-mah] Central American nation, location of canal. Formerly Colombian; independent, 1903. Cap.: Panama City. Native: Panamanian. Currency: balboa.

Panama Canal Zone Under U.S. control, to be turned over to local authorities 1999. The Canal Zone; BUT the canal.

Pan-American Games, Pan-American Highway.

panegyric [pan-nuh-JEER-ihk] formal eulogy.

panel —led, —ling.

panel Cap. for organizations. Atomic Energy Panel. Labor-Management Relations Panel (federal), etc.; the Panel.

panful (pl.) —fuls.

panhandle a narrow strip of land. Usu. refers to Texas: Texas Panhandle, the panhandle. Also Oklahoma, Idaho.

panic —icky, —icked.

panic-stricken (adj.).

panoply [PAN-uh-plee] full suit of armor; hence, any excessive show of power. (pl.) —plies.

pantheism (from Gr. "all-god") belief that the universe, plus its laws, comprises God. See **atheism, polytheism.**

pantryman

pants Use pl. verb. *These green pants are mine.*

paperback —boy, —cutter, —hanger, —mill, —weight, —work (n., all one word); paper-thin (adj.); paper pulp.

papers Woodrow Wilson papers, etc.; the papers. BUT white paper; construction paper.

papier-maché [pa-PYAE mah-SHAE; (angl.) PAE-per muh-SHAE].

paprika [pap-PREE-kuh] (from Hungarian "Turkish pepper").

Papua New Guinea [PAH-poo-ah, GIH-nee] E half of island of New Guinea, in SW Pacific. Formerly Australian and U.N.; independent, 1975. Capital: Port Moresby. Native: Papuan, Melanesian. Currency: Kina.

papyrus [pap-PIE-ruhs] (pl.) —ri.

par established or nominal value; common level.

parable a short illustrative story designed to make a single point, usually to teach a lesson.

paradigm [PAR-uh-diem] model; pattern.

paradisiacal [par-uh-dihs-SIE-uh-kal] heavenly. Pref. to *paradisiac.*

paradox (n.) in rhetoric, a seeming contradiction which is nonetheless somehow true. (adj.) paradoxical.

paraffin [PAR-uh-fin] petroleum wax used for sealing jars.

¶. abbr.: **paragraph.**

paragraph 4 Lowercase.

PARAGRAPHS Used to break up a text into apprehensible thoughts. The length depends on the level of the reader, the type of material, and the degree of formality. Technical material permits longer paragraphs.

Paraguay [PAR-ah-guie or -guae] landlocked nation in South America. Independent, 1811. Cap.: Asuncion. Native: Paraguayan. Currency: guarani.

parakeet

parallel —ed, —ing, —llelism.

parallelism, parallel structure in rhetoric, a technique of placing ideas in the same grammatical construction so as to emphasize their similarity. *''We cannot dedicate—we cannot consecrate—we cannot hallow this ground.''*

paralyze (v.); paralysis (n.). (pl.) —ses.

paramount supreme. NEVER *most paramount.*

paranoia [par-uh-NOI-yuh] (n.) mental illness involving delusions of persecution. Hence, any intense fear. (adj.) —noid.

paraphernalia [par-uh-fehr-NAE-lih-uh, -NAEL-yuh] personal belongings, usu. unimportant.

paraplegia [par-uh-PLEE-juh] paralysis of lower half of body. paraplegic.

parcel —led, —ling.

parcel post

parchment-covered (adj.), parchment paper (n.).

PARENTHESES Used in pairs: (1) To enclose words not intended to be part of the sentence, where confusion might arise from the use of other punctuation. *New York (population about 8,400,000) is the second largest city in the world. Jones (reading from his notes): This is Q (referring to the exhibit).*

(2) To enclose a clause that takes a tangent thought. *They spoke in a language (if you could call it a language) that only their friends understood.*

(3) To enclose an explanation not part of the statement. *The Springfield (Massachusetts) census showed a population increase.*

(4) To enclose numbers or symbols designating items in a series: *(1), (B),* etc.

(5) To enclose figures confirming numbers given in words, when the double form is used: *delivery to be made in sixty (60) days.*

A parenthetical statement within a sentence takes neither an initial capital nor a final period, even if it is a complete statement. Question marks and exclamation points, however, may be used if the statement calls for them. *His home (he lived there for about ten years) is next to the store. His store (did you know he had one?) is . . . His store (he has a wonderful location!) is at . . .*

When the parenthetical statement is at the end of the sentence, the same rule applies. The closing period of the main sentence goes outside the parenthesis. *His home is next to the bank (he uses another bank, though). His home is next to the bank (isn't he foresighted?) . . . to the bank (he has a wonderful location!).*

A period goes inside the parenthesis only when the parenthetical statement is an independent sentence not standing with another. Such cases also take an initial capital.

Parenthetical expressions within parenthetical expressions are placed in brackets.

Parenthetical material exceeding one paragraph is written with an opening parenthesis at the beginning of each successive paragraph and a closing parenthesis at the end of the last.

parenthesis [pah-REHN-thee-sihs] (n.) sing. form of *PARENTHESES.* (adj.) parenthetic, parenthetical.

paresis [pae-REE-sihs] partial paralysis.

par excellence [pahr EHK-suh-lahnss] (Fr.) preeminent.

parfait [pahr-FAE] (Fr.) frozen whipped cream dessert.

pariah [pah-RIE-uh] lowest Hindu caste; hence, any outcast.

parish area served and field of activities of a local church. In Britain, sub-division of a county. In Louisiana, a county.

parity [PAH-rih-tee] equality of price between two markets.

park Fairmount Park; the park. See **national.**

parkway George Washington Memorial Parkway, the memorial parkway; the parkway.

Parliament, Houses of the Parliament; Parliamentarian.

parlor, parlormaid, parlor car. Br. —our.

parmesan [PAHR-mehz-an] hard, sweet Italian cheese.

parsec [PAHR-sehk] astronomical unit of measure = 3.262 light-years, = 1.917×10^{13} miles, = 3.09×10^{13} kilometers.

part less than the whole.

PORTION a specific part.

SHARE a receiver's portion.

PROPORTION the ratio to the whole.

PERCENTAGE the fraction of the whole in hundredths.

partial affecting a part only: *partial eclipse.* Usu. adjective. Opposite of *complete* or *total.*

PARTLY in some measure: *partly full.* Usu. adverb.

part-finished, part-Japanese, part-time (adj.); part-timer (n.); part owner, part way.

part 2, A, II BUT cap. if title: *Part 2: Iron and Steel Industry.*

parti- prefix meaning divided: *parti-colored, partitive.*

partially in part; or showing partiality. AVOID use which may be ambiguous. NOT: *The debate was partially documented.*

PARTICIPLE Verbal adjective, also used to form verbal phrases. In English, the present participle (or active participle) is formed by adding —ing to the simple form of the verb: *write, writing.* The past participle is usually formed by adding —ed or —en to the simple form of the verb: *written.*

Both participles are used to create compound verbs. The perfect form has the auxiliary *have: having written.* The present participle refers to an action in progress. *Writing every day, he should finish by the end of the month.* See *TENSE.*

The past participle is used with *have* in making completed tenses past, present or future. *Having written every day since summer, he finished in December.* See verbal.

Participles may be used as adjectives: *shouting spectators.*

Participial phrases contain a participle and are used as adjectives. *The cakes, baked on Tuesday, were still fresh.*

PARTICIPLE MODIFIERS may be a single word. *Divorced, she is the mother of three children.*

participating preferred stock. See **stock.**

particular. See **special.**

partisan [PAHR-tih-san] a supporter of a particular faction; or a guerilla fighter.

PARTS OF SPEECH words are classified by their function in a sentence: noun, pronoun, verb, adjective, adverb, preposition, conjunction, interjection.

party in legal forms, signifies *person.*

partymaking, party line.

parvenu [PAHR-vee-nyoo] (Fr.) newly rich or powerful; often used disparagingly: an upstart.

pass (p. and p.p.) —ed. But (adj.) past; passable.

pass Cap. if part of name: Brenner Pass; the pass.

passageway

passbook, —key, —port, —way, —word (n.). pass out (v.).

passé [pa-SAE] antiquated; past prime.

passenger-mile measure of railroad passenger carried 1 mile. (pl.) passenger miles: sum of distance traveled by each passenger on a carrier.

passer-by, passerby (pl.) passers-by, passersby.

passible in theology, susceptible to feeling or suffering.

PASSABLE able to pass.

passim [PAH-sihm] (Lat.) (adj.) here and there. Usu. italicized.

Passion (cap.) Refers to the suffering of Christ.

passion-driven (adj.) passionfruit (n.); Passion play.

Passover Jewish holy day. See **Feast of the Passover.**

past (n.) time gone by.

   PASSED (v.) (p.) moved along.

pasteboard, —pot, —up (n. and adj.) (all one word).

pastel [pas-TEHL] pale color.

Pasternak, Boris [PAHS-tirh-nahk] (1890–1960) Rus. writer (*Doctor Zhivago*); Nobel prize, 1958.

Pasteur, Louis [pahs-TEUR] (1822–1895) Fr. chemist, immunologist.

pasteurize [PAS-tuhr-iez] (v.); —ization (n.).

past history is a tautology.

pastiche [pas-TEESH] literary or musical work composed of parts of others. See **collage.**

pastime [PAS-tiem] diversion.

pastor clergy member in charge of a church. Adj., *pastoral*, refers especially to care of the personal problems of the congregation such as visiting the sick: pastoral duties.

pastoral [PAS-toh-ral] in theology, relating to the care of souls. (n.) —ism. *Pastorale* is a music term.

pastryman, pastry cook.

pastureland

patchwork, patch test.

paté [pah-TAE] meat paste; *paté de foie gras,* paste of goose liver and truffles.

patent [PAT-ehnt] (n.) in law, a grant of exclusive rights. (adj.) evident, obvious.

paterfamilias [PAE-tuh-fam-IHL-ih-as] (Lat.) head of a family. (pl.) paterfamilias.

pathbreaker, —finder, —way (all one word).

pathos [PAE-thahss] quality that elicits pity or sympathy.

patio [PAT-ih-oh; PAH-tee-oh] paved area adjoining building.

patois [PAT-wah] (sing. and pl.). See **language.**

patriot [PAE-tree-aht] (n.); —ic (adj.).

patrol, patrolman; patrol wagon. —led, —ling.

patron [PAE-trun]; —ess, —ize; patronage [PAT-rah-nihj].

patternbook, —maker.

Pavlov, Ivan [PAHV-luhf, ee-VAHN] (1849–1936) Rus. psychologist; developed concept of conditioned reflex.

Pavlova, Anna [PAHV-luh-vah]

(1885–1931) Rus. ballerina.

pawnbroker, pawnshop.

pay (p. and p.p.) paid.

paycheck, —day, —dirt, —load, —master, —off, —roll, —sheet (n. and adj., al one word); pay envelope.

P.B.S. (abbr.) Public Broadcasting System. BUT: *your local public broadcasting station.*

p.c., P.C. personal computer. Also, informally, *politically correct.*

P.C.P. (abbr.) animal tranquilizer, used as illegal hallucinogen.

pct. (abbr.) percent.

peagreen, pea-sized (adj.); pea soup.

peacemaker, —monger, —time (all one word); peace-loving (adj.); peace pipe.

peaceable not inclined toward war.

PEACEFUL not at war.

peacock (m), peafowl (f.).

peaked [peekt] pointed.

PEAKED [PEEK-ehd] wasted; thin.

pecan [pee-KAN].

peccadillo [pehk-uh-DIHL-oh] a small sin. (pl.) —oes, —os.

peck (abbr.: pk.) unit of capacity; (1) U.S. = 1/4 bu. = 8 dry qt. = 16 dry pt. = 8.80961. = 537.605 cu. in. =

8.8096.1.; (2) Brit. = 1,0320 U.S. pk. = 554.84 cu. in. = 9.09191.

peculiar

pecuniary [pee-KYOO-nih-ehr-ih] refering to money.

pedagogy [PEHD-uh-goh-jee] the art of teaching.

pediatric [pee-dee-AT-rihk] concerning the health of children.

peek to spy furtively.

PEEP *Webster's* lists as a synonym to *peek.*

peephole, peepshow.

peer equal. NOT superior. Also, a nobleman.

peerless without equal.

pegboard, pegleg.

Pei, I.M. [pae] (b. 1917) Chinese-American architect.

pejorative [PEH-joh-ruh-tihv] depreciatory.

Peking [pee-KIHNG], also, Beijing [bae-ZHIHNG] cap. of People's Republic of China (mainland, Communist China).

Pekingese or **Pekinese** breed of dog.

pekoe [PEEK-oh; (Br.), PEK-] tea leaf of India or Sri Lanka.

pellmell, pell-mell frantically; rushed and confused. See **pall-mall.**

pellucid [peh-LYOO-sihd] easy to understand; also translucent.

P.E.N. Poets, Essayists, and Novelists; international organization founded 1922.

penal [PEE-nal] (adj.); penalize [PEEN-uh-liez] (v.).

pence (abbr.: p.) Br. currency, 1/12 shilling.

penchant [PEHN-chant] strong inclination.

penholder, penknife, —manship, —point (n.); pen name.

pencilholder, pencil-pusher (n.); pencil box.

penciled —ing.

pendant (n.) a hanging thing.

    PENDENT (adj., arch.) hanging; pending.

    PENNANT (n.) flags or nautical rigging.

    PENNON (n.) banner, military or heraldic.

    GUIDON small flag for identification.

pendulum (pl.) —ms.

penicillin [pehn-ih-SIHL-ihn].

peninsula (n.); peninsular (adj.): the Peninsular War.

Peninsula, Upper In Michigan; also Lower; the peninsula.

penitentiary [pen-ih-TEHN-sharrih] Albany Penitentiary, the penitentiary.

pen name. See **nom de plume.**

Pennsylvania U.S. state. abbr.: PA. Cap.: Harrisburg. Native: Pennsylvanian.

Pennsylvania Dutch people and habits of German and Swiss descent now living in Pennsylvania. Also, Amish.

penny U.S. currency, 1¢. (pl.) pennies.

penny (abbr.: d) Unit of nail measurement, originally price per hundred; now indicates length: 4d = 1 1/2 in.; 6d = 2 in.; 10d = 3 in.; 20d = 4 in.; 40d = 5 in.; 60d = 6 in.

pennywise, pennyworth.

pennyweight (abbr.: dwt.) unit of weight = 0.05 oz. troy; or ap. = 1.2 scruples = 24 grains = 1.5552 grams.

pentameter in poetry, verse of five metrical feet.

Pentateuch [PEHN-tuh-tuook]. See **Torah.**

Pentecost [PEHN-tih-kawst] Christian holy day in late spring, a/k/a Whitsunday. (adj.) Pentecostal.

penthouse (n.); pent-up (adj.).

penultimate [PEHN-uhlt-ih-mat] (adj.) next to last.

penurious stingy.

people (sing. and pl.) BUT for people of several nations use *peoples: Aramaic-speaking peoples.*

Pepys, Samuel [peeps] (1633–1703) Eng. diarist. (The family name is now pronounced PEHP-ihs).

per (Lat.) in business writing, means "by" or "by means of."

per capita (Lat.) "by the head;" from each person; average per person; *average per capita* is a tautology.

per annum *yearly* is pref.

percent (abbr.: pct.) Never use % in a text: *75 percent, one-half of 1 per cent,* BUT *seven percentage points.*

percentage, percentile; per annum, per centum. See **part.**

per curiam (Lat.) by the court.

per diem (Lat.) by the day.

per se (Lat.) by itself. *Though we've lost the receipt per se, we still have a copy.*

père [pair] (Fr.) father or senior: *Dumas père; Dumas fils.*

peremptory [peur-EHMP-toh-ree] final, destructive.

  PREEMPTORY [pree-] preferential.

perennial active throughout the year, or for a long time.

perestroika [PEH-rehz-TROI-kah] (Rus.) "reorganization," "reconstruction." General term for **U.S.S.R.** re-

forms begun by **Mikhail Gorbachev** in 1985. See **glasnost.**

Pérez de Cuellar, Javier (PEH-rehz deh KWAE-yahr, HAH-vee-eh) (b. 1920) Peruvian statesman; U.N. Secretary-General, 1982–1992.

perfect complete; flawless. NOT *more* or *most perfect;* use *more nearly perfect. —ible.*

Pericles [PEH-rih-klees] (c.495–429 B.C.) Athenian statesman who ruled at height of city's prestige and power.

perigee [PEH-rih-jee] in astronomy, point at which an Earth satellite is closest to the Earth. See **apogee.**

perihelion [-HEE-lee-uhn] point in an orbit around the sun which is nearest to the sun. (For the earth, 91,500,000 miles.) See **aphelion.**

peril —led, —ling. (adj.) perilous.

periodic sentence a sentence which leaves its principal verb to the end. *If John loves Mary, they should be married.*

periodontics [PEH-ree-oh-DAHN-tihks] dentistry on the gums.

permanence the fact of continued existence.

  PERMANENCY the quality of permanence.

permeate [PUHR-mee-aet] to pass through the pores. (adj.) —meable.

permissible

pernicious   [puhr-NIHSH-uhs] highly injurious.

perorate (v.) conclude and summarize, esp. in a speech; also harangue. (n.) peroration.

perpendicular [puhr-pehn-DIHK-yoo-lur]. Use with *to*.

perpetrate to commit. *He planned to perpetrate a crime.*

PERPETUATE to make enduring. *He provided a scholarship fund to perpetuate his memory.*

persecute to harass with unjust attacks. *Minority groups have been persecuted in the course of history.*

PROSECUTE to follow through to an end. *The district attorney prosecuted the legal action to conviction.*

Persephone [puhr-SEHF-foh-nee] Greek goddess of springtime, held captive in Hades throughout each winter.

Persepolis [puhr-SEHP-oh-LIHS] ancient Persian capital city.

Perseus [PUHR-see-uhs] Greek hero, slew Medusa.

person, -person Often a good substitute for traditional sexist constructions using *man*. Instead of *chairman*, for instance, *use chairperson*. Instead of *to the last man*, use *to the last person*. In grammar, *person* affects verb formation: first person, second, third. (pl.) persons, -persons. See: *SEXIST LANGUAGE*.

PEOPLE Usually both singular and plural. BUT when speaking of groups, use *peoples: English-speaking peoples*. See: **people.**

person of color See: **color, person of.**

persona [puhr-SOHN-uh] Implies a social facade. *Dramatis personae; persona non grata.* (pl.) —ae.

personal [PUHR-suhn-n'l] (adj.) private: *personal letters.*

PERSONNEL [puhr-suhn-NEHL] (n.) persons employed; also the department handling them: *government personnel. Insurance is handled through the personnel office.*

personification in rhetoric, metaphoric attribution of personality. *The fog came in on little cat feet.*

perspective (n.) view.

PROSPECTIVE (adj.) expected.

perspicacity insight. (adj.) —cious.

PERSPECUITY clarity of an idea; lucidity.

persuade (v.); —dable or —suasible (adj.).

Peru nation in NW South America, on the Pacific. Independent, 1824. Cap.: Lima [LEE-mah]. Native: Peruvian. Currency: Intl.

peruse [peh-ROOS] to study.

pervertible

pesthole (n.) pest-ridden (adj.)

pestle [PEHS-s'l] tool to crumble material in a mortar.

petaled

petard [peh-TAHRD] an explosive or firecracker. *Hoist with his own petard* means "blown up by his own bomb." See **hoist.**

petit- [peh-TEE] (Fr.) prefix meaning small: *petit-fours, petitgrain.* See **petite, petty.**

petite [peh-TEET] (adj.) small; dainty. (n.) a size in women's clothes.

Petrarch (Francesco Petrarca) [PEH-trark] (1304–1374) It. poet and humanist, famed for love sonnets.

petrel [PEHT-rehl] sea bird related to the gull: *stormy petrel.*

    PETROL [PEHT-rohl] Br., gasoline.

petty [PEHT-ih] small; mean; subordinate: *petty larceny.*

peyote [peh-YOH-tee] cactus found in SW U.S., produces powerful hallucinogen (**mescaline**).

pF. (abbr.) water energy (p,logarithm; F, frequency).

Pfc. (abbr.) private, first class.

PG, PG13 See **movie ratings.**

pH. (abbr.) hydrogen-ion concentration, used in expressing acidity and alkalinity in a range of 0-14: 0 = highest acidity, 7 = neutrality, 14 = highest alkalinity.

P.H.A. (abbr.) Public Housing Administration.

phalanx [fae-LANKS] ancient military formation of interlocked shields; by extension, any united group. (pl.) —xes.

phallus [FAL-uhs] the penis, or a facsimile. (pl.) —li. (adj.) phallic.

phantom a visible illusion; something seen.

    PHANTASM a fantasy; may be only a mental image.

phantasmagoria [fan-TAS-mah-GOH-ree-ah] (sing.) changing succession of imaginary things.

Pharaoh [FAE-roh].

Phar. D. (abbr.) doctor of pharmacy.

Pharisee ancient orthodox Jewish sect. —saic, —saism.

pharmaceutical

phase [faez] Verb combination is *phase out.* NOT **faze.**

Ph.D. Doctor of Philosophy.

phenomenal [fuh-NAH-mih-nuhl] (adj.); phenomenon (n.), (pl.) —ena.

phenomenology major 20th-C. philosophy, attempting to define human consciousness by its perceptions of phenomena. Best-known exponent is Edmund Husserl (1859–1938).

Phi Beta Kappa [FIE BAE-tah KAP-puh].

philately [fihl-AT-ehl-ih] stamp collecting. —ist: stamp collector.

—phile [fiel] suffix meaning "lover of:" *Anglophile, bibliophile.* The related prefix is *philo-: philosophy, Philadelphia.*

philharmonic [FIHL-ahr-mon-ihk] literally "love of harmony."

Philippine Islands island republic in W Pacific. Formerly Spanish, then U.S.; independent, 1946. Old cap.: Manila, new cap.: Quezon City. Native: Filipino. Currency: peso.

philistine [FIHL-ihs-teen] in Bible, cap., barbarians; hence, anyone without culture.

philo- See **phile.**

phlegm [flehm] mucous secretion.

phlegmatic [flehg-MA-tihk] sluggish.

—phobia (from Gr.) suffix meaning irrational fear; **agoraphobia.**

Phoenicia [fuh-NIHSH-ih-ah] ancient seagoing empire based in area of present Lebanon (fl. 1200 B.C.). Created first alphabet.

phoenix in Egyptian myth, bird which rises from its own ashes.

phonetics [fuh-NEH-tihks] the science of word sounds.

phony NOT *phoney.*

phosphorus [FAH-fohr-uhs] (n.) the stone.

phosphorescence [-EH-sehnz] (n.) the glitter.

photocell, —copy, —electric, —montage.

PHRASE in grammar, a group of related words without subject or predicate.
 A phrase may function as a noun, an adjective, an adverb, or a verb. They are classified as prepositional, participial, gerund, or infinitive.

phrasebook, phrasemaker.

phraseology [frae-zee-OL-uh-jee] way of speaking or writing.

phylogeny. See "**Ontogeny recapitulates phylogeny.**"

phylum [FIE-luhm] a primary biological division. (pl.) phyla.

physician medical professional.
 DOCTOR Holds a doctorate degree.
 SURGEON Performs operations.
 HOMEOPATHIC PHYSCIAN Attempts to cure by introducing small doses of disease virus.
 OSTEOPATHIC PHYSICIAN Attempts to cure by manipulation of tissue, muscle, or bone.

physics [FIH-sihks] science dealing with laws of inorganic matter and energy. (Sing., *physic,* is archaic for medicine.)
 PHYSIQUE [fih-ZEEK] (n.) body structure.
 PSYCHIC [SIE-kihk] (adj.) of the mind; also, occult.

physiognomy [fihz-ih-AHG-noh-mih] face. See **countenance.**

physiology science dealing with functions of living things.

pi Greek letter π. In mathematics, the ratio of the circumference of a circle to its diameter = to a constant of 3.1415926 or approximately 3 1/7.

pianist [PEE-ah-nihst].

piano [pih-AN-oh] musical instrument. (pl.) —os.

PIANO [pih-AH-noh] musical direction: softly.

pianoforte, pianoplayer.

piazza [pee-AH-tza] (It.) public square.

pica [PIE-kah] printer's measure of 12 points or 1/6 inch. See **type size.**

picaresque [pih-kah-REHSK] (from picaro, a rogue) Usu. applies to stories full of bohemian adventure: *a picaresque novel.*

PICTURESQUE pleasing to see: *picturesque scenery.*

Picasso, Pablo [pee-KAH-soh, PAH-bloh] (1881–1973) Sp. painter, sculptor.

picayune [pihk-uh-YOON] trifling.

piccolo (pl.) —os.

pickax., —lock, —off, —pocket, —up (n. or adj., all one word).

pick-me-up, pickmeup (pl.) —ups.

pickerel the fish.

picket (v.) —eted, —eting; picket line.

picnic —icking, —icked.

picturesque See **picaresque.**

pidgin English [PIH-jihn] spelling NOT *pigeon.*

piebald [PIE-bald] (adj.) of different colors spotted with black and white.

piecrust, piemaker, piepan; pie-eyed (adj.); pie plate, pie tin.

piece any standard length of a woven cloth.

piecemeal piecework; piece goods, piece rate.

pièce de résistance [PYEHS-de rae-see-TAHNZ] (Fr.) the most substantial dish of a meal; something outstanding.

pier no. 1 Lowercase. Also, pier head; pier dam, pier table.

pierce —ceable; pierced; piercing, —ly; piercer.

pietà [pee-AE-tah] picture of Mary mourning over Christ's body. Cap., usu. refers to sculpture by **Michelangelo.**

piety [PIE-eh-tee] piousness; devoutness. NOT *pity.*

pigeonhole (n. and v.); pigeon-toed (adj.); pigeon breast.

piggyback Rarely *pickaback*.

pigmy, pygmy

pile driver, pile hammer, pile-up (n. and adj.); piledriving (adj.).

pilfer —ered, —ering.

pillowcase, pillowslip.

pilot (v.) —ed, —ing.

pilothouse, —man; pilot boat, pilot burner, pilot light.

Pilsudski, Jozef [peel-SOOT-skee, YOO-zehf] (1867–1935) Pol. general, statesman.

pince-nez [PANSS-nae] eyeglass clipped to nose by a spring.

pincers (pl.) gripping device.

pinchpenny, pinch-hit, pinch-hitter.

pinochle [PEE-nuh-k'l].

pint (1) Unit of liquid measure = 1/2 liq. qt. = 16 liq. ou. = 28.875 cu. in. = 128 fl. drams.
(2) Unit of dry measure = 33.61 cu. in. = 0.55061. = 16 ou. = 1/2 dry quart. (3) British imperial pint = 34.68 cu. in. = 20 fl. oz. = 1.032 U.S. dry pt. = 1.2009 U.S. liq. pt. = 34.6775 cu. in. = 0.56821.

pipe unit of capacity = 1/2 tun = 126 gal. = 476.952 l.

piquant [pee-KAHNT] (arch.) pro-

vocative: *a piquant face.* Also, tart or pungent: *a piquant taste.* (n.) piquancy [PEE-kahn-see].

pique [peek] to nettle, offend.
PIQUE [pee-KAE] cotton fabric with raised ribbing.

pirouette [PEER-oo-EHT] in ballet, a spin.

pis aller [pee za-LAE] (Fr.) (lit.) "Go worst." Only course possible.

Pisces [PIE-seez] born Feb. 19–Mar. 19. See **Zodiac.**

Pissarro, Camille [pee-SAH-roh, kah-MEEY] (1830–1903) Fr. painter.

pistachio [pihs-TAH-shee-oh; pihs-TASH-ih-oh] a nut; the flavor; the yellow-green color (pl.) —os.

pitchblende shiny black uranium-based mineral.

piteous [PIHT-ee-uhs] exciting pity or sympathy.
PITIABLE exciting pity or contempt.
PITIFUL feeling and deserving pity or contempt.

pitter-patter

Piute [PIE-yoot] Native American tribe. (pl.) Piute or —s.

pizzicato [pihts-sih-KAH-toh] (music) plucked. (pl.) —os.

pk. (abbr.) peck.

pl. (abbr.) plural.

placard [PLAK-ahrd].

placate [PLAE-kaet] to appease; pacify. (adj.) —cable.

    IMPLACABLE [ihm-PLAK-uh-bl].

place (v.); —ceable (adj.).

place Cap., spell out if part of name: Pioneer Place, the place.

placebo [pla-SEE-boh] harmless medical prescription given to placate a patient; (fig.) a soothing remark.

placecard

PLACEMENT OF WORDS To avoid confusion, place modifiers as close as possible to the words they modify.

    Incorrect placement of a word may radically alter the meaning of a sentence. Words most commonly misplaced are *alone, at least, even, only.* Examples: *I alone can do it.* (Nobody else can.) *I can do it alone.* (I do not need any help.) *Only he can read a book a day.* (No one else can.) *He can only read a book a day.* (He cannot do anything else.) *He can read only a book a day.* (He cannot read any more.)

PLACE NAMES (1) Two generally accepted authorities are *The World Almanac* and the *Columbia Lippincott Gazetteer of the World.* Often, English publications replace the Egyptian *j* with *g*; the French *dj* with *j* and *ou* with *w*.

    (2) Avoid the repetition of geological formations in names where the foreign name includes the geological designation: *Rio Grande*, NOT *Rio Grande River; Sierra Nevada*, NOT *Sierra Nevada Mountains.*

placer [PLASS-uhr] system of mining.

plague [plaeg] —guable, —guing, —guy.

plagueproof, plague-infested (adj.).

plaid [plad]; Scot. [plaed].

plain —nness.

plainclothes —clothesman, —hearted, —work, —woven (all one word); plain-looking (adj.), plainspoken (adj.).

Plains The Great Plains. Usu. Kansas, Nebraska, Missouri, Iowa; sometimes the Dakotas and Oklahoma.

plaintiff in law, one bringing suit. The plaintiff makes a *declaration*, the defendant, a *plea*; the plaintiff's reply is a *replication*, to which the defendant makes a *rejoinder*. The plaintiff then files a *surrejoinder*, the defendant a *rebutter*, and the plaintiff, a *surrebutter*. Case name usually printed in italics in legal writings. *Brown vs. Smith.*

plait [plaet or pleet]; Br. [plat] a braid.

pleat [PLEET] a fold.

plan Lowercase Colombo plan, 5-year plan, Marshall plan; BUT Reorganization Plan No. 6 (Hoover Commission); plan no. 1.

Planck, Max [plahngk, mahks] (1858–1947) German physicist. Planck's constant.

planeload

planetarium Hayden Planetarium, the planetarium.

planets Mercury, Venus, Earth, Mars, Jupiter, Saturn, Uranus, Neptune, Pluto; possibly Planet X. See **heavenly bodies.**

plangent [PLAN-jehnt] loud and reverberating.

plantain [PLAN-tihn] a weed.

plant Rockford Arsenal Plant; the plant. BUT Savannah River (A.E.C.) plant, United States Steel plant.

plaque [plak].

plaster board, plasterwork; plaster of paris.

plate 2, A, II BUT Cap. Plate 2, when part of a title: *Plate 2.—Rural Structures.*

plateau (pl.) —s.

plate glass

platitude (n.); —dinous.

plausible reasonable.

plaza [PLAH-zuh] Union Station Plaza, the plaza.

plead (p. and p.p.) pleaded. (RARELY pled), —ing.

pleasurebound, pleasureseeking or pleasure-seeking (adj.); pleasure boat.

plebeian [pleh-BEE-yan] (n.) one of the common people. (adj.) pertaining to common people, vulgar.

plebiscite [PLEHB-ih-siht] vote of the people.

Pleiades [PLEE-ah-dees] in Gr. myth, seven daughters of Atlas; in astronomy, cluster of seven small stars in Taurus.

plenary [PLEHN-uh-ree] entire, complete: *a plenary Congress.*

plenitude abundance.

pleonasm (n.) more than enough. In grammar, redundancy.

plethora [PLEHTH-awr-uh] (n.) excess. In medicine, an excess of red corpuscles. (adj.) —ic.

pleurisy [PLEU-rih-see] inflammation of chest lining.

plexus (pl.) —uses.

pliable [PLIE-uh-b'l] flexible.

pliant [PLIE-ehnt] bending; easily influenced.

P.L.O. (abbr.) Palestine Liberation Organization.

plover [PLUHV-uhr] a shore bird.

plow Pref. to *plough.*

plumb [PLUHM] lead on a string used to determine the height or the depth. —er, —ing; —line.

PLURALS (1) Usually form plural of nouns by adding *s.* Nouns ending in o preceded by a vowel add *s*. If preceded by a constonant, they generally add *es*. BUT there are many exceptions. See **—o, —i.**

(2) Nouns ending in **y** (except most names) change **y** to *ies: babies, bellies, Alleghenies, Sicilies.*

(3) In compound nouns, the significant word takes the plural. Where only one word is a noun, the noun is pluralized; where no word is a noun, the last word takes an s: *passersby, bystanders, go-betweens.*

(4) Nouns ending in *-full* change to *fuls: 3 cupfuls* (1 cup filled 3 times). BUT: *3 cups full of whiskey* (3 separate cups).

(5) Some words invariably or occasionally take Latin plurals, changing the final *-a* to *-ae*, *-is* to *-es*, *-um* to *-a*, and *-us* usually but not always to *-i*. A typical exception is *hiatus*, the pl. of which is *hiatus or hiatuses.*

(6) Letter abbreviations and symbols form plurals by adding the apostrophe and *s: 2's, T's, Y's, etc.* BUT contractions sometimes are treated as words: *co-ops, AMVETS, hets.*

(7) Some plurals have the force of singular: *pains, means, news, measles, gallows, gymnastics, a harvest of good fruit, fruits of Florida, boatload of fish.* See *COLLECTIVE NOUNS.*

p.m. (abbr.) post meridiem; afternoon. When printed, small caps, PM.

pneumatic [noo-MAT-ihk].

P.O. (abbr.) petty officer.

pocketbook, pocket-size, pocket-veto, pocket knife.

pockmark; pock-marked

podium [POH-dee-uhm] dais (pl.) —ia.

LECTERN raised speaker's table.

poet-artist, poet-musician; poet laureate.

pogrom [POH-gruhm] organized massacre.

poignant [POIN-yuhnt], Brit. [POInant] keen, affecting, touching.

poinsettia [poin-SEHT-ee-uh] a tropical American plant popular at Christmas-time.

point Cap. and spell out if part of a name: *Outlook Point.*

point unit of measure = 1/100 carat. In printing, 1/72 inch. See **type size.**

pointblank, point-blank

points of the compass Spell out in ordinary text, abbr. without periods in technical material. Otherwise N., NE., NNE. See **compass, directions, latitude.**

Poitier, Sidney [pwoi-TYAE] (b. 1924) African-American actor, film maker.

Pol Pot [pohl paht] (b. 1928) Cambodian revolutionary and leader of **Khmer Rouge**; Prime Minister 1975–79.

Poland nation in NW Europe, on Baltic Sea, since Middle Ages. Cap.: Warsaw. Native: Pole. Currency: zloty. See **Polish.**

Polaris U.S. intermediate range missile designed to be fired with nuclear warheads from a submerged submarine. Also, North Star, **Pole Star**.

Pole North Pole, South Pole, the pole; subpolar.

polemic (n.) controversy. (pl.) —s.

POLEMICAL (adj.) controversial.

Pole Star, North Star; Polaris.

police (v.) —cing, (adj.)—ceable.

policeman, police car, police dog; Capitol Police.

policyholder, —maker; policy racket.

Polish of Poland: *Polish sausage, Polish workers.*

polite *more polite, most polite* are pref. to *politer, politest.*

politic (adj.) expedient, discreet. *He did not think it would be politic to tell his boss about the errors.* (adv.) —ly.

POLITICS (n.) the science of government. *She went into politics because she wanted to serve the public.* (adj.) political. (adv.) —cally.

politicial parties and adherents Cap. if part of name; BUT *N.Y. Times* and wire services lowercase party: Democratic party, the party; Communist Party, a Communist; Conservative Party, a Conservative; a Democrat, a Republican, an Independent, a Progressive.

The Republican Party is the Grand Old Party.

Lowercase unorganized groups: *conservatives, liberals, socialists.*

polity form of government or a government.

POLICY a line of action.

pollination

poltergeist [PAWL-tuhr-geist] noisemaking ghost.

polygamy [puh-LIHG-uh-mee] the practice of having more than one wife or husband.

POLYANDRY [PAHL-ih-an-drih] the practice of having more than one husband.

polyglot [pah-lee-GLAHT] (adj.) of many languages.

Polynesia [pahl-ih-NEE-zhah] group of SW Pacific islands. Native: Polynesian. See **Oceania.**

polynomial [pol-ih-NOH-mee-al] in algebra, an expression of two or more terms.

polyphony [puh-LIHF-uh-nee] multiplicity of sounds.

polysyllabic [pahl-ee-sih-LAHB-ihk] having many syllables.

polytheism belief in many gods. See **atheism.**

pommel, pummel [PUHM-mehl] (n.) (usu. *o* spelling) rounded knob, as on sword handle or saddle. (v.) (*u* spelling only) to beat. —meled, —meling.

pompadour [PAHM-peh-dawr].

Pompeii [pahm-PAE-ee] ancient city SE of Naples, Italy; buried in eruption of volcano Vesuvius A.D. 79.

Ponte Vecchio [POHN-teh vehk-YOH] Old Bridge, Florence.

pontificate (v.) to lecture self-importantly (as if a pontiff).

pontoon [pahn-TOON] portable float or boat. pontoon bridge.

pool Northwest Power Pool; the pool.

poolroom, pool table.

Pope ADDRESS: His Holiness the Pope, Vatican City, Rome; His Holiness, Pope John Paul II. SALUTATION: Your Holiness; Most Holy Father.

Popocatepetl [poh-poh-kah-TAE-peht'l] volcano in SE Mexico.

p.o.r. (abbr.) pay on return.

porous [PAWR-uhs] with many pores.

porphyry [POR-fuh-ree] feldspar-based rock with crystals.

port [pohrt] in seamanship, left side when looking towards the bow of a ship. Formerly *larboard.*

STARBOARD right side.

port city containing a harbor.

HARBOR place where ships may be accommodated.

port Cap. if part of name: Port of New York Authority (See **Authority**), the port. BUT Baltimore port; port of Baltimore.

portal-to-portal System of payment under which travel and other time spent (including time for wash-up, dressing, etc.) on company property is included in the work day.

Port-au-Prince, Port au Prince [pohrt-oh-PRIHNSS] cap. of Haiti.

porte-cochère [pohrt koh-SHAIR] (Fr.) large gate and cover for vehicles.

portentous ominous. NOT spelled -tious.

porterhouse steak choice cut from thick end.

portfolio portable case for keeping papers. (pl.) —os.

portico (pl.) —os.

portmanteau [pohrt-MAN-toh] (n.) traveling bag (pl.) —s (adj.). of more than one use.

PORTMANTEAU WORDS expressions coined by combining two or more words: *brunch, cinemajestic, sci-fi.*

Porto Rico See **Puerto Rico.**

Portugal nation on W coast of Iberian Peninsula. Since 12th C. Cap.: Lisbon (Lisboa). Native: Portuguese. Currency: escudo.

Poseidon [poh-SIE-dihn] in Gr. myth, god of the sea.

poseur [poh-ZOOR] *Poser* is pref.

posse [PAHS-ee] (Lat.) a legal armed band.

POSSESSIVES In English, possessive forms remain to some extent in flux. The following is a summary of the most widely-accepted conventions at the end of the 20th century.

(1) The possessive of a noun ending in any letter other than s is formed by adding 's. This applies to both singular and plural: *man's, men's; child's, children's.*

(2) Where the noun ends in s, the possessive is formed by adding an apostrophe only: *Charles'; hostess', hostesses'; princess', princesses'.* NOTE that the rule no longer depends on how the word is sounded. Words that end with an s sound but no s take 's: *prince's,* NOT *prince'.* BUT *princes,* plural, ends in s and so takes the apostrophe only: *princes'.*

(3) In the same way, the sound of the possessive does NOT dictate its form: *Robert Burns' poetry; the boss' daughter.*

BOTH points (2) and (3) are not universally accepted. *Chicago Manual of Style,* for instance, follows the old rule of apostrophe—plus -s after singular words ending in s: *Charles's, hostess's.* This older rule applies only with singular words ending in s, and only in those institutions which elect to follow it.

(4) Compound nouns add the 's to the element nearest the object possessed, the last word in the compound: *Ivan the Terrible's beard; attorney general's brief; John D. Brown, Sr.'s money.*

(5) To show joint possession, place the apostrophe on the last element of the series. Individual possession requires an apostrophe with each element of the series: *Brown and Smith's store* (the store owned by Brown and Smith); *Brown's and Smith's stores* (the store of Brown and the store of Smith); *soldiers and sailors' home, John and Mary's home* (one home); *men's, women's, and children's clothing; Reagan's and Bush's administrations; Mrs. Smith's and Mrs. Allen's children; master's and doctor's degrees.*

(6) In general, possession is attributed only to animate things. After names of countries or other organized bodies, use no apostrophe: *United States legislature, United Nations committee, Teamsters Union, teachers college.* Use an *of* to form the possessive of inanimate things: *The sale of drugs.*

(7) For geographic, trade, organization or institution names, or book titles, use the form established: *Harpers Ferry; Court of St. James's; Hells Canyon; Hinds' Precedents; International Ladies' Garment Workers' Union.*

(8) Use an *of* phrase to avoid piling up of possessives. NOT *John's mother's sister's coat.* Also use *of* to form the possessive of compound names: *The meeting of the Daughters of The American Revolution.*

(9) Sometimes both phrase and possessive are needed to express meaning accurately. *This is a picture of the Mayor* means: this is his portrait. *This is a picture of the Mayor's* means: this picture is his property.

(10) The possessive case is not used in expressions in which one noun modifies another: *day labor* (la-

bor by the day), *quartermaster stores, state prisoner, city employee.*

(11) Possessive personal pronouns take no apostrophe: *its, theirs. Your, our, and my clothing.* NOT: *Yours, ours,* and *my clothing.* BETTER: *Your clothing and ours are here.*

NOTE that *it's,* with the apostrophe, can only be a contraction, meaning "it is."

(12) BUT possessive indefinite or impersonal pronouns require an apostrophe: *each other's pockets, someone's pen, somebody else's proposal, anyone's boat, anyone else's boat.*

(13) Singular possessive case is used in general terms such as *author's alterations, cow's milk, printer's ink.*

(14) The possessive is often used in lieu of an objective phrase, even when actual ownership is not involved: *one day's labor* (labor for 1 day), *two hours' travel time, a stone's throw, two week's pay, for charity's sake.*

(15) A possessive used in an adjective sense still requires the addition of possessive form. *He is a friend of John's. The auction's merchandise.*

(16) If a possessive is followed by an appositive or an explanatory phrase, form the possessive on the explanatory word. *This was Mr. Keating, the Senator's, proposal.* If the appositive is set off by commas, the possessive may be formed on both the main word and the explanatory word. *Here is John's, my teacher's, wallet.* OR: *Here is John, my teacher's, wallet.*

(17) Possessives with participle take possessive. *The American Society's representative's joining the conference is a significant step forward.*

(18) Abbreviations follow rules for other words, with the apostrophe and *s* following the period: *the M.D.'s case, Smith Bros.' product.*

(19) A noun or pronoun immediately preceding a gerund is in the possessive case. A participle, which may have the same form as a gerund, functions as an adjective; its subject is in the objective case. *His being early upset the schedule. Tom's coming here made her nostalgic.*

(20) DO NOT use the possessive case for the subject of a gerund unless the subject immediately precedes the gerund. If subject and gerund are separated by other words, the subject must be in the objective case. *I could see no reason for him, with all his money, returning the merchandise. I can see no reason for a man with his background failing to pass the test.* BUT: *She could see no reason for the lady's returning.*

(21) There are no possessive forms for the demonstrative pronouns *that, this, these,* and *those.* When these words are used as subjects of a gerund, they do not change their form. *He could not be certain of that* (NOT *that's) being received.*

possible, possibly

postdate (v.) to date a document later than the current date.

post diem (Lat.) after the day.

poste restante [pohst rehs-TAHNT] (Fr.) general delivery.

postern [POHST-uhrn] (adj.) at the back or side.

posthaste, —mortem (nonlieral, —graduate.

posthumous [PAHS-choo-muhs] after death.

Postmaster General (pl.) Postmasters General.

Postmodern Also PostModern, Post-Modern, post-Modern; may be adj. or n. Art and culture since W.W. II. In general, Postmodern work recycles art from the past and reveals its own inner makings, thus demystifying the artist.

Still in flux, this developing culture has been identified in work as different as dramas by Samuel Beckett, shopping-mall architecture, and rap music. See **Modernism.**

P.O. Box Cap. if part of address.

postprandial after dinner.

postscript [pohst-skrihpt] (abbr.: p.s.).

postulate [PAH-styoo-leht] prerequisite or assumption in an argument.

Potemkin, Grigori [puh-TYAWM-kihn, grihch-GAW-ryih] (1739–1791) Rus. marshal, statesman. Gave name to battleship featured in 1925 film by **Sergey Eisenstadt.**

potency [POH-tehn-see] power.

POTENTIAL [poh-TEHN-shuhl] possibilities.

potful (pl.) —s.

pothole, potlatch.

potpourri [poh-poo-REE] mixture; medley.

poultry (sing. or pl.) NEVER use with a numeral: *4 poultry.*

pound (abbr.: lb.) (pl.) pounds (lbs.): *ten pounds.* BUT: *a tenpound turkey.*

pound, avoirdupois (abbr.: lb. avdp.) unit of weight = 16 oz. = 1.215 lb. troy or apothecaries = 256 drams advp. = 350 scruples = 7000 grains = 543.592 grams.

pound, troy or apothecaries. (abbr. lb. t. or lb. ap.) unit of weight = 12 oz. t. or ap. = 0.822286 lb. advp. = 96 drams t. or ap. = 240 dwt = 288 scruples = 5760 grains = 373.242 grams.

pound keeper, pound-foot; pound-foolish (adj.).

pound (£) (orig. 1 lb. of silver.) Write, £12 16s. 8p. NOT 12/16/8. One pound was 20 shillings = 240 pence = 2.48828 grams of gold (1963). Indefinite sums and round numbers are usually spelled out. Spell out shillings and pence when used alone: *7 shillings, two pence; ten thousand pounds.*

British decimal system now £1 = 100 pence.

pour to cause to flow.

PORE (v.) to gaze intently: *Pore over a book.* (n.) a minute opening.

pousse-café [poos-kah-FAE] liqueurs of different specific gravities which form layers of different colors in a glass.

poverty Means "poorness," when referring to money or property.

P.O.W. (abbr.) prisoner of war.

powers Cap. if part of name: Allied Powers, Axis Powers, Big Four Powers. BUT European powers. SEE **alliances.**

p.p. (abbr.) past participle.

p.p.i. (abbr.) policy proof of interest; in printing, pages per inch.

p.p.m. (abbr.) parts per million.

PR (abbr.) Puerto Rico.

practicable feasible, capable of being put into practice.

PRACTICAL useful; capable of being used profitably. *Television was practicable for many years before production techniques made it commercially practical.*

practically (adv.) almost; also, in a practical sense.

practice (n.) a lawyer's practice. (v.) to practice the piano.

pragmatic skilled in law or business; practical.

prairie chicken, prairie dog, prairie schooner.

praiseworthiness —worthy.

prandial [PRAN-dee'l] pertaining to a meal, esp. dinner.

pre- prefix meaning before. When placed before *e,* or a proper noun, or to avoid a possible misconception, hyphenate: *pre-eminent, pre-arranged, pre-Columbion, pre-position.*

precarious [preh-KAIR-ee-uhs] hazardous; insecure.

precede to go before.

PROCEED to go ahead. *Ladies precede gentlemen into a room, but both must proceed on foot.*

precedence [preh-SEED-ehns] priority. *Matters of health must take precedence over matters of money.*

PRECEDENTS [PREHS-ih-dehnts] instances that serve as authority or justification for future similar actions. *Legal precedents influence judicial decisions.*

precinct first precinct, 11th precinct.

preciosity [prehsh-ee-OSS-ih-tee] excessive fastidiousness.

PRECOCITY [pree-KAH-sih-tee] early development.

precipitate [pree-SIHP-ih-taet] (adj. and v.). —itable.

precipitous steep.

précis [prae-SEE] (sing. and pl.) a statement of the gist. See **abbreviation.**

predate (v.) to date a document prior to current date.

predecessor [preh-dehs-SEHS-uhr; PREE-].

predicate [PREHD-ih-kaet] (v.) to proclaim publicly; predict; imply. (v.) —ted, —ing; (adj.) —cable; (n.) —cation.

predicate [PREH-dih-kiht] (n.) in

grammar, the part of a clause containing the verb and its complements.

predicate, complement, predicate noun or predicate adjective Noun, pronoun, or adjective used after a linking verb to complete its meaning. Tom is *a good boy*.

PREDICATE NOMINATIVE A word following any form of the verb *to be* (except the infinitive, in certain cases; see below) must be in the nominative, the same case as the word before the verb: *I am he. Is that he?* NOT: *Is that him?* The verb *to be* has the same function as the equals sign in mathematics.

With the infinitive *to be*, a noun or pronoun following the verb is in the nominative only if the infinitive has no subject: *His sister was thought to be I.*

In cases of double pronouns, decide which case would be appropriate if one pronoun were the simple subject or predicate nominative, and then use the same case for both. *The tellers selected are he and I.* Reverse positions: *He and I are the tellers selected.*

preface (n.) statement preceding a text, usually by the author. (adj.) —cable. Also a verb: to preface.

FOREWORD statement preceding a text, usually by another.

INTRODUCTION An introduction differs from a foreword or a preface in that it is the initial part of the text. If the book is divided into chapters, it should be the first chapter.

prefect [PREE-fehkt] high official or

administrator. (adj.) —orial.

prefer —ring, —rred, —ence.

prefer . . . than *He preferred to go out drinking rather than assume the responsibilities of his father's business.*

preferable [PREHF-ehr-uh-b'l] *more preferable, most preferable* acceptable.

preferential [prehf-uhr-ehn-sh'l].

prefix letters or syllables attached to the beginning of the word. (v.) *prefix to*; NOT *with* or *by*.

AFFIX (v.) to attach.

SUFFIX letters or syllables attached to the end of a word.

PREFIXES AND SUFFIXES Ordinarily these combine into unbroken words. A few are hyphenated under special circumstances.

(1) Words ending in -*like* and -*smith* are written solid except when the *l* or *s* would be tripled, or when the first element is a proper name: *lifelike, girllike, bill-like, Florida-like; tinsmith, bass-smith, fender-smith.*

(2) Use a hyphen when the prefix ends in the same vowel with which the root begins: *semi-invalid, semi-intellectual.*

(3) Use a hyphen to join duplicated prefixes: *re-redirect, sub-subcommittee, super-superlative.*

(4) Use a hyphen to avoid ambiguity: *re-sort* (to sort again), *re-treat* (to treat again), *re-creation* (second creation), *un-ionized* (without ions).

(5) Unless usage demands otherwise, use a hyphen to join a prefix or combining form to a capitalized

word: *pro-British, un-American.* BUT: *overanglicize, transatlantic.* See **HY-PHENS.**

prehensible [pree-HEHN-sih-b'l] capable of being laid hold of.

PREHENSIBLE [-sie'l] adapted for grasping.

prejudgment a judgment made before hearing evidence.

prejudice preconceived attitude, usu. unfavorable; bias. Use *prejudice against, in favor of;* NOT *to* or *towards.*

prelate [PREHL-iht] a church dignitary.

prelude [PREH-lood] an introductory event. In music, cap. in a title: *Gershwin's Prelude in B flat; the Prelude to the Second Act of ''Pelleas et Melisande.''*

premature [pre-muh-TYOOR] before the usual time.

premier [PREE-myeer, PREHM-] (adj.) chief or principal. (n.) first minister of state, prime minister. See **foreign cabinets.**

PREMIERE [preh-MEER] first performance of a show.

premise [PREHM-ihs] (n.) proposition assumed before argument. (v.) [preh-MIEZ] to explain before discussion.

PREMISES [PREHM-ihs-ihz] property conveyed in a deed.

premium (pl.) —s.

premonition [pree-moh-NIHSH-uhm] a forewarning; foreboding.

preparation [prehp-uh-RAE-shuhn].

preparatory [PREH-prah-TAW-ree].

prepare [pree-PAER]. preparable [pree-PAER-uh-b'l].

PREPOSITION A word used to relate a noun or pronoun to another word in the sentence: *at, on, by, from, toward.*

Repeat preposition before the second of two connected elements. *He seemed interested in us and in our problems.*

A preposition at the end of a sentence is NOT necessarily incorrect. The placement should not destroy the sentence's rhetorical impact. Winston Churchill was once criticized for ending a sentence with a preposition, and he replied: "That is the sort of impertinence up with which I will not put!"

prepositional phrase The number of the noun in the phrase controls the number of the verb. BUT a preceding verb indicates the number in the following prepositional phrase. *Some of the paper has been written. Some of the books have been read. Has some of the material been used?*

prerequisite [pree-REH-kwih-siht] (n.) something needed to accomplish a task. See **requirement.**

presage [PREH-sij] (n.) portent. [preh-SAEJ] (v.) to portend.

Presbyterian [PREHS-bih-TEHR-ee-ehn], presbytery.

prescience [PREE-shih-ehns] (n.) foreknowledge of events. (adj.) prescient [PREE-shih-ehnt].

prescribe (v.) to lay down a plan of action. *A physician prescribes medicines, a lawyer prescribes lawsuits.* (n.) prescription; (adj.) —ible.

PROSCRIBE to condemn; prohibit. *Under the Eighteenth Amendment, the sale of liquors was proscribed.*

presentation [prehs-en-TAE-shuhn] a showing or a giving. *Presentation of a gift to the departing president is customary.*

presentiment [prih-ZEN-tih-mehnt] premonition. *They had a presentiment of danger ahead.*

PRESENTMENT [prehz-EHNT-mehnt] presentation. *The grand jury handed down a presentment of its findings.*

preserve Wichita National Forest Game Preserve, Wichita Game Preserve, Wichita preserve.

president Cap. for President of the United States, the Chief Executive, the Commander-in-Chief, the President-elect, ex-President, former President; also the Presidency.

Also cap. references to chief executive of any other country: the President of Brazil. Cap. with federal or international unit. BUT: president of the Erie Railroad, president of

George Washington University, the president.

president-elect (pl.) presidents-elect.

president pro tempore (of the Senate).

president of a college or university ADDRESS: Robert F. Goheen, Ph.D., President of Princeton University, Princeton, N.J.; or Dr. Robert F. Goheen, President of Princeton University; or (if he holds no doctor's degree) President Robert F. Goheen, Princeton University.

SALUTATION: Dear Sir; Dear President Goheen.

president of state senate ADDRESS: The Honorable Stanley Storm, President of the State Senate of Maryland, The State Capitol. SALUTATION: Sir.

president of the United States. ADDRESS: The President, The White House, Washington, D.C.; or The President of the United States; or President George Bush, Washington, D.C.

SALUTATION: Sir; Dear Mr. President.

presidential assistant, authority, order, proclamation. BUT: presidential candidate, election, timber, year.

president's wife ADDRESS: Mrs. Barbara Bush, The White House, Washington, D.C. SALUTATION: Dear Mrs. Bush. *Ms.* is also appropriate.

presidium [preh-SIHD-ee-uhm].

pressure 1 lb. per sq. in. = 0.070302 kg. per cm.^{2} 1 kg. per sq. cm.^{2} = 14.223 lbs. per sq. in.

prestidigitation [prehs-tih-dij-ih-TAE-shuhn] sleight of hand; magic tricks.

prestige [prehs-TEEJ; —TEEZH] power to command admiration.

prestissimo in music, very quick. (pl.) —os.

presto in music, quick.

presume [pree-ZOOM] to take for granted (with confidence).

   ASSUME to take for granted (with less confidence).

Pretender, the

pretense [PREE-tehns], —ension [pree-TEHN-shuhn], —entious.

preterit(e) [PREHT-uh-iht] past, former. Also, outcast.

preternatural [pree-tehr-NACH-ehr-al] strange and inexplicable; outside natural possibility.

prevaricate [pree-VAR-ih-kaet] to equivocate, quibble. NOT lie. —tor; —tion.

prevent —able pref. to —ible; —ive preferred to —tative.

previous going before, preceding in time or order.

   PREVIOUS TO Use *before*.

PRIOR Refers to time only, particularly when more important because earlier. (n.) priority.

pricelist, price-cutting, price-fixing, price-support (adj.); price cutter, price fixer, price index.

prie-dieu [pree-DYOO] (Fr.) "Pray God." Convertible desk or chair suitable for kneeling at prayer.

priest ADDRESS: The Reverend; or Reverend Charles B. Stone; or Reverend Father Stone, St. Andrews Church, etc. SALUTATION: Reverend Sir; Dear Reverend Father; Dear Father Stone.

prima donna [PREE-muh DAH-nah] (pl.) donnas.

prima facie *(N.Y. Times* spells *primafacie)* [PRIE-muh FAE-shee] (adj.) on first appearance.

prima facie evidence in law, sufficient to prove the case unless contradiction is offered.

primarily [prie-MEHR-rih-lee] in the first place.

primary colors in painting: red, yellow, blue; in lighting: orange-red, green, blue. Minor colors: magenta, orange, green.

primate [PRIE-maeht] In zoology, cap. (pl.) —s.

Prime Minister See **foreign cabinets.**

prime-ministerial (adj.) -ministership, -ministry.

primer [PRIH-muhr] elementary textbook.

primeval [prie-MEE-val] of the earliest times.

primitive

princehood, prince-priest; prince regent.

Prince Edward Island (abbr.: P.E.I.) island province in Canada. Cap.: Charlottetown.

prince of the royal blood ADDRESS: His Royal Highness Prince Albert. SALUTATION: Sir.

princess [PRIN-sihs (before a name); PRIN-sehs (as an independent noun)]. ADDRESS: Her Royal Highness Princess Anne. SALUTATION: Dear Princess.

principal chief, most important. (n.) the principality.

PRINCIPLE a fundamental cause, a truth, a rule: *the principle of relativity.*

principal of a school ADDRESS: Ms. Helen Hill, Principal, Teaneck High School, Teaneck, N.J. SALUTATION: Dear Principal Hill; Dear Ms. Hill.

prior to Use *before.*

prise (v. only) to force.

PRIZE (v.) to value. (n.) an award.

prison Auburn Prison, the prison.

prisonbound, prison-free, prison-made (adj.).

prisoner of war (abbr.: POW) (pl.) prisoners of war. (adj.) prisoner-of-war camp.

pristine [PRIHS-teen] primitive; hence, uncorrupted.

privilege [PRIH-vlihj].

privy [PRIH-vee] (adj.); privily (adv.).

privy council. See **council.**

prizefight —fighter, —holder, —winner (n.); —worthy (adj.); prize crew, prize ring.

prize Nobel Prize, Pulitzer Prize; the prize.

pron. (abbr.) pronoun.

pro-choice pro-Sandinista; pro-term-limitation; pro forma, pro rata, pro tem, pro tempore.

probable NEVER use *probable to: Such a result is probable. The probable score will be. . . .*

probate in law, testing; applies esp. to wills and to courts which examine wills.

probity [PROH-bih-tee] Uprightness, not merely honesty.

problematical [prah-bleh-MA-tih-k'l].

proboscis [proh-BAHS-ihs] a long, flexible snout. (pl.) —ses.

proceed [proh-SEED] (v.) to advance. See **precede.**

PROCEEDS (only pl.) amount realized from a sale.

process [PRAH-sehs].

procès-verbal [proh-SEHSS veh-BAHL] report of verbal statements; minutes of a meeting. (pl.) procès-verbaux.

Proclamation Presidential Proclamation No. 24; Proclamation No. 24; the proclamation. BUT: Presidential proclamation.

procurator [PRAH-kyoo-rae-tawr] in law, an agent; in ancient Rome, a government fiscal agent.

prodigy [PRAHD-ih-jee] an extraordinary person; a wonder.

produce [(n.) PRAHD-oos; (v.) proh-DOOS].

Prof. (abbr.) professor. Cap. in a title.

professedly [proh-FEHS-ehd-lee].

professor in a college or university ADDRESS: Professor Gerald Fitzgerald, Ph.D., English Department (or Department of English), Boston University, Boston, MA; or Gerald Fitzgerald, Ph.D., Professor of English, Boston U. SALUTATION: Dear Professor Fitzgerald.

Do not use the title *professor* for all college teachers. Many are instructors, or hold other ranks.

proffer [PRAHF-uhr] to offer. —ering, —ered.

proficient Use with *in* or *at.*

profitmaking, profit-and-loss, profit-sharing (adj.).

pro forma (Lat.) "according to form." In accounting, a statement as it would appear if a merger, financing, or other specified change should occur.

prognosis [prahg-NOH-sihs] to forecast. (pl.) —oses [—eez].

prognosticate [prahg-NAH-stih-kaet] —tor.

program [(v. or n.) PROH-gram] in computer science: programmed, programmer, —ming; programmatic [proh-gram-MA-tihk].

progress [(n.) PRAH-grehs; (v.) proh-GREHS].

progressive [proh-GREHS-sihv] in politics, favoring social change. See **conservative, liberal.**

progressive average the figures from each period added to those of the previous period.

progressive tax System that taxes higher incomes more heavily than lower. Also, *graduated tax.*

prohibit from doing NOT *prohibit to do.*

prohibition [proh-ih-BIHSH-uhn].

prohibitive [pro-HIH-bih-tihv] (adj.), tending to prohibit or restrain. Pref. to *prohibitory.*

project [PRAHJ-ehkt] Central Valley project, Manhattan project, McNary Dam project, Rochester atomic energy project.

Prokofieff, Sergei [prohk-KAWF-yehf] (1891–1953) Russian composer.

prolific [proh-LIH-fihk] fruitful, productive, fertile.

prologue [PROH-lahg] (n.; rarely used as v.).

promenade [PROM-uh-nahd; PROM-uh-naed] Both n. and v. imply public display, walking to be seen.

Prometheus [proh-MEE-thee-uhs] in Gr. myth, stole fire from the gods and brought it to humans. Condemned to have his liver eternally consumed by vultures.

promise —sor (legal), —ser; —ssory.

the Promised Land

promote *Promote to the presidency, to be president.* NOT: *promote to president.*

promptbook

promulgate [PRAHM-uhl-gate] *Publish* or *issue* is pref. —tor.

PRONOMINAL ADJECTIVES pronouns which are also used as adjectives: *all, any both.* Sometimes also *his, her their, my.* Place these before other adjectives in a series.

pronounce [proh-NOUNS] —ceable, —cedly, —cement.

PRONOUN (abbr.: pron.) a substitute for a noun.

(1) Every pronoun must have a clear antecedent, preferably nearby, to which it refers. Antecedent and pronoun must agree in number, case, person, and gender.

(2) Place a pronoun as close as possible to its antecedent. NOT: *He told his friend he was feeling better.*

(3) Avoid changing the person of pronouns referring to the same antecedent: *When one is young, it seems that everyone* (NOT *you* or *he*) *is young.*

There are six classes of pronouns: (1) personal: *I, we, me, us, my, ours;* (2) relative: *who, whom, which, that, whoever, whomever, whatever;* (3) interrogative: *who, whom, which, what;* (4) indefinite: *another, anyone, each, either, everyone, no one, nothing;* (5) demonstrative: *those, these;* and (6) intensive and reflexive: *myself, yourself, himself, themselves, ourselves, herself.*

A personal pronoun changes to show which person is the subject. First person: *I, we, me, us, my, mine, our ours;* second person: *you, your, yours;* third person: *he, she, it, they, his, hers, its, theirs, him, her, them, their.*

The relative pronoun takes the place of a noun in the clause it introduces and connects its clause with the rest of the sentence. It must agree in number, person, and case. *Ms. Hill is the only woman who dared to come forward.*

The interrogative pronoun is the same in form as the relative pronoun, but asks a question.

Demonstrative pronouns may also serve as adjectives to point out or refer to a substantive which has been clearly expressed or implied: *Give these toys to the children.* But it may not otherwise be used as an adjective.

Intensive pronouns intensify meaning. *She herself will bring the book* (no commas). Reflexive pronouns serve as subject, direct object, or antecedent. *She gave herself a holiday.*

pronunciamento [proh-nuhn-shih-uh-MEHN-toh] proclamation. (pl.) —os.

pronunciation [proh-nuhn-sih-AE-shuhn]

proof applied to liquors, the percentage of alcohol multiplied by two. 100 proof = 50% alcohol.

proofread proofreader, proofsheet (all one word). proof paper, proof press, proof spirit.

propaganda (pl.) —s.

propel —lling, —lled.

propellant (n.). propellent (adj., fig.).

propensity [proh-PEHN-sih-tih] natural inclination. *propensity to —*, *propensity for —*.

proper nouns or adjectives in grammar, those which apply to a particular person or thing: *American, John.*

property (pl.) —ties. (adj.) —tied.

prophecy [prahf-eh-see] (n.) prediction.
Compare to

PROPHESY [PRAHF-eh-sie] (v.) to predict.

propitiate [proh-PIH-shih-aet] to appease, conciliate. —tor, —tion [proh-pih-shih-AE-shuhn].

propjet —wash.

proportion Refers to a ratio. AVOID use where *part* will do. *A large part of the class passed. Next year a still larger proportion will pass.* —able, —al.
Write: 2 to 7; 1: 4725; 1-3-5. See **part.**

proportions. See **dimensions.**

proposal offering, plan, bid. The proposal of marriage is colloq.

PROPOSITION originally, formal statement of truth to be demonstrated or discussed, as in math or logic. Now widely used as a business proposal.
Also (colloq.) an immoral suggestion. *She expected a proposal but got a propostion.* In this meaning, usage allows as v. *He propositioned her.*

proprietary pertains to ownership.

PROPRIETORY conscious of ownership. Also, *proprietor:* owner.

pro rata [proh-RAE-tuh] (Lat.) "according to the rate." In proportion.

prorogue [proh-ROHG] parliamentary term meaning to discontinue meetings; for example, at the end of a session. Adjourn for a recess; dissolve at termination. —ed, —guing.

prosaic [proh-ZAE-ihk] of prose; hence, commonplace.

proscenium [proh-SEEN-ih-uhm] part of stage in front of curtain, sometimes framing curtain. (pl.) —ia.

proselyte [PRAHS-eh-liet] (n.) new convert. (v.) —tize [-lih-tiez].

prosody [PRAHS-oh-dih] the science of writing poetry.

prosthesis [prah-STHEE-sihs] artificial limb; sometimes other substitute body parts. Also, prosthetics [-STEH-tihks].

prostrate [PRAHS-traet] with face down.

    PROSTATE [-taet] muscular-glandular body organ.

protagonist in theater, leading character, hence, any leader or active participant. NEVER chief protagonist.

protean [PROH-tih-an] versatile, changeable. In Gr. myth, Proteus assumed different shapes when seized.

    PROTEIN [PROH-teen] amino acids essential for life; contain carbon, hydrogen, oxygen, nitrogen, etc.

protegé [PROH-teh-zhae] person under the protection or sponsorship of another. (pl.) —s.

pro tem, pro tempore (Lat.) temporarily; for the time being.

Protestant [PRAHT-ih-stehnt] a Christian not of the Roman Catholic or Eastern Orthodox Church. Some Anglican churches do not accept this designation. During 17th C., only Lutherans and Anglicans. Protestant Reformation.

protestation [PROH-tehs-TAE-shuhn].

protocol [PROH-tah-kahl] rules of etiquette, esp. regarding procedure. Also, preliminary memorandum or first draft.

prototype the first model. See **archetype.**

proton [PROH-tahn] subatomic particle carrying positive electric charge. See **atom, electron, neutron.**

protozoa [PROH-tah-ZOH-ah] one-celled animals.

proudhearted, proud-blooded (adj.).

Proudhon, Pierre-Joseph [proo-DAW(n)] (1809–1865) French socialist philosopher.

Proust, Marcel [proost, mahr-SEHL] (1871–1922) French Modernist novelist (*Remembrance of Things Past*).

prove (p.) proved. (p.p.) proved or proven.

provenance [PRAHV-eh-nehns] place of origin.

providing Use *if* instead where appropriate.

province Cap. if referring to an adminstrative subdivision: Ontario Province, Province of Ontario; Maritime Provinces (Canada); the Province. (adj.) provincial.

proving ground Aberdeen, etc.; the proving ground.

proviso [pro-VIE-zoh] a clause in a law or a contract in which a condition is introduced. (pl.) —os.

provocative [proh-VAH-cuh-tihv] serving to incite.

provost [PRAH-vuhst; (mil.) PROH-vohst] an official head. Military, a military police officer.

provost marshal (pl.) —marshals. provost marshal general, generals.

proxy [PRAHK-sih] power to act for another, esp. to vote.

prudent having wisdom and discrimination.

    PRUDENTIAL considered prudently.

prurience [PROOR-ih-ehns] tendency to lascivious longings.

P.S. (abbr.) post scriptum, postscript.

psalmbook [SAHM-buk].

pseudo- [SOO-doh] prefix meaning false: *pseudo-Messiah, pseudomorph, pseudonym.* See **nom de plume.**

p.s.f. (abbr.) pounds per square foot.

p.s.i. (abbr.) pounds per square inch.

psilocybin [sih-lo-SIE-bihn] hallucinogens found in certain mushrooms. See **mescaline.**

psittacosis [siht-uh-KOH-sihs] disease of birds, esp. parrots.

psoriasis [saw-RIE-ah-sihs] skin disorder.

P.S.T. (abbr.) Pacific standard time.

psychic [SIE-kihk] having supernatural mental powers. Also, *psychical.* See **physics.**

Psyche [SIE-kee] in Gr. myth, beautiful princess loved by Cupid.

    PSYCHE (not cap.) the life-essence: mental, emotional, spiritual. Exists in the body, but distinct from it.

    PSYCHEDELIC [SIE-kih-DEH-lihk] mind-altering.

psychiatry [sieh-KIE-uh-tree] medical specialty dealing with mental disorders. (adj.) psychiatric [sie-kee-AHT-trihk].

    PSYCHOLOGY [sie-KAH-loh-jee] science of the mind.

psycho- [SIE-koh] prefix meaning life, soul, mind: *psychodrama, psycho-organic, psychosis.*

psychopathic [-PAH-thihk] subject to severe mental disease or disorder; usu. entails illegal antisocial behavior.

    PSYCHOSIS severe mental derangement, but not necessarily legal insanity. (adj.) psychotic.

    NEUROTIC subject to a nervous disease.

psychosomatic [SIE-koh-soh-MAT-ihk] functional interrelationship between mental disorder and physical illness.

pt- Pronounce as t: *Ptolemy, ptomaine.*

pt. (abbr.) part; pint.

P.T. (abbr.) Pacific time.

P.T.A. (abbr.) Parent-Teachers' Association.

ptero- [TEHR-oh] prefix meaning wing, feather: *pterosaur.*

Ptolemy [TAHL-eh-mih] (fl. 2nd. C.) Greek-Egyptian astronomer, mathematician. Also, ancient Egyptian dynasty.

ptomaine [TOH-maen; toh-MAEN] alkaloid formed by putrefactive bacteria. *ptomaine poisoning.*

puberty [PYOO-buhr-tee] period of reaching sexual maturity.

pubic of the pelvic region.

Public Act 26, Public Law 9, Public 37, Public Resolution 3. BUT: public enemy No. 1.

public-minded, public-spirited (adj.); public words.

Public Printer the Government Printer, the Printer.

Public Res. (abbr.) public resolution.

Puccini, Giacomo [poot-CHEE-nee, JAH-koh-moh] (1858–1924) It. opera composer.

pueblo [PWEHB-loh] from Native American tribe in SW United States, stone or adobe village; also, individual dwelling.

puerile [PWEHR-ihl] immature; childish.

Puerto Rico [PWHER-toh REE-koh] Caribbean island; voluntary association with U.S. Cap.: San Juan. Native: Puerto Rican.

pugilism [PYOO-jihl-ih-zm] boxing.

puissant [PWIH-sant] potent. (n.) puissance.

Pulitzer, Joseph [PUH-liht-suhr] (1847–1911) Hungarian-American publisher, established Pulitzer Prize.

pullback (n. and adj.); —on, —out, —over, —up (n. and adj.); pull back, pull through, pull out (all v.).

pulley (pl.) —eys.

pulmonary [PUHL-muhn-air-ee] of lungs.

pulque [POOL-keh] fermented Mexican drink.

pumice [PUHM-mihs] light volcanic glass used for polishing.

pummel (v.) to beat. See **pommel.**

pumphandle —house, —room; pump drill (n.).

punctilio a fine point of ceremony; a trifling formality. (pl.) —os. (adj.) punctilious.

punctureproof (adj.).

pundit [PUHN-diht] (from Hindu) wise writer or teacher.

punitive [PYOO-nih-tihv].

pupa chrysallis stage of insect life. (pl.) —ae.

pupil one who is taught.

   STUDENT one who seeks knowledge.

puppet doll with movable parts for stage presentation.

   MARIONETTE puppet manipulated by strings.

pureblood —blooded, —bred.

puree [pyoo-RAE] strained pulped food.

Puritan 16th–18th C. Protestant based in England, Netherlands, and New England.

   PURITAN (not cap.) (n.) a person overly strict in religious principals, usu. derogatory. (adj.) puritanical.

purport [PUHR-pawrt] (n.); [puhr-PORT] (v.) See **import.**

pursue

pursuance [pehr-SOO-ehnz].

purview scope, range. *Religion is not within the purview of the law.*

pushbutton —cart, —over (n. and adj.); push-pull (adj.).

pusillanimous [pyoo-sih-LAN-ih-muhs] (adj.) cowardly. (n.) —nimity [pyoo-sih-luh-NIHM-ih-tih].

pussycat —foot.

put (p. and p.p.) put.

putout, put-on (n. and adj.); put-put (n.).

putsch [PUCH] a petty rebellion.

putter to dawdle; busy oneself with trifles.

Pvt. (abbr.) private.

PX. (abbr.) post exchange.

pygmy. Pref. to *pigmy.*

pyjamas. See **pajamas.**

pyramid Cap. the Pyramids of Egypt.

Pyrenees [PIH-reh-nees] mountains between France and Spain.

pyrites [PIE-riets] minerals which strike fire; for example, metallic-looking sulphides.

pyro- [PIE-roh or PIH-roh] prefix meaning fire: *pyrochemical, pyrotechnical.*

pyromania [pie-roh-MAE-nee-uh] See **mania.**

pyrotechnic [pie-roh-TEHK-nihk] fireworks display; science of fireworks. Hence, any extravagant display. (pl.) —s.

Pyrrhic victory [PIHR-rihk] a victory so costly it amounts to a defeat.

From ancient Greek king (318?–272 B.C.) who won such victories against Rome.

Pythagoras [pih-THAG-oh-ruhs]

(Died c. 470 B.C.) Greek philosopher, mathematician. (adj.) Pythagorean [-REE-ehn].

python [PIE-thahn].

Q

Quaddafi, Muammar [kah-DAH-fee, MOO-ah-mahr] Also Khaddafy, Kaddafi, Ghaddafi. (b. 1942) Libyan general, statesman; dictator since 1969.

Qatar [KAH-tuhr] Persian Gulf nation. Formerly Br.; independent, 1971. Cap.: Doha [DOH-hah]. Native: Qatari. Currency: Riyal.

Q-boat Q-fever, Q-ship.

q.e.d. (abbr.) *quod erat demonstrandum* (Lat.) "that which was to be demonstrated." In geometry, a statement following the proof of a theorem; hence, any logical deduction.

Also (abbr.), quantum electrodynamics.

ql. (abbr.) quintal.

Q.M. Gen. (abbr.) quartermaster general.

qt. (abbr.) quart.

qua in the character or capacity of. Use only when comparing the same person or thing in two different settings. *Qua husband he is tender; qua financier he is hard.*

quadrant [KWAH-drant] 1/4 circle = 90°.

quadrennial [kwah-DREHN-ee-ehl] occuring every four years; also, lasting four years.

quadrille [kwah-DRIHL] a square dance for four couples.

quadrillion 1000 trillion. See *NUMBERS.*

quagmire [KWAG-mie-uhr] marsh.

quaint [KWAENT] strange but attractive.

qualified expert is redundant.

quality Usage allows as adjective meaning "of quality."

qualm [kwalm] sudden nausea; faint-heartedness or fear.

quandary [KWAN-dar-ee] state of perplexity.

quantitative quantity. See *NUMBERS.*

quarantine [KWAHR-an-teen] isolation to avoid contagion.

quark [kwahrk] mysterious subatomic particle, theorized but unsubstantiated. Hence, any small mystery.

quarrel —ling, —led.

quart liquid measure (abbr. liq. qt.) (1) U.S. = 0.833 Brit. qt. = 1/4 gal. = 2 liq. pt. = 8 gills = 57.75 cu. in. = 0.94631; (2) Br. or imperial = 1.032 U.S. dry qts. = 1.2009 U.S. liq. qts. = 2 Br. pints = 69.35 cu. in. = 1.1365 liters.

quart, dry (abbr.: dry qt.) unit of capacity; (1) 1/8 peck; 1/32 bu. = 2 dry pt. = 67.201 cu. in. = 1.012 U.S. = 0.969 Br. or imperial qt.

quarter (1) U.S. = 8 bushels; (2) Br. 8 imperial bu. = 8.2564 Winchester bu.; (3) 1/4 ton; (4) 1/4 mi.

quartermaster general (pl.) quartermaster generals; quartermaster-generalship; quartermaster sergeant.

quartet a group of four.

quarto (abbr.: 4to) book size, approx. 9 × 12 in. (pl.) s.

quatrain [KWAH-traen] four-line stanza.

Quasimodo [KWAH-see-moh-doh] title character in Victor Hugo's novel *The Hunchback of Notre Dame* (1831). Hence, an ugly person.

quay [kee, kae] paved bank or loading place beside water.

Quebec (abbr.: Que.) province in Canada. Cap.: Quebec City.

queen ADDRESS: Her Gracious Majesty, the Queen, To Her Royal Highness Queen Elizabeth, or The Queen's Most Excellent Majesty. SALUTATION: Your Royal Highness; Madam.

querulous [KWEH-ruh-luhs, -roo-]. complaining, peevish.

QUESTION MARK Indicates to the reader that a question is being asked or that a doubt exists. The meaning rather than the form of the sentence determines whether the question mark is required.

If more than one question is raised, while the rhetoric remains that of a single sentence, each subordinate phrase may carry its own question mark: *Will it grow? or just wither? or perhaps be destroyed by rodents?* BUT this tactic is nearly always limited to poetry or poetic prose.

questionnaire

queue [kyoo]. Pigtail; waiting line. See **cue**.

quid pro quo (Lat.) "something for something."

quiescence [kwie-EHS-ehns] state of rest. (adj.) quiescent.

quiet Indicates the state of silence. *The hall was quiet.*

    QUIETNESS Indicates the quality. *Her step had a rare quietness.*

    QUIETUDE Indicates the habit. *He loved the quietude of his study.*

    QUIETUS [kwie-AE-tuhs] extinction. *The earthquake put the quietus on talk of drilling for oil.*

quinine [KWIE-nien] antimalarial medicine.

quintet a group of five.

quintillion 1000 quadrillion (18 zeros). See *NUMBERS.*

quintuplet [KWIHN-tuhp-leht] a collection of five of a kind. Each of five children born at one birth. (pl.) —s.

quisling [KWIHS-lihng] a traitor.

(from Norwegian army officer [1887–1945] who collaborated with Nazis).

quit (p. and p.p.) quit.

quitclaim legal release of a right or title to property. (v.) (p.) —ed.

quite completely; positively. *He is quite sane.* Meaning "to a considerable degree" is colloq. *They made quite a fuss.*

quiver [QUIHV-uh].

qui vive [kee VEEV] (Fr.) "Who goes there?" Hence, *on the qui vive* means "on the alert."

QUOTATION MARKS Used to enclose a direct quotation. Each part of an interrupted quotation must begin and end with quotation marks. *"Never!" he said. "No," he said, "I won't go."*

A quotation within a quotation is indicated by single quotation marks. Where double and single quotations coincide, the single mark goes inside the double one. *Mary reported: "Mother said, 'Go to the bakery.'"* OR: *Mary reported: "'Go to the bakery,' Mother said."* A quotation inside a single quotation takes a double quotation mark. *"He called loudly: 'Ship Ahoy! I see the "Battersea" off the rocks.'"*

Quotation marks are usually required following words like: said, replied, responded, entitled, the word, the term, marks, endorsed, signed. *He wrote a story entitled "Rise and Shine." After the word "peace," the* group applauds. The note was signed "John Brown." BUT quotation marks do not generally follow the words *called* and *so-called.*

In quoting more than one paragraph, a quotation mark is placed at the beginning of each paragraph but at the end of the final paragraph only.

Quotation marks are used to enclose misnomers, slang expressions, or ironic use. *They called for Johnny "Red" Jones. Most Mondays he called in "sick."* BUT avoid using quotation marks simply for emphasis or to indicate questionable material.

Quoted material that is indented or set in smaller type does not require quotation marks. Letters reproduced with date and signature require no quotation marks.

The comma and the final period are always placed inside the quotation marks. Other punctuation is enclosed only if it is a part of the matter quoted. *Mary pleaded, "Please stay." She asked, "Why?"* BUT: *John says her story is "bunk"? He called her "darling"! He wrote under "Announcements": "Be sure to vote today!"*

Cap. the first word of a direct quotation if it would be capitalized if standing alone, but not the first word of a fragmentary or indirect quotation. *He objected "to the phrasing," not to the ideas. Everyone knows about the sort of thing that "gathers no moss."*

Qu'ran [ku-RAN] Islamic holy book. See **Koran.**

q.v. (abbr.) *Quod vide.* (Lat.) "Which see."

R

-r, -rr-. Words of one syllable ending in *r*, if preceded by a single vowel (but not a diphthong), double the *r* when adding a suffix beginning with a vowel: *starring, charring*.

Words of more than one syllable double the r only when the accent falls on the last syllable: *interred, entered*. BUT *confer, infer, prefer, refer, transfer* all double the *r*.

R. (abbr.) Réaumur. See **temperature**. Also, a **movie rating** meaning Restricted.

rabbet (n.) slot or groove. (v.) to cut such a slot. —ing, —ed. NOT *rabbit*.

rabbitskin, rabbit's foot.

Rabelais, Fransçois [RAB-eh-lae] (c. 1495–1553) Fr. satirist and fabulist (*Gargantua, Pantagiruel*).

RABELAISIAN (adj.) exuberant, with extravagant imagery (not necessarily indecent).

rabbi Refer to Rabbi Joseph Cohen, Dr. Joseph Cohen. Among Jews, the title *Rev.* may be applied to a cantor or shochet, but is eschewed by rabbis.

ADDRESS: Rabbi Joseph Cohen; Rev. Dr. Joseph Cohen, Dr. Joseph Cohen. SALUTATION: Dear Rabbi Cohen; Dear Dr. Cohen.

rabies [RAE-bees] virus disease of animals (dogs, squirrels) transmitted to humans via a bite.

raccoon

Rachmaninoff, Sergei [ruhk-MUH-nyih-nuhf, syihr-GAE] (1873–1943) Rus. pianist, composer, conductor.

RACIST LANGUAGE Appropriate designations for racial and ethnic groups have changed throughout the century. *Black* was a derogatory term for *Negro* until the 1960s, and then after *black* enjoyed public favor for twenty years or so, it was slowly superseded by *African-American*.

No doubt such redefinitions will continue. Current usage prefers appelations with the suffix **-American:** *Asian-American, Hispanic-American. Native American*, meaning an indigenous American Indian, is not hyphenated.

In general, calling attention to skin color or idiosyncracies of facial features is at the very least colloquial and, at worst, insulting. Usage allows *black* in good writing, but never *darky. Redskin* or *slope* are always inappropriate.

Person of color is an acceptable general term for anyone not of white northern European extraction.

These expressions can result in ungainly phrasing: *A collection of poems of persons of color . . .* Good writing both avoids the appearance of prejudice and communicates effectively.

rack and pinion (n.); rack-and-pinion (adj.) steering.

racket Pref. to *raquet* in all meanings, even for tennis.

raconteur [rah-kahn-TEUR], (fem.) —teuse [tooss] storyteller.

radar (abbr.) radio detection and ranging. Also **radarman, radarscope.**

radiator [RAE-dih-ae-tawr].

radio (v.) —ed, —ing.

radio frequency, radioisotope; radio amplifier, antenna, channel, communication, engineer, link, range, receiver, set, spectator, transmitter, tube, wave (all separate words).

radio waves Wave length of radio signals is expressed in kilocycles (KC), classified by FCC as:

VLF—Very low frequency—10 to 30

LF—Low frequency—30 to 300

MF—Medium frequency—300 to 3000

HF—High frequency—3000 to 30,000

VHF—Very high frequency—30,000 to 300,000

UHF—Ultra high frequency—300,000 to 3 million

SHF—Super high frequency—3 million to 30 million

radio stations Abbreviate and omit periods: *WABC.* But for broadcasting networks, *N.Y. Times* uses periods: *N.B.C., A.B.C.*

radium therapy

radius [RAE-dih-uhs] (pl.) radii, radiuses.

R.A.F. (abbr.) Royal Air Force.

raffle The verb uses *off. We raffled off the car.*

ragout [rah-GOO] a stew.

raillery [RAEL-ehr-ee] banter, especially satirical.

railroad Figuratively, to *railroad through* is to force into being, without allowing the opposition to be heard.

rainbow-colored (adj.); rainbow chaser (n.).

raise (p. and p.p.) raised. A transitive verb which requires a direct object. *He raised his hat.*

RISE (p.) rose; (p.p.) risen. An intransitive verb which cannot take a direct object. *She rose as he entered.*

raison d'être [REH-zohn DAET-ruh] (Fr.) reason for being. *Writing and performing new songs is his raison d'être.*

rajah or raja [RAH-jah] Hindus use *raj*, title of Indian king, prince or chief.

raku [rah-KOO] lead-glazed earthenware.

ramjet, —line, —rod, —shackle.

rampant (v.) in heraldry, to rear or leap; (adj.) unrestrained.

Ramses, Rameses [RAM-eh-seez] royal dynasty in Egypt, at time of Old Testament Exodus (1292 B.C.–1167 B.C.).

ranchhouse, ranch hand.

rancor NOT —our.

range Cascade Range (mountains), the range.

rangefinder

ransack (v.) —ing, —ed.

Raphael [RAH-fah-ehl] Raffaello Santi [RAHF-fah-ehl-loh-SAHN -tee] (1483–1520) It. painter.

rapier [RAE-pyeer].

rapine [RAPP-ihn] pillage, NOT necessarily sexual rape.

rapport [rap-PAWR] harmony.

rapprochement [ruh-prawsh-MAHN] return to harmonious relationship; requires a prior falling out.

rapt (originally from *raped,* carried off) intensely concentrated; enraptured.

rarebit a delicacy, NOT *rabbit.* BUT *Welsh rabbit* is correct.

rarefy rarefied. BUT rarity. *Webster's* accepts sp. *rarify.*

rarely Use *rarely if ever;* NOT *rarely or ever.*

rase Use *raze.*

raspberry [RAZ-buhree].

Rasputin, Grigori [ras-PYOO-t'n, gryih-GAW-ryih] (1871–1916) Rus. scholar and monk who exerted dan-

gerous control over the Czar; hence, any shady manipulator.

ratable taxable real property.

ratbite, ratcatcher (n.); rat-infested, rat-tailed (adj.); rat race (n.).

rate holder a small advertisement run in a periodical to qualify for a lower rate earned on multiple insertions.

ratemaker, ratefixing, rate-setting, rate-cutting, rate-raising; rate base.

ratemeter instrument for measuring rate of radiation absorption.

ratio [RAE-shih-oh] (pl.) —os. relation between things.

ratiocinate [rash-ih-AHS-ih-naet] (v.) to think carefully. (n.) ratiocination [RASH-ee-ahs-ih-NAE-shuhn].

ration [RAE-shuhn] allowance; share.

rationale [rash-uhn-AL] a motive, esp. one that's contrived. *Their rationale is that they want to help the community, but the real reason is that they want the property for themselves.*

rattan [rat-TAN] long-stemmed palm tree used for making walking sticks, wicker furniture.

raucous [RAW-kuhs] disagreeably harsh.

Rauschenberg, Robert [ROU-shenberg] (b. 1925) American Pop artist, famous for multi-media collage.

ravage [RAV-ihj] (v.) to devastate; destroy violently. —ged, —ging.

> RAVISH (v.) to abduct; by extension, to rape.
>
> RAVISHING (adj.) inspiring delight: *ravishing beauty.*

ravel —led, —ling.

Ravel, Maurice [rah-VEHL, maw-REES] (1875–1937) Fr. composer famous for "Bolero."

ravine [ruh-VEEN] steep depression, larger than a gully, smaller than a valley.

raving frantic, irrational.

Rawalpindi [RAH-vahl-PIHN-dee] city in Pakistan.

rawboned, rawhide (n.); raw-edged, raw-looking (adj.).

razzle-dazzle

Rd. (abbr.) road.

R. & D. (abbr.) research and development.

R. & R. (abbr.) rest and relaxation.

re- prefix meaning again. Use hyphen before an *e: re-enlist;* use optionally before other vowels: *re-assess.*

Also hyphenate to avoid confusion in meaning: *re-cover;* not *recover; re-count,* not *recount;* or before a simple word: *re-do, re-ice, re-ink;* or to avoid mispronunciation: *re-create* (create again); *re-cross-examination.* See *HYPHENS.*

re, in re legalese and commercialese for *in the matter of.*

-re Br. ending for many words spelled -er in U.S.: *theater, theatre; center, centre.*

R.E.A. (abbr.) Rural Electrification Administration.

reactionary in politics, conservative; reacting against progressive thought.

read [reed] (p. and p.p.) read [rehd]; reading, readable.

reading room

ready-made (adj.); ready room.

Reaganomics [RAE-gehn-ahm-ihks] conservative economic policies associated with U.S. presidency of Ronald Reagan (1980–88), and with worldwide movements of the time.

-related Informal usage allows as suffix meaning "pertaining to:" *a drug-related homicide.*

realize in business, to convert property or paper profit into cash.

Realpolitik [reh-AHL-poh-lee-TEEK] (Ger.) "realist politics." Policies dependent on the threat of military power.

Realtor [REE-al-tehr] a member of the National Association of Real Estate Boards. Cap. if title, but not as job description: *She works as a realtor.*

realty [REEL-tee] real estate. *Invest-*

ments in realty usually bring excellent re-turns.

> REALITY [ree-AL-ih-tee] something real; the quality of being real. *His dream became a reality after he inherited a fortune.* (adj.) realist.

ream 500 sheets of paper = 20 quires (25 sheets each).

Rear Adm. (abbr.) rear admiral.

rear guard, rearmost, rearview; rear end.

the reason is because Avoid, redundant. Use *the reason is that.*

Réaumur (abbr.: R.) thermometric scale; 0° is freezing, 80° boiling point of water. Invented by R.A. Réaumur.

rebel (v.) —lling, —lled.

rebellion Cap. if part of name: Boxer Rebellion, War of the Rebellion, Whiskey Rebellion; the rebellion.

rebuke (v.); —kable (adj.).

rebus [REE-buhs] riddle which uses pictures to represent syllables.

rebut —tting, —tted.

rebuttal refutation.

recalcitrant [ree-KAL-sih-tr'nt] (from "kicking backwards") objecting to restraint.

> INTRANSIGENT (from not coming to an agreement) uncompromising.

recapitulate —tor.

receipt [ree-SEET] evidence of payment.

receive receivable.

recession [reh-SEHSH-uhn] Usage allows as a general term for a slowdown in the economy.

recherché [reh-shehr-SHAE] (adj.) exquisite, choice.

recidivist [ree-SIHD-ih-vihst] one who reverts to antisocial behavior. (n.) —vism, (adj.) —vistic.

recipe [REHS-ih-pee] prescription; esp. for cooking.

reciprocal [reh-SIH-proh-k'l] shared by both sides. (v.) reciprocate. (adj.) —cable.

recitative [reh-SIH-tah-TIHV] narrative; esp. set to music.

reckon —ing; —ed.

reclamation [rehk-luh-MAE-shuhn] act of reclaiming.

recluse [reh-KLOOS] one who lives in seclusion; hermit.

recognizance [reh-KAHG-nih-zehns] in law, "released on his own recognizance" means released without posting bail.

recollect to remember after searching memory. Hyphenated, *re-collect*, means to gather together again.

> REMEMBER to know from previous learning.

RECALL to bring back to memory.

recommend

reconcile [REHK-ahn-sie'l] —lable; —liation. *The marriage counselor worked to bring about a reconciliation.*

recondite [REHK-uhn-diet, ree-KAHN-diet] (adj.) abstruse; concealed.

reconnaissance [ree-KAHN-ih-sans] (n.) a survey. *A patrol was sent on reconnaissance to determine the number of the enemy in the area.*

reconnoiter [ree-kah-NOI-tuhr] to examine or survey. —tering.

Reconstruction period Following U.S. Civil War: 1865–1880.

record *All-time record, new high record,* etc. are redundant.

recordbreaker, —keeper, —maker, —making (all one word).

recount (v.) to narrate.

RE-COUNT (v.) to count again. —ing, —ed. May appear without hyphen and as n.

recourse [REE-kawrs] (n.) a turning to something for help. *Luckily, he had recourse to a VISA account number.*
Also, the source of help itself. *That 7–11 store was our recourse in times of need.* In this meaning, *resort* can be a synonym. *That 7–11 store was our last resort.*

RESOURCE [REE-sawrs; ree-SAWRS] a source of help, informa-

tion, etc. Can be adj.: *resource book.*

recover, re-cover Hyphen changes meaning.

recreation, re-creation Hyphen changes meaning.

recrudesce (v.) to break out again. (n.) recrudescence: renewed morbid activity. *The recrudescense of this plague.*

recti-, rect- prefix meaning right, straight: *rectifiable.*

rectilinear Formed by straight lines. Pref. to —neal.

recto- prefix meaning rectal: *rectoscope.* Without hyphen, side of manuscript to be read first; usu. in combination with **verso,** meaning to read right side first, then left. Hence, recto-verso, *reverse.*

recuperate [reh-KOO-pehr-aet] (v.) to recover. (adj.) —rable.

recur Pref. to *reoccur.*

RECURRENT For scientific, technical use.

RECURRING For non-scientific use.

red, reddish

CRIMSON blue red, low brilliance.

FUCHSIA [FYOO-shuh] pink-purple-red, medium brilliance.

MAGENTA purplish fuchsia.

PINK light red, high brilliance.

MAROON medium yellowish red, low brilliance.

SCARLET hard yellow-red, medium brilliance.

VERMILION softer yellow-red, medium brilliance.

redact [ree-DAKT] to rearrange, edit. —or, —ion.

Red Cross, American

redeemable Refers to practical matters. *Is this coupon redeemable for cash?*

redemptible Refers to the spiritual: *a redemptible soul.*

redolent [REHD-oh-lehnt] (adj.) odorous. Use with *of.*

redoubtable [rih-DOUT-ih-b'l] formidable.

redressible [ree-DREHS-ih-b'l] able to be set right.

reductio ad absurdum [ree-DUHK-tih-oh ad ab-SUHR-duhm] (Lat.) "reduction to absurdity." In logic, proving a proposition by connecting its denial to other accepted propositions until a contradiction is reached. Hence, any argument that extends certain assumptions until they appear ridiculous.

redundancy superfluous repetition.

TAUTOLOGY needless repetition of meaning in other words: *visible to the eye.*

re-entry

re-enforce See **reinforce.**

refectory [ree-FEHK-toh-ree; (Monastic) REF-] a dining hall.

refer [ree-FUHR] (v.) —red, —ring. (n.) reference [REHF-uh-rehns]. See **allude.**

referee

referendum (pl.) —s or —da.

reflectible, reflexible capable of being thrown back.

REFLEXIVE PRONOUNS Include *myself, himself, herself.* Commas isolating such pronouns are not correct. *I myself couldn't stand it. I hurt myself.*

Usage allows *He is as fast as myself;* BUT *He is as fast as me* is pref.

AVOID as subject or direct object. NOT: *My wife and myself went.* (Use *I*). NOT: *The letter came for my son and myself* (Use *me*).

reform, re-form Hyphen changes meaning.

reformation [reh-fawr-MAE-shuhn] Cap., the Reformation, when referring to 16th-C. religious revolution which divided Christendom into Catholics and Protestants.

reformatory Elmira Reformatory, the reformatory.

refuge Blackwater Migratory Bird Refuge, Blackwater Bird Refuge, Blackwater refuge.

refund [(v.) ree-FUHND; (n.) REE-fuhnd].

refutable [reh-FYOO-tuh-b'l] capable of being disproved.

regalia [reh-GAEL-yah] (n. pl.) royal emblems; hence, any ostentatious display.

regard When used to mean *consider,* requires *as. He considers it scandalous.* BUT: *He regards it as scandalous.*

Never follow with infinitive. NOT: *She regards it to be an insult.* The terms *with regard to, in regard to* mean *with reference to. As regards* means *as far as it relates to.* AVOID *regarding, in regard to* for introducing a subject.

As noun, use plural, *regards,* only in the formal expressions: *Give my regards to your sister.*

regatta [reh-GAHT-tah] organized rowing competition.

Regency Period in English arts and decor, 1811–1820. Identified with classical motifs (Greek, Roman), including use of brass, rosettes.

regime [rae-ZHEEM] mode of rule. *Ancien regime,* from pre-French Revolution, now any abolished government.

region north-central region; first region, 10th region, mid-continent region; region 3; regionwide.

register —trable, —trar.

Register of Copyrights City Register; Register of the Treasury, the Register.

regress (n.) [REE-grehs; (v.) ree-GREHS].

regretful showing or feeling regret.

REGRETTABLE causing regret.

The riot was a regrettable incident, for which I am regretful.

Regular Army Regular Navy; a Regular. See **Officer.**

regulation ceiling price regulation 8; regulation 56 (Navy); supplementary regulation 22; Veterans Regulation 8, (BUT veterans regulations); Regulation W.

Reign of Terror In France, 1792. Period of mass excecutions by guillotine, following Fr. Revolution.

reindeer (sing. and pl.).

reinforce [REE-ihn-fawrs] (v.) to strengthen. As adj.: *reinforced concrete.* As n.: *troop reinforcements.*

RE-ENFORCE (v.) to enforce again. (adj.) —ceable.

re-join, rejoin *He re-joined* (reunited) *the links of the chain. He rejoined the party.*

rejoinder [ree-JOIN-duhr] (n. only) See **answer, plaintiff.**

rejuvenate —ting, —ted, —nable.

relative Can apply to any relationship: *relative facts.*

RELATION person connected by blood or marriage.

KIN one of same stock, race, or family.

RELATIVE CLAUSE a dependent clause introduced by a relative pronoun (who, which, that).

RELATIVE PRONOUNS. See *CON-*

NECTIVES, PRONOUN.

relativity theory theory that the universe follows equivalent physical laws, such as gravity, throughout all its frames of reference. Developed by Albert Einstein (1879–1955).

relegate to banish; remove. —ting, —ed, —gable.

relevance [REHL-uh-vans] pertinence.

relic [REH-lihk] something surviving from the past, esp. associated with a saint.

RELIQUARY place of safekeeping for a holy relic.

reliction extension of land due to withdrawal of a body of water. *He acquired the property by reliction.*

Religions Bahai; Baptist; Brahman; Buddhist; Catholic, Catholicism, BUT catholic (universal).

Christian; Christian Science; Evangelical United Brethren; Judaism; Latter-day Saints, Moslem; New Thought; Protestant; Roman Catholic; Seventh-Day Adventist; Seventh-Day Baptist; Zoroastrian.

religious terms Cap. all words denoting the Deity except *who, whose,* and *whom;* all names for the Bible and other sacred writings; all names of confessions of faith (*the Apostles' Creed*), of religious bodies and their adherents (*the Presbytery of the Cascades*), and words specifically denoting Satan. See **Bible.**

R.E.M. rapid eye movement, during deep sleep.

remainder what is left when something is taken away. Used in arithmetic and in practical situations.

RESIDUE, RESIDUARY Used in law.

RESIDUUM Used in chemistry. (pl.) —dua. (adj.) residual.

BALANCE Used in bookkeeping.

Rembrandt van Rijn [REHM-brant vahn RIEN] (1606–1669) Classic Dutch painter.

remedial [reh-MEE-dee-al] designed to cure.

REMEDIABLE [reh-MEE-dih-uh-b'l] curable.

remediless [REM-eh-dee-lehs] having no remedy.

remembrance   [reh-MEHM-brehnse].

reminisce [reh-mih-NIHS] (v.) to give oneself up to recalling the past. NOT to remember. (n.) —iscence; (adj.) —iscent.

remit —tting, —tted, —ttal, —ttance.

remissible, remission

remodeler

remonstrate [ree-MAHN-straet; REH-mehn-] to say in protest; urge reasons opposed. —strance, —stration.

remove —ving, —ved, —vable.

remunerate —ted, —rable, —ration, —rative. NOT renumerate.

renaissance [reh-neh-ZAHNS] rebirth; revival: *a renaissance of poetry.*

the Renaissance Roughly 1350–1600. Named for renewed interest in achievements and values of ancient Greece and Rome, characterized by great vitality in the arts and sciences. Can be adj.: *Renaissance architecture.*

renascence [ree-NAES-ehns] (n.) rebirth. (adj.) renascible.

rend (n.) a tear, as in clothing. (v.) (p.) rent.

rendezvous [RHAN-deh-voo] (n. sing. and pl.) meeting place; a meeting. (pl.) —vous [vooz]. (v.) to meet. (p.)—voused [vood], (pres. part.) — vousing [vooing].

renege [ree-NEHG] to deny; renounce. In card playing, fail to follow suit. —neged, —neging.

Renoir, Pierre Auguste [reh-NWAHR, aw-GOOST] (1841–1919) Fr. impressionist painter.

   Renoir, Jean, [zhuh(n)] (1894–1979) Fr. filmmaker (*Grand Illusion*), son of the painter.

renounce —cing, —ced, —ceable (n.) renunciation [ree-NUHN-sih-ae-shuhn]. (adj.) renunciatory [-shih-a-toh-rih].

repairman, repair shop.

reparable [REHP-uh-rabl] (adj.) able to be repaired. Pref. to *repairable.* Opp. of *irreparable.*

repartee [reh-pahrt-TEE, NOT — TAE]. See **answer.**

repatriate [ree-PAE-tree-aet] to return to one's own country.

repeat (v.) to say over again.

   REITERATE (v.) to say or do over again, usu. for emphasis.

repel —lling, —lled, —llent.

repercussion [ree-puh-KUHSH-uhn].

repertoire [REHP-ehr-twahr].

repertory theatre

repetition of sounds Avoid if not in deliberate parallel structure. NOT: *The session discussed several September dates. Long strings are wrong for John.*

repetitive, repititious [reh-PEH-tih-tihv; reh-peh-TIH-shuhs] *Webster's* lists as synonyms.

replace (v.); —ceable (adj.).

replenished filled again.

replete [ree-PLEET] filled up. DO NOT use in negative. NOT: *The house is not replete with antiques.*

   COMPLETE whole.

reply See **answer.**

report Cap. if part of name (with date or number); Annual Report of the Secretary of Defense for the year ended June 30, 1990; Hoover Commission Report on Paperwork. BUT Hoover Commision report, Hoover report; task force report; the annual report.

repoussé [reh-poo-SAE] art work in relief, esp. metal work.

reprehensible [re-pree-HEHN-sih-b'l] culpable; connotes extreme wrongdoing. —sibleness, —sibly, —sion.

representative. Representative at Large (U.S. Congress); Representative-elect.

representative in Congress ADDRESS: The Honorable Les AuCoin, The House of Representatives, Washington, D.C.; or Representative Les AuCoin, The House of Representatives, Washington, D.C.; or (if sent to his home) The Honorable Les AuCoin, Representative in Congress (followed by postal address). SALUTATION: Dear Congressman AuCoin; Dear Representative AuCoin; Dear Mr. AuCoin; Dear Sir; Sir.

representative at large BUT, for a specific person with title; Representative at Large John Jones.

repress (v.); —ssible (adj.).

reprise (n.) in law [ree-PRIEZ], annual charge or rent. In music [ree-PREEZ], a repetition.

reproduce (v.), —cible (adj.).

reptile [REP-tiel] class of cold-blooded animals; includes snakes,

crocodiles, salamanders, turtles.

repudiate [ree-PYOO-dih-aet] (v.) to renounce. (adj.) —diable.

repugnant [rih-PUHG-nant] (adj.) distasteful; also, incongruous, contradictory. (n.)—ce.

republic Cap. if part of name; cap. standing alone if referring to a specific government: French Republic; Irish Republic; Republic of Panama; Republic of the Philippines, Philippine Republic; United Arab Republic; the Latin American Republics, South American Republics, the Republics.

Republican member of Republican party.

requiem [REH-kwih-ehm] mass for the dead.

requirement a need. *Her qualities meet our requirements.*

REQUISITE (adj.). *He lacks the requisite degrees.*

PREREQUISITE (n.). *Biology 101 is a prerequisite for any advanced medical studies.*

INDISPENSABLE (adj.) Indicates that without it (the thing being described) something else cannot be done. *Biology 101 is a prerequisite for medical school; good study habits are indispensable for staying there.* See **essential.**

requite [rih-KWIET] (v.) to repay. (adj.) —table.

rescind [reh-SIHND] (v.) to annul. (n.) rescision.

research [re-SUHRCH pref. to REE-suhrch]. n. and v.; can also be an adj.: *research study, research worker.*

resentment Used with *against, at,* or *of.* NOT *to, towards.*

reservation (wildlife, military, or Native American) Cap. if part of name: Great Sioux Reservation, Siletz Wildlife Reservation; the reservation.

Reserve Cap. if part of name: the Army Reserve; the Reserve; Active Reserve, Air Force Reserve.

Federal Reserve Board; Civil Air Patrol Reserve, Reserve components; Enlisted Reserve; Reserve Establishment; Naval Reserve officer; Officers' Training Corps Reserve; Ready Reserve; Retired Reserve.

reservedly [ree-ZUHR-vehd-lih].

Reserves, the, a reservist.

reservoir [REHZ-uhr-vwahr].

residents those living in a place.

RESIDENCE a home; act of living there.

RESIDENCY official residence, esp. of a diplomat.

residual [reh-ZIHD-yoo-uhl] remaining. (n.) residue.

res ipso loquitur [rehs IHP-so LAH-kwih-tohr] (Lat.) "the thing speaks for itself." In law, doctrine under which the defendant in certain cases must prove that an accident was not caused by his or her negligence.

resilience [reh-ZIHL-yehnss] elasticity, hence, strength of character. *He showed resilience in meeting adversity.* Also, —cy.

resin [REHZ-zihn] Term used for liquid, chemical.

ROSIN [RAH-zihn] Used for commercial product.

resist (v.); —tible (adj.). Opposite of *irresistible; unresisting.*

resoluble, resolvable Opposite of *unresolvable, irresoluble.* BUT *irresolvable.*

resolution Cap. with number: House Joint Resolution 3; Public Resolution 6; Resolution 42; Senate Concurrent Resolution 18. BUT: Kefauver resolution.

resolutions The first word following *Whereas* in resolutions, contracts, and the like is not cap.; the first word following an enacting or resolving clause is capitalized.

Resolved itself is italicized. *Whereas the Consitution provided . . .; and Be it enacted, That ***** WHEREAS, we are dedicated to liberty; therefore be it Resolved, That . . .*

resonance [REHZ-uh-nehnss] act of resounding.

resource [ree-SAWRS, REE-sawrs] source of aid. See **recourse.**

respective, respectively each in the order given. AVOID except where necessary. NOT: *The corporation was sold and each stockholder received his respective share.*

WITH RESPECT TO Also *in respect of, to.* AVOID.

respite [REHS-piht] (n. and v.) delay.

responsible

restaurateur [rehs-toh-rah-TEUR] NOT *restauranteur.*

restless, —room; rest cure.

restive [REHS-tihv] resisting control.

resume or **résumé** [REH-zeu-mae] written summary of job experience.

VITA (from *curriculum vitae*) an academic resume.

resurrect [rehz-uh-REHKT] to restore to life.

resuscitate [reh-SUHS-ih-taet] to revive. —tating, —tated.

retaliate [ree-TAHL-ee-aet] —ating, —ated.

reticent [REH-tih-sehnt] reserved in speech. (n.) reticence.

retina (pl.) —s or —ae.

retrace to go back. —cing, —ced, —ceable.

retrieve (n.) retrieval; BUT *beyond retrieve.*

retroactive [REHT-troh-ah-tihv] effective in a prior time.

retrogress (v.) to move backwards, from better to worse. (n.) —gression;

—gradation. (adj.) retrograde.

Reuters [ROI-terhs] international news agency.

Rev. (abbr.) reverend. Honorary title for clergymember. Must be followed by *Mr., Dr,* or a first name. See **reverend, clergy.**

revaluate —ting, —ted, —ation. Pref. to *re-evaluate.*

reveille [REHV-ehl-ih] in military, bugle call at sunrise.

revel [REH-vehl] (v.) to celebrate noisily. —ling, —led. (n.) Usually pl.: *Our revels now have ended.*

revenge (v. & n.) See **avenge.**

reverberate —ting, —ted, -rable, —tor.

reverend *Reverend* (before a name), Rev. John Brown; the Rev. Mr. Doe; the Rev. Dr. Doe; Rev. and Mrs. Brown; Rev. Brown, Doe, and Jones; Rev. A.J. Brown, D.J. Doe, and J.S. Jones. BUT NOT Rev. Doe. See **clergy, minister, priest, abbot.**

reverie [REHV-eh-ree] a daydream. Pref. to —*ry.*

reverse (v.) to turn upside down or completely about. —sing, —sed. (adj.) —sible; opposite of *unreversable* or *irreversible.*

REVERT to go back.

revoke —king, —ked, —vocable; —vocation [REHV-oh-kae-shuhn].

revolt [ree-VOHLT].

revolution, revolutionary Cap. American, French, English Revolution. See **war.**

revue [ree-VYOO] (n.) musical or stage spectacle with little or no plot.

REVIEW (n.) a re-examination. (v.) to re-examine.

Reykjavik [RAEK-yah-veek] seaport capital of Iceland.

RF. (abbr.) radiofrequency.

R.F.D. (abbr.) rural free delivery.

rhapsody [RAP-soh-dee].

rheostat [REE-ah-stat] device that regulates flow of electric current.

rhetorical question a question with no apparent answer. *Who can tell what time will bring?* Also, one that needs no answer: *Wouldn't you love to be rich?*

rhinestone [REIN-stohn] colorless, high-lustre paste or glass.

rhinoceros (sing. and pl.) Pl. also —ceri.

Rhode Island U.S. state. (abbr. RI). Cap.: Providence. Native: Rhode Islander.

Rhodesia [roh-DEE-zhah]. See **Zambia, Zimbabwe.**

rhombus (pl.) —buses or —bi. See *SHAPE.*

rhyme common sounds in line endings.

rhythm in poetry, the meter created by stressed and unstressed syllables. In prose, a more general affect of speed or slowness, choppiness or fluency. (adj.) rhythmical, rhythmic.

RHYTHM AND BLUES Rarely use -*'n'*-.

RI (abbr.) Rhode Island.

ribald [RIHB-ld] scurrilous, usu. with sexual content.

riboflavin Vitamin B2, from eggs, green vegetables, milk.

rice-throwing, rice paper, rice water.

riches wealth. Takes a plural verb; there is no singular.

ricochet [RIHK-oh-shae] —eting, —eted.

rickets Takes a singular verb.

rickety [RIHK-ih-tih] shaky.

rickrack

rid (p. and p.p.) rid or ridden; ridding.

ride (p.) rode; (p.p.) ridden; riding.

rider additional clause attached to an agreement.

riffraff [RIHF-RAFF] rabble.

right correct; also, the direction.

RITE ceremony.

WRITE to inscribe.

—WRIGHT (suffix) A worker: *shipwright*.

right angle 90°.

right bank orientation determined when looking downstream.

right, rightist, rightwing (adj.) In politics, means conservative: *a rightwing group; a member of the right wing.* See **left, leftist, leftwing.**

right stage orientation determined from the actor's view.

righteous [RIE-chuhs] pertaining to that which is right.

right-of-way (pl.) rights-of-way.

right-to-work law Forbids requirement of membership in a union as a requisite of employment.

rigmarole or **rigamarole** foolish, confused talk or action.

rigor Pref. to —*our.* Also, rigorous, rigor mortis.

Rilke, Rainer Maria [RIHL-keh, RAE-nihr mah-REE-ah] (1875–1926) Modernist Austro-German poet *(Duino Elegies).*

Rimbaud, Arthur [ram-BOH, ar-TOOR] (1854–1891) Fr. surrealist poet *(Illuminations)* and adventurer.

rime (n. or v.) white frost. (adj.) rimy, rimier, —iest.

Rimski-Korsakov, Nikolai [RIHMM-skee KUHR-suh-kawf, nyih-kuh-LIE] (1844–1908) Rus. composer.

ring (v.) to make noise (p. and p.p.) *rang* is pref. to *rung;* ringing.

RING to encircle. (p. and p.p.) ringed; ringing.

Ring of the Niebelung [NIH-beh-luhng] cycle of 5 operas based on Nordic myth, by Richard Wagner, 1876. Includes "The Valkyrie" and "Gotterdammerung (Twilight of the Gods)."

Rio de Janeiro [ree-oh deh zhuh-NAE-roh] seaport in Brazil.

Rio [REE-oh] Means "river;" thus, NOT Rio Grande River. Cap. in names: Rio Grande, Rio Bravo, Rio de la Plata.

riot —ting, —ted.

riposte [rih-POHST] quick retort; from fencing.

Rip van Winkle in a story by Washington Irving, a man who slept for 20 years. Hence, anyone out of touch with events.

rise (p.) rose; (p.p.) risen; rising.

risible [RIHZ-ih-b'l] causing laughter.

risqué [rihs-KAE] verging on indecent; implies sexual risk.

rival —led, —ling.

riven [RIH-vihn] torn apart. Past part. of the verb *rive.*

Rivera, Diego [ree-VAE-rah, DYAE-goh] (1886–1957) Mexican painter, muralist; husband of **Frida Kahlo.**

riverbank —bed, —front, —side, (all one word); river bottom.

rivet —eted, —eting, —eter.

Riviera [rih-vee-EH-rah] Fr. and It. Mediterranean coast, famed for beaches, resorts, etc.

road Cap. if part of name: Benning Road; the road.

roadbed, roadrunner, road show.

roan [ROHN] brown or tan horse with gray markings.

roast *roast beef, roast chestnuts. Let's make a roast.* BUT *roasted coffee.* (p. and p.p.) roasted; roasting.

rob in law, to take property feloniously. (p. and p.p.) robbed, robbing.

STEAL More general: *steal a kiss.*

Robespierre, Maximilien François de [deh ROHBZ-pyair; mahk-see-mih-LYANN frahn-SWAH] (1758–94) Fr. revolutionary.

robot [ROH-baht] (from *nove R.U.R.,* by Karl Capek) mechanical person.

robust [roh-BUHST] in vigorous health.

rockaby rock-bottom (nonliteral), rock-bound.

rock'n'roll Also *rock and roll.*

Rockefeller [RAHK-eh-fehl-uh]. John Davison (1839–1937), U.S. oil tycoon. Grandson Nelson (1908-1979), Governor of New York and U.S. Vice President (1974–76).

rococo [roh-KOH-koh] (n.) Baroque decoration; (adj.) baroque.

rod unit of length = 25 links = 1/40 chain = 5.5 yds. = 16.5 feet = 1/320 mi. = 5.0292 m. = 1 perch.

rodeo [ROH-dee-oh (more common); roh-DAE-oh (more correct)].

roentgen, rontgen [RUHNT-jehn] unit of x-ray measurement. 600 is universally lethal, 500 lethal to half of those exposed, 300 is lethal to some.

Roentgen or **Rontgen, Wilhelm Konrad** [RUHNT-gehn] (1845–1923) Ger. physicist.

Roget's Thesaurus [roh-ZHAE] (after Peter Mark Roget [1779–1869] British physicist-scholar) Reference book listing synonyms.

role actor's part; hence, any defined social function: *your role as a father.*

ROLL Spelling for all other meanings.

rollback, rolltop, rollup; roll call; call the roll.

roll, wallpaper unit of length = 16 yds.

rolling stock wheeled property of a railroad.

ROMAN NUMERALS May be in capitals or small letters. (1) I; (2) II; (3) III; (4) IV or IIII; (5) V; (6) VI; (7) VII; (8) VIII; (9) IX or VIIII; (10) X; (11) XI; (14) XIV or XIIII; (15) XV; (20) XX, (21) XXI; (40) XL or XXXX; (42) XLII; (50) L; (100)C; (101) CI; (400) CD or

CCCC; (500) D; (600) DC; (1000) M; (1600) MDC; (1800) MDCCC; (1900) MCM or MDCCCC; (1950) MCML; (2000) MM.

In general, use Arabic numbers. Use Roman numerals in small caps or lowercase for preliminary pages of a book, and where Roman numerals are used in tabulations.

Use Roman numerals in capitals for (1) title of a ruler or prince: *Elizabeth II, Pope John XXIII*; (2) where customary to distinguish other persons in a series: *Miss America VI; Marshall Field II*; (3) for periodical chapters, plates,graphs, volume numbers, etc: *Vol. XXI, Map Plate II, Chart IV* (no periods). BUT use Arabic numbers for text illustrations: *Fig. 3*; (4) for primary subdivisions: *Chapter VII; II. The Tertiary Era*; (5) common nouns used with Roman numerals are not capitalized: *book II, chapter II*. BUT cap. complete heading, in titles: *Book II: Modern Types; Part XI: Early Thought*.

romance languages derived from the Latin of the Roman Empire.

Romanesque art and architecture of 11th–12th C.

Romania [roh-MAEN-yah] (Pref. to Rumania) Eastern European nation since 1871; in Soviet bloc, 1945–1990. Cap.: Bucharest. Native: Romanian. Currency: leu.

romantic novels popular stories involving stylized high passions and extravagant situations.

Romanticism 19th-C. artistic movement, particularly literary. Empha-

sizes free expression of personality, connection with transcendant nature. Br. Romantic writers include: Byron, Keats, Wordsworth. Americans: Emerson, **Thoreau**, Poe. See **genre, transcendental.**

roman type upright type with shaded stroke. See **italics.**

rondeau, rondo poem of 13 (or 10) lines, plus refrain, with recurring words or lines and fixed rhymes.

RONDO (this spelling only) a musical form.

RONDEL poem similar to rondeau, 14 or 13 lines.

RONDELAY short simple song with a refrain.

roof garden, rooftop

roomful (pl.) —s.

roominghouse

roomkeeper —mate; room clerk.

Roosevelt [ROH-zeh-vehlt, formerly ROOS-eh-vehlt].
Eleanor (1905-1962): niece to Theodore, wife to Franklin Delano; U.S. representative to U.N., 1949–52.
Franklin Delano (1882–1945): U.S. President, 1933–45.
Theodore (1858–1919): U.S. President 1901–09.

root [root, not ruht].

Roquefort cheese [ROHK-fihrt].

Rorschach Test [RAWR-shak] Examines free-association reactions to ink blots, developed by Herman Rorschach, Swiss psychologist, to appraise personality and diagnose mental illness.

rosary [ROH-zuh-ree] string of beads used in prayer, or the prayers themselves. See **Mass.**

roseate [ROH-zee-aet] like a rose, esp. in color.

Rosh Hashanah Jewish spiritual New Year (literally, "Days of Awe"), in September or October. Also *Rosh ha-Shana.*

Rosicrucians brethren of the Rosy Cross. Mystical Christian reformers who use science to interpret religion.

rosin [RAH-zihn]. See **resin.**

roster [RAH-stehr, RAW-stehr].

rostrum [RAHS-trum] (pl.) —s.

rotary Can be synonym for traffic circle.

Rotary Club local association of businessmen; promotes service and goodwill.

R.O.T.C. Reserve Officers' Training Corps.

rotisserie [roh-TIHS-uh-ree] restaurant where meat is roasted on a spit in view; home device with same use.

rotogravure intaglio printing process.

rotten —nness, rottenhearted.

rotund [roh-TUHND] round; rounded out.

Roualt, Georges [roo-AL, zhawrzh] (1871–1958) Fr. painter, printmaker, ceramicist.

roué [roo-AE] debauched bon vivant.

roughen (v.) BUT for "treat roughly" or "harden," use *rough: rough up a new baseball, rough in a sketch, rough a lens, rough it on a camping trip.*

roundabout (n. and adj.); round robin.

round trip (n.); roundtrip (adj.). In baseball, *a roundtripper* is a home run.

rouse Pref. for literal use: *He roused himself at 8.*

AROUSE Pref. for abstract use: *His anger was aroused.*

Rousseau, Henri [roo-SOH, ohn-REE] (1844–1910) Fr. painter, famed for "naive" or primitive style.

Rousseau, Jean-Jacques [zhahn-zhak] (1712–1778) Fr. philosopher, helped inspire French Revolution.

rout [rout] (v.) to set into flight. *Our cannons routed the enemy.*

ROUTE [root, rout] (n.) a way or course. *The shortest route is not always the easiest.*

route route No. 12466, mail route 1742, railway mail route 1144. BUT: cap. Route 66, State Route 9 (highways).

routine [roo-TEEN] —tinism, —tinist.

rowboat

royalty payment for use of a copyright or patent.

r.p.m. (abbr.) revolutions per minute.

R.R. (abbr.) railroad.

R.R.B. (abbr.) Railroad Retirement Board.

R.S.V.P. (abbr.) *respondez s'il vous plait* (Fr.) please respond.

Rt. Rev. (abbr.) right reverend.

Ruanda. See **Rwanda.**

Rubai'yat of Omar Khayyam [roo-bie-YAHT, kae-YAHM] (from *ruba 'iyat*, an Arabic poem in quatrains) 11th-century love poems, translated by Edward Fitzgerald in 1859. See **Omar Khayyam.**

rubberband, —necker, —proofed, —stamp (nonliteral), rubber-lined, rubber-stamped; rubber plant, rubber stamp.

rubdown, rub-a-dub.

ruble U.S.S.R. currency unit. See **kopek.**

rucksack [RUHK-sak] small backpack.

KNAPSACK

rule 21 Cap. when part of title: *Rule 21: Renewal of Motion.*

rule of thumb (n.) BUT adj.: *rule-of-thumb decisions.*

rules Rules of the House of Representatives, BUT rules of the House; Standing Rules of the Senate, BUT rules of the Senate.

Rumania [roo-MAEN-yah]. See **Romania.**

rumba, rhumba [RUHM-buh].

rumor (n. and v.), rumored (p. and p.p.), rumormonger (n. and v.).

rumpus room

rumrunner, rumrunning, rumshop.

run (p.) ran; (p.p.) run; running.

runabout —around, —away, —down, —over, —through (all n. and adj.), —way; run-in, run-on (both n. and adj.).

run-on sentence two or more sentences combined without connectives or sufficient punctuation. *Some people like pepper others like salt.* IMPROVE by separating the clauses with a semicolon or inserting a comma, an *and*, or a *but.*

ruse [ROOZ] (n.) trick.

russet reddish brown.

Russia [RUHSH-ah] largest republic in former **U.S.S.R.**; part of **Commonwealth of Independent States,** 1992. Extends from E Europe to Siberian Pacific coast. Cap.: Moscow. Native: Russian.

Boris Yeltsin first freely elected president, 1989.

Russia, Russian are also general terms, referring to entire former U.S.S.R., its peoples and projects.

rustproof

Rwanda [ruh-WAN-duh] landlocked republic in E central Africa. Formerly Belgian (**Ruanda**); independent, 1962. Cap.: Kigali. Native, Rwandan, Rwanese. Currency: franc.

S

s. (abbr.) shilling.

S. (abbr.) south; Senate bill (with number); in chemistry, sulfur.

S-bend, S-brake, S-shaped, S-trap, S-wrench.

's See *POSSESSIVES.*

S.A. *Sturmabteilung* (Ger.) Nazi military-political organization, 1923–34, a/k/a Brown Shirts, storm troopers. See **S.S.**

Saar [zahr], Saarland [ZAHR-lant] territory along border between France and Germany, often disputed.

Sabbath. Sabbath Day. The Sabbath is observed on Saturday by Jews and Seventh Day Adventists, on Friday by Moslems, on Sunday by Christians.

sabbatical [sah-BA-tih-k'l] (from "sabbatical year," when Israelite fields lay fallow) any leave of absence.

Sabra native-born Jewish Israeli.

S.A.C. (abbr.) Strategic Air Command.

Sacagawea, Sacajawea [sa-kah-jah-WEE-ah] (c. 1786–1812) Native American woman of the Shoshone tribe who helped guide Lewis and Clark expedition, 1804–05.

saccharin [SAK-uh-rihn] (n.) sugar substitute; saccharine (adj.) overly sweet.

sacerdotal [sas-uh-DOH-tal] relating to priesthood.

sachem [SAE-chehm] Native American chief; hence, any leader or official.

sachet [sa-SHAE] small packet, usu. perfumed. See **cachet.**

sacrifice [SAK-rih-fies].

sacrilegous [sak-rih-LIH-juhs] (from "sacred") (adj.) stealing or desecrating sacred things.

sacrosanct [SAK-roh-SANKT] inviolable; used esp. ironically.

el-Sadat, Anwar [suh-DAHT, AN-wahr] (1918–1981) Commonly referred to as *Sadat.* President of Egypt 1971–81. Helped author first Arab peace agreements with Israel, 1978; assassinated, 1981.

Sadducee [SAD-yoo-see] sect of ancient Jews.

Sade, Marquis de [deh sahd] (1740–1814) Full name: Comte Donatien Alphonse Francois de Sade. French erotic writer, philosopher. See **sadism.**

sadism [SAE-dizm] (n.) delight in cruelty, from the sexual perversion which is satisifed by cruelty. sadist [SAD-] (adj.). See **Sade.**

S.A.E. (abbr.) Society of Automotive Engineers (sets product standards).

safari [suh-FAH-ree] expedition, especially for hunting.

saga [SAH-guh] epic story.

sagacious [suh-GAE-shuhs] keen in perception.

Sagittarius [saj-ih-TAIR-ee-uhs] Born Nov. 22–Dec. 21. See **Zodiac.**

Sahara AVOID *Sahara Desert*; "desert" is in the name.

said Possible substitute words: answered, asked, cried, continued, denied, groaned, replied, shouted, whispered.
AVOID: grimaced, smiled, frowned, hissed, laughed. NOT: *"I accept," he laughed.*

said, same In law, used for *aforesaid.* Otherwise, avoid.

same See **just as.**

Saigon [sie-GAHN] capital city of South Vietnam before unification in 1975; after that, **Ho Chi Minh City.**

saint (abbr. St.; pl. Sts., sometimes SS.; Fr., Ste.). Usu. abbreviate before a name: *St. Louis, St. James's Palace, St. Vitus Dance.* Omit St. in connection with apostles, evangelists, and Church Fathers: *Luke, Paul, Augustine.*

St. Christopher (St. Kitts) and Nevis [NEE-vuhs] Also, St. Christopher Nevis. Island nation in E Caribbean Sea. Formerly Br., independent, 1983. Cap.: Basseterre [bas-TEHR]. Native: Liamuigans. Currency: E. Caribbean dollar.

Saint-Laurent, Yves [eev saen law-RUHN] (b. 1936) Fr. fashion designer; later a brand name.

Saint Lucia [LOO-shah] island nation in E Caribbean. First Fr., then Br.; independent, 1979. Cap., Castries [KA-streez]. Native: Saint Lucian. Currency: E Caribbean dollar.

St. Paul See **Minneapolis, MN.**

St. Petersburg See **Leningrad.** Citizens voted to restore old name, 1991.

Saint-Saens, Charles [san-SAENS] (1835–1921) Fr. composer.

Saint Vincent and the Grenadines [greh-neh-DEENZ] island nation in E Caribbean. Formerly Br., independent, 1979. Cap.: Kingstown. Native: Grenadinian, St. Vincentian. Currency: E Caribbean dollar.

sake [SAH-kee] Japanese rice wine.

salable [SAEL-a-bl] capable of being sold. (n.) salability.

salad days Means good times, usu. in youth.

Saladin [SAL-ah-dihn] (1138–1193) Muslim sultan and hero, famous for chivalric resistance against the Crusades.

salesperson, salesman, saleswoman. AVOID saleslady.

salient [SAE-lee-ehnt] conspicuous,

noticeable. (n.) —ce or —cy.

saline [SAE-lien] containing salt.

salmon [SAM-uhn].

salmon-colored, salmon-red (adj.); salmon fishing.

Salome [sal-LOH-mee] in New Testament, niece of Herod; received the head of John the Baptist as a reward for dancing.

> SALOME [SAH-loh-mae] 1896 drama by Oscar Wilde; 1905 opera by Richard Strauss.

salon exhibition hall, esp. for artwork; hence, any gathering of artists and celebrities.

saloonkeeper, saloon deck.

salt Use for table salt.

> SALTS Use for chemical salts, bath salts, Epsom salts, smelling salts.

saltbox —cellar, —peter, —water; salt cake, salt glaze.

salubrious [sa-LOO-bree-uhs] conducive to good health.

salutations. See **dear**, and individual titles of people.

Salvador. See **El Salvador.**

salve [sahv] healing ointment.

salvable [SAL-vuh-b'l] (adj.) able to be salvaged.

salvage [SAL-vehj] (n.) rescued merchandise.

salver [SAL-vuh] tray.

salvo [SAL-voh] a series of shots at intervals; or a simultaneous discharge of shots or bombs. (pl.) —os.

S.A.M. (abbr.) surface-to-air missile.

Samaritan [suh-MAR-ih-t'n] (from Christ's parable in Luke) a generous and helpful person.

same DO NOT use meaning "the above mentioned." NOT: *It is imperative that same be delivered immediately.*

same identical redundant. *Same* means *identical.*

Samoa Since 1900, U.S. island territory S of Hawaii.

Samson [SAM-s'n] Biblical hero; hence, anyone of great strength.

samurai [SA(M)-moor-ie] Japanese warrior class, under feudal system; hence, any belligerent person.

sanatoriaum (pl.) -s. See **sanitarium.**

sand, sands Both are mass nouns. See *COLLECTIVE NOUNS.*

sandaled —ing.

Sandinista [sahn-dih-NEE-stah] Nicaraguan revolutionaries of 1970s, named for guerrilla hero César Sandino (1893–1934). Overthrew dictatorship, 1979; ruling political party till 1989.

sandy-bottomed, sandy-red (adj.).

sang-froid [SAHN-frwah] (Fr.) "cold blood." Coolness under pressure.

sanguinary [SANG-gwih-nehr-ee] bloody, bloodthirsty: *a sanguinary tribe of savages, a sanguinary code of justice.*

SANGUINE confident, hopeful; also cheerful, warm.

Sanhedrin [san-HEE-drihn] supreme council and tribunal of ancient Jews.

sanitarium place for healing. Pref. to *sanitorium.* (pl.) —s.

sanitary (adj.) hygienic. (n.) sanitation.

San Marino [san-mah-REE-noh] tiny republic in central Italy, since 4th C. Cap.: San Marino. Native: Sanmarinese. Currency: lira.

San Martin, José de [sahn mahr-TEEN hoh-sae] (1778–1850) Argentine soldier, statesman; worked with Simon Bolivar to liberate South America.

sans serif type [san seh-REEF] simplified print; letters without embellishments at the end of a line.

de Santa Anna, Antonio Lopez [dae SAHN-tah AH-nah] (1795?–1876) Mexican general and president; famous for attack on the Alamo.

São Tome and Principe [SA-oo tah-MAE, PRIHN-sah-pah] island nation off W Africa. Formerly Port.; independent, 1975. Cap.: Sao Tome. Native: Sao Tomean, Principean. Currency: Dobra.

sapphire [SAF-ier].

Sappho [SAF-foh] (fl. 6th C. B.C.) Greek woman poet; her work suggests a preference for partners of her own sex. Hence, Sapphic (adj.) and Sapphism (n.) refer to female homosexuality.

Sarajevo. See **Serajevo.**

sarcophagus [sahr-KAHF-a-guhs] ancient coffin. (pl.) —i or —uses.

sarsparilla [sass-pah-RIHL-uh; sahr-suh-puh-].

Sartre, Jean-Paul [SAHRTR, zhahn pohl] (1905–1980) Fr. philosopher and writer *(Nausea)*; helped define **Existentialism.**

S.A.S.E. (abbr.) self-addressed stamped envelope.

Saskatchewan (abbr.: Sask.) province in Canada. Cap.: Regina.

sassafras [sa-sah-FRAS].

Satan [SAE-tan] Lucifer, the Devil, His Satanic Majesty; BUT a devil, the devils. (adj.) Satanic.

satellites Discoverer IV; Explorer II; Sputnik I. BUT do not cap.: weather satellite; telecommunications satellite.

satiate [SAE-shi-aet] to fully satisfy. —tiable, —ation.

satiety [seh-TIE-eh-tee] in science,

the point at which an animal ceases food intake.

Sato Eisaku [SAE-toh ai-SAH-koo] (1901–1975) Japanese statesman, prime minister 1964–72. Oversaw Japanese re-emergence as world power; Nobel Peace Prize, 1974.

satrap [SAE-trap; SAT-rap] ancient Persian or Indian ruler.

saturate [SAT-yuh-raet] to impregnate completely. (adj.) —rable.

Saturday (abbr.: Sat.).

Saturnalia (sing. and pl.) raucous year-end festival of ancient Rome; hence, any celebration. (adj.) Saturnalian, saturnalian.

satyr [SAT'r; SAET'r] demigod with tail and ears of a horse, famous for lasciviousness. Hence, a sexually active man.

Saudi Arabia [SAW-dee] kingdom on Arabian peninsula. Formerly Turkish; independent, 1932. Cap.: Riyadh (ree-YAHD). Native: Saudi Arabian or Saudi. Currency: riyal.

sauerbraten [SOU-ihr-BRAH-tehn].

sauté [soh-TAE] quick-fry in hot fat.

savable [SAE-buh-b'l] Also *saveable*. (n.) saver.

savant [sa-VAHNT] wise person. NOT an **idiot savant.**

save and except A legal expression.

save face

savings a mass noun, but takes plural verb. See *COLLECTIVE NOUNS.*

savings bank NOT **saving.**

savior BUT cap. for the Saviour (Christ).

Savonarola, Girolamo [sah-voh-nah-ROH-lah, jee-RAW-lah-moh] (1452–1498) It. religious reformer.

savory [SAE-vuhr-ih] (n. and adj.) herb.

Savoyard (from Savoy Theatre, London) any Gilbert and Sullivan production company. Also, a native of Savoy, in France.

saw (p. and p.p.) sawed; sometimes (p.p.) sawn; sawing.

saxophone [SAKS-eh-fohn] usage allows *sax.*

say tell, relay information. *She said so.* (p. and p.p.) said.

> STATE (v.) to set forth formally; make a declaration. *He stated his point of view for the record.*

say-so (n.)

S.B.A. (abbr.) Small Business Administration.

SC (abbr.) South Carolina.

scalawag a rascal. Sometimes *scallawag.*

scallop [SKAHL-uhp] —ed, —ing.

scan Originally meant to analyze poetry, read painstakingly. Now often used for the opposite: to skim (col-loq.).

scandalmonger.

Scandinavia Norway, Denmark, and Sweden, sometimes Iceland or Finland.

scansion To scan poetry. (1) divide into two-syllable "feet:" five feet (10 or 11 syllables) are pentameter, six are hexameter, etc.; (2) indicate the meter of each foot by the rhythm of emphasis, such as iambic (1 short or unaccented syllable, 1 long or accented syllable), trochaic (1 long, 1 short), etc.

The most famous English meter is Shakespeare's iambic pentameter, or blank verse:

Tommorrow, and tomorrow, and tomorrow
Creeps in this petty pace from day to day
To the last syllable of recorded time;
. . . .

scant Pref. to *scanty*, except regarding clothes.

scapegoat

Scaramouch [SKAHR-uh-mouch] (from novel by Rafael Sabatini) boastful buffoon.

scarce Usage allows for *scarcely. We had scarce begun.*

scarcely Followed by *when* NOT *than. He had scarcely washed when dinner was announced.* Avoid double negative. NOT: *He could scarcely depend on*

no help. NOT: *without scarcely.*

scarf (pl.) —s or —ves.

scarface (n.); scar-faced (adj.).

Scarlatti, Alessandro [skahr-LAHT-tee, ah-lehs-SAHN-droh] (1659–1725) It. composer.

Scarlatti, Domenico [doh-MEH-nee-koh] (1685–1757) son of Alessandro; Italian-Spanish composer.

scarlet fever

scatterbrain, —ed; scatter rug.

scenario [sehn-NAIR-ih-oh] synopsis of a play; hence, any summary. AVOID as bureaucratic: *worst-case scenario . . . , best-case scenario . . .*

scenic [SEEN-ihk] like a stage setting; picturesque.

scepter, sceptre sovereign's staff of authority.

schedule [SKEHD-yool; (Br.) SHEHD-yool].

schedule 2, A, 11 BUT cap. *Schedule 2,* when part of title: *Schedule 2: Open and Prepay Stations.*

schema [SKEE-muh] diagram or outline. (pl.) —mata.

scherzando [SKAER-tsahnd-doh] (Ital., "joke") a musical direction, meaning "playful," usu. allegretto tempo. (pl.) —os.

> SCHERZO [SKAER-tsoh] a musical piece, playful, surprising. Usu. triple-time. (pl.) —os.

Schiaparelli, Elsa [skyahp-ah-REHL-ee] (1896–1973) Fr. dress designer.

schism [SIHZ'm; SKIHZ'm; NOT shihz'm] a division; the offence of producing one.

schizoid [SKIHZ-oid] resembling schizophrenia.

schizophrenia [SKIHZ-oh-free-nih-uh] psychosis. From Gr. for "split personality," but usage allows as a general term.

school Cap. if part of name; capitalize any school of U.S. Army or Navy: Hayes School, the school, school district. See **district.** Cap. the proper names or other designations: *De Witt Clinton High School, Columbia University.*

Do not write or abbreviate No. in school names: *School 5, P.S. 5, Public School 5.*

school colors Cap. when designating school: *Crimson Tide.*

Schopenauer, Arthur [SHOH-pehn-hou-ahr, AHR-toor] (1788–1860) Ger. philosopher.

Schubert, Franz [SHOO-buhrt] (1797–1828) Austrian composer.

sciatica [sie-AT-ih-kuh] backache.

science a study or discipline characterized by knowing facts.

ART Generally associated with skills, doing, individual workmanship: *science of paints; art of painting.*

scintilla [sihn-TIHL-uh] the slightest trace. (pl.) —lae.

scion [SIE-uhn] detached plant shoot; hence, any descendant.

scissors Always plural. Refers to a single tool, BUT takes pl. verb in most cases. In a few constructions, sing. v. is permissible. *Here is your scissors.*

Usage allows *pairs of scissors.* In a compound, the singular form is pref.: *scissorhandles.* Also true for other two-pronged instruments: *shears, tongs, calipers, clippers.*

S.C.L.C (abbr.) Southern Christian Leadership Conference.

S. Con Res. (with number) (abbr.) senate concurrent resolution.

score (n.) group or set of 20: *Four score and seven years* (87 years); *scores of trains went by every day.*

scoreboard, scorecard, scoresheet.

scores Write in numerals. *The Red Sox won, 12 to 4.* BUT spell out play-by-play. *They scored their ninth, tenth, and eleventh runs on Wade Boggs' third double of the game.* See **sports.**

Scorpio [SKAWR-pee-oh] born Oct. 23–Nov. 21. See **zodiac.**

Scotch tape. Trademark (by Minnesota Mining & Mfg. Co.).

Scotch-Irish.

scot-free (adj.)

Scotland Native: Scot(s), Scotsman,

Scotch (collective). (adj.) Scotch, Scottish.

Scotch plaid, tweed, whiskey, terrier.

scour [SKOU-'r].

scoutcraft, scoutmaster.

scream high-pitched emotional cry.

SHRIEK higher pitch, more emotion.

SCREECH higher pitch, animalistic; may be comic.

screwdriver, screwworm; screwdriven; screw fastener.

scrimmage football play. In rugby, use *scrum.*

Scripture, Scriptures Holy Scriptures. See **Bible.** Takes singular verb. *Holy Scriptures remains our guide.*

scroll work

scruple unit of apothecaries' weight = 20 grains = 1/3 dram = 1/24 oz. = 0.04166 oz. = 1.2959 grains.

srupulous [SKROO-pyoo-luhs] Opposite of *unscrupulous.*

scull oar used at stern of boat for propulsion.

SKULL cranial bone.

scurrilous [SKUHR-eh-luhs] coarse, obscene.

scuttlebutt rumor, gossip.

scythe [sieth] mowing tool with long blade, long handle.

SICKLE short, curved blade, short handle.

SD (abbr.) South Dakota.

S. Doc. (abbr.) with number, Senate document.

SE (abbr.) southeast. Also S.E.

Seabees Navy construction battalion, est. 1941.

seaboard Atlantic seaboard, eastern seaboard, etc.

SEALS Navy mobile strike force. See **Special Forces.**

scance [SAE-ahns] meeting to communicate with the dead.

seasonable coming at the right time: *A seasonable arrival.*

SEASONAL connected with a season: *seasonal employment.*

S.E.A.T.O. (abbr.) Southeast Asia Treaty Organization. Defunct, 1976. See A.S.E.A.N.

Seaway See **geographic terms, authority, corporation.**

sec. (abbr.) secant, second, section.

S.E.C. (abbr.) Securities and Exchange Commission.

secede (v.); secession (n.).

2d Lt. (abbr.) second lieutenant.

secondhand (adv. and adj.); second-class, second-rate, second-degree (adj.), second-guess (v.), second in command, second sight (n.).

Second World War. (abbr.: W.W. II) See **war.**

secondary education high school.

secretary

secretary Cap. if head of national governmental unit: Secretary of Defense, Secretary of State, and so on; the Secretary of the Smithsonian Institution, the Secretary, also the Assistant Secretary, the Executive Secretary;

BUT: secretary of the Interstate Commerce Commission; secretary of state of Iowa.

secretary general (pl.) secretaries general.

secretaryship, secretary-generalcy, secretary-generalship, secretary-treasurer; secretary general.

secretary-treasurer (pl.) secretaries-treasurers.

secretive [SEE-crih-tihv].

secretmonger, secret service, secret society.

section 2, A, II BUT cap. part of title: *Section 2: Test Theory.* Abbreviate after first use: *Section I . . . Sec. 11.*

section crew, section gang, section man.

section of land unit under U.S. land

laws = 1 sq. mi. = 1/32 township = 640 acres.

securityholder

seder [SEH-duhr] passover meal.

seducible [see-DOOS-ih-bl].

see (pl.) saw; (p.p.) seen; seeing.

seesaw

seeing that Avoid as conjunction meaning "since," "inasmuch as." NOT: *Seeing that she was finished, she put away her tools.*

seek (p. and p.p.) sought.

seem Often creates confusion about tense. Distinguish between time for the verb and time for the complementary clause. *I seem to understand what he says now.* OR . . . *what he said.* OR . . . *what he will say.* BUT: *I seemed to understand yesterday, though I may have been wrong.*

This seems to be the case all the time. Only if they approved, as seems to be the case, would the settlement be appropriate.

seer [seer] prophet; mystic.

seismic [SIEZ-mihk] pertaining to geologic activity, earthquakes. *seismograph.*

seldom Use *seldom or never.* NOT: *Seldom or ever.*

selectman

self-addressed stamped envelope abbr. S.A.S.E.

self-collected, self-evident AVOID as redundant: *collected, evident* are better, except for exceptional emphasis. *We hold these truths to be self-evident.*

self-determination the right of peoples to establish their own national identity and homeland, and the process by which that is accomplished. Part of United Nations Charter.

self-liquidating premium premium for which the charge to the purchaser pays the cost.

sell (p. and p.p.) sold.

sellers' market occurs when demand exceeds supply.

selloff (n. and adj.); sellout (n. and adj.).

selvage in sewing, finished fabric edge.

SALVAGE (n.) rescued merchandise.

semantic [seh-MAN-tihk] pertaining to word meanings. Suggests trivial. *The candidates wasted time arguing over semantics, rather than getting into the issues.*

semen [SEE-m'n] fluid containing spermatozoa.

semester [seh-MEHS-tihr] originally six months; now one of two periods of instruction in academic year. See **trimester.**

semi- prefix meaning half: semiannual, semiarid, semicircular; semi-Christian, semi-idleness, semi-truck.

SEMICOLON (1) Used to connect independent clauses (complete sentences) that belong together logically or rhetorically. *I love her; she loves Bob Dylan. I sing to her; she turns up "Blood On the Tracks."* By far the most common usage.

(2) To separate dependent clauses or phrases complex enough to require such a clarifying break. *In 1861, Lincoln took over a nation that faced a bloody internal turmoil, a war that would set brother against brother, and that might ruin the Union forever; while Franklin Roosevelt, 80 years later, headed a country that faced destruction from without, a war no less devastating but nonetheless easier to commit to.*

semiotics [seh-mee-AH-tihks] study of signs and their use. Refers not only to words, but to signs in culture generally

Semite (from Noah's son Shem, forefather in Biblical mythology) Technically, all Middle Eastern peoples. BUT usu. refers to Jews, esp. in suggesting prejudice against: anti-Semitism, anit-Semitic. Also, Semitism, Semitic. See **Jew.**

the Senate

senate (U.S.) Cap. titles of officers standing alone. Cap.: Chaplain, Official Reporter(s), President of the Senate, President pro tempore, Presiding Officer, Secretary.

senate (State) Ohio State Senate, etc.; the senate.

Senator ADDRESS: The Honorable Harrison Williams, United States Senate, Washington, D.C.; or Senator Harrison Williams, The United States Senate, Washington, D.C.; or (if sent to a home address) The Honorable Harrison Williams, United States Senator.

SALUTATION: Sir; Dear Sir; Dear Senator Williams.

Senator, senator. Cap. for U.S. Congress, lowercase for state senator unless preceding a name.

senatorial

send (p. and p.p.) sent; sending

sendoff (n. and adj.).

Senegal [sehn-ee-GAHL or SEH-] nation on W African coast. Formerly French Sudan; independent, 1960. Cap.: Dakar. Native: Senegalese. Currency: franc (CFAF).

senility [SEE-nih-lih-tee] mental impairment caused by aging. (adj.) senile.

señor [sen-YAWR] Sp. for Mr.

SEÑORA [sen-YAWR-ah] Sp. for Mrs.

SEÑORITA [sen-yaw-REE-tah] Sp. for Miss.

sense in Pertains to reason or logic.

SENSE OF Pertains to perception or meaning. *There is no sense in staying together—at least, not in the sense of sleeping together.*

sensible perceptible to the senses;

also, having good sense.

SENSIBLE OF (arch.) aware; responsive to emotion.

SENSIBLENESS good sense.

SENSIBILITY acuteness of feeling; often plural. Also, a person's intrinsic nature, esp. in artistic matters.

sensitive (adj.) responding to sensation. (n.) sensitivity.

SENSITIVE ABOUT emotionally responsive; defensive. *He's sensitive about his hair.*

SENSITIVE TO physically responsive. *My skin is sensitive to strong sunlight.*

sensuous appealing to the senses.

SENSUAL Appealing esp. to sexual appetites.

SENTENCE In grammar, a group of words complete and independent in themselves, containing subject and predicate expressed or understood.

A sentence may be a statement (declarative), a command (imperative), or a question (interrogative).

A complex sentence contains at least one dependent clause. A compound contains at least two independent clauses.

sententious [sehn-TEHN-shuhs] containing too many maxims; pompous.

sentient [SEHN-shuhnt] conscious, receptive of sensation.

sentinel anyone on watch. Sentineled, —ing.

> SENTRY guard, esp. soldier on watch.

separate

Sept. (abbr.) September.

septillion 1000 sextillions. See *NUMBERS.*

septuagenarian [sehp-chu-uh-juh-NAIR-ee-uhn].

septum separation between nasal cavities. (pl.) septa.

sepulcher [SEHP-uhl-kuhr] burial vault. Pref. to —re.

seq., et. seq. (abbr.) *et sequentes* (Lat.) the subsequent lines. *f., ff.* are more widely used.

SEQUENCE OF TENSES The tense of a subordinate clause must take the tense of the principal clause. *I know he is here.* BUT not in a quotation. *I said, "He is here."* And NOT in a parenthetical expression. *I thought, even as I think now, I was right.* See *SUBJUNCTIVE MOOD.*

sequester [seh-KWEH-stihr] in trial law, separating a jury from the public, to keep their deliberations free of prejudice.

seraglio [sihr-AH-lyoh] harem. (pl.) —os.

Serajevo [SAH-rah-yeh-voh] Also Sarajevo. Cap. of Bosnia and Herzegovina, now in Yugoslavia. Site of assassination of Archduke Ferdinand, which sparked W.W. I.

seraph [SEHR-aff] angels. (pl.) seraphs or seraphim.

Serbia See **Yugoslavia.**

Sergeant at Arms. (U.S. Senate or House).

sergeant at arms (pl.) sergeants at arms.

sergeant major (pl.) sergeants major.

serif embellishment in a typeface. See **sans serif type.**

Sermon on the Mount Christ's discourse (Matthew V, VI, VII; Luke II).

serum (pl.) —rums.

service (n.); —ceable (adj.).

service Lowercase most: airmail service, Army service, consular service, customs service, (see Bureau), diplomatic service, employment service (state), general delivery service, Navy service, postal service, railway mail service (See **division**), rural free delivery service, special delivery service, star route service.

Service Cap. if referring to Federal unit: Employment Service, Extension Service, Fish and Wildlife Service, Foreign Service (See Foreign Service), Forest Service, Immigration and Naturalization Service, Internal Revenue Service, National Park Service, Secret Service. See also **System.**

BUT selective service, in general sense; selective service classification 1-A, 4-F.

serviceman, service stripe; service-connected (adj.).

serviceable

servile [SUHR-vihl]

sesame [SEHS-uh-mee] herb, seed, from E India.

sesqui- prefix meaning one and a half: *sesquicentennial.*

session a sitting of a public body. *The court was in session.*

> CESSION a giving up. *France's cession of the Sudetenland became a symbol of appeasement.*

> SECESSION a withdrawal: *the secession of the Southern states.*

> CESSATION a stopping: *a cessation of hostilities.*

set a transitive verb which requires a direct object. *I set the plate on the table.* (p. and p.p.) set; setting, setter.

> SIT (p.) sat, (p.p.) sat; sitting. An intransitive verb: *He sat. Sheila sat down. I sat on the chair.*

settler In law, *settlor.*

Seurat, Georges [suh-RAH, ZHAWRZH] (1859–1891) French impressionist painter, famous for "pointillism."

Seuss, Dr. [soos] (1904–1991) Pen name for Theodore Seuss Geisel, author and illustrator of children's books, such as *The Cat in the Hat.*

sever —ered, —ering.

several three or more, but not many. Takes plural verb.

sew (p.p.) sewed or sewn; sewing.

sewage refuse for sewers.

> SEWERAGE removal of sewage; a sewer system.

sextet group of six.

SEXIST LANGUAGE Good contemporary usage avoids rhetoric rooted in out-of-date assumptions about the gender of a given job or authority. Executives may be women, and their secretaries may be men. AVOID: *A secretary should never leave her phone unattended.* OR: *An executive is expected to be at his desk promptly every morning.*

Changing such expressions may cause problems. Historically, the pronoun *he* has stood for both sexes, as has the noun *man: to boldly go where no man has gone before.* Substituting *he or she* or *man or woman* in order to avoid sexism can make for less powerful rhetoric.

Find the least clumsy substitutes: *to boldly go where no one has gone before.* OR: *Secretaries should never leave their phones unattended.* OR: *Now is the time for all good people to come to the aid of their country.*

Most job-related expressions now have non-sexist alternatives: *salesperson* instead of *salesman, insurance agent* instead of *insurance man, supervisor* instead of *foreman, work hours* instead of *manhours*, *postal carrier* instead of *mailman*.

Feminine designations should also be avoided. NOT: *authoress*, *songstress*, etc. BUT some remain appropriate: *abbess*, *actress*, *adultress*, *duchess*, *goddess*, *governess*, *hostess*, *princess*, *waitress*, etc.

Ms. is now accepted usage for female address: (pl.) *Mses.* The title is also used for a wife addressed simultaneously with her husband: *Mr. James Brown & Ms. Helen Gurley Brown.* See **Ms., person,** *RACIST LANGUAGE.*

Seychelles [SAE-shehl, -shelz] island nation in W Indian Ocean. Formerly Br.; independent, 1976. Capital: Victoria. Currency: rupee.

Sfc. (abbr.) sergeant, first class; seaman, first class.

sforzando [sfawr-TSAHN-doh] in music, strong, accented.

Sgt. (abbr.) Sergeant.

shagbark, —tail; shag-haired (adj.).

shake (p.) shook; (p.p.) shaken; shaking, shakable.

Shakespeare, William. The great poet and playwright lived 1564–1616, and wrote roughly between 1590 and 1610. (adj.) —earian.

shaman [SHAH-man] medicine man.

shambles a scene of destruction.

shame, (n. and v.); —mable (adj.).

shanghai [shang-HIE] (after the city in China). (v.), to take someone by force, esp. humorously. —aied; —aing.

Shangri-La (from James Hilton's novel *Lost Horizon*) faraway utopia.

SHAPE Words indicating shape include: aliform (wing); alveolate (honeycomb), arciform (arch); bacillary (rod); bicorn (crescent); campanulate (bell); capsular (capsule); claviform (club); cochleate (snail-shell); crenate (scalloped); crescent (first-quarter moon); cordate (heart); cruciate (cruciform cross); cuneate (wedge); cystoid (bladder); deltoid (triangle); dentiform (tooth); domical (dome); helical (spiral); helicoid (snail-shell); herbaceous (leaf); ichthyomorphic (fish); lunate (crescent); luniform (moon); mammillary (breast); navicular (boat); olivary (olive); ovate, ovoid (egg); pediform (foot); pisciform (fish); reticular, reticulate (net); rotate (wheel); rhombic (diamond); scutate, scutiform (shield); semilunar (halfmoon); spheroid (earth); stellate (star), tabulate (table); trapeziform (trapezium), pyramid (triangle); undulant (wavy); vermicular (worm).

ALSO diamond, lozenge, rhombus, oblong, rectangle, parallelogram, rhomboid, trapezoid (foursided figure with two sides parallel). See —**gon;** —**hedron.**

shapeup (n. and adj.)

share. See **part.**

sharecrop, sharecropper, shareholder

shave (p.) shaved, (p.p.) shaved or shaven; shaving.

shavehook, —tail.

she Nominative case. Objective and possessive: her.

sheaf (pl.) —yes.

shear to cut hair; to deviate. (p.p.) —led or shorn; shearing.

SHEER (adj.) transparent; perpendicular; utter: *sheer stocking, sheer cliff, sheer folly.*

shears. See **scissors.**

sheathe [sheeth] (pl.) —s [sheeths].

shed (p. and p.p.) shed.

sheer. See **shear.**

sheerline, —off, —up (n. and adj.).

sheik [SHEEK, SHAEK] Pref. to *sheikh.*

shelf (pl.) —ves; (v.) —ve; (adj.) —ved. shelf-full.

shellac —cked, —cking.

shepherd [SHEHP-uhrd] herder of sheep.

S.H.F. (abbr.) superhigh frequency.

shibboleth [SHIHB-oh-lehth] (from Old Testament story) watchword, criterion, test.

shillelagh, shillalah [shi-LAE-luh or-lee] Irish cudgel.

shilling. (abbr.: s.) = 5 pence = 1/2 florin.

shilly-shally

shinbone, shinplaster.

shine (intransitive) (p. and p.p.) shone; shining.

shine (transitive) (p. and p.p.) shined; shiny, shining.

shingle (pl.) —s; (adj.) shingly.

ship. See **boat.**

shipping master, shipping office, shipping room.

ships' names Require an article beforehand: *the Serapis, the Bon Homme Richard.* In U.S. Navy, full name requires *U.S.S.,* abbr. for United States' Ship: *the U.S.S. Tambourine.*

Merchant vessels have international identification numbers, used in business and law. Their names may be combined with company names for clarity: *the Exxon Valdez.*

In U.S. Navy usually aircraft carriers are named for historical vessels or battles; battleships for states; cruisers for cities; destroyer leaders for admirals; destroyers for naval personnel, members of Congress, or inventors; destroyer escorts and transports for naval personnel killed in action during World War II; submarines for marine creatures; and ballistic missile submarines for historical figures.

Shiva. See **Śiva.**

shoe (p. and p.p.) shoed or shod; shoeing.

shoot (p. and p.p.) shot.

short circuit (n.); short-circuit (v.).

shorthand, shorthorn, shortlived [-lieved], shortwave; short-range, short-tailed; short story. BUT: short-story writer.

shortsightedness a problem in thinking: failing to fully understand future contingencies. Sometimes hyphenated.

> NEARSIGHTEDNESS a medical problem: inability to see distances.

> FARSIGHTEDNESS inability to see close objects.

> MYOPIC nearsighted.

> ASTIGMATISM blurred vision; generally used for nearsightedness.

Shoshone [shoh-SHOH-nee] Indian tribe in the Rockies.

Shostakovich, Dimitri [shoss-tah-KOH-vihtch, dee-MEE-trcc] (1906–1975) Rus. composer.

shot As collective for "ammunition," takes sing. verb.

shotgun, —put, —putting.

should In formal English, belongs with *be glad, be inclined, care, like, prefer: I should like to be there.* BUT usage allows would: *I would like to be there. I would prefer coffee.*

should, would, will. (1) To express the idea that something will happen, or is expected to happen: (a) Use *should* with the first person. *I (we)* *should go to school.* (b) Use *will* or *would* with the second or third person. *He (you, they) will.*

(2) To express determination, command, promise, desire, or willingness. (a) Use *will* or *would* with the first person. *I (we) will do or die.* (b) Use *should* with the second or third person. *He (you, they) should do or die.*

(3) The verb *shall* is archaic; it has the same rules as *should.*

(4) In a question, use should or will according to which is expected to be used in the reply. *When will I be permitted to drive? (Answer: You wil be permitted to drive when you . . .) Should we be doing this? (Answer: We should.)*

should have NOT *should of: He should have stayed home.*

shoulder-high (adj.); shoulder blade, shoulder strap (n.).

shovel —ed, —ing.

show —ed, shown; —ing.

shred (p. and p.p.) *shredded* is pref. to *shred.* —dding.

shriek. See **scream.**

shrink, shrank, shrunk; shrinking (adj.); (p.p.) shrunken or shrunk.

shrivel —ed, —ing.

shuffleboard

shut (p. and p.p.) shut.

shutaway, shutdown, shuteye, shutoff, shutout (all n. and adj.), shutup (adj.); shut-in (n. and adj.), shutmouthed (adj.).

shuttlecock

shy shyer, —est; —ish, —ly, —ness.

Sibelius, Jean [sih-BAE-lih-uhs, zhan] (1865–1957) Finnish composer.

sibilant in phonetics, a hissing sound, like *s, z,* or *sh.* Avoid sibilants in close sequence.

sibyl fortune teller. (adj.) sibylline.

sic. (abbr.) (Lat.) "thus." Inserted in brackets after a quotation which may appear to be incorrect. See **brackets.**

sick ill. Use *more* or *most* for comparison.

sickbed, —hearted, —list, —room; sick bay, sick call, sick leave.

sideboard, sideburns, sideward; side horse.

sidle —led; —ling.

siege

Siegfried [SIHG-freed] hero in Norse myth; featured in Wagner's operas **Ring of the Nibelung.** Also Sigurd.

Sierra Leone [sih-EHR-uh lee-OHN] nation on W African coast. Formerly Br.; independent, 1961. Cap.: Freetown. Native: Sierra Leonean. Currency: leone.

Sierra Nevada [see-EHR-uh ne-VAH-duh] mountains in CA. Sierra means mountain; AVOID Sierra Nevada Mountains.

signal (v.) —ed, —ing. DO NOT confuse with *single.*

signalman, signal tower.

sign painter

significant

signor [see-NYAWAR] signora [see-NYAWRuh], signorina [seen-yawr-EE-nuh] It. for Mr., Mrs., Miss.

silage [SIE-lihj] winter fodder preserved in a silo.

silhouette [SIHL-oo-eht].

silly sillier, silliest, sillily (adv.); silliness.

silt, —pan, —stone.

simile a metaphor in which similarity is expressed using *like* or *as: hearts that click like taxi meters.*

> METAPHOR a figure of speech that describes or illuminates by comparison. Comparison is usu. between abstract and concrete. *In the cathedral of my heart, a candle always burns for you.*

simon-pure (adj.) genuine; often ironic. (n.) simon pure.

simony [SIHM-oh-nih] Trading in church honors.

simple-minded (adj.).

simpleness Implication is derogatory; use *simplicity.*

simulacrum [sihm-yoo-LAE-kruhm] imitation. (pl.) —cra.

simultaneous [sie-muhl-TAE-nee-uhs; (Br.) sihm] at the same time.

since Avoid the redundant use with *ago*. NOT: *It is six months ago since she arrived.* See also **because.**

sincerely

sinecure [SIE-nee-kyoor, SIHN-ee-] position which requires little responsibility, yet is secure.

sine curve, sine wave.

sine die [SIE-nee DIE-ee or SEE-nae DEE-ae] (Lat.) without setting a date: *Adjourned sine die.*

sinc qua non [SIH-nae kwae NAHN; SIE-nee kwae nahn]. (Lat.) "without which not." Indispensible thing. (pl.) sine quibus non.

sing (p.) sang; (p.p.) sung.

Singapore [sihng-uh-PAWR] port city, nation at tip of Malay peninsula, SE Asia. Formerly Br., then Malaysian; independent, 1963. Native: Singaporan. Currency: dollar.

singe (p.p. and p.) singed; singeing.

Singer, Isaac Bashevis [bah-SHEH-vihs] (1904–1991) Polish-American writer (*"Gimpel the Fool"*), worked in Yiddish; Nobel Prize, 1978.

Singhalese of Ceylon (from Sinhala, a local language).

singsong

sinister (from Lat. for left.) in her-

aldry, on the left of the person bearing a shield. See **dexter.**

sink (p.) sank or sunk, (p.p.) sunk; sinking. (adj.) sunken.

Sinn Fein [shihn-faen] Irish nationalist party.

Sino- [SIE-noh] prefix meaning Chinese: *Sino-Soviet Pact.*

sinus (sing. and pl.) Pl. also —uses.

Sioux [soo] (n. or adj.) Native American tribe.

siphon [SIE-fihn].

Siqueiros, David Alfaro [see-KAE-rohs] (1896–1974) Mexican painter, famous for work's political content.

sir for a knight or baronet, the title is placed before the Christian name: *Sir Lancelot,* NOT *Sir Du Lac.*

Sirius [SIHR-ih-uhs] the Dog Star in constellation Canis Major; brightest star in N Hemisphere.

sirocco [sih-RAHK-oh] hot wind out of the Sahara. (pl.) —os.

Sister (adherent of religious order) ADDRESS: Sister Maria Therese, Convent of the Sacred Heart. SALUTATION: Dear Sister; My dear Sister Maria Therese.

sisterhood, sister-german, sister-in-law.

sit (p. and p.p.) sat.

sitdown (n. and adj.); sit-in (n.).

site a place or a piece of land: *Site for a 20-story building.* NEVER: *a 20-story site.*

sitting room

Śiva [SEE-vah] most powerful of Hindu gods. Also *Shiva.*

S.J. Res. (with number) (abbr.) Senate joint resolution.

skeptic one who questions; doubter. (adj.) —tical.

sketchbook, sketch plan.

skewbald. See **piebald.**

ski [skee]. (pl.) skis; (v.) ski; skied; skiing, skier.

ski lift, ski jump.

skid road, skid row *Webster's* lists as synonyms. The worst part of town, the area frequented by vagrants and criminals. Orig. a logging term.

skillful

skim milk

skindiver, skintight; skin-graft (v.); skin test.

skins, sheepskin, calfskin. May be separate: goat skin.

skirt around Use is redundant. *Skirt* is sufficient.

skulduggery [-DUH-gihr-ee] trickery.

skullcap

sky blue (n.); (adj.) sky-blue.

skyscraper

slack (v.) to relax. Also, slack-off, slacking.

slacken (v.) to abate, slow down; become negligent.

slalom [SLAH-luhm] ski race, usu. zigzag, against time.

slam-bang

slander in law, false and malicious defamation uttered orally.

LIBEL [LIE-b'l] false and malicious defamation published or broadcast. NOT **liable.**

Slang. See **language.** This text includes many entries that, strictly speaking, are slang.

slantwise, slant-eyed (adj.).

slapstick

SLASH Generally limited to use within certain disciplines: business, military writing, advanced scholarship.

(1) Indicates word omitted in certain expressions. *B/L (bill of lading); L/C (letter of credit).*

(2) Used between *and* and *or: Pay in pounds and/or dollars.*

(3) Combines two related principles: *ordnance/tactics problems; critical/academic hegemony.*

See *DIAGONAL LINE, VIRGULE.*

slash-and-burn agriculture

slaveholder, —owner, —ownership (all one word); slave-born (adj.); slave labor, slave market, slave trade.

slay (p.) slew, (p.p.) slain; NOT slayed, slaying.

sleazy [SLEE-zih] degrading; morally dubious. sleazier, —iest.

sledge-hammered (adj.); sledge hammer (n.).

sleep (p. and p.p.) slept.

sleight [sliet] skill, deftness: *sleight of hand.*

> SLIGHT [sliet] (adj.) slender, frail. (v.) to treat lightly; ignore. Also n., in this sense.

sleuth [slooth] detective.

slide (p. and p.p.) slid.

sling (p. and p.p.) slung; NOT slang.

slingshot (n. or v.).

slink (p.) slunk; NOT slank.

slit (p. and p.p.) slit.

sloop. See **boat.**

slosh, slush, sludge Listed in order of increasing viscosity.

sloth [slawth] (n.) laziness. (adj.) slothful, (v.) —ully, (n.) —fulness.

slough [slou] (n.) bog: *slough of despond.* (v.) [sluhf] shed or cast off.

Slovakia. See **Czechoslovakia.**

Slovenia See **Yugoslavia.**

slovenly [SLUHV-ehn-lee] lazy and slipshod.

slow Usage allows as an adverb. *Drive slow.*

sluice [sloos] (n.) passage or channel for water (adj.) —ceable. Also sluice-box, —way; sluice gate.

slumberous Pref. to —brous.

sly —er, —est; —ly, —ness, —ish.

Small Business Administration BUT *small-business loans* differentiates from small loans for purposes of business.

smallpox —talk, —time (n.), —town (adj.); small-minded, small-scale (adj.); small-claims court; small arms.

smite (p.) smote; (p.p.) smitten.

Smithsonian Institution. See **institution.**

smog smoke plus fog.

smolder

smorgasbord [SMAWR-gahs-bawrd] Swedish buffet.

smudge pot (n.).

snackbar

snafu [SNA-foo] (n.) "Situation normal: all fouled up."

sniperscope [SNIE-pehr-skohp] attachment on rifle.

sniveled, —ing.

snowmobile (n. and v.), —led, —ling.

snuffbox —maker, —making (n.); snuff-stained (adj.).

s.o. (abbr.) seller's option.

sobeit (n. and conj.); so-and-so, so-called (adj.), so-seeming (adj.).

sobersided, sober-minded (adj.).

sobriquet [SOH-brih-kae; -keht] nickname.

so-called (adj.) *My so-called friend attacked me in a letter.*

SO CALLED In predicative use: *The Happy Warrior, so called because of his . . .*

sociable (adj.) pleasant to be with.

social pertaining to society, friends.

socialism economic and political system, emphasizing state control, (adj.) socialist, -tic. Cap.: Socialist Party, a Socialist. Compare **Communism**.

society. Cap. if part of name; the society: American Cancer Society, Inc. Boston Medical Society.

sociopath. See **Psychopathic.**

Socrates [SAH-krih-teez] (c. 470–399 B.C.) Greek philosopher, teacher of Plato.

sodajerk, soda granite, soda pop, soda water.

sodden [SAHD-'n] soaked. (colloq.) drunken.

Sodom and Gomorrah. [SAH-duhm, gah-MAWR-rah]. In Bible, cities destroyed by God for wickedness.

software computer program capable of transfer on **floppy disk.** A noun only. *Can we get the software? Do it through the software.* Opposite of hardware, the computer itself.

soiree [swah-RAE]

sojourn [SOH-juhrn] to dwell in temporarily.

sol [sahl] the sun. [sohl] musical note.

solace [SAH-lihs] comfort, alleviation of grief.

solder [SAH-duhr] (n.) metal used to join. (v.) to join by melting.

soldierly (adj. and adv.). NOT *soldierlily.*

solecism [SAH-lih-sihsm] grammatical error; hence, incorrect behavior.

solemn [SAH-lehm] solemnity [sah-LEHM-nih-tee].

Solicitor for the Department of Commerce; the Solicitor; Solicitor General; Solicitors General.

soliloquy [soh-LIH-lo-kwee] In drama, the speaking of thoughts aloud at some length.

solo (pl.) —s.

Solomon Islands [SAH-luh-muhn] nation in W Pacific. Formerly Brit.; independent, 1976. Cap.: Honiara [HOH-nee-AH-ruh] Native: —Islander. Currency: Dollar.

solon [SOH-lahn] (from Athenian lawgiver) a wise man; (colloq.) a legislator.

soluble, insoluble, dissolvable. Use for substances.

SOLVABLE, SOLUBLE, INSOLUBLE, UNSOLVABLE Use for problems.

Solzhenitsyn, Aleksandr [sohl-zihn-NEET-sihn, ah-lehk-ZAN-d'r] (b. 1918) Russian writer (*The Gulag Archipelago*), persecuted for attacks on Stalinist tyranny. Nobel Prize, 1970.

Somalia [soh-MAH-lee-uh] Formerly Italian and British Somaliland. Independent, 1960. Cap.: Mogadishu [mah-uh-DIHSH-oo]. Native: Somali. Currency: shilling. See **Afars and Issas.**

somber Pref. to —bre in U.S.

sombrero [suhm-BRAE-roh].

some AVOID use for "somewhat." NOT: *The rain let up some.*

some Meaning approximately, should precede only round numbers. NOT: *some 476 persons were present;* NOR *some 400-odd persons.*

some of us The possessive pronoun which follows should be *our*, unless the speaker is not involved. *Some of us get our just desserts.* BUT to a child: *Some of us don't obey their parents.*

someone a person.

SOME ONE one person, or thing.

somersault

something of a fool. Pref. to *somewhat of a fool.*

some time (adverbial phrase) a considerable period. *He waited for some time.*

SOMETIME (adv.) at some indefinite occasion. *Sometime I will stay longer.*

SOMETIME (adj.) former: *a sometime sheriff.*

SOMETIMES an undetermined number of times. *He sometimes came early.* (A rare plural adv.)

someway AVOID this spelling. Instead: *There must be some way.*

somewhere NOT *somewheres.*

Somme River [suhm] Fr. river; battle site in W.W. I.

somnolent [SAHM-noh-lehnt] sleepy. (n.) somnolence, (adv.) somnolently.

somnambulism [som-NAM-byoo-lihzm] sleepwalking.

Somoza [soh-MOH-sah] family ruling Nicaragua from 1937 till Sandinista revolution, 1979; hence, any dictator.

son-in-law, sons-in-law.

sonic boom explosive sound of aircraft breaking the sound barrier (moving faster than speed of sound waves).

sonnet rhyming poem of 14 lines in iambic pentameter. Most famous are those by **Petrarch**, **Shakespeare**, and Milton.

Son of Man New Testament, Jesus. Old Testament, a prophet.

sonorous [soh-NOH-ruhs] resonant, full of sound.

soot [sut (as foot)].

S.O.P. (abbr.) standard operating procedure.

Sophocles [SAH-fuh-klees] (c. 496–406 B.C.) Greek playwright, authored **Oedipus** tragedies.

sophomore [SAHF-mour] technically, second-year student (rarely cap.). Hence, anyone with shallow learning.

soporific [soh-pawr-RIHF-ihk] sleep-inducing.

soprano (pl.) —s.

Sorbonne [sawr-BUHN] university in Paris.

sorehead (n. and adj.), —headed, —hearted, —eyed (adj.); sore throat.

S O S (spaces, no periods) code signal for distress; not an abbreviation.

so that No comma after *that*.

sotto voce [SOH-toh VOH-chae] (It.) in an undertone: *a comment uttered sotto voce.*

soufflé [soo-FLAE] delicate spongy mixture of egg whites.

sough [suhf, sou] sighing sound, as of wind.

soupçon [SOOP-sawn] a small amount.

sourcebook

source . . . from Use is redundant. NOT: *The only source of water was from the Nile.* Instead: *The only source was the Nile.*

Sousa, John Phillip [SOO-suh] (1854–1932) American composer of marches.

south For rules on cap. see **east.**

South South American Republics, South American States, South Atlantic, South Atlantic States, Deep South (U.S.), South Korea, Midsouth (U.S.), South Pacific, South Pole, the South (section of United States); Southland.

South Africa republic on southern tip of continent. Formerly Dutch, then British; independent, 1961. Cap.: Pretoria, seat of administration; Cape Town, seat of legislature. Native: Afrikaner(s) (from original Dutch or Huguenot immigrants; hence, of white stock). Currency: rand.

SOUTH-WEST AFRICA U.N. name: **Namibia.** Formerly German; under South African control since 1915.

southern Comparative: more southern; superlative: southmost, southernmost.

South Carolina U.S. state. Abbr.: SC. Cap.: Columbia. Native: South Carolinian.

South Dakota Abbr. SD. Native, South Dakotan. Cap., Pierre [peer].

southeast (abbr.: SE) —eastern, —going, —land, —lander, —paw, —ward, —west, —bound (adj.), —wester (all one word); south-central (adj.), south-sider, south-southeast (abbr. SSE); south end, south side.

southerly southern, southerner.

Southern Christian Leadership Conference. (abbr. **S.C.L.C.**) Established by Martin Luther King, 1957; instrumental in U.S. Civil Rights movement.

Southern United States Alabama, Florida, Georgia, Kentucky, Mississippi, Louisiana, North Carolina, South Carolina, Texas, Virginia. Sometimes: Kentucky, Tennessee, West Virginia. a/k/a the South, the Old South.

Southwest U.S. Arizona, New Mexico, Texas, southern California. Sometimes: Nevada, Utah, Oklahoma.

South-West Africa. See **South Africa, Namibia.**

sovereign [SAHV-r'n].

soviet [soh-vih-EHT] a council.

SOVIET UNION See **Union of Soviet Socialist Republics.**

sow (p.) sowed, (p.p.) sown.

sowback —backed, —belly, —bug.

Soyinka, Wole [shaw-YIHN-kah, WOH-leh] (b. 1934) pen name of Nigerian playwright (*Kongi's Harvest, The Road*) , novelist, essayist. Actual name Akinwande Oluwole. Nobel Prize, 1986.

SP (abbr.) Mil., shore patrol. Proofreading, spelling error.

Sp. (abbr.) Spanish.

spa [SPAH] a mineral spring or nearby resort.

spacious with ample space.

SPECIOUS plausible but false.

spadeful (pl.) —s.

Spain nation in SE Europe, since Middle Ages. Cap.: Madrid. Native: Spaniard, Spanish. Currency: Peseta.

span unit of length = 9 inches = 1/8 fathom = 22.86 cm.

Spanish Spanish-born, Spanish-speaking (adj.): Spanish American. See **-American.**

Spanish-American War See **war.**

Spanish Names See **names.**

sparerib, spare-bodied (adj.); spare room.

spasm involuntary muscle tremor. (adj.) spasmodic [spahs-MAH-dihk].

SPASTIC characterized by spasms: *spastic, paralysis.*

speak (p.) spoke, (p.p.) spoken; speaking.

speak-easy (n.)

Speaker of the House of Representatives ADDRESS: The Honorable Tom Foley, Speaker of the House of Representatives, Washington, D.C.; or The Honorable, The Speaker of the House of Representatives; or The Speaker of the House of Representatives.

SALUTATION: Sir; Dear Sir; Dear Mr. Speaker.

special distinctive. See **unique.**

PARTICULAR As adj., more special.

INDIVIDUAL As adj., peculiar to one of a group.

SPECIFIC definitive. *The specific qualities of silver ore . . . The specific charges were . . .*

special forces U.S. Army guerrilla units, a/k/a Green Berets. See **Coins, Seals.**

specie [SPEE-shih] coin, not paper money.

species [SPEE-sheez or sees, SPEE-shihz] (pl.) biological group between genus and sub-species. Print name in *italics. Lepomis* (genus) *gibbosus* (spe-

cies). See **Classification of Animals and Plants.** (sing.) specie.

specious [SPEE-shuhs] deceptively attractive; feasible but fallacious: *a specious argument.*

specter Spelling pref. —re.

spectro- prefix meaning visible: *spectrograph.*

spectrum (pl.) —*tra* pref. to —*s.*

speech. See **address.**

speed (p. and p.p.) sped. Usage allows: speed up, speeded up.

speedboat, —way, —writing; speed trap.

spell —lled; spelling.

spelunking [SPEE-luhn-kihng] cave exploration.

spend (p. and p.p.) spent.

spermatozoon [spuhr-muh-tuh-ZOH-uhn] sexual cell. (pl.) —zoa.

sp. gr. (abbr.) specific gravity.

sphere area of surface = $4\pi r^2$, volume = diameter $3 \times .536$.

sphinx In Greece, woman's head and bust, lion's body and wings. In Egypt, lion with head of man. (adj.) sphinxlike. (pl.) —es. By extension, any mysterious person.

spice —ceable.

spill (p.) spilled.

spinach [SPIH-nihtch].

spin-off in finance, sale or distribution of stock of a subsidiary company to shareholders of a parent company.

Spinoza, Baruch (Benedict de) [spihn-OH-zuh, bah-ROOK] (1632–1677) Dutch Jewish lensmaker, philosopher.

spiraea [spie-REE-uh] shrub with white or pink flowers.

spit (p. and p.p.) spat. Use *spit 'n' image* or *spitting image: the spit and image of someone.* NOT: *spittin' image.*

splendor Pref. to Br. —*our.*

splice —eable.

SPLIT INFINITIVES An adverb may split an infinitive if required by natural position, or if another position would lead to ambiguity. *It would be wise to at least call. No teacher has the right to needlessly destroy a student's ego.*

SPLIT VERBS adverbs normally fall between auxiliary and verb, and after all auxiliaries if there are more than one. *They will not be seriously threatened.*

spoiled Pref. to *spoilt.*

spoilsport

spokesman

spoliation [NOT spoil—] authorized plundering.

spongecake, sponge-diver (n.);

sponge-diving (adj.), sponge-shaped (adj.); sponge bath.

sponsible worthy of credit.

spontaneity Pref. to —*eousness.*

spoonerism (from Oxford's Rev. W.A. Spooner [1844–1930]) accidental transposition of sounds and letters of words. *I am gleased and prateful.* (for pleased and grateful).

spoonful (pl.) —fuls.

sports Use figures for **scores.** *Celtics 103, Lakers 99; Red Sox 5, Mets 0.* Spell out numbers of runs, touchdowns, baskets, goals, etc. when less than 10, but use numerals for larger numbers. *The Red Sox got their fifth run when Ellis Burks hit his 36th home run.*

Time is written in figures: 2:25. A figure less than a minute is written: *0.59.3; 2 minutes 4.3 seconds, 2:04.3.*

Cap. names of sports events, stadiums, bowl games: *Polo Grounds, Rose Bowl game, World Series.* Titles should precede a proper name when a position is appointive or elective: *Coach Chris Ford.*

spouse [SPOUS] husband or wife.

spring the season.

SPRING (v.) p. *sprang* is pref. to p.p., *sprung.*

sprint (n.) short race. (v.) to run fast.

SPURT (n. or v.) increase in pace.

spry, spryer, —ryest; —ly, —ness, —ish.

Sp3c. (abbr.) specialist, third class.

spurious [SPYOOR-ih-uhs] not from a reliable source; illegitimate.

spyboat, spyglass.

sq. in. (abbr.) square inch.

sq. mi. (abbr.) square mile(s).

squad. See *ARMY ORGANIZA-TION.*

squalor, squalid [SKWAHL-lawr, —ihd] of filth.

square Lafayette Square, Washington Square; the square.

square —rable, —rish. NEVER *more or most square.* BUT *more nearly square.*

square building unit = 100 sq. ft. = 9.29 m².

S. Rept. (with number) (abbr.) Senate report.

S. Res. (with number) (abbr.) Senate resolution.

Sr. (abbr.) senior.

Sri Lanka island nation off Indian coast. Originally Ceylon. Name changed 1972. Cap.: Colombo, Native: Ceylonese, Cingalese, or Singhalese. Currency: rupee.

S.S. (abbr.) steamship.

S.S. (abbr.) Schutzstaffel (Blackshirts), Nazi German elite guard under Heinrich Himmler.

S.S.A. (abbr.) Social Security Administration.

S. Sgt. (abbr.) staff sergeant.

S.S.T. Supersonic transport plane. (1800 m.p.h.)

St. (abbr.) Street. Usu. abbreviated in news media and in lists. Also abbreviate Ave., Blvd., Terr., BUT NOT Drive or Road. In a directory, St. is often omitted to save space, but Ave., Rd., etc. are included.

St., Ste., SS. (abbr.) Saint, Sainte, Saints.

stable —bility, —bilize.

stadium Pl. —*iums* pref. to —*dia.*

Stael, Mme. de (Anne) [deh stahl] (née Necker) (1766-1817). Fr. writer *(On German Romanticism).*

staff (pl.) —s; (pl. for music), staves; archaic pl. for *sticks.* For a group use a singular verb. *The support staff feels . . .*

staff foreign service. See **foreign service.**

stage —geable, —gy.

stained-glass window BUT *a panel of stained glass.*

stalactite [stuh-LAK-tiet] calcium deposits hanging from overhead, usu. in a cave.

STALAGMITE [stuh-LAG-miet] calcium deposits formed from the floor.

Stalin [STAH-lihn] Original name, Joseph Vissarionovich Dzhugashvili

(1879–1953). Russian dictator, 1924–1953.

Stalingrad [stah-lyihn-grad; stal-] city on Volga River, U.S.S.R., scene of 1942 turning-point battle in W.W. II. Formerly Tsaritsyn; now Volgograd.

stanch. See **staunch.**

stand standby (n. and adj.), —down (adj. and n.), —fast (n. and adj.), —off (n. and adj.), —offish (n. and adj.), —pat, —pipe —still (n. and adj.), -up (n. and adj.) (all one word). stand-in (n. and adj.). (p. and p.p.) stood.

standard time. See **time.**

staple basic commodity; or wire device for holding papers together.

starboard right side of a ship (looking forward).

Star Chamber proceedings originally, legal ploys of English kings, esp. Henry VIII and Charles I, ignoring rights of accused. Hence, any unfair decision-making.

stark mad (adj.), stark naked (adj.), stark raving (adj.).

starlit (adj.) Pref. to *starlighted.*

Starr, Ringo (b. 1940) Drummer for **Beatles.** Actual name, Richard Starkey.

stars. See **heavenly bodies.**

Star-Spangled Banner. See **flag, U.S.**

startup (n. and adj.).

Stat. (abbr.) in law, Statutes at Large.

—stat suffix meaning stationary: *thermostat, gyrostat.*

state Lowercase when referring to the federal government, the body politic, foreign states: church and state, state of the Union message, statehood, statehouse, stateside, statewide, state's evidence, tristate, upstate, welfare state. Also, out-of-state (adj.).

State government State legislature (See **legislature**), State line, Ohio-Indiana State line; New York State, State of Israel, State of Veracruz; State prison; States rights. State-aided; State-owned (adj.).

state groupings Cap. complete regional groups: *New England States, Mid-Atlantic States.* BUT: some of the mountain states.

stated that use before a noun. *He stated his demands.* NOT: *He stated he wanted more money.*

State Representative ADDRESS: The Honorable John J. White, The House of Representatives, The Sate Capitol, Jefferson City, MO.
    SALUTATION: Sir; Dear Sir; Dear Mr. White.

States. Arab States, Balkan States, Baltic States, Communist States, Eastern States, BUT eastern industrial States.

East North Central States, Eastern Gulf States, Eastern North Central States, etc.; Far Western States, Gulf States, Gulf Coast States, Lake States, Latin American States, Middle Atlantic States, Mid-Atlantic States, Middle Western States, Midwestern States, Mountain States, New England States, Northern States, Northwestern States.

Organization of American States; Pacific States, Pacific Coast States; South American States; Southern States, the six States of Australia, Thirteen Original States; West South Central States, Western States, but western Gulf States; western farming states.

State's attorney state's evidence, States rights.

State Senator. ADDRESS: The Honorable Roger Howards, The State Senate, Trenton, NJ; or Senator Roger Howards, The State Capitol. SALUTATION: Sir, Dear Sir, Dear Senator Howards.

station. Cap. if part of name: Grand Central Station, Key West Naval Station (see **naval**), Nebraska Experimental Station, Syracuse Air Force Station; the station.

Lowercase if referring to media: television station SWYR-RV; WRC station, station WRC, broadcasting station WRC; station 27; substation A.

stationman —master; station house, station wagon.

stationary fixed, not moving. *A tree is stationary.*

STATIONERY writing materials. *The e in envelope reminds one of the e in stationery.*

statism [stae-tih-s′m] concentration of power in the government. (adj.) statist.

statue sculpture.

STATURE height.

STATUTE law.

Statue of Liberty, the statue.

status [STA-tuhs, STAE-] position of affairs.

STATUS QUO (Lat.) as things are.

Statutes at Large (U.S.) Revised Statutes.

staunch to stop the flow of. Pref. to *stanch.*

stave [staev] (n.) (pl.) —s.

stave (v.) (p. and p.p.) staved or stove.

std. c.f. (abbr.) standard cubic foot (feet).

steadfast

steal (p.) stole; (p.p.) stolen.

steamerload, steam line, steamship (abbr. SS., U.S.S.), His or Her Majesty's Ship (H.M.S.). See **ship's names.**

steerageway sufficient ship speed to permit steering.

Steichen, Edward [STIE-kuhn]

(1879–1973) American photographer, pioneer of the art form.

stevedore one responsible for taking cargo on and off ship; usu. employs longshoremen. May be verb.

stele [STEE-lee] shaft.

St. Elizabeths Hospital (no apostrophe).

Stendhal [stann-DAHL] Pseudonym of Marie Henri Beyle [bael]. (1783–1842) Fr. novelist (*The Red and the Black*).

steno- prefix meaning narrow, small: *stenograph, stenotic*.

stentorian [stehn-TOH-ree-uhn] very loud.

steppingstone, stepping-off (adj.).

step up (n.) improvement. (v.) increase. Only the adj. has a hyphen: *You need a step-up valve.*

—ster suffix meaning one who does something, or is of a type: *gangster, punster.*

stere unit of volume = 1 m³ = 35.314 cu. h. = 1.308 cu. yds.

stereotype NOT **prototype** (the original model) but a predictable copy. *Bob Dylan is the prototype for singer-songwriters. By now any musician in that vein has to avoid seeming like a mere stereotype.* (adj.) stereotypical.

sterile [STEHR-ihl] not fertile. (n.) —ility.

sterling silver 92.5 percent silver. Technically, "silver" is redundant.

stern rear end of a vessel.

steroids technically, chemical compounds important in biology. In general use, drugs used to enhance muscle mass.

stet (Lat.) Let it stand. Direction to printers to ignore correction made.

stethoscope

stick (p. and p.p.) stuck.

stick-in-the-mud (n. and adj.), stick-to-itiveness (n.).

Stieglitz, Alfred [STEEG-lihts] (1864–1946) American editor, photographer.

stiffnecked, stiff-necked (adj.).

stifling [STEIF-lihng] stopping the breath.

stigma (n.). brand; mark. In Christian theology, Christ's wounds are *stigmata.* (pl.) —s.

stigmatize (v.) Used with *as*. *He was stigmatized as a liar.*

stiletto [stih-LEHT-oh] Slender dagger. (pl.) —os.

still life (n.), still-life (adj.).

still remains Redundant. Use *remains.*

stimulate to excite, spur on. —lable, —tor.

stimulus [STIHM-yoo-luhs] that which excites. (pl.) —li.

STIMULANT temporary exciter.

sting (p. and p.p.) stung.

stink (p.) stank or stunk; (p.p.) stunk.

stipend [STIE-pehnd] compensation for service.

stirabout porridge.

stirrup [STIHR-uhp pref. to STUHR-uhp].

stir up (v.). *Don't stir up trouble.*

stock shares in a corporation.

COMMON STOCK Represent basic ownership.

PREFERRED STOCK Holder entitled to shares of profit (usually fixed) before common stock.

CONVERTIBLE STOCK May be converted from preferred to common stock under specified conditions.

CUMULATIVE   PREFERRED STOCK Dividends accumulate if they are not paid.

stockpile

stogie [STOH-gee] cigar. Spelling pref. to *stogy.*

Stokowski, Leopold [stoh-KAWF-skee] (1882–1977) British-American conductor.

STOL aircraft (abbr.) Short (dis-tance) takeoff and landing, such as a helicopter.

stomachache

stone unit of weight = 14 lbs. = 6.35 kg.

Stone Age May be lowercase. See *AGES.*

stop, stay *Stop* is temporary, *stay* more permanent. *He is stopping by my house on his way to the Mallory, where he is staying for the weekend.*

storage room

story a narrative. (pl.) —ies. (adj.) —ied.

STOREY the floor of a building. (pl.) —s. Also, *story.*

St. Peter's Church

Stradivari, Antonio [strah-dee-VAH-ree] (1644–1737) It. violin maker. The violin: Stradivarius.

strafe [STRAEF].

straight (adj. and adv.) direct; uninterrupted.

STRAIT (adj.) tight, narrow: *strait-jacket; straitlaced; straitened circumstances.* (n.) narrow place: *Straits of Magellan; in dangerous straits.*

straightaway, —edge, —forward, —way (adj.); straight-backed, straight-legged, straight-up-and-down (adj.).

strait. See **straight.**

stranglehold

strata [STRAH-tuh] See **stratum.**

stratagem [STRAT-ajehm] ruse, deception, especially in war.

strategic [stra-TEE-jihk].

strategy (general) plan for overall victory.

TACTIC (particular) plan for immediate objective.

Stratford-on-Avon English town, birthplace and gravesite of William Shakespeare.

stratosphere part of earth's atmosphere, above troposphere, free of weather phenomena. See **atmosphere.**

stratum [STRAT-'m] in geology, layer of earth. (pl.) strata.

Strauss, Johann [shtrous, YOH-hahn] father, 1804–1849; son, 1825–1899. Austrian composers; son, "The Waltz King."

Strauss, Richard [shtrous, REEK-ahrt] (1864–1949) German composer, no relation to Austrian **Strauss.**

Stravinsky, Igor [strah-VIHN-skee, EE-gohr] (1882–1971) Russian-American Modernist composer.

straw-hat circuit summer theatres.

streamlined designed to cut wind resistance; hence, faster, operating more smoothly.

Stream, Gulf. See **geographical terms.**

street Cap. if part of name: I Street (not eye); Fifteen-and-a-Half, 110th Street; the street.

street cleaner (n.), street-cleaning (adj.), street-walker or streetwalker (n.), street-legal (colloq., adj.), street-length (adj.).

streptococcus [strehp-toh-KAHK-uhs] microorganism which occurs in pairs or chains.

stress physical or psychological pressure. A prepositional object: *He suffered from stress. The rod broke under stress.* Usage allows as prefix: *a stress-induced disorder.*

STRAIN change created by stress.

strew (p.) strewed; (p.p.) strewn or strewed.

striated grooved: *striated muscle.* p. of striate. (n.) striation.

stricken (p.p.) of strike. Avoid adj. use for *afflicted.*

stride (p.) strode; (p.p.) stridden.

strike (p.) struck; (p.p.) struck or stricken. *The comment was stricken from the record.*

strikebreaker, —breaking, —out.

Strindberg, August [STRIHND-bihrg] (1849–1912) Swedish playwright (*The Ghost Sonata*) and novelist.

string (p. and p.p.) strung.

stringed having strings: *Stringed instruments:* BUT: *high strung.*

striped [STRIEPT] having stripes.

strip-mining, strip-mined.

strive (p.) strove; (p.p.) striven.

strongbox —hold, —point, —room (n., all one word), strong-arm (adj. and v.), strong-backed, strong-minded (adj.).

strong opinion words Certain words should not be used in a neutral context: admirable, disgraceful, excellent, exemplary, incredible, remarkable, stupendous, tremendous. NOT: *Please bring me two remarkable steaks and two excellent books.* BUT: *He brought two excellent books from Paris.*

Structuralism or **Structural Linguistics** system of linguistic and cultural analysis. Sometimes lowercase.

strychnine [STRIHK-nien] poison; may be a stimulant.

strung. See **stringed.**

stubbornness

stuck up, stuckup. (n. and adj., either form).

student one who studies.

SCHOLAR Implies intense study.

PUPIL Use for anyone attending school.

studio (pl.) —s.

Stuka [SHTOOK-ah] German W.W. II dive bomber.

stunt man, stuntman

stupefy

stupendous wonderful; astounding.

stupor [STOO-pehr] insensibility; lethargy.

Sturm und Drang [shtoorm-oont DRAHNG] (Ger.) storm and stress; also, 18th-C. literary movement.

sty pig sty. (pl.) sties.

STYE swollen gland on the eyelid. (pl.) styes.

style mode.

STILE passage.

stylebook manual of uniform typographic forms, including spelling, capitalization, etc.

stylus pointed metal writing device used on stencils, tablets, etc. Also, phonograph needle. (pl.) —uses or styli.

stymie [STIE-mee] (v.) to interfere with; stop. (adj.) stymied, —ying.

styptic [STIHP-tihk] astringent; stopping bleeding.

Styx in Gr. myth, river bordering Hades.

suasible [SWAES-a-bl] capable of being persuaded.

suave [swahv] urbane; smoothly pleasing.

sub- prefix meaning under, inferior. Usu. without hyphen in U.S.: subcommittee, subcutaneous, subma-

chinegun, substandard; sub-Hima-
layan; sub rosa, sub specie.

subaltern [suhb-AWL-tuhrn] subordinate.

subcommittee. See **committee.**

subdivisible

SUBJECT OF A SENTENCE the
word or group of words that names
the thing, person, place, or idea
about which a statement is made in
the sentence.

subject-object, subject-objectivity.

SUBJUNCTIVE MOOD In English,
three forms exist: (1) The present
subjunctive, indicating a statement
concerned with an idea rather than
with a fact. (2) The past subjunctive,
indicating an uncertain or improba-
ble statement. (3) The past perfect
subjunctive, indicating past tense.

Present subjunctive is marked by
two constructions. The first places *be*
directly with a subject. *They demanded
that the motion be tabled.* The second
takes the third person singular without the *s* ending. *I insisted that he call
me every day.*

Past subjunctive is indicated by
the same form as the past indicative,
but expresses a present or future
event. *If she studied all next week, she
would still fail. If they (or she) were 90
pounds lighter they (or she) would still
be too heavy. (Were is used for both
sing. and pl.).*

Past perfect subjunctive is formed
by *had* — past participle in the indicative mood — but here implies that the
facts are contrary. Words which mark

this construction are *if, suppose, although, unless,* and the auxiliary verb
placed before the subject: *If he had
been there; had he been there . . .*

Several auxiliary verbs have subjunctive meanings: *may, must, shall,*
etc. *They demand that he come. I wish he
would stay.*

The degree of probability is expressed in the subjunctive thus (a
probable event with the present subjunctive): *though he speaks well; though
he should speak well.*

A positive statement is expressed
in the indicative mood. *Inasmuch as he
spoke well,* (any tense may follow) *I
will honor him.*

An unlikely event is expressed in
the past subjunctive. *Even if he ran a
three-minute mile,* (past subjunctive)
*we might not honor him. If he had spoken
well last week,* (past perfect subjunctive) *I might have honored him.*

sublimate [SUHB-blih-maet] deflect
emotional drives from primitive
channels to socially acceptable ones.

subliminal [suhb-BLIH-mihn-al]
(adj.) below the threshold of consciousness. *Subliminal advertising
reaches the consumer without his knowing it.*

submersible [suhb-MIHR-sih-b'l]
capable of functioning under water,
NOT merely of going under.

subordinate in grammar, dependent
and less important.

**subordinate (or subordinating)
conjunction** Used to introduce a dependent clause and join it to the main

clause: *as, before, since, unless.*

subpar

subpoena [suh-PEE-nah] legal writ requiring one to appear in court. Usu. served in person. (v.) —naed, —naing.

subsequent to Use *after.*

subservience Pref. to —cy.

subsistence [suhb-SIHS-dehns] existence.

subsidy [SUHB-sih-dih] financial gift in aid. (pl.) —dies.

substantiate [suhb-STAN-shih-aet] to verify; prove. (adj.) —tiable, (n.) —tiation.

substantive in grammar, any word or group of words used as a noun.

substitute (v.) *You replace A with B when you substitute B for A.* Also a noun: substitution.

subtle [SUH-t'l] —tler, —tlest; —tly. (n.) subtlety [SUHT-t'l-tee].

subtropical. subtropic(s). See **tropical.**

subversive (adj.); subversion (n.); subvertible.

succeed

successful achievement Avoid use; redundant.

succinct [suhk-SIHNKT] concise.

succor [SUHK-ehr] (n. or v.) aid. Pref. to *succour.*

Succoth Jewish Feast of Tabernacles, usu. in October. Also Sukkot.

succubus demon; in myth, assumes human form to have sex with humans in their sleep. Technically, *-bus* ending is masc; (pl.) *-bi.* fem, *-ba,* (pl.) *-bae.*

such when meaning *the above described,* or *those, it, them,* etc., this word should be avoided. NOT: *The bylaws prohibit drinking on the premises, and such drinking is in poor taste.*

such Avoid use for *which, who, where, that.* Generally incorrect. NOT: *He selected such fabrics which he felt would be suitable.* (Eliminate *such.*)

suchlike INCORRECT.

sucrose [SOO-krohs] natural sugar in cane and beets. See **fructose.**

Sudan [soo-DAN] republic in NE Africa. Formerly Anglo-Egyptian; independent, 1956. Cap.: Khartoum [kar-TOOM]. Native: Sudanese (sing. and pl.). Currency: Sudanese pound.

Sudan, French Became (with Senegal) Federation of Mali (1959–1960). Since 1960, Republic of Mali.

suddenness

suds There is no singular form.

sue sued, suing, suable.

suede [swaed] tanned skin with flesh

rubbed into nap to produce a rough surface.

Suez Canal [soo-EHZ].

suffer from, sufferable.

sufficient. See **enough.**

suffix an abstract element attached at the end of a word which alters its meaning or denotes derivation, formation, or inflection, usually without a hyphen: *tenfold, colonization.*

BUT —*elect,* —*odd,* —*wide,* are usu. hyphenated. —*like* is sometimes hyphenated. See **prefix.**

suffocate to choke, stifle, NOT necessarily fatally.

suffuse (v.) —ed, —sing, (adj.) —sable.

suggest, suggestible.

suicide (n.) NOT a verb.

Sui generis [SOO-ee jeh-NEH-rihs] (Lat.) of its own kind. In a class to itself.

sui juris (Lat.) of his own right. Entitled to act for himself.

suit [soot], **suite** [sweet] Both from Middle English, "a set." Use *suit* with clothes, cards, armor, sails; use *suite* with rooms, attendants, furniture.

Sukarno [soo-KAHR-noh] (1901–1970) leader of Indonesian independence movement, first president (1950–1967). First name, Ahmed (rarely used).

sukiyaki [soo-kee-YAH-kee] Japanese dish.

Sukkot. See **Succoth.**

Suleyman, the Magnificent [seu-lae-MAHN], also Soliman, Suleiman [suhl-ih-MAN] (1496–1566). Sultan at height of Ottoman empire.

sulfur pref. to —*phur.*

sullenness

sumac [SOO-mak].

Sumatra [soo-MAH-trah] Indonesian island. (adj.) Sumatran.

summarily [suh-MAH-rih-lee; SUHM-ma-].

summary. See **abbreviation.**

SUMMERY like summer.

summertime the season.

summit meeting

sun Lowercase unless with names of planets, other stars.

Sunday [SUHN-dih] abbr.: Sun.

sundry several, various. *All and sundry* means each and every one.

sundries miscellaneous small items or articles.

sunk. See **sink.**

Sun Yat-sen [soon YAHT-SEHN] (1866–1925) Chinese statesman. Overthrew last Imperial dynasty;

served as first modern president (1911–1912).

Sup. Ct. (abbr.) Supreme Court Reporter.

superannuated

supercargo agent of shipper on board ship.

superfluous [soo-PUHR-floo-uhs] more than needed.

superintendent. (abbr.: Supt.) Cap. if head of federal unit: Superintendent of Documents (Government Printing Office), Superintendent of the Naval Academy.

superintendent of schools ADDRESS: Superintendent Harold Scribner, Teaneck Public Schools, Teaneck, NJ; or Mr. Harold Scribner, Superintendent of Teaneck Public Schools, Teaneck, NJ. SALUTATION: Dear Sir; Dear Dr. Scribner.

Superior of Sisterhood (Roman Catholic) ADDRESS: The Reverend Mother Superior, Sisters of Notre Dame; or Sister Superior, Sisters of Notre Dame. SALUTATION: Dear Reverend Mother, My dear Reverend Mother; Dear Mother Superior; Dear Sister Superior.

superior to NOT *than.*

superlative forms Often misused where the positive or comparative form is correct. NOT: *He is in closest contact with the situation.*

supernumerary [soo-puhr-NOO-muhr-ehr-ee] (adj.) exceeding pre-

scribed amount. (n.) employee beyond those needed.

supersede

supervise

supine [soo-PIEN] (adj.) lying on back, face up.

supp. (abbr.) supplement.

suppertime

supple [SUHP-ihl] (adj.) flexible when bent. Adv., supplely [SUHP-lih]. (n.) suppleness.

supplement. See **complement.**

supply and demand Usage allows standing alone: *It is simple supply and demand.* Otherwise, use hyphens: *Considering supply-and-demand formulas. . . .* supply-side economics.

suppress, —ible, —ssor.

supra [SOO-pruh] (Lat.) above; previously cited.

supra- prefix meaning above in position.

supreme NEVER use *more* or *most supreme.*

Supreme Court (U.S.) the Court, High Court; cap. titles of officers standing alone: Associate Justice, Justice, Chief Justice, Clerk, Marshal, Reporter.

Supt. (abbr.) superintendent.

surcease [suhr-SEES] (n.) cessation; end.

sure-fire, sure-footed (adj.); sure enough, sure thing.

surely

surety [SHOOR-eh-tee; SHUR-tih] one who makes himself liable for performance or payment by another.

Surgeon General the Army, Navy, and Public Health Service.

surgeon general (pl.) surgeons general.

Suriname [SOOY-rih-nahm] nation on Caribbean coast of South America. Former Dutch Guiana; independent, 1975. Cap.: Paramaribo [PAR-uh-MAR-uh-boh]. Native: Surinamian. Curency: guilder.

surly (adj.); surlily (adv.).

surmise [suhr-MIEZ] to guess. (adv.) surmisedly [-MIE-zehd-lih].

surplice [SUHR-plihs] white clergical robe.

surprise (n. and v.); surprisedly [suhr-PRIEZ-ed-lee] (adv.).

surreptitious [suh-rehp-TIHSH-uhs] (adj.) clandestine, stealthy. (adv.) surreptitiously [-TIH-shuhs-lee].

surrogate [SUH-roh-geht] (n. or adj.) substitute. *Jack went as my surrogate. She is a surrogate parent for her sister's child.*

surround *surround on all sides* is redundant.

survey Cap. if part of name of federal or state unit: Coast and Geodetic Survey; Geological Survey, the survey.

surveillance [suhr-VAEY-lanss] (n.) close supervision. (n. or adj.) surveillant.

survivors Best use in passive and the specific. *He is survived by one son and two daughters.* Other forms tend to be misleading. *They had three children* implies that the children are dead.

susceptible [suhs-SEHP-tih-b'l] (adj.) easily affected. (n.) —tibility. (adj.) —tive.

suspendable Pref. to *suspensible.*

suspenders One strap is a suspender.

suspense mental uncertainty.

SUSPENSION state or action of being suspended: *He awaited the decision in great suspense. The suspension of his license was a great blow.*

suspensible capable of being held up.

suture [SOO-tyuhr] (n.) thread used to close surgical incisions. (v.) to sew shut such a cut.

svelte [svehlt] slender.

Svengali [svehn-GAH-lee] (from *Trilby,* 1894 novel by Georges du

Maurier) evil manipulator.

SW (abbr.) southwest.

swam Past of *swim.*

swampland, swamp fever.

swansong a swan's fabled outburst of song before death; hence, a last artistic work.

swap (n. or v.). Pref. to *swop.*

swarm [swawrm] (n. or v.).

swarthy [SWAWR-thee] of dark complexion.

swastika [SWAHS-tihkuh] a symbol: Greek cross with ends bent at right angles. Official emblem of **Nazi** Third Reich.

swath [swahth], also **swathe** [swaeth] a row or strip cut by a scythe. Hence, devastation.

swayback (n. and adj.), sway-backed (adj.); sway-brace (v.).

Swaziland [SWAH-see-land] land-locked nation in SW Africa. Formerly Brit.; independent, 1968. Cap.: Mbabane [ehm-bow-BAWN]. Native: Swazi(s). Currency: Lilageni.

swear (p.) swore; (p.p.) sworn.

swearword

sweat p. and p.p., sweat pref. to *sweated.*

sweatband, sweatbox, sweatshop, sweatshirt; sweat gland.

Sweden Scandinavian nation, since early Middle Ages. Cap.: Stockholm. Native: Swede, Swedish. Currency: krona.

Swedenborg, Emanuel [SWEE-d'n-bawrg] (1688–1772) Swedish scientist, philosopher; famous for writings on angels.

sweetbriar, sweet potato.

swell (p.) swelled; (p.p.) swollen.

swim (p.) swam; (p.p.) swum.

swimsuit, swimwear.

swine (sing. and pl.); swinish (adj.).

BOAR wild swine, esp. male.

SOW female swine.

HOG usu. male; domestic swine for market.

PIG young swine. A piglet is a baby.

swing (p. and p.p.) swung.

Switzerland [SWIHT-sur-l'nd] land-locked mid-European nation, since Middle Ages. Cap.: Bern. Native: Swiss. Currency: franc. Poetic, archaic: *Helvetia.*

swivel —led, —ling.

swivel chair

swordbearer, swordfish, —play. BUT swordsman.

sybarite [SIHB-uh-riet] (from Sybaris) sensualist. (adj.) —itic [sihb-uh-RIHT-ink], —itical.

sycophant [SIHK-oh-fant] flatterer, esp. for favors.

syl- See **syn-**.

syllable one or several letters that form one sound.

syllabus (pl.) —buses or —bi.

sylvan of the woods. Pref. to *silvan*.

sym-. See **syn-**.

symbols

symphony (pl.) —nies. (adj.) symphonic.

symposium (pl.) symposia. See **forum**.

symptom indication, sign. (pl.) —s.

syn- prefix meaning with, associated, like: *synchronize, synagogue, syntax. Syn-* becomes *sym-* before *p, o,* and *m (symptomatic), sy-* before *l (syllogism).*

synagogue [SIH-nah-gahg] Jewish house of worship.

synapse [SIH-naps] junction of nerve endings, esp. in the brain. (adj.) synaptic.

syncretic [sihn-KREH-tihk] bringing together different cultures. (n.) syncretism.

synecdoche [sihn-NEHK-doh-kih] using a part to indicate the whole. *He had fifty head on his ranch.*

synergy [SIH-nihr-jee] in chemistry, improved reaction caused by bringing together independent substances. Hence, any combination that results in better outcome.

synod [SIHN-uhd] council, usu. ecclesiastical.

synonym word having the same meaning as another. (n.) synonymity.

SYNONYMOUS WITH of identical meaning. See **homonyms.**

synopsis (pl.) synopses. See **abbreviation.**

syntax in grammar, the arrangement of word forms in a sentence, showing their relationship and meaning.

synthesis combining of parts to form a whole. (pl.) —theses.

syphilis [SIH-fih-lihs] venereal disease.

Syria Middle Eastern nation. Formerly Turkish and French; independent, 1941. Cap.: Damascus. Native: Syrian. Currency: pound. Alphabet, language: *Syriac.*

syringe [SIHR-ihnj] small hand pump.

system Cap. if referring to federal or state unit: Alaska Communication System, the system; Federal Credit System, Federal Home Loan Bank System; National System of Interstate Highways; Interstate Highway System, the Interstate System, the National System, the system. BUT highway system, Federal road system, Postal Savings System; Selective Service System (see also **service**).

BUT Pennsylvania Railway system, Pennsylvania system; Bell system, the system.

systematic Pref. to *systemic* except in physiology.

systematize Pref. to *systemize*.

systemwide

systole [SIHS-toh-lee] contraction of the heart.

Szechwan [SEHSH-wahn] province of SW China, known for spicy cuisine.

T

t Silent after s when followed by l or n sounds: *chasten, fasten, listen, epistle, jostle, bustle.*

-t, -tt- Double the *t* with a monosyllable ending in *t* and preceded by a single vowel (NOT a diphthong or double vowel), before a suffix beginning with a vowel. Polysyllables follow the same rule if the accent is on the last syllable.

-t or **-ed** bereaved, bereft; burned, burnt; dreamed, dreamt; kneeled, knelt; leaped, leapt; learned, learnt; spilled, spilt; spoiled, spoilt. Written usage tends towards *-ed,* pronunciation towards *-t* (burnt). *Bereaved* has a more emotional connotation than *bereft.*

T-beam, T-iron, T-shape, T-square, T-man, T-scale.

tabernacle in Judaism, portable sanctuary. May be cap.

tableau (pl.) —eaux.

table d'hôte [TAH-b'l DOHT] restaurant meal at set price. Opposite of **à la carte.**

table tennis Ping-pong, more common, is a trade name.

table 2,11,A Lowercase, but *Table 2,* when part of title: *Table 2. Degrees of Land Deterioration.*

table a motion to suspend discussion of the motion till later.

taboo [ta-BOO] (p. and p.p.) —ooed.

tabula rasa [TAH-byoo-la RAH-sah] (Lat.) "scraped tablet." Clean surface on which to write; hence, an uneducated mind.

tabulate (v.); —lable (n.).

tacit [TASS-iht] implied but not expressed: *tacit consent.*

Tacitus, Cornelius [TAS-ih-tuhs] (A.D. 55–117) Roman historian.

tack in sailing (v.), to change direction. Hence (n.), direction. *He tried another tack.*

TACT ability to deal with others.

tactician [tak-TIHSH-'n] a skillful maneuverer.

tactics. See **strategy.**

tactile [TAK-tie'l] capable of being felt, or of feeling.

Tadzhikistan [TAHD-zihk-stahn] republic in former **U.S.S.R.**; in **Commonwealth of Independent States,** 1992. In SE, bordering China and Afghanistan. Cap.: Dushanbe [dyoo-SHAM-buh]. Natives: Tadzhiks.

taffeta [TAH-feh-tah] smooth, shiny weave of silk or rayon.

taffy NOT a synonym for toffee.

Tahiti [tah-HEE-tee] Fr. S Pacific island, symbol of carefree living.

Taipei [tie-PAE]. See **Taiwan**.

Taiwan [tae-WAHN] Democratic China, as opposed to Communist China (See **China**). Established 1949 on Formosa Island off SW Chinese coast. Cap.: Taipei [tai-PAE]. Native: Taiwanese. Currency: New Taiwan dollar.

Taj Mahal [TAHZ muh-HAHL] mausoleum for wife of Shah Jahan, built 1632–1643, at Agra, India. Symbol of grandeur.

take (p.) took, (p.p.) taken; taking.

takedown —off (also take off), —out, —over, take-all, take-home, take-in.

take-home pay wages after all deductions.

talent (1) innate ability; (2) ancient weight and money unit.

talisman [TAH-lihs-man] engraved figure charm. (pl.) —s. (adj.) talismanic.

talkfest

talking-to (n.). *She gave him a talking-to.*

Talmud [TAHL-muhd] (Heb.) Jewish lawbooks and Biblical commentary. (adj.) Talmudic, (n.) —dist.

Tanganyika [tan-gan-YEE-kuh]. See **Tanzania**.

tangelo [tan-JEH-loh] hybrid tangerine-grapefruit. (pl.) —os.

tangible [TAN-jih-b'l] capable of being touched, realized or appraised: *tangible assets.*

Tanzania [tan-ZAE-nee-ah] republic on E coast of Africa. Formerly German and British. Tanganyika independent in 1961, then combined with Zanzibar and Pemba 1964. Cap.: Dar es Salaam [DAHR ehs-LAHM]. Native: Tanzanian. Currency: E Africa shilling.

Tao [dow] (Chin.) "road" or "way." Ancient Chinese philosophy of ethics. (n.) Taoism (adj. and n.) —ist. See **Lao-tzu**.

taper [TAE-pehr] (n.) a candle.

TAPIR [TAE-puhr] South American animal.

Tarawa [tah-RAH-wah] island in SW Pacific, scene of bloody W.W. II battle, 1943.

Tarot [ta-ROH] card deck used in fortune-telling.

tarragon [TAR-uh-gahn] a spice.

tassel —led, —ling.

tattler revealer of secrets, esp. to make trouble.

TATTLETALE A synonym for *tattler.*

tattoo (v.) to mark skin by pricking with coloring. —ed, —ing. Also a noun.

taupe [TOHP] tannish yellow.

Taurus [TAW-ruhs] born April 20-May 20. See **Zodiac**.

tautology [taw-TAHL-uh-jee] repetition in different words. *We'll have a better income if we make more money.* (adj.) —logical. See **redundancy**.

taxi (pl.) —s. (v.) taxied, —iing, or — ying; taxicab, taxi meter.

TB. (abbr.) tuberculosis.

tbs. (abbr.) tablespoonful.

Tchaikovsky, Peter Ilich [chie-KAWF-skih, PYAW-tuhr ihl-YEHCH] (1840–1893) Russian composer.

teach (p. and p.p.) taught.

teammate, —work, team play.

tear [taer] (p.) tore; (p.p.) torn; tearing.

teardrop, —out, —sheet, —stain; (n.) tear-stained (adj.); tear gas (n.).

technical

technique [tehk-NEEK].

tedious [TEE-dee-uhs, TEED-yuhs, TEEjuhs] tiresome.

Te Deum [tee DAE-uhm, DEE-] (Lat.) "Thee, God." Ancient Gregorian chant, full name "Te Deum Laudamus."

tedium [TEE-dee-uhm] (n.). boredom.

teenage (adj.); teenager (n.). AVOID *teenaged*.

tee shirt, T shirt, T-shirt.

teetotaler [tee-TOH-t'l-uhr] one

who abstains entirely from alcohol.

Tel Aviv-Jaffa [tehl ah-VEEV] seaport in Israel. Jaffa (also Heifa, Joppa, Yafo) is the older city, Tel Aviv former suburb.

tele- prefix (from Gr., "far") meaning covering a distance: *telegraph, telepathy, telescope.*

Telemachus [tih-LEHM-uh-kuhs] son of **Odysseus**.

Telemann, Georg Phillip [TAE-luh-mahn, GAE-awrg] (1681–1767) Ger. composer.

televise (v.) to transmit or receive.

TELECAST (v.) to broadcast by television.

television station. See **station**.

telltale

temerity boldness. *He had the temerity to ask for a raise when the business was failing.*

TIMIDITY shyness. *Timidity prevented her saying no.*

tempera [TEHM-p'rah] a paint.

TEMPURA [tehm-POO-rah] Japanese cooking sauce.

temperature See **fahrenheidt, Kelvin, Réamur**.

tempus fugit [TEHM-puhs FYOO-jiht] (Lat.) Time flies.

tendentious [tehn-DEHN-shuhs] having a tendency with a purpose, usu. to make a change. *Looking over* *his voting record, we discovered a tendentious leaning toward the right.*

tender (n.) an offer: *legal tender.* (v.) to make an offer.

tenfold —penny (nail), —pins.

tenebrous [TEHN-uh-bruhs; TEHN-nehb-rih-uhs] gloomy.

tenement [TEH-neh-mehnt] city building.

tenet [TEHN-eht, -iht] a central philosophic principle.

Tennessee [tehn-eh-SEE] abbr.: TN. Cap.: Nashville. Native; Tennessean, Tennesseean.

Tennyson, Alfred Lord [TEHN-ihs-sehn] (1809–1902) English poet *(Idylls of the King).*

tenor in music, high male voice. Also, usu. abstract, the nature of something. *What was the tenor of the conversation?*

TENURE [TEHN-yoor] period in office.

TENSE In grammar, tense is the property that describes the time of an action or state of being. English has three simple tenses: present, *talk*; past, *talked*; and future, *will talk.* It also has three compound or perfect tenses which show that an action has been perfected or completed: present perfect *have* or *has talked*; past perfect, *had talked*; and future perfect, *shall* or *will have talked.*

In addition, there are progressive forms of each tense which indicate that the action is continuing. The progressive forms are made up of the present participle, *talking*, and a form of the auxiliary verb, to be: present progressive, *I am talking*; past progressive, *I was talking*; future progressive, *I will* (or *shall*) *be talking*; present perfect progressive, *I have been talking*; past perfect progressive, *I had been talking*; future perfect progressive, *I will* (or *shall*) *have been talking.*

Tense is indicated both by changes in the verb and by auxiliary verbs. Verb forms that indicate tense are called the principal parts: infinitive or present, *talk*; past, *talked*; past participle, *talked.* The past participle is always used with an auxiliary verb.

When actions occur at the same time, the same tense may be used, but if a series of actions is interrupted by an action that either occurred earlier or will occur later, the tense must be changed to show this change in time.

The past tense is usually formed by adding *-ed* to the present tense form. See **irregular verbs.** The habitual past of most verbs is formed by the auxiliary *used to. She used to read every book she could find.* The emphatic past is formed with the auxiliary *did. She did read it.* Simple past tense is also used for completed action. *He spoke to me. He came here.* Past perfect progressive is also used to show habitual past action. *I had been teaching for many years.*

In the subjunctive mood, the simple past tense, used as the past subjunctive, refers to either present or future. *If he performed well today or to-*

morrow, he could win. BUT the past subjunctive of *to be* requires *were* in both singular and plural: *If I were you* . . . Use of *was* or *were*, followed by a *to* infinitive, refers to either the present or the future. *If she were to say no* . . . BUT when followed by any other form, this construction refers only to the present. *If they were near, we could see them.* To show that something is not a fact, *were* and *had* may be used without *if*. *Had you been ten feet tall, and were I as strong as Hercules, still we could not have defeated them.* A verb in the past tense may be used with *if* to refer to the past in the simple indicative mood. *If he went, he will tell me about it.*

Tense in a subordinate clause is past if the principle clause is past; but it may be in any tense, according to the sense to be expressed, if the principle clause is in the persent or future tense. This rule does not apply to verbs expressing habitual action. In clauses of result or purpose, introduced by such conjunctions as *in order that*, or *so that*, if the verb in the principal clause is in the past or past perfect tense, use one of the past auxiliaries (*might, could, would*) in the subordinate clause. *He walked* (or *had walked*) *to the store, so that he could have rolls for breakfast.*

tensible [TEHNS-suh-b'l] (adj.) capable of being extended. (n.) —bleness, tensibly, tensibility.

tensile strength resistance to pulling lengthwise.

tenterhooks hooks used to hang drying cloth. Hence, *on tenterhooks,*

waiting helplessly. NOT *tenderhooks*.

tenure. See **tenor**.

tepee [TEE-pee] Pref. to *teepee*.

tepid [TEHP-ihd] (adj.) lukewarm (n.) —ity, (adv.) —ly, (n.) —ness.

tequila Mexican liquor.

Ter- Preceding a name. See **Le-**.

terazzo or **terrazzo** [tehr-AHT-soh] polished flooring of marble chips set in cement.

tercentenary [tehr-sehn-TEHN-ehr-ee] 300th anniversary.

terminal bus or train station.

> TERMINATE [TUHR-mih-nate] (v.) to end; have its end. (adj.) — nable, (n.) —tor.

> TERMINUS end of line. (pl.) termini.

Terpsichore [tuhrp-SIK-eh-ree] in Gr. myth, Muse of dance and song; thus dance. (adj.) terpsichorean [-KAWR-ree-uhn].

terra-cotta (adj.); terra cotta (n.); terra firma.

terrarium [teh-RAER-ee-uhm] glass enclosure. (pl.) —ums.

terrestrial [teh-REHS-tree'l] earthly. NOT *terrestial*.

terrible [TEHR-ih-bl] afflicting severely; exciting terror.

terrified. See **afraid**.

territorial Cap. if a political subdivision.

territory Cap. if part of name: Northwest Territory, the territory; Trust Territory of the Pacific Islands, Pacific Islands Trust Territory. BUT: trust territory, gang territory, territory of Guam.

terror-stricken

tertiary [TUHR-shih-ehr-ee] of third order; minor importance.

tertiary era the Cenozoic period. See **time**.

test Otis Mental Ability Group Test, the group test; the test.

testator [tehs-TAE-tehr] person who leaves a will.

testosterone [tehs-TAWS-teh-rohn] masculinizing hormone.

testimony Write: *Q: Did she arrive? —A: Yes.*

tête-à-tête [TAET-uh-TAET] (Fr.) "head to head." Private or confidential conversation.

tetralogy four connected artistic works.

Texarkana [tehk-sahr-KAN-uh] border city, area between Texas and Arkansas.

Texas U.S. state. Abbr.: TX. Cap.: Austin. Native: Texan.

textile [TEHKS-tihl] woven fabrics.

Thailand [TAE-land] nation in SE Asia; formerly Siam. Cap.: Bangkok. Native: Thai(s) [TIE]. Currency: baht.

thalamus [THAL-uh-muhs] part of forebrain. (pl.) —mi.

thalidomide [thuh-LIH-doh-mied] sedative which, taken by pregnant women, resulted in deformed children.

than (coordinating conjunction). Use only with *other, rather, else,* and the comparative form of an adjective or adverb. *They arrived sooner than we expected.* BUT: *Scarcely had they arrived when we started.*

than, as If the word following is the subject of a clause, even if part of the clause is understood, that word must be in the nominative case. *I have more money than she (has).* But if the word following is not the subject of a clause, it must be in the objective case. *I know him better than (I know) her.*

thanking you in advance AVOID; assumes that a favor will be granted.

Thanksgiving Day Otherwise, no cap.: thanksgiving.

Thant, U [THAHNT, OO] (1909–1974) Burmese educator, diplomat, acting U.N. Secretary-General (1961–1962), Secretary-General (1962–1972).

that (adj. adv.) to such an extent. AVOID: *that section which is involved* and other uses where *the* or *very* will do as well. NOT: *He was that rich.*

NOT: *After examining the arm, the surgeon removed that part infected.* USE *the part infected* or *the part which had been infected.*

that Possessive form is *whose. That store is the one whose advertisements look best.*

that (relative pronoun). *This is the world that man has made.* NOT with a question: *I question that, had he been well, he would have done better.* USE *whether.*

that When *that* or *which* introduces a series of parallel clauses, the conjunction should be repeated for each clause. *They recalled that seven persons were present and that six wore wigs.*

that (conj. omitted) *I knew* (that) *he was here.* Good usage allows omission of *that*, esp. with such verbs as *believe, presume, suppose, think, assert, aver, calculate, conceive, learn, maintain, reckon, state, suggest.*

BUT *that* is seldom omitted after *acknowledge.*

that in place of *who.* Usage allows *that*, esp. when no one specific is mentioned. *The first governor that ordered police protection . . .*

that . . . that. AVOID: *All of us know that he would live up to the promises that his mother had made for him.* USE *that . . . which,* or omit second *that.*

that, which *That* is pref. as a defining relative in all cases. *Which* or *who* is used as a defining or non-defining relative pronoun.

Although *who* is used for individual persons, *that* may be used for a group, class, or type. *Any groups that were on active duty may be relieved.*

A non-defining clause is set aside by parenthetical commas. *This house, which I built with my own hands, is one of the most beautiful in town.*

the Cap. only when it is a part of the name: The Hague, BUT the Hague Conference; *The Times* (of London), BUT the *Times* article; The Dalles (in Oregon), BUT the Dalles Dam, the Dalles region.

the- and the- *The first and the second classes have 30 pupils* (meaning each). *The first and second classes have 60 pupils* (meaning together). *The blue and red flags* (flags of two colors). *The blue and the red flags* (flags of a single color); BETTER: *The blue flags and the red.*

Usually repeat *the* with each adjective except after *some.* With two nouns, elimination of the second *the* indicates a single, combined quality. *The strength and the courage of the people is of historic importance. The strength and the courage of the people are of historic importance.*

the—in question AVOID. Use *this* or *that. This hat is mine.* NOT: *The hat in question is mine.*

theatergoer, —going, theater-in-the-round.

their possessive form of *they, them.* Make certain the antecedent is clear. Do not confuse with *his* or *its. They spoke their thoughts. Each to his own* *choice. Everyone* (everybody) *has his faults.*

theirs *This prize of theirs. The book is theirs. Theirs is the winner.* NOT *their's.*

theirselves INCORRECT. Use *themselves.*

theism [THEE-ihz'm] belief in a deity, and in supernatural revelation. See **atheism.**

thence [thehnss]. See **hence.**

thenceforth, thenceforward For sense of "from then on," use alone. NOT *from thenceforth.*

then-existing

theoretical Pref. to *theoretic.*

there Use as anticipatory expletive. Except after verb *to be,* omit *there* as part of a verb in an inverted position. *It was evident that whatever* (there) *remained belonged to him.*

thereabout(s), —above, —after, —among, —at, —by, —for, —fore, —from, —in, —inafter, —into, —of, —on, —to, —tofore, -unto, —upon, —with (all one word).

thereat, therein, thereof AVOID except in law.

thereby AVOID use before an unattached present participle. NOT: *The horse ran last, thereby losing our bet.*

therefor [thair-FAWR] (adverb or adjective phrase) a legalism for the words *for that. He was paid therefor.*

THEREFORE [THAIR-fawr] (adverbial conjunction) for that reason. Commas before *therefore* accent the preceding word. AVOID *therefore* after *and, it,* and other weak words.

thesaurus sourcebook for words. (pl.) —ruses, —ri. See **Roget's Thesaurus, dictionary.**

these *This kind, these kinds.*

thesis [THEE-sihs] proposition; central idea. In academics, a long paper written for a degree. (pl.) —es [eez].

T.H.I. temperature-humidity index. Weather Bureau ratio designed to measure discomfort (hence, Discomfort Index). At T.H.I. 75, 50% of the population is uncomfortable.

thiamine [THIE-ah-mehn, -meen] B-1 vitamin.

thine, thy. (arch.) possessive of *thou.*

things— *Things American,* etc. is an affectation; avoid except for special uses.

think that *I think* (that) *he is bright.* Omit *that* after think.

think to do AVOID use.

thinness

third-hand (adv. and adj.); third-class, third-degree, third-rate (adj.) thirdrater; third house.

Thirteen Colonies See **Colonies.**

Thirteen Original States

thirties. See *NUMBERS.*

this *This two months is . . .* acceptable grammatically if the period is a unit.

Thomas Aquinas, Saint [ah-KWIEN-uhs] (1224–1274) It. saint, famous for systematic theology.

thorax [THOH-raks] in insects, part of body between neck and abdomen. (pl.) thoraxes or —ces.

Thoreau, Henry David [THAW-roh] (1817–1862) American writer *(Walden),* philosopher.

those *Those persons who are selected. The persons selected. Those selected.* NOT: *Those persons selected.*

though, although (conj.) *Although* is more formal.

as though *She wooed as though she had to win.*

thrall bondage, usu. emotional. *His witty asides held her in thrall.* (v.) enthrall; (n.) thralldom.

thrash Use for animals, people.

　　THRESH Use for grain.

three, 3, III, thirteen, thirty. See **four**.

3-D Advertising shorthand: three-dimensional.

threefold, —penny (nail), —score, —some; three-bagger, three-cornered, three-dimensional; three-in-hand, three-ply, three-spot, three-square.

three quarters (n.). *A yard and three quarters.*

　　THREE-QUARTER (adj.). *He wore a three-quarter coat.*

threnody [THREHN-oh-dih] dirge. (pl. —dies). (adj.) —dic.

threshold [THREHSH-ohld] the structure under a door; hence, entering point.

thriftbox

thrive (p.) thrived or throve; (p.p.) thrived.

throughout the whole of is redundant.

throw (p.) threw; (p.p.) thrown; throwing.

thru AVOID this spelling.

thruway, New York Thruway, the thruway.

Thucydides [thoo-SIHD-dih-dees] (fl. 5th C. B.C.) Greek historian.

Thurs. (abbr.) Thursday [THUHRZ-dih].

thus AVOID use before a present participle. NOT: *thus making himself important.*

thusly AVOID.

thwart [THWAWRT] placed across something else.

thy. See **thine**.

thyme [tiem] seasoning related to mint.

thyroid [THIE-roid] gland near larynx that influences growth.

tiara [tee-AH-rah] decorative headband. Originally, three-tiered crown.

Tibet [tih-BEHT] Himalayan nation currently occupied by Communist China. Cap.: Lhasa [LAH-sah]. Native: Tibetan.

tidal wave

tidbit Pref. to *titbit.*

tiddlywinks [TIHD-lee-WIHNKS] game with objective of snapping small disks into cup.

tie-dye —dyed, —dying. May be a noun. *She wore a spectacular tie-dye.*

tie-in attachments to a deal. (pl.) tie-ins.

Tienanmen Square [TYEH-nih-mehn] Central Square in **Beijing,** China, site of riots and massacre, May–June 1989.

Tierra del Fuego [TYEHR-uh del FWAE-goh] islands at southern tip of South America; hence, any place out of touch.

till, until *Until* is more formal. NOT til; AVOID 'til.

timber [TIHM-buhr] wood.

TIMBRE [TAM-br] resonance.

Timbuktu or **Timbuctoo** [tihm-BUHK-too] city in Mali; symbol of a place both faraway and fabulous.

time *The years 1957–1961. The club meets Monday through Friday at 9 o'clock.* The short dash is substituted only for *through* or *to,* BUT also removes need for introductory *from.* NOT: *From May-September 1960.* See **days, weeks, months, years, decades, century, Ages, Numbers**.

TIME CAPITALIZATION Atlantic time, Atlantic Standard time, central time, central standard time, mountain standard time, Pacific time, Pacific standard time, universal time, atomic time.

COMPUTATION Noon in New York City (Eastern Standard Time) is 11 A.M. in Chicago (Central Standard Time); 10 A.M. in Denver (Mountain Standard Time); 9 A.M. in San Francisco (Pacific Standard Time); 7 A.M. in Nome and Honolulu (daylight saving time is 1 hour later).

Similarly, 5 P.M. in Greenwich, London, Paris = 6 P.M. in Berlin = 7 P.M. in Moscow, Bucharest, Istanbul = 2 A.M. the following day in Tokyo.

FORM *12 noon; 12 p.m.* (midnight); *3: 40 p.m.; 7 o'clock; 7 p.m.* (BUT NOT *7 o'clock p.m.); half past 7; 4h 30m or 4.5h* (in scientific work); *0025, 2359* (in astronomy). *6 hours 8 minutes 4 seconds. four centuries. three decades.* See also **dates, years**.

timebound —card, —clock, —keeper, —killer, —lock, —out, —piece, —proof, —saver, —server, —sheet, —span, —table, —taker, —waster, —work, —worn (all one word); time-consuming, time-honored.

timid Applied to people, animals. See **temerity**.

> TIMOROUS Also, applied to ideas, actions, animals: *a timorous program.*

tin Sometimes used for can (the container), esp. in Britain.

tinfoil, tintype; tin-glazed.

tinderbox, tinder-dry.

tinge [tihnj] —geable, —inged, —ging.

tinsel —seled, —ing.

tiptoe tiptoed, tiptoeing.

tirade [TIE-raed; tie-RAED] long speech, esp. angry.

tire (n. or v.) tired; tiring.

tissue [TIH-shoo].

titan [TIE-t'n] (from Titan, giant in Gr. myth) (n.) one that is gigantic in size or power.

titanium [tih-TAE-nee-uhm] metal used in high-speed aircraft.

titbit Use **tidbit**.

tithe [tieth] (Old English) "a tenth." (n.) amount given to charity. (v.) to give to charity. (p.) tithed; tithing.

Titian [TIHSH-ihn] Tiziano Vecellio (1477–1576) It. painter.

title in law, proof of ownership.

titleholder, —winner; title-holding (adj.), title-winning (adj.); title page.

title 2, II, A lowercase; BUT *Title 2,* when part of title: *Title 2: General Provisions.*

titled Use *entitled.* BUT: *a well-titled novel, a titled family.*

TITLES Capitalize principal words. The rule applies to titles of: acts, addresses, articles, books, captions, chapter and part headings, documents, editorials, essays, headings, headlines, motion pictures and plays (including TV and radio programs), papers, pamphlets, performance pieces, short poems, reports (not annual reports), songs, subheadings, subjects, laws, treaties, and themes.

In printing, titles are set in italics for books, essays, plays, motion pictures, symphonies, operas, pamphlets, published documents, newspapers, magazines, and collections of paper; BUT NOT in long lists of these. *N.Y. Times* places these titles in quotation marks.

Cap. both parts of compound words: *Record of First-Class Merchants Club.*

Also cap. titles of heads of state, governmental units, members of the diplomatic corps, princes and rulers. BUT NOT officers of the armed forces, professors, corporate officers, or nonofficial titles.

Hyphenate a double title, but not a civil or military title denoting a single office: *ambassador at large. sergeant at arms.* BUT: *secretary-treasurer.*

Abbreviate a civil, military, or naval title and honorable, reverend, monsignor, mister, mistress, messieurs when followed by a Christian name or initial: *Lt. A.B. White; Insp. Gen. Black.*

Italicize the titles of legal cases (except the verb), BUT NOT titles of legal reports: *John Doe v. Richard Roe.* See *CAPITALIZATION.*

The capitalization of the titles of books, etc., written in a foreign language conform to national practice in that language: *Cien anos de soledad (100 Years of Solitude).*

title search examination of records to determine ownership of property.

titular [TIHT-yoo-lahr] of a title; in name only.

t.m. (abbr.) true mean.

T-man treasury investigator.

T.N.T. (abbr.) trinitrotoluol, or trimtrotolouene.

today, tomorrow, tonight; to-and-fro, to-do (n.); to wit.

-to lean-to, stand-to, etc.

tobacco (pl.) —s.

tobacco-growing (adj.); tobacco shop.

Tabago. See **Trinidad and Tobago**.

Tocqueville, de, Alexis [duh-TAWK-vehl, ah-LEHK-see]. (1805-1859) Fr. writer (*Democracy in America*), statesman.

tocsin [TAHK-sihn] alarm.

TOXIN poison. (adj.) -ic.

toffee a candy; NOT *taffy*.

tofu [TOH-foo] (Jap.) protein-rich bean curd.

toga flowing wrap worn in Imperial Rome.

Togo [TOH-goh] nation on SW coast of Africa. Formerly Fr. independent, 1960. Cap.: Lomé [loh-MAE]. Native: Togolese. Currency: CFA franc.

toilet [TOI-leht] Formal use allows *bathroom, restroom, lavatory.* Other terms, colloq. but not obscene, include *can, head* (naval jargon), *john, W.C.* (for water closet).

toilette [twah-leht] lady's bath, hairdressing, and other preparations for public appearance.

Tokyo [TOH-kyoh] capital city of Japan.

tolerance allowable deviation from the standard specification in a manufacture.

tolerant *of* or *towards*.

toll Take a toll; inflict a toll; suffer a toll. NOT *have*.

tollhouse, —keeper, —master, —payer, —taker (all one word); toll bridge, toll line, toll road.

tomato [toh-MAE-toh, -MAH-] (pl.) —oes.

tomb Grant's Tomb, the tomb; Tomb

of the Unknown Soldier, Unknown Soldier's Tomb, the tomb. See also **Unknown Soldier.**

tombstone, tomb-strewn.

ton (not abbreviated.) unit of weight: (1) U.S. = 2000 lbs. avoirdupois = 907.2 kilograms; (2) Brit., gross or long ton = 2240 lbs. = 1016 kilograms; (3) displacement ton, unit for ship size measurement = 35 cu. ft. = volume of 1 long ton of water; (4) measurement ton, unit for ship charges = 40 cu. ft. = vol. use of 1 long ton of average cargo; (5) metric ton = 1000 kilograms = 2,204.6 lbs. avoirdupois; (6) registered ton, a unit of ship measurement = 100 cu. ft. of internal space.

The adj. is always sing: *three-ton load.* (pl.) —s.

Tonga [TAHN-guh] island nation in SW Pacific. Formerly Br. independent, 1970. Cap.: Nuku'alofa [NOO-kuh-wuh-LAW-fuh]. Native: Tongan. Currency: Pa'anga.

tongs. See **scissors.**

tonguetied, tonguelash, tongueshaped, tonguetwisted, tonguetwisting, tongue twister, tonguetwister.

tonsil (pl.) —s. Also tonsillitis: inflammation of the tonsils; tonsillectomy: removal of the tonsils.

tonsorial of a barber or barbering.

too When *too* qualifies a following adj. or adv. it means "more than is desirable:" *too big, too slowly.* BUT

never use with a comparative or superlative form.

When used to mean "in excess," use only as an intensive. *He was only too happy to join us.* BUT avoid use without *only.* NOT: *It was too wonderful.*

too much Usage allows *too much,* meaning "very" to modify a verb: *Too much concerned with;* NOT: *too concerned with.* Watch, esp., use with negative adverbs. See **very.**

topmost

topography [tah-PAH-gra-fee] physical features of an area.

TOPOLOGY algebra used for measuring surfaces.

topsy-turvy

Topsy fictional character who "jes' grew."

Torah [TOH-rah] in Judaism, first five books of **Bible** (the **Pentateuch**). In broader sense, divine law and its interpretation. See **Talmud.**

torchbearer, —light, —lighted, —lit; torch song.

torment —ntor, —inter.

tornado [tawr-NAE-doh] (pl.) —oes, os.

torpedo (pl.) —oes.

torpor [TAW-pehr] suspended animation; sluggishness.

torque [tawrk] rotational force. Instrument: torquemeter.

Torquemada, Tomás de [taw-kae-MAH-dah, toh-MAHS] (1420-1498) Sp. inquisitor; famous as torturer.

tort [twart] in law, a private, actionable injury, such as vehicular negligence or libel.

tortilla [tawr-TEE-uyh] thin, unleavened flat cakes.

tortoise [TAWR-tuhs], tortoiseshell.

tortuous [TAWR-tyoo-uhs] twisting or winding. *The road followed a tortuous course.*

> TORTUROUS [TAWRT-yoor-uhs] (from torture). *The barbarians employed torturous rituals.*

> TORTIOUS involving a tort.

Toscannini, Arturo [TOHS-kah-nee-nee, ahr-TOO-roh] (1867-1957) It. conductor.

toss (p. and p.p.) tossed.

tosspot, tossup, toss-up, (n. and adj.).

total —ize, —ity, —ed, —ing, —ly. AVOID *a total of* except as a device to avoid beginning a sentence with a number.

total effect of all is redundant.

totalitarian [toh-tal-ih-TAIR-ee-uhn] pertaining to an oppressive centralized government; "total" in that it exerts total control.

totally destroyed AVOID, redundant.

totem Can refer either to icon (*totem pole*) or to animal-spirit. *The wolf was his totem.*

touché (n.) hit, esp. at sensitive spot.

Toulouse-Lautrec, de, Henri [too-LOOZ loh-TREHK] (1864-1900) Fr. painter, famous for paintings of "can-can" dancers.

toupée [too-PAE]. Pl. -s. A small wig.

tour de force [(Fr.) anglicized as tawr-dih-FOWRS] feat of strength, skill, ingenuity.

tourney [TOOR-nee].

tourniquet [TOOR-nih—keht] noun only: *apply a tourniquet.*

tousle [TOU-z'l] —led, —sling.

toward [(adj.) TOH-ahrd; (prep.) tohrd]. Usage allows more formal *towards* for prep.

towboat, towline, towrope; towheaded, tow car.

toweled —ing.

tower Cap. if part of name: the Eiffel Tower.

townfolk, —gate, —house, —ship, —site, town-bred (adj.); town clerk, town crier, town hall, town meeting.

townsboy, —fellow, —man, —people.

township Cap. if part of name: Township of Union.

toxemia

toxin See **tocsin**.

trace (v.); —ceable (adj.).

trachea [TRAE-kee-uh] Windpipe. (pl.) —eae [-ee].

trademark, trade-in, trade-off, (n. and adj.); trade fair, trade name, trade school, trade union, trade wind.

tradesfold, —people.

trade union (pl.) trade unions.

trade wind a dry wind, easterly near the equator.

trading stamp a stamp redeemable for merchandise.

traduce (v.) to slander; defame. (adj.) —cible.

traffic —icked, —icking, —icker.

trafficway, traffic-mile.

tragedian [tra-JEE-dee-uhn] writer or actor of tragedy.

tragedy Applies to all art, not just drama. When referring to life, usu. applies in the borader sense: *a tragic figure* or *a tragic existence*. For a particular person or instance, use *bad luck, misfortune, setback, disaster, calamity,* etc.

TRAGIC (adj.) Pref. to tragical.

TRAGICO-, TRAGI- combining form meaning tragedy: *tragicomical, tragical, tragicomedy, tragicomic.*

trailblazer, —blazing, —breaker, —side, —site, (all one word); trail-marked, trail-weary; trail head.

training camp, training ship

traipse [traeps] to trudge. Spelling pref. to *trapse.*

trait [traet] characteristic; peculiarity.

traitor (n.); —torous (adj.).

Trajan [TRAE-jan] (c. A.D. 53-117) benevolent Roman ruler, 98-117; oversaw empire's farthest expansion.

tramcar, —line, —load, —man, —rail, —way, —wayman, —yard.

trammeled —ing.

tranquil (adj.); —ize (v.). tranquility (n.).

transcendental (adj.) visionary, beyond experience. Cap., describes writings of 19th-C. Americans like Emerson and **Thoreau**. Also, Transcendentalist. See **Romanticism**.

transfer, —ferred, —ferring, —ferrer, —ferable, —ference; —feree (who receives). In law, —feror (who conveys).

transfuse [trans-FYOOZ] (v.) to pour, transfer: *transfuse blood.* (adj.) —sible.

transgress [trans-GREHS] (v.) to go

beyond limits; esp., break the law. (n.) —essor.

transient (n.) someone or something passing through. (adj.) transitory.

TRANSITIVE VERBS verbs that require a direct object. *Hit the ball! He put his gun away.* See *INTRANSITIVE VERBS, VERBS.*

translate to reproduce meaning.

> TRANSLITERATE to reproduce sounds in a different alphabet.

> CONSTRUE [kuhn-STROO] to understand or explain the gist. *Rereading his note, I construed him to mean the woman was gone.* Also, to show grammatical structure, esp. of something that requires translation.

translucent —cence, —cency, —cently, See **transparent**.

transmit to send from one person or place to another. Destination should be indicated, NOT merely implied. *He sent the letter. He transmitted the letter to Dr. B.*
> —mitted, —mitting, —mittance, —mitter, —missible, —mittible.

transom crosspiece over door. Hence, the window above.

transparency Preferred to —ce.

transparent able to be seen through: *transparent glass.*

> DIAPHANOUS [die-A-fuh-nuhs] fine-textured, translucent, but not perfectly transparent: *diaphonous chiffon.*

PELLUCID [peh-LOO-sihd] clear, easy to understand: *pellucid logic.* Opposite of **turbid**.

TRANSLUCENT diffusing light so objects cannot be seen clearly: *translucent tortoiseshell.*

transpire (v.) Commonly means occur, and implies previous secrecy. *It transpired that he had looted the pension fund.* Also means exhale.

transplant (n.) (pl.) tranplants. (v.) —ted, —ting.

transpose (v.) to change in order. (n.) —sition; this form pref. to *transposal.*

trapezoid four-sided polygon. (pl.) —s.

trauma [TRAW-mah] (Gr.) a wound or blow, esp. psychological. (adj.) traumatic.

travail [TRA-vael] (v.) to toil, esp. with great effort. (n.) painful or laborious work.

travel [TRA-vehl] —led, —ler, —ing.

travelogue or **travelog**

travesty ludicrous distortion; usu. literary or artistic in nature.

trawl boat, —net.

trayful (pl.) —fuls.

treacle [TREE-kl] molasses; old remedy against poison.

tread (p.) trod; (p.p.) trodden; (pres.

p.) treading, NOT *trodding.*

treadboard, —mill.

treasurer the Assistant Treasurer, BUT assistant treasurer of New York, etc.

Treasury of the United States. General Treasury, National, Public; Treasury notes, the treasury.

treaty Cap. if part of name: Jay Treaty, North Atlantic Treaty, Treaty of Versailles; the treaty. BUT treaty of 1919.

treaty bound

treble [TREH-b'l] triple; in music, highpitched. (adv.) —bly.

trecento [trae-CHEHN-toh] (It.) the 1300s. In art, 1300-1399; guattrocento, 1400-1499; cinquecento, 1500-1599.

trek —kked, —kking.

trellis (n. and v.). —ed; trellis-work, trellis-covered (adj.).

tremendous. See **strong opinion words.**

tremolo (pl.) —os.

tremor [TREH-mer].

trepan [tree-PAN] In surgery, to saw through skull. —nned, —nning.

trespass (n. pl.) trespassers. (v., pres. part.) —ing.

triad [TRIE-ad] related group of

three; trinity. See **groups.**

trial [TRIE-'L] a test; a formal civil or criminal examination.

TRAIL [TRAEL] a path.

tribesman, —people.

tribunal [trie-BYOO-nal] court.

tribunal Cap. standing alone only in specific, offical reports; also High Tribunal, the Tribunal (Supreme Court).

tricentenary Use *tercentenary.*

triceps (sing. and pl.).

Tricolore or **Tricolor** the French flag.

trillion 1000 billion in U.S. and France; 1 million billion in Britain and Germany. See *NUMBERS.*

trillium [TRIH-lee-uhm] purple woods flower.

trilogy in lit. and music, three associated works by same author.

trimester [trie-MEH-stehr, TRIE-meh-] period broken into three parts, esp. a woman's pregnancy or a school year.

Trinidad and Tobago [TRIH-nih-dad, toh-BAE-goh] island nation off coast of Venezuala. Formerly Br.; independent, 1962. Cap.: Port-of-Spain. Natives: Trinidadian(s), Tobagan(s). Currency: dollar.

Trinity In Christianity, God the Father, God the Son, and God the Holy Spirit.

tripartite [trie-PAHR-tiet; TRIHP-uhr-tiet] (adj.) divided into three parts. Also, tripartible.

Triple A name for any group abbreviated with 3 A's: American Automobile Association.

tripod [TRIE-pohd] a stand with three legs.

triptych [TRIHP-tihk] three-part folded picture.

trireme [TRIE-reem] Ancient galley. See **boat**.

Tristan und Isolde [TRIH-stahn oond ee-SAWL-deh] epic Ger. love story, 1856 Richard Wagner opera.

triumphal [trie-UHM-f'l] (adj.) in celebration of victory.

TRIUMPHANT [—fuhnt] victorious, exultant.

triumvirate [trie-UHM-vihr-eht] a rule of three officials; originally during Roman Republic. (pl.) —s. (adj.) triumviral.

trivia [TRIHV-ih-uh] Appears in plural form only.

troche [TROH-kee] medicinal lozenge.

TROCHEE [TROH-kee] poetic foot with one long, one short beat. See **scansion**.

troika [TROI-kah] (Rus.) "three." Russian cart drawn by three horses; hence, any ruling group of three.

trolleycar, trolleybus; trolley line.

trompe l'oeil [TR(h)AHMP loi] (Fr.) "trick the eye." In painting, representation that somehow fools the viewer.

troop a company, especially military.

TROUPE a company of actors.

trope [TROHP] figure of speech in which words are used in unusual sense. *Two incipient chandeliers hung from her ears.* Suggests trickery over meaning. *That sounds profound, but it's merely a clever trope.*

tropical neotropical, subtropical; the Tropics of Cancer, Capricorn.

Tropic of Cancer area from the Equator to 23° 27′ N lat.

Tropic of Capricorn area from the Equator to 23° 27′ S lat.

troposphere lowest layer of **atmosphere**.

Trotsky, Leon [TRAWTS-kih] Born Lev Davydovich Bronstein. (1877-1940) Russian Communist revolutionary, theoretician. Worked with **Lenin**, assassinated on **Stalin's** order.

troubadour [TROO-buh-dawr] lyric singer, 11th-13th C.

troublemaker —making, —proof, —shooting, —some (all one word); trouble-free (adj.), trouble-shooter (n.).

trounce [trounss] to thrash —ced, —cing, —ceable.

trousseau [troo-SOH, TRR-soh] bride's personal clothes and accessories. (pl.) —eaux or —eaus.

trout (sing. and pl.).

troweled —ing.

troy weight system of measurement for precious stones and metals. 5760 grains = 1 lb. = 12 oz. = 240 penny-weights.

trucebreaker, truce-seeking.

truculent [TRUHK-yoo-lehnt] (adj.) fierce; savage (adv.) —ly. (n.) truculence, —lency.

true facts is a tautology.

Truffaut, François [troo-FOH, fran-SWAH] (1932-1984) Fr. film maker (*The 400 Blows*), actor.

Trujillo Molina, Rafael [troo-HEE-yoh moh-LEE-nah, rah-fah-EHL] (1891-1967) Dominican Republic dictator, general. Symbol of dictatorial excess.

truly

truncheon [TRUHN-ch'n] a short stick, esp. policeman's. Orig., low-wheeled cart.

trundle [TRUHN-d'l] (v.) to move laboriously. *The children trundled off the bed.*

> TRUNDLE BED. On wheels, fits under adult bed.

trunkful (pl.) —fulls.

trust

BENEFICIAL TRUST Trustee is a beneficiary.

CONSTRUCTIVE TRUST a trust created without a formal writing, implied in a situation and declared a trust by a court.

INTER VIVOS TRUST [IHN-tehr VEE-vohs] "between living persons." Living trust; a gift from one person to another.

LIVING TRUST voluntary trust created without consideration, usually for a person's support.

trust terrritory See **Territory**.

tryst [trihst] meeting, esp. of lovers.

tsar [(t)zahr]. See **czar**.

Tschaikovsky, Peter. See **Tchaikovsky**.

tsetse [TSEH-tsih] fly that carries sleeping sickness.

T. Sgt. (abbr.) technical sergeant.

tsp. (abbr.) teaspoonful(s).

T-square. See **tee shirt**.

tsunami [tsoo-NAH-mee] tidal wave.

tuberculosis [too-BUHR-kyoo-loh-sihs] lung disease.

tuber [TOO-buhr] (n.) any fleshy root, like potatos. (adj.) —ous.

tubful (pl.) —s.

Tuesday [TOOZ-dih] abbr.: Tues.

tugboat, —boatman; tug of war.

Tuileries [TWEE-luhr-eez] garden and park in Paris.

tulle [tool] a fine net for veils.

tumbrel or **tumbril** [TUHM-br'l] (from French Reign of Terror) cart carrying prisoners to execution.

tumescence [too-MEH-sehns] swollenness, esp. of sex organs. (adj.) tumescent, opposite of detumescent.

tumor [TOO-mehr] May be benign or, if cancerous, malignant.

tumultuous [tum-MUHL-too-uhs] *tumultuous applause, tumultuous seas.* NOT *tumultus.*

tun large wine cask; unit of capacity measure = 252 wine gallons = 953.9 1 tun = 2 pipes = 8 bbls.

tuna, tunafish; tuna oil.

tundra [TUHN-drah] artic plain.

tungsten [TUHNG-stehn] metal filament in electric lamps.

Tunisia [tyoo-NEEZ-ih-ah] country in Mediterranean Africa. Formerly Fr., independent, 1956. Cap.: Tunis [TOO-nihs]. Native: Tunisian(s). Currency:dinar.

tunnel (v.) —led, —ling; tunneler (n.).

tunnel Cap. if part of name: Lincoln Tunnel, the tunnel. BUT lowercase irrigation tunnel, railroad tunnel etc.; tunnel no. 1.

turbid confused, muddy. (n.) turbidness is perf. to —ity.

turbine [TUHRB-bin pref. to -bien] rotary engine driven by fluid (esp. water), or by teated air, as in a jet.

tureen [tuh-REEN; too-REEN] soup serving-bowl.

turf (pl.) —s.

Turgenev, Ivan Sergeevich [toor-GEHN-yehf, ee-VAHN] (1818-1883) Russian novelist (*Fathers and Sons*).

turgid swollen; vainly ostentatious. See **turbid.**

Turkestan, -istan [tuhr-keh-STAN] Central Asian region, including parts of former U.S.S.R., China, and Afghanistan.

Turkmenistan [tuhr-MEHN-ih-stan] republic in former **U.S.S.R**; part of **Commonwealth of Independent States**, 1992. In S Central Asia, bordering Iran. Cap.: Ashkabad [ASH-kuh-bad]. Native, Turkemeni(s).

Turkey country between Aegean Sea and Black Sea; empire in Middle Ages. Cap.: Ankara [an-KAH-rah]. Native: Turk(s), Turkish. Currency: lira.

turnover (n.); verb compound is *turn over.*

turquoise [TUHR-kwoiz] blue-green color; semi-precious stone.

AQUAMARINE more green than blue.

turret a little tower. (adj.) —eted.

Tutankhamen [toot-ahngk-AH-mehn] (c. 1358 B.C.) boy-king of Egypt; tomb discovered untouched, 1922.

Tuvalu [TOO-vah-loo] tiny island nation in SW Pacific. A/k/a/ Ellice Islands, formerly Br.; independent, 1978. Cap.: Funafuti [FOO-nah-foo-tih]. Native: Tuvaluan. Currency: Australian dollar.

TV (abbr.) television. NOT: T.V.

T.V.A. (abbr.) Tennessee Valley Authority.

twelfth (pl.) **-s.**

twenties See *NUMBERS*.

twentyfold, —penny (nail); twenty-first, twenty-one.

twice-born (adj.); twicetold (adj.)

twilit Preferred to —*lighted.*

twinborn twin-engined, twin-jet, twin-motor, twin-screw (adj.); twin boat, twin ship (n.).

Twin Cities Minneapolis and St. Paul, Minnesota.

twins A pair of twins is four people.

two (pl.) twos.

twofold, two-penny (nail), two-score, twoseater, twosome; two-a-day (n. or adj.), two-decker (n. or adj.), two-faced, -fisted, -piece, -ply, -way (all adj.); two-party system, two-

spot (n.), two-step (dance), two-wheeler (n.).

TX Texas

tying

tyke a dog, (colloq.) a boy. Pref. to *tike.*

tympani kettle drum. (adj.) tympanic. One who plays the instrument is a *tympanist.*

tympanum [TIHM-puh-nuhn] Ear drum. (pl.) —s.

type *O-type blood.* BUT NOT *intellectual-type person.* BETTER: *intellectual type of person;* or *the intellectual type.*

typecast —casting, —cutter, —cutting, —face, —script, —set, —setter, —write, —writer; type metal, type page.

type size System based on 72 points = 1 inch. Type faces are manufactured in 5, 5 and 1/2, 6, 7, 8, 9, 10, 11, 12, 14, 16, 18, 24, 30, 36, 42, 48, 60, and 72 points. 1 pica = 12 points = 2 nonpareils.

typhoid fever *typhus* is another name for same disease.

typhoon tropical seaborne cyclone.

typhus. See **typhoid fever.**

typify [TIH-pih-fie] (v.) to embody characteristics of. —fied, —fying.

tyranny [TIH-rah-nee] Despotism. (n.) tyrant: despot. (adj.) tyrannical.

tyro [TIE-ruh] beginner. (pl.) —s.   **tzar** See **czar** (pref.).

U

U Symbol for uranium.

U-2 or U2. U.S. spy plane.

U-boat, U-cut, U-magnet, U-rail, U-shaped, U-tube.

U.A.R. United Arab Republic, a/k/a/ Egypt.

U.A.W. (abbr.) United Auto Workers.

Ubangi [yoo-BANG-(g)ee] Name of River, people in central Africa.

ubiquitous [yoo-BIHK-wih-tuhs] (adj.) everywhere.

u.c. (abbr.) uppercase, capital letters. See l.c., lowercase.

Uccello, Paolo [oo-CHEH-loh, PAH-OH-loh] (1397-1475) Florentine painter.

U.C.M.S. (abbr.) University of Chicago Manual of Style. Also referred to as C.M.S., Chicago. Manual of style.

Uganda [yoo-GAN-duh] landlocked African nation west of Kenya. Formerly Br.; independent, 1962. Cap.: Entebbe [ehn-TEHB-beh] Currency: shilling.

U.H.F. (abbr.) ultra-high frequency.

ukase [yoo-KAES] (arch.) official decree.

Ukraine [yoo-KRAEN] republic in former U.S.S.R., part of Common-wealth of Independent States, 1992. In E central Europe on Black Sea, famous for farming. Cap.: Kiev [kee-EHV]. Native: Ukrainian.

ukulele [YOO-kuh-LAE-lee] small guitar, usu. associated with Hawaiian music.

ulna inner of forearm bones. (pl.) — nae.

ultimate [UHL-tih-miht] (from Latin, "last".) Adjective means unsurpassable, best. *Climbing Everest is the ultimate challenge.* Noun is colloq.: *Man, she's the ultimate.*

  ULTIMATUM [uhl-tih-MAE-tehm] final offer or condition.

ultra- prefix meaning beyond, excessively. Usu. in one word except preceding a vowel: *ultra-ambitious, ultra-exclusive, ultra-high-speed (adj.); ultramodern, ultrareligious (adj.).*

ultra-high frequency (abbr.: U.H.F.) radio or television range 30 to 300 megacycles.

ultraviolet light Also called "black light;" causes radiation damage.

ululate [OOL-yoo-laet] (v.) to howl. —lated, —lating, —lation.

Ulysses [yoo-LIH-sees] Romanizing of Gr. Odysseus, hero of Odyssey. Also, 1922 novel by James Joyce.

umber brown.

umbilicus [um-BIHL-ih-kuhs] navel. (pl.) —ci.

umbrage [UHM-brihj] shadow; resentment.

umlaut [OOM-lout] two dots over a vowel to indicate pronunication change caused by another vowel in the same syllable, esp. in German: ä, ö, or ü. See **DIACRITICAL MARKS.**

un- prefix meaning not: un-American, uncalled-for, unheard-of, unlooked-for, un-ionized, unselfconscious, unsent-for, unthought-of, ununiformity, unaided, unbearable. See **in-.**

U.N. (abbr.) United Nations.

unable not able; not usu. incapable.

INCAPABLE lacking capacity. *She is unable to come because she has guests; he is simply incapable of finding this place by himself.*

unadmissible INCORRECT; use *inadmissible.*

unanimous [yoo-NAN-ih-muhs] with consent of all. Never *more* or *most* unanimous.

unappeasable implacable.

unapt not likely to; unsuitable.
    INEPT backward, lacking skill.

unartistic not interested in art.
    INARTISTIC not a work of art.

unauspicious *Inauspicious* is pref.

unaware (adj.) ignorant, not know-

ing. *They were unaware of his presence.*

UNAWARES (adj.) without preparation, suddenly. *The troops moved forward unaware of their objective: they came upon the enemy unawares.*

unbeliever one who does not believe, esp. in Islam.

unbeknownst [uhn-bee-NOHNST] AVOID.

unbiased [uhn-BIE-uhsd] unprejudiced.

unceasing (adj.) incessant, continuous. (adv.) —ly.

uncertainty principle in physics, effect of observation on nuclear particles; exact velocity and location are impossible to ascertain. Discovered 1927 by Ger. physicist Werner Heisenberg.

uncomparable cannot be compared. *Pens and mice are uncomparable.* AVOID; awkward.

INCOMPARABLE [ihn-KAHMP-rabl] unequalled, *An incomparable athelete.* Pref. to *uncomparable.*

unconscious In psychology, a noun: *the unconscious.*

unconscionable [uhn-KAHN-shuhn-uh-b'l] (adj.) without conscience.

uncontrollable Pref. to *in-.*

uncorruptible *Incorruptible* pref.

unctuous [UHNG-choo-uhs] oily;

hence, falsely ingratiating.

undependable

under, underneath See **below.**

underage [UHN-deh-ehj] (n.) (rare) deficit.

    UNDERAGE   [uhn-dehr-AEJ] (adj.) not old enough.

underground Implies anti-establishment, subversive.

under secretary (pl.) under secretaries.

under secretary Cap. if federal officer: the Under Secretary of Agriculture, of State, of the Treasury.

Under Secretary of State ADDRESS: The Under Secretary of State, Washington, D.C.; or The Honorable David K. Bruce, Under Secretary of State. SALUTATION: Sir; Dear Sir; Dear Mr. Bruce.

under the counter (adj.) surreptitious.

underwrite agree to accept the risk, as in insurance and security flotations.

undigested (adj.); BUT *indigestion.* (n.).

undisciplined Pref. to *in-.*

undiscriminating not discriminating, esp. in art; usu. applies to abstractions: *undiscriminating tastes.*

    INDISCRIMINATE showing no sense of discrimination; usu. ap-

plies to actions: *indiscriminate spending.*

undisposed Not disposed of. See **indisposed.**

undissolvable *Indissoluable* pref.

undistinguishable *In-* is pref.; BUT undistinguished.

undue Avoid double negative. NOT: *no need for undue fear.*

uneconomical bad for business. Pref. to *uneconomic.*

unequaled, unequalled

unescapable *in-* Pref.

UNESCO (abbr., no points) United Nations Educational, Scientific, and Cultural Organization. Sometimes Unesco.

unessential *In-* is pref. See **essential.**

unexhaustible *In-* is pref.

unexpressible *In-* is pref.

unfrequented [uhn-free-KWEHNT-ehd] Not infrequented. BUT infrequent. *The bar remains unfrequented, but my infrequent visitors speak of it fondly.*

unguent [UHNG-gwehnt] salve; ointment.

unhuman not a human being.

    INHUMAN lacking in civilized human behavior.

uni- Prefix meaning one: *united, uniform, universal.*

UNICEF (abbr., no points) United Nations Children's Fund. (*International* and *Emergency* have been dropped from the name, but not from the acronym.) Sometimes Unicef.

Uniform Code of Military Justice See **code.**

unimproved property property in the natural state, with no construction, sewers, sidewalks, or other development.

unintelligible [uhn-ihn-TEHL-ih-jih-b'l].

union Cap. if part of proper name; cap. standing alone if synonym for United States or for an international unit: European Payments Union, the Union; International Typographical Union, the Typographical Union, the union; Pan American Union; Union Station; Teamsters Union, the Teamsters, the union; Universal Postal Union, the union; Western Union; Woman's Christian Temperance Union. BUT: a painters union, printers union.

un-ionized Not ionized.

Union of South Africa name for **South Africa** while a British protectorate, 1910-1961.

Union of Soviet Socialist Republics (abbr.: U.S.S.R.) 20th C. name for huge Eurasian nation, begun in Middle Ages. Cap.: Moscow. Native: Russian(s), Soviet(s). Currency: ruble.

Empire of **Russia**, under **czar**, till Russian Revolution of 1917; Communist state till 1992. Dissolved to become **Commonwealth of Independent States.**

See also the 12 republics: **Armenia, Azerbaijan, Byelorussia, Georgia, Kazakhstan, Kirghizia, Russia, Tadzhikistan, Turkmenistan, Ukraine, Uzbekistan.**

See also **Gorbachev, Lenin, Stalin.**

RUSSIA Ancient name for **U.S.S.R.**, still a general reference; also name of the largest Commonwealth state.

SOVIET Cap. if part of name; cap. standing alone if referring to central governmental unit: Soviet Government, BUT Communist government; Moscow Soviet, National Soviet, Soviet of Labor and Defense. BUT a soviet (meaning council).

Union Jack See **flags, foreign.**

unionman, union-made, union card, union shop.

unique technically, the only one of its kind. Colloq. usage allows sense of "rare:" *rather, more, most,* or *somewhat unique.* (*Webster's* lists *rare* as a synonym).

BUT *almost, truly, certainly, perhaps,* or *in many ways unique* are strictly correct: *truly one of a kind.*

unit Cap. if a federal or state branch: Alcohol Tax Unit, Income Tax Unit, the Unit; BUT Pasco unit.

Unitarian [yoo-nih-TAR-ee-an] Protestant church founded 16th C., esp. popular in New England (U.S.).

United Arab Emirates nation on S shore of Persian Gulf. Formerly Brit.; unified and independent, 1921. Cap.: Abu Dhabi [AH-boo DAH-bee]. Native: Arab. Currency: dirham.

United Arab Republic (abbr.: U.A.R.) Union of **Syria** and **Egypt**, 1958-1961; **Egypt** retained name till 1971.

United Kingdom (abbr.: U.K.) Formal name for **Great Britain**, island country off NW Europe. Since 17th C. composed of **England, Scotland**, Wales, and Northern **Ireland**. Cap.: London. Native: English, British. Currency: pound (£).

United Nations United Nations Charter, the charter; United Nations Children's Fund (UNICEF), the Fund; United Nations Conference on International Organization, the Conference; United Nations Economic and Social Council, the Council; United Nations Educational, Scientific, and Cultural Organization (UNESCO); United Nations General Assembly, the Assembly; United Nations International Court of Justice, the Court; United Nations International Labor Organization; United Nations Assembly, the Assembly; United Nations Permanent Court of Arbitration; Secretary General of the United Nations; United Nations Security Council, the Council; United Nations Trusteeship Council, the Council, World Health Organization (WHO), the Organization.

See also **court, organization.**

United States (abbr.: U.S.) Takes singular verb.

United States Cap. Republic, Nation, Union, Government only in specialized use; BUT Federal usu. cap.

United States of America (abbr.: U.S.A.) Since 1776. Cap.: Washington, D.C. Native: American(s). Currency: dollar. See **American, United States.**

unit fraction, unit price.

units of measure When a number appears with a plural noun as a unit of measurement (fractions, money, time, etc.) use singular verb EXCEPT when the term is considered to be made of individual parts. *Here is $20. Here are two tens.*

unity, dramatic In *Poetics* of **Aristotle,** good drama observes three unities: time, place, and (a more complex matter) appropriateness of the action.

university Cap. part of name: Stanford University, the university. See **college.**

unknown quantities are represented by lower case letters, usu. italicized; *(a + b)/c.* BUT NOT abbreviations or representations of persons' names: *A sold B two items.*

Unknown Soldier Unknown Soldier of World War II, World War II Unknown Soldier; the Unknowns. See also **tomb.**

unlearned

unlisted security security not traded on a registered securities exchange.

unmaterial *Immaterial* is pref. for all meanings.

unmoral See **amoral.**

unnavigable

unparalleled

unpractical *Impractical* is pref.

unquiet

unredeemed

unresponsible not responsible (implies no blame).

    IRRESPONSIBLE unwilling to assume responsibility (implies blame).

unsanitary lacks sanitation (implies no blame).

    INSANITARY Implies dangerous neglect. *It's an unsanitary job, but you don't work under insanitary conditions.*

unsolvable Not capable of being solved.

unstable [uhn-STAE-b'l] (adj.); instablility (n.).

unsusceptible

until See **till** (note double *l*). AVOID *until such time as.*

untoward [uhn-TOH-uhrd] Perverse; awkward; inconvenient.

unwieldy [uhn-WEEL-dee] unmanageable. unwieldiness.

Upanishads [yoo-PAN-ih-shads] ancient Hindu scriptures (c. 1000-600 B.C.). See **Vedas.**

upbeat (n. and adj.); upcountry (adv. and adj.); upend, upgrade (v.); upgrading, upkeep (n.); upstairs, upstate, upstream (adj. and adv.); upswing, uptake, uptown (adj. and adv.); upturn (n.); up-and-coming, up-over (adj.), up-river, up-tend, up-to-date or up to date (adj.); up anchor (command), up and up, up oars.

upon, on *On* is pref. to avoid two unaccented syllables; *upon* is pref. at the end of a sentence.

Upper Cap. if part of name: Upper Colorado River Basin, Upper Egypt, Upper Peninsula; BUT upper House of Congress.

uppercase (n.) in printing, capital letters. (adj., v.) uppercased.

upperclassman, uppermost; upper crust, upper class, upper deck, upper hand.

Upper Volta [VAHL-tuh] See **Burkina Faso.**

upward(s) See **backwards.**

upwards of Means "more than;" AVOID.

uranium 235 BUT U^{235}, Sr^{90}; $92U^{234}$.

Uranus [YOOR-uh-nahs] the planet.

URANOUS containing uranium.

urban characteristic of or pertaining to a city.

URBANE suave. *Her urbane manner and sophisticated clothes impressed the naive visitor.*

uremia [uh-REE-mih-uh] toxic condition caused by insufficient urine secretion.

ureter [yoo-REE-tuhr] duct from kidney to bladder.

URETHRA duct that carries urine from the bladder.

urethane [you-REH-thaen] foam plastic.

urinalysis [yoo-ruh-NAH-lih-sihs] analysis of urine, esp. to detect drug use.

Uruguay [OO-ruh-gwie, -gwae] South American country, on S Atlantic coast. Cap.: Montevideo [mahn-tih-vih-DAE-oh] Native: Uruguayan(s). Currency: peso.

us (objective); we (nominative). *They know as much as we* (know); or . . . *more than we. We Americans can join . . . Let us join.* BUT formal grammatical rules may be breached in this respect in conversation.

U.S.A. (abbr.) United States of American. Also, U.S. Army.

U.S.A.F. (abbr.) U.S. Air Force.

usage In grammer, customary practice.

U.S.C.G. (abbr.) U.S. Coast Guard.

U.S. Congress

use As a noun: *Put this to good use. Sorry, that's not for use.*

U.S.I.A. (abbr.) U.S. Information Agency.

U.S.M.C. (abbr.) U.S. Marine Corps.

U.S.N. (abbr.) U.S. Navy.

U.S.-owned

U.S.S. (abbr.) U.S. Senate; U.S. ship.

U.S.S.R. (abbr.) Union of Soviet Socialist Republics.

usually Place immediately before or after verb. *She's usually in bed by nine. We usually wait another hour.*

usurp [yoo-ZUHRP] (v.) to sieze without right.   ed,   ing.

usury [YOO-zhyoor-ree] (n.) the charging of illegally high interest. Hence, any greedy and unfair dealings (adj.). usurious [yoo-ZHOOR-ee-uhs]

UT Utah.

Utah [YOO-taw] (abbr.: UT.) Cap.: Salt Lake City. Native: Utahan.

uterus (n.); uterine (adj.).

U Thant See **Thant, U.**

utilize *Use* is pref.

utmost Pref. to *uttermost.*

Utopia [yoo-TOH-pee-ah] (From Gr., "no place;" title of 1516 book by Thomas More.) Perfect society. (adj.) utopian.

uxorious [uhks-OH-rih-uhs] flattery and submissiveness, esp. to a wife.

Uzbekistan [uhz-BEHK-ih-stahn] republic in former **U.S.S.R.**; part of **Commonwealth of Independent States,** 1992. In S Central Asia, by Aral Sea. Cap.: Tashkent [tahsh-KEHNT]. Native: Uzbek(s).

V

v. (abbr.) versus, against. Esp. in law: *the case of Roe v. Wade.*

v. (abbr.) verb; volt.

V-1, V-2 airborne weapons developed by Germans at end of W.W. II. V-1 was "Buzz Bomb," V-2 first true missile.

V-boat, V-curve, V-8, V-neck, V-shaped, V-type.

VA (abbr.) Virginia.

V.A. (abbr.) Veterans Administration.

vacation See **holidays.**

vaccine [VAK-seen] (n.) substance for preventive innoculation. (v.) vaccinate. (n.) vaccination: the act of vaccinating.

vacillate [VASLih-laet] to waver.

vacuous [VAAK-yoo-uhs] (adj.) empty. (n.) —cuity, —cuousness. See **vapid.**

vacuum [VAK-yoo-m] (pl.) —s.

vagary [YAE-gih-ree] eccentric action. (pl.) —ies.

vagrant [VAE-grant] a homeless wanderer; vagrancy: the state of homelessness or wandering.

vain (adj.) without value; also, conceited. (adv.) —ly.

VANITY that which is meaningless or useless, esp. in Biblical book of Ecclesiates: *All is vanity.* Also, excessive pride: *The artist's vanity.*

IN VAIN without result. *Our efforts were in vain.*

vainglorious [vaen-GLOH-rih-uhs] (adj.) boastful. (n.) vainglory.

***Valdez* oil spill** [val-DEEZ; -DEHZ] See **Exxon Valdez disaster.**

valence [VAEL-ens] (n.) in chemistry, combining power. Hence, colloq., the attractiveness of any goal.

Valéry, Paul [vah-leh-REE] (1871-1945) Fr. essayist, poet ("A Cemetery by the Sea").

valet [val-LAE] man servant. (v.) —eted, —eting.

Valhalla [val-HAL-uh] in Norse myth, Hall of Odin, for dead heroes.

Valkyrie [val-KIH-ree, -KIE-ree] in Norse myth, angels who guide heroes to Valhalla. 1876 opera by Wagner (See **Ring of the Nibelung**). (pl.) —ries. (adj.) Valkyrian.

valley Shenandoah Valley, the valley; BUT the valleys of Maryland and Virginia.

valor (n.) pref. to —*our.* (adj.) valorous.

value monetary worth. *Of what value is that? It has got no value any longer.* (adj.) valuable.

VALUES (pl.) beliefs, principles. *A*

senator who remains friendly with the Mafia has dubious values.

vandal from barbarians who sacked Rome. (n.) desecrator; destroyer. (v.) to vandalize; to commit such acts.

vanguard, vanload, vanpool.

van Gogh, Vincent See **Gogh.**

Vanuatu [veh-NOO-eh-TOO] island nation in SW Pacific. Formerly Br. and Fr. New Hebrides; independent, 1980. Cap.: Vilah [vih-LEH]. Native: Vanuatuan. Currency: Australian dollar and Vanuatu franc.

vapid [VAP-ihd] (adj.) lifeless, dull; See **vacuous.** (n.) vapidity pref. to —*ness.* (pl.) —ities.

vapor Pref. to —*our.* —orless, —ory; vaporific, —rize, —izer.

variable [VAR-ih-uh-B'L] (adj.) subject to change; (n.) variability. Variable. (n.) in algebra means an unknown quantity.

> VARIANCE [VAR-ih-ans] (n.) a difference or exception, esp. in law: *a variance from the zoning code.*

> VARIANT anything different from the norm.

> VARIATION a slight difference; in music, repetition of a theme, with modifications.

> VARIETY many variations and choices: *a variety show.* Also, the smallest classification in biology or geology: *a variety of Mollienesia caucana.*

varicolored

variegate [VAIR-ee-eh-gaet] to diversify.

variorum [vaer-ee-OR-uhm] classical text with notes.

various Usage allows as "several:" *various odds and ends.*

vase [vaeze, vahz].

vasectomy [va-SEHK-toh-mee].

Vatican City [VA-tih-kihn] sovereign state within city of Rome, Italy; legal jurisdiction of Catholic Church.

vaudeville [VAWD-vihl].

vault room in which safe deposit boxes and valuables are kept; NOT a safe. Also, a mausoleum.

V.C.R. (abbr.) video cassette recorder.

VD (abbr., rarely with points) venereal disease.

Vedas [VAE-duh; VEE-duh] Hindu sacred texts; includes **Upanishads.**

V-E Day, V-J Day. See **holidays.**

vehicle [VEE-ihk'l].

vehicular [vee-HIHK-yoo-lahr] of a vehicle.

Velázquez, Diego (Rodríguez de Silva y) [vae-LAHS-kaeth, DYAE-goh] (1599-1660) Sp. painter.

veld [VEHLT] African grassland. Pref. to —*dt.*

vellum prepared skin of a lamb, kid, or calf used for bookbinding; also, paper in imitation of vellum. (pl.) —s.

venal [VEE-nal] capable of being bought or bribed.

> VENIAL SIN [VEE-nih-al] in Christian theology, a minor offense, as opposed to *mortal sin.*

vend —ible.

vendee (buyer); vendor (seller). Vendor is pref. to —*er,* esp. when contrasted with buyer. *Caveat vendor: "Let the seller beware."* See **emptor.**

Venezuela [veh-neh-ZWAE-lah] in NE South America, on the Caribbean. Independent, 1830. Cap.: Caracas [kah-RAH-kas]. Native: Venezuelan. Currency: Bolivar.

vengeance retribution, punishment.

> REVENGE retaliation; returning evil for evil.

venial [VEE-nih-al] See **venal.**

veneer thin sheet of overlay, especially of fine wood.

venous [VEE-nuhs] (adj.) of veins. NOT *veinous.*

ventilate (v.); —lator (n.).

ventral abdominal; in humans, front.

venue [VEHN-yoo] place of a trial.

Venus the planet. Also, Roman love goddess. (pl.) —es; (poss.) —us's.

> VENUS DE MILO ancient, armless statue now in Louvre Museum, Paris.

Vera [VEE-rah] Name from Latin for "truth."

veracious [veh-RAE-shuhs] habitually truthful.

veranda [veh-RAN-dah] porch. Pref. to —*ah.*

VERB in grammar, a word or group of words which expresses being or action. The **subject** either commits the action or receives it. The verb, its modifiers, and its complements constitute the predicate of a sentence. Every sentence must have a verb.

Verb form may vary according to person (1st, 2nd, 3rd), number (sing. and pl.), tense (past, present, etc.), voice (active, passive), mood (indicative, subjunctive, imperative), and —a relatively complex concept —aspect (the intention of tense revealed by context). See **number, person, tense,** etc.

A **transitive verb** has a direct receiver of the action (an object). *He smelled the incense. He lay* (in the sense of "put") *the corpse on the table.* An **intransitive verb** does not have an object. *The incense stank. The corpse lay* (in the sense of "lie still") *among the broken furniture.*

An intransitive verb (or copulative verb) joins two ideas without the action of one or the other. *He was a regular Hitler. She seems bright. The girl felt chilly.* BUT: *He felt his sweetheart's hair against his cheek.*

verbal in grammar, a word that can be modified like a verb: gerund, participle, and infinitive (not necessarily preceded by *to*). BUT these words funciton as nouns, adjectives, or adverbs — NOT as verbs.

Laughing out loud, Amy left the room (gerund verbal as adj. phrase). *To break our record will be hard* (infinitive verbal as subject noun).

Verbals may serve as subject complement, or modifier, but cannot act as verbs.

Verbals express time only in relation to the time of the main verb in the sentence; they may show that an action occurred at the same time or at an earlier time. *Charlie chased him up the street, almost catching him twice.*

verbal of words. A verbal promise is one made out loud.

ORAL of or with the mouth.

AURAL of hearing.

verbatim [ver-BAE-t'm] in the same words.

verboten [vehr-BOH-t'n] (Ger.) forbidden.

Verdi, Giuseppe [VAIR-dee, joo-ZEHP-pae] (1813-1901) It. composer, famous for operas.

verdigris [VUHR-dih-gree] greenish, poisonous pigment created by the effect of acetic acid on copper.

Vergil See **Virgil.**

verily [VEHR-ih-lee] truly. Archaic except in *I verily believe.*

Vermeer, Jan [ver-MEHR, jahn] Jan van der Meer von Delft (1632-1675) Dutch painter.

vermilion, vermillion [vehr-MIHL-lyuhn] bright red.

vermin [VUHR-mihn] (sing., pl., and collective) disgusting insects or animals.

Vermont U.S. state. (abbr.: VT.) Cap.: Montpelier. Native: Vermonter.

vermouth [vehr-MOOTH] flavored white wine.

vernacular See **language.**

Verne, Jules [vehrn] (1828-1905) Fr. author of early science fiction novels like *Twenty Thousand Leagues Under the Sea.*

Verrazano-Narrows Bridge [vair-a-TSAH-noh] In N.Y.C., longest bridge in world. After 15th-C. Florentine navigator Giovanni da Verrazano.

Versailles [ver-SAEZ, ver-SIE] City near Paris, site of Louis XIV palace, beginnings of French revolution, and treaty of 1918.

versatile [VUHR-suh-tihl] capable in many areas.

verse metrical composition in general. Takes sing. verb.

FREE VERSE without rhyme or meter. (Fr.) *vers libre.*

STANZA a group of metrical lines. (pl.) stanzas.

VERSO [VIHR-soh] See **recto.**

vertebra [VUHR-teh-bruh] a segment of the spinal column. (pl.) —brae (in biology); —s.

vertex (pl.) —es or —ices.

vertigo [VEHR-tih-goh] dizziness. (pl.) —os.

very, very much Adverbs can modify verbs, adverbs, or adjectives. BUT in formal English, *very* can modify only adjectives and adverbs.

Difficulties arise in the case of participles when a participle is used as an adjective, *very* can properly modify it. *She is very pretty* (modifying an adjective). *He is very comfortably situated* (modifying an adverb). *The very drunk man in the corner is the president of the company* (modifying a participle used as an adjective).

BUT in formal usage, when a participle is part of the verb, *very much* must be used. *He is very much distressed* (modifying a participle that is part of the verb). NOT: *He is very distressed.* A fairly reliable rule of thumb is: Wherever *much* can be used, *very* by itself cannot be; wherever *much* cannot be used, *very* alone is correct.

Casual usage now allows *very* as an adverb. *She's very tired.*

vesper, (pl.) vespers. Late afternoon or evening services. Usu. in plural form with pl. verb.

Vespucci, Amerigo [vehs-POO-chee, ah-MEH-ree-goh] (1451-1512) It. explorer and mapmaker; gave name to America.

vessel boat; internal conducting tissue (blood vessel); utensil for serving or holding.

vestige [VEH-stihj] (n.) small remainder; leftovers. (adj.) vestigial [veh-STIH-jee-uhl]. In biology, a degenerate body part with no apparent use.

Veterans Administration

veterinarian (n.); veterinary (adj.).

veto (n. or v.) (pl.) vetoes, vetos.

V.H.F. (abbr.) very high frequency.

via [VIE-ah] by way of. *He came via I-5.*

viable [VIE-uh-b'l] (adj.) acceptable; able to be done. (n.) —ability.

viand [VIE-and] food; usu. plural. (pl.) —s.

vicarious [vie-KAIR-ee-uhs] experienced at one remove; substituted for the actual. *He got a vicarious thrill from watching his friend score.*

vice-chairman (pl.) vice-chairmen.

vice president For capitalization rules, See **president**. (pl.) vice presidents. BUT hyphen for vice-presidency.

Vice President of the United States ADDRESS: The Honorable Dan Quayle, Vice President of the United States, Washington, D.C.; or The Vice President, Washington, D.C.

SALUATION: Sir; Dear Sir; Dear Mr. Vice President.

vice versa [vies VUHR-sah] reversed; conversely. *The family has a child problem, or rather, vice versa: a problem child.*

Vichy [VEESH-ee] city in S France, source of famed mineral water, cap. of Nazi-run French government, W.W. II.

vichyssoise [vee-shee-SWAHZ, vih-shih-] Cold leek soup.

vicious [VIH-shus] cruel.

    VISCOUS [VIHS-kuhs] Gummy.

vicissitude [vih-SIHS-ih-tood] changeableness; unexpected, affecting event.

vicuña [vie-KYOO-nah] fur-bearing animal of Andes mountains.

victual [VIH-t'l] food, esp. already prepared. Also, victualer: keeper of a restaurant or a handler of provisions for army, navy, or ship.

vide [VEE-dee; (sometimes angl.) veed] (Lat.) Refers to example in another text. *The King was adamant; vide the 1651 statute.*

video May be n. or adj.

Viet cong, Vietcong [VEE-eht kahng] North Vietnamese guerrillas in conflict with S Vietnam and U.S., 1950s-70s.

    VIET MINH [mihn] N Vietnamese guerillas in conflict with Japanese and French, 1940s-50s.

Vietnam [vee-eht-NAHM; -NAM] in SW Asia, on Pacific coast. Formerly Fr.; independent as North and South Vietnam 1954-75, then unified. Cap.: Hanoi [heh-NOI]. Native: Vietnamese. Currency: Dong.

viewfinder, viewpoint.

vigilante [VIH-jih-LAN-tee] volunteer or group of volunteers organized for protection, esp. against crime.

vignette [vihn-YEHT] small decorative illustration. In printing, a picture which shades into background.

Viking [VIE-kihng] Pirate Norsemen, 8th-10th C. NOT a generic term like **vandal.**

vilify [VIHL-ih-fie] to debase; defame.

Villa, Pancho (Francisco) [VEE-yah, PAHN-choh] (1877-1923) Mexican bandit, revolutionary.

villain [VIHL-ihn].

Villon, François [vee-YAWNN, frahn-SWAH] Pesudonym of François de Montcarbier (1431-c.1463), Fr. poet ("*Where are the Snows of Yesteryear?*")

vinaigrette [vinn-ae-GREHT] originally, ornamental container for vinegar or smelling salts. Also, tangy sauce.

Vinci, Leonardo da [dah VEEN-chih, lae-oh-NARHR-doh] (1452-1519) Florentine genius in arts and engineering.

vindicate to justify; defend successfully. *By proving the charges were spurious, he was vindicated.*

    VINDICTIVE vengeful. *Let us encourage a merciful attitude rather than a vindictive one.*

vineyard [VIHN-yehrd].

viola [vie-OH-luh; vee-OH-luh] the instrument. [VIE-uh-luh] the flower.

violate (v.); —lable. (adj.), —tor (n.).

violoncello [vee-oh-lahn-CHEHL-oh; vie-] See **cello.**

V.I.P. (abbr.) very important person.

virago [vih-RAE-goh] woman of strength; quarrelsome woman.

Virgil or **Vergil** [VUHRjihl] (70-19 B.C.) Roman epic poet, full name: Publius Vergilius Maro. See **Aeneid.**

Virginia U.S. State. (abbr.: VA.) Cap.: Richmond. Native: Virginian.

Virgin-Islands U.S. territory in West Indies. (abbr.: V.I.) Three chief islands: St. Thomas, St. Croix [saen-KROI], and St. John. Cap.: Charlotte Amalie [SHAHR-laht uh-MAHL-yuh].

Virgo [VIHR-goh] Born Aug. 23 - Sept. 22. See **Zodiac.**

VIRGULE See *SLASH, DIAGONAL LINE.*

virile [VIH-rihl].

virtu [vehr-TOO] love of objets d'art; also objets d'art collectively: *A piece of virtu.*

VIRTUE moral excellence.

virtually in essence, but not in fact. *Virtually does not mean very nearly or almost. In 1942, Hitler was virtually the ruler of France, although Petain was*

nominally the chief of state.

virtuoso [vehr-choo-OH-soh] (pl.) —s or —si. Outstanding performer in any field.

virulent [VIH-roo-lent] (adj.) deadly, malignant. (n.) virulence.

virus [VIE-ruhs] microscopic infection. (pl.) —es.

visa [VEE-zuh] (n.) stamp passport to allow entry. (v.) —ed, —ing.

VISA (Cap., no points) credit card.

visage [VIHZ-ahz] the face.

vis-à-vis [vee-zah-VEE] face to face.

viscera [VIS-ihr-uh] internal body organs.

viscid, viscous [VIHS-ihd, VIHS-kuhs] (adj.) Sticky; gummy. (n.) viscosity. NOT vicious.

viscount [VIE-kount] noble with rank between earl and baron, courtesy title for earl's eldest son. See **nobility.**

vise a gripping tool.

visibility (n.) ability to see; often referred to in descriptiions of light and weather conditions. (adj.) visible. Also, (n.) visibleness: abiltiy to be seen.

vision sight. Also, supernatural foresight.

visit AVOID *visitation* except for prisoners' rights or supernatural events.

Visnu, Vishnu [VIHS-noo] Hindu deity.

visor [VIE-zuhr pref. to VIHZ-uhr] eye shade; helmet piece.

VISTA (no periods) Volunteers in Service to America.

vita [VEE-tah] (from *curriculum vitae,* (Lat.) "course of life.") **resume,** esp. in academics.

vitiate [VIHSH-ih-aet] (v.) to corrupt; invalidate. (adj.) vitiable.

vitrify (v.) to change to glass by heat. (adj.) —fiable or vitrescible, vitreous. (n.) vitrification.

vitriol [VIHT-ree-uh] a caustic acid; hence, angry speech.

vituperate [vie-TYOO-puhr-aet] to censure severely; berate. (adj.) —rative.

vivace [vee-VAH-chae] in music, lively.

vivacious [vih-VAE-shuhs; vie—] lively, spirited.

Vivaldi, Antonio [vih-VAHL-dee, an-TOH-nee-oh] (1678-1741) It. Baroque composer.

viva voce [VEE-vuh VOH-see, -chae] (Lat.) spoken: *a vote viva voce.*

viz. (abbr.) videlicet [vih-DEHL-ih-seht] namely. Always precede with a comma or semicolon.

vizier [vih-ZEER; VIHZ-yehr] official in Islamic countries, esp. Turkish empire. (adj.) —ial, —irial.

V.L.F. (abbr.) very low frequency. See **radio frequency.**

vocabulary High school students have an average vocabulary of 4500 to 8000 words in speech; college graduates use 15,000 to 25,000 words in speech, and write with fewer, but may understand as many as 50,000 before they graduate. By contrast, Shakespeare used only 24,000 words.

voice In a verb, indicates whether subjects is agent or receiver of action. Active voice: *I hit him,* passive voice: *I was hit.*

voice-mail (n.) recorded messages via telephone.

voilà [vwah-LAH] (Fr.) There! Behold!

vol. (abbr.) volume.

volatile [VAHL-uh-tihl; -tiel] of a liquid, readily vaporized; hence, of a person, fickle.

vol-au-vent [vahl-loh-VAHNN] (Fr.) meat pie made with rich puff paste.

volcano [vahl-KAE-noh] May be active, dormant, or extinct. (pl.) —oes. (adj.) volcanic.

Volgograd [VOHL-goh-grad] See **Stalingrad.**

volition [voh-LIH-shuhn] free choice. *People in repressive countries cannot leave of their own volition.* (adj.) —nal.

Volkswagen [VOHLKS-wah-gehn].

volley. (pl.) —s.

volleyball, volley fire.

Voltaire [vahl-TAER] pen name of François Marie Arouet [ah-RWEH] (1694-1778) Fr. writer, philosopher.

volume 2, A, II Lowercase; BUT *Volume 2,* when part of title: *Volume 2: Five Rivers in America's Future.*

voluminous [vah-LOO-mih-nuhs] of many books; hence, of great length.

Vonnegut, Kurt, Jr. [VAH-nih-guht] (b. 1922) American author.

vortex [VAWR-tehks] whirlpool. (pl.) —es or —tices.

votable, voteable of voting, or of being submitted to a vote.

vote-getter, vote-casting, vote-getting (adj.).

vouch to pledge one's word. *He was prepared to vouch for my honesty.*

vouchsafe [vouch-SAEF[to grant as true.

vox populi [vahks PAHP-yoo-lie] (Lat.) voice of the people.

voyeur [voi-YUHR]; —ism [VOI-yuhr-is'm].

VT. Vermont.

VTOL (abbr.) Vertical takeoff and landing, as in the operation of a helicopter.

vying [VIE-ihng] vie, vied; —ly.

W

W west.

w. watt.

W-engine, W-sharped, W-type.

WA Washington (the state).

W.A.C. (abbr., arch.) Woman's Army Corps; a WAC.

wacky slang for eccentric. NOT whacky.

W.A.F. (abbr. arch.) Women in the Air Force; a WAF.

waft [waft] (v.) to move lightly, as if on air. (n.) the thing moved in this manner.

wage (pl.) —s; wages sometimes accepted as singular.

SALARY Implies steadier, higher level of employment and pay than wages: a day's wages; a year's salary.

Wagner, Wilhelm Richard [VAHG-nehr, VIHL-hehlm] (1813-1883) Ger. composer famous for operas.

wagon-lit [va-gawn-LEE] (Fr.) sleeping car.

Waikiki Beach [WIE-kih-kee] a beach in Hawaii.

wainscot [WAEN-skuht] wood molding usu. three or four feet above floor. wainscoting, -scotting; —ted, —tted.

waistcoat [WAEST-koht] vest.

wait He waits to hear from you. NOT: He awaits.

AWAIT Must have an object. We await your arrival.

Waiting for Godot [goh-DOH]. 1952 play by Samuel Beckett; helped define Existentialism, Postmodernism, Theatre of the Absurd.

waive to abandon; forgo. We waive our right to counsel.

WAVE The physical motion.

waiver (n.) reliquishing of a right. A waiver of immunity would leave him open to prosecution.

WAVER (v.) to hesitate; also, totter. He will not waver in his efforts to clear your name.

wake (p.) woke, sometimes waked; (p.p.) waked, wakened, woke, or woken. NOT awaked, awoken; See awake.

Waldheim, Kurt [VAHLD-heim] (b. 1918) Austrian, U.N. Secretary-General 1972-1982. President of Austria since 1986.

Wales Native: Welsh (collective pl.). See Celts, Gallic.

walkie-talkie

Walkyrie. See Valkyrie.

wallop —ed, —ing, —er.

wallpaper

Walpurgis Night [vahl-PUHR-gihs] Eve of May Day, Witches Sabbath.

walrus [WAWL-ruhs].

waltz Ger. *valse's* sometimes used in programs.

wan [WAHN] pallid, sickly; hence, faint: *wan hopes.*

wanderlust [WAHN-dehr-luhst] impulse to wander.

wanton [WAN-tuhn] (adj.) unrestrained, unchaste. (n.) —ness.

War of Independence any anti-colonial war: Algerian War of Independence (1950s–60s), American War of Independence (1775–83).

War Between the States U.S. Civil War (1861-65)

war Cap. if part of name: First World War, World War I (W.W.I), Great War; Second World War, World War II; French and Indian War (1754-63); Mexican War; War of the Nations; War of the Rebellion (BUT the rebellion); War of 1812 (BUT war of 1914-18).

War Between the States, Civil War; Philippine Insurrection; Revolutionary War; Seven Years War; Spanish-American War;

Korean War; Vietnam War; Gulf War.

The two World Wars; post-World-War.

ALSO: cold war, hot war, European war, French and Indian wars, Indian war, war in Korean; third world war, world war III, war with Mexico, war with Spain.

-ward(s) [-wehrd, -wehrds] suffix meaning direction to or motion towards.

ward 1, 2, 3 lowercase; first ward, 11th ward, and so on.

Warhol, Andy [WAR-huhl] Actual name Warhola. (1930-1987) American artist; developed Pop Art.

warmed-over (adj.)

warp [wawrp] (n.) threads that make the length in a loom. See **woof.** Hence (v.), to bend, twist.

warrant, —y (agreement), —or (maker), —ee (receiver), See **guarantee.**

Warsaw Pact former military alliance of **U.S.S.R.** and Eastern European allies (Poland, East Germany, etc.). Dissolved 1989.

was, were *Was* is 1st and 3rd person sing., past of the verb *be.* NOT *we was, they was;* USE *were.*

Were, plural past, is also used in the singular with you. *You were here yesterday.*

Were is sometimes used in the past subjunctive of *be* after *if, suppose,* and *wish,* and in hypothetical statements: *I wish I were home now. If I were home now. . .* BUT *was* may also be used in these constructions. *Were* is pref. in *If I were you. . .* and is required if the verb precedes the subject. *Were I to go to school. . .*

In a statement about the past expressing uncertainty, use *was*. *If Tom was late, I would find out about it.*

Washington U.S. state. Abbr.: WA. Cap.: Olympia. Native: Washingtonian.

Washington's Birthday The holiday is Presidents Day (Washington's and Lincoln's birthdays combined).

wassail [WAHS-'l; WAHS-ael] (n.) a Christmas toast; sweet, spiced alcoholic drink. (v.) to drink a wassail.

waste (n.) Tech. use allows *wastage*. (adj.) wastable.

wastrel [WAES-trehl] spendthrift; profligate.

watercolor

Watergate scandal, Watergate break-in, coverup. Colloq. usage allows -*gate* as suffix indicating any scandalous political machinations: *Irangate, Contragate.*

waterway inland waterway, intercoastal waterway, etc. BUT: Intracoastal Waterway.

watt unit of electric power.

Watteau, Jean Antoine [wah-TOH, zhahn, ahn-TWANN] (1684-1721) Fr. painter.

Waugh, Evelyn [WAW, EEV-ehl-ihn] (1903-1966) English writer. (*Brideshead Revisited*)

wavy

wax (adj.) make of wax: *wax candles.*

WAXEN appearance of wax: *a waxen face.*

waybill official list of goods in a shipment.

—ways, —wise Both suffixes are correct, and have the same meaning. Usage has established one suffix with some words, the other with others: *sideways, clockwise.* When improvising, —*wise* is pref. See **-wise**.

W.C. (abbr.) water closet: bathroom.

W.C.T.U. (abbr.) Women's Christian Temperance Union.

weal [WEEL] (arch.) wealth, use only in *public weal, commonweal.*

wear (p.) wore; (p.p.) worn.

weatherbeaten —blown, —board, —glass, —man, —proof, —proofed, —proofing, —strip, —tight, —worn (all one word); weather-marked (adj.), weather-stain (v.); weatherwise; weather-bound; weather eye, weather gauge.

weave (p.) wove or weaved; (p.p.) woven or weaved. BUT: *He weaved his way through the land mines.*

web fabric on a loom.

wed (p. and p.p.) wed.

wedge (v.), wedgeable (adj.).

Wedgwood china

Wednesday [WEHNZ-dih] abbr.: Wed.

weedkiller —killing; weed-choked (adj.).

week Cap. for specific occasion: Fire Prevention Week, etc. See *DATES* and *NUMBERS.*

weft [wehft] Cross threads in loom. also See **warp, woof.**

weigh [wae] Nautical, to hoist: *weigh anchor; anchors aweigh.* BUT: *The ship is under way.*

weightlifting

weird [WEERD] (adj.) strange; unearthly. (adv.) —ly, (n.) —ness.

welfare state

as well as *The U.S. as well as Britain is in need of increasing exports.* NOT a synonym for *besides* or *only.*

well-nigh (adj.) nearly. Best used with adjectives of time. *The house is well-nigh 200 years old.*

WELL PLUS PARTICIPLE Hyphenate when an attributive adj. *His well-heralded approach.* BUT DO NOT hyphenate predicate adj.: *His approach was well heralded. Well-trained schoolteachers are necessary for all schools, and his teachers were well trained.*

Welles, Orson [AWR-s'n] (1915-1985) American actor and film maker, famous for *Citizen Kane.*

welsh [WEHLSH] (Slang) to avoid payment of a debt. (n.) welsher. Pref. to welch [WEHLCH].

WELSH Cap. pertains to Wales or inhabitants.

welterweight

weltgeist (Ger.) spirit of the age. —politik, —schmerz.

Welty, Eudora [yoo-DAWR-rah] (b. 1909) American writer. (*"Why I live at the P.O."*)

were See **was, were.**

werewolf

west western, more western, westernmost.

West Coast. BUT west coast also allowed, esp. in U.S.; West End, etc. (section of city); West Europe (political entity); Far West, Far Western States; West Germany (political entity); Middle West (U.S.), Midwest; West South Central States, etc., the West (section of U.S. or world political entity).

westbound westmost, westward; west-central (adj.), west-facing (adj.), west-northwest, west-sider; west end, west side.

Western civilization Western countries; Western Europe (political entity); Western Hemisphere, the hemisphere; Western North Central States, Western Powers; Western States; Western Union (See **alliances**). BUT far western; western farming states (U.S.).

Western Samoa [sah-MOH-ah] island nation in SW Pacific. Former property of New Zealand, independent, 1962. Cap.: Apia [uh-PEE-uh]. Native: Samoan. Currency: Tala.

West Germany See **Germany**.

West Virginia U.S. State. Abbr.: WV. Cap.: Charleston. Native: West Virginian.

westward (adj. or adv.); —s (adv. only).

wet-nurse (v.); wet nurse.

wharf [hwawrf] (pl.) —ves; Br., —s.

wharfage fee for use of dock.

Wharton, Edith [HWAWR-t'n] (1862-1937) Am. writer. (*House of Mirth*)

what [hwaht].

WHATEVER, whatnot (n.), whatsoever (adj.); (slang) whaddyacallit (n.).

WHATEVER all that. *They have whatever they need. Whatever you say, don't tell.*

WHAT EVER AVOID as the emphatic of *what*. NOT: *What ever did he say?*

WHATSOEVER Formal for whatever.

when AVOID using *when* to introduce a definition unless time is involved. NOT: *Success is when you make money.*

whence [hwehns] from where. *Let them return whence they came.* See **hence**.

WHITHER (arch.) to what place.

WHENCESOEVER (arch) from what place (or cause).

when ever Colloq. emphasis of where. *When ever will they get here?*

WHENEVER (conj.) at whatever time. *They visit us whenever their ship is in port.*

WHENSOEVER Use *whenever* instead.

where AVOID to introduce a definition except when place is involved. NOT: *A book where the hero dies is called a tragedy.*

whereabouts —as, —at, —by, —for, —from, —in, —into, —of, —on, —soever, —to, —upon, —with, —withal (all one word).

wherever at or to whatever place. *He goes wherever help is needed.* AVOID colloq. use as emphatic of *where*.

whether or not *Or not* is essential. *Just tell me whether or not you'll come home with me.*

whether, as to AVOID use. NOT: *The question as to whether he would come was posed.*

which [hwich] Clarify antecedent by placing close by : *the book which. . .*

Which can introduce a defining clause (in which case no punctuation is used), but is better used in nondefining clauses (in which case commas enclose the clause). *This magazine, which was dated March 1986, arrived for Christmas 1991.*

One of the greatest books which have (NOT *has*) *ever been written.* (*The greatest books* determines the number of *which*, the subject here.) See **that . . . which**.

whichever which ever.

while (conj.) (*whilst* is arch.) during the time that. Also, whereas. AVOID use with unattached particples. NOT: *Tears streamed down his face while reading the story.* USE: *. . . while he was reading the story.*

AVOID use to introduce a definition not involving time, or as a substitute for *though, although, whereas, and,* or *but.* NOT: *While he does not recall the agreement, he will pay the bill.* Use *although*.

whimsy or **whimsey**

whip, the of a political party in Congress, legislator appointed to enforce discipline.

whiplash May be v. *She was whiplashed in the accident.*

whippoorwill

whir buzzing sound. *Motion picture cameras may whir but TV cameras are silent.*

whirlybird a helicopter.

whisk (v.) *He whisked the children away.* Also, (n.), whisk broom; egg whisk.

whisky (pl.) —ies. Pref. to *whiskey*. Bourbon, Scotch, Irish.

Whisky Rebellion. See **rebellion**.

whistle stop (n.), BUT *whistle-stop tour,* (adj.).

white-collar worker Person at executive or management level of employment. Not a manual laborer. See **blue-collar**.

white elephant overexpensive and useless.

White House, Blue Room, East Room, Red Room, Oval Office, State Dining Room. White House Police.

whiten —ed, —ing.

Whitsunday, Whit Sunday, Whitsuntide 7th Sun. after Easter. The Feast of Pentecost. NOT Whitsun Day.

whiz (n. pl.) whizzes. (v.) whizzed, —zing.

who, whom *Who* is nominative; *whom* objective. But *who* is often acceptable at the beginning of a sentence where *whom* is grammatically correct. *Who are you looking for?* BUT generally, use *whom* after *to, for, from, with,* and *than. He is a man who. . .* is redundant (except for emphasis).

who (agreement) The verb must agree in person and number with the antecedent of who. *To him who has everything . . . For us who have* (NOT *has*) *nothing.*

who (interrogative pronoun) *Who* and *what* are used in reference to an unlimited group, *who* for persons and *what* for inanimate things, animals, and in reference to persons' status, interests, and so on. *Who is he? What did you get? What are his interests?*

who (relative pronoun) Avoid use for inanimate objects unless personifcation has been established previously. NOT: *Canada, who sold wheat to China* (use *which*).

Who is pref. if the antecedent is a person or personal pronoun. *Which* refers to inanimate things but may refer to persons in an impersonal way, as in official reports. *He spoke of the child which was killed in the wood.*

That is used to refer to an unidentifiable person and is ordinarily used to refer to either a person or a thing. See **that, which**.

Who and *whom* are perferred for introducing nondefining clauses; *that* for defining clauses. *The man, whom I think you know, was here. He knew John, who was a bright boy. We expected John, whom he liked. The boy that was here yesterday was John.* See **whom**.

who Meaning *whoever*, is archaic. NOT: *He who comes on Monday,* BUT: *Whoever comes on Monday. . .*

W.H.O. (abbr.) World Health Organization.

whoever. Use *whoso, whosoever* only in formal documents.

wholehearted

wholesale —saling.

wholly [HOH-lee] fully.

whom (relative pronoun) *Whom* is required after *than: Lincoln, than whom*

no man earned more respect, was a humble man; although *who* is actually the correct form.

Who is required as the subject when it is placed before a verb.

Whom may be used as the subject of a verb when a parenthetical clause intervenes. A classic example is Shakespeare's: *Arthur, whom they say is killed tonight. . .*

Use *whom* as the object of a preposition. *The girl to whom you gave the book. . .* BUT the object of a verb requires *that* if possible, and *whom* only where necessary, such as after an identified person. *The teacher that he knew best, Ms. Jones, whom you recall. Who* is also acceptable in this construction.

whomsoever (arch.).

whooping cough [HWOOP-ihng cawf].

whose poss. of who, but may apply to things as well as people. *The company whose stock we bought.*

WHO'S who is. May refer to animate or inanimate objects. See **who**.

w.-hr. (abbr.) watt-hour.

WI Wisconsin.

—wide. See **suffix**.

wide See **broad**.

wide awake (n.); wide-awake (adj.).

widow in printing, a word or short line carried alone over to the top of the next page. See also *NAMES, FIL-ING*, **divorcee**.

widow If no preference is expressed, address by former title: Ms. (or Mrs.) John Brown, NOT maiden name.

wild cat untamed cat.

WILDCAT wild animal native to U.S.; lynx.

will (v.) to intend to have come to pass. *She willed her father to cross.* (v.) wills, willed. (adj.) willable. (pres. part.) willing.

Willamette River [wih-LAM-eht] a river in Oregon.

willful Pref. to wilful.

will-o'-the-wisp (pl.) —wisps.

willy nilly also willy-nilly, willynilly.

wilt-resistant

win (p. and p.p.) won.

wind [(v.) wiend, (n.)wihnd] (v.) to twist. (p. and p.p.) wound [wound]. (n.) movement of air.

wireless

Wisconsin U.S. state. Abbr.: WI. Cap.: Madison. Native: Wisconsinite. Nickname: Badger State.

—wise, nowise, clockwise, dollarwise, lengthwise. *He's a great star videowise, but musicwise, he's mediocre at best.* Hyphenate more complex constructions. *Sweeps-month-wise, it's*

poor primetime programming.

wishbone

wisteria [wihs-TEER-ih-uh] Pref. to *wistaria* [-TAER-].

withdraw, withhold.

without not with. Meaning "outside," this word is archaic. AVOID use for *unless.* NOT: *No representative should vote for this measure without he first sees the deplorable conditions involved.*

with reference to with regard to. *About* is pref.

witness Avoid use meaning "see" except in legal sense.

Wittgenstein, Ludwig [VIHT-gehn-stein, LOOT-vihg] (1889-1951) Austrian-British philosopher.

wizened [WIHZ-'nd].

W.O. (abbr.) warrant officer.

woebegone

wolf (pl.) wolves; (v.) wolf, wolfed, —fing.

Women's Army Corps. See **corps**.

wont [wuhnt, wohnt] (adj.) accustomed to. (n.) custom; habit. *He got a double caffé latté, as was his wont.*

WON'T [WOHNT] will not.

wooden (adj.) pref. to *wood.* (n.) —enness

woodsman

woof cross threads on a loom. See also **weft**.

woofer loudspeaker for low acoustic frequencies.

wool woolen (adj.); wooly.

Woolf, Virginia [wuhlf] b. Virginia Stephen (1882-1941) Br. author. (*To the Lighthouse*)

word processing (n. and adj. only) *I work in word processing, so I need a good word processing program.*

work (p.) and (p.p.) worked; wrought (arch.).

world New World, Old World.

World Series

World War W.W. I, W.W. II. See **War**.

worndown (adj.); worn-out (adj.).

worrywart

worsen (v.) to become or make worse.

worship (v.) —ed, —ing.

worsted [WUHS-tid] hard-twisted wool yarn and its cloth.

worthwhile (n., adj., adv.), (n.) —ness.

would, should See **should, shall**.

wrack (n.) destruction; remnants after destruction. (v.) to wreck; torment.

wrangle (v.) —ed, —ing.

wraparound, wrap-around, wrap-up, wrap-up (n. and adj.).

wrath [rath] (n.) anger, *the king's wrath.* (adj.) —ful.

    WROTH [rawth] (adj. arch.) angry.

wreathmaker, —work (n.); wreath-crowned (adj.).

wring (p. and p.p.) wrung.

writ court order to perform a specific act.

write (p.) wrote; (p.p.) written. *I wrote her yesterday. I've written her a letter.*

write down (v.) in accounting, to reduce the value of an asset on the books of account. (n.) writedown: The reduction.

write-in (n. and adj.): *a write-in vote* (adj.).

write off (v.) in accounting, to remove the value of an asset from the books of account. (n.) writeoff: the amount removed.

write up (v.) in accounting, to increase the value of an asset on the book of account. (n.) writeup: the amount increased.

wrong (adj.) *His work was done wrong.* (adv.) wrongly: *He did his work wrongly.*

wrongdoer, wrongdoing; wrong-ended (adj.), wrong-minded (adj.), wrong-thinking (adj.).

wrought. (arch.) See **work**.

wrought iron handcrafted malleable iron.

wry wrier, wriest; wryly, wryish.

WV West Virginia.

W.W. I, II. (abbr.) World War I, II.

WY Wyoming.

Wyoming [wie-OH-mihng] U.S. state. Abbr.: WY. Cap.: Cheyenne. Native: Wyomingite.

X

—x French words ending in —*eau* or —*eu* usually take —*x* for a plural: *beau, beaux* (or *beaus*). Exception: *adieus, plateaus.*

X U.S. Air Force symbol for *experimental* in numbering aircraft: *X-15.*

X, XXX movie ratings. Both indicate explicit sexual content, but XXX was never more than a marketing ploy of adult theatres. See **movie ratings.**

x-body, x-shaped, x-virus.

Xanthippe [zan-TIHP-ee] (5th C. B.C.) wife of Socrates, famous for criticizing the philosopher.

Xavier, Saint Francis [ZAH-vih-ehr] Francisco Xavier (1506-1552). Spanish Jesuit, missionary; Apostle of the Indies.

xenophobia [zehn-oh-FOH-bee-uh] fear of foreigners.

Xenophon [XEHN-uh-f'n] (c. 434-355 B.C.). Greek historian, soldier.

Xerxes I [ZUHRK-seez] (519?-465 B.C.) King of Persia, famous for defeats against Greece.

—**xion** This suffix is common in Britian; in U.S., —*ction* is pref.

Xmas Christmas.

X-ray, X ray (n.) electomagnetic wave with radiation wavelength of 0.1 to 2.0 angstroms. (v.) X-ray. (adj.) X-ray: *an X-ray photograph.*

xylophone [ZIE-loh-fohn] percussion instrument.

Y

Y-chromosome, Y-joint, Y-shaped, Y-tube.

y endings There are three conventions for adding a suffix to a word ending in y. (1) If *y* is preceded by a consonant, change *y* to *i*: *beauty, beautiful, beautify.* (2) If the suffix begins with *i*, retain the *y*: *satisfy, satisfying.* (3) If *y* is preceded by a vowel, retain the *y*: *enjoy, enjoying, enjoyable.*

yacht [YAHT], yachtsman; —manship.

Yahwch [YAH weh] Old Testament Jehovah. Orig. consonants only, YHWH; God's name was not supposed to be spoken.

Yangtze River YANG-tsee] principal river in China.

Yankee New Englander. Hence, in Southern U.S., a northerner; abroad, any American.

Yankee Doodle

yard unit of length = 3 ft. = 36 in. = 0.9144 meter.

yardarm, yardstick (both n.); yard-long; yard-wide (both adj.).

yd. (abbr.) yard.

yea [YAE] yes, esp. in parliamentary voting.

year period of 365 days (366 in a leap year.) Calendar year begins January 1; fiscal year may begin at any time selected.

Year International Geophysical; the Geophysical Year, the Year.

years Use dash to indicate periods of two or more years: *1907-17; 1898-1902; 1900-1902.* BUT indicate individual years by number only. *They corresponded in 1897, 1900, 1902, and for the last time in 1905.*

Use *From 1901 through 1906,* or *between 1921 and 1923,* or *1937 to 1945 inclusive.* NOT *between 1901-1906.*

Spell out dates as needed: *the year nineteen hundred and sixty-three.* Or use distinctions for before and after Christian year: *193 B.C.; A.D. 1888.* (A.D. and B.C. may be printed in small caps.) See **time.**

Yeats, William Butler [YAETS] (1865-1939) Irish poet, (*"The Second Coming"*) dramatist. Nobel Prize, 1923.

Yeltsin, Boris (b. 1931) Rus. politician, statesman. Winner of first free elections in old **U.S.S.R.**, 1989, making him President of Russia (former **U.S.S.R. republic**).

Leader in forming **Commonwealth of Independent States**, 1991-92, and first chairman of its ruling body.

Yemen [YEH-mehn] two nations, North Yemen and South Yemen, at SW corner of Arabian peninsula. Natives in both, Yemenis.

NORTH YEMEN Mostly on Red

Sea. Formerly Turkish; independent, 1918. Cap.: Sanaa [SAN-ah]. Currency: Rial.

SOUTH YEMEN Mostly on Indian Ocean. Formerly British Aden; independent, 1967. Cap.: Aden. Currency: Dinar.

yeoman [YOH-m'n] freeborn man, but subordinate.

yes man, yessir.

yesterday, yesteryear.

Yevtushenko, Yevgeny [YEHV-too-SHEN-koh, yehv-GEH-nee] (b. 1933) Rus. poet, spokesman for artistic freedom.

Yiddish language of middle European Jews; from Hebrew, German, and Slavic. See **Hebrew.**

yin-yang [yihn yang] in Chinese philosophy, two basic principles of life; any two complementary approaches to a subject. *The yin of wanting to make art is balanced by the yang of needing to make a living.*

Y.M.C.A. Young Men's Christian Association.

Y.W.C.A. Young Women's Christian Association.

yoga [YOH-guh] in Hinduism, mental and physical exercises to achieve higher consciousness. Can also mean the physical exercises alone: *I practice yoga to stay in shape.*

YOGI [YOH-gee] yoga teacher.

yogurt

yoke (n.) pair of draft animals; wood frame by which they are connected. (v.) to connect as if by yoke.

yolk [yohk] yellow of an egg.

Yom Kippur [yohm KIHP-uhr] Jewish Day of Atonement; in Sept. or Oct.

Yosemite National Park [yoh-SEHM-ih-tee] park in California.

you-all, y'all (slang) U.S. Southernism. Takes pl. verb.

your (poss.); you're (you are).

your *Your and our and my* (his, her) *books.* NOT: *yours and ours and my books.* BETTER: *Your books and ours and mine;* BUT: *her and his books.*

Your Excellency, Your Honor, Your Majesty.

youth [yooth] Esp. refers to males. (pl.) —s. (adj.) —ful.

yr. (abbr.) year; your.

Yugoslavia [yoo-goh-SLAH-vih-ah] nation on Adriatic Sea. Formerly Turkish, then Austro-Hungarian; 1918, Kingdom of the Serbs, Croats, and Slovenes; 1945, Yugoslavia. Cap.: Belgrade [BEHL-grad]. Native: Yugoslav(s). Currency: dinar. In 1990-92, Yugoslavia suffered civil war among four constituent states: Croatia, Slovenia, Bosnia-Hazogovina, and Serbia (Yugoslavia).

SERBIA [SUHR-bee-ah] Claims title and central authority of Yugoslavia. Landlocked, occupies much of east. Cap.: Belgrade.

CROATIA [kroh-AE-shah] Occupies central coast. Seeks independence. Cap.: Zagreb [ZAH-grehb].

SLOVENIA [sloh-VEE-nyah] NW corner, coast. Seeks independence. Cap.: Ljubljani [LOO-bih-AH-nah]

BOSNIA-HERZOGOVINA [BAHS-nee-ah-HEHR-soh-goh-VEE-nah] SW corner, with tiny coastline. Seeks independence. Cap.: **Serajevo.** (See).

yuletide yule log.

Y.W.C.A. See **Y.M.C.A.**

Z

zabalione [zah-BAHL-yoh-neh] It. dessert of eggs, wine, creamed fruit.

Zaire [zah-EER] Central African nation. Formerly Belgian Congo; the Republic of **Congo** 1960-1971. Cap.: Kinshasa [kihn-SHAH-sah], formerly Leopoldville. Native: Zairian(s). Currency: zaire.

Zambia [ZAM-bee-ah] Landlocked SE African nation. Formerly Br., then Northern **Rhodesia**. Independent 1964. Cap.: Lusaka [loo-SAH-kah]. Native: Zambian(s). Currency: kwacha.

zany [ZAE-nee] mildly insane. Comp.: zanier, —iest.

Zarathustra [zah-rah-THOO-strah] (adj.) —trian. A/k/a Zoroaster [ZAWR-oh-ASS-tihr] (adj.) —trian. mystic, founder of ancient Persian religion.

zealot [ZEHL-uht] zealous person; in Hebrew history, fanatical anti-Roman.

zenith [ZEE-nihth] sky overhead; hence, highest point.

zephyr [ZEHR-ihr] gentle wind.

zero (pl.) —os.

Zero hour starting moment.

zeugma [ZYOOG-muh] figure of speech: one word modifies or affects two others, taking a different meaning in each case. *The Senator picked up his hat and his courage. He sometimes took counsel, sometimes tea.* (pl.) —ata or —as.

Zeus [zooss] chief Greek god.

zigzag —gged, —gging.

zillion an undefinably large number.

Zimbabwe [zihm-BAHB-wae] landlocked nation in SE Africa. Formerly Brit., then Southern **Rhodesia**. War of independence, 1965-80. Cap.: Harare [hah-RAHR-ree]. Native: Zimbabwean(s). Currency: dollar.

Zionism [Zie-ahn-ihz'm] movement first to establish Jewish homeland, then to provide support. (adj.) —ist.

zither [ZIH-thuhr].

zloty [ZLAH-tih] Polish currency.

zodiac [ZOH-dee-ak] 12 constellations, each rising above horizon in a different month, forming basis of astrology: **Aries, Taurus, Gemini,** etc. (adj.) zodiacal [zoh-DIE-uh-k'l].

Zola, Émile [ZOH-luh, ae-MUHL] (1840-1902) Fr. novelist.

zone Cap. if part of name: British Zone; Canal Zone (Panama), Canal Zone Government.
　　Arctic Zone; Eastern Zone; Frigid Zone; New York Foreign Trade Zone; Foreign Trade Zone No. 1, BUT the foreign trade zone; Zone of Interior (see Command), Temperate Zone,

Torrid Zone, BUT the zone; Trizonia, trizonal.

Also, eastern standard time zone, polar zone, tropical zone.

zoning municipal control of types and use of structures in specified areas.

zoological park Cap. if part of name: National Zoological Park, the zoo; the park.

Zouave [zoo-AHV] French infantry group with flamboyant costumes, later imitated in U.S. during Civil War.

zweibach [TSWEE-or SWIE-] toasted biscuit.

zygote [ZIE-goht] cell formed by two mature sex cells; the maturing individual thus produced.